GREEK MUSIC IN AMERICA

GREEK MUSIC
in AMERICA

Edited by Tina Bucuvalas

University Press of Mississippi / Jackson

The University Press of Mississippi is the scholarly publishing agency of the
Mississippi Institutions of Higher Learning: Alcorn State University, Delta
State University, Jackson State University, Mississippi State University,
Mississippi University for Women, Mississippi Valley State University,
University of Mississippi, and University of Southern Mississippi.

www.upress.state.ms.us

The University Press of Mississippi is a member
of the Association of University Presses.

Publication of this volume was made possible in part by a generous donation from the
AMS 75 PAYS Endowment of the American Musicological Society, funded in part by
the National Endowment for the Humanities and the Andrew W. Mellon Foundation.

First printing 2019
∞

Library of Congress Cataloging-in-Publication Data available

ISBN 978-1-4968-1970-3 (hardcover)
ISBN 978-1-4968-1971-0 (paperback)
ISBN 978-1-4968-1972-7 (epub single)
ISBN 978-1-4968-1973-4 (epub institutional)
ISBN 978-1-4968-1974-1 (pdf single)
ISBN 978-1-4968-1975-8 (pdf institutional)

British Library Cataloging-in-Publication Data available

Dedicated to George Soffos. Αιωνία του η μνήμη.

CONTENTS

Contents

PART FOUR: PROFILES

Contents

ACKNOWLEDGMENTS

There are many people to thank for their generous contributions of time and information. First and foremost, this book could not have been written without the profound knowledge, guidance, and efforts of Stavros K. Frangos. Not only did he prove to be a constant and reliable sounding board regarding content and ideas, but his writings compose a substantial part of this work. Since graduate school, we have periodically conducted joint forays into wildest Greek America and have been richly rewarded with experiences and laughter. In many ways, this is his book too.

Meletios Pouliopoulos has been a true treasure. Not only does he have a deep and encyclopedic knowledge of Greek music and recordings but, miraculously, he is willing and able to discuss issues and supply essential data at the drop of a hat. And he has munificently supplied numerous, if not the majority of, images of record labels, album covers, sheet music, and artists from his remarkable Greek Cultural Resources archive.

I am immeasurably indebted to several other friends and colleagues who have imparted their expertise. Over several years, many collaborative concerts, and innumerable bouzouki workshops, Leonidas Zafiris and Elias Poulos have taught me an enormous amount about the history, genres, and artists of Greek music. My ethnomusicologist/musician colleagues were of great help: Michael G. Kaloyanides reviewed and provided helpful suggestions regarding the introduction, Panayotis League assisted with thorny transliteration and dialect issues, Michalis Kappas ably advised on genre references, and Laurie K. Sommers shared her knowledge about the scope of ethnomusicology scholarship. I also profited greatly from the insights of musicians Jim Stoynoff and Parry Tsangaris.

Special thanks go to Emily Papachristou, Katerina Papagika, Ethel Raim (Center for Traditional Music and Dance), Elaine Eff, Tom Pich, Alan Govenar (Documentary Arts), George Johann (Angry Mom Records), Tom Diamant (Arhoolie Records), and Dimitri Matsis for supplying me with images and artist contacts.

As always, it was a great pleasure working with Craig Gill, director of the University Press of Mississippi, who not only demonstrates an ongoing commitment to knowledge in the fields of music and traditional culture but also provided strong support and encouragement from the beginning to the end. I am very appreciative of the excellent editorial work done by Emily Bandy and other members of the press team. And special thanks to amazing copyeditor Norman Ware, who rapidly learned enough about Greek and Turkish music to pinpoint and correct numerous issues for a dozen different writers.

I would also like to thank my wonderful daughters, Alexandra and Chloe Curran, who have always bemusedly tolerated their mother's unusual research propensities. And Alexandra proved to be an enabler through her assistance in scanning slides.

Most of all I must acknowledge my enduring gratitude to the late George Soffos, who was the inspiration for this volume. In addition to being a remarkable musician, during our years together he generously shared his encyclopedic knowledge of Greek music acquired through forty years in the business. After his death, it was through the process of coproducing a CD featuring his work that I recognized the need for a book on this topic.

GREEK MUSIC IN AMERICA

INTRODUCTION

—Tina Bucuvalas

Even before the waves of mass immigration to the United States in the late nine-teenth and early twentieth centuries, Greeks are known to have accompanied Spanish explorers and British colonists to the New World.[1] Along with many other cultural elements, they brought their treasured music. Despite a substantial history, there has been little written about Greek music in America outside of a limited number of essays in relatively ephemeral or obscure sources. This volume is intended to provide a foundation for understanding the scope, practice, and development of Greek music in America through essays and profiles written by many of the principal scholars in the field.

Greek communities encompass a wide range of distinctive social phenom-ena—one of which is shared acoustic traditions, such as music. As composer/ scholar Barry Truax posited, acoustic communities are those "in which acoustic information plays a pervasive role in the lives of the inhabitants. . . . The commu-nity is linked and defined by its sounds. To an outsider they may appear exotic or go unnoticed, but to the inhabitants they convey useful information about individual and community life" (1983, 58). Greek acoustic communities are now and have long been transnational in nature—physically, emotionally, and cultur-ally. "Sounds move, cross borders, and link bodies that might otherwise not be linked, that might otherwise be divided from each other. But sounds also stay put, engendering familiarity and intimacy, creating spaces of shared identity."[2] Thus, in our diaspora communities, music is an essential component of most social activities—linking the past to the present, the distant to the near—saturat-ing the acoustic community with an intricate web of information and memories. And, as Kip Lornell and Anne Rasmussen observed, for many whose roots are outside the United States, "music *invents* homeland" (2016, 20).

In recent years, an increasing number of music scholars and vintage record collectors have discovered Greek regional music and especially *rebetika*, the genre best known by outsiders. While the recognition is long overdue, the over-emphasis on early rebetika neglects not only the remarkably varied and complex range of other genres and artists but also the natural stylistic evolution and many of the acoustic community contexts that ascribe cultural significance. In other instances, a particular artist or regional genre is acclaimed as the pinnacle of skill and emotional expression.[3] I am always puzzled at these pronouncements, for my experience with both recorded historic and live contemporary Greek music is that there is an astounding number of performers who, as a matter of course, rip your heart out with the beauty, depth, and power of their art. Perhaps a factor contributing to the current interest in this music is that Greeks are not reluctant to explore the dark, passionate, or mournful corners of the human condition—indeed, as their music attests, they excel at it.

The Essays

Despite the richness, diversity, and longevity of Greek music in America, there has been relatively little published on the subject. A few pioneering scholars in the mid-twentieth century wrote about vernacular and ethnic music, but it was not until the 1970s that books on diverse music traditions regularly appeared. While there are numerous works dealing with other types of ethnic music, this seems to be the first that addresses Greek music in America. Most often, the topic of ethnic music is addressed through works that focus on specific groups or the musical genres associated with those groups, such as blues, salsa, Cajun, klezmer, or polka (Lornell and Rasmussen 2016, 18).[4] Such studies have emerged from a wide range of disciplines such as folklore and ethnomusicology as well as in studies of migration, identity, place making, and the recording industry.[5] Many of them have posited that "[e]thnic and community identity are fluid, vigorous, and to a certain extent voluntary, and it is through and with music that processes like exposure, enculturation, and embodiment, all of them key to the formation of identity, are set into motion" (Lornell and Rasmussen 2016, 23).

Although several significant scholars have written essays on Greek music in America since the 1970s, most of their work has appeared in publications that are difficult to access. Thus, this volume includes several of their pioneering essays, as well as recent and previously unpublished work from contemporary specialists. It is important to note that major technological advances have vastly increased the availability of original commercial recordings, record catalogs, sheet music, ephemera, oral histories, and other documentation—often resulting in scholarship with a more solid foundation than was possible in the past.

The essays brought together in the section titled "Musical Genre, Style, and Content" are intended to cover a wide range of Greek music. Little has been written about the considerable changes in sacred music in America—although this this is one of the earliest and most frequently performed types of Greek music. The late Frank Desby (1922–1992) offers an excellent overview of this important topic in the chapter "Growth of Liturgical Music in the Iakovian Era." Based at Saint Sophia Cathedral in Los Angeles, Desby was part of a second generation of academically trained Greek Orthodox Church musicians who created a westernized body of liturgical music (Lingas 2013).

In 1981, writer Roderick Conway Morris penned a comprehensive review of the early development and interrelationship of the *café aman* and rebetika urban musical forms in "Greek Café Music." His detailed exposition of the development of such components as social context, instrumentation, musical composition and performance styles, accompanying dances and dancers, song themes, and commercial recordings takes us from origins in Asia Minor to elaborations in America. Of particular interest is his attention to café aman, about which relatively little has been written.

Although Gail Holst-Warhaft is best known for her groundbreaking work *Road to Rembetika*, in "*Amanes*: The Legacy of the Oriental Mother," she tackles a genre that has rarely been discussed in English-language essays. She deftly delineates the earliest known appearances of the emotionally intense amanes and its ties to other Greek musical traditions. This is a much-needed examination of the genre, which I frequently see performed in Florida by male and female vocalists from mainland and island folk traditions.

With an impressively large and comprehensive body of work examining myriad aspects of rebetika, Australia's Stathis Gauntlett is arguably the topic's most knowledgeable scholar today. "*Rebetika*, the Blues of Greece—and Australia" not only delineates the lengthy history of rebetika in Greece and Greek communities in Australia but also traces its ties to the American recording industry (including its construction as a genre by that industry) and its comparisons to the blues. Although this book focuses primarily on America, developments in Australian diaspora communities provide fascinating and relevant points of reference due to the powerful similarities between the two countries and the lives of diaspora Greeks.

There is probably no more prolific writer on Greek American culture and history than anthropologist Stavros K. Frangos. His essays span many realms of culture, but the body of work regarding early Greek American recordings is particularly strong. His chapter titled "George Katsaros: The Last *Café-Aman* Performer" examines early Greek musical forms and transformations as documented by the recording industry. By using the career of iconic musician Katsaros as an example, he finds a reflection of the collective Greek American experience and illustrates that Greek music must be viewed through the lens of music history to ascertain whether certain genres are created traditions.

In "'Health to You, Marko, with Your Bouzouki!' The Role of Spoken Interjection in Greek Musicians' Imagined Performance World in Historical Recordings," Michael Kaloyanides categorizes and analyzes the role of *tsakismata*, the common verbal interjections in Greek music performances, both live and recorded. Not only is the world of the recording studio a topic rarely explored in terms of Greek music, but the ubiquitous verbal interjections are likewise rarely illuminated. As a music scholar who was raised in and also performed in Greek diaspora communities, Kaloyanides is unusually well equipped to interpret the differences in usage between such interjections in live community events as opposed to recording studio conventions.

Through information about specific recordings and musicians, Joseph Graziosi's chapter, "Turkish Music in the Greek American Experience," delineates how many immigrants from the former Ottoman Empire embraced Turkish music and song as a familiar aspect of their home culture. This again challenges theories promoted by some twentieth-century scholars who portrayed Greek music as highly differentiated from that of surrounding musical cultures—and perhaps harking back to a glorious ancient past. Many of those theories assume the continuing purity of Greek musical forms, genres, or contexts—yet when we honestly examine any musical lineage, it is clear that it changes and evolves in response to a variety of influences.

In the "Places" section, authors interrogate the musical culture of specific Greek American communities. Long America's premier port and urban center, New York City has always been a fulcrum of musical expression. In "Survival of Greek Folk Music in New York," esteemed ethnomusicologist and musician Sotirios (Sam) Chianis sets the stage by ably delineating the many forms of Greek music, then tracing the long history of music, musicians, venues, and instrument makers in the city.

Longtime Baltimore resident Anna Caraveli unraveled the complex of social and musical forms and their meanings in the city's Karpathiot diaspora community. In addition, she journeyed multiple times to Olymbos, Karpathos—widely believed to be one of Greece's most strongly traditional villages—where she documented the effect of the diaspora on traditional culture. Although the two essays on which the chapter "Communities Born in Song" was based were published originally in 1985, Caraveli's work remains an outstanding ethnographic study on transnational musical bonds.

Around the turn of the twentieth century, hundreds of Greek sponge fishermen and their families settled in Tarpon Springs, Florida. Their relatively large numbers combined with a continuing stream of immigration created a community that has carefully preserved a large part of its culture. In 1999, Anna Lomax Wood undertook a labor of love: recording the music of Kalymnian *tsambouna* player and National Heritage Fellow Nikitas Tsimouris and his family, with whom she shared bonds of friendship and fictive kinship. "Musical Practice and Memory on the Edge of Two Worlds: Kalymnian *Tsambouna* and Song Repertoire in the Family of Nikitas Tsimouris" is a sensitive and carefully delineated contextual exploration of the social, lyrical, and ethnomusicological dimensions of an ageless but increasingly rare musical tradition.

A descendant of one of its early Greek families, rising ethnomusicologist and musician Panayotis League has strong roots in Tarpon Springs. In a two-part essay on Kalymnian music and dance, "Alternate Resonances: Kalymnian Traditions in Tarpon Springs, Florida," he interweaves several perspectives to create a multilayered, highly textured assessment. The first part, "Living the Dance: Imaginative Journeys and Musical Movement in Tarpon Springs, Florida," presents the topic as an expression of ethnic affiliation and belonging. The second part, "Interrogating 'Authenticity' in the Kalymnian Diaspora," explores music and dance as highly fluid identity markers dependent upon specific social contexts.

The section titled "Delivering the Music: Recording Companies and Performance Venues" examines the ways that Greek music was made accessible in the United States. Recording companies not only created documentation of musical expression, they were a source of great pleasure and consolation through their distribution of music as well as an enormous influence on the tastes of the public. Dick Spottswood is revered by scholars, record collectors, and music enthusiasts for his groundbreaking work in documenting sound recordings of ethnic music from 1893 to 1942. His essay here focuses specifically on "Greek Record Making in the Early Days, 1896–1937." In "Greek Music Piano Rolls in the United States," knowledgeable collector Meletios Pouliopoulos presents important research on some of the earliest recordings of Greek music in America. Player pianos were popular in the late nineteenth and early twentieth centuries, and piano roll companies, like record distributers, issued significant quantities of Greek piano rolls to target the ethnic market.

In Greek culture, music is an integral part of special events and often daily life—and the specifics of those contexts may affect the music itself in terms of what is presented, and how. As such, it is important to explore the venues in which the Greek diaspora experienced music. In "Encountering Greek American Soundscapes," respected dance scholar and choreographer Anthony Shay investigates the context of Greek musical performances based on his experiences as a young international folk dancer in California in the period from the 1950s to 1970s. Similarly, journalist Nick Pappas explores in detail the social and economic dimensions of Greek club and restaurant presentations in New York during the 1980s in "Bouzoukis and Belly Dancers, Drinkers and Dreamers: A Look at Greek Nightlife at the Crossroads."

The "Profiles" section consists of short sketches of noteworthy individuals or entities that shaped the course of Greek music in America or contributed through their talents to its allure and perpetuation. It is in no way intended to be a comprehensive listing—that would require another volume. Rather, it is an admittedly somewhat random selection based on the research interests of the authors. Nevertheless, the stories presented in this section further illuminate the distinctive history and myriad permutations of Greek music in the United States. Subjects range from artists who lived in the early twentieth century to those who still perform, from instrument makers to record company founders to club kids. The section is organized more or less chronologically.

Finally, as a boon to researchers and enthusiasts, the appendix contains a guide to collections of recordings and related materials that are available to the public. In "Greek Music Collections in the United States," Stavros K. Frangos reviews the known holdings that contain all types of traditional and popular music, commercial and field recordings, and both amateur and professional performances, as well as liturgical music, oral history interviews, notes, and manuscripts.

Note on the Transliteration

To say that it has been difficult to ensure consistent transliteration from the Greek to the Latin alphabet would be a gross understatement. Not only have styles in the rendering of Greek into English changed over centuries and even decades, but Greek itself has changed. And when you throw regional dialects into the mix, the undertaking becomes a miasma of confusion. Music recordings present a particular problem because often the artists' names or song titles were originally incorrectly transliterated, or the spelling shifted, sometimes in both Greek and English, on different recordings. Naturally, then, the authors in this volume presented their references in a wide variety of styles.

I have tried to navigate this issue by combining the most common and easily recognizable transliteration of words (e.g., *rebetika* rather than *rempetika*) with guidelines established by the International Organization for Standardization, the United Nations, and the American Library Association–Library of Congress.[6] For the most part, I have not included the syllable stresses used in Greek but have retained diacriticals that change pronunciation (e.g., the umlaut in Smyrneïka). In addition, I have honored the authors' own transliteration system when I judged the result to be fairly standard and universally understandable. Most titles of existing recordings are given as they originally appeared. Suffice it to say that the result is in no way perfect—but there simply is not a perfect system.

Notes

1. According to the 2010 census, more than 1,315,775 Americans claim Greek heritage. The first to arrive was Teodoro in the expedition to Florida led by Álvar Núñez Cabeza de Vaca in 1528, followed by two Greeks who were part of Pedro Menéndez de Avilés's 1565 expedition and five more who joined the 1566 Sancho de Archiniega expedition (J. Michael Francis, e-mail message to the author,

March 31, 2018). From the eighteenth to the late nineteenth centuries, a limited number of Greek sailors and merchants settled throughout the country. In 1768, about five hundred ethnic Greeks were among the indentured colonists brought to work on a British plantation in New Smyrna, Florida. Many of their descendants remain in nearby Saint Augustine, where their history is commemorated at the Saint Photios National Shrine. Greek residents of New Orleans founded the first Greek Orthodox church in the Americas in 1864.

2. John D. Calandra Italian American Institute, May 10, 2016, e-mail communication/call for papers for the conference titled Italian Sonorities and Acoustic Communities: Listening to the Soundscapes of Italianità, April 27–29, 2017, Queens College, City University of New York.

3. See, for example, the excellent essays by journalist Amanda Petrusich (2014) on *epirotika* or collector Christopher King (2014) on violinist Alexis Zoumbas.

4. Laurie K. Sommers, e-mail message to the author, October 30, 2016.

5. See Lornell and Rasmussen's introduction to *The Music of Multicultural America* (2016) for an overview of the scholarship on ethnic music.

6. See the useful entry on the romanization of Greek in Wikipedia, at https://en.wikipedia.org/wiki/Romanization_of_Greek, accessed April 29, 2017.

References

King, Christopher. 2014. "Talk about Beauties." *Paris Review*, September 22. At http://www.theparisreview.org/blog/2014/09/22/talk-about-beauties/. Accessed June 16, 2016.

Lingas, Alexander. 2013. "The Divine Liturgy of St. John Chrysostom, Liner Notes, Part Three: A Second Generation of Greek American Church Musicians." Cappella Romana, November 26. At http://www.cappellaromana.org/tag/frank-desby/. Accessed April 23, 2016.

Lornell, Kip, and Anne K. Rasmussen, eds. 2016. *The Music of Multicultural America: Performance, Identity, and Community in the United States.* Jackson: University Press of Mississippi.

Petrusich, Amanda. 2014. "Hunting for the Source of the World's Most Beguiling Folk Music." *New York Times Magazine*, September 24. At http://www.nytimes.com/2014/09/28/magazine/hunting-for-the-source-of-the-worlds-most-beguiling-folk-music.html?_r=0. Accessed June 6, 2016.

Truax, Barry. 1983. *Acoustic Communication.* Westport, CT: Greenwood Press.

Zoumbas, Alexis. 2014. *A Lament for Epirus, 1926–1928.* Angry Mom AMA-004. Angry Mom Records, New York.

OVERVIEW OF GREEK
MUSIC IN AMERICA[1]

—Tina Bucuvalas and Stavros K. Frangos

Greeks have developed a rich variety of traditional, popular, and art music. Traditional music reveals historical influences from ancient Greece, Byzantium, the
Ottoman Empire, and the Balkans. There are two streams of traditional Greek
music that share many influences and elements: Byzantine ecclesiastic music used
in the Greek Orthodox Church, and folk (*dimotika* or sometimes *paradosiaka*)
music, including both rural and urban traditions.

Greek music varies enormously in style, meter, and instrumentation. In many
areas of Greece, there is a substantial repertoire of nonmetrical instrumental and
vocal compositions without a regular beat, as well as some vocal genres, like the
amanes, *miroloi*, and *rizitiko* traditions, that use the natural textual rhythm to
create a free-flowing rhythmic structure.[2] Mainland folk music often features
unrhymed verses, musical scales utilizing microtonal intervals (intervals smaller
than a Western sharp or flat), and the 2/4 or 4/4 meters of the *syrtos* and 7/8
meter of the *kalamatianos*.[3] The standard *kompania* ensemble typically included
clarinet, violin, *laouto*, *santouri*, and *defi*. The islands and coastal areas favor musical scales with microtonal intervals, rhymed verses, and two-beat dance rhythms,
as well as the nine-beat *zeibekiko* and *karsilamas* originally from Asia Minor.[4]
Island ensembles (*ziyia*) often feature violin, *laouto*, and santouri, with *lyra* and
tsambouna on some islands. The bouzouki and the related *tambouras* were widespread throughout Greece, although particularly prominent in the Peloponnese
and the eastern Aegean islands (Kourousis 2013, 23–24, 28–36). Popular and art
music often combine traditional Greek musical elements with Western forms
and instrumentation.

Members of the diaspora brought with them to America a taste for all the
permutations of music in Greece. During the early twentieth century, a flood of
immigration combined with commercial record production generated unparalleled documentation of ethnic music. From May 1896 to 1942, more than one
thousand Greek recordings (Gauntlett 2003, 28) in many genres were recorded
in the United States on Victor, Columbia, Odeon, and other labels large and

Figure 1. Open Heart *kafeneio*, Greektown, Salt Lake City, Utah, 1920. Used by permission, Utah State Historical Society.

small (Spottswood 1990)—and thousands more have appeared since then. The recordings encompass not only Greek traditional music from all regions but also emerging urban genres, stylistic changes, and new songs of social commentary.

Ethnic recordings are invaluable documents of community musical practices and preferences in America.[5] Commercial recordings represented the daily lives of immigrants and the perils that afflicted them. Songs dealt with numerous pressing issues, both within and outside the community. In addition to its social importance to the community, music was also one of its most prized and enduring creations. Historian and poet Dan Georgakas asserted: "Music, in fact, proved to be the most important cultural legacy of the immigrants" (1987, 17). Greeks who arrived in the massive waves of immigration also had an enduring influence on the musical culture of Greece and other diaspora communities. What Gail Holst-Warhaft noted regarding one genre was true of many: "The history of *rebetika*, both as a recorded and live genre, has always been closely linked to the émigré communities in the United States" (2001).

1880–1918

From the late 1880s to the early 1920s, between four hundred thousand and five hundred thousand Greeks immigrated to the United States (Kitroeff 2015).[6]

Figure 2. New York City Greeks returning to Europe to fight in the Balkan Wars, October 1912, Bain Publishing. Courtesy of the Library of Congress.

Most came because of agricultural failures in Greece and an economy overburdened with refugees from the Balkan Wars (1912–1913) and the Greco-Turkish War (1919–1922). They were over 90 percent male, and the vast majority never intended to stay in the United States (Kourvetaris 2008, 560). The men found work in cities across the nation, as well as in railroad construction and the mines and factories of the West. In the early days, when they had virtually nothing, the immigrants still had music, which helped them cope emotionally with the separation from their families and homeland.

Although thirty thousand Greek Americans returned to fight for Greece during the Balkan Wars (Kourvetaris 2008, 560), the vast majority returned to the United States. Their intention to build their lives and communities in America provided the impetus for the increased immigration not only of women but also of many more of their countrymen.

In the late nineteenth and early twentieth centuries, the two most common types of Greek music performed were Byzantine and dimotika. Byzantine chants were performed as part of the Greek Orthodox liturgy. However, in America, priests and others began to compose new liturgical music, some of which abandoned the traditional Byzantine modes and single vocal line. The new music with European scales was often presented in a westernized style through choirs accompanied by organs. Among those associated with this progressive style was Father George Anastassiou of Tarpon Springs, who formed the Damaskenos Byzantine Choir.

Regional folk music was the other widespread performance genre. Through sounds that resonated of home, Greek immigrants revisited their villages, towns, or cities and their memories of loved ones left behind. Migratory work and separation were not new to Greeks, who had endured centuries of outmigration to improve their lives or escape persecution. The song tradition centered around *xenitia* (foreign lands or exile) arose from the ongoing economic need to migrate and expresses a sense of loss and desolation. With the recent collapse of the economy propelling new waves of Greek immigration, this genre has acquired renewed relevance.

The first singers and instrumentalists in America were undoubtedly drawn from the ranks of those who sought temporary work or to establish a new life (Frangos 2013). Yet professional musicians and other traveling performers soon traveled to Greek enclaves, labor camps, and coffeehouses (*kafeneia*) to entertain the weary and isolated men. They later also entertained at weddings, picnics, religious festivals, and name-day celebrations. By 1910, the *café aman* tradition took root in major urban areas as places where immigrants could socialize, eat, drink, and enjoy music and dance. Respected musicians of the time were paid generously by those who danced to their music (Chianis 1983, 3).

Traditional instrument makers arrived in America in the first waves of immigration. In 1903, luthier Anastasios Stathopoulos (1863–1915) established a workshop on Manhattan's Lower East Side, and later a showroom and factory at 247 West Forty-Seventh Street. Sometime before 1910, Theodoros P. Karabas founded I Neolaia instrument workshop near Eighth Street and First Avenue in New York. By 1910, Dimitrios Grachis and his son George had launched the Terpandros instrument workshop in Chicago's Greektown. Over the years it produced superb mandolins, laoutos, violins, and more than three hundred bouzoukia—clearly indicating the popularity of the instrument in America.[7] By 1933, another luthier, Alexandros Politis, had established himself in New York.

Thomas Edison invented the phonograph for the mechanical recording and reproduction of sound in 1877. On May 4, 1896, tenor Michael Arachtingi recorded the first eight documented Greek commercial records in New York City for the Berliner label. Song titles such as "Smyrna Serenade," "Great Constantinople Song," and a piece with Turkish lyrics, "Cozaghaki Song," reveal Arachtingi's familiarity with music from Asia Minor (Frangos 2007b).

The early record companies manufactured and sold record players in addition to creating recordings. Because they engaged in cultural niche marketing, European and later American-based record companies soon began to send field agents around the world to record music. By providing Greeks and other ethnic groups with their music, they intended to encourage continued purchases of both music

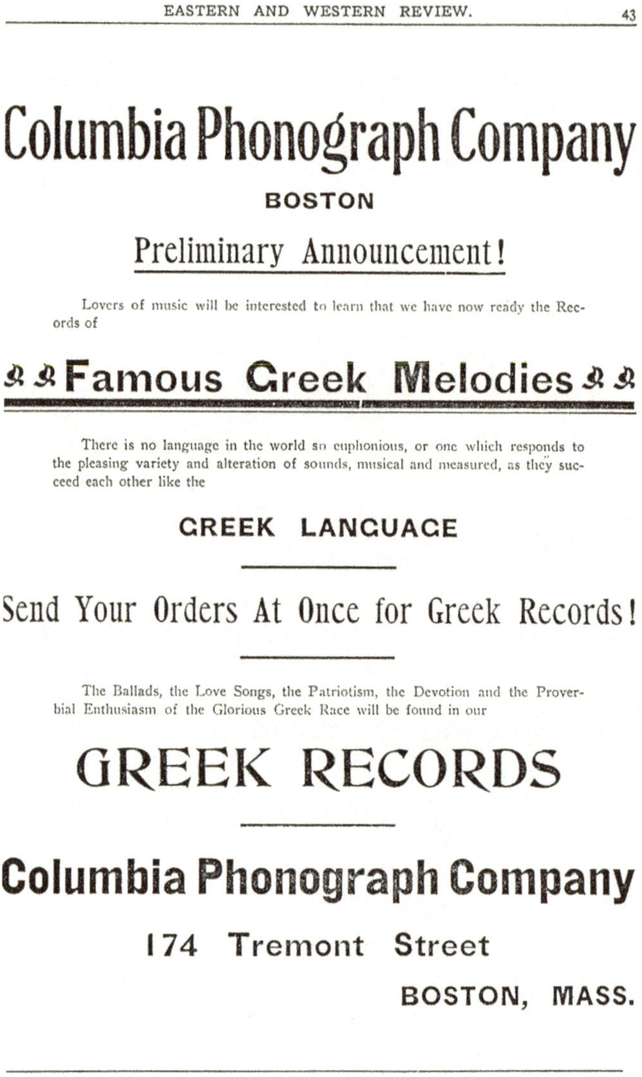
EASTERN AND WESTERN REVIEW. 43
Columbia Phonograph Company
BOSTON
Preliminary Announcement!
Lovers of music will be interested to learn that we have now ready the Records of
Famous Greek Melodies
There is no language in the world so euphonious, or one which responds to the pleasing variety and alteration of sounds, musical and measured, as they succeed each other like the
GREEK LANGUAGE
Send Your Orders At Once for Greek Records!
The Ballads, the Love Songs, the Patriotism, the Devotion and the Proverbial Enthusiasm of the Glorious Greek Race will be found in our
GREEK RECORDS
Columbia Phonograph Company
174 Tremont Street
BOSTON, MASS.

Figure 3. Advertisement, *Eastern and Western Review*, January 1910, 43. Courtesy of Stavros K. Frangos.

and gramophones (Gronow 1981, 274). An advertisement for Greek commercial records appeared as early as 1910 in *Eastern and Western Review* from Boston.[8]

With the development of new technologies, the commercialization of traditional Greek music took many forms. Music cylinders and records were the first innovations available to an avid consuming public. Mechanical music machines such as music boxes and player pianos were soon equipped with Greek music.

Figure 4. Mme. Koula, "Garoufalia," 1916. Panhellenion 4007B.
Courtesy of Meletios Pouliopoulos.

Figure 5. Marika Papagika, "Eleftheria (Over There)," 1919. Columbia
Graphophone Company E5187. Courtesy of Meletios Pouliopoulos.

Piano roll companies such as QRS issued long lists of traditional and newly composed Greek musical favorites, such as Lukianos Cavadias's performances of "Ti se meli esenane" (QRS WF9166) and "Arapiko eipto" (QRS F8862). The popular piano rolls were fundamentally an American, not Greek, phenomenon.[9]

In late 1916 or early 1917, Kyriaki Antonopoulou (ca. 1880–1954) recorded thirty-four songs in Greek and sometimes in Turkish for Columbia Records in New York. Known as Mme. Coula or Kyria Koula, her recordings ignited the boom period of Greek recording in America. By 1918, Columbia issued a *Greek Record Catalogue* featuring both domestically recorded and imported 78-rpm records. At the same time, the Apollo Greek Musicians Union was established in Chicago.

Greek immigrant participation in World War I was a complicated mix of patriotic feelings for both America and Greece. With the US entry into the war, some sixty thousand Greeks volunteered to serve with the American Expeditionary Forces. Many more returned to fight in the Greek military. Greeks joined in large numbers because they believed that the Megali Idea, which promoted the creation of a Greek nation-state encompassing much of Asia Minor, would be achieved with the defeat of the Ottoman Empire. The song "Eleftheria" (Freedom), performed by Marika Papagika (1890–1943) and many other Greek vocalists, was based on George M. Cohan's "Over There." The altered lyrics encouraged Greek American doughboys to plant the Greek flag on Agia Sofia in Constantinople (Frangos 1994, 50–51).

1918–1933

The turmoil, loss, and tumultuous energy of the era from 1918 to 1933 can be heard in the music created or consumed by Greek immigrants. The end of World War I marked the triumph of American aspirations. Offsetting the Allied victory in Europe, the burning of Smyrna and the expulsion of indigenous Greek populations from Asia Minor in 1922 signaled the end of most ambitions for a greater Greece. Nevertheless, Greek musicians in North America realized that they had a relative freedom of cultural expression that was not permitted in the Old World (Gauntlett 2003, 29). Coupled with the relative wealth that American Greeks enjoyed, it made them a major audience for the arts—one that consumed records more than most other ethnic groups in the United States.

Several events marked the establishment of a major American market for Greek music. By the early 1900s, advertisements in Greek and American magazines showcased imported Greek 78-rpm records. The growing demand also

Figure 6. Picnic with a phonograph in Gary, Indiana, 1930. Photo by Basil Hatziminas. Courtesy of Stavros K. Frangos.

was demonstrated by the appearance of sheet music, beginning with musician Spyros Becatoros's 1914 collection. In 1920, the nationally distributed newspaper *Atlantis* published *Terpsichori*, a Greek sheet music album. Founded in 1923, the Apollo Music Publishing Company of New York City would issue sheet music for decades to come. Sheet music was consumed by those providing entertainment for picnics, theatricals, and informal home gatherings, as well as by choirs and musicians.

The QRS Music Company of Chicago remained the major provider of Greek piano rolls. In 1923, they issued a separate Greek catalog with light classical, contemporary, and popular music. They offered traditional songs such as "O gero Dimos," "Maria Pentagiotisa," and "Kato sto yialo," as well as patriotic marches. The Hellenic Phonograph Company, under the trademark Alector, also issued piano rolls.

Immigrants soon established independent Greek record companies. The Panhellenion Phonograph Record Company was founded by laouto player Andreas Antonopoulos (d. 1927) and his wife Kyriaki in New York in 1919 (Frangos 2007a). Violinist George Grachis and santouri and cimbalom player Spyros Stamos (1894–1973) owned Chicago's Greek Record Company, which was

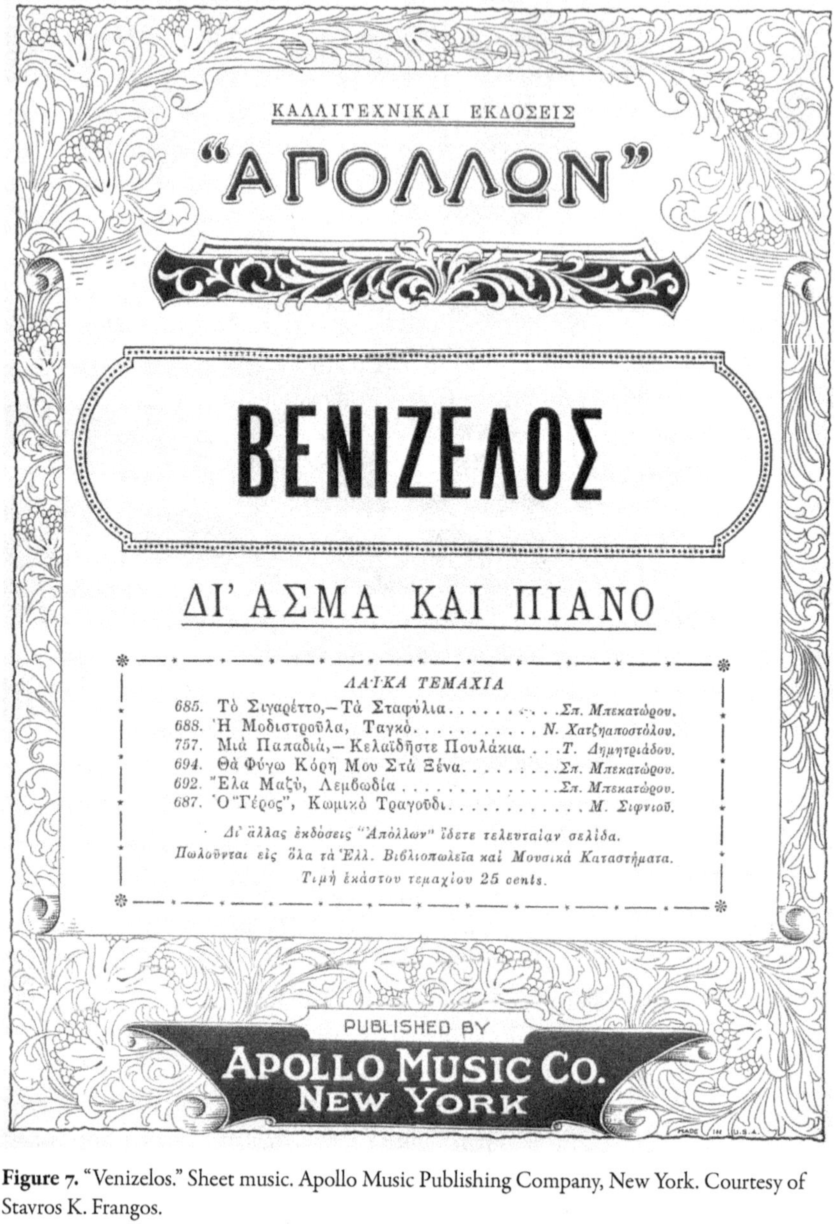

Figure 7. "Venizelos." Sheet music. Apollo Music Publishing Company, New York. Courtesy of Stavros K. Frangos.

Figure 8. Theodotos "Tetos" Demetriades (1897–1971), "Misirlou," 1927. Columbia 56073F. Courtesy of Meletios Pouliopoulos.

established in 1922–1923. In addition, the Greek Musicians' Union of America formed in New York in 1921.

Music released during these years consisted of traditional and popular songs, serenades, songs from operas and operettas, comical pieces, and religious music. Record companies, performers, and promoters often targeted specific niches within the broader collective of diaspora Greeks through performances of different regional genres. Perhaps the most widely known Greek song of the era, "Misirlou," was copyrighted by immigrant musician Nicholas Roubanis in 1927, and Tetos Demetriades made the first recording in the same year. In addition, newly composed songs commented on American social realities such as the Roaring Twenties. In the 1927 sensation "To cigaretto" (The Cigarette), Tassia Demetriades sang about doing as she pleased, bobbing her hair, and smoking in public (*Discography of American Historical Recordings*).

By 1925, Marika and Gus Papagikas had opened a nightclub in New York on West Thirty-Fourth Street near Eighth Avenue. Marika's was arguably the first multinational café aman in the United States. Greek music shared many characteristics with Balkan and Middle Eastern musical traditions, so the establishment attracted not only Greek patrons but also Albanians, Arabs, Armenians, Bulgarians, and Turks. Moreover, the musicians who have played in Greek music ensembles past and present have never solely been Greek—they have frequently

Figure 9. Marika Papagika (1890–1943), "Armenaki," 1926. Greek Record Company, 511-B. Courtesy of Meletios Pouliopoulos.

included Armenians, Sephardic Jews, Macedonians, and Albanians. In her club, Marika Papagika was known for singing the traditional song "Armenaki" with mixed Greek and Armenian lyrics.[10]

Singer, orchestra leader, and record company executive Theodotos "Tetos" Demetriades (1897–1971) had a major impact on Greek music. Originally from Constantinople, he became the director of RCA Victor Orthophonic's International Division. From March 1930 through December 1931 he made more than two hundred recordings in Greece, focusing on instrumentalists and singers from Asia Minor and Athens, including Roza Eskenazi, Rita Abatzi, Antonis Diamantidis (Dalgas), and many others. The recordings not only made the performers household names in America, they also showcased musical genres and mixed language lyrics, gypsy musicians, and topics such as drug use and free love that were marginalized in Greece. Acutely attuned to niche markets in America, Demetriades carefully crafted records to appeal to wide audiences—often by combining a song from one genre on the first side of a record with one from another on the reverse.[11] He also translated popular American songs to fit Greek sensibilities.

In Columbia Records' New York studios in January 1932, Ioannis Halikias (Jack Gregory) recorded two bouzouki instrumentals with Sophocles Mikelides accompanying on guitar: "To mistirio" and "Minore tou teke." In 1933 he recorded "Raste tou teke" and "Mourmouriko." Not only were these the first

Figure 10. Jack Gregory (Ioannis Halikias) and Sophocles Mikelides, "Minore tou teke," 1932. Columbia 56294F. Courtesy of Meletios Pouliopoulos.

widely popular recordings of bouzouki in Greece and America, but Halikias's musical interpretation became a significant influence on music subsequently recorded in Greece.

1933–1945

Music of the interwar era resounded with the deep uncertainties plaguing Greek Americans. Half of those who journeyed to America had already returned to Greece. Among those who remained, only half ever married—resulting in predominately male communities. Some expressed dismay with the Great Depression by rejecting the obligations of everyday life and turning toward hedonism. Their lifestyle, filled with gambling, drinking, and a desire for freedom from responsibility, was given voice on commercial records. The genre most associated with this lifestyle was rebetika, and songs that typified it included "Mes' ton teke tis Marigos" (At Marigo's Teke, 1934) by Takis Nicolaou (aka Tetos Demetriades) and "Oli mera pezei zaria" (All Day Playing Dice, 1928) and "O Vangelis o bekris" (Vangelis the Drunk, 1938) by George Katsaros (1888–1997).

Figure 11. Takis Nicolaou (aka Tetos Demetriades), "Mes' ton teke tis Marigos," 1934. Orthophonic S-344-A. Courtesy of Meletios Pouliopoulos.

Figure 12. George Katsaros, "Mana mou ime fthisikos," 1935. Columbia 56358-Fl. Courtesy of Meletios Pouliopoulos.

The loss of their homeland and exile to the xenitia, as recorded on dozens of records by Asia Minor Greeks, found a ready market outside Greece. The common experience of exile linked all diaspora Greeks and contributed to the widespread popularity of the genre. Often, songs of xenitia were coupled with those commenting on other social problems. The ravaging illnesses of tuberculosis and black lung experienced by Greeks, some of whom labored in American mines under harsh conditions, were so prevalent that they generated songs by noted performers of the day, such as Katsaros's "Mana mou eimai fthisikos" (Mother Mine, I Am Sick, 1935).

Other songs of the era dealt with returning to Greece in hopes of escaping the deepening American economic crisis. Simultaneously, music hall–style songs recorded in Greece spoke of the arrival and unexpected trials experienced by those who returned. Although they fled an American society by which they felt rejected, many returnees found that they no longer fit into Greek society.[12]

By the end of the 1920s, it was nearly impossible to find someone without access to a radio. In the 1930s, far from being ignored, immigrant groups listened to their traditional music and sometimes music hall–style entertainment on the radio. In metropolitan areas, Greek Hour radio programs broadcast regularly. Aside from music, the programs were extremely popular—especially during the war years—as the only local, national, and international news source for an audience often monolingual in Greek or illiterate and thus unable to read newspapers.

Amateur vocalists and traditional musicians were scattered throughout Greek America, but weddings, baptisms, and holidays often required the services of professional musicians who toured the nation. Whether the musicians were brought by individual café owners or the widespread circuit of Greek promoters, Greek communities large and small were rarely without music. During the 1920s and 1930s, Greek American promoters and owners of candy stores, movie theaters, amusement parks, and vaudeville houses provided entertainment for American and Greek audiences across the country.[13]

Among the foremost touring artists of the era were Spyros Becatoros (violin), Mme. Koula (vocalist), Konstantinos Filis (clarinet), Gus Gadinis (clarinet), John K. Gianaros (accordion), George Grachis (violin), George Katsaros (guitar/vocals), Marika Papagika (vocals), Ioannis Sfondilias (santouri), and many others. In addition to cafés and local church events, musicians and singers performed at Greek resorts, such as the Sunset Springs Hotel in the Catskill Mountains (Gianaros 1986).

In January 1930, members of the premier Greek fraternal organizations, the Greek American Progressive Association (GAPA) and the American Hellenic Educational Progressive Association (AHEPA), visited Greece via organized excursions. While the express purpose of the predominately male members was to honor the enduring bonds between Greece and America, for many the real

Figure 13. "Mi me stelnis manna," 1936. Sheet music. Apollo Music Publishing Company, New York. Courtesy of Stavros K. Frangos.

Figure 14. Fotis Argyropoulos and D. Zatta, "Vre Mourgo Mousolini," January 20, 1942. Sheet music. Orthophonic S-577/Colonial Music. Courtesy of Stavros K. Frangos.

purpose was to find brides. This practice, often referred to as the pursuit of "picture brides," generated mixed emotions. Songs produced in Greece, such, as "Mi me stelnis mana stin Ameriki" (Mother, Please Don't Send Me to America, 1934), written by violin virtuoso Dimitrios Semsis and sung by Rita Abatzi, rejected and lampooned the returnees. The song was so popular that many artists in the United States recorded it.

As World War II engulfed Greece, Greek Americans rallied as never before. The Greek military repelled the Italian invasion of Greece begun on October 28, 1940, but were eventually defeated by the German army in April 1941. Archbishop Athenagoras's call for a Greek war relief effort was answered by thousands of Greek Americans. Their war rallies, home relief work, and sales of war bonds were occasions for music and dance. Anti-Axis songs recorded in Greece, such as "Koroido Mussolini" (1940) by Nikos Gounaris and "Pedia tis Ellados pedia" (Children of Greece, 1940) by famed singer Sofia Vembo (1910–1978), were played on many such occasions. Accompanying sheet music was released by American companies such as Colonial Music Publishing.

1945–1960

The devastation wreaked by World War II and the Greek Civil War precipitated a second wave of Greek immigration. Between 1947 and 1965, an estimated seventy-five thousand Greek immigrants arrived legally on American shores (Moskos 1989, 156). In addition, more than thirty thousand Greek sailors jumped ship from 1957 through 1974 (Moskos 1989, 55).[14]

Recordings after World War II reflected a wide range of musical tastes, but the popularity of traditional music (dimotika) and European forms such as the tango, foxtrot, and *roumba* expanded greatly. Liberty Records in New York City was the largest independent Greek record company. Among their earliest releases were recordings of *mandolinata* (mandolin bands) performing traditional and European music. In 1955, the release of "To bouzouki stin Ameriki," performed by Nikos Pourpourakis (bouzouki) and Thodoros Kavourakis (vocals), signaled the escalating importance of the instrument in America. And, as they had for decades, artists released works that combined Greek and American musical forms—such as the swing version of the traditional kalamatianos, "Tria pedia voliotika" (Attikon 452-B, Chicago, ca. 1948),[15] sung by Nikos Gounaris with John Raptis and his Aragon Orchestra.

Although the technology to produce long-playing record albums (LPs) became available in 1948, the first major Greek LPs appeared in the late 1950s. Many of the first albums were simply compilations of previously released 78-rpm records. Eventually, Greek promoters and musicians based in the United States

Figure 15. Pan-Hellenic Mandolinata, Ipswich, Massachusetts, late 1940; the ensemble performed from the late 1940s to the mid-1950s. Left to right, James George (mandolin), Spiros Aloupis (banjo and mandolin), Fotis Sotiropoulos (mandolin), William Kokoras (accordion), Arthur Sotis (guitar), and Andrew Giannakakis (drums). Courtesy of Spiros Aloupis and Meletios Pouliopoulos.

Figure 16. Nikos Pourpourakis, New York City, ca. 1953. Press photo by Acropolis, New York. Courtesy of Meletios Pouliopoulos.

Figure 17. Nikos Gounaris, and John Raptis and his Aragon Orchestra, "Tria pedia voliotika." Attikon 452-B. Courtesy of Meletios Pouliopoulos.

began to release a flood of new music ranging from the traditional to the modern. Producers embraced the "concept album" format, with songs bound together by a single theme. Striking album covers sometimes turned bland records into best sellers, while poorly designed ones could doom outstanding music to oblivion. Liner notes, which were developed during this period, are sometimes the only information available regarding artists, companies, promoters, or clubs.

The first Greek-owned company to release an LP was the Nina Record Company in New York, founded by George Valavanis. He and the company's second owner, guitarist/vocalist Nicos Tseperis (1923–2010), brought musicians from Greece to record. The musicians then played in the New York clubs. Nina's rival and musical opposite was New York's Liberty Records, which specialized in traditional musicians and genres. Sofia Vembo, whose repertoire included island music, was the most popular Greek vocalist on early Liberty LPs. In time, both Nina and Liberty began to release whatever genres and artists would attract a buying public. Nina issued *Festival in Greece* (1959) and the compilation *Mysteries of Eleusis*. Early Liberty LPs included *A Night in a Greek Tavern* and *The Songs of Eva Styl*. Similarly, Demetriades recorded the musicians playing in New York clubs on his Colonial label. He also released LPs with music from Greece, sing-along albums, and compilations of unreleased recordings from the 1930s.

Numerous other labels emerged. Steve Zembillas founded Grecophon Records, based in Gary, Indiana, and initially recorded island music (*nisiotika*). Zembillas and his wife hailed from Tarpon Springs, Florida, and he began by making recordings at his studio near the Sponge Docks before moving north (Galoozis 2016; Ioannidis 2016).[16] Later, he expanded to include rebetika and artists such as guitarist/vocalist George Katsaros, guitarist/vocalist Mitsakis Orfanidis, and Cretan lyra player Harilaos Piperakis. In New York, Metropolitan Records recorded Virginia Magkidou singing Asia Minor songs with Markos Melkon on *outi*, Nikos D. (Nick Doneff) on violin, and Theodoros Kappas on *kanonaki*. An Armenian from Smyrna, Melkon also sang Asia Minor–style songs in Greek, Turkish, and Armenian.

Venues

During the postwar era, music was presented in a range of venues. *Horoesperides*, variety shows with music and dancing, were popular in Greek communities. Cultural and fraternal organizations held regular dances and outdoor picnics that featured live music, such as that of Chicago's Zakynthos Brotherhood in November 1959. Hotels and music venues such as Chicago's Aragon Ballroom presented popular Greek nights. Several resort hotels in the Catskills, such as the Greek-owned Sunset Springs Hotel and the Monte Carlo Hotel, hosted music and dance programs with acclaimed vocalists and musicians (Belasco 1954; Karras n.d.).

Greek nightclubs emerged from the *tavernas* that had long featured various forms of entertainment. The dominant club music was bouzouki-based, although some clubs would set aside a period for visiting musicians to play their own styles and genres (Georgakas 1987, 17). In New York City, clubs were concentrated in a few blocks along Eighth Avenue. Among the most popular were the Port Said Café, Britania Café, Egyptian Gardens Café, Ali Baba, and Grecian Palace Café. They usually operated until 1:00 a.m. but often stayed open all night for private parties. In addition, hotel shows sometimes offered Greek music. Shows frequently featured two bands: one playing Greek, ballroom, and international music and another playing exclusively Greek music. On March 8, 1953, for example, Roza Eskenazi and Agapios Tomboulis appeared with Virginia Magkidou and the Kalos Diskos Orchestra at New York's Capitol Hotel—in addition to the John Degaïtas Orchestra playing Greek, American, and Spanish dance music.

The reach of the Greek American acoustic communities was extended via the media of the day. Greek radio programs proliferated in all major metropolitan areas and presented the latest recorded music. In the 1940s, many radio stations had house orchestras that not only performed sets but also provided background

Figure 18. Greek orchestra at the Port Said Café, 257 West Twenty-Ninth Street, just east of Eighth Avenue, New York City, 1959. Tasos Sofopoulos (bouzouki) and Nikos Doneff (violin). Photo by Demetrios Kesoglides. Retrieved from the Library of Congress, at https://www.loc.gov/item/2005691943/.

music during the announcements. Audiences also experienced Greek music in restaurants, clubs, bars, and sweet shops through jukeboxes. In 1959, *Billboard* magazine reported an increasing demand for foreign-language records in Gary, Indiana, with Rena Dalia and Michalis Thomakos among the most popular Greek artists on the jukeboxes (Klein 1959).

Artists

In the 1950s, bouzouki music became the dominant form in Greek nightclubs. Popular bouzouki players who performed in the clubs, recorded, and toured nationally included Giannis Papaioannou (1913–1972) and Giannis Tatasopoulos (1928–2001), who recorded on Nina, and Nikos Pourpourakis on Kalos Diskos.

Celebrated musicians included those with long histories in America as well as recent arrivals. Among those popular during the early 1950s were violin players Nick Doneff (Nikos D.), Antonis Loris, and Andreas Poggis; accordion players John K. Gianaros and Demetris Frantzeskakis; and clarinet players Kostas (Gus) Gadinis, Peter Mamakos, and Kostas Sevastakis. Nikos Gounaris (1915–1965), Nicos Tseperis, and Eleni Bartseri were noted singers.

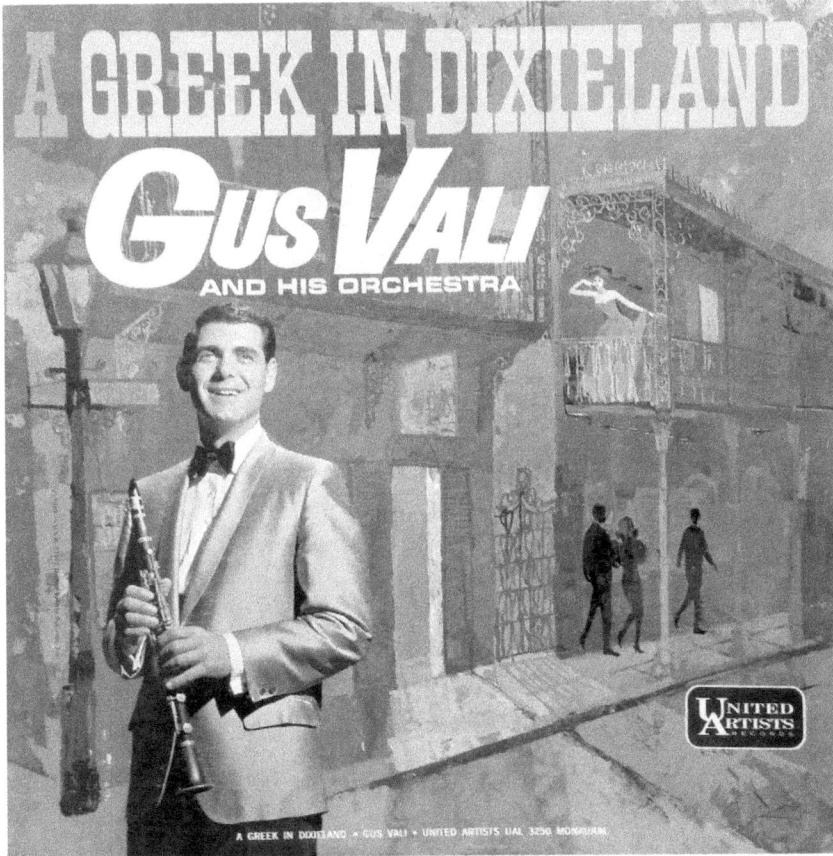

Figure 19. Gus Vali and His Orchestra, *A Greek in Dixieland*. United Artists, 1962. Courtesy of Meletios Pouliopoulos.

In 1958, Greek American clarinetist and orchestra leader Gus Vali recorded the first Greek LP on a major label, *The Greeks Had a Song for It* (United Artists), with the popular Greek folk singer Milton (Miltiades) Stamos. Vali's parents were from Asia Minor, and he grew up in New York. As a young man, he performed in some of the most popular big bands of the time, such as those of Artie Shaw and Louis Prima. In the late 1950s, he established a band with musicians Luis Barreiro, Chet Amsterdam, John Yalenzian, and Norman Gold, which played Greek, American, Middle Eastern, and fusion dance music. Their 1962 LP *A Greek in Dixieland* devoted one side to such standards as "Saint James Infirmary" and "When the Saints Go Marching In." Vali and his orchestra enjoyed great popularity and played at major events for more than a decade.

Figure 20. *Never on Sunday.* United Artists, 1960. Original soundtrack music. Courtesy of Stavros K. Frangos.

1960–1975

With the passage of the Immigration and Nationality (Hart-Celler) Act in 1965, the United States eliminated quotas on European immigrants, generating a stream of 160,000 new arrivals from Greece between 1966 and 1979 (Moskos 1989, 156). At the same time, Americans developed a renewed interest in their various ethnicities—resulting in a recharged sense of identity among Greek Americans of the 1960s and 1970s. Most Greeks in America opposed CIA support of the 1967 Greek military junta and the 1974 invasion of Cyprus by the Turkish military. Despite common causes, differences between the newcomers and long-established Greek Americans were sometimes reflected in musical preferences and the places they gathered to hear music. Often, the recent immigrants took control of fraternal organizations, while churches remained the bastion of established diaspora communities.

Figure 21. Louis Fatimus Orchestra, ca. 1961. Fatimus is playing bouzouki on the right. Courtesy of Frances Fatimus Mastorides.

In the 1960s, new forms of instrumental music, song styles, and dance emerged. *Laïko*, a type of urban traditional music with an orientalized style, was popular during the 1950s and 1960s. A lighter version, *elafro laïko*, was performed in musicals and restaurants. *Entechno laïko*, or art music infused with folk rhythms and melodies, surfaced in the late 1950s. By the 1960s, films featured soundtracks by entechno composers such as Manos Hadjidakis (*Never on Sunday*, 1960) and Mikis Theodorakis (*Zorba the Greek*, 1964). Before *Never on Sunday* became a major box office hit, few Americans were familiar with bouzouki music. *Zorba the Greek* was so popular that a musical version opened on Broadway in 1968 and was revived in 1983. Extensive national tours showcased music interpreted by skilled bouzouki player Fotis Gonis, who specialized in *elafro laïko*.

Another popular musical form consisted of trios with a sound that fused Latin American trio and early twentieth-century Ionian Islands *kantada* styles. Trio Kitara and Trio Bel Canto were widely popular with American audiences during the 1960s. Already established in Greece, Trio Kitara did some of their best work in the United States, including four LPs—the first three with piano and accordion accompaniment and the last with bouzouki. Trio Bel Canto, the most sought-after Greek vocal band of the 1960s, performed music popular in Greece for American audiences. Celebrated singer Nikos Gounaris performed with them during the early years, and they later recorded with the George Stratis

Figure 22. Panayiotis Haliyannis (1935–2013).
Courtesy of Meletios Pouliopoulos.

Orchestra. In 1971, Michael Matheos left and was replaced by the brilliant bouzouki player Takis Elenis.

Bouzouki-based popular music dominated the 1960s—to the extent that a
severe shortage of bouzouki players was reported in the press in 1961.[17] However, Greek American audiences still wanted to hear traditional music. Thus,
many orchestras included both bouzouki and clarinet musicians. For example,
bouzouki virtuoso Manolis Hiotis and singer Mary Linda toured America and
recorded for Grecophon. Hiotis not only pioneered a new bouzouki sound by
adding a fourth set of strings, but he and Linda also brought a modern sensibility
to the music. Yet, to please American audiences, they continued to perform traditional songs during live performances. Trio Bel Canto also added reinterpreta-
tions of folk standards to their repertoire.

In addition to nationally and internationally known bands, dozens of local and
regional groups performed during every era. Outstanding regional groups of this
time included the Louis Fatimus Orchestra (Ohio, Pennsylvania), the Greek Lads
(Chicago), the Grecian Lads (Ohio), the Kastorians (Chicago and Indiana, who
sang in Greek and Macedonian), the Grecian Keys (Ohio and New England),
the Chris Kalogerson Orchestra (Minnesota), and Meraklides, T'Adelphia, and
Apollo's Children (California). In Los Angeles, celebrated Armenian violinist
Hrach Yacoubian led a widely popular orchestra that played Greek, Armenian,
Middle Eastern, and classical pieces from the 1950s to the 1980s.

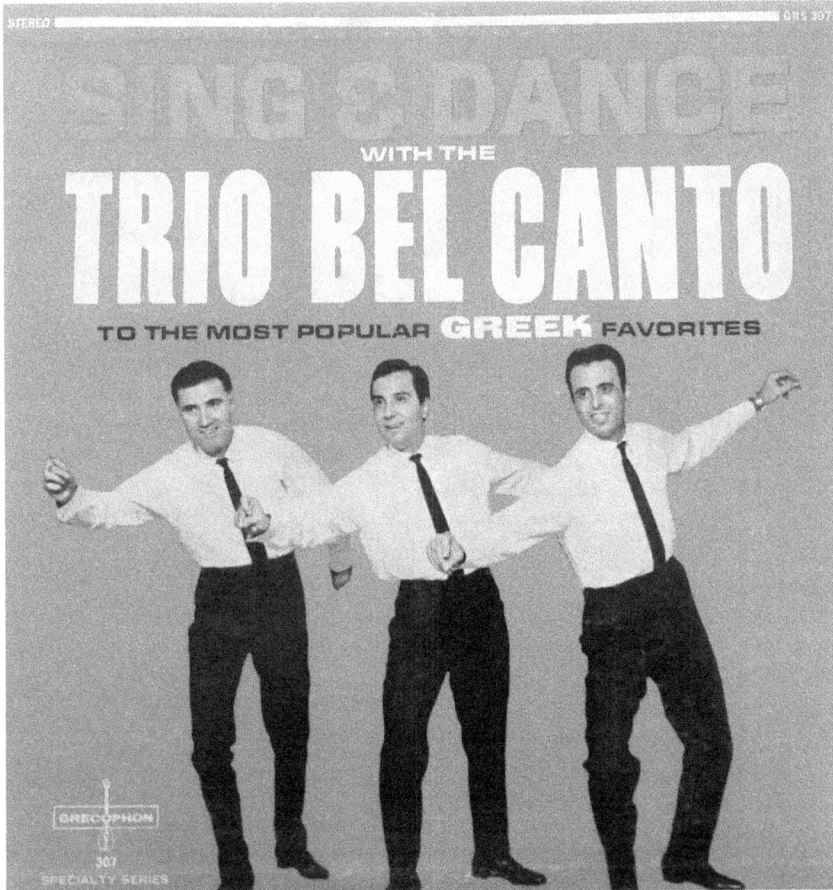

Figure 23. *Sing and Dance with the Trio Bel Canto*, 1966. Courtesy of Meletios Pouliopoulos.

The record industry underwent significant changes. While earlier recordings were predominantly folk music with a variety of instruments, later ones focused on popular bouzouki music. In the early to mid-1960s, Demetriades's Colonial and Standard record labels produced LPs featuring New York regulars such as clarinetist Panayiotis Haliyannis, as well as sing-along and dance-along albums appealing to Greek Americans and others. Popular dance albums included *Diplopennies* (The Greeks Have a Dance For It, 1965), *Dance the Greek Lads* (1967), and *Sing and Dance with the Trio Bel Canto* (1966). Alector Records released the acclaimed *Greek Town USA* albums, showcasing the bouzouki of Dimitris "Bebis" Stergiou and Tassos Halkias on clarinet, as well as *Concerto for Bouzoukee* with Anestos "Gyftos" Athanasiou and singer Anna Chrysafi. Still the largest independent company in the Greek American market, Liberty's Fiesta and Grecophon labels featured Trio Bel Canto, Nikos Gounaris, Manolis Hiotis, and

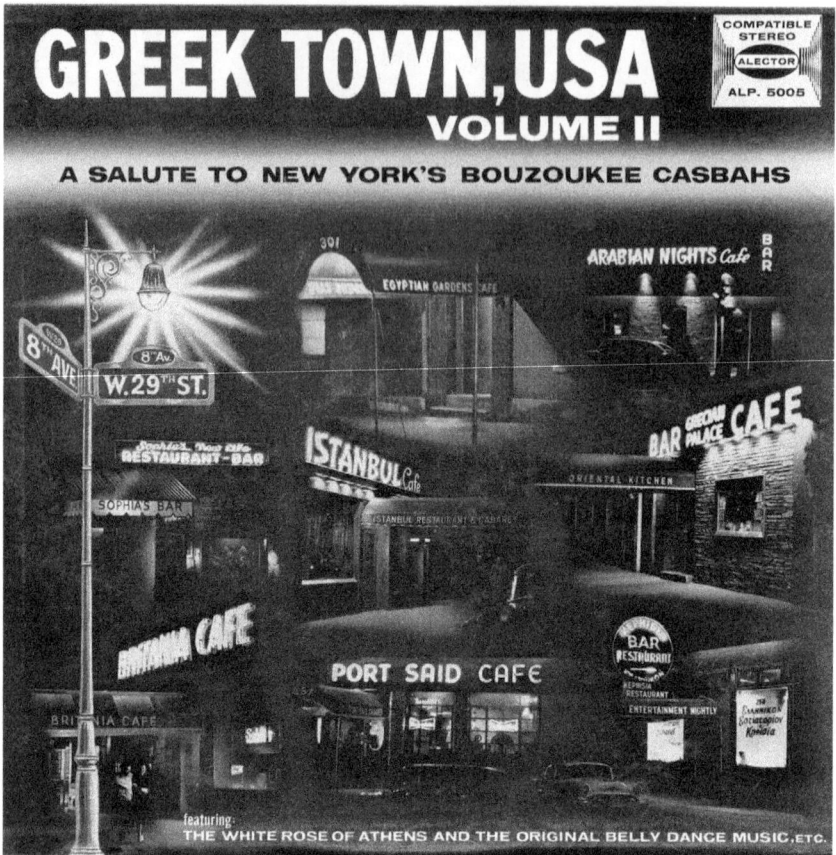

Figure 24. Bebis Stergiou and the Alector Anatolian Ensemble, *Greek Town USA*, vol. 2: *A Salute to New York's Bouzoukee Casbahs*, 1960. Alector ALP 5005. Courtesy of Meletios Pouliopoulos.

Mary Linda. Nina Records also specialized in recording visiting Greek artists. Peters International bought as many Greek record labels as they could and subsequently issued Greek, Turkish, and Balkan LPs.

Songs like "Misirlou" and "Never on Sunday" became as much a part of 1960s American pop music as the Greek nightclub scene. "Misirlou" was widely featured in albums of many genres. Lebanese American guitarist Dick Dale's classic 1963 surf rock version was enormously influential, inspiring performers throughout the world and in Greece—as illustrated by the note-for-note guitar rendition with vocals by pop star Anna Vissi at the 2004 Summer Olympics in Athens.[18] "Never on Sunday" was recorded by Eartha Kitt, Bing Crosby, Lena Horne, Doris Day, Andy Williams, Connie Francis, Herb Alpert, the Ventures, and a plethora of other American artists.

There was a resurgence of the Greektown club scene across America. The hit motion pictures *Never on Sunday* (1960), *Zorba the Greek* (1964), and *Z* (1969) generated strong mainstream interest in Greek food, music, and clubs. Greeks continued to frequent the clubs and restaurants to hear bouzouki and clarinet, and the growing popularity among American audiences created more work for musicians. *Bouzoukia* (Greek nightclubs) offered several different genres of Greek music. Many included traditional music geared toward participatory dance, but celebrity vocalists singing Europeanized songs were the primary draw. Although some scholars believe that rebetika died out during this era, in actual practice it was simply incorporated into the varied repertoire of dance bands and performed in an updated style.[19] In addition, belly dancers were a popular attraction who appealed to both American and Greek audiences, and to accompany their performances bands played long, improvisational pieces with a Turkish flavor.

1975–1990

Modern *laïka* emerged as an urban style in the early 1980s and became the predominant popular Greek musical style. Many songs were sentimental ballads with rock and folk instrumentation, sometimes similar to Western dance pop. Laïka is often associated with nightclub performances, and the main dances accompanying it are *tsifteteli*, *zeibekiko*, and *hasapiko*.

By 1975, a significant quantity of music was imported from Greece via albums pressed there or recordings made in Greece and pressed in America. Grecophon Records and Peters International started releasing albums recorded in Greece. Recent immigrants were the primary consumers of this type of music. Peters also was among the first to provide Greek satellite/cable television and sell Greek VHS videos in the United States.

As indicated by their numbers, American-based companies such as Liberty, Nina, Peters International (later Odeon-Peters International), Fiesta, Standard, Ariston, Attikon, Flogera, Panhellenic, Alpha, Hellas, and Balkan (which issued subtitled specialty labels like Metropolitan and Me-Re) maintained strong sales in the Greek record market. They continued to release recordings that appealed to the divergent musical tastes of the regional communities.

When the Greek military junta ruled from 1967 to 1974, the music of Mikis Theodorakis gained enormous popularity as a form of protest against the dictatorship. In addition, there was a revival of rebetika in its many forms—from *mikrasiatika* (music of Asia Minor) to *peraiotika* (music from Piraeus) to the postwar music of musician/composer Vassilis Tsitsanis (1915–1984), who was instrumental in transforming the genre by connecting it to modern music. With

Figure 25. Freddy Elias Ensemble with Nick Kokoras, George Kokoras, Arthur Chingras, and Richard Bayrouty. Courtesy of Meletios Pouliopoulos.

its rebellious lyrics, rebetika was perceived as a way to express opposition to the repressive regime.

Exceptional Greek American musicians and vocalists entertained tens of thousands over many years—each bringing his or her own distinctive mélange to the music scene. The most famous recording band of the 1960s, Trio Bel Canto, became the most popular touring band of the 1970s and 1980s. In addition to their contemporary hits, they integrated traditional standards into their repertoire. Gus Vali included elements from American idioms such as jazz into his style, and he sometimes alternated Greek and American songs in performances. In New York and then Washington, DC, Greek-born Giannis (John) Tatasopoulos was a stellar bouzouki musician and composer. He not only performed Greek music but also melded it with Latin rhythms and Middle Eastern music. In the latter instance, he often played with Greek American musicians George Kokoras, Nick Kokoras, and Arthur Chingras, and with the great Lebanese American violinist Fred Elias. Younger musicians who played at clubs and events, such as bouzouki prodigy George Soffos, began to incorporate rock and roll elements during this era. Takis Elenis dazzled audiences with performances that drew inspiration from sources that included jazz, rock and roll, flamenco, and Indian music. Other outstanding bouzouki players, such as Alekos Galas, began

Figure 26. Apollo's Children, San Francisco, ca. 1975. Ari Harmandas (guitar), Panos Lemonidis (drums), and George Soffos (bouzouki). Courtesy of Tina Bucuvalas.

Greek Music Tour
Sponsored by the National Endowment for the Arts and the Ethnic Folk Arts Center
Winter 1982 – Spring 1983

Figure 27. Greek Music Tour. Sponsored by the National Endowment for the Arts, the Ethnic Folk Arts Center, and the Greek Ministry of Culture. Winter 1982– Spring 1983. Courtesy of Tina Bucuvalas.

their careers performing in Greek clubs, but their music gradually evolved into a jazz/Greek fusion directed to wider audiences. Most instruments were amplified, and musicians experimented with the wah-wah pedal and other electronica.

Traditional music was sustained by various Greek societies, folk dance troupes, and traditional musicians—in fact, diaspora musicians sometimes preserved older musical forms that had changed in Greece (Georgakas 1987, 18). Regional organizations held regular dances, which stepped up the demand for traditional music. Often they hired musicians based in the United States, but sometimes they invited notable bands and dance troupes from their regions of origin. The Greek Music Tour, sponsored by the National Endowment for the Arts, Ethnic Folk Arts Center, and Greek Ministry of Culture, presented concerts by outstanding musicians in ten major cities during 1982–1983. Among the participating American-based musicians were the Halkias Family Orchestra playing *epirotika*; outi player Kostas Kamanis from Chios; Pontian lyra player Ilias Kementzides; Cretan lyra player Kostas Maris and laouto player Antonios Kokonas; and Sotirios (Sam) Chianis on santouri and cimbalom.

Venues

Greek churches and societies continued to hold regular dances with live bands, but the picnics generally gave way to large Greek festivals that served as fundraisers for them. These events offered the mainstream public a chance to enjoy Greek food, music, and dance performances by local troupes, and to buy imported items. Bands usually were hired for several days and played a repertoire of popular hits combined with local favorites.

Greek nightclubs continued to flourish in major metropolitan areas. Bouzouki bands, often with two lead players, frequently played traditional mainland and island music, as well as laïka. Although belly dance performances lingered, they were no longer the same focal point as in previous decades. Even when many clubs started to cater more to American tastes, there were a few that featured primarily traditional or avant-garde Greek music (Georgakas 1987, 17–18). Among the major New York–area clubs of this era were Molfetas in New Jersey and the Grecian Cave and Skorpios in Astoria, New York.

New York seems to have been the primary locale where small, intimate music clubs called *boites* flourished. Mirroring a trend in Greece, they offered an "informal sing along atmosphere, high quality, natural sounds that do not pierce your eardrums played on authentic, non-electric instruments, meaningful lyrics and high quality ear-pleasing melodies" that appealed to young people of the era (Maninakis 2009). From 1979 to the early 2000s, places like Mikrokosmos and Acroama Boite in Astoria and Thiasos in Manhattan featured a repertoire of predominantly entechno, rebetika, and some regional and political protest songs.

Figure 28. Deni's Den Ensemble, Chicago, 1981. George Papadatos (drums), Vasilios Gaitanos (piano and vocals), Vasilis Roussis (bass guitar), and Alekos Galas (bouzouki). Photo by Mark Mamalakis for the album *Vasilios Gaitanos Sings*, VAM Records, 1981. Courtesy of Meletios Pouliopoulos.

On the West Coast, entertainer Lewis Gundunas's Balkan Village in Los Altos attracted crowds that included many celebrities. The Greek Village and Athenian Gardens were important stops in Los Angeles, as was the Mad Greek in La Jolla. These clubs were patronized not only by Greeks but also by members of the local Armenian and Jewish communities. In Los Angeles, dancer and Loyola Marymount University professor Athan Karras (1927–2010) helped popularize Greek dance and music through university classes, theater, festivals, dance camp classes, and the international folk dance movement. His club, Intersection, was an international folk dance institution for two decades.

With its large Greek community, Chicago supported a thriving music scene. Singer Deni Dimitreas established Deni's Den around 1968, and it became the artistic hub of those who opposed the junta in Greece and the Turkish invasion of Cyprus. The club regularly brought musicians from Greece and around the United States, such as Vasilios Gaitanos, who offered a mix of traditional songs, choral singing, modern pop hits, and entechno. In the early days, Deni's Den also offered lectures, poetry readings, and discussions on cultural topics. Chicago's Greektown boasted large bouzouki clubs and restaurants catering to dancers, such as Neon Greek Village, as well as sophisticated restaurant/clubs featuring entechno. Audiences comprised Greeks and Greek Americans along with other admirers of Greek food and music.

Figure 29. Amalia Baka, *Amalia! Old Greek Songs in the New Land, 1923–1950*, 2002. With Markos Melkon, Alexis Zoumbas, Gus Gadinis, and John Pappas. Arhoolie ARHCD 7049. Courtesy of Meletios Pouliopoulos.

1990–2015

In the 1990s, the live presentation of Greek music underwent a major shift. Many who had left inner-city communities turned increasingly to American music or became less familiar with Greek music. As demand decreased, the number of bouzoukia also diminished—and, with them, jobs for musicians. Clubs and restaurants often switched to "Greek Nights," offering live Greek music only one or two nights each week. In order to survive, most bands changed their focus from clubs to events such as festivals, weddings, baptisms, and dinner dances.

Times became difficult for working musicians who, in the past, had counted on performances for their income. As their compensation decreased along with

1. Ali Pasha
2. Kala Kalaya Bakar
3. T' Asteri To Lambro
4. I Thalassa
5. Apo Mikros Stin Xenitia
6. Paramana Cuna Cuna
7. Haido Syrto
8. Pes Mou Ti Tha Katalavis
9. I Vlaha I Emorfi
10. Thelo Na S'Alismoniso
11. Agrilamas ke Psarades

12. Horis Elpida Na Zo
13. Apo Ta Mikra Mou Hronia
14. To Mnima Mou Hortariase
15. Mavromata
16. Smyrneikos Balos
17. Den Mou Lete Ti Na Kamo
18. Mi Me Dernis Mana
19. Ego Yia Sena Tragoudo
20. Tora Ta Poulia
21. Smyrneiko Majore

demand, so did the number of musicians in Greek bands. Keyboards often replaced the rhythm section (guitar, bass, drums) and lead instruments like the clarinet. Bands that once performed as a four- or five-piece orchestra were reduced to three pieces. The tradition of throwing money to show appreciation for the band, singer, or dancers—once a major source of income for musicians—became less frequent and could not be relied upon as a steady source of income. With an inherent versatility that allowed them to play a variety of music on demand, including American and the latest Western-influenced Greek pop, disc jockeys co-opted many of the gigs that previously required live music.

As Kip Lornell and Anne Rasmussen observed, "It is difficult to overstate the impact of twenty-first-century digitally based media on the flow of music,

Figure 30. Alexis Zoumbas, *A Lament for Epirus, 1926–1928*, 2014.
Cover art by R. Crumb. Angry Mom AMA-004. Courtesy of Angry
Mom Phonograph Record Company and Meletios Poulioupoulos.

because such technology enables not only the broadcasting of music but also communicating about music among musicians and their publics. YouTube.com helped revolutionize the ability to post all sorts of video material, from archival historic recordings to entire 'channels' devoted to artists" (Lornell and Rasmussen 2016, 8). Indeed, the digital age and the advent of CDs, mp3s, and the Internet dramatically changed the Greek music industry. Consumers readily duplicated CDs at home, and the mp3 format allowed sound files to be compressed and easily distributed over the Internet. In contrast with the early days, when major record companies sought top artists whose music would sell their records, musicians now can produce and sell their music with minimal investment. Broadcast radio stations were once the only way Greek communities could hear a wide variety of music, especially new releases. With the Internet, it became possible to listen to Greek music that was being broadcast in another part of the country or the world.

Technological advances drastically transformed the way that people experienced music. Through the 1960s, most homes had only one centrally located radio and phonograph player, so family and friends listened, and often sang or danced, together to the same music. With multiple digital music players in most modern homes and the ability to carry music with them, people now frequently listen to music individually and in separate spaces.[20]

Figure 31. Drómeno: Christos Govetas (*zournas*), Bobby Govetas (drums), and Eleni Govetas (*zournas*), Seattle, ca. 2014. Photo by Tom Marks Photography. Courtesy of Christos Govetas.

Despite the changes precipitated by shifts in technology and social structure, in recent decades there has been an increasing demand for older recordings of urban and regional music to be released in new formats. One example is Arhoolie's 2002 CD *Amalia! Old Greek Songs in the New Land, 1923–1950* (Amalia 2002); another is the 2014 CD of recordings by violinist Alexis Zoumbas from the period 1926–1928 (Zoumbas 2014), with a label design by R. Crumb based on Mme. Koula's Panhellenion labels. The demand is often fulfilled through postings of historical recordings on the Internet. Ironically, this music once denigrated by government officials and the social elite as criminal or "peasant" is now revered by Greeks of all status as among the most beautiful manifestations of the Greek spirit (King 2014; Petrusich 2014). Yet in actual practice, Greek traditional music has always maintained widespread popularity in the United States. Modern urban music, while popular, seldom attained the same level of demand as that for traditional music. Most often, contemporary dance bands perform a

Figure 32. Leonidas Zafiris and Elias Poulos teach a bouzouki workshop for the city of Tarpon Springs, 2013. Photo by Tina Bucuvalas.

mix of the two—although the composition of a particular audience determines which genres predominate.

Beginning in the late 1960s, there was a growing recognition that the Greek music produced in the United States, and/or imported for Greeks in America, constituted a unique body of art. Record collectors, academics, and even Greek government agencies issued vinyl LP, eight-track tape, and then CD compilations of Greek American recordings—sometimes without proper authorization. One such example is the Greek-produced CD *Port Said Café* with American-based musicians Giannis Tatasopoulos on bouzouki, violinist Fred Elias, George Kokoras on accordion and organ, guitarist Nick Kokoras, and percussionist Arthur Chingris (Tatassopoulos and Elias 1997) performing at the Washington, DC, club. The reissuing on CDs of Greek music recorded or released in America is now a regular occurrence in the realm of world music.

Greek Americans are now largely perceived as fully assimilated into mainstream American culture, but the persistent performance of Greek traditional and popular music in diaspora communities contradicts this notion. Modest music venues, often associated with restaurants, continually emerge in metropolitan and suburban areas across America. Among those that preserve traditional music, Olymbites in Baltimore still celebrate traditional *glendia* (holidays) by composing *mantinades*, an improvisational form of lyrical folk poetry that comments on important community events. In Boston, the resurgence of interest in rebetika that began in Greece in the 1970s is reflected in the popularity of old-style rebetika revival bands such as Rembetoparea;[21] and Panagia Soumela offers young people opportunities to learn Pontian music, dance, language, and Pontian lyra making. In Seattle, clarinet and *zournas* player Christos Govetas from eastern Macedonia leads Drómeno, a Greek and Balkan music group specializing in the music of northern Greece. For several years, the city of Tarpon Springs, Florida, has sponsored workshops that teach Greek bouzouki and Kalymnian violin technique as well as a traditional repertoire to young community members.

Another important element contributing to the preservation of musical traditions is the vast network of dance groups. In the 1970s, dance directors, including Tarpon Springs's John Lulias, created a model in which dance groups attend and host dance conferences and competitions. This became a significant force as Greek dance, taught through numerous churches and fraternal organizations, increased in popularity. Moreover, national and regional Greek folk dance competitions such as those sponsored by Greek Orthodox Metropolises in San Francisco, Atlanta, and New Jersey hire outstanding traditional musicians to play Greek folk music—such as Kalymnian tsambouna player Manolis Houlis from Long Beach, California.

A recent phenomenon contributing to the perpetuation of Greek musical culture has been noted by veteran scholar Sotirios (Sam) Chianis, who writes:

> There is a movement in Greece among the young generation to perform the old repertoire of Greek folk music from the mainland and various islands of Greece. The young musicians are listening to old 78 rpm records (both dimotika and rebetika music) and actually performing this style and repertoire in clubs in Athens and other large cities of Greece.[22]

This is mirrored among rising young musicians in the United States such as Vasilis Patrikis (violin) in New York, Kostas Revelas (bouzouki) in Ohio, Eleni and Bobby Govetas in Seattle, and Savvas Ferekides, Costas Garoufalidis, and George Makris in Tarpon Springs.

Even more recently, the economic crisis in Greece is precipitating a revitalization of Greek musical culture within the diaspora. As the crisis has diminished their opportunities to perform, an increasing number of Greek artists are giving more frequent concerts in diaspora communities throughout the world—thus bringing outstanding contemporary Greek music and artists to the attention of these communities. Interestingly, this is similar to the situation in the 1950s and early 1960s, when the post–World War II and Greek Civil War economic miasma brought the cream of Greek music (e.g., Giannis Tatasopoulos, Manolis Hiotis, and Stelios Kazantzidis) to perform or live in America.[23]

Notes

1. This overview is an expansion of the text of the 2015 exhibit, *Greek Music in America*, which Tina Bucuvalas curated for the city of Tarpon Springs, Florida. Although Bucuvalas was the editor and coauthor of the exhibit text, much of the knowledge was contributed by Stavros K. Frangos and Meletios Pouliopoulos, two leading authorities on Greek music in the United States who ably served as consultants. While Frangos and Bucuvalas—especially Frangos—contributed the majority of the exhibit text, Pouliopoulos provided substantial information for the postwar section and many if not most of the visual images throughout the exhibit.

2. Thanks to Michael G. Kaloyanides for elucidating this point in an e-mail communication, March 20, 2017.

3. When referring to this and many other dances, we will imply a connection with the word for dance, i.e., *o horos kalamatianos* rather than *to kalamatiano*. However, there are some cases when the name of a dance never appears with a final *s*, e.g., *sousta* or *hasapiko*.

4. Thanks to Sotirios (Sam) Chianis for his input regarding the structure of Greek music.

5. See also Gauntlett 2003 about how Greek Australian recordings reveal not only the artists' cultural practices but also their involvement in the Australian economy as producers, consumers, and traders of cultural artifacts.

6. Exact immigration figures are difficult to assess, since many ethnic Greeks emigrated from areas then held by the Ottoman Empire or Italy and were thus recorded as Turkish or Italian.

7. See Chianis's profile of Grachis for further information.

8. The advertisement was for the Columbia Phonograph Company, 174 Tremont Street, Boston, advising: "Send Your Orders at Once for Greek Records!" It appeared in the January 1910 issue of *Eastern and Western Review*, when Telemachus Thomas Timayenis (1853–1918) was the editor.

9. See the chapter by Meletios Pouliopoulos, "Greek Music Piano Rolls in the United States," in part 3 of this volume for more information on this topic.

10. For more information on Papagika, see Frangos 1994. Some of his information on Papagika comes from his interviews with musician John K. Gianaros, who worked as a musician for more than forty years.

11. Demetriades's mixing of genres was initially demonstrated to Frangos by music collector Dino Pappas.

12. See Stavros K. Frangos's chapter, "George Katsaros: The Last *Café-Aman* Performer," in part 1 of this volume for more on this topic.

13. For example, as owner/operator of the Ramona Amusement Park in Grand Rapids, Michigan, Alex Demar booked both Greek and American acts from Chicago and elsewhere, who then continued on to other locations.

14. See also Kitroeff 2015 and Kourelis 2016 for recent discussions of Greek illegal immigration.

15. Thanks to Meletios Pouliopoulos for background information on the recording.

16. Sevasti Smolios Galoozis and Anna Smolios Ioannidis were young friends of the Zembillas family who visited the studio and the shop as children.

17. Reports appeared in newspapers around the country, such as the New Orleans *Times-Picayune* of August 23, 1961.

18. See https://www.youtube.com/watch?v=AURm7GY-Uj4 for Anna Vissi's performance of "Misirlou" at the 2004 Olympics in Athens. It is interesting that one of the ways that Greece chose to represent its musical culture at the Olympics was through the performance of this song, which was not only first recorded in America but reinterpreted through the uniquely American musical surf rock genre.

19. This updating of rebetika is based on my observation of innumerable performances by many different musical groups at events ranging from dinner dances to *glendia* and clubs in venues from Florida to Boston, as well as on discussions with musicians such as George Soffos, Elias Poulos, and Leonidas Zafiris.

20. Meletios Pouliopoulos, conversation with the author, March 18, 2015.

21. This is similar to the resurgence of interest in klezmer music among American Jews since the mid-1970s. See Lornell and Rasmussen 2016, 8.

22. Sotirios (Sam) Chianis, e-mail message to the author, April 13, 2016. In another email communication, ethnomusicologist Michael G. Kaloyanides also noted that he "observed musicians holding 'sessions' in kafeneia and tavernes, in Greece in recent years. Like Irish sessions, they are not primarily intended to entertain patrons, but, rather, to provide a venue for musicians to preserve, learn and disseminate these traditions. The musicians are not compensated for these performances." Michael G. Kaloyanides, e-mail message to the author, March 18, 2017.

23. Special thanks to Vasilia Kourtis-Kazoullis from the University of the Aegean, Rhodes, who brought this to my attention in a conversation in Rhodes on September 14, 2016.

References

Amalia. 2002. *Amalia! Old Greek Songs in the New Land, 1923–1950*. With Markos Melkon, Alexis Zoumbas, and John Pappas. Arhoolie ARHCD 7049. Arhoolie Records, El Cerrito, California.

Belasco, John. 1954. "Sunset Springs Hotel." *Athene* 15, no. 1 (Spring): 28–29.

Chianis, Sotirios (Sam). 1983. "A Glimpse of Greek Music in America." In *Greek Music Tour*, 3–4. New York: Ethnic Folk Arts Center.

Discography of American Historical Recordings, s.v. "Victor Matrix CVE-40235. To cigaretto / Tassia Demetriades." At http://adp.library.ucsb.edu/index.php/matrix/detail/800014466/CVE-40235-To_cigaretto. Accessed June 6, 2016.

Frangos, Steve. 1994. "Marika Papagika and the Transformations in Modern Greek Music." *Journal of the Hellenic Diaspora* 20, no. 1: 43–64.

———. 2007a. "Madame Koula: The Kanarini of Ameriki." *National Herald*, November 5. At https://www.scribd.com/doc/48081513/Steve-Frangos-Madame-Koula-The-Kanarini-Of-Ameriki. Accessed December 3, 2016.

———. 2007b. "The Very First Greek Records in Old Ameriki." *National Herald*, December 17.

———. 2013. "Everyday, Non-Celebrity Traditional Greek Musicians in North America." *National Herald*, March 28.

Galoozis, Sevasti Smolios. 2016. Interview with Tina Bucuvalas, Tarpon Springs, Florida, June 8.

Gauntlett, Stathis. 2003. "Greek Recorded Sound in Australia: A Neglected Heritage." In *Greek Research in Australia: Proceedings of the Fourth Biennial Conference of Greek Studies, Flinders University, September 2001*, edited by Elizabeth Close, Michael Tsianikas, and George Frazis, 25–46. Adelaide: Flinders University Department of Languages.

Georgakas, Dan. 1987. "The Greeks in America." *Journal of the Hellenic Diaspora* 14, nos. 1–2 (Spring–Summer): 5–53. At http://www.kalami.net/2012/omogeneia/Georgakas_greeks_usa.pdf. Accessed June 5, 2016.

Gianaros, John K. 1986. Interview with Steve Frangos, Tarpon Springs, Florida, April 13. Audio recordings in the State Archives of Florida, Series S1708, tapes 19–20.

Gronow, Pekka. 1981. "The Record Industry Comes to the Orient." *Ethnomusicology* 25, no. 2 (May): 251–84.

Holst-Warhaft, Gail. 2001. "Rebetika Born in the USA." Review of *Mourmourika: Songs of the Greek Underworld 1930–1955*, Rounder CD-1120, and *Women of Rembetika*, Rounder CD-1121. Greekworks, October 15. At http://www.greekworks.com/content/index.php/weblog/print/rebetika_born_in_the_usa/. Accessed March 30, 2017.

Ioannidis, Anna Smolios. 2016. Interview with Tina Bucuvalas, Tarpon Springs, Florida, December 12.

Karras, Athan. N.d. "Trio Bel Canto: The Next Generation." Hellenic Communication Service. At http://www.helleniccomserve.com/trionextgeneration.html. Accessed June 3, 2016.

King, Christopher. 2014. "Talk about Beauties." *Paris Review*, September 22. At http://www.theparisreview.org/blog/2014/09/22/talk-about-beauties/. Accessed June 16, 2016.

Kitroeff, Alexander. 2015. "Greek-American History and Unauthorized Immigration." *National Herald*, October 15, 13.

———. N.d. "The Story of Greek Migration to America." The Journey: the Greek American Dream. At http://www.thejourneygreekamericandream.org/historical.htm. Accessed June 6, 2016.

Klein, Joseph. 1959. "Gary's Juke Ops Cater to Nationality Tastes." *Billboard*, no. 88 (August 10).

Kourelis, Kostis. 2016. "Undocumented Greek Migrants." Objects-Building-Situations, September 21. At http://kourelis.blogspot.com/2016/09/undocumented-greek-migrants_21.html. Accessed November 28, 2016.

Kourousis, Stavros. 2013. *From Tambouras to Bouzouki: The History and Evolution of the Bouzouki and Its First Recordings (1926–1932)*. Athens: Orpheum Phonograph.

Kourvetaris, George A. 2008. "Greek Americans." In *Encyclopedia of Race, Ethnicity, and Society*, edited by Richard T. Schaefer, 559–62. Thousand Oaks, CA: Sage Publications.

Lornell, Kip, and Anne K. Rasmussen, eds. 2016. *The Music of Multicultural America: Performance, Identity, and Community in the United States*. Jackson: University Press of Mississippi.

Maninakis, Grigoris. 2009. "Musical History: N.Y.'s Music 'Boxes'; The Memorable Greek American Boites." *National Herald*, November 28–December 4, 7.

Moskos, Charles. 1989. *Greek Americans: Struggle and Success*. 2nd ed. New Brunswick, NJ: Transaction Publishers.

Petrusich, Amanda. 2014. "Hunting for the Source of the World's Most Beguiling Folk Music." *New York Times Magazine*, September 24. At http://www.nytimes.com/2014/09/28/magazine/hunting-for-the-source-of-the-worlds-most-beguiling-folk-music.html?_r=0. Accessed June 6, 2016.

Saloutos, Theodore. 1973. "Causes and Patterns of Greek Emigration to the United States." *Perspectives in American History* 7: 381–437.

Spottswood, Richard K. 1990. *Ethnic Music on Records: A Discography of Ethnic Recordings Produced in the United States, 1893–1942*. 7 vols. Urbana: University of Illinois Press.

Tatassopoulos, Giannis, and Fred Elias. 1997. *Port Said Café*. Great Bouzouki Soloists series. ΠΜΕ A-260. Anodos, Athens.

Zoumbas, Alexis. 2014. *A Lament for Epirus, 1926–1928*. Angry Mom AMA-004. Angry Mom Records, New York.

PART ONE

Musical Genre, Style, and Content

Growth of Liturgical Music in the Iakovian Era[1]

—Frank Desby

Seldom has an art form been subjected to as strong a changing influence as the music of the Orthodox Church when it was brought to America. Since the beginning of the twentieth century, our music has been seriously impacted by the art and ethos of the New World. True, there was great influence of the Moslem world on our music after the late fourteenth century. This influence introduced some alterations in the scales upon which the melodies were constructed and rhythmic elements as well. Yet the basic concept of a single melodic line, without a background harmony, prevailed until the twentieth century. The Slavonic Church, on the other hand, developed a harmonic-contrapuntal choral idiom in the seventeenth century, while the Greek and Antiochian Orthodox retained the single melodic chant line, save for the held tone of the *isokratai*.

Harmonized choral music for the church did not originate in America. Greeks living in France and Germany experimented with harmonizations. Eventually, at the turn of the century, attempts at harmonized Byzantine chant were introduced by John Sakellarides.

Outside of Greece, one would expect to find choral music without much opposition, so it is no surprise that on Easter Sunday in 1844 in the Orthodox Church of the Holy Trinity in Vienna, John Haviaras led a choir of twenty-four male singers in a four-part setting of the liturgical music. At the end of the nineteenth century, Spyro Spathis settled in Paris. He offered the Greek community harmonized settings for mixed chorus. Criticism of this early pioneer's work lies in the fact that the subtleties of Byzantine scales are theoretically not adaptable to Western major-minor tonality. It is not our purpose here to discuss the possibilities of adapting one type of musical thought (Byzantine) to another (European) except to state that compromises, once believed unworkable, are possible.

In Athens, the influence of John Sakellarides on the musical habits or customs of the Greeks was minimal; it was in America that his influence became enormous. As an opera coach and music teacher at a number of schools, and also trained thoroughly as a *psaltis* (a precentor, or chanter), Sakellarides came into contact with a large number of musicians of varying backgrounds. In the 1920s he met Henry J. Tillyard, of England, who was with the British School at Athens. Tillyard became quite interested in Byzantine music and secured Sakellarides as his teacher. Together they explored some of the earlier layers of melodic tradition, noting that the melodic style and, indeed, the tonality had been subjected to several transformations. Music before the Turkish conquest (1453) was different, and every 150 years or so thereafter the melodies were subjected to "interpretations," which the Byzantine composers called "exegesis." The last transformation occurred during the last half of the eighteenth century, culminating in 1814 with a revision of teaching methods. Also, for the first time, in 1820, it became possible to engrave and print Byzantine music.

With this vehicle of mass reproduction, it was unfortunately only the latest style that became universally established. Little of the music of the older *melourgoi* survives today except in manuscripts. Furthermore, what melodies had survived had become decorated to the point of corruption. Sakellarides studied the early examples, combed out many ornaments, and produced a kind of classical reform. This purging upset his contemporaries. However, many of his simplified versions became standard, but not his harmonic versions.

With the migration of Greeks to the United States, beginning at the turn of the twentieth century, came some of Sakellarides's students. They offered their services as *psaltes* and even as instrumentalists for community entertainment. The creation of language schools for the first generation of Greek American children created new demands from the church. In many instances, the local precentor was also the local Greek schoolteacher.

The influence of public school choral music, and its existence in local non-Greek churches, was strong enough to introduce in our churches some experimentation with choral music and a participating group—the choir. Separated from the Mother Church, the Greek church in the United States was not under the watchful eye of anyone objecting to innovations. So, in the first quarter of the twentieth century, the Greek church of the New World introduced choral music on a permanent basis.

Early Contributors

No one knows for sure where and when the first choir was formed in America's Greek churches, or when organ accompaniment was introduced, but many have laid claim to being the originators. Among the early choir directors are the Sakellarides group, especially those who had their training under the Athenian master. These include Christos Vrionides and Angelos Desfis. Others who had come under Sakellarides's influence were Nicholas Roubanis, George Anastassiou, and

MOYΣIKO-EKKΛHΣIAΣTIKH BIBΛIOΘHKH NIK. HΛ. POYMΠANH

TETAPTH EKΔOΣIΣ   FOURTH EDITION
ΕΠΗΥΣΗΜΕΝΗ   O P . V I

HELLENIC ORTHODOX CHURCH
2606 Riggs Ave.
DALLAS 1, TEXAS

Η
ΘΕΙΑ ΛΕΙΤΟΥΡΓΙΑ

Y Π O
ΝΙΚ. ΗΛ. ΡΟΥΜΠΑΝΗ

—⟡⟡⟡—

THE GREEK LITURGY
B Y
N. ROUBANIS

—⟡⟡⟡—

Published by
N. ROUBANIS
265 W. 41st Street
New York

PRINTED IN THE U. S. A.

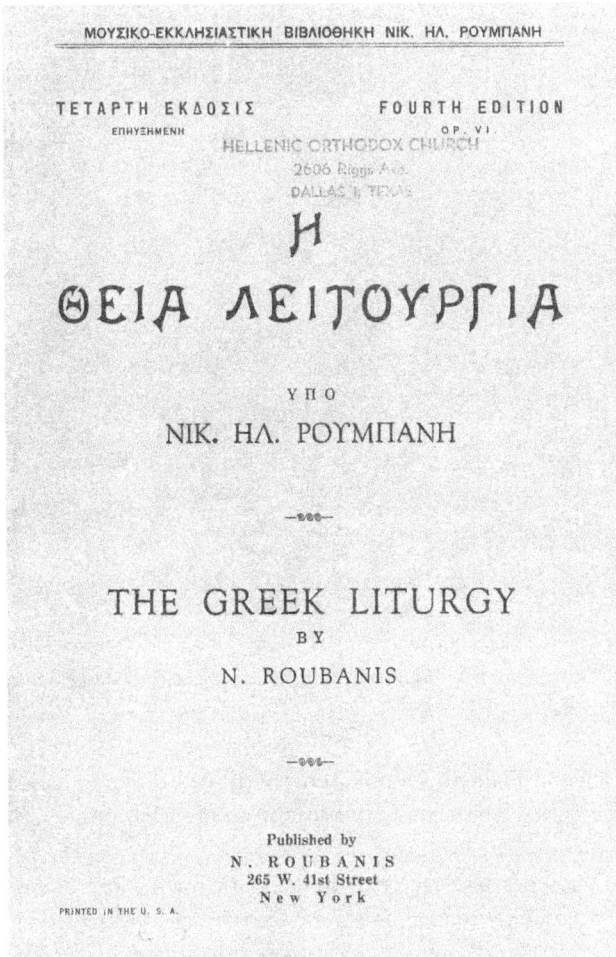

Figure 33. Nicholas Roubanis, *I Theia Leitourgia: The Greek Liturgy.*
Photo by Tina Bucuvalas.

Athan Theodores. These few were singled out because they contributed published material to our churches.

In each of the large cities, the precentors organized choral groups to take part in the liturgy and occasionally other *akolouthiae* for Holy Week and major feast days. The inclusion of young girls and women seemed to raise no objection by either the faithful or the clergy. Indeed, this seemed to be another vehicle for preserving the heritage, while in Greece the inclusion of women in church services is still not acceptable. The music brought to this country had been written for four-part male ensemble. It was soon discovered that with women now part of the choir, such writing was unsuitable. Rewriting was inevitable, as was the

Figure 34. The Damaskenos Byzantine choir, directed by Father George Anastassiou, Tarpon Springs, Florida, 1934. Courtesy of Esther Raptis.

influence from non-Hellenic sources. Some of the new directors had received full formal training in Western music in addition to their Byzantine training. Here are brief profiles of these leading choir directors:

Christos Vrionides had received diplomas in the United States as well as Greece, was thoroughly trained on several instruments, and served as conductor of a number of symphony orchestras. By appointment of the federal government, he founded and conducted the Long Island Symphony in Babylon, New York. Vrionides was recognized in the 1951 *Who's Who of Music*. Later, he became the music instructor at Holy Cross Seminary, teaching both Byzantine music and the formal music of the West. He wrote the first US-published treatise on Byzantine chant.

Nicholas Roubanis came to the United States in the twenties from Alexandria, Egypt, as a French horn player. He was active in Chicago for a number of years before moving to the East Coast, becoming involved with the musical growth of several communities. His "Divine Liturgy for Mixed Voices" was to become immensely popular due to its simplicity and effective part writing. His song "Misirlou" became an international hit in the popular music field. He was active in the church all his life; his final position was as a choir director in New Jersey.

George Anastassiou was a student in Cyprus of the famous Stylianos Chourmouzios but studied the choral settings of Sakellarides with great diligence when

56

he immigrated to the United States and formed a choir in Tarpon Springs, Florida. Eventually he moved to Philadelphia, where he was the *protopsaltis*, directed the choir, and became a greatly respected music teacher. Anastassiou, like others about him, realized that the four-part male choir setting of Sakellarides could not be used with mixed voices. Therefore, he composed his own music for the Divine Liturgy. While the work of Anastassiou was similar to the liturgies of Vrionides and Roubanis, it introduced some additional material, contained both a major and minor version of the liturgy, and included information for use of the organ. Most valuable was an appendix of the special hymns needed throughout the ecclesiastical year. This material, appearing in Western staff notation, makes this volume indispensable. Probably no choir director even today is without one.

Athan Theodores's and Angelos Desfis's contributions consisted mostly of separate hymns of the liturgy, such as the Cherubic and Communion hymns. Privately published, their circulation was not extensive. In 1947, Desfis on a visit to Greece secured the publishing rights to Sakellarides's Western notation liturgical book, *Hymns and Odes*, which explains how so important a transition work came to be printed in America.

Father Demetrios Lolakis studied at the Conservatory of Athens, becoming proficient in the piano and violin, which he played all his life. He came to the United States about 1927 and was active mostly in the Midwest. He transcribed an enormous amount of Byzantine music into staff notation and recorded much of this on tape. This contribution has proven to be quite valuable to priests and psaltes alike. After his ordination in 1922, his musical activities grew rather than becoming subordinate to parish duties; yet, as a parish priest, he was always highly esteemed. After his retirement, he continued his musical activities with undiminished interest and vigor.

The Postwar Period

At the outbreak of World War II, most churches had a choir of mixed voices, ages ranging from fifteen to twenty-five. They also had an organ of some kind, either a harmonium with pedals to pump the bellows or a simple electric instrument, and a choir director who might also be church secretary, psaltis, language teacher, or all three.

When the service members returned home, they displayed a new spirituality and renewed interest in their ethnic roots. This resulted in a welcome renaissance for the church. The returning military entered colleges and joined musical organizations there. As they participated in their local choir, they required the church to offer more challenging musical fare. In many cases, the liturgical repertoire remained identical to the prewar music, but standard choral music was added so that church-sponsored programs offered the community a broader selection. Many second-generation Greeks also majored or minored in music; therefore, as the original directors retired, the positions were filled by well-trained newcomers. As a result, more challenging types of music became manifest.

It should be mentioned that all of the archbishops of these periods, despite their traditional upbringing, encouraged the adaptation of choral music and inclusion of an accompanying instrument. A little-known but interesting piece of information concerns the introduction of a pipe organ to the church on the island of Kerkyra (Corfu) by then Metropolitan Athenagoras (later, archbishop of North and South America and, in 1949, ecumenical patriarch). Whenever a new prelate takes over, there is naturally some anxiety on the part of the clergy and laity as to whether progress will be maintained. It was therefore exceptionally fortunate for the Orthodox Church in America to have Archbishop Iakovos elevated to this post in 1959. Our new archbishop, extensively educated and cultured, was well aware of the worldwide religious situation. He was up to date on all facets of community life, education, spirituality, music, art, and architecture. Having traveled widely, he was not given to snap decisions nor did he impede progress in any field. With his encouragement and participation, the musical life of the communities flourished for many years. It was our good fortune to have a prelate who possessed experience and wisdom combined with good judgment.

Musical Styles

Some discussion of prewar and postwar (World War II) musical style is necessary to clarify the position of both the musical contributors and the hierarchy. The single-line melody of Byzantine chant (monophony) of the Church of Greece was rendered by two groups of precentors, explicitly guided by the rubrics or red-printed directions in the service books and the Typicon. Services in the early American churches (Annunciation, Chicago, 1893; Holy Trinity, New York, 1902; Holy Trinity, Boston, 1903) were followed by others, reaching fifty-two by 1962. The service music was certainly supplied by a right and left psaltis plus volunteers when available, carrying on the tradition of the Mother Church. Yet, here too, a kind of melting pot was created. Because not all psaltes came from Athens or the Peloponnese but from all over Greece and Asia Minor, a mixture of various styles was absorbed at large in the New World.

In 1902, the first edition of Sakellarides's *Sacred Hymnody* was published in Byzantine notation in Athens. This was of little use to the American-based church except that the author had managed to write, for the first time, two- and three-part harmonizations in this notation, thereby giving Athenian congregations a taste of harmony. In 1930, he published this music in European staff notation. It was this music that was used by our earliest choirs. One can imagine that in America the Sunday School children were taught the melodies at first and introduced to harmonized versions soon after. Sakellarides's music was reprinted in bootleg editions in those early days by Greek American newspaper publishers.

What was this music like? It consisted of the melody in the top (tenor) voice and a follower a third lower, over a simple bass line, easy to sing and learn. The addition of a piano in the Sunday School or language classroom made the learning process faster. The transfer of a keyboard instrument into the church itself was inevitable. This simple style of music prevailed for at least twenty years. Everyone knows that singing a round is a simple form of polyphony, or counterpoint, as it is technically known. As choirs improved, a few composers began to experiment with polyphony in a limited manner.

Shortly before World War II, James Aliferis became among the first Greek Americans to earn a doctoral degree in music. His activity in the church resulted in the first publications of Byzantine hymns for mixed-voice choir by the established New York publishing house of Witmark and Sons. Aliferis's publication must be considered an important landmark in the development of our choral music. A more advanced style was on its way, and we find this in the music produced by Athan Theodores and Thomas Regas. Unfortunately, their work was not published and was known only locally. A priest-musician who also contributed simple choral music was Father E. Chrysoloras, whose three-part writing was designed to be expandable to more parts.

In all these versions, the traditional melodic line was adhered to, but the harmonizations were simple major-minor key associations. Even the last phase of Byzantine chant was based on the ancient modal system, in which several scales and tonalities were in use. One argument against the "westernization" of Byzantine melody was the fact that the West had only one tonality and two scales, rendering the two systems incompatible. However, modal treatment in harmonic and polyphonic music had already been achieved in the West as early as the fifteenth century with the adaptation of Gregorian chant to choral music.

With the return of the service members in 1946, the church was to expand in all directions, resulting in larger congregations, new churches, American-born parish and community leaders, and musical innovation. The first person to introduce music for liturgical use at this time was Anna Gerotheou Gallos, daughter of a Greek priest and married to Reverend George Gallos. Presvytera Gallos had a thorough musical education, beginning in her childhood and culminating in her graduation with a master's degree from the Eastman School of Music in Rochester, New York. Her teaching experience spans the public school and the university; in the 1960s, she was for a time a music instructor at Holy Cross Seminary in Brookline, Massachusetts. She published four liturgies, some folk songs, and music for the organ. She headed Evangeline Press, a Greek music publishing firm. At present, Presvytera Gallos is preparing liturgical music in each of the eight ecclesiastical modes.

The question after World War II was whether modality could be applied in the choral settings of Byzantine melody. Some evidence of such experimentation also appeared in one or two examples of Vrionides's first setting. When I became choir director at the Church of Annunciation in Los Angeles in 1948, this notion produced successful experimentation with Byzantine hymns. The eight modes of this music were quite easily adaptable to harmonic and polyphonic treatment. The first attempt was a musical setting for the Divine Liturgy published by the Greek Sacred and Secular Music Society in 1951. This early success at modal treatment aroused the interest of other composers including Anna Gallos, whose second and subsequent liturgies are modally based. Other early successes were those of Tikey Zes, Demetrios Pappas, and Theodore Bogdanos. Byzantine choral music had found its voice. By 1960, the work of these Greek Americans was beginning to find adherents and admirers even in Greece.

At this point, it becomes necessary to resolve a stubborn conflict in the identification of our musical heritage. Byzantine chant, or music, is simply vocal music with a single melodic line, sometimes assisted by a particular sustained tone, also vocal. There is not, and has never been, Byzantine choral part music. In the West, Gregorian chant is also single-line melody only, vocal music without even the *ison*, or sustained tone. No one listens to a mass by Palestrina, for example, based on a Gregorian chant and calls it Gregorian music. It is simply vocal music based on a preexisting melody.

So it is with our choral music. It is not "Byzantine music" at all, but a sacred music composition based on a Byzantine chant melody! We have heard that so and so's music is more "Byzantine" than another writer's. Such a remark makes no sense. Some composers of Orthodox service music at present do not even use traditional chant melodies, nor do they try to imitate them. It is hoped that the public at large will understand the difference between the nature of our choral music and that of the traditional method of rendering chant.

Organizations and Societies

The Seminary

Undoubtedly one of the most important events in the history of the Greek American church was the establishment of Holy Cross Orthodox Seminary in 1937 at Pomfret, Connecticut, later moved to Brookline, Massachusetts, as part of Hellenic College.

In 1937, Ambrose Giannoukos formed the first seminary choir—a highly successful venture. Giannoukos was at the time finishing a master's degree in music. An accomplished pianist and organist, his interest in Orthodox music resulted in 1938 in his ordination in the priesthood. Under his direction, the seminary choir achieved wide fame and recognition throughout New England. After leaving the seminary, he served as professor of music at various universities and also as pastor to many parishes. At present, Father Giannoukos is pastor of Saint Nicholas Church in Corpus Christi, Texas.

At the time of Archbishop Iakovos's enthronement, the musical instruction at the seminary was in the hands of Christos Vrionides, whose vast experience in all phases of music was invaluable to the seminarians, who were fortunate to study under him. The students were brought face to face not only with Byzantine chant, in which Professor Vrionides was an authority, but also with the musical traditions of all other religious faiths, symphonic and operatic music, and a vast store of Greek folk songs.

With the passing of Vrionides in 1962, the archbishop invited Savas Savas to teach Byzantine music at the seminary. Born in Greece, Professor Savas was trained in Athens, and served as protopsaltis and music director of the city's cathedral. He taught Byzantine music at the University of Athens, the Theological School, and the Athens Conservatory as well. Before coming to the United States, he directed choirs in Paris and Munich.

At Holy Cross Seminary, Professor Savas felt a need for a basic aid in the English language, and in 1965 he published *Byzantine Music in Theory and Practice*. This book and another published a few years later, *The Hymnology of the Orthodox Church*, are the basic textbooks of his efforts at the School of Theology. They inspire and continue to inspire our seminarians to penetrate more deeply into the content of our hymns and their musical interpretation.

Professor Savas has also contributed articles to many important musical periodicals. His knowledge extends even to art and archaeology. In 1959, Patriarch Benedictos of Jerusalem presented him with the Golden Cross of the Patriarchate. In 1976, he was knighted by the ecumenical patriarch as Archon Didaskalos and selected as Outstanding Educator in America.

It seems that the musical education of our priests has been entrusted, from the beginning, to the most outstanding men in the field. Professor Savas continues his dedication by constantly updating his materials and techniques, as evidenced by his employment of audiovisual equipment in his instruction.

Byzantine music has always been the exclusive property of the male singer, although in convents some women have learned this art. Since Kassiani of Byzantine times, there has not been any recorded female contribution to the repertoire. It comes as a first for the seminary then, to have Professor Savas train women to read and chant our music. Two young women, Jessica Suchy and Valerie Karras, have become quite successful protégés of Master Savas. Suchy has served as a psalta at Saint Sophia Cathedral in Los Angeles and is presently in Indianapolis serving the church there.

Choir Schools

Finding qualified musicians to train our choirs will always be a major concern. One cannot expect a young person to take a four-year college degree in music only to fulfill the requirements of a part-time job. Realizing this, Anna Gallos and Arthur Kanaracus originated the first choir school in 1946, wherein a person could spend a few weeks during the summer in specialized subjects such as conducting, accompanying, repertoire, and some theory designed around Byzantine music characteristics. The idea worked so well that Archbishop Iakovos has supported the choir school organizations with much enthusiasm. At present, choir schools often function with the annual conference of the regional choir federations.

I mentioned above that Professor Savas trained the first women to be precentors, but other women have also taken part, although not American trained. Janet Christopoulos Webster migrated to the United States from Jerusalem after World War II. She had been her father's psalta in the Holy City, where he was an Orthodox priest. She, too, has served at Saint Sophia Cathedral in Los Angeles.

It is no wonder, then, that women as well as men in America are at present seeking to learn to perform the music as well as study it as musicologists. On the academic level, Greek Americans are also entering the musicological fields. At Saint Louis University, Diane Touliatos is contributing articles on important research in early phases of Byzantine chant. Touliatos was trained in Thessaloniki by the famous Christos Patrinelis. In Vancouver, Australian-born Dimitri E. Conomos has become internationally known for his Byzantine music scholarship and is at present editor of the journal *Studies in Eastern Chant*.

Choir Federations

At the time of Archbishop Iakovos's elevation, there were a few choir federations throughout the country, each one covering several churches. The main purpose of these organizations will be presented, with their special contributions noted. In 1984, there were eight choir federations—one in each diocese and in the Archdiocesan District. Four issue periodic newsletters containing information on activities and articles of interest by a wide range of contributors. Some have the means to publish and sell choral music. Each of the regional federations sponsors an annual conference, where the focal point is a hierarchical liturgy offering the music of a special composer. New music is also reviewed and sung. In addition, lecturers offer seminars and workshops. These are interspersed with social events and a formal banquet, and sometimes a well-prepared concert is included. The annual affairs have done much to help the cause of Greek Orthodox music in the United States. The influence has reached the Sunday School classroom, helping foster younger groups, the junior choirs. Most important, the federations have encouraged a higher standard of performance by individual choirs. The federations have been the major factor in providing new musical settings of our music to the public. They have also been responsible for preserving some valued traditions, such as Byzantine chant of earlier periods. The organ has become a required item in the choir loft, with expert organists giving workshops through federation sponsorship, which have borne fruit in the form of a growing number of fine players.

Other Choral Organizations

Specialists who are conductors, composers, and performers always desire a vehicle of expression that is of the highest caliber. Therefore, when a parish can afford it, a professional group may be retained.

The Archdiocese

Such a choir was always available to the Archdiocese Cathedral in New York City. For thirty years, its conductor was Nicholas D. Iliopoulos. This group has also presented special programs and oratorios and has featured the music of several composers. In 1976, the choir was taken over by Dino Anagnost, whose vigorous leadership has not only carried out the fine work of Iliopoulos but has added to the repertoire and in other ways contributed to the prestige of the cathedral.

Metropolitan Chorale

A choral group of professional ability to represent the archdiocese was organized in 1962, the first director being James Stathis. In 1968, Dino Anagnost assumed its directorship and brought it to national attention. Since 1978, the chorale has been under the directorship of George Tsontakis, who has continued to enlarge both its scope and its audience. Works of exceptional perception and prominence are being written for and presented by this group, which promises to be an important musical showcase for our church.

Both Anagnost and Tsontakis are representatives of the finest musical development of this generation. Both have been professionally groomed and have already caught the attention of a discerning musical public.

Chicago Chorale

The Midwest has recently organized another such group in Chicago at the suggestion of Archbishop Iakovos, with Georgia Mitchell as director. Mitchell has been very active and influential in this area for many years. She is an accomplished pianist of virtuoso status and is equally accomplished on the organ.

The Pacific Northwest

In the Northwest, Panos Vlahos at Lewis and Clark College organized a group that not only served the Holy Trinity Church in Portland, Oregon, in the late 1950s but also presented concerts throughout the area that brought enthusiastic comments from critics. Unfortunately, this group was disbanded.

After taking part in the World Council of Churches Ecumenical Liturgy in Vancouver in August 1983, plans for a Northwest Byzantine chorale are under way. Organizers are George Lendaris of Portland; Rose Munson, choir director; Jerry Mulinos; Father Homer Demopoulos of Seattle as spiritual adviser; and myself as musical director at the initial stages. The repertoire will consist of Byzantine chant of various periods, and both sacred and folk choral music.

California

For a number of years, two professional-caliber groups existed in California, the Bay Area Chorale, with Pericles Phillips as conductor, and the Byzantine Chorale of Los Angeles, where I am the conductor. The Bay Area group has been reorganized and is now known as the Dorian Singers with Tikey Zes as conductor. These groups have performed extensively, recorded, and toured. Members of both groups were part of the 1974 Archdiocesan Chorale that toured Greece.

The Archdiocesan Chorale was organized by Ernest Villas and Pericles Phillips in 1972. Membership in the chorale was drawn from a large area, and the chorale met in Fresno, California, once a month for rehearsals to prepare for a major pilgrimage and concert tour of Greece and to present a memorial to the late Patriarch Athenagoras in his hometown of Vasilikon in northwestern Greece. In July 1974, after a year's delay due to political events in Greece, the chorale was on its way, giving concerts on the islands and in Egypt, and liturgies in Athens and Thessaloniki. Father Spencer Kezios was spiritual adviser; Thomas Lappas and Thomas Pallad, tour directors; myself, conductor; Tikey Zes, assistant; and Xenia Anton Desby, accompanist. On hearing a tape of the chanted (men's voices) portion of the memorial music, Simon Karas in Athens was amazed that Americans were able to perform this very difficult music, with its tricky intonations, in such an expert manner. Karas is an undisputed leader in Byzantine music in Greece and has trained a large number of psaltes.

The Byzantine Chorale in Los Angeles has issued a number of recordings in which both choral music and ancient chant are offered. The oldest extant Christian hymn, transcribed by Egon Wellesz, appears on one of the disks.

The National Forum of Greek Orthodox Church Musicians

It soon became evident that the various federations and independent church choral organizations needed an integrating national voice. For many years, the National Choir Committee of the Greek Orthodox Youth Association (GOYA) served such a purpose, but increasing requirements led to the formation of the National Forum. In this way, an organization with a full staff represents our choral organizations and musicians, including choir personnel, clergy, psaltes, and music educators.

The growth of musical activities on the local and national levels was due largely to Archbishop Iakovos's desire to see the musical situation upgraded in all aspects. In 1976, the forum became official; its first chairman was Niki Kalkanis. A graduate of Wayne State University (Detroit) in science and business administration, Kalkanis is also a talented organist and conductor, having served not only churches in the Detroit area but as guest lecturer and administrative leader of the Mideastern Choir Federation. His critical four years in office established the forum as the major organization of church musicians the archbishop envisioned.

George Demos succeeded Kalkanis as national chairman in 1980. In addition to his training to become a distinguished otorhinolaryngologist, he took advanced courses in music and conducting. His involvement in the church stems from a very early age and is evidenced by an enormous enthusiasm for its musical heritage. He has conducted in various parts of the country and was instrumental in forming many musical organizations for the church.

While chairman of the National Forum, Demos inaugurated the National Choir Music Endowment Fund, assisted by Niki Kalkanis. He also initiated the Xenia Desby Memorial Scholarship. He has encouraged many musicians to contribute compositions to the liturgical repertoire. With the Western Federation East, he has spearheaded the publication of the works of our outstanding composers.

Since 1982, Vicki Pappas, educator and researcher at Indiana University, has chaired the National Forum. Pappas has excellent organizational talents as well as being a well-trained musician and choir director. She accomplished the early work in originating a charter and organizational plan for the forum. At present, she is in constant contact with all her committee personnel, oversees the various projects, stays in frequent contact with the archdiocese and the Holy Synod, and still continues her local church and choir commitments. During her tenure, she focused national attention on the work of the forum, culminating in the publication of musical education materials for youth and a symposium on church music cosponsored with Holy Cross School of Theology.

Projects of the forum include:

1. *The Liturgical Guidebook*, issued annually to choir directors at a nominal cost. This booklet contains the order of Sunday services and some special

feasts from January to the beginning of the moveable season in the following year. There is also an annotated bibliography of related materials. The *Guidebook* was introduced in 1956 as a GOYA Choir Committee project at the request of Anna Gallos. Since its inception, I have been the manual's author. When the forum assumed responsibility for publication, Peter Vatsures of Columbus, Ohio, became editor.

2. *Publications.* In addition to the *Guidebook*, this committee oversees educational materials, makes available survey reports, and is considering the preservation of the music of early contributors. Peter Vatsures (chairman), Thomas Lappas, James Maniatis, Harry Booras, and Gerald van de Bruinhorst make up the committee.

3. *Cantonal Training Manual.* This is a complete treatise with recorded examples for clarification, aimed toward the training of future psaltes. The text is by myself, with recorded examples by Theodore Bogdanos.

4. *Children's Hymn Series.* Mary Jo Cally of Chicago and Vicki Pappas selected musicians trained in composition to prepare selected liturgical hymns in Greek and English versions. Included also are teaching suggestions regarding the meaning of the hymns, their spiritual roots and relation to a selected icon, and meanings of key Greek words. Aimed for instruction in Sunday School, the series promises to have broader application to retreats, camps, and adult education. In a similar vein, Nicolas and Connie Maragos of Rochester, Minnesota, are compiling an Orthodox youth songbook for use at informal gatherings.

5. *Archives.* Tina Vratimos of California compiled and maintains a library of historical and biographical archives. Tina, originally a very vital part of the music situation in the Midwest, is now active in choral development in the Bay Area.

6. *Other Activities.* John Tsokinos (Cleveland) and Dean Limberakis (Boston) coordinate the presentation of the Saint Romanos the Melodian Award to outstanding church musicians each year.

Publishers

Early publications were often the product of the composers themselves, privately printed and distributed. Unfortunately, such organizations tend to be one-generation firms, resulting in the eventual loss of creative work. One of the goals of the National Forum is to create a music archive of these out-of-print works.

At present, there are a few publishers that supply liturgical music and some folk music. The Greek Sacred and Secular Music Society publishes Orthodox service music and folk songs; several composers are represented. Thomas Lappas serves as its president. Evangeline Press publishes, in addition to liturgical and folk, organ music based on Byzantine hymns. Anna Gallos is publisher and editor of Helicon Press, for which Arthur S. Kanaracus oversees the printing of liturgical and folk music. The Federation of Western States East Publishers represents several composers of liturgical music, especially hymns of feast days. George Demos is its publisher and editor. And, finally, Holy Cross Orthodox Press, as the official archdiocese press, publishes music as well as didactic, theological, and historical material.

Musical Composition in America

At the end of World War II, there was a mere handful of composer-arrangers of choral literature. The roster has since grown to more than two dozen, producing printed music as well as recordings. This postwar renaissance was especially aided by two factors: professional, advanced training sought by our new generation, and the encouragement of the archdiocese, especially since the 1960s.

Compositions are by nature three types: (1) based on traditional chant melody, modal in concept; (2) traditional chant in free harmonization; and (3) entirely new melodic material. Most composers have indulged in all three methods; some prefer one idiom for most of their work.

First and foremost of the postwar contributors is Anna Gallos, whose background as a thoroughly trained musician and conductor was influenced by a family involved in the church. Above, all Gallos's interest in fostering the music of her colleagues is unmatched in this country. Her own output is considerable, and her untiring efforts in establishing choral organizations, schools, and events has pushed our music forward at a greater pace than would have been otherwise possible.

In California, the liturgical lyre has been tuned modally. Contributors here include myself, Tikey Zes, and Theodore Bogdanos. Zes and I were trained concurrently at the University of Southern California, which has a sacred music department. Both of us have made trips abroad to seek out new material. We have been, in a sense, an influence on each other. Inspired by the "new" modal and polyphonic technique, Bogdanos began contributing to this type of repertoire. The efforts of these modal pioneers surfaced because of the contributions of several people on the scene at the time. They must be remembered because without their assistance any significant changes would never have become known.

An organization was founded to promote the works of the new composers, the Greek Sacred and Secular Music Society. The original staff consisted of Thomas and Anthony Lappas, George and James Bonorris, Pericles Caiopoulos, Helen Kostelas (now Georgilas), and, later on, Constantine Lappas and Xenia Anton Desby. The first president was George Bonorris; at present, Torn Lappas heads the organization. Charles Hirt and Pauline Aldermann of the University of Southern California, and Lauren Petran of the University of California at Los Angeles, are advisers for the group. An editorial board examines all music submitted.

At this same time, Pericles Phillips and John Reckas, both of Oakland, were the first to recognize the quality of the new music. On the East Coast, Anna Gallos almost single-handedly created a demand for this music and encouraged budding composers to continue producing. Working in the East at this time was Demetrios Pappas. He introduced a liturgical setting with an occasional separate organ part, not merely a reproduction of the vocal parts. Pappas's knowledge of traditional Byzantine melody was unusual, having grown up listening to his father, a protopsaltis for the archdiocese. He began early, starting to direct at the age of seventeen. For thirteen years, he sang with the prestigious Robert Shaw Chorale. In addition to two liturgies, a number of recordings with his Amphion Choir are to his credit. Their two Yassou recordings have reached international prominence.

More recently, a new wave of composers has come to the fore. Some adhere to traditional melody and modality, but many write in an "implied" melodic and modal style, using more modern techniques. This is not to be condemned, for no art form should remain static; there is a certain freshness to these sounds that still manages to capture an essence of Byzantium, much as Béla Bartók did with much of the ethnic music he collected throughout his travels.

Ernest Villas has devoted a lifetime to the church. He has taught music and in the 1950s was musical director of Hormel Caravan, a choral and instrumental ensemble that toured the country and made weekly broadcasts. During these tours, Villas visited as many Greek communities as possible to talk to the younger generation and form youth clubs. He was the founder of GOYA and headed the organization in its initial stages. He was also responsible for forming the Metropolitan Chorale and for a time directed the group. He published a liturgy for unison voices that is now used in many communities as a means to encourage congregational participation of the Sunday liturgy. It was this work that was presented to the congregation at the 1983 World Council of Churches Ecumenical Liturgy.

In Madison, Wisconsin, Professor Mike Petrovich, conductor of the Greek Orthodox Church of Assumption, not only introduced some exceptionally fine music of his own, often based on traditional melodies, but was quite an inspiration to the young people in his choirs. Nicolas Maragos, one of his protégés, has become an important contributor to Orthodox service music and has written a complete liturgy and many other hymns in Greek and English.

I mention here others who have recently contributed music of interest and value: Steve Cardiasmenos, San Francisco area; Neal Desby, Los Angeles; Dimitri Futris, Skokie, Illinois; William Harmand, Syracuse, New York; Christopher Kypros, Norfolk, Virginia; Georgia Tangeres, Baltimore; Peter Tiboris, Plymouth,

New Hampshire; Mike Pallad, Northridge, California; Steve Phillips, New York; Alex Lingas, Portland, Oregon; John Revezoulis, Milwaukee; and George Raptis, Detroit. While this roster is admittedly incomplete, it points out the fact that fully trained musicians now supply our church with first-rate choral music.

Those Who Make It Happen

We have singled out the composers, and their contributions have given them celebrity, but their "workers" at the scene are seldom honored. It is this latter group who have the genius for recognizing talent, the faculty for promotion, and the stamina for administration and implementation.

Pericles Phillips of California is an excellent conductor, has been a professional musician, and is an impresario second to none. He organized the Archdiocesan Choir that toured Greece in 1974. While president of the Western Federation from 1951 to 1954, the organization was enlarged to take in all of the western states. At present, he is entertainment editor for the *Oakland Tribune* and director of the Ascension Choir in Oakland. He founded the Bay Area Chorale, whose performances all over the West have received praise from critics. Most important is his ability to recognize talent and promote the works of new composers.

George Dimopoulos was the most influential leader in the Midwest. In Chicago, he was a psaltis, conductor, composer, and teacher. Archbishop Iakovos conferred on him the highest ecclesiastical musical honor in 1955, that of Archon Protopsaltis. George Raptis in Detroit and John Tsolainos in Cleveland have spent most of their lives furthering the cause of our music, both on the organizational level and as conductors. They took part in the early stages of the formation of the National Forum of Greek Orthodox Musicians and have been the vital nerve center of the Mideastern Choir Federation. They have discovered singers, conductors, and composers; established a valuable archive of sacred and folk music; and in general been surging forces in the growth of Orthodox music.

In the southern states, John Demos, active in the Georgia State University instrumental and choral departments, has used his expertise in the Atlanta Church of Annunciation and for the Southern Federation. Choral groups under his direction always achieve a high degree of musical presentation.

At the Conservatory of Cincinnati, Ann-Marie Koukios is an instructor in choral directing and a doctoral candidate at the University of Cincinnati. She has formed performing groups of university students to present Orthodox choral music, Byzantine chant, and Greek folk songs. She directs the choir of Holy Trinity and has introduced this group to the music of various composers. Her talent in developing a flowing, expressive sound in a choral group is (to this listener) unsurpassed. A brilliant future is anticipated for this unusually talented young woman.

Also behind the scenes, but very important, are Evelyn Mickles, Joan Petrakis, Maggie Bovis, George Lendaris, George Haikalis, Jeffrey Economou, Rose Munson, Cathy Zarbis, George Georgantas, Agi Grigoriadis, Bill Bobolis, Paul Pronoitis, Bonnie Lozos, Adrianna Kolandranos, Dimmie Efstathiou, Athena Tsougourakis, Connie Speronis, Harry Booras, Nick Chimitras, Jane Patsakos, John Douglas, Tom Pallad, Jim Economou, Anna Marakas Counelis, Mike Hadgis, Chris Calle, James Counelis, Steve Bournos, Lois Pappademos, and Dean Limberakis. There are many others dotted throughout our continent. On a local level, these people keep up the enthusiasm, find supporters, raise funds, and make arrangements for travel, housing, transportation, and countless other necessary details to keep choral organizations afloat, but they get little recognition.

In closing, one vital force should be recognized as having made such tremendous progress possible. This force is the Holy Synod, with its diocesan bishops and their clergy. In each area of the United States, our bishops have provided the best possible support, encouragement, and spiritual guidance. This is real trust, and the hierarchy apparently has always had confidence in the musical leadership. Such an attitude, of course, stems from the top, our own Archbishop Iakovos. It is from him that the course of choral development has been charted and expanded. It is from him that a network now extends—of dedicated, trained, talented, and energetic church musicians working locally, regionally, and nationally to preserve and extend the rich heritage of Byzantine music and Orthodox worship.

Notes

1. Editor's note: This essay was originally published in *History of the Greek Orthodox Church in America*, compiled and edited by Reverend Miltiades B. Efthimiou and George A. Christopoulos (New York: Greek Orthodox Archdiocese of North and South America, 1984), 303–23, and has been lightly edited for this volume. The author originally extended his gratitude to the National Forum of Greek Orthodox Musicians for its research assistance in preparing this chapter and the special contributions of Vicki Pappas, national chairperson.

Greek Café Music[1]

—Roderick Conway Morris

The Origins of Greek Café Music

During the second half of the nineteenth century, there emerged in the seaports of western Asia Minor and the Aegean a distinctive form of Greek urban popular music. It was the product of the lower levels of Greek-speaking society and flourished in the haunts of the criminal underworld—hashish and gambling dens, cheap wineshops, brothels, and low-class musical cafés—and among the humblest participants in commercial life: sailors, fishermen, workers in the meat, vegetable, and fish markets, stevedores, small café owners, and traders. The musical institutions where this music could be heard ranged from makeshift hashish dens to somewhat better appointed but, in terms of clientele, hardly more socially elevated Eastern-flavored *cafés chantants*.

Musical entertainment and displays of dancing were already well-established features of the taverns and cafés of the Ottoman Empire by the seventeenth century. The entertainers themselves were usually Greeks, Armenians, Jews, or Gypsies rather than Turks; the Turkish traveler and writer Evliya Çelebi, in his *Seyahatname*, gives an exhaustive account of these popular musicians and dancers as they appeared in the great procession of the trade guilds of Istanbul held for Sultan Murad IV in 1638. The dancing boys alone are numbered at 5,705 (Çelebi 1846, 240–41). Foreign travelers and residents in the Near East provide many descriptions of the music and dancing boys in the taverns and cafés of Asia Minor and Istanbul, often drawing attention to the dominant role played by Greek performers. As François Charles Pouqueville, for example, writes:

> In the taverns, of which there are an infinite number in the capital of the *true believers*, there are commonly a sort of dancers called *yamakis*. They are Greeks from the islands of the Archipelago, elegantly dressed, with bracelets and necklaces of precious stones, and with very rich shawls. They have long flowing hair, are perfumed with essences, and highly rouged. The indolent Turks are extremely fond of these dancers: they encourage them by large presents of money: and each fixing upon a

favorite, they will often finish even by fighting to maintain the superiority of such and such a *yamaki*. The guard then interposes, and separates the combatants by rolling the empty barrels in among them; for the barrels and the drinkers are pell-mell together in the same place. After this the tavern is shut up, and the master cannot obtain permission to open again without paying some piasters. (1813, 290)

Indeed, the frequent rioting resulting from the inflamed passions and rivalries among the spectators at the displays of the dancing boys in public places often necessitated the intervention of the authorities and even the sultan himself (Tott 1785, 2:132), and finally led to a decree banning their performances altogether (And 1976).

During the nineteenth century, dancing girls (Turkish, *çengi*), who, in keeping with the Muslim practice of restricting the appearance of women in public, had for the most part previously performed at private gatherings, began to perform more openly, although once again the dancers were usually Greeks or Armenians. Along with other general changes in social conditions, another factor that rendered it acceptable for women to appear in public in this manner was their inclusion in the *tulâat* (improvised popular theater acted on a small stage) and in a kind of musical interlude, called a *kanto*, in which female singers performed songs, dancing and enacting the words with appropriate gestures. This new form of popular theater, which began to displace the traditional *ortaoyunu* (improvised folk theater in the round), seems itself to have elements derived from the French and Italian cafés chantants that were occasionally set up in Turkey by visiting European troupes of entertainers in the late nineteenth century.

Therefore, we can see that by the 1870s the old style of café and tavern performance, with dancing boys in the center of the floor and musicians among them or off to one side, has given way to women dancing and singing (often on a small raised platform called a *palko*) at one end of the room, with the musicians behind them.

The music in these establishments was, like the music that accompanied the dancing boys, *ala turka*: that is, music based on the *makam* system of Turkish classical music (as opposed to *ala franka*, European or European-style music). Also, the repertoire consisted of Turkish songs and dances, although when these cafés were established in the midst of an almost exclusively Greek population, there was a tendency to introduce Greek lyrics into the Turkish songs (without, however, altering the ala turka nature of the music) and to include a number of Greek island and mainland *dimotika* (folk music) pieces.

In Greece itself these cafés acquired the name *café aman*, probably because of the frequent occurrence of the word *aman* (alas! mercy!) in the Turkish songs that were their distinctive hallmark, but possibly, as Dimitrios Vikelas suggests, in order to distinguish them from the café chantant, where Western-style music

Figure 35. Hashish smokers and musicians with *baglamas* and *tzouras* being arrested by the Greek police, ca. 1930. Photographer unknown. Courtesy of Roderick Conway Morris.

was played: "[O]n voit sur la scène une troupe de caféaman, comme on dit pour le distinguer du caféchantant. C'est un concert de musique turque, entremêlé de ballets egalement turque" (1885, 247). Vikelas witnessed this touring café aman company in Pirgos during the 1880s, but there appears to have been a permanent café aman in Athens at least as early as 1874 (Stasinopoulos 1963, 117). These musical establishments became very numerous in Greece after the defeat of the Greek invasion of Turkey in 1919 and the subsequent exchange of populations after 1922, when some 1.5 million Asia Minor Greek refugees came to Greece. Indeed, with some notable exceptions, Asia Minor Greek musicians proceeded to dominate the urban popular musical scene in mainland Greece for the following two decades.

Although the café aman was a favorite resort of prostitutes and ruffians and was frequented by the lower strata of society generally, there were a number of more strictly cabalistic criminal venues that fostered their own style of Greek urban music and song. This music—usually referred to nowadays as *rebetika*—drew upon and contributed to the café aman but retained a number of distinctive features. This type of musical expression was especially the product of the hashish dens (*teke*) and the prisons, the connection between the two institutions effectively nurtured by the fact that the habitués of the former frequently became inmates of the latter.

In both Greece and Turkey, smoking hashish was an established communal urban low-life activity usually accompanied by music, played on a *baglamas* or bouzouki; songs often consisted of a series of improvised or semi-improvised couplets. The baglamas or bouzouki could also provide diverting interludes of instrumental improvisation (*taximi*) or offer musical accompaniment for dance. Similarly, music and hashish smoking were a regular feature of prison life encouraged by the enforced idleness, communal lifestyle, and lack of supervision over the inmates. The nexus between hashish music and prison music is attested not least by the blending of hashish and prison motifs in many of these low-life songs.

The Music

The principle of composition and performance in Greek café music was the Turkish *makam*, which itself derives substantially from the Arabo-Persian musical system. In outline, the makam (pl. *makamlar*) provides the musician with a melodic framework for both improvisation in free time and rhythmic composition, and consists of a prescribed starting note, an ascending and descending scale with certain distinctive melodic contours, and particular notes that should be emphasized. The makam, sometimes called the *dromos* (literally road, way) by Greek musicians, finds its closest Western counterpart in the concept of mode in early European music. Whereas a number of café aman musicians received some training in classical Turkish music, which gave them a familiarity with a wide range of makamlar, most bouzouki players worked with a more restricted number.

The normal practice in performance, as in Turkish classical music, was to play a series of songs or instrumental pieces of the same makam in succession without intervals, usually prefaced by a passage of solo instrumental improvisation. When a new set of songs in another makam was introduced, they were once again preceded by a taximi in that makam. All the musicians would play the same melody in unison but would add their own embellishments and individual ornamentation within the limits set by the melodic and rhythmic modes, so creating a heterophonous effect. Except in the case of the taximi—played in free time—the rhythmic structure was provided by a rhythmic mode (*usûl*). Most of these consist of combinations of twos and threes, with the nine rhythm, divided into various permutations, being particularly favored.[2]

The vast majority of café musicians were completely unversed in Western musical notation and, even when sheet music very occasionally exists from the period,[3] it represents music composed in a makam transcribed into Western notation, rather than music composed according to European canons. Indeed, the entire concept of "composition" in the context of café music is problematic. First, the most prized form of purely instrumental creation was the taximi, in which the player would improvise within the melodic parameters set by the makam; here, the act of improvisation constituted composition. Second, musicians drew upon a large stock of traditional melodies from tavern and musical café songs, folk tunes, dervish music, and Turkish classical music. Naturally enough, the absence of fixed notation and the practice of extensive ornamentation during the performance encouraged variations and developments of the received material, which formed the basis for "new" compositions. Thus, before the advent of recorded sound, musical virtuosity and creativity in performance, especially in improvisation, were more highly esteemed than the claim to a particular composition.

With the beginning of commercial recording, however, the appearance of an author's or composer's name on the label of a disc became the source of previously unavailable financial and personal rewards. In fact, earlier recordings (ca. 1905–1920) seldom bear a claim to composition of the music; subsequently, such a claim became more usual, although often it is unclear whether it refers to the music and/or the lyrics. Therefore, claims to the origination of music should be treated with some caution and skepticism.

Panayotis Toundas, for example, who was one of the most energetic promoters of Greek café music and a prodigious discoverer of musical talent, is frequently cited as the composer on the labels of discs recorded in the 1920s and 1930s. However, in many cases where it has been possible to trace particular melodies to an earlier period, these turn out to be traditional Greek or Turkish tunes, hence revealing Toundas, in Western musical terms, as more an arranger than a composer. Moreover, a number of surviving musicians of the period bear witness to Toundas's practice of searching out traditional pieces and his dexterity at arranging them for the purpose of recording.

This brings us to the final obstacle in establishing the composer of any given piece preserved on disc. Although surviving musicians are a valuable source of information on the music, songs, personalities, and lifestyle of the period, even allowing for the length of time that has elapsed, they frequently manifest the distressing inability to be consistent or truthful. This derives from a number of motives—self-aggrandizement, partisanship, and jealousy—and has caused a considerable amount of confusion and disagreement. It is not uncommon for two or three musicians to claim musical authorship for themselves or their friends for a single piece. In conclusion, bearing in mind the essentially traditional quality of the music and the practice of variation and improvisation in performance, even in those cases where it is possible to establish some responsibility for a composition, it still may not be an entirely individual composition in the Western sense.

Giambattista Toderini, who resided in Istanbul in the late eighteenth century and took a scholarly and informed interest in the indigenous music, both classical and popular, observed: "La musique cultivée par les Grecs d'aujourd'hui à

Constantinople, excepté la musique d'église et la romeque qui ne vaut pas grande chose, est de la musique toute turque" (1789, 224). ("La romeque" refers to the *syrtos/kalamatianos* circle dance.) Similarly, a manuscript dating from the early nineteenth century recently discovered at the Greek Orthodox Patriarchate in Istanbul records a number of popular songs in Greek, and above each is given the Turkish makam and usûl. So, too, the music of the late nineteenth-century café aman, with the exception of the Greek dimotika pieces that found their way into the repertoire, still falls within the tradition of Turkish popular music.

However, as early as the beginning of the twentieth century, certain Western musical influences can be detected, as, for example, in the popularity of the Italian mandolin, the guitar, and the accordion, which, being unable to reproduce microtones, are unsuitable for a proper rendering of certain makamlar. Nonetheless, this influence could be described as superficial and did not become radical until the third decade of the twentieth century, when the creation of music based on Turkish makamlar declined and with it the ability to improvise. An index of this process can be found in the rise to fame, as a popular urban musician and bouzouki player, of Vassilis Tsitsanis, who was born in Trikala (a provincial town in central Greece), completed a high school education, learned to play Western music and European notation, had no links with low-life activities, and was wholly ignorant of the makam system. Indeed, Tsitsanis has remarked that there are only two modes: major and minor.

The Instruments

The instruments employed in the café aman were those of the classical and popular urban Turkish ensembles. Collectively, these were sometimes referred to in Turkish as *incesaz* or "fine orchestra," denoting sophisticated chamber instruments, as opposed to *kabasa* or "crude orchestra," describing a rougher rural ensemble usually consisting of a *davul* and *zurna*. Greek musicians commonly referred to the former type of ensemble as a *kompania*, although the label of one of the discs in the British Institute of Recorded Sound (BIRS)[4] collection, Markos Melkon's *Sakramento–Boston–Nea Yorki* (Balkan 822-A), describes the ensemble as *psila organa*, a literal translation of the Turkish incesaz.

The primary instruments of the kompania were the *outi* (Turkish, *ud*), a short-necked, unfretted plucked lute with five pairs of strings (and sometimes an additional single string); the *kanonaki* (Turkish, *kanun*), a board zither resembling a psaltery with twenty-six courses of strings in sets of three, which is rested on the player's knees and plucked with two plectrums attached to the index fingers by rings; the *santouri* (Turkish, *santur*), a trapezoidal-shaped dulcimer with twenty-four courses of strings in sets of four, which is suspended from the player's neck

Figure 36. Markos Melkon, "Σακραμεντο–Βοστον–Νεα Υορκη" (Sacramento–Boston–New York). Balkan Phonograph Records, Balkan 822-A. Courtesy of Meletios Pouliopoulos.

Figure 37. Lambros Leondaridis (*lyra*), Roza Eskenazi (*defi*), and Agapios Tomboulis (*outi*). Athens, ca. 1930. Photographer unknown. Courtesy of Roderick Conway Morris.

and shoulders by a leather strap or rested on a table, and struck with two light wooden hammers tipped with cotton pads; the *lyra* (sometimes called by its Turkish name, *kemençe*), a short-necked bowed lute with three strings, which are stopped by pressing the fingernails against the strings rather than pressing them down onto the fingerboard as with the violin; the *defi* (Turkish, *def*), a circular frame drum with metal jingles, very similar to the tambourine; and the *zilia* (Turkish, *zil*), pairs of metal finger cymbals attached to the thumbs and index fingers of each hand and struck together.

The lyra was very commonly replaced by the Western violin, and the outi was sometimes replaced by the *cümbüs*, which is strung and played in exactly the same way but has a metal, instead of a wooden, resonator with a goatskin sound table and a longer neck than an outi. The kanonaki and santouri were never played in the same kompania. The two main percussion instruments—the defi and the zilia—were played exclusively by women, the zilia particularly while dancing. The zilia were sometimes replaced by pairs of wooden spoons—*koutalia*—played like castanets. It is worthy of note that all the stringed instruments were capable of rendering makamlar with the correct microtones, either by virtue of the absence of frets on the fingerboard or the presence of a large number of strings that could be tuned to the given makam and plucked or struck open.

The characteristic instruments of the hashish dens and prisons were the bouzouki and its smaller relations: the *tzouras* (Turkish, *cura*) and the baglamas (like the Turkish *bağlama* in form, but much smaller). The bouzouki is a long-necked lute with three pairs of strings played with a plectrum. At the beginning of the twentieth century, it was still indistinguishable from the Turkish *buzuk*, with a carved wooden or gourd bowl, moveable gut frets, and wooden tuning pegs. However, more recently, the bouzouki's body has been carvel-built like a *laouto* or mandolin, and it has acquired fixed metal frets and metal machine tuning heads. The tzouras has a very small carved wooden bowl, but a neck equal, or nearly equal, in length to that of a bouzouki, and the baglamas is a miniature version of the bouzouki.

These instruments were particularly favored by hashish smokers and prisoners, not least because they are relatively cheap and simple to construct and repair; they can be played quietly in order to avoid attracting attention from outsiders; and they can easily be concealed. The periodic need for concealment arose from the strong associations that the bouzouki, tzouras, and baglamas had with hashish smoking and the criminal underworld. This association led to the instruments themselves becoming a focus for police persecution in the 1930s, particularly during the Ioannis Metaxas dictatorship after 1936. Greek police files of the period contain photographs of seized hookahs used by hashish smokers and confiscated musical instruments, side by side (Stringaris 1964, plate 3).

The Dances

Dance played an indispensable and integral role in Greek café music, and, as travelers of the eighteenth and nineteenth centuries observed, the Greeks stood out as being keen dancers, even in the Middle East, where it was so generally popular as a pastime. The dance that characterized the performances of both dancing girls and female singers in the café aman was the *tsifteteli*, a form of belly dance found all over the Middle East. The term "tsifteteli" derives from the Turkish *çiftetelli* ("with double strings"), since it was common for the lyra or violin player to tune two strings of the instrument together in order to enhance the undulating and wailing effect of the music to complement and encourage the erotic movements of the dancer (Mazaraki 1959, 49).

The single most popular male dance, both in the café aman and in the more exclusively criminal haunts, was the *zeibekiko*. This was originally a male martial dance, versions of which were performed throughout western Asia Minor, but it was particularly identified with the irregular troops and brigands of the mountains of the Aydın-İzmir region—the Zeybeks. It was introduced to the Greeks through the large Greek population in western Anatolia, especially in İzmir (Smyrna) and its environs, and its popularity in other Turkish cities with Greek communities outside the Anatolian region where it originated. The steps of the dance are for the most part improvised on a basic circling pattern, punctuated by the dancer's leaping, crouching, spinning, and kneeling, and his striking the ground with the palms of his hands. As in the original martial version, the style offers a fine opportunity for the dancer to display his physical prowess and agility; in addition, its loose, spontaneous form allows for highly idiosyncratic styles of performance and stimulates self-projection and expression. The zeibekiko was commonly danced in confined spaces—between the tables in small cafés and taverns, in hashish dens, in prison cells, and, by sailors, on board ship—and, perhaps as a consequence, even when more space is available the dancer tends to move within a very restricted area of the floor. In its urban setting, zeibekiko became the dance par excellence of the *mangas*, the habitué of the criminal underworld and the self-conscious profligate who lived in defiance of the moral code of society.

Whereas the zeibekiko was a solo dance—indeed, to step onto the floor while another man was dancing constituted a challenge to a fight—the second most popular male dance, the *hasapiko*, was danced by two or three men linked together with their arms over one another's shoulders. The hasapiko (Turkish, *kasap*—butcher) is reputed to have been the dance of the old butchers' trade guild in Istanbul and in its present form is clearly related to certain country dances still found in northern Greece and Serbia. A number of Greek dimotika dances were also sometimes performed in the café aman, including dances in which the couple face each other—the *karsilamas* and the *ballos*—and the Panhellenic circular chain dances: the *syrtos* and the *kalamatianos*. However, these dances did not develop distinct urban versions, as did the zeibekiko, hasapiko, and tsifteteli, and were of secondary importance in these nonrural milieus.

The Songs

The songs of the Greek musical cafés embrace a wide range of subjects and occasions. The café aman offered songs in praise of the mangas, alluring love songs spiced with sexual innuendo and, perhaps most common of all, complaints about the perversity of fate, faithless lovers, exile, poverty, drunkenness, drug addiction, and the general injustice of life. Hashish and prison songs narrate events both dramatic and inconsequential in the life of the underworld and sometimes consist of a string of tenuously connected or even totally unrelated couplets encapsulating protests, threats, banalities, jokes, and whimsical flights of fancy. Others relate to activities such as preparing the hookah, lighting it and passing it around, drinking, throwing gambling dice, playing music, and dancing. Others again derive from the provocative and mocking verses that were habitually exchanged between pugilists and bravos as a prelude to brawling.

The question of authorship of lyrics presents very much the same problems encountered in attributing particular pieces to a single composer. Performers drew upon a reservoir of traditional song material, poetic formulas, and emotional clichés. It should also be remembered that it was the practice in performance to run one song into another without pause and that the singers, like the instrumentalists, did not subscribe to the notion of a fixed text. On the contrary, rather than attempting to give identical renderings of a particular song, they would deliberately change words and introduce whole verses from other songs for the sake of variety.

Nevertheless, the emergence of commercial sound recording provided both the incentive for performers to claim authorship of existing traditional songs and to create variations of them and new songs based on their central themes to satisfy the demands of the recording companies. Consequently, as is the case with the music, claims to authorship have to be treated with care, and disputes between individuals and factions are even more common and vituperative than disagreements over melodic compositions.

Apart from songs played to different dance rhythms, one type of song in particular that was extremely popular in Turkish musical cafés and later introduced into the Greek repertoire is worthy of mention. Usually known among the Greeks as an *amanes*, this kind of song is the vocal equivalent of the instrumental taximi, consisting of virtuoso vocal improvisation in a particular makam.

It is normally introduced by a short instrumental improvisation establishing the outline of the makam. Then one or more couplets are sung in free time beginning with, and extended and embroidered by, frequent interpolations of the word *aman* (alas! mercy!) and sometimes other Turkish words of similar import, such as *meded* (mercy! aid!) and *yara* (sorrow!). In most cases, the singer pauses during the song, and the leading musician plays a refrain or a passage of improvisation. The couplets cover many subjects, but usually they concern disappointed love or make generalized, pessimistic statements about the impermanence of things and people's helplessness in the face of destiny.

The Turkish word for this kind of song is *gazel* or *manî*. The Greek word *amanes* (an *aman* song) clearly derives from the frequent occurrence of the word "aman" in the song but also has associations with the Turkish manî: indeed, early gramophone record labels often describe such a song as a "Greek Mane."

The Commercial Recording of Greek Café Music

The fragmentary nature of material documenting the commercial recording of Greek urban popular music makes it very difficult to date individual discs accurately. However, a certain amount of information can be extracted from sales catalogs, artists' recording sheets, advertisements, and contemporary accounts; these, in conjunction with a number of key events in phonographic history (such as the replacement of the picture of an angel by the famous dog on the labels of Gramophone Company discs in 1909 and the introduction of electric recording in 1925), provide an overall, if general, dating framework.

The first commercial recordings of Greek café music appear to have been made in Istanbul and İzmir during the early years of the twentieth century. Master copies were recorded locally by visiting engineers, the discs manufactured in England and Germany and then exported to the Eastern Mediterranean and Middle East. The prominent companies of this pioneer period were the Gramophone Company, Zonophone, Odeon, and Orfeon, and their labels frequently bore the name of the recording locality. The recording of Greek music also commenced in the United States around this time, probably around 1910. Victor produced separate catalogs of Greek discs from at least as early as 1913 and Columbia (USA) from at least as early as 1915. Recording in Greece itself did not commence until about 1920. The recordings were still made in temporary studios, including rooms in the Hotel Tourist and the German Club in Athens, and the masters sent to Europe for manufacture. Purpose-built studios and a factory were finally set up in 1930 at Rizoupolis on the outskirts of Athens. Although constructed by Columbia, they were used by all the companies recording in Greece, including Odeon, HMV, Parlophone, and Decca.

Figure 38. "Smyrneïkos manes," 1906. Zonophone X-108003, Istanbul. Courtesy of Roderick Conway Morris.

Figure 39. Recording session, Athens, probably late 1920s. Right to left, Dimitris Arapakis (*sandouri*), Dimitrios Semsis (violin), unknown singer, Antonis (Dalgas) Diamantidis, and Yannis Davos (mandola). Courtesy of Roderick Conway Morris.

Meanwhile, the 1920s and 1930s were a period of great activity in the recording of Greek popular music in the United States. Established companies continued to add Greek discs to their lists in increasing quantities. New labels such as Kaliphone/Kaliphon, Metropolitan, and Orthophonic (Victor) appeared specifically for Greek and Turkish music; even some personal labels emerged, for example Gadinis for Kostas Gadinis and his ensemble, and Virginia for Virginia Magkidou. Whereas the lyrics on discs recorded in America never appear to have been subject to any kind of official control, in Greece itself Metaxas introduced strict censorship in 1936. References to hashish and low-life activities, and sexual innuendo, were banned. Also, Turkish songs and ala turka music generally were discouraged as undesirable alien imports. Thus, both café aman musicians and bouzouki players suffered severe restrictions that affected not only their personal fortunes but also the ultimate survival of the genre.

The Collection at the British Institute of Recorded Sound

Despite its modest size, the BIRS collection of 78-rpm recordings of Greek café music, which now forms part of the British Library Sound Archive in London, gives a remarkably balanced picture of the range of discs made from the earliest days of the commercial recording of Greek café music at the beginning of the twentieth century up to the years following the Second World War, when the tradition lost its vitality. Fortunately, most of the discs are in good condition.

The music of café aman is very well represented. There are fifteen songs by the most celebrated female singer of the 1920s and 1930s in Greece, Roza Eskenazi, including her first disc, "Lili i skantaliara." Eskenazi began her career as a dancing girl in the café aman, where she was discovered by the musician and entrepreneur Panayotis Toundas. Second only to Eskenazi in the period was another Toundas protégée, Rita Abatzi. There are eleven pieces sung by her in the BIRS collection, including two of her best-known recordings, one on the theme of reluctant emigration, "Mi me stelneis mana stin Ameriki," the other a hashish song, "Ta hanoumakia." Most of the important male café aman vocalists also appear: Antonis Diamantidis, Giorgos Kavouras, Spyros Peristeris, Stellakis Perpiniadis, Kostas Roukounas, and, along with Eskenazi on "O Mylonas," Kostas Marselos. These discs also bear witness to the virtuosity and inventiveness of the café aman instrumentalists, notably the outi player Agapios Tomboulis, the lyra player Lambros Leondaridis, and the most renowned Greek ala turka violinist, Dimitrios Semsis, who is also represented by four classic, purely instrumental pieces. In addition, there are some fine examples of amanedes by Roza Eskenazi, Marika Papagika, Lefteris Menemenlis, and Yiorgos Tsanakas.

Perhaps the most interesting single feature of the BIRS collection is the extensive number of discs made in America by Greek emigrants from Asia Minor and Greece. These include the female vocalists Victoria Hazan, Virginia Magkidou, Amalia Matsa Baka, and the supremely gifted and much-recorded Marika Papagika. As for male vocalists and instrumentalists, we have the Armenian outi player Markos Melkon (who, like some of the other performers, recorded songs in both Greek and Turkish), the Kostas Gadinis ensemble, the Cretan lyra player Harilaos Piperakis, and the guitar player and singer George Katsaros.

George Katsaros exercises a peculiar fascination over scholars of Greek urban music, not only because of his highly idiosyncratic and engaging vocal and instrumental style but also because of the breadth of his repertoire, which embraces hashish songs—"Chthes to vradi stou Karipi," "Dervisaki," "Mes tou Manthou to teke," and "Pou pas Memeti"—as well as Italian-style *kantades* such as "Ean den isouna kakia" and "Mana mou ime fthisikos." The collection contains a substantial proportion of the known Katsaros recordings, most of which are in virtually mint condition. Finally, there are a number of interesting discs of the bouzouki as played by the most famous "Piraeus-style" musician, Markos Vamvakaris—"Mi me peismatoneis" and "O Yannis o koumbaros"—and by the post–World War II popular rebetiko exponents Vassilis Tsitsanis (accompanying Ioanna Georgakopoulou) and Nikos Pourpourakis.

Glossary of Terms and Instruments

akordeon	Western accordion
ala turka	Popular urban music based on the *makam* system of Turkish classical music
amanes	A piece of vocal improvisation adorned and extended by the word "aman"
andikrysto	Another name for *karsilamas* dance
baglamas	Long-necked plucked lute
ballos	Facing-couple dance in duple time, particularly popular in the Aegean islands
bouzouki	Long-necked plucked lute
café aman	Café offering *ala turka* musical entertainment
daouli	Large double-headed cylindrical drum
darabuka	See *toumbeleki*
defi	Circular wooden-frame drum with metal jingles (similar to a Western tambourine)
dromos	Greek term for *makam* (literally "road," "way")

gazel	Originally a love poem, but also used as a synonym for *amanes*, especially when the lyrics are in Turkish
hasapiko	Male line dance in duple time
kalamatianos	Circular chain dance for men and women in 7-time
kanonaki	Plucked board zither
karsilamas	Facing-couple dance in 7- or 9-time
koutalia	Wooden or metal spoons struck together in pairs as a percussion instrument
laouto	Long-necked fretted lute with four pairs of strings, plucked with a goose-feather plectrum; although widespread in rural areas, it rarely appears in urban ensembles
lyra	Short-necked, bowed lute with three strings
makam	A Turkish musical system of modes and tonal intervals
mandola	Large mandolin
manes	See *amanes*
mangas	An urban ruffian, spiv, or habitué of the criminal underworld
minore	An *amanes* in which a Western minor scale is employed as a base for vocal improvisation
outi	Short-necked plucked lute; oud
rebetika	Popular urban Greek music originating in Aegean seaports among lower economic classes
rebetis	An urban ruffian (or *mangas*)
santouri	Greek subtype of hammered dulcimer
saz	Turkish term denoting any plucked stringed instrument, but particularly with reference to the family of long-necked Turkish lutes
sousta	Facing-couple dance in duple time, particularly popular in the Aegean islands
syrtos	Circular chain dance for men and women in duple time, danced in various forms throughout the Greek-speaking world
taximi	Instrumental solo in free time improvised within the framework of a specific *makam*; Turkish, *taksim*
toumbeleki	Hourglass drum made of brass or clay with goatskin stretched across one end
tsamikos	Male chain dance in 6-time
tsifteteli	Greek version of belly dance
tzouras	Long-necked plucked lute with a very small carved wooden bowl, but with a neck equal, or nearly equal, in length to that of a bouzouki

violi	Western violin
zeibekiko	Male dance in 9-time
zilia	Finger cymbals

Acknowledgments

I would like to thank Stathis Gauntlett of the University of Melbourne, Hector Catling of the British School of Athens, Markos Dragoumis of the Center for Asia Minor Studies in Athens, Theodore Petrides and Yannis Soulis of Athens, and V. L. Ménage and Margaret Bainbridge of the School of Oriental and African Studies in London for their generous help and encouragement.

Notes

1. This chapter was first published in *Recorded Sound: Journal of the British Institute of Recorded Sound* 80 (July 1981): 79–117, and is available online at http://www.roderickconwaymorris.com/Articles/415.html. The text has been lightly edited for the purposes of this republication.

2. In the Greek repertoire, for example: *vari zeibekiko* (2 + 2 + 2 + 3), *aptaliko zeibekiko* (3 + 2 + 2 + 2), and *karsilamas* (2 + 2 + 2 + 3).

3. There are some examples in the Ilias Petropoulos Archive in the Gennadius Library, Athens, such as mss. 1400-A, 1400-B, 1401-A, and 1401-B.

4. Since 1983, the BIRS has been part of the British Library Sound Archive.

References

And, Metin. 1976. *A Pictorial History of Turkish Dancing, from Folk Dancing to Whirling Dervishes, Belly Dancing to Ballet.* Ankara: Dost Yayinlari.

Çelebi, Evliya Efendi. 1846. *Narrative of Travels in Europe, Asia and Africa.* Translated by Joseph von Hammer. London: Oriental Translation Fund of Great Britain and Ireland.

Mazaraki, Despina. 1959. *To laïko klarino stin Ellada me eikosi mousika paradeigmata.* Athens: Galliko Institouto Athinon.

Pouqueville, François Charles Hugues Laurent. 1813. *Travels in the Morea, Albania and Other Parts of the Ottoman Empire.* London: Henry Colburn.

Stasinopoulos, Epameinondas. 1963. *I Athina tou perasmenou aiona (1830–1900).* Athens: n.p.

Stringaris, Michalis G. 1964. *Hashish.* Athens: n.p.

Toderini, Giambattista. 1789. *De la litterature des Turcs.* Paris: Chez Poincot.

Tott, François de. 1785. *Memoirs of Baron de Tott.* 2 vols. London: J. Jarvis.

Vikelas, Dimitrios. 1885. *De Nikopolis a Olympie, lettres a un ami.* Paris: P. Ollendorff.

Amanes: The Legacy of the Oriental Mother[1]

—Gail Holst-Warhaft

In his *Journey to the Morea: Travels in Greece*, Nikos Kazantzakis writes: "In the taverns, at festivals, on holidays, when they have drunk a little, the small business-men and infantry officers [of the Peloponnese], so logical and selfish, break into melancholy eastern *amanedes* [sing. *amanes*], into a sudden longing; they reveal a psyche completely different from their sober everyday one. A great treasure, a deep longing" (Kazantzakis 1965, 325).[2]

Further on, Kazantzakis expands on the bifurcating nature of the contem-porary Greek of his day: "What has the dually descended modern Greek taken from his father, what from his mother? . . . He is clever and shallow, with no metaphysical anxieties, and yet, when he begins to sing, a universal bitterness leaps up from his oriental bowels, breaks through the crust of Greek logic and, from the depths of his being, totally mysterious and dark, the Orient emerges" (1965, 326).

In these two passages, Nikos Kazantzakis articulates a common Greek atti-tude to a late Ottoman musical tradition, and in particular to the vocal improvi-sations called *amanedes*.

The Amanes

The amanes became emblematic of a style of music that was both admired for its emotional intensity and rejected for its association with the oriental and feminine side of the modern Greek psyche. Kazantzakis's description of the Greek split personality reflects a dichotomy noted by many foreign observers of Greece, beginning with Patrick Leigh Fermor's "Helleno-Romaic Dilemma" (1966, 96–147) and most subtly delineated by Michael Herzfeld (1987, chs. 4–5). Like all dichotomies, the division is not a clean one, and there are areas of overlap, but the interesting point is that such a dichotomy has been widely perceived in the Greek personality not only by outside observers but by Greeks themselves. As Herzfeld notes, the dichotomy is itself both a European notion and a literate device (1987, 96). It tends to reinforce stereotypes, especially about gender and the privileged position of the European versus the Oriental. Influenced by nineteenth-century accounts of the Orient, the European-educated Kazantzakis, like Nerval and Flaubert, aligns the Orient with the female, but not in the sense Edward Said notes of pure, inarticulate femininity (Said 1979, 186–88). As a Greek, and more importantly as a Cretan, Kazantzakis saw himself as uniquely capable of synthesizing Hellenism and the Orient.[3] His Apollonian/ Dionysian divide between West and East may be secondhand, but he employs the dichotomy not in order to privilege the Hellenic side of the Greek character but rather to honor his maternal inheritance, the mysterious, dark, and oriental soul embedded in the otherwise pragmatic Greek personality.

Not surprisingly, in this context, Kazantzakis describes the modern Greek as being "Digenes" (dually descended, twy-born). Digenes Akritas, hero of the eponymously titled epic Byzantine poem and of numerous folk songs, is, in the epic version, the son of an Arab father and a Greek mother. But, as Herzfeld (1987, 104) remarks, in many of the folk song texts, he becomes the son not of an oriental father but of a mother who is of marginal or outsider status. As guardian or baron of the Byzantine Empire's Mesopotamian borders, Akritas is geographically as well as socially marginalized. His feats of bravery, his capture by an Arab leader, and his ultimate recognition as a hero provided Greeks with an ideal myth of Greekness that was exploited by nineteenth-century nationalists.[4] Herzfeld compares the character of the redeemed outsider Digenes with the hero of the shadow puppet theater, Karagiozis, also a trickster figure, who successfully uses his wits to reverse his lowly status as a *raya* (chattel) of the Ottoman Empire. Both the ethnically ambiguous hero of the folk songs and epic poem, and the low-born hero of the puppet theater, triumph over their origins as well as their enemies. So the Digenes texts become an apt metaphor "for a nation struggling to obliterate a recent history that the tutelary West deemed degrading" (Herzfeld 1987, 106).

The fashioning of Greek nationalism in the nineteenth century was achieved under the gaze of a "tutelary West" that was so invested in the rebirth of an idealized Hellenism that it sent thousands of volunteers to fight for it. In response, Greeks were initially prepared to present an ideal image of themselves to their supporters. This did not mean that they were unaware of how little the image matched reality. The tension between the expectations of European philhellenism and the reality of an oriental past helped stereotype both the European and the Oriental as extreme poles of the Greek character. This polarization was played out in the *glossiko zitima*, or language question, in which *katharevousa* ("pure" language) came to stand for the European vision of a pure, revived Greekness and *dimotiki* (current language) for the recognition and celebration of an eclectic, heterogeneous past that gives richness to the Greek language without sacrificing its national character. Besides the language question, folklore was probably the most important area in which issues of national purity and eclecticism were played out.[5] Like the texts, music itself became the nexus of opposed views, and folklorists become leading figures in the struggle to claim folk song as the single most important link between ancient and modern Greece. The fact that many Greek folk songs conform to modal types described by ancient Greek theorists of music appeared to confirm a continuous tradition of melodic composition from the ancient to the modern period. The music of the Orthodox Church, which preserved some of the ancient modes, could also be invoked as an intermediary source.

Debate over the origins and character of Greek folk music originally focused exclusively on regional traditions or *dimotiki mousiki*, but from the 1880s onward urban music joined rural as part of the broader nationalist controversy.[6] At the center of the discussion about urban music was a disagreement about the relative merits of the "oriental" music performed in the *cafés aman* and the "European" music of the *cafés chantants*. This discussion needs to be placed against the background of a double-descended myth of nationalism that reflected a genuine ambiguity in the Greeks' perception of themselves. On the one hand, what the café aman music, especially the amanes, represented was the oriental side of the modern Greek inheritance. On the other, in contrast to the light and superficial music of the café chantant, it was recognized by many Greek intellectuals and musicians to be musically more profound, capable of expressing pathos and grief in a way that western European popular song did not.

For those Greeks like Kostis Palamas (Gauntlett 1989, 13; Kazantzakis 1965, 325; Phaidros 1881, 2–26), who recognized the depth and passion of a form of music that was non-European in origin, the problem became one of reclaiming it as an essentially Greek phenomenon. How was this to be done? Kazantzakis's association of the amanes or song of bitter grief with the contemporary Greek's oriental and maternal inheritance gives us at least a point of departure. Just as the mother, rather than the father, of Digenes Akritas becomes the outsider or marginal figure in the folk song tradition, so the song of pain or amanes is ascribed to the Greek's maternal inheritance. Thus the dark, mysterious, oriental strain of the Greek character is linked to the feminine through the art of lament. As a sort of stylized lament, the amanes is associated, in the Greek tradition, with the female voice. In rural Greece, as in most preindustrial societies, it is women who sing the laments for the dead, and not only women who are the immediate kin of the deceased but those who are regarded to be especially skilled in the art of expressing the pain of the community through the improvisation of an artful song.[7]

In Greece, as a number of researchers have observed (Alexiou 1974, 10–35; Auerbach 1987, 25–43; Caraveli 1986, 169–92; Seremetakis 1991, 99–158; Holst-Warhaft 1992, 14–97, 98–126), both laments (*mirologia*) and the women who sing them (*mirologistres*) have been regarded, throughout history, with some ambiguity. They may be considered essential at the time of death, but otherwise they are often avoided, even shunned by Greek men. Moreover, there is a long line of thought in Greece, beginning in antiquity and continuing through the Byzantine period, that associates lament, especially excessive lament, not only with the female but with the Orient, namely with Asia Minor (Holst-Warhaft 1992, 130–33). This long association appears to be reflected in the controversy about amanedes in the Athenian press summarized by Thodoros Hatzipantazis (1986) and Stathis Gauntlett (1987, 1989). In the debate, which centered on the Greekness or otherwise of music performed in the cafés aman, the term "oriental music," as Gauntlett notes, is often synonymous with amanes. As the musical form in which the oriental voice—the lamenting (female) voice—is showcased, the amanes stands for what is, according to which side of the debate the writer is on, the least or the most Greek genre in the Asia Minor repertoire. The debate highlights the ambiguity that Greeks, more precisely Greek men, feel toward what Kazantzakis saw as the oriental and female side of their own inheritance.

A more extreme attempt to claim the amanes as essentially Greek is found in one of the most important documents we have on the subject: Yiorgos Phaidros's article "Pragmateia peri tou smyrneikou mane i tou par' arxaiois manero" (Treatise on the Smyrna Manes Known to the Ancients as Maneros), written in Smyrna in 1881. Phaidros traces the origin of the amanes to the ancient lament for Linos. Following Herodotus into error, he claims that Linos is called "Maneros" by the Egyptians.[8] The lament, the origin of song itself, was invented, according to Herodotus, to be sung in honor of the first Egyptian king's son, whose name was Maneros. Phaidros links the ancient Greek song for Linos or Ailinos to modern Greek and Egyptian folk laments. His attempt to derive *manes* from Maneros is etymologically far-fetched and dictated by his desire to claim the genre as Greek, via Egyptian lament rather than Turkish. While he demands that his own hypothesis of the ancient origin of manes not be rejected, he claims: "It is, on the other hand, absurd for anyone to call the contemporary manedes Turkish strains. They are clearly Greek strains that we have inherited from our forefathers and we must guard this inheritance forever" (Phaidros 1881, 18).

Notice how, in contrast to Kazantzakis, Phaidros insists that this inheritance is paternal, not maternal. Still more revealing, as Phaidros pursues his etymology, are his remarks about the nature of Turkish *makamia*:

The Turks have various monotonous melodies called makamia which mostly belong to Arabia or Egypt. These usually begin with the exclamation "Yiar Aman!" which means "merciful beloved" or "have mercy." Some foolish people added the letters "es" to the word Aman, and then left off the initial "a," forming the word Manes. But among the Ottomans, neither the word *Amanes* nor Manes occurred, nor did they sing the strain in the Minor key (*Minore*). The aforementioned Aman Yiar remains, according to the opinion of the writer, inexplicable and cannot be categorized. (Phaidros 1881, 20)

Phaidros reveals here his ignorance not only of Ottoman music but also of Greek. The modal types of the *minore* and *matzore* were certainly influenced by European music, but they do not indicate merely that a song is written in major or minor key—rather, that it is based on melodic material common to major or minor scales. The majority of amanedes were sung on Ottoman melodic types (*makamlar* in Greek is *makamia*). To call the *makam* "mode" is somewhat misleading. The scale is not the only determinant of the improvisations performed in each makam. There are also melodic progressions (Turkish, *seyir*) that characterize the makam and include an emphasis on particular notes. The interchangeable use of the terms *gazel*, manes, amanes, and *gazeli*, sometimes hyphenated, on record labels suggests that the recording companies and presumably the musicians themselves made no distinction between them. As a lyric form, it is possible to characterize the Ottoman gazel as a stylized romantic genre of poetry, composed in quatrains.

Musically, however, gazel simply came to mean the vocal equivalent of a *taksim* (Greek, *taximi*). The Ottoman singer would often take a quatrain from the classical Ottoman poetic repertoire and improvise a gazel that seemed to suit the mood of the lyrics (Aksoy 1997, 45). The gazel/amanes became a vehicle for the singer to display his or her musical talents, a showpiece for the sophisticated artist, just as the taksim was for the instrumentalist.

Within the genre of amanes, there are various subgroupings according to the musical mode of the particular amanes or to a song type such as *Tzivaeri*, *Galata*, or *tabahaniotika*.[9] Since each makam is not a scale but a group of melodic passages on one or more tone levels, the particular makam will dictate the melodic contour of each amanes. We may also be able to speak of an association of a particular group of makamlar with Greek amanedes. Of the entire range of makamlar, the *sabak*, *nihavent*, *hidzaz*, and *houzam* seem to have been among the most commonly used by Greek singers. There are also subgroupings of the amanedes according to the rhythm of the introduction and finale, which may be in the dance rhythms of *tsifteteli*, *ballos*, *syrtos*, and so on. In the faster rhythmic finales to the amanedes, there are even examples of tango and waltz, which change the mood of the piece to something quite lighthearted, but that does not alter the fact that the dominant mood, at least of the Greek amanes, is tragic. In fact, it may be a deliberate device to break the despairing tone of the piece.[10]

As a form of stylized lament, as Phaidros correctly noted, the amanes has links to Greek folk laments and, by association, to a feminine genre. This does not mean to say that it was necessarily sung by women, as we know from numerous male recordings, but that it was a form that Greeks may consciously or unconsciously have felt was particularly suited to the female voice because of the association with laments. In Phaidros's article about the manes, it is curious that the first example he uses to support his assertion that the mane or amanes is derived from ancient Greek lament is not a lament but another genre dominated in the folk tradition by women. It is a lullaby that he says was still being sung in Smyrna at the time he was writing his article (Phaidros 1881, 1–2):

> *Na mou kamni naniiii nani to moro mou naniii*
> *O ilios vyen' is ta vouna*
> *k'e perdike es ta dasi. . . .*
> *(1) kimisou (2) haidemenon mou*
> *ton ipnon na hortasis*
> *E to moro mou, e, e, e, e, e, e*

> So my baby can go hush-a-bye,
> The sun comes out on the mountains
> and the partridges from the forests.
> (1) Sleep (2) my dearest
> so you'll have all the sleep you want.
> Eh, my baby, eh, eh, eh, eh.

Phaidros may have chosen his example simply for the repeated *e* sounds or the melismatic vocal style, but there is interesting support for his association of lullaby with laments and with amanedes in general in a recording by Marika Politissa made in Athens between 1929 and 1931 on the Odeon label. The title given is the original Turkish ("Nini"), and it is designated as a manes.[11]

> *O-o . . . Ach*
> *Kimisou orfano pedi*
> *ke dakria mi hinis, aman!*
> *Stin tihi sou itan grafto*
> *orfano na min ise, aman!*
> *Kimisou orfano moro, naaaani*

> Ooh! Aah!
> Sleep, orphan child,
> And don't you cry, aman!
> It wasn't written in your fate
> For you to be an orphan, aman!
> Sleep, orphan baby, hush-a-byeeee!

The coupling of amanedes both with laments and lullabies confirms their association with the female voice. The association of lullaby with lament is not unique to Greece. In the Finnish-speaking region of Karelia, formerly occupied by Russia and later part of the Soviet Union, laments/lullabies for girls, whose inevitably miserable lives were considered a fate worse than death, were common (Nenola-Kallio 1982, 101). Similarly, laments for brides, usually sung by their mothers and female relatives, are a common phenomenon not only in Greece but in China and many other societies (see, for example, Blake 1979, Danforth 1982, Kligman 1988). What emerges from the cross-cultural comparative studies of laments is that with very few exceptions they, like lullabies and most other songs that mark rites of passage or stages in the life cycle, are not only women's songs but associated with a certain emotional intensity that may be admired, even sought out, by men in times of crisis but at other times may be considered unmasculine, overemotional, even threatening.

Refugees and the Music of Nostalgia

The revival of interest in Asia Minor music and the proliferation of cafés aman in Athens after the Greco-Turkish War of 1919–1922 with its consequent exchange of populations is hardly surprising. The sheer numbers of refugees created an audience for the music, and there were also many musicians among them. More importantly, the already established association of the amanedes with laments, articulated in Phaidros's essay, made them an ideal vehicle for the expression of the refugees' nostalgia for their lost homeland. Amanedes were still showpieces for the vocalists, but they were also, as Kazantzakis correctly observed, cries of bitterness that arose from their innermost being and represented, to singer and audience, the Orient they had been forced to abandon.

For the newly arrived refugees, the cafés aman of Athens were places to gather and collectively mourn the loss of their homeland while at the same time enjoying the fine musicianship of the artists who had emigrated from Istanbul or Smyrna. These artists soon made a large impact on the local Greek musical scene. Bülent Aksoy (1998, 4) notices an acceleration of borrowed melodies from Turkish music in rebetika songs of the post-1922 period; at the same time, many recordings were made of amanedes with Greek or a mixture of Greek and Turkish words. Although the cafés aman themselves were at their height of popularity in the years immediately following the war, recordings of café aman–style music, including amanedes, remained popular during the 1930s. Whereas Turkey and the United States had been the centers of the recording industry for Asia Minor music before the exchange of populations, from 1922 on, Athens became an important center of recordings. Even before the major studios were set up in

Figure 40. Rita Abatzi. Photo from *Rita Abatzi*, 1995. Lyra CD-0165/66, Athens. Courtesy of Meletios Pouliopoulos.

Greece, the Gramophone Company (later HMV) had sent a team to Greece, where they recorded various types of Greek music, none of it in the Asia Minor style. By 1924, when Odeon sent another team of talent scouts to Greece, the musical scene had changed dramatically. Using a Thessaloniki firm as their agent, Odeon conducted eight recording sessions in Athens during 1924–1925. The success of their recordings prompted three other recording companies (Gramophone, Columbia, and Polydor), to join the competition, making recordings in Athens and other Greek towns. Of the recordings made between 1925 and 1929 by these companies, approximately 30 percent were in the Asia Minor style. The Gramophone Company characterized and marketed these recordings as "rebetika" as well as "manes Constantinople" and "manes Smyrna."

Initially, Gramophone and Odeon each used a male refugee singer to perform Asia Minor or, as it was termed, "Anatolian"-style music. Yiorgos Vidalis, a refugee from Smyrna, became the chief vocal artist for Odeon, while Antonis Diamantidis, or "Dalgas," a native of Istanbul, was the mainstay of the Gramophone label. Both of these singers used the amanes to display their formidable skills. It was not until the 1930s that the male singers of amanedes were joined, in the Greek studios, by younger female performers like Rita Abatzi, Roza Eskenazi, and Marika Kanaropoulou.

These singers worked closely with other refugee musicians, reproducing the ensembles that had dominated the popular musical world they had left behind in Smyrna and Istanbul. The most earthy and perhaps the most distinctive of the Greek female vocalists of the 1930s, Rita Abatzi made a series of outstanding recordings of amanedes. She is accompanied by the brilliant Asia Minor–style violinist Dimitrios Semsis in several of these recordings. On an HMV recording of "Manes karip hetzaz" made around 1935 (OGA-285B, AO 2306),[12] she sings an amanes that seems uniquely adapted to the plight of the refugees and close in spirit and sentiment to the many Greek folk songs about *xenitia* (foreign lands). These songs often concern the loss of sons, husbands, or other male kin who have gone abroad.[13]

Aaaaaaaa, Aaaaaaaa, Aman!
Otan ftohini o anthropos, aman, aman!
Aman! O anthropos ine kaimos megalos.
Aaaaaaaaa!
Aman, aman!
Ine kaimos megalos mete kemile
Aman, aman!
Ton thanato tou karteri, aman, karteri,
yiati den ehi tharos.
Aaaaman!

Aaaaaaaaa, Aaaaaaaaa, Aman!
When a man grows poor, aman, aman,
Aman! A man, it's a great sorrow.
Aaaaaah!
Aman, aman!
It's a great sorrow *mete kemile*
Aman, aman!
He waits for death, aman, he waits
because he has no courage.
Aaaaman!

Another amanes that is close not only in spirit but in verse to a traditional *miroloi* is "Gazeli Neva Sebah," again recorded by Abatzi in Athens (this recording is included in Schwartz 1991 and dated by him as ca. 1935).[14]

Aman, aman
Prepi na skeftete kanis, aman aman . . .
tin ora tou thanatou, aman, aman . . .!

oti tha bi sti mavri yis, aman, . . . sti mavri yis [sic]
kai svini t'onoma tou, aman!

Aman, aman
A man must think, aman aman . . .
at the hour of his death, aman, aman . . .!
that he'll go into the black earth, aman, . . . into the black earth,
and his name will be erased, aman!

To anyone familiar with the Greek folk tradition, it is impossible not to see this bleak amanes as a form of lament. Despite the wide variety of music performed and recorded by the Asia Minor musicians in the decade following the exchange of populations, the fact that amanedes became synonymous with the music of the café aman (Gauntlett 1989, 13–15) suggests that they had become emblematic of what Greeks either admired or disliked about the music performed in these establishments. The melismatic style of the amanes was not unknown in Greek music (the same artists who recorded amanedes often recorded *kleftika*—heroic songs about brigands who fought the Turks that were also characterized by vocal ornamentation—and there were obvious parallels in the music of the Orthodox Church), but it was quite foreign to the light, popular music imported from Europe and to the music of the cabarets and musical theater becoming popular in Athens. It had more in common, indeed, with what could legitimately be called traditional Greek music than it did with European, but it came at a time when many bourgeois Greeks looked to Europe for their cultural models. It may also have reinforced the prejudice of local Greeks toward the newcomers as representatives of a somewhat different form of Greekness, one that had ties to a past they preferred to forget.

The debate that arose in the columns of the newspaper *Ta Athinaika Nea* in 1934 over whether amanedes should be banned in response to a rumor that the Kemalist government had banned them in Turkey made the association of these songs clear (Gauntlett 1989). The Turkish ban was said to be part of a campaign of modernization and Europeanization. Greeks now had to face the issue of whether Greece could afford to be considered less European than its eastern neighbor by allowing the offending oriental dirges to be sung in its public cafés. The response to a survey conducted by the newspaper was a spirited defense of the genre by "experts" such as the composer Manolis Kalomiris on the grounds that amanedes were derived from ancient Greek music via Byzantium. Either Phaidros's article had borne fruit, or the interviewees reflected the tendency of Greek nationalists to accept their "oriental" heritage provided it was passed through the filter of antiquity. In either case, the experts consulted recognized the amanedes as intrinsically more interesting than the music presented in the rival establishments—the cafés chantants. Despite the championing of the music of the cafés aman by respected figures in the music world of Athens, there were calls from the newspaper's own music critic for the banning of the amanedes and for raising taxes on imported recordings of such music from the United States.

The desire of local urban Greeks to establish a form of popular music that was firmly based in Greece rather than Asia Minor may have contributed to the success of Piraeus-style rebetika. Some of the refugee musicians were attracted to the low-class music of the Piraeus *manges* and joined ensembles that featured the bouzouki as their principle instrument. At first, these rebetika songs, especially in their instrumental solos, had much in common with the Asia Minor music, and there was considerable cross-fertilization between the two styles. The refugee musician Stratos Pagioumtzis, for example, recorded both rebetika songs and amanedes, and other refugees moved between one style and the other, although the orchestration of the two remained distinct. By 1935, however, bouzouki-style rebetika had begun to attract a wider audience at the expense of the café aman style. The reasons for the success of the all-male Piraeus-based rebetika take us back to Greek perceptions of the nature of the amanes and the fact that the bouzouki appears to have become, for many Greeks, symbolic of a new hybrid style of urban music.

Debate continued in the Athenian press about what would probably now be called the "political correctness" of various types of urban music, but the bouzouki-backed rebetika songs of the so-called Piraeus style gradually took center stage as the amanes faded from the repertoire, its traces still evident in the interpolated exclamations of *aman! aman!*, which continued to be a common feature of rebetika as well as of other types of Greek folk music. The censorship imposed by Prime Minister Ioannis Metaxas on rebetika, followed closely by World War II and the German occupation of Greece (which resulted in widespread starvation, particularly in the urban centers), turned rebetika into a form of covert protest.[15] At a time when most Greeks were united in their resentment toward the occupying power, Piraeus rebetika, with their generally unsentimental lyrics, their strident combination of bouzouki and baglamas, and their male dances, seemed more suited to represent the public mood of suppressed anger than the nostalgic Asia Minor amanedes.

The Asia Minor Style in the United States

To the Greek refugees of Asia Minor, many of whom eventually settled in the United States, the tragic history of Greece during the 1940s must have been viewed as a second catastrophe that mirrored, in many ways, the period of the 1920s. During the war and subsequent civil war, communication with Greece

Figure 41. Marika Papagika, "Manes in fa matzore," 1919. Columbia 85458. Courtesy of Meletios Pouliopoulos.

was greatly reduced, and the refugees felt twice displaced. As Dino Pappas, a son of refugees and a collector of Asia Minor music, wrote: "We Greeks from Asia Minor, displaced after 1922 and later, no longer had a place to think of as home. . . . [F]or us [it was] *xenitia* [living in a foreign land] with an extra dose of bitterness" (1995, 10). It is not surprising to find that there appears to have been a brief revival of the Asia Minor music during this period. Although it is impossible to make any definitive statements about the reasons for the revival, it is tempting to surmise that the increase in the number of recordings of songs during the 1940s in the United States, in particular of amanedes recorded by women singers, reflects a mood of despair and nostalgia in the refugee communities.

This revival needs to be placed in context. Asia Minor refugees had been recording in the United States since the early part of the twentieth century. A notable feature of the recordings of the teens and twenties is their stylistic innovation. A recording made in 1919 (Columbia 85358) of "Manes fa matzore" by Marika Papagika, for example, could almost be music for a silent movie. Like many of the early recordings she made with her cimbalom player husband Gus, it shows signs of having been "modernized." The Greek musician Tetos Demetriades, who became head of the Victor Company's Greek-Turkish label Orthophonic, influenced the musicians of his generation to adapt their music to the new culture. He himself made recordings of American songs with Greek words and westernized backing during the 1920s and 1930s. At the same time, as the person responsible for selecting material for the large Greek record-buying public, Demetriades did not hesitate to choose several recordings on the Turkish Sahibinin Sesi label for his reissues (Pappas 1995, 12). As Ole Smith (1995, 129–31) notes, Greek musicians may have adapted their music to their new environment, but they did not, on the whole, venture beyond their community into the American musical scene. What Smith ignores, however, is that Greek musicians had a much broader audience than the members of their own community. Stavros K. Frangos (1994, 43–63) argues that the live audience for Asia Minor music performed by Greek singers was made up of Armenians, Egyptians, Syrians, Jews, Bulgarians, and a few Turks. What this audience had in common was an appreciation of a musical tradition that had developed during the late Ottoman period. Whatever their attitude toward Turkey, they appreciated the artistry of singers and musicians skilled in that tradition. The most successful of the Greek émigré musicians, Marika Papagika, began recording Asia Minor music and Greek folk songs in New York in 1918, and continued to record a mixture of the two styles for most of her career. Born on the island of Kos, just off the Turkish coast, she also recorded songs in Turkish.[16] Significantly, in the year of the Smyrna disaster (1922), she recorded both a group of patriotic Greek songs and two songs in Turkish (Spottswood 1990).

It has been noted by various observers that the Asia Minor–style songs were popular not only with audiences in New York but in the Greek émigré communities all over the United States. Most of the Greek communities were not made up of refugees from Asia Minor, but all were composed largely of young men without families: "The loss of home that the Asia Minor Greeks sang of so eloquently must have struck a chord in those young men who also lived far from where they were born" (Frangos 1994, 46).

Nostalgia for the lost Greek, Armenian, or Turkish homeland was probably the strongest shared emotion among immigrants to the United States, and the music of the café aman, particularly the amanes, was perfectly suited to express it. Moreover, the absence of female family members undoubtedly made the associations of amanedes with women's musical forms still more poignant.

Despite their occasional experiments with modern sounds or lyrics, most of the Greek recording artists either remained conservative or reverted to a more conservative style. By the end of the 1920s, the two leading female vocalists of the Asia Minor style, Papagika and Coula Antonopoulou (Kyria Koula), had stopped recording, but among Papagika's last recordings were songs in the Asia Minor style that showed little trace of American influence. During the 1930s, recordings made in Greece became, for the next decade at least, more popular than local recordings, and the market for American Greek recordings of this type seemed to have been exhausted. During the 1940s, however, there was a brief

ΓΕΝΙΚΟΣ ΚΑΤΑΛΟΓΟΣ ΦΩΝΟΓΡΑΦΙΚΩΝ ΔΙΣΚΩΝ ΤΗΣ
"METROPOLITAN PHONOGRAPH RECORDS"

GENERAL CATALOG
"METROPOLITAN"
PHONOGRAPH
RECORDS

ΒΙΡΓΙΝΙΑ ΜΑΓΚΙΔΟΥ   ΑΜΑΛΙΑ

(Βιργινία Μαγκίδου—'Οριεντάλ ΤΡΙΟ)
(Νίκος Δ. Βιολί.)

150 Α — ΕΥΖΩΝΑΚΙΑ-ΕΥΖΩΝΑΚΙΑ
(Συρτός)
150-Β — ΔΕΝ ΜΠΟΡΩ ΝΑ ΚΑΤΑΛΑΒΩ
(Τσιφτὲ Τέλλι)
151-Α — ΣΚΛΑΒΙΑ ΤΗΣ ΜΑΝΑΣ
(Ζεϊμπέκικο)
151-Β — ΤΟ ΑΧ ΝΑ ΜΗ ΤΟ ΠΗ ΚΑΝΕΙΣ
('Αμανές)
152-Α — ΧΗΡΑ ΜΟΥ ΜΕ ΤΑ ΜΑΥΡΑ ΣΟΥ
(Συρτὸ)
152-Β — ΜΑΥΡΟΜΑΤΑ ΜΟΥ ΜΙΚΡΗ
(Χορὸς Πεταχτὸς)

153-Α — ΣΥΡΕ ΣΤΗ ΜΑΜΑ ΣΟΥ (Συρτὸ)
153-Β — ΣΑΝ ΤΑ ΜΑΤΙΑ ΣΟΥ
(Τσιφτὲ Τέλλι)

154-Α — ΕΛΑ ΔΩ ΜΑΡΙΚΑΚΙ ΜΟΥ
(Καρσιλαμὰς)
154-Β — ΠΑΡΑΜΑΝΑ ΚΑΙ ΒΑΡΚΑΡΗΣ
— Καλαματιανὸς —

Οἱ κάτωθι Δίσκοι μόλις ἐξεδόθησαν μὲ λόγια πλή-
ρη εἰς τὴν παραπλεύρως Σελίδα.

165-Α — Η ΝΟΣΟΚΟΜΑ ΜΑΝΝΑ
(Τζιορτζίνα Τέμπο)
165-Β — Η ΜΟΙΡΑ ΤΟΥ ΜΟΥΣΟΛΙΝΙ
(Συρτὸ)

166-Α - ΣΟΥ ΤΟ ΕΙΠΑ ΒΡΕ ΚΑΚΟΥΡΓΑ
(Ζεϊμπέκικο)
166-Β — ΠΑΣΧΩ ΝΑ ΕΒΡΩ ΜΙΑ ΚΑΡΔΙΑ
(Νέο Τσιφτὲ Τέλλι - 'Αμανές)

167-Α — Μ' ΑΓΑΠΑΕΙ ΕΝΑΣ ΝΕΟΣ
ΩΜΟΡΦΟ ΠΑΙΔΙ - Κάντο
167-Β — ΔΩΟ ΧΡΟΝΑΚΙΑ ΠΕΡΑΣΑΝ
ΠΟΥ ΧΩΡΙΣΑΜΕ - Συρτὸ

(Τουρκικοί, Βιργινία — 'Οριεντάλ ΤΡΙΟ)
2003-Α — BIR KANATLI KUSH OLSAN
2003-Β — MIHNETI DUNIAILE - Gazel

('Αμαλία)
('Ιωάννης Πάππας, κλαρίνο)
('Οριεντάλ 'Ορχήστρα)

160-Α — ΚΑΛΛΙΟΠΑΚΙ - Ζεϊμπέκικο
160-Β — ΣΜΥΡΝΕ·Ι·ΚΟΣ ΜΠΑΛΟΣ
161-Α — Μ' ΕΙΠΕΣ ΝΑ ΓΙΝΩ ΜΑΓΚΑΣ
(Δικελὶ Ζεϊμπέκικο)
161-Β — ΤΑ ΜΑΤΑΚΙΑ ΣΟΥ ΠΟΥΛΙ ΜΟΥ
(Τσιφτὲ Τελλὶ)
162-Α — ΑΔΑΝΙΩΤΟΠΟΥΛΑ
(Ζωηρό Τσιφτὲ Τέλλι)
162-Β — ΔΟΣΕ ΜΟΥ ΤΗΝ ΕΥΧΗ ΣΟΥ
(Συρτὸ)
(ΒΙΚΤΩΡΙΑ ΧΑΖΑΝ - 'Οριεντάλ Τρίο)
156-Α — ΩΜΟΡΦΟ ΜΟΥ ΧΑΡΙΚΛΑΚΙ
(Τσιφτὲ Τελλὶ)
156-Β — ΝΑ ΣΕ ΧΑΡΩ ΧΑΣΑΠΑΚΙ
(Συρτὸ)

('Ισπανο-'Ισραηλιτικοί - ΒΙΚΤΩΡΙΑ ΧΑΖΑΝ)
Μὲ Τουρκικὴν Μελωδίαν

3001-Α — ME KEMI Y ME INFLAMI
3001-B — NON RIYAS CON MI
3002 A — UN ANIO AY
3002-B — MIS PENSERIOS - GAZEL
3003-A — UN DIA YO BEZI
3003-B — TODAS MIS ESPERANSAS
3004-A — LAGRIMAS VERTERE
3004 B — SEDA AMARILLA SON
3005-A — CANTE POR LA VICTORIA
(Victory Song)
3005-B — SABAH GAZEL - NO AY LUZ
('Ελληνικοί)
156-A — OMORFO MOU HARIKLAKI
156-B — NA SE HARO HASAPAKI
(Τουρκικοί, Βικτ. Χαζὰν -- 'Οριεντάλ Τρίο)
2002-A — GARIP HICAZ CIFTE TELLI GAZEL
2002-B — GORDUM BEN SENI - CANTO

(Ζητήσατε ἀπὸ τοὺς δήλερς τὸν Σπέσιαλ κατάλο-
γον τῶν ἄνω Δίσκων μας.)

Figure 42. Metropolitan Phonograph Records General Catalog. 78 Strofon, page 2. Courtesy of Meletios Pouliopoulos.

revival of locally produced Asia Minor music, including a number of amanedes recorded by women artists.

The establishment of three new recording companies in the United States devoted largely to producing Asia Minor music seems to indicate a revival of interest in the genre. In 1942, the Metropolitan label began producing recordings of singers resident in the United States. Soon after came the Balkan and Kaliphon companies, established immediately after the war. Virginia Magkidou, Katina Karras, Amalia Baka (a Greek Jew from Ioannina), and Victoria Hazan (also a Sephardic Jew, who recorded in Greek, Turkish, and Ladino) all sang splendid amanedes on the Metropolitan label during those years.

What is interesting about the 1940s recordings is that, despite their late date, they seem to be performed in a style that pays no lip service to their American environment. Magkidou's recording of the amanes "Pascho na vro mia kardia" (I Struggle to Find a Heart) with oud player Markos Melkon, violinist Nick Doneff, and either Kanuni Garbis or Theo Kappas playing *kanonaki* (Metropolitan 166-B);[17] Amalia Baka's recording of "Smyrneïkos ballos" (Metropolitan 160); her daughter Diamond Baka's recording of "Smyrneïko matzore" (Balkan 808); and Victoria Hazan's "Huzam-gazel" (Metropolitan 2001-A) give some idea of the recordings of amanedes made during the years that corresponded to the German occupation of Greece and the Civil War. It is surely significant that Greek Jews and Armenians were leading performers of a genre that was the product of a hybrid, heterogeneous society.

The quantity and quality of this last flowering of the Asia Minor music performed by Greeks and non-Greeks for a largely Greek audience in the United States suggest that there was a renewed demand for traditional Asia Minor music, particularly for amanedes. It is tempting to see this increase in demand as a response to the events of the times. For the displaced Greeks, many of them twice removed from their homeland in Asia Minor, the 1940s was a period in which laments were appropriate. For, while the gazel may have been a showpiece for the vocalist in Ottoman music, and for cultural reasons more often performed by men than women,[18] its associations in Greek were affected by different cultural attitudes, musical traditions, and political events. The association of amanes with miroloi and with what was perceived to be the non-Western, deeply emotional side of the Greek personality, as I have pointed out, caused the genre to be at once popular and suspect. In some ways, like most immigrant communities, the Greeks of Chicago, Ohio, and New York were more conservative than their compatriots at home. They preserved many of the customs that were dying out in the urban centers of Greece, including the traditional laments for the dead.

The voices of women singers performing amanedes reminded Greeks of their maternal and oriental heritage, the "universal bitterness" that was, at the same time, "a great treasure" from which they had been cut off. Revivals of the amanes coincided with tragic events in Greek history, particularly with the loss of what was popularly referred to as *Smyrna-Mana* (Mother Smyrna). Of the repertoire of Asia Minor songs, it was the gazel-amanes that demanded the greatest musical skill from the singer. By the 1960s, most of the generation of musicians born in the centers of eclectic Ottoman music who were skilled in improvisation had died or were no longer performing. As a new generation of Greek performers takes an interest in the music of Asia Minor, it remains to be seen whether the musical treasure of the tradition will regain its prominence, and if so, how it will be perceived by an audience far removed from the events that made the amanes speak so eloquently to the Greek soul.

Notes

1. This chapter originally appeared in *Music and Anthropology: Journal of Musical Anthropology of the Mediterranean*, no. 5 (2000), and is available online at https://www.umbc.edu/MA/index/number5/holst/holst_o.htm. The word *amanes* (singular) is pronounced with the accent on the last syllable, and, in *amanedes* (plural), the accent remains on the third syllable.

2. Author's translation.

3. A good account of Kazantzakis's personal philosophy, which he called "the Cretan Glance," is given in Kimon Friar's introduction to *The Odyssey: A Modern Sequel* (Kazantzakis 1958, xviii–xx).

4. As Herzfeld notes: "The nationalists' Digenes emerged from an act of preordained miscegenation whose subsequent recurrences were to be regarded as corruptions of the Hellenic ideal, affronts to the national honor (*ethniko filotimo*)" (1987, 107). By this logic, orientalizing elements in Greek culture are seen to be subsumed in a timeless past and become undesirable if they are present in the creating of a historical "beginning." Herzfeld is using Edward Said's (1975) terminology here, as he makes a distinction between beginnings and origins, between a timeless and passive past or "origin" and a historical struggle for identity or "beginning" (Herzfeld 1987, 108).

5. Again, Herzfeld (1982) is an important commentator on this question. From Adamantios Koraes, through Claude-Charles Fauriel, Spyridon Zambelios, Dora D'Istria, Nikolaos Politis, Panagiotis Aravandinos, and many others, numerous commentators saw the songs as important repositories of Greek identity, supplying an otherwise absent link with an ancient past.

6. The earliest phase of the debate centering on the music of the café aman is documented by Thodoros Hatzipantazis (1986) and reviewed by Stathis Gauntlett (1987). This phase and the post–Asia Minor Catastrophe period are further discussed by Gauntlett (1989).

7. There is a burgeoning bibliography on laments; the largest cross-cultural study remains Rosenblatt, Walsh, and Jackson (1976), which deals with lament in seventy-eight cultures. Even in those cultures where men also lament the dead, the authors observe that women tend to weep longer and louder and compose more structured laments.

8. As A. R. Burn notes, neither the name "Linos" nor "Maneros" is Egyptian (1954, 159). Herodotus's own question about the origin of the song may be a reflection of some Greek confusion about rituals that involved dying gods.

9. See "Galata manes," a well-known amanes named after the Galata quarter of Istanbul sung by Marika Papagika with Alexis Zoumbas on violin, Markos Sifnios on cello, and Kostas Papagikas on cimbalom, recorded in New York in July 1926. It appeared on the CD *Marika Papagika: Greek Popular and Rebetic Music in New York, 1918–1929*, 1994, ACCD-802, Alma Criolla Records, with liner notes by David Soffa; the song can be accessed on YouTube.

10. If this is so, it would correspond with many examples of comedy, games, satire, and farce that followed laments or tragic genres in other cultures. The satyr plays that followed trilogies of ancient tragedy are an obvious example, and the wake games that followed the singing of laments in Ireland and many other European countries are another (Holst-Warhaft 2000, ch. 2).

11. See "Nini," an amanes recorded between 1929 and 1931 by Marika Politissa accompanied by unnamed lyra and outi players on Odeon GO-1539. It can be heard on YouTube at https://www.youtube.com/watch?v=FRTmYQc3IoQ, accessed April 22, 2017.

12. For this and other recordings I am grateful to the late Dino Pappas, who generously made his large collection of Greek and Turkish music available to me on tape as well as supplying me with information based on his deep knowledge of the Greek American music scene.

13. Rita Abatzi, "Karip hetzaz manes," HMV, ca. 1935, at https://www.amazon.com/Karip-hetaz-manes/dp/B001ASOMQY, accessed April 22, 2017.

14. Rita Abatzi recorded the amanes "Gazeli neva sabach" in Athens around 1935 with Lambros Savaidis on *kanonaki* and Dimitrios Semsis on violin. It was later released on the CD *Greek-Oriental Rebetica: Songs and Dances in the Asia Minor Style; The Golden Years, 1911–1937*, Arhoolie/Folklyric 7005, and is available online at https://www.youtube.com/watch?v=_6io7rrnJyY.

15. On this aspect of the rebetika, see Kostos Takhtzis's article, "Zeibekiko, 1964: An Essay," in Holst 1977, 202–9.

16. Steve Frangos notes that other Greek female vocalists recorded in Turkish as well as Armenian, Ladino, Syrian, and "mixed language" between 1911 and 1933 (1994, 45). Examples can be heard at https://www.youtube.com/watch?v=CIoMmfeF9eo.

17. The Metropolitan series begins at number 150, so this recording is probably from 1942.

18. Both Muslim and non-Muslim women recorded gazels. Bülent Aksoy (1997, 46) mentions seven of the better-known female artists including Hikmet Riza, Güzide, and the Thessaloniki-born sisters Lale and Nerkis Hanimlar.

References

Aksoy, Bülent. 1997. "Ottoman Classical Music and the Art of Improvisation." Liner notes to *Gazeller: Ottoman-Turkish Vocal Improvisations on 78-rpm Records*. Kalan CD no. 067. Kalan Müzik, Istanbul.

———. 1998. "Turkish Songs in the Rebetika Repertoire." Paper presented at the International Conference on the Contribution of Asia Minor to the Development of Greek Music, Nikaia, Greece, July 2–5, 1998.

Alexiou, Margaret. 1974. *The Ritual Lament in Greek Tradition*. Cambridge: Cambridge University Press.

Anoyanakis, Fivos. 1991. *Greek Popular Musical Instruments*. Athens: Melissa.

Auerbach, Susan. 1987. "From Singing to Lamenting: Women's Musical Role in a Greek Village." In *Women and Music in Cross-Cultural Perspective*, edited by Ellen Koskoff, 25–43. Westport, CT: Greenwood Press.

Blake, Fred. 1979. "The Feelings of Chinese Daughters toward Their Mothers as Revealed in Marriage Laments." *Folklore* 90, no. 1: 91–97.

Burn, A. R., ed. 1954. *The Histories*, by Herodotus. Translated by Aubrey de Sélincourt. Harmondsworth, England: Penguin.

Caraveli, Anna. 1986. "The Bitter Wounding: The Lament as Social Protest in Rural Greece." In *Gender and Power in Rural Greece*, edited by Jill Dubisch, 169–94. Princeton, NJ: Princeton University Press.

Danforth, Loring. 1982. *The Death Rituals of Greece*. Princeton, NJ: Princeton University Press.

Frangos, Steve. 1994. "Marika Papagika and the Transformations in Modern Greek Music." *Journal of the Hellenic Diaspora* 20, no. 1: 43–63.

Gauntlett, Stathis. 1987. "Apomythopiisi tis rebetikis proistorias." *Diavazo* (Athens) 177: 62–65.

———. 1989. "Orpheus in the Criminal Underworld: Myth in and about Rebetika." *Mantatophoros* 34: 7–48.

Hatzipantazis, Thodoros. 1986. *Tis Asiatidos mousis eraste: I akmi tou athinaikou kafe aman sta chronia tis vasileias tou Yiorgiou A'.* Athens: Stigmi.

Herzfeld, Michael. 1982. *Ours Once More: Folklore, Ideology, and the Making of Modern Greece.* Austin: University of Texas Press.

———. 1987. *Anthropology through the Looking-Glass: Critical Ethnography in the Margins of Europe.* Cambridge: Cambridge University Press.

Holst, Gail. 1975. *Road to Rembetika: Music of a Greek Sub-Culture.* Athens: Denise Harvey.

———. 1977. *Dromos yia to rebetiko.* Athens: Denise Harvey.

Holst-Warhaft, Gail. 1992. *Dangerous Voices: Women's Laments and Greek Literature.* London: Routledge.

———. 2000. *The Cue for Passion: Grief and Its Political Uses.* Cambridge, MA: Harvard University Press.

Kazantzakis, Nikos. 1958. *The Odyssey: A Modern Sequel.* Translated by Kimon Friar. New York: Simon and Schuster.

———. 1965. *Taxidevontas: Italia, Aigiptos, Sina, Ierousalim, Kypros, O Moreas.* Athens: Eleni Kazantzakis.

Kligman, Gail. 1988. *The Wedding of the Dead: Ritual, Poetics, and Popular Culture in Transylvania.* Berkeley: University of California Press.

Kounadis, Paniotis. 1981. "To Smyrneiko minore: I amanedes tis Smyrnis." *Mousiki* 48: 30–39.

Nenola-Kallio, Aili. 1982. *Studies in Ingrian Lament.* Helsinki: Suomalainen Tiedeakatemia.

Pappas, Dino. 1995. "Tetos Demetriades: Blending Greek and American Music." *Laografia* 12, no. 2.

Phaidros, Yiorgos. 1881. *Pragmatia peri tou Smyrneikou mane i tou par archaiois Manero: Anevreseos tou ailinou kai Ellinikon ithon ke ethimon diasozomenon iseti para to Elliniko lao.* N.p.: n.p.

Rosenblatt, Paul C., R. Patricia Walsh, and Douglas A. Jackson. 1976. *Grief and Mourning in Cross-Cultural Perspective.* New Haven, CT: Human Relations Area Press.

Said, Edward. 1975. *Beginnings: Intention and Method.* New York: Basic Books.

———. 1979. *Orientalism.* New York: Vintage Books.

Schwartz, Martin. 1991. Liner notes to *Greek-Oriental Rebetica: Songs and Dances in the Asia Minor Style; The Golden Years, 1911–1937.* Arhoolie/Folklyric 7005. Arhoolie Records, El Cerrito, California.

Seremetakis, C. Nadia. 1991. *The Last Word: Women, Death and Divination in Inner Mani.* Chicago: University of Chicago Press.

Smith, Ole. 1995. "Cultural Identity and Cultural Interactions: Greek Music in the United States, 1917–1941." *Journal of Modern Greek Studies* 13, no. 1: 125–37.

Soffa, David. 1994. Liner notes to *Marika Papagika: Greek Popular and Rebetic Music in New York, 1918–1929.* ACCD-802. Alma Criolla Records, Berkeley, California.

Spottswood, Richard K. 1990. *Ethnic Music on Records: A Discography of Ethnic Recordings Produced in the United States, 1893–1942.* 7 vols. Urbana: University of Illinois Press.

Tolbert, Elizabeth. 1990. "Women Cry with Words: Symbolization of Affect in the Karelian Lament." *Yearbook for Traditional Music* 22: 80–105.

Torp, Lisbet. 1993. *Salonikios: The Best Violin in the Balkans.* Copenhagen: Museum Tusculanum Press.

Rebetika, the Blues of Greece—and Australia

—Stathis Gauntlett, University of Melbourne

Comparisons of Greek *rebetika* songs with American blues date from at least the 1970s. One of the first scholars to remark publicly on the similarities between the two genres, while not underplaying the differences, was the late Argyris Fatouros, professor of international law at Indiana University at the time, in a paper titled "Night without Moon: A Glimpse of the Rebetika" (1970), which he presented at the third annual seminar of the Modern Greek Studies Association. Five years later, the Thessalonian jazz musician Sakis Papadimitriou tabulated the broad characteristics of blues and rebetika in parallel columns in a small composite volume titled *Rebetika* (1975), which was published in English in Athens for the guidance of visiting young Americans inter alios.

Soon thereafter, the simile "rebetika *are like* blues" was inflated into a metaphor "rebetika *are* the Greek blues," as in the title of the 1982 English-language documentary film *Rebetika, the Blues of Greece*. Although narrated by actor Anthony "Zorba" Quinn in a markedly ethnic American brogue, his script was actually written, and the film was produced, by Australians, and it duly declared Melbourne to be one of world's main centers of rebetika. Around the same time, the Australian mainstream media became aware of rebetika, referring to them as "Piraeus Blues" and even domesticating them as "Greek bodgie songs" (bodgies being an antipodean version of "Teddyboys").

It was only a matter of time before practitioners of rebetika and blues joined in, producing fusion performances of the two genres, some of which were recorded for posterity, notably the 1994 collaboration of Stelios Vamvakaris and Louisiana Red in Athens (Gauntlett 2001, 135).

Although quite well established by now, the equation of rebetika with blues is not uncontested: it has been criticized, not unreasonably, as reductive. I have chosen to use it in the title of this chapter because, from the outset, it usefully brings America into the same frame as Greece and Australia, which will form my primary focus. It also allows me to note the historical importance of the physical contiguity of the blues with rebetika from the late 1920s onward, when they were both being recorded in the same studios in the United States. At a time when

Figure 43. "Apo kato ap'tis domates" (Greek Bum Song). Columbia 56137-F. New York, 1928. Courtesy of Stathis Gauntlett.

blues musicians were redefining standards of commercial musicianship, Greek Americans were gaining access to recording technology and, unfettered by metropolitan Greek cultural taboos, were making a signal contribution to the construction of rebetika as a genre and to the establishment of the term "rebetiko" as a commercial genre-descriptor. In illustration of this point, figure 43 shows the label of an American-produced gramophone record that provides an important clue about what *rebetis* actually meant in the 1920s: *rebetiko zeibekiko* is translated "Greek bum song." ("Bum song" would have been a synonym of "vagabond song"—or perhaps "hobo blues.")

Above all, the comparison with the blues supplies any newcomers to rebetika reading this chapter with a conveniently familiar (and not seriously misleading) starting point. There are many similarities in the typical mood of the lyrics: both blues and rebetika are basically songs of complaint, full of grumbling about everything from the behavior of one's lover to the weather—one of the best-known rebetika is titled "Cloudy Sunday." And the grumbling doesn't stop there: one song deplores, "You bitch of a life, you cheat of a world, and you wicked society"—a fairly comprehensive indictment of most things. (All the translations from Greek in this chapter are my own unless otherwise attributed.)

Blues complain of such things too. Indeed, there's an old saying that if you play blues *backward*, your woman comes home, you get out of jail, and your dog comes

Figure 44. Nikos "the Nutter" Mathesis.
Courtesy of Stathis Gauntlett.

back to life. What would happen if you played rebetika backward? I suspect you'd give up alcohol or drugs with the help of the woman who drove you to them; people would stop picking on you; and your mother would smile for the first time since the day you were born. This gives the newcomer to rebetika a preliminary idea of some of the main themes of the genre and also introduces its mythology, which centers on the protagonist of most songs, the prodigal rebetis, his fickle woman, and his long-suffering mother. The core cast of rebetika also includes Death personified—Charos, the modern Greek "grim reaper." All rather ominous and potentially depressing, but the capacity of rebetika and blues for generating fun is not to be overlooked: indeed, paradoxically, the music of rebetika tends to be quite upbeat and jaunty, however morbid the lyrics. The distinctive crystalline sound of the bouzouki (a long-necked lute) plays a large part in achieving this uplifting effect. This is not the place to analyze in detail the trajectory of the bouzouki from instrument of ill repute, mainly heard in hashish dens and prisons, to the national instrument of Greece. The bouzouki story and the catalytic role of Greek Americans in its ascendancy in Greece itself are accessible in several publications (most recently Kourousis 2013). It suffices to note here briefly that in the early twentieth century the bouzouki was mostly associated with low-life characters known as *manges* or *rebetes*. Figure 44 depicts a legendary example of this species, Nikos Mathesis, better known as Trellakias ("Nick the Nutter"), a small-time thug with a stall in the Piraeus fish market. Significantly, Mathesis did not actually play any musical instrument and was just posing for a photograph with a bouzouki, because in the 1930s it was as much a part of a macho's regalia as the gangster hat. Mathesis fancied himself a cartoonist and poet, and wrote this rebetiko song about himself, proclaiming his pedigree as a macho:

> Do you know him, boys, Nick the Nutter?
> He's a fine lad but a bit of a troublemaker.

The verses proceed to describe his weapons of choice, to flaunt his credentials as a tough guy, and to explain that he earned the nickname "Nutter" by reserving a prison cell for whenever it's needed!

Both blues and rebetika sing about some fairly offbeat characters and antisocial fringe dwellers—indeed many of the early composers and performers of both rebetika and blues were marginal types. This marginality has affected the way in which both genres have been received, contributing both to their condemnation and to their appeal, as we shall see. Rebetika in their interwar heyday expressed the world view of people such as Nick the Nutter, which has been hyped up by commentators into a whole philosophy of life that might be called *rebetia*, the abstract essence of being a rebetis. Rebetia is a display of waywardness, a performance of nonconformity and unreliability. Its adherent, the rebetis, presents himself as the polar opposite of the *noikokyris*, the responsible family man, the law-abiding, compliant citizen. How prodigal and intractably antisocial the rebetis has to be in order to qualify for the title varies between commentators: some have defined rebetis as an underworld spiv or sociopath like Nick the Nutter, a primitive anarchist; others, as a lovable rogue, a harmless fun lover, a bohemian—a noikokyris just taking an evening off and enjoying a therapeutic time-out on the wild side. From what I have read and observed over more than half a century, being a rebetis is basically about opportunistic posturing, dressing in a certain style, posing for photographs, and singing about being tough; it's more about myth and display than about crime—although we might note that in the interwar years rebetes tried to dress like American mafiosi as portrayed by Hollywood. Both rebetis and its antonym noikokyris are ultimately terms denoting roles that people choose to act out from time to time. As such, they are rhetorical constructs rather than scientific descriptions of actual people, and they are infinitely variable. Rebetia is ultimately a matter of style, and its essential nucleus is the display of indifference to conformity and conventional respectability. It follows that rebetika are songs with lyrics depicting the anticonformist style and mythical mindset of rebetes. Several commentators have failed to recognize all this, and "rebetology" has been preoccupied with the romantic sociology of myth instead of analyzing the texts as art and artifice.

Figure 45. Roza Eskenazi. Courtesy of Stathis Gauntlett.

How this discourse plays out in the Greek diaspora is particularly interesting and will become the primary focus of this chapter, but first a few more introductory observations are needed regarding the characteristic content and style of rebetika at their source—on both sides of the Aegean. These aspects of the genre have affected its fortunes wherever it has taken root.

Many rebetika might be termed love songs, mainly morose complaints or seduction songs. Experts in gender discourse might diagnose rebetika overall as highly androcentric texts: the male protagonist is usually the discursive subject and the female is the eroticized object, often the victim of cunning seduction or even physical violence. Rebetika can be seen as monuments of hypermasculinity and products of a competitive, theatrically macho society.

"Macho and morose" also describes the tenor of the most remarkable dance accompanying rebetika, the *zeibekiko* or dance of the Zeybeks, a fierce nomadic tribe of Asia Minor. Greeks were so impressed with the legends of the Zeybeks that they not only adopted a version of their dance but would also dress up as Zeybeks at carnival time. The zeibekiko time signature is 9/4 or 9/8, and the dance has no fixed steps; it is performed by a solitary male with a glum look of serious concentration on his face. It involves improvising ponderous movements within a small space, turning on the spot, swooping, balancing, and displays of strength. The zeibekiko dance has been aptly described as "the choreographic embodiment of defiant masculinity" (Cowan 1990, 153). Another favorite dance of the rebetes was the *hasapiko*, the so-called butcher's dance, a short-line dance for two or three men in duple time; it has precise geometric steps and requires strict coordination. Magisterial descriptions of performances of both these dances are given in superb English prose by the late Patrick Leigh-Fermor in his travelogue *The Broken Road* (2013, 241ff.). These macho dances used to be danced only by men; women were assigned a type of belly dance called *tsifteteli*, among whose professional exponents Roza Eskenazi excelled well into her eighties. Her talents as a singer of rebetika and dancer are celebrated in a recent Israeli documentary film titled *My Sweet Canary*.

The instrumentation and choreography of rebetika foreground the fact that the songs are permeated by a strong flavor of the Levant. Indeed, the commercial recording of rebetika was initially monopolized by exponents of the so-called Smyrna style of performance, playing fiddles, dulcimers, and various lutes other than the bouzouki. Many of these musicians were refugees from Asia Minor, where they had honed their musicianship in musical cafés known as *cafés aman* (the oriental equivalent of the Parisian *café chantant*). Their professionalism initially made them more acceptable than local Helladic exponents of rebetika to the multinational recording companies operating in Greece, as did their more cultivated singing voices (both male and female). The Asia Minor disaster of 1922 and the ensuing exchange of minority populations with Turkey helped to make rebetika in the Smyrna style broadly popular in Greece—and in America, as other chapters and artist profiles in this volume reveal.

However, the oriental features of the Smyrna style struck a raw nerve with many Western-minded Greeks and drew rebetika into a long-running controversy in Greek cultural politics over whether Greece belongs to the West or to the East. Self-image and self-definition ("identity politics") are at issue here. Those Greeks looking to the West have tended to play down Greece's oriental legacy from the Ottoman and even the Byzantine period. For them, rebetika were an embarrassing oriental relic or even an "illegal immigrant" from the East. This attitude culminated famously in the censorship of rebetika in September 1937 by the dictatorship of Ioannis Metaxas: the genre was banned from the recording studios and stage performance (nominally, rather than effectively) not just on account of the low-life content of its verses but also because of its oriental music. Ironically, Metaxas may have been taking a lead from Turkey, where the Kemalist government had earlier banned Ottoman music as part of its campaign of Europeanization. It followed that Greece, the font of European culture, also had to ban such songs in the interest of progress and civilization. The issue of oriental music had been hotly debated in the Athenian press since the 1880s, but not all commentators had condemned it. Some had argued that the origins of music and songs now known as rebetika could be traced back via Byzantium to ancient Greece. This speculative line of argument did not convince Metaxas in 1937, but it has been periodically revived ever since, and strenuous efforts have regularly been devoted to legitimizing modern reality by connection with the Hellenic past (Gauntlett 2015). This has usually been in the context of moral panic periodically whipped up by the custodians of Helleno-Christian civilization in Greece, as in 1968 when the military junta of the day imprisoned the author of the first substantial monograph on rebetika for obscenity and contravening its censorship regulations. Perversely, the colonels' disapproval of rebetika actually helped to fuel the revival of rebetika in the 1970s, when the genre came to be seen as a form of defiance of an oppressive regime. Rebetika carried vague connotations of heroic resistance to Metaxas, to the junta, then to Konstantinos Karamanlis's conservatism, to the European Economic Community (which Greece joined in 1981), and to Western cultural imperialism in general. It should be noted, however, that the Stalinist cadres of the Greek Left also disapproved of rebetika and regularly denounced the genre as an antiproletarian bourgeois conspiracy. The diaspora has also not been immune to various types of backlash against rebetika, as we shall see.

The scandal and controversy surrounding rebetika has been amply documented and analyzed, as has the evolution of the revival of the genre in reaction to the junta's disapproval into an all-pervasive *rebetomania* under the populist Andreas Papandreou administrations of the 1980s. So strong was Papandreou's love for rebetika perceived to be, that the neologism *tsiftetelokratia* ("belly-dance-ocracy") was coined to describe his style of government (Gauntlett 1991). By the 1990s, the airwaves, Greek print media, and cinema were saturated with rebetika. There were countless reissues and cover versions of recorded rebetika in every imaginable format from vinyl to CDs, mp3s, video clips, and even ring tones for mobile phones. Live performances of rebetika abounded in venues both large and small, from *barakia* and dedicated *rebetadika* to sports stadiums. Every imaginable kind of book and article about rebetika was produced in great profusion, from works of scholarship to fiction, comics, and even a cookbook. An index of the recognition value of rebetika is the large number and range of advertisements based on well-known songs; they have been used to promote everything from beer to insecticide. By the 1990s, the adjective *rebetikos* had become a fashionable but rather meaningless buzzword, guaranteed to draw a consumer's attention. Rebetika fatigue inevitably ensued toward the end of the 1990s, when Greece was entering a period of postcharisma politics. Rebetika enjoyed one last charisma-fueled political fling in 2001, when the last active member of the dynasty, George Papandreou Jr. (at that time foreign minister of Greece), performed a transcultural zeibekiko for his Turkish counterpart, İsmail Cem, at a media event, by way of cementing the Greco-Turkish rapprochement.

Meanwhile, rebetika musicians in Greece were also moving with the times and courting not just politicians but also the corporate sector. From 1992 onward, a group of veteran rebetes, supplemented by young revivalists, gave matinee performances on weekdays in the Central Meat Market of Athens in a venue called the Arcade of the Immortals. The niche market they targeted was the businessman's long lunch, and in no time the venue was being booked out not only by stockbrokers from Sophocleous Street but also by parliamentarians from across town. Both groups often treated overseas visitors to a lunchtime walk on the wild side *à la grecque.*

More changes of government followed the turn of millennium, and the tide of rebetomania ebbed further in Greece, but rebetika still featured prominently in the opening ceremony of the 2004 Olympic Games in Athens, which incorporated tableaux from Costas Ferris's 1983 film *Rebetiko* into the pageant of Greek culture from antiquity to the present. It is, of course, paradoxical that antiestablishment rebetika should be thus promoted by the Greek establishment and that they are even represented in official schoolbooks. Rebetika musicians, once sent into exile as sociopaths and misfits, are now celebrated as national heroes, with prime ministers issuing official condolences when they die. Explaining how and why rebetika moved from being persecuted and reviled into a position of national prominence requires a more detailed history lesson than can be accommodated here. One obvious and succinct answer might be that the verses and the music of rebetika have continued to speak profoundly and undeniably to the condition of large numbers of ordinary Greeks—it's just taken some Greeks a long time to admit it. In this regard, the fortunes of rebetika since the current economic crisis afflicted Greece should make interesting reading when properly documented. Anecdotal evidence suggests a downturn in all forms of the commerce of rebetika. Also, historical songs about previous crises have been recycled, such as Kostas Roukounas's "The Crisis" of 1933:

> Everyone's at their wits' end and muttering deliriously
> and cursing this crisis every single day.

Likewise have Vassilis Tsitsanis's compositions from the Greek Civil War, such as "Driven away from My Mother" of 1948, which strives to salvage some traces of dignity:

> Even if all my beauty has died off,
> my spirit and nobility are not lost.

Predictably, rebetika are also being commonly parodied into satire of contemporary events—an Athenian friend riffed on some verses by Vangelis Papazoglou to commemorate finance minister Yanis Varoufakis's closure of Greek banks and limitation of ATM withdrawals in the summer of 2015:

Με εξήντα μόνο γιούρα
μήτε διακοπές στα Γιούρα!

On just sixty euros
you can't even holiday on Youra! [formerly an exile island]

Since the 1990s, another international opportunity for marketing rebetika has been provided by World Music. *The Rough Guide to Rebétika* was duly released in London in 2004 on the World Music Network label, featuring "Greek songs of hash and heartache." And, of course, websites for rebetika in both Greek and English, and YouTube clips of original and cover performances, have proliferated exponentially on the Internet since the 1990s.

And so to the diaspora and the intriguing parallels and divergences of rebetika trajectories between metropolis and diaspora. Other chapters and artist profiles in this volume amply cover the American experience and allow me to invest the limited space left to triangulating the geographic focus to include Australia.

The Australian connection of rebetika predates the invention of World Music and derives from the presence down under of up to half a million Greeks in the postwar period—the majority of them are now Australian born. Recordings of rebetika have been sold in Greek record shops in Australian cities and heard in Greek clubs and tavernas and on Greek radio since the mass migration of Greeks to the antipodes started in the 1950s. Many of these recordings were imported from the United States and pressed on the Apollo label to circumvent the Australian monopoly of EMI (Gauntlett 2003, 34ff.). In 1960, an advertisement in the Melbourne newspaper *Neos Kosmos* heralded the arrival of *live* bouzoukia at a taverna in Melbourne as "incredible but true." By 1962, the bouzouki was sufficiently acclimatized in Australia to sustain the first of a long sequence of visits by leading exponents of rebetika and rebetika derivatives. Australia is still a lucrative touring ground for metropolitan artistes, but, as in the United States, there is also a resident contingent of exponents of rebetika, and some locally produced songs are claimed to be rebetika (see Stavros K. Frangos, "George Katsaros: The Last *Café-Aman* Performer," in this volume).

One of the pioneers of rebetika in Melbourne was the bouzouki player Thymios Stathoulopoulos. He died in Melbourne in 1992 after almost thirty years of playing at private and public functions (both Greek and multicultural) and in

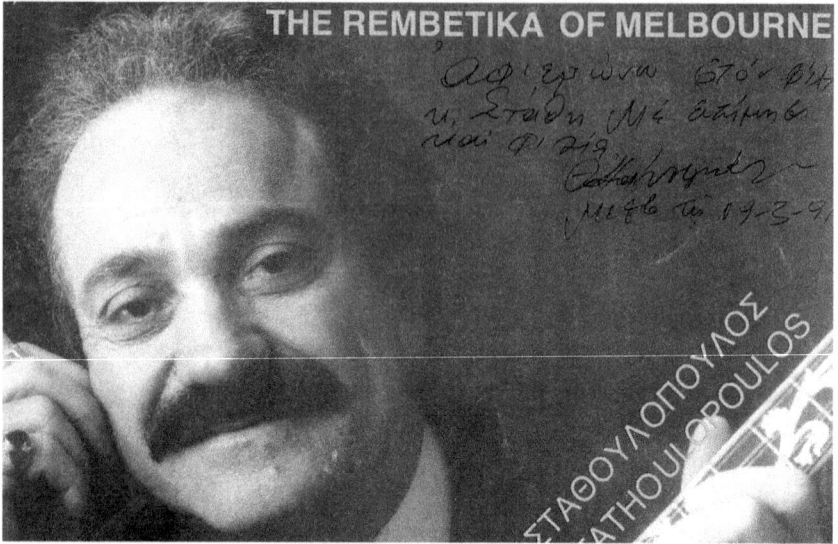

Figure 46. Thymios Stathoulopoulos, *The Rembetika of Melbourne*, 1985. Courtesy of Stathis Gauntlett.

Greek clubs and tavernas. Thymios also composed and recorded rebetika in Melbourne and about Melbourne, such as the song "The Bouzouki in Melbourne" from his LP, *The Rebetika of Melbourne*:

> In Melbourne's lovely evenings now,
> in clubs and tavernas the bouzouki plays.
> And people dance and live it up in the purely Greek way,
> getting merry on Aussie wine and breaking all the plates.

Thymios is singing here in Greek about Australia to Australians—perhaps he did this in deference to the record's sponsors, having received a grant from the Australian Arts Council to produce the LP. Or perhaps he intended it ironically, because this good-times song is quite unrepresentative of the overall content of the album; most of the songs paint a very bleak picture of desolation and despair in the diaspora, consistent with the traditional Greek discourse of "black exile." This is well illustrated in the song "Alone and Suffering in Exile," which has as its refrain:

> I stay out all night, all alone and careworn,
> I'm in a foreign land and I'm always a foreigner.

The alienation expressed here stands in stark contrast to the "commitment to Australia" extolled by Australian politicians when they hold up the Greek community as an exemplar of successful integration into Australian society. There is a striking contrast between all the forlorn antiheroes of *The Rebetika of Melbourne* and the irrepressible, all-conquering Greek migrant of the official narrative.

Thymios's verses also refer to the fascination of non-Greek Australians with rebetika. By the 1980s, rebetika were being promoted to the broader Australian public by the multicultural arts industry in festivals and on mainstream television and radio programs. Multiculturalism was first institutionalized in Australia in 1972 by the Labor government headed by Gough Whitlam, and it remained the official policy of most Australian governments thereafter. At a rather crude level, the rise in popularity of rebetika in Melbourne might be seen to reflect the spread of gastronomic multiculturalism; since the 1970s, there has been a spectacular proliferation of Greek tavernas with live Greek music. But over the years, successive generations of Greek Australians have increasingly pushed rebetika to the forefront of the musical showcase through which they proclaim their Greekness. Rebetika have become the musical staple of almost every kind of secular festive event staged by Greek organizations in Melbourne. Audiences of more than six hundred are reported to have attended rebetika concerts in Melbourne at the turn of the millennium. And rebetika are often performed live to rolling audiences of many thousands at the street party with which the annual Greek Festival is launched in downtown Melbourne. By the 1990s, rebetika bands had become an almost obligatory ornament at every kind of multicultural event in Melbourne, notably the very popular ensemble Apodimi Compania, former students of modern Greek studies at Melbourne University and all Australian born. They went on to make recordings in both Australia and Greece, where they have now resettled. Although they are essentially a rebetika revival band, they have also experimented with fusions of Greek and Celtic music. Indeed, Australian multiculturalism has brought about some weird and wonderful hybrids of rebetika music: some bands have introduced the aboriginal didgeridoo into performance of rebetika. There have also been attempts to link the myth of the rebetis to that of the Australian larrikin, the embodiment of the defiance of authority, dating from Australia's early history as a penal colony. The Melbourne band Rebetiki Compania has appeared on national television performing rebetika in the Old Melbourne Gaol under a photograph of the most notorious rebetis or larrikin to be hanged there, Ned Kelly, the Irish-Australian bushranger. Figure 47 depicts a somewhat irreverent impressment of Ned Kelly's iconic homemade helmet into a project of Australianizing rebetika. There has even been some speculation about the earliest transplantation of rebetika into the sonic landscape of Australia: perhaps the first Greeks to arrive in Australia (in 1829) might have brought with them "proto-rebetika" of some kind. They were, after all, seven young "pirates" from Hydra, transported in chains to the penal colony of New South Wales, and they would have been well qualified to inaugurate down under the oral traditions of the dark underside of Aegean seaports.

Figure 47. Rebetiki Compania musician playing the *baglamas* as Ned Kelly in his iconic helmet. Courtesy of Stathis Gauntlett.

However that may be, in the late 1990s, far from showing signs of rebetika fatigue, the educated young Greeks of Melbourne were reported by the local Greek press to be in the grip of an "epidemic" of enthusiasm for rebetika. The young professionals interviewed by one reporter enthused about the authenticity of rebetika and their capacity to evoke powerful passions. These young Melburnians also saw parallels between the plight of the refugees and other outcasts described in rebetika and that of immigrants in Australia, like their parents. They further claimed that rebetika are "the thinking Greek's songs of choice" and that the capacity to appreciate rebetika is an index of Greekness. The journalist felt reassured that his youthful interviewees were not lost to Greek culture through assimilation; but he was also slightly alarmed that these future leaders of the Greek community should primarily attach their cultural identity to a popular subculture of dubious origins. There was nothing new in these misgivings; over the years there have been numerous letters to the editors of Melbourne's Greek newspapers denouncing "bouzouki music" as corruptive and even as a betrayal of the Greek War of Independence. The moral panic and embarrassment of such commentators are heightened by the apparent benevolence shown toward rebetika by Anglo-Australian officialdom. And indeed, anyone who understands the lyrics cannot fail to see the incongruity of many of the songs (with their male machismo, drugs, male domination of women, and other politically incorrect attitudes) amid the political correctness of the events at which they are often performed (Gauntlett 2009).

So it could be argued that the accommodation of rebetika within Australia's official multiculturalism is yet another form of paradoxical institutionalization of what was once antiestablishment song. And yet, one Anglo-Australian sociologist has claimed that it is exactly because of these inherent ambiguities and dubious origins that rebetika have a special power to transcend their ethnic community of origin and to be embraced by other Australians as their own cultural capital, in that great imagined musical community that is multicultural Australia (Gauntlett 2009, 272). This might explain why in 1995 the Melbourne Antipodes Festival staged a musical play titled *The Rebetes*, written in English by an Anglo-Australian woman (a non-Greek speaker), who claimed in a press interview: "This play is not about the trendy 'pseudo-rebetes' who have surfaced in recent years. It is about the real life experiences . . . of those free spirits, the rebetes of Yarraville [a working-class suburb of Melbourne]." So it seems that even non-Greeks in Melbourne are able to relate to rebetika passionately, even protectively (Gauntlett 2009, 276). Again, in both 2009 and 2011, a musical titled *Café Rebetika!* was staged in Melbourne and at the Sydney Opera House, written and directed by an American married to a Greek Australian; he doesn't speak Greek but claims some experience of Broadway (see www.caferebetika.com).

Rebetika seem to have become an emblematic music of the Greek Australian community both in its own self-image and in the expectations of the host society—and perhaps an emblematic music of multicultural Australia at large. It could be that what appeals to Australians about rebetika is the kindred spirit of larrikinism or rebetia and the defiance of authority expressed in the verses. The appeal of low-life songs might also hold some voyeuristic and even prurient attraction; rebetika have been said to offer a taste of forbidden fruit. And, of course, the best way to make people curious about something is for officialdom to ban it—the resilience of the popularity of rebetika in Greece is partly due to the very actions of those who have sought to suppress or destroy it. Also attractive to some is the apparently unaffected directness of the songs—they can appear aesthetically primitive, especially as played by revivalist bands. This can appeal to those seeking an alternative to the commercialized and mass-produced popular music of the West. In reality, of course, the marketplace has drastically shaped the development of rebetika, as we have seen, so it is advisable to take a balanced approach in trying to explain the complex—and now globalized—allure of "the Greek-American-Australian blues."

References

Cowan, Jane. 1990. *Dance and the Body Politic in Northern Greece*. Princeton, NJ: Princeton University Press.

Fatouros, Argyris A. 1970. "Night without Moon: A Glimpse of the Rebetika." Paper presented at the third annual seminar of the Modern Greek Studies Association.

Gauntlett, Stathis. 1991. "Folklore and Populism: The Greening of the Greek Blues." In *Proceedings of the Fourth National Folklore Conference, November 1990*, edited by Margaret Clarke, 85–91. Canberra: Australian Folk Trust.

———. 2001. *Rebetiko Song: A Contribution to a Scholarly Approach* [in Greek]. Athens: Eikostou Protou.

———. 2003. "Greek Recorded Sound in Australia: A Neglected Heritage." In *Greek Research in Australia: Proceedings of the Biennial International Conference of Greek Studies, Flinders University*, edited by Elizabeth Close, Michael Tsianikas, and George Frazis, 25–46. Adelaide: Flinders University Department of Languages.

———. 2009. "The Diaspora Sings Back: Rebetika Down-Under." In *Greek Diaspora and Migration since 1700: Society, Politics and Culture*, edited by Dimitris Tziovas, 271–84. Farnham, Surrey, England: Ashgate.

———. 2015. "Antiquity at the Musical Margins: Rebetika 'Ancient' and Modern." *Byzantine and Modern Greek Studies* 39, no. 1: 98–116.

Kourousis, Stavros. 2013. *From Tambouras to Bouzouki: The History and Evolution of the Bouzouki and Its First Recordings (1926–1932)*. Athens: Orpheum Phonograph.

Leigh-Fermor, Patrick. 2013. *The Broken Road: From the Iron Gates to Mount Athos*. London: John Murray.

Papadimitriou, Sakis. 1975. "Rebetika and Blues." In *Rebetika: Songs from the Old Greek Underworld*, edited by Katharine Butterworth and Sara Schneider, 34–37. Athens: Komboloi Press.

George Katsaros: The Last *Café-Aman* Performer[1]

—Stavros K. Frangos

The study of modern Greek music can no longer ignore the early history of the international recording industry. The collection and production of world music by the major international record companies offers critical information missing from current studies on Greek music. The history of the international recording industry unintentionally documents Greek musical forms and transformations more precisely than current writing on this musical tradition. These existing non-Greek studies also provide a chronology and the wider social context for Greek music, which is not yet part of the existing literature.

In order to assess the complex documentation available on the international record industry, and the information relative to Greek music since 1900, three thematic areas will be presented. First, I will present basic documentation from the international recording industry that attests to the systematic collection of Greek music. Next, as a case study, to understand how closely these wider events are reflected in the life and career of one especially notable Greek musician, I will examine the recording career of George Katsaros. Finally, to demonstrate that the study of modern Greek music must be examined within the wider context of modern music history, I will review folklore and ethnomusicological arguments that discuss created traditions within certain world musics.

The International Music Industry[2]

In the early years of the twentieth century, cylinders and 78-rpm records were cutting-edge technologies in sound recording. Their influence and distribution were not limited to Europe and North America but rather took place on a worldwide scale. The phonograph was invented in 1877, and only twenty-odd years later, anyone in the Ottoman Empire could order a gramophone from a London-based company (Gronow 1981, 252). In the early 1890s, all the major international record companies were using the techniques they had pioneered earlier in the century in the production of foreign-language products, with the successful

119

innovation of target marketing in the sales of old-time and race records. "All companies used the same business strategies. . . . [T]hey manufactured both recordings (disks and cylinders) and record-playing equipment (gramophones, phonographs), and tried to market them worldwide" (Gronow 1981, 276).

From our perspective in history, the music documented on these cylinders and records is the principle artistic legacy of these companies. Yet preserving rare and, at times, obscure music traditions was far from the original intent. "Recordings of the smallest group were not made in hopes of large record sales, but to help the sale of gramophones, which were manufactured by the same companies" (Gronow 1981, 254). By 1907, the largest companies had divided the world between them: "Victor got the Americas, China, Japan, and the Philippines, while Gramophone got the rest of the world" (Gronow 1981, 254; Racy 1976, 23). Commercial companies even before 1907 had sent engineers around the world to record virtually every musical tradition on the planet.

The record companies relied on local middlemen who acted as talent scouts. These men were often merchants who spoke European languages and were familiar with their region's musicians and musical preferences. Economic motives—never aesthetic judgments—propelled these early commercial recordings. As Pekka Gronow emphasizes: "[T]he record industry did not set out to change musical traditions. It recorded whatever it thought could be sold, seeking its artists from the opera houses as well as the music halls. . . . But the artists had to be professionals in their own fields performing in the urban centers where the industry operated" (Gronow 1982, 5).

As far as traditional Greek and Anatolian musical recordings are concerned, Dick Spottswood explains:

> [T]he Gramophone Company of England sent an engineer, W. Sinkler Darby, to Constantinople in July 1900. The company sponsored further visits in 1903, 1904 (twice), 1905, 1907 and 1911. Another expedition is known to have stopped in Smyrna in 1910. Records made on these trips served the company well. Not only were they available in Greece and Turkey, but the best were routinely reissued on Victor in the United States, forming the bulk of the Greek catalogs. (1979, 255)

To gain some perspective on what all these field trips generated in terms of Greek and Anatolian music, between 1900 and 1910 the Gramophone Company collected 1,925 recordings in Constantinople and Smyrna alone (Gronow 1981, 255). To fully appreciate the success of these early Ottoman recordings, we should note that they were the third largest in overall production in a list of sixteen regions in Asia and North Africa. The resounding significance of this number is all the more noteworthy when we realize that the first- and second-place regions of field collections were the entire subcontinent of India, with 4,410 recordings, and the whole of the Far East, with 4,265 recordings (Gronow 1981, 255). With so much invested in these field recordings, it is not surprising that the record companies actively sought to advertise their newly acquired music inventory. In the early 1900s, record catalogs were published in a host of languages and sent around the world; they were also target-marketed to immigrant groups throughout North America.[3] The efforts of these companies to educate the public and inform them about which foreign music traditions were available on records were not limited solely to the newly arriving American immigrants but to American-born retailers as well.

The following hypothetical scenario is taken from the May 1918 issue of the *Voice of Victor*, a commercial record publication expressly issued to record store owners. This particular feature story is entitled "The Buyer of Foreign Records":

> To the Victor Dealer... [are]... offered... opportunities in starting a foreign record department. Many dealers, no doubt, have felt they would like to get some of the foreign business, but have been a bit hesitant, fearing the complexities which might arise.
>
> A careful analysis of the subject clarified conditions materially. It is not as hard as it seems. You ask how to proceed? It is really easy if you but take a little time to work out the details.
>
> Tony Andrianopoulos shyly enters your store, hat in hand, and asks if you have some Greek records. Of course you have none, and in the past have simply told him so and turned away from him. He slinked out of the store. You soon forgot the whole incident. Now, had you invited Tony into your office, inquired from him about how many Greeks, for instance, lived in your city, and put it to him squarely if he thought it would be profitable for you to carry Greek records, you might sit up surprised that you had wasted some wonderful opportunities. (Spottswood 1979, 220)

While Gramophone eventually secured primacy of market share in musical traditions hailing from the Balkans and Anatolia, it was far from the only company issuing such recordings. Greek, Balkan, and Turkish records were systematically produced from approximately 1902 through the 1930s by a host of different international record companies. To cite only a few of the most important, we should note Odeon, International Zonophone (which became Blumenthal Frères and later the International Talking Machine Company and Odeon-Blumenthal), and finally Victor, which, after 1929 and the merger with the Radio Corporation of America, became RCA Victor.

In the whirl of international mergers and buyouts, even the Gramophone Company eventually merged, with His Master's Voice (HMV). As the labels themselves indicate, such early recordings (while field-collected in places like

Smyrna, Constantinople, and Thessaloniki) were ultimately pressed and mass-produced in factories located in Austria, Germany, France, and Switzerland.[4]

Greek Commercial Recordings, 1896–1965

The broad historic sequence of Greek commercial recording is no longer in doubt. The first documented commercial records of Greek music were made in New York City in 1896. From at least 1902, recordings were made simultaneously in western Anatolia and North America. From 1900 until approximately 1922, commercial field recordings in Constantinople and Smyrna were actively collected and regularly released.

From 1916 until the end of World War II, the Greek recording industry in North America ultimately produced such an extensive series of recordings that by 1940 Greek music ranked fifth in the nation in terms of records produced for ethnic groups (Gronow 1982, 23).[5] This is especially noteworthy given that, at this time, the US Census Bureau counted 273,520 Greeks, making them only the thirteenth-largest ethnic group in the country. It is generally accepted that the musical competition between Mme. Koula (Kyriaki Antonopoulou, ca. 1880–1954) and Marika Papagika (1890–1943), which began in 1916–1917 with Mme. Koula's first commercial recordings, ignited this unexpected surge in record sales.

Greek music and musicians followed and were influenced by the diaspora. As Sotirios Chianis relates:

> By the 1920s there were many Greek emigrants, from both the mainland and the islands, in the Congo and Abyssinia and especially in the Egyptian cities of Alexandria, Suez, Port Said, Zagazid and Ismailia. The majority, however, settled in such cities as New York, Boston, Detroit, Chicago, San Francisco, and Los Angeles. Wherever they settled, these immigrants established strong Greek communities, zealously guarding and perpetuating their religion, language, social customs, and especially their regional folk music and dances. By 1920 each community had several coffee-houses and at least one café aman, where one could hear (and dance to) live Greek music. (1988, 682)

In 1925, Marika's, the first fashionable *café aman* in New York City, opened in a walk-up at Thirty-Fourth Street between Seventh and Eighth Avenues. The owner was the top-selling commercial record vocalist Marika Papagika. During extended interviews, John K. Gianaros (1904–1998), one of the senior generation of fellow musicians, recalled that this club catered to a wide array of ethnic groups: Arabs, Armenians, Bulgarians, Greeks, Yugoslavs, and even Turks (Frangos 1991; Frangos 2002, 223–39).

Figure 48. George Katsaros, "Pezo poka, pezo pinokli," 1929. Victor
V-58046-B. Courtesy of Meletios Pouliopoulos.

In 1926, the opening of commercial recording studios in Athens met with sustained success. Record production in the United States was such that by 1940 more than a thousand records had been issued with Greek materials (Gronow 1982, 23). This figure does not include Greek records imported to North America. From 1945 to 1965, the growing postwar economy of North America, along with a number of other factors, led to a renaissance in Greek and Balkan music recorded in North America. Having learned the lessons of target marketing from the international companies, a vast number of small record companies began to appear that were even more tightly focused in terms of musical styles and specialized niche market appeal.

Complicating this entire chronology is the 1930–1932 RCA Victor–sponsored field trip to Greece made by music executive Tetos Demetriades (ca. 1897–1971) (Chianis 1988, 42).[6] Released only in North America under RCA Victor on the Standard Orthophonic label, the approximately two hundred recordings document an incredible array of musicians, vocalists, and musical styles. Demetriades's unique field collection was produced at a highly critical moment. The post-1922 exchange of populations between Greece and Turkey led to a situation in which whole genres of music were outlawed by both countries. Demetriades's commercial venture unintentionally amassed the single greatest collection of traditional urban and folk Greek and western Anatolian music recorded during this era.

The success of Orthophonic is simultaneously a commentary on that regrettably ignored facet of the international commercial record industry, the status of imported records. As already noted, the pattern of the international music companies was established before the substantial waves of immigration from the eastern Mediterranean around the turn of the twentieth century. However, once immigrants from any ethnic group arrived in sufficient numbers to constitute a buying market, the companies began to record or import music traditional to that group.

The first waves of immigrants arriving from the Balkans and Anatolia were predominantly men with newfound money and a nostalgic taste for homeland traditions. No discography or other publicly available tabulation currently exists that documents the full array of Greek, Balkan, and Anatolian records imported to North America. It is important to stress that the target-marketing strategies of the international record companies were not limited to the urban centers of North America but reached practically everywhere on the planet.[7] The strong traditions of music and dance from the Balkans and Anatolia were showcased by consummate musicians who could adapt to the new demands of performance on commercial records and were willing to travel the world to perform.

A Life in Brief

George Katsaros was born Yiorgos Theologitis on December 19, 1888, in the village of Agia Marina on the island of Amorgos. In 1913, Katsaros left his mother and sister, who then lived in Athens, and traveled to New York City. He was soon playing regularly in an array of venues under his stage name, Katsaros ("curly"). As he recalled, he learned of the outbreak of the First World War (July 28, 1914) just as he was stepping off the train in San Francisco.

During the years of World War I and into the 1920s, Katsaros followed the touring patterns typical of Greek and Balkan performers of the era. He traveled a seasonal route throughout the United States, performing and composing traditional Greek music. In 1919, he began wintering in Tarpon Springs, Florida, where he was assured both a relaxing winter and a full schedule of engagements. Due to his growing popularity, in 1928 Katsaros began recording for the Victor Talking Machine Company at their main studios, then located in Camden, New Jersey.[8]

Given Victor's promotional efforts and their target marketing to potential Greek audiences around the world, Katsaros began to tour to Greek diaspora colonies (and to perform for wealthy individuals around the world) sometime in the 1930s. Katsaros was neither the first nor the last traditional Greek musician to travel such worldwide circuits. Mme. Koula and Marika Papagika are both

Figure 49. George Katsaros, ca. 1940s. Courtesy of
Stavros K. Frangos.

known to have traveled back and forth between North America and Greek colonies in Egypt, as did other performers.

Paradoxically, while producing one hit song after another, Katsaros (for reasons he never discussed with me) experienced considerable trouble in the recording studio. And here we have the unsolved mystery behind Katsaros's recording career. Record company documentation reports that while Katsaros was acknowledged far and wide as an extremely popular musician, his studio recordings were often rejected and not released. Consequently, record companies would only release two of Katsaros's songs (i.e., one record) per year. Yet at the same time these very same companies have documentation evidencing Katsaros's ongoing commercial popularity. As a case in point, Katsaros's songs were often simultaneously released on both a ten-inch record and a 45-rpm record. Then, once again without explanation, after 1938 Katsaros no longer recorded for any of the large international companies.

Such was Katsaros's enduring popularity that he continued to record, working with a variety of independent record companies such as Grecophon and

Figure 50. George Katsaros, "O Panterimos," ca. 1947. Grecophon 9B. Courtesy of Meletios Pouliopoulos.

Metropolitan, until the late 1950s. During the Second World War and for some time thereafter, Katsaros based himself primarily around Boston, except for the winter months, which he spent in Florida. Curiously, this era was also one of general decline for the type of music Katsaros played. While remaining a major name in the field, Katsaros began to appear on records more often as the composer or backup artist rather than the lead performer.

The overall decline in the number of performance venues led to Katsaros's semiretirement in Tarpon Springs, Florida. Even during this period, Katsaros was regarded locally with considerable admiration and was periodically called upon to perform. During the 1960s, Katsaros performed as an honored senior musician at the annual Tarpon Springs Epiphany Celebration. Nevertheless, more broadly in North America, where Katsaros had established his career, he was virtually forgotten from the 1960s through the 1980s. Yet in Greece, during this same period, his most notable songs appeared in one anthology of rereleased music after another. It is not surprising, then, that in 1988 renewed interest by music scholars in Greece led eventually to Katsaros being honored by a special national radio program devoted to his life and career, a concert tour replete with medals from the concert-tour cities of Athens, Piraeus, and Thessaloniki, and the release of a special two-disc CD (Gauntlett 1997).

Since the late 1980s, the recognition Katsaros has received has not been limited to Greece. In North America, various academic articles, numerous newspaper

Figure 51. Musicians George Katsaros (right) and John K. Gianaros (left) at the Tarpon Springs Centennial, March 1987. Courtesy of the City of Tarpon Springs.

accounts, and an array of appearances on Greek American television and radio programs only increased awareness of his considerable role in the history of modern Greek music. In 1990, Katsaros was the recipient of a Florida Folk Heritage award. The interest in his career continued apace with the release in 1994 of two CDs of his original 78-rpm records: *Dervisaki* (Eros Music A. E.) and *Giorgos Katsaros: Rempetika and Folk Songs; USA Recordings 1920–1950* (Vintage Music).

Just one year before his death, Katsaros's renewed fame saw expression in the media well beyond the life of dark cafés, lost loves, and excess so often heard in his songs. A photograph of Katsaros, guitar in hand, appeared on the title page of *Greek Americans*, a volume in Benchmark Books' Cultures of America series (Phillips and Ferry 1996). The series, which is aimed at a juvenile audience, presents Katsaros to American schoolchildren as the very epitome of a "beloved . . . composer and performer of tavern music" (Phillips and Ferry 1996, 50). On June 22, 1997, George Katsaros died in his home in Holiday, Florida, and was buried in Tarpon Springs at Cycadia Cemetery.

Three Songs, One Tradition

George Katsaros's compositions provide an especially suitable vehicle for the study of modern Greek music. While Katsaros certainly receives recognition as a noted musician and composer, the full range of his themes is ignored. Roderick Conway Morris's observation, focusing on the European motifs in Kastaros's songs rather than expressions of the Greek American experience, is typical of this general pattern: "Georgios Katsaros exercises a peculiar fascination over scholars of Greek urban music, not only because of his highly idiosyncratic and engaging vocal and instrumental style but also the breadth of his repertoire, which embraces hashish songs . . . and Italian-style *kantades*" (1981, 89–90).

As we shall see, the selective responses to Katsaros's full range of musical themes parallels the general neglect of the activities of the international record industry. In 1934, Katsaros recorded "Me tis tsepes adeianes" (With Empty Pockets) and "Pitzames" (Pajamas) (Columbia 56345-F A/B). Both songs became colossal hits.

The lyrics to "Me tis tsepes adeianes" have especially interested scholars:

> *Ti tha kanoume, vre filoi stin katastasin afti,*
> What are we to do, friend, with a catastrophe like this,
> *pou hamenoi pame oli m'edo stin Ameriki.*
> we are lost altogether here in America.
> *Opou ftoheia ehei pesei kai den vriskoume douleia*
> Where poverty has befallen us all and we can't find jobs.
> *Kai ta eksoda den vgainoun kai travoume symfora.*
> and we can't meet our expenses and we're suffering.
> *Me ta moutra kremasmena me tis tsepes adeianes,*
> With our faces hanging out, with our pockets empty,
> *Perpatoume mes' stous dromos. Hoover ti mas ekanes?*
> We walk in the streets. Hoover, what have you done to us?

In "Rebetika in the United States before World War II," Ole Smith asserts:

> [T]his song is a purely American product in text and music. It reflects the Depression experience, and there are no particular Greek values and norms in the song. It would be difficult to understand for Greeks living in Greece. We see here on a small scale the adaptation to American standards, values, and culture. (1991, 148)

While the definition and precise parameters of rebetika as a distinct musical genre remain a matter of debate, all possible definitions concur that such compositions are ultimately "songs of the people" (Butterworth and Schneider 1975; Holst 1975; Gauntlett 1982–1983). Coupled with that core element, the notions of pain and loss are equally within the broadest definitions of rebetika. Logically, then, why are Katsaros's best-selling records, which focus directly on the everyday experiences of the Greeks in North America, not really rebetika? It is also ahistorical to assume that Greeks, in the 1930s, whether they were living in the rural countryside or in an urban setting, had never heard of the American

Great Depression. Katsaros often wrote of the troubles and lives of Greeks in North America. That scholars today overlook at best and at worst deliberately omit these songs from consideration, focusing instead on Katsaros's hashish songs and kantades, does not lessen their initial impact or their lasting historical significance.

To cite one other example of Katsaros's ability to identify and express in song the experiences of his Greek American audience, we turn to his 1935 recording, "Mana mou ime fthisikos" (Mother I Have Consumption) (Columbia 56358-F B). It has long been recognized that the 1890–1924 Greek immigrant generation's greatest initial fears as general laborers were job-related injury and lung disease. It is important to note that, as Katsaros sings this song, he continually coughs between verses. A point of some interest to Greek speakers is the fact that Katsaros also plays with the words *fthisikos*, consumption, and *ftisikos*, spitting.

Mana mou eimai fthisikos, eho megali ftisi,
Mother, I am consumptive, mother I've got consumption,
Fila ton allo mou adelfo, mana na mi' kollisei.
Take care of my other brother, mother, so he doesn't catch it.
S'arachniasmeno spilaio tha' pa' na katoikiso,
In a cobwebbed cave I will go to live,
Osotou na' rthei i stigma, mana, na xepsihiso.
Until the moment comes, mother, to die.

Is this a *laïko* song or a *xenitia* song? Certainly, in 1935, this was not a Greek American song. The majority of Greeks thought that their time spent in America was only a temporary sojourn. Demographically, half of all Greeks who immigrated to North America between 1880 and 1924 returned to Greece. In point of fact, from 1908 to 1931 Greeks were fourth among all ethnic groups who left the United States to return to their country of origin (Saloutos 1956, 29).

Aside from repatriation, a recognized phenomenon of the diaspora experience is the temporary return trip back to one's family and home village or town. An as yet unexplored feature of the Greek American experience is the exceptionally high number of individuals and newly established families who returned to Greece in the 1930s. Today, these trips are often recalled as a time of indecision. Many Greeks who fully intended on returning permanently to Greece, for whatever reasons, ultimately did not and so made the trip back to America. Others who only went to visit stayed on for an extended period.

Many experienced a strange sense of double and even triple alienation. An often heard remark from the senior generation of immigrants is that they never considered themselves true Americans. Yet once they returned to Greece they soon realized they had also become something other than simply Greeks. For others who made the trip back to the United States, the feeling of never really belonging fully to either Greek or American society came as a deep and lasting realization.

It seems reasonable, then, that in 1935 "Mana mou ime fthisikos" was considered a xenitia song and not one that designated one's identity as a Greek living permanently in the United States. In keeping with the xenitia songs of the hard life away from family and home, most of the anti-emigration reports seen in Greece during this period (produced by the Greek government to keep citizens in the country so as to strengthen the domestic situation) focused on the dangerous work conditions and the poor health care overseas that Greeks were subjected to on a daily basis. "Mana mou ime fthisikos," given this overall context, was another tremendously popular record.

Repatriation and temporary return trips in the 1900–1930 era are also relevant to our discussion because the common Greek, whether in the countryside or in an urban setting, did not simply hear or read about Greeks in America. Given the overall demographics involved, it would have been extremely rare for a Greek not to have spoken directly with someone who had been in America, or at least known of someone who had. The interpretive evaluation of any Katsaros song must be informed by both American immigrant history as well as the history of the Greek diaspora.

Even though, after August 12, 1938, Katsaros never recorded again for either the Columbia or RCA Victor companies, his recording career was far from over. He was yet to record many songs in the hashish and kantades vein now praised by scholars. But Katsaros was also to record top-selling songs with enduring historical import that do not fall into easily defined categories. One such song is "I Saltadori" (The Jumpers), which was recorded in 1945 (Standard Records F-9025A):

> When the Germans go by they put on all airs,
> I jump up on their cars and steal everything from them.
> I'll jump up and jump up, *vre'* and I'll break even again.
> Gasoline and petrol we are after,
> Because it brings us a lot of money and we have a good time.

Katsaros is writing of the Greeks during World War II who stole all manner of supplies from the fascist occupying forces. Based on the Italian verb "to jump" (*saltare*), the Saltadori were (from the fascist perspective) thieves who stole off the back of military supply trucks while these vehicles were in transit, jumping onto them to take food, weapons, gasoline, and other items, and then quickly jumping off again. Extensive networks of children were employed as a warning system during such raids.

Given the current definitions of rebetika and xenitia songs, in 1945, when "I Saltadori" was first released, how would it be categorized? Other questions that naturally suggest themselves are: How did Greeks living in North America during the 1940s learn of these "jumpers," especially given that they were designated by an Italian slang term? Given that this song was released by an independent music company, how did Greek Americans learn of it such that it became a top-selling record? And so how do we properly refer to a Greek composer writing about events in Greece while living in far-off Boston?

Created Traditions

Musical traditions can serve contemporary political purposes that the original musicians, record company executives, and their intended audience could not have anticipated. The political factors are diverse. The final downfall of the Ottoman Empire between 1911 and 1922 initially curtailed, then stopped, all export of records from anywhere in the Balkans, Anatolia, or elsewhere in the broader empire. The dismemberment of the Ottoman Empire at the end of the First World War was only the political, not the final cultural outcome.

Every Balkan nation-state following the war sought to completely disavow any connection to the Ottoman past. Among the cultural manifestations of this ideologically inspired position was the total and systematic eradication of anything perceived as Ottoman: architectural sites (including mosques and grave-yards), language, place-names, written script, music genres, dances, and so on.

The Balkan political and cultural leaders deemed these actions crucial to their very survival as distinct sovereign nations. Politically dependent on the Great Powers, the Balkan statesmen realized that cultural forms often determined the geopolitical boundaries agreed upon at Versailles. All major political figures of the region believed that the realpolitik conditions that prevailed after the First World War meant not simply political change but cultural transformation.

In Greece, the cultural sanctions on music were rigorously enforced. Recording studios were not established in Athens until the mid-1920s. By the late 1920s, government restrictions completely excluded certain musical genres from being recorded commercially. Entire genres, individual musicians, specific ethnic groups, certain subject matter (drugs, criminal activities, and political subversion), mixed-language recordings, and even particular musical instruments were actively targeted for suppression.

All of these conditions are generally well understood in the field of modern Greek studies. What is not so readily recognized is that other Balkan countries, including Turkey, imposed their own sanctions on these shared musical traditions for exactly the same reasons—they were foreign to an idealized "national" form.

Yet, by whatever name, this matrix of popular music persisted in the region, albeit in forms said to be exclusive to the nation-state in which it was played and recorded.

Beginning in the 1970s, across the former Ottoman territories, these suppressed musical forms were rediscovered and then labeled as part of a unique ethnic musical tradition. This occurred with a number of nationality-specific genres such as rebetika, neo-klezmer, *gazino* (what is today called Turkish "music hall"), and other Balkan and Anatolian music traditions. The rerelease in North America of music originally found on 78-rpm records from 1900 to 1965 that document these once pan-Ottoman genres is now offered as the cultural property exclusively of one or another group.

What is missing from the wider study of Greek and pan-Balkan/Ottoman musical recordings since 1890 is the influence of, first, European- and then American-based recorded music. Music traditional to all peoples and cultural traditions indigenous to the Balkans, Greece, the eastern Levant, North Africa, and the Ottoman Empire in general was, at one point or another, collected by international record companies. Some of the only examples ever recorded of many musical traditions, genres, and musicians were released in America but not in their countries of origin. In addition, immigrant musicians in North America, independent record companies, and ethnic consumers from this broad geographic-cultural zone—all free of repression—put on record anything and everything they found entertaining regardless of the changing political landscape back in their home region.

These original records still constitute a creative feedback loop of music. It should be quickly noted that this feedback was/is itself part of an ongoing historical process. In terms strictly of Greek music (but the implications for other traditions should be obvious), restricting the study of musical influences solely to what is acceptable within the nation-state of Greece cannot offer a historically or culturally accurate presentation of Greek music since 1890.

This renewed interest in these common pan-Balkan/Ottoman music genres could well serve scholars of modern Greek music by helping to situate the tradition(s) they study within the wider scheme of world history and research. Debates in American folklore over the ongoing influence of scholars in the transformation of hillbilly into country music mirror many of the same alterations and created traditions of rebetika, neo-klezmer, and gazino (Rosenberg 1991; Slobin 1984). The collection and production of world music by the major international record companies along with the unique legacy of Orthophonic Records attests not only to time-honored Greek-specific musical genres but also to the shared music traditions of the Balkans, western Anatolia, and beyond. Greek recorded music and the recollections of musicians in North America provide a rich but largely unexplored field of study for this wider nexus of traditions that were systematically eliminated or severely suppressed.

Figure 52. George Katsaros singing in front of a sponge boat in Tarpon Springs. Courtesy of the City of Tarpon Springs.

Katsaros's description of the various instrumentalists, dancers, and singers with whom he routinely toured is especially instructive in noting the original performative setting that helped to perpetuate these outlawed traditions in North America:

> By the time I came to the United States [1913] I found in every city: San Francisco, Salt Lake City, Chicago, Detroit, Cleveland, Philadelphia, Boston, New York over fifty, sixty bands . . . in every city! . . . [D]uring those early years there were eleven or twelve cabarets in every city. Greek musicians and dancers, Armenians, Turkish girls, Egyptian all playing at the same clubs.
>
> We'd play Turkish music. We'd play Armenian music, Greek music, everything. And those musicians they had to be experienced! Oh, yes, because not only Greeks went into those clubs. Syrians, Armenians, and Turks came to those clubs. In my *kompania* I had to be careful to have an oud player to sing a little Turkish and then another fella to sing a little Arabic for the Syrian customers. See that's the reason I had to have six sometimes seven musicians with me. You had to have them! I had to have a cimbalom player, a clarinetist, a violinist, me on guitar, and an oud player just to play for the different customers.[9]

While this quotation focuses exclusively on the conditions in major cities, Katsaros reported (as did other senior-generation musicians) that these same mixed kompanias were also necessary in small towns and rural areas. Such recollections (along with the existence of commercial records) illustrate that no substantial change in the attention musicians devoted to pleasing their audiences took place in North America. In the Aegean and Adriatic seaports of the Balkans and Anatolia, the population was mixed and the musicians had to perform to an ever-changing audience. In North America, given the relative demographics between Balkan and Anatolian immigrants and the general American population, having a mixed ensemble ensured that all the various musical genres could be performed regardless of the musical preferences of any given evening's audience.

George Katsaros's career clearly documents the power of the international record companies in the movement of traditional musics around the planet. Further, the full range of Katsaros's compositions also attests to the role of music in speaking of the Greek collective experience in America from the 1900s to the 1960s. Only by correlating the history of the international record industry with the specific activities of traditional Greek musicians and promoters can we ever hope to learn the actual history of Greek music since the 1890s.

Notes

1. This chapter first appeared in the *Journal of Modern Hellenism*, nos. 12–13 (Winter 1995–1996): 239–56. Because this account appeared before Katsaros's death, I have amended it accordingly. I have also tried to tighten my historical arguments. My enduring thanks to Neni Panourgia, Pamela J. Dorn-Sezgin, and Dan Georgakas for their input on my earlier version and to Tina Bucuvalas for hers on this one.

Copies of my oral history interviews with Katsaros are under ATL #89-049-C/F at the Archives of Traditional Music (hereafter ATM) at Indiana University. Other Katsaros oral history collections and original 78-rpm records are held by the State Archives of Florida, the National Hellenic Museum, the Helen Z. Papanikolas Oral Histories Collection at the University of Utah (Marriott Library), and the British Institute of Recorded Sound.

I will refer to the artist as George Katsaros because that was the legal name on his death certificate, and it also appears on many record labels.

2. For a more complete discussion of this topic, see Racy 1976, 23; Frangos 1991; and Racy 1977, 58–94.

3. The more than fifty Albanian, Greek, Syrian, and Turkish record catalogs in various ATM collections provide a comparative base for future research. To give some sense of the time frame involved, the oldest Greek catalog in the ATM collection is the 1911 Columbia record catalog, while the oldest full-page advertisement for Greek records found there is from the *Eastern and Western Review* 2, no. 8 (January 1910): 43.

4. The history of academic musical field recordings of Balkan and Anatolian music traditions has yet to be resolved. We do know that while commercial recordings were being made in Constantinople and Smyrna, European musicologists were simultaneously sporadically documenting music traditions throughout the Balkans and western Anatolia.

Currently, only the most basic information about these first field recordings is available. Existing references report that the first field recordings of Greek folk music were made by French scholar Hubert Pernot on the island of Chios in 1898–1899. Paul Kretschmer recorded three discs on the island of Lesbos in 1901, Felix von Luschan in 1901–1902 recorded a number of cylinders in Turkey, music is known to have been recorded in Albania in 1903, an unspecified number of cylinders were collected in the Balkans during 1905–1910, and Béla Vikár (sometime before 1911) recorded five cylinders in Constantinople (Krader 1993, 185–86; Gillis 1984, 322–55). Not all traditional Ottoman music was recorded where one would expect. Perhaps the most famous example is that of Benjamin Ives Gilman recording Ottoman (perhaps Egyptian) musicians in 1893 at the World's Columbian Exposition in Chicago (Racy 1977; Frangos 1991). Obviously, to arrive at a full historical and aesthetic understanding of Balkan and Anatolian music at the turn of the last century, the commercial records and the academic field recordings must be compared.

5. For the sake of clarity, while the production of Greek records was recognized as the fifth largest among ethnic group record production, that number was in point of fact an academic assumption in the early 1980s. Enough documentation was readily available at that time to demonstrate that Greek records were fifth in sales for Columbia Records. For RCA Victor, they were in fact thirteenth in documented sales. The assumption made was that the approximately two hundred recordings on the RCA Victor Standard Orthophonic label—for which at that time no public documentation existed—could be added to the existing RCA Victor figure, which would then place their Greek material into that company's fifth place as well (Gronow 1982; Smith 1991). Since the 1980s, various collectors and archival materials on the Orthophonic label have confirmed this earlier supposition.

6. Chianis's statement that Demetriades had a "two year stay (1930–1932)" to gather his field collections has been confirmed. Dick Spottswood's discography notes that Demetriades (who was an extremely active vocalist) recorded "Rempetiko," "Night Blues," and "Oh! Baby" sometime in March 1930 and did not resume recording until January 15, 1932 (Spottswood 1990, 3:1159).

7. The circulation of Greek music produced in North America back to Greece and diaspora colonies elsewhere is generally recognized but little understood.

8. Katsaros asserted to me (and others) that he first began to record for commercial record companies in the United States at a very early time, citing at various times years such as 1911 and 1919 (Frangos 1991; Smith 1991). But I have never seen any public documents that confirm these early dates. Dick Spottswood lists 1928 as the first year Katsaros successfully recorded. Collectors often make claims to owning unique recordings. But unless these records are made public in some manner or evidence is presented in the form of company documents, record catalog citations, or some other source material, I believe that the only prudent course is to follow Spottswood.

9. Katsaros 2B ATL 89-049-C/F.

References

Butterworth, Katharine, and Sara Schneider, eds. 1975. *Rebetika: Songs from the Old Greek Underworld*. Athens: Aiora Press.

Chianis, Sotirios (Sam). 1988. "Survival of Greek Folk Music in New York." *New York Folklore* 14, nos. 3–4: 682.

Frangos, Steve. 1991. "The Many Traditions of Greek Music." *GreekAmerican*, March 23–April 6.

———. 2002. "Marika Papagika and the Transformations in Modern Greek Music." In *Readings in Greek America: Studies in the Experience of Greeks in the United States*, edited by Spyros D. Orphanos, 223–39. New York: Pella.

Gauntlett, Stathis. 1982–1983. "*Rebetiko Tragoudi* as a Generic Term." *Byzantine and Modern Greek Studies* 8.

———. 1997. "Obituary: George Katsaros." *Independent*, July 6, 1997. At https://www.independent. co.uk/news/people/obituary-george-katsaros-1249521.html. Accessed April 17, 2018.

Gillis, Frank J. 1984. "The Incunabula of Instantaneous Ethnomusicological Sound Recordings, 1890–1910: A Preliminary List." In *Problems and Solutions: Occasional Essays in Musicology Presented to Alice M. Moyle*, edited by Jamie C. Kassler and Jill Stubington, 322–55. Sydney: Hale and Iremonger.

Gronow, Pekka. 1981. "The Record Industry Comes to the Orient." *Ethnomusicology* 25, no. 2: 252.

———. 1982. "Ethnic Recordings: An Introduction." In *Ethnic Recordings in America: A Neglected Heritage*. Washington, DC: American Folklife Center, Library of Congress.

Holst, Gail. 1975. *Road to Rembetika: Music of a Greek Sub-Culture*. Athens: Denise Harvey.

Krader, Barbara. 1993. "Greece." In *Ethnomusicology: Historical and Regional Studies*, edited by Helen Myers, 185–86. New York: W. W. Norton.

Lecoeur, Sheila. 2009. *Mussolini's Greek Island: Fascism and the Italian Occupation of Syros in World War II*. London: Tavris Academic Studies.

Morris, Roderick Conway. 1981. "Greek Café Music with a Listing of Recordings." *Recorded Sound* 80 (July): 79–117.

Phillips, David, and Steven Ferry. 1996. *Greek Americans*. New York: Benchmark Books.

Racy, Ali Jihad. 1976. "Record Industry and Egyptian Traditional Music, 1904–1932." *Ethnomusicology* 20, no. 1: 23.

———. 1977. "The Impact of Commercial Recording on the Musical Life of Egypt, 1904–1932." *Essays in Arts and Sciences* 6: 58–94.

Rosenberg, Neil V. 1991. "Collecting Our Thoughts." *Journal of American Folklore* 104, no. 411 (Winter): 92–102.

Saloutos, Theodore. 1956. *They Remember America*. Berkeley: University of California Press.

Slobin, Mark. 1984. "The Neo-Klezmer Movement and Euro-American Musical Revivalism." *Journal of American Folklore* 97, no. 383 (January–March): 98–104.

Smith, Ole L. 1991. "Rebetika in the United States before World War II." In *New Directions in Greek American Studies*, edited by Dan Georgakas and Charles C. Moskos, 143–51. New York: Pella.

Spottswood, Richard K. 1979. "Do You Sell Italians?" *John Edwards Memorial Foundation Quarterly* 15, no. 56: 255.

———. 1990. *Ethnic Music on Records: A Discography of Ethnic Recordings Produced in the United States, 1893–1942*. 7 vols. Urbana: University of Illinois Press.

"Health to You, Marko, with Your Bouzouki!": The Role of Spoken Interjection in Greek Musicians' Imagined Performance World in Historical Recordings Made in America and Abroad[1]

—Michael G. Kaloyanides

OK, let's get in the mood! *Opa! Aïde! Aman. Mannam. Olé.* Po po po po po! Ooof! *Yashar, Ela*, Allah, *Isia. Trava. Yiassou*, Michael with your article!! Greeks call these terms and phrases *tsakismata*.

Historical 78-rpm gramophone recordings of Greek music from the early twentieth century document a remarkable variety of tsakismata, interjections or interpolations common to the performances of Greek song forms. As noted by Sam Chianis in his monograph *Folk Songs of Mantineia, Greece*, the tsakismata (sing. *tsakisma*) in rural Greece's table songs, songs of the road, wedding songs, laments, and dance songs commonly take the form of short, extralyrical, sung exclamatory phrases or words such as *more* (you!), *kale* (good friend), *mannam* (mother), and *aïde* (come on!) (Chianis 1965, 6). Urban Greek traditions such as *rebetika* and *Smyrneïka* also employ tsakismata, both sung and spoken. The impact of tsakismata is so significant that the most celebrated of the Smyrneïka song forms, the *amanes*, takes its name from its characteristic tsakisma: *aman* (alas!). The pervasiveness of these tsakismata—not only the traditional short sung examples but also spoken interjections ranging from a single word, to short exchanges between musicians, to twenty-second-long dialogues between musicians or between a musician and an audience member—in Greek music recorded in the United States, Greece, Constantinople, and elsewhere during the first half of the twentieth century testifies to their importance to the traditions. In this chapter, I will examine the use and function of spoken tsakismata in contextualizing rebetika and Smyrneïka recordings' shellac soundscape and imagined performance world as well as in defining and validating the identity and status of performer, audience, and musical genre.

What drew me to this topic was the ubiquity of these spoken interjections in the commercial recordings of Greek urban music traditions I encountered both in the United States and in Greece. As a Greek American growing up in a Greek and Armenian immigrant community and regularly participating in social events that included music making, I was certainly aware that musicians, dancers, and other participants at celebrations would occasionally contribute tsakismata to the event. As a performer in Greek American ensembles for four decades, I often hear the typically occasional shouts of *opa!* or *aïde!* at performance events such as a church festival, *glendi* (party), or wedding. But since the 1990s or so, hitherto unavailable historical recordings of Greek music have been released on CD. In that time, I have listened to hundreds if not thousands of recordings of primarily Greek urban music by both Greek and Greek American performers and have been struck by how common the inclusion of tsakismata is on the corpus of recorded work. In contrast to the occasional use of these interjections in live performances I have observed, fully two-thirds of the historical recordings I have examined include one or more tsakismata. More contemporary and humorous evidence of their systematic utilization is the website tsakismata.rebetiko.org featuring the trademarked Tsakismata Automatic Generator, which functions like a cross between a Magic 8 ball and monkeys on typewriters, "producing randomously [*sic*] 11,688,200,277,601 different original tsakismata" (RMRDBD 2003). It is apparent that the performers and producers of the historical recordings consciously intended that they include tsakismata. Why? What were the uses and functions at work here?

In undertaking this research, in addition to examining hundreds of recordings, I have drawn on the expertise of Greek musicians and dancers, collectors of historical recordings on their original media, scholars of these musical traditions, academics in modern Greek studies, and enthusiasts of Greek music of all sorts. Since the use of tsakismata was most common on recordings of rebetika and Smyrneïka, I have chosen to focus on these traditions and recordings.

The terms "rebetika" and "Smyrneïka" are used to identify Greek urban music genres that arose sometime between the end of the nineteenth and the beginning of the twentieth century in urban communities in Greece, the Ottoman Empire, and the Turkish republic. Most associated with the development of these traditions were the Greek communities of Constantinople, Smyrna, Thessaloniki, Athens, and Piraeus. By the end of the nineteenth century, music venues or nightclubs called *cafés aman* had become well established in Ottoman Constantinople and Smyrna. Because they offered secular musics linked with the profanities of alcohol, eroticism, and dance, for the most part only Greek, Jewish, Armenian, and Roma musicians were comfortable inhabiting that world. The café aman, the café of sighs, took its name from the song form amanes, which in turn took its name from its signature opening text of *Aman!*, a tsakisma or interjection that can be translated as "Alas!" or with a sigh. The amanes, very similar musically to the Turkish *gazel*, was a featured song form of the café aman, speaking of deep emotions, passions, and world-weariness. Dance songs such as the *zeibekiko* and *tsifteteli* were also part of the café aman repertoire. Given its association with the city of Smyrna, this genre became known as Smyrneïka. The *outi, santouri, kanonaki, toumbeleki*, violin, *lyra*, finger cymbals, and *defi* were the instruments of the tradition.

The Balkan Wars, World War I, the Smyrna catastrophe of 1922, and the subsequent Treaty of Lausanne precipitated a massive exchange of populations on an unprecedented level between Greece and Turkey. With the negotiating governments distinguishing Greek from Turk on the basis of religion, 1.5 million Greek Christians were repatriated to Greece in a remarkably short period of time. Although the Greek government hoped to settle the immigrants in villages, the dearth of rural space resulted in their relocation to essentially squatters' camps and ghettos in the Greek seaports of Piraeus and Thessaloniki. Unwanted, ill treated, and seemingly too foreign to the resident Greek population, a segment of the new immigrant population created a criminal underworld society. This was a macho, violent, antiestablishment, antisocial world of drug use and dealing, prostitution, petty theft, scams, cons, and black marketeering. And it was in this world, in its illegal cafés aman hidden in factory basements, that a new urban musical tradition developed, based in part on the Smyrneïka musics arriving with the new refugees from Asia Minor. This tradition became known as rebetika, taking its name from the *rebetes*, the members of this underworld. The rebetes, accompanying themselves on bouzouki, *baglamas*, guitar, and shot glasses on worry beads, performed songs that both celebrated and despaired of the rebetes' life, songs of drug use, addiction, tuberculosis, betrayal, run-ins with the police, prison life, revenge, and death.

Beginning as early as perhaps 1910, Smyrneïka and rebetika made their way onto gramophone recordings in Greece, Turkey, and the United States. And the golden years of these two related traditions were documented on shellac recordings made primarily between 1918 and 1946. The first half of the twentieth century marked the birth of a thriving Greek American music industry, particularly in New York City, with Greek American–owned music retailers like the Prodromidis Company; music publishing companies such as Attikon Music, Hermes Music Publishing, and Apollo Music; and record companies including Nina, Grecophon, and Alector providing sheet music, recordings, and instruments to the community. This era also produced the first generation of well-known Greek American recording artists: singers Kyria Koula, Marika Papagika, and Amalia Baka; bouzouki player Ioannis Halikias (aka Jack Gregory), and bandleaders Gus Vali and Peter Kara (Kaloyanides 2013). In listening to the recordings of this era, one sees the ways Smyrneïka and rebetika composers, performers, and producers adapted to the new medium. A template of performance and recording practice emerged: four-minute performances that included a set composition, space for one or more improvisational *taximia*, and more often than not one or more tsakismata interjections.

The tsakismata took four distinct forms, each with their own distinct uses and functions:

1. *Kefi* Call: a short one- or two-word exclamation:
    Opa!
    Och!
    Bravo!
    Aïde!
    Allah!
    Aman!
    Ela!
    Isia!
    Trava!
    Po, po, po!

2. *Yiassou* Shout-out: a personalized toast/praise phrase:
    Yiassou, Marko, with your *bouzouki*
    Yiassou, Jack
    Yiassou, Margaroni, with your *kanonaki*
    Yiassou, Niko, with your *violi*
    Yiassou, Strato, *tembeli*
    Yiassou, Artemi *mou*, with your lovely picking
    Yiassou, Menelae, my dervish

3. Keepin' It Real Phrase: the soundscape/imagined performance world phrase:

Gemis to dolario, dervisi	Give him plenty of bucks, dervish
Sti banda ta doumania	Put aside the dope
Ouzo stous batsous	Ouzo for the cops
Hara sto prama moudzourothike i giftissa	Big deal, the gypsy woman got dirty

4. Extended Dialog

Let's look at each of these interjection forms in terms of their use and function in the recordings. Here I am using Alan Merriam's applications of the terms (1964).

Form 1, the short exclamation, which I name the *kefi* call, seems primarily to consist of a word or phrase associated with the Greek concept of kefi: a feeling or emotion of enthusiasm, a sense of positive, excited spirit, often associated with social events particularly involving music and dance.

Eho kefi!	I have kefi, I have enthusiasm, I am excited, I'm in great spirits!
Den eho kefi	I don't have kefi. I'm not enthused, I'm not in the mood.

For example, the terms that have English equivalents or are understood include:

Opa!	Opa! (you must know this one)
Ela!	Come on!
Bravo!	
Isia!	Right on!
Trava!	Keep going!

Like these, the majority of terms used in kefi calls on the historical recordings were in Greek, but we do occasionally encounter kefi calls in Ladino, Turkish, and other languages. For example, in the song "Evraiopoula," legendary singer Roza Eskenazi shouts "vámos! vámos!" in response to the male singer's call of "pame!" The terms *keyf* in Arabic and *keyif* in Turkish have meanings, contexts, and implications similar to the Greek term "kefi." And in flamenco tradition, the *jaleo*, shouts of encouragement such as *olé*, has similar value in invoking *duende* (spirit).

So, clearly, one purpose of the short exclamation is to express kefi. But it is also intended to encourage or create kefi. Anna Caraveli, in her article "The Song beyond the Song: Aesthetics and Social Interaction in Greek Folksong," notes the "occasional audience participation through the repetition of certain tsakísmata, meant to encourage and stimulate the singer: ópa, yásou, éla, áinde, etc." (1982, 153). Musicians have commented that, in the early years of recording in particular, recordings were made in rather sterile and kefi-killing environments such as hotel rooms and warehouses. So kefi exclamations were clearly of value in encouraging enthusiastic performances, particularly in a tradition that sought to present deep emotions and encourage passionate improvisations as in the taximia. Nick Laggis, an outi player, told me that musicians, in making these recordings, were cognizant of and intent on producing two channels of kefi transmission and creation: one from musician or producer to musician in the recording session and a second between the shellac and the imagined audience.[2] Tony Klein, a performer and collector of rebetika and Smyneïka, agreed that these tsakismata were "done for the gallery, the imagined future audience."[3] Both were considered crucial to an aesthetically and commercially successful recording.

Also, it is apparent that one reason tsakismata appeared in the earliest recordings of rebetika and Smyrneïka as they did in live performances of the era was the absence of a bright line distinguishing the aesthetics and norms of recording studio performances from those of live performances. That is, studio recordings were, in part, thought of as just a "record" of what a performance in a traditional context would be like. As recording evolved, tsakismata would be created and used for reasons particular to the recording context and perhaps distinct from their role in live performance.

What may also be at work here is the function of tsakismata to legitimize these mediated performances. In his article on the music of the Congo Pygmies, Steven Feld invokes Walter Benjamin as he discusses the transformation of a performance from unique to plural existences, as in the case of the mediation of recordings and their duplication. The risk here is that recordings of performances may lose the "aura" of the authenticity or legitimacy of the original performance. Feld says that "this 'aura' frames the consequent status of the 'copy,' particularly as regards contestation of its 'authenticity' or 'legitimacy' vis-à-vis an 'original'" (1996, 14). Clearly, tsakismata, including the short kefi exclamations, are part of the live performance world of rebetika and Smyrneïka, and their inclusion on recordings can be seen as an attempt to maintain the "aura" and authenticate or legitimize the recordings.

Tsakisma form 2 is what I call the *yiassou* shout-out. It typically consists of three components: first, the word *yiassou*, which translates as "to your health"; second, the name of the person addressed in the shout-out; and, third, a qualifying term.

Clearly, the word *yiassou* is intended as a toast or to praise a participant in the recording. Although it literally means "to your health," yiassou has many applications. It is used as a word of greeting or farewell; it is used as a drinking toast; it is used to praise someone's skill, as in the phrase *yia sta heria sas* (health to your hands) directed by the diner to the cook who has prepared a delicious meal. It is in this last context, a praise phrase, that yiassou is ostensibly used in these shout-outs.

The second component of the yiassou shout-out, the name, identifies the recording participant being addressed. Called by a given name, surname, professional name, or nickname, the addressee is typically, in descending frequency, the singer; a featured instrumentalist who gets a shout-out either for his general performance on the recording or for a fine taximi; or some other engaged participant in the conversation. In this last instance, someone (other than a performer) participating in or attending the recording session may also receive a shout-out in reply after offering a shout-out to one of the performers.

The third component is the qualifying term or phrase. It may identify the instrument being played (bouzouki, violin, santouri, outi); the particular skills evinced (golden double-picking, for example); or an associative term, honorific or not-so-honorific, such as *Samiotaki*, little one from Samos; *Politaki*, little one

142

Figure 53. Amalia Baka, daughter Diamond Baka Papachristou, and musicians. Courtesy of Emily Papachristou.

from Constantinople; *merakli*, passionate one; *dervisi*, dervish; *mangas*, wise guy; or *hasiklis*, dope-head.

The yiassou shout-out is clearly the most common of the tsakismata phrases found on the historical rebetika and Smyrneïka recordings. At first glance, it is apparent that the yiassou shout-out, like the kefi call, is intended to encourage, acknowledge, or create kefi. And, of course, its purpose is to praise or toast an artist in a way authentic and "aura"-preserving to the tradition. Certainly in live music making, musicians and other participants use the shout-out to recognize a fellow musician for a spirited performance.

But it is interesting to note that well over half the recordings I examined included at least one shout-out, and at times they seem to be nearly obligatory elements of the recording. Some are spoken enthusiastically; some offered perfunctorily, like the phrase, "Do you want fries with your order?" There is clearly other value and meaning to the yiassou shout-out.

Perhaps the most significant function of the yiassou shout-out is the identification of performers and composers. As an example, in the 1929 recording of the *karsilamas* dance-song "Thelo na s'alismoniso" (I Want to Forget You) by Amalia Baka, a male, ostensibly one of the accompanying instrumentalists, loudly shouts, "Yiassou, Amalia mou!" after she sings the second verse of the song. Amalia, in turn, acknowledges violinist Nishan Sedefjian: "Y'Allah, och, yiassou, Nishani, yiassou." (Note that this tsakisma combines a kefi call—"y'Allah, och"—with a yiassou shout-out). In their text *Hasiklidika Rebetika*, Suzanne Aulin and Peter Vejleskov recognize this identification function: "Moreover we record interjections that do not constitute part of a song at all, by which we often can ascertain the identity of the singer, and in certain cases also of the instrumentalist" (1991, 34).

During the heyday of these recordings in the first half of the twentieth century, a considerable proportion of the Greek population and the Greek diaspora was still functionally illiterate. According to Aris Anagnostopoulos, a practicing rebetiko musician: "Since most of the musicians in surviving recordings were professionals, working within a cash economy, these exclamations largely evolved as a form of advertising addressed to a largely illiterate public that knew the song but could not, or could not be bothered to, read the label on the record."[4] So it was through the shout-outs that the singers and instrumentalists were identified to the audience, recorded credits as it were. Often the musicians were also the composers, and the shout-out served as a means to establish ownership of the songs, the performances, and the recording itself. Record companies commonly identified performers on the disc's label with only a stereotyped blanket term like "Greek Popular Orchestra," so the shout-out assured the musicians that the shellac audience would know their names and roles. On some recordings, artists resorted to praising and thereby identifying themselves; thus Rita Abatzi's "Yiassou Rita" and Giorgos Kavouras's "Yiassou Kavoura." This form of recorded identification is certainly not without precedent, particularly in the Anatolian environment, where the *aşik*, Turkey's famed minstrel, composed and performed his songs. In the *aşiklar*, the songs of the aşik, the last verse would include the aşik's name, identifying him as the author of the song.

It is important to note the role of Greek *fonografidzides* in the insertion of the shout-out in the recordings. The fonografidzides were itinerant phonograph players who, in addition to working as buskers of sorts, often represented phonograph companies. They functioned as marketing and test-marketing agents, A&R men who attempted to determine what artists and musics would sell. Because the village and city audiences wouldn't be able to see credits on the labels, having credits in the recording itself served as a practical tool for identifying performers and the record companies as well. Some recordings began with an announcement such as "An Odeon Record!" In addition, performers and composers benefited from this additional form of publicity. Markos Vamvakaris, one of the most famous rebetika musicians, first came to the public's attention in 1933 through the effort of fonografidzides playing two of his hash-smoking songs.

Some musicians on the recordings clearly were annoyed by the de rigueur shout-out. Aris Anagnostopoulos recalls a recording by vocalist Kostos Nouros, who responds to a shout-out with his own tsakisma of "Na pethaneis, pousti!" (Die, you fag). Songwriter, bouzouki player, and singer Vassilis Tsitsanis laconically replied to a tsakisma of a female singer with "Skase mori" (Shut up, you).[5]

Of particular interest is the third component of the shout-out, the qualifier. Its use is clear when it identifies the instrument the musician is playing. But sometimes a guitarist is praised for his bouzouki playing, or a santouri player is toasted for his kanonaki work. This could be a simple mistake, but more likely it serves to authenticate the recording as part of a particular genre with characteristic defining instruments. So, although Spyros Peristeris may be playing a guitar on a rebetiko recording, calling it a bouzouki may give the recording more legitimacy as a rebetiko performance. Or it may be that what is being identified here is not the instrument itself but rather its "instrumentness." So the santouri is identified as a kanonaki because of its kanonakiness, or a guitar as a bouzouki by its bouzoukiness. A modern parallel would be a synthesizer player performing a clarinet-like taximi using a clarinet setting and being praised for his clarinet playing. Tony Klein mentions another theory (advanced by Nicholas Pappas, but which Klein feels doubtful about):

[T]his "pseudobouzouki" was a means for the Asia Minor immigrant musical community (who did not seem to have used the bouzouki in their original environment, and who were, according to Pappas, somewhat discriminated [against] by the local Greek population) to "hijack" a local phenomenon during a period when their musical star was losing its ascendance in favor of the bouzouki-centered music which became standard by the end of the 1930s.[6]

When the qualifier is an honorific or less-than-honorable honorific such as *dervisi* (dervish), *asikis* (aşik), *mangas* (wise guy), *dais* (gangster), *hasiklis* (hash-head), *alaniaris* (drifter), or *alitis* (bum), it serves the function of establishing what one might call the musician's street cred. So she is not just a musician recording a song about life as a hash-head, she *is* a hash-head. And he is not just a rebetiko singer, he is a dervish mystic in his *teke* monastery. This is legitimizing the performance not just as an original piece of art but also as one that is authentic to the genre and to the society it represents.

Tsakisma form 3 is the "keepin' it real" phrase. It typically consists of an imperative sentence or fragment that encourages and describes actions that might occur in the venues where rebetika and Smyneïka were performed, or that are part of the creatively romanticized public imagination fantasy narrative of life among the rebetika gangster heroes. This tsakisma form serves to craft an appealing soundscape of life in the underworld, populated with stoners, con men, corrupt police, and sirens.

For example, in the 1933 recording of "Mourmouriko zeibekiko," a bouzouki solo by Ioannis Halikias, an additional figure makes his presence known on the recording. He snaps his fingers and makes occasional comments: "Fill him with dollars, Dervish! Put aside the dope! Right on, keep going! Ouzo for the cops!" Here we are presented with a performance in an imagined *teke*, a dervish monastery but a term also used in the rebetiko world for illegal speakeasies. Halikias

'Η ΡΟΖΑ ΕΣΚΙΝΑΖΗ καὶ ἡ ὀρχήστρα ἀπὸ ψιλὰ ὄργανα σὲ Δίσκους «BALKAN»

Figure 54. Roza Eskenazi and ensemble. Balkan Records flyer. Courtesy of Meletios Pouliopoulos.

is addressed as a dervish. The recording venue is a place littered with hash-filled waterpipes, where musicians are tipped for their performances and police are bought off with free ouzo.

In a 1934 recording by Roza Eskenazi entitled "I'm a Snorter" (as in snorting heroin and cocaine), a listener interjects twice with "Och, I'll snort dope, brother, until the resurrection!" and "Roza, for you I became a dope snorter!" Here we have a temptress who extols the virtue of hard drugs and drags her suitors into addiction.

And in the 1930 recording of "Sousta politiki" (Constantinople Sousta) by Antonis Diamantidis (Dalgas), a participant provides the hat trick: yiassou shout-outs for Dalgas, the singer, and Antonis Amiralis (Papatzis), the accordion player; a kefi call; and an enthusiastic "keepin' it real" phrase. The entire sequence translates as follows: "Yiassou, my Dalgas, yiassou! Opa! Man, what a fine party this is! Yiassou my Papatzis, with your accordion, Och, po po po po po po po po! May I enjoy you, my City!" The enthusiastic participant depicts a wonderful evening of merriment with music performed by great masters of the tradition somewhere in Constantinople. In all three examples, the tsakismata establish both a physical and a social place where the performance is imagined to occur.

Tsakisma form 4 is the extended dialog. It is almost always found at the beginning of the recording as a prologue to the song or instrumental piece and takes the form of a short conversation between two individuals, one of whom may be the primary vocalist or instrumentalist. In every dialog I have examined, one or both of the characters could be considered a grossly stereotyped mangas: a lovable scoundrel high on hash, doped-up silly, looking for some fun, or in a stoner chasm bummed out with existential angst. The dialog functions as a setup for the piece that follows, as an invitation for the mangas either to tell his tale or to set the imagined stage, a rebetiko environment, for the piece to exist in.

The 1936 recording of "Pente chronia dikasmenos" (Sentenced to Five Years), subtitled "The Voice of the Waterpipe," by Vangelis Papazoglou and Stellakis Perpiniadis begins with the bubbling of a waterpipe and a riff on a santouri. Vangelis addresses Stellakis:

– Yiassou, Stellaki, my friend.
– Health and joy to you, Vangelis.
– What's that you're holding?
– A waterpipe.
– A waterpipe?
– What do you want me to hold, an ocean liner?
– But for ages, brother Stellakis, whenever I seek you out, I find you holding a waterpipe.
– Ach, brother Vangelis, you're right, but if you knew what sorrows and torments I have, you wouldn't scold me.
– Can't you tell me your troubles so I can learn from them?
– Listen, my dear brother Vangelis, so you can console me.

Stellakis then sings of five years locked up in prison, resorting to smoking hash to forget his sorrows like his fellow jailed manges. Here, the dialog serves as a device to elicit Stellakis's confessional tale of the road to addiction.

The audience for these prefaced pieces would have found the dialogs familiar. Similar comedic dialogs could be found in the Karagiozis shadow puppet tradition and the satirical *epitheorisi* revue, the most popular theatrical genre in Greece between approximately 1894 and the early 1930s, the same era as of the great rebetika and Smyrneïka recordings.

Finally, if we look at these four tsakismata forms collectively, it becomes apparent that there is a commonality, if not a synergy, to their function in the 78-rpm soundscape. This corpus of recordings constructs a virtual rebetiko/Smyrneïko world, a shellac locus inhabited not only by musicians but also by an appreciative, encouraging, flawed, and certainly idiosyncratic audience that addresses the performers by name; an imagined Greek underworld *Cheers*, "where everybody knows your name" (Portnoy and Hart Angelo 1982).

Notes

1. This article evolved from a paper I presented at the 2008 Society for Ethnomusicology conference at Wesleyan University, Middletown, Connecticut, and a talk in 2009 at the Yale Hellenic Studies Program, New Haven, Connecticut.

2. Nick Laggis, personal communication, 2007.

3. Tony Klein, personal communication, 2007.

4. Aris Anagnostopoulos, personal communication, 2007.

5. Ibid.

6. Tony Klein, personal communication, 2007.

References

Aulin, Suzanne, and Peter Vejleskov. 1991. *Hasiklidika Rebetika.* Copenhagen: Museum Tusculanum Press.

Caraveli, Anna. 1982. "The Song beyond the Song: Aesthetics and Social Interaction in Greek Folksong." *Journal of American Folklore* 95: 129–58.

Chianis, Sotirios (Sam). 1965. *Folk Songs of Mantineia, Greece.* Berkeley: University of California Press.

Feld, Steven. 1996. "Pygmy POP: A Genealogy of Schizophonic Memesis." *Yearbook for Traditional Music* 28: 1–25.

Kaloyanides, Michael G. 2013. "Greek American Music." In *The Grove Dictionary of American Music.* 2nd ed. Oxford: Oxford University Press.

Merriam, Alan P. 1964. *The Anthropology of Music.* Evanston, IL: Northwestern University Press.

Portnoy, Gary, and Judy Hart Angelo. 1982. Theme from *Cheers* ("Where Everybody Knows Your Name").

Radical Movement for Rebetiko Dechiotification and Bouzouki Detetrachordization (RMRDBD). 2003. At tsakismata.rebetiko.org. Accessed January 6, 2016.

Turkish Music in the Greek American Experience

—Joseph G. Graziosi

In February 1925, the prominent New York recording company Columbia published a catalog of 78-rpm records for the Greek American immigrant market.[1] The catalog cover featured a painting of three male musicians dressed in the traditional mainland *fustanella* playing *laouto*, *santouri*, and violin, with a female singer dressed in the formal attire of the Attica villages. The catalog is titled *"Δισκοι Ελληνικοι (Greek-Turkish) Records."* The inside page announces, *"Καταλογος Ελληνικων και Τουρκικων Διπλων Δισκων Φωνογραφου Columbia (Katalogos Ellinikon kai Tourkikon Diplon Diskon Fonografou Columbia, Catalog of Greek and Turkish Double-Sided Phonograph Discs Columbia)."* That Columbia should give equal weight to both Greek- and Turkish-language songs in this early catalog directed to a Greek market might seem incongruous to some people today, especially given the long 1912–1922 decade of war between Greece and the Ottoman Empire (the First and Second Balkan Wars, World War I, and the 1919–1922 Greco-Turkish War with its subsequent Mikriasiatiki Katastrofi or Asia Minor Catastrophe). It did not seem so at the time, as the following personal recollections will show.

Among the thousands of 78-rpm records in the vast collection of the late Dino Pappas (Constantine Papakonstantinou) of Detroit, pride of place belonged to a very rare disc, "Kiaghidkane,"[2] an instrumental *tsifteteli/çiftetelli* with Zurna Naci Bey accompanied by *nakkara* drums, recorded circa 1910 on the Odeon label in Istanbul (at the time still officially known as Constantinople/Konstantiniyye). This record was among the very few personal possessions brought to the United States by Pappas's mother when she emigrated from the Samatya/Psomathia district of old Stamboul around 1919. Her own parents had been internal migrants from the Turcophone Greek community of Urgup/Prokopi in Cappadocia. Although known primarily as the owner of the largest collection of recorded Greek music in the United States, Pappas had also amassed a huge collection of Turkish recordings, both songs recorded among immigrants in the New World and songs recorded in the Old World.

Columbia

ΔΙΣΚΟΙ ΕΛΛΗΝΙΚΟΙ
(GREEK-TURKISH)
RECORDS

Figure 55. "Δισκοι Ελλινικοι (Greek-Turkish) Records," 1925. Catalog, Columbia Phonograph Company, New York. Courtesy of Joseph Graziosi.

While living in New York City in the 1980s, I came across several collections of old 78s that belonged to elderly and deceased Greek American immigrants that included several discs of Turkish vocal and instrumental pieces. While perusing the white elephant table at a Greek festival at the Annunciation Church in Manhattan's Upper West Side, I came across several 78s recorded in the United States, including a few Turkish sides, some written in old Ottoman script, with the Armenian violinist and singer Kemany Minas. Upon inquiring, I learned that these recordings had belonged to a recently deceased prominent member of the church and past Philoptochos president, who had been born on the island of Tenedos (now Bozcaada), Turkey.

About the same time period, I found and bought at the festival of the Saint Barbara Greek Orthodox Church of New Haven, Connecticut, an old 78 with the songs "Aman Doctor" (*sheba* or *saba canto*) and "Neva chifte telli gazel" (an *amanes*) in Turkish, recorded by the singer and oud player Tom Stathis or "Kirkilisiotes" in New York City on the Columbia label in June 1921. As his artistic nickname makes clear, he was an immigrant from the town of Kirk Kilise (Saranda Ekklisies in Greek, now Kirklareli) in Turkish Thrace—which is also the hometown of my maternal grandfather. Interestingly, the original founding families of the Saint Barbara community were monolingual Turkish speakers from the town of Permata/Bermede in the Aksehir region of central Anatolia.[3]

As a final note, I was allowed to record onto cassette from several discs that had belonged to George Cardamenis, an immigrant from Constantinople who first settled as a confectioner in Indiana and later ran a coffeehouse/social club in Los Angeles. The latter was frequented by Greeks from the greater region of Constantinople (including the Marmara islands and both the Thracian and Asia Minor shores of the Propontida, or Sea of Marmara). According to his son, Fedon Cardamenis (my aunt's husband), these old 78s were kept at the coffeehouse and played by the patrons on an old jukebox. Perhaps 40 to 50 percent of the discs contained Turkish songs. Unfortunately, these cassettes warped beyond easy listening before they could be digitized, and my cousin, who inherited the original collection, threw them out with the trash during one season's spring cleaning—the fate of a large percentage of family record collections.

The above personal recollections demonstrate that among early Greek American immigrants, or at least a substantial percentage of them, Turkish song and music were held in high regard. For many immigrants from former Ottoman Turkey—whether Anatolia or Thrace, urban or rural—Turkish songs were a familiar aspect of home culture. For these Greeks, whether monolingual or bilingual Turkish speakers or monolingual Greek speakers, Turkish songs and their accompanying music were familiar and recognizable, often more so than the rural songs of mainland Greece that immigrants brought from the Morea, Roumeli, Epirus, or Thessaly.

It was not just the Anatolian Greek who might have an affection for Turkish song. It seems that Turkish and Ottoman music was known and widely popular in late nineteenth- and early twentieth-century Greece. In June 26, 1886, the demoticist[4] Athenian newspaper *Rambagas* published an article "Αι Αθηναι διασκεδαζουν" (Athens Entertains), in which the writer describes how the Constantinopolitan Greek female singer "Hanende" Foteini had captured the attention and excitement of Athens nightlife—especially with her rendition of the Turkish song "Memo." The article includes the refrain in Turkish of the main song and describes how the song became a great hit among Athenians in general. Significantly, Foteini is accompanied by an orchestra of clarinet, violin, santouri,

COLUMBIA TURKISH DOUBLE RECORDS   **15**

10-Inch—75c.   (Instrumental, cont'd)

ΜΕΛΩΔΙΑΙ ἐπὶ ΒΙΟΛΙΟΥ
VIOLIN SOLOS

E 4526
Ταξὶμ Οὐσάκ, διὰ βιολίου, ὑπὸ ᾿Αθαν. Μακεδόνα.
Taxim Oushak, violin solo.
Ζεϊμπέκικο, ᾿Αϊβαλῆ, διὰ βιολίου, βιολονσέλου καὶ κυμβάλου.
Zeibekiko Aivali. Violin, 'Cello and Cymbal.

ΜΕΛΩΔΙΑΙ ΕΠΙ ΒΙΟΛΟΝΣΕΛΟΥ, ὑπὸ Χ. Σάντπη
'Cello Solos, by H. Sandby

E 3476
᾿Εσπερινὸ τραγοῦδι. Esperino trayoudi.
᾿Αντάτζιο. Adagio.

ΦΥΣΑΡΜΟΝΙΚΑ ὑπὸ Μ. ΤΣΠΤΑΝΙΔΟΥ
Accordion Solos

7001 F
᾿Η Κρητικιά. E Kretikia.
᾿Η Βλάχα. E Vlaha.

─────────

Turkish Records

M. PAPAGIKA, Soprano, Oriental Orchestra accompaniment

12-Inch—$1.25   (Folk Songs)

E 5283
Chanacale. Canto.
Sinanai. Canto.

E 5272
Kioutsouk Hanoum.
Memo. (Minas Effendy).

10-Inch—75c.

E 9030
Ben Yarimi Giordoum.
Dareldime Tzitzim Bana.
(M. Steele).

E 4878
Ne itsoun saidin.
Hetzaz taxim. Violin Solo.

KEMANY MINAS EFFENDI, Oriental Orchestra accompaniment

12-Inch—$1.25

E 5272
Memo. (Kemany Minas E-fendy).
Kioutsouk Hanoum.
(Papagika).

E 5169
Mavili Cantosou.
Sheker Oglan Cantosou.

E 5168
Halima Cantosou.
Tsifte Telli Ghazel, Nenny
(Garabet Eff.)

Figure 56. "Δίσκοι Ελλινικοι (Greek-Turkish) Records," 1925. Catalog, Columbia Phonograph Company, New York, 15–16. Courtesy of Joseph Graziosi.

and laouto played by well-known Peloponnesian musicians of the time. The above article is included in the appendix to Thodoros Hatzipantazis's 1986 book *Tis asiatidos mousis erastai* (The Lovers of the Asian Muse), subtitled *The Flourishing of the Athenian Café Aman in the Years of the Reign of George I: A Contribution to the Study of the Prehistory of Rebetika*. It describes in detail the long-term, twenty-year popularity of the musical nightclubs known as *cafés aman* in the last two decades of the nineteenth century. These clubs, named after the highly melismatic couplets sung to a variety of Ottoman and Arabic named modes (*makams*) and featuring the exclamation "aman," hosted traveling singers and musicians

16   COLUMBIA TURKISH DOUBLE RECORDS

10-Inch—75c.   (Folk Songs, cont'd)

E 4696 { Denizli Cantosou. / Bulbul Olsam (Garabet Eff.)   **E 3786** { Bulbul Cantosou. / Oushak Gazel.

E 4250 { Karshuda Kurd Evlery. / Nazarimda Yine Afak.   **E 3745** { Conialy Cantosou. / Nine Nine Cantosou.

E 4249 { Eghin Havassi. / Seni Giordukje.   **E 3744** { Sabah Ghazel, Tambourile. / Ispahan Sharki. (Garabet / Eff.)

M. MARIE STEELE, Soprano, Oriental Orchestra accompaniment

E 7171 { Shemi Husnun Sharki. / Nare.   **E 7422** { Severim Tzanim Kibi. Can- / to. / Yeni Tsifte Telli.

E 9030 { Dareldime Tzitzim Bana. / Ben Yiarimi Giordoum. (M. / Papagika).

V. BOYAJIAN, tenor, clarinet and Oud accompaniment

32000 F { Darelmadja Yiok. Canto. / Martinim Omouzoumda. / Canto.   **32001 F** { Neva Gazel. / Telegrafin Tellerine. / Canto.

TOM STATHIS, KIRKILISSIOTIS, tenor, Oud accompaniment

E 7364 { Aman Doctor. / Neva Tsifte Telli Ghazel.

M. COULA, Soprano, Oriental Orchestra accompaniment

12-Inch—$1.25

E 5153 { Hovarda Cantosou. / Hidzaz Canto, Koymazmi- / sin.

10-Inch—75c.

E 3387 { Hiouzam Canto, Merhamet. / Kesik Kerem Ghamzadeyim.   **E 3327** { Zabekiko Vary. / Chifte Telli.

from the port cities of the Ottoman Empire. These troupes were composed of a variety of ethnicities—Greek, Turkish, Armenian, Arab—accompanied by female professional singers who often doubled as *defi* (tambourine) players and costumed dancers. These visiting musicians were also on occasion joined by local Greek musicians. The café aman would feature songs typical of the urban traditions of the Ottoman Empire, most often sung in Turkish but also supplemented with songs learned locally sung in Greek and even Albanian.

Returning to the 1925 Columbia catalog, Turkish songs and instrumental pieces take up three and a half pages just before the index. The abovementioned song "Memo" is listed on E-5272 as sung by the Armenian violinist Minas Effendy. The reverse side is "Kioutsouk hanoum," sung by the well-known and prolific recording artist Marika Papagika, accompanied by her husband, hammered dulcimer (cimbalom) player Gus Papagikas, with Nikolaos Rellias on clarinet and Markos Sifnios on cello. Reflecting the multiethnic personnel who played, composed, and supported Ottoman urban music in its home milieu, the recording artists featured in this catalog include the Greeks Marika Papagika (originally from the island of Kos), Mme. Koula (Kyriaki "Koula" Antonopoulou, originally from Constantinople), Tom "Kirkilisiotes" Stathis (originally from Saranda Ekklisies, or Kirk Kilise in Thrace), and Marie Steele; the Armenians Kemany Minas, Vahan Boyajian, Karekin Proodian, Hanende Sinem Effendi; and others.

Although not included in the 1925 Columbia catalog, the female singer Amalia Baka, a Romaniote Jew originally from Ioannina in Epirus, is included as among the three most famous Greek recording artists in the United States along with Marika Papagika and Kyria Koula. She started her recording career as Amalia Hanoum, with six Turkish songs for the Armenian-owned independent Pharos label in the early 1920s (Baka 2002, liner notes).

Among these early songs recorded by Greek artists were several that were widely known and popular: "Chanacale, canto" and "Ben yarimi giordoum" by Marika Papagika; "Dareldime tzitzim bana" by Marie Steele; "Aman doctor, sheba [sabah] canto" by Kirkilisiotis; and "Gamzedeyim, sarki" by Amalia Baka (Kyria Amalia or Yianiotissa) on the independent Greek Record Company label out of Chicago. "Chanacale" was inspired by the Dardanelles campaign during World War I and quickly spread in popularity among many ethnicities of the former Ottoman Empire. Today it is treated in republican Turkey as a patriotic anthem, which makes it ironic that this recording, one of the very earliest of the song, features a Greek singer and Greek musicians. Greek lyrics were later added both with a meaning parallel to the original Turkish, in a folk version preserved in Thrace, and a later 1940s Greek American recording "Dos mou tin efhi sou" with Amalia Baka. In October 1940 in New York, the clarinetist Kostas "Gus" Gadinis and the accordionist John Gianaros would record an instrumental version, "Tsanakale," as a *syrtos*. In the 1930s in Greece, the song was recast with Greek lyrics and more *rebetiko*-type content; as "Katinaki mou yia sena," it was recorded by several of the era's top vocalists and became a major success.

Marie Steele's "Ben yarimi giordum," a *karsilamas*-dance type, would later be recorded in Greece in Turkish by the oud player Agapios Tomboulis (of Constantinopolitan Armenian origin), and then, circa 1955, in Athens with Greek lyrics by Duo Stamboul. "Dareldime tzitzim bana" would enjoy great success later in 1930s Greece with the addition of Greek lyrics, recorded as "Hariklaki" by both Roza Eskenazi and Rita Abatzi, and today it is still among the best-known tunes in the so-called Smyrneïka genre. "Aman doctor" would also enjoy great success both in its original Turkish version and with the early addition of Greek lyrics parallel in meaning to the Turkish. It appeared on several Greek American recordings by Marika Papagika, Amalia Baka, George Katsaros, and, in the 1940s, with Virginia Magkidou, in recordings titled "O yiatros" or "Ah yiatre mou."

These songs are usually described on the labels as *canto*, a term most associated in Turkey with the songs, music, and style of playing of the European-inspired musical theaters that began to flourish in late nineteenth-century Constantinople. Most of the theater owners, managers, and singers were of Greek or Armenian ethnicity. In the early American recordings, the term is used more broadly: it seems to refer to urban-style songs in general, those not strictly associated with Ottoman art music. This later would be most frequently represented in American-based Turkish recordings by the song type *sharki*, which developed in the mid-nineteenth century. It was associated with music clubs often called *gazino*, in which suites called *fasil* were introduced by an instrumental classic Ottoman form, a *peshrev*, followed by a series of sharki songs (with or without *taxim* and *gazel* [amanes] interludes), and finishing with another instrumental form called *saz semai*. Unusual among Greek American recordings of Turkish songs is Amalia's "Gamzedeyim," a famous sharki composition by the Armenian Tatyos Efendi.

The years subsequent to Columbia's 1925 catalog would see the meteoric rise of the most successful Greek recording artist for Turkish music in America. Achilleas Poulos, born in 1893 in Balıkesir in western Anatolia, immigrated to the United States in October 1913 and first settled in New York City. Trained as a tailor, Poulos was a singer and oud player of high caliber and, though relatively short, 1926–1929, his recording career as a featured artist produced approximately ninety sides in Turkish, along with several others in Greek, and these mostly in the urban Ottoman style. He recorded for Columbia and Victor as well as the Armenian-owned Parsekian and Pharos labels. Poulos collaborated closely with other practitioners of Ottoman music, including the Armenian violinist Nishan Sedefjian and the oud player/vocalist Markos Melkon (born Melkon Alemsherian), who was also an immigrant from western Anatolia—Smyrna (İzmir) in this case—and with whom he developed a close friendship.[5]

Poulos recorded in many genres, including sharki ("Seouyletmen beni," "Ashta gel rizam"); kanto/canto ("Djivali giorvedjin," "Cahve yemeni," "Bolshevik kizi," "Yeni halime,"); *turku*, a form indicative of village/rural folk song ("Kioroglou turkiosou," "Emine"); and gazel, usually titled by the musical mode in which it develops ("Mahour," "Segiah," "Sirf hidjasker").

One of Poulos's most famous pieces was "Nedem geldum americaya" (Why Did I Come to America?), which was recorded twice on different labels. Musically, it is more characteristic of eastern Anatolia than his native western Anatolia; the time signature, *curcuna* (10/8), would have been quite familiar to his Armenian colleagues, although it also appears in Ottoman classical and semiclassical pieces. In fact, Poulos recorded several tunes of eastern Anatolian and Armenian-Kurdish origin, such as "Palandygen-Harpoot"—the town and region of Harput being the place of origin of many Armenian immigrant musicians. One of the most popular Turkish songs that Poulos recorded was "Adalar saedine," which also exists in Arabic, and some believe that the tune originated in the Syrian city of Aleppo. In the same time period as Poulos's recording, the song appeared in Greece as "Matia mou," first recorded by the Constantinople-born Dalgas (Antonis Diamantidis). The tune was adopted and stylistically adapted to an urban Cretan Rethymno genre that flourished in the interwar years, nowadays usually called *tabahaniotika*. On Crete, the melody is known as either "Halepianos manes" or "Ta vasana mou herome," from the famous recording by the *boulgari* player Stelios Foustelierakis.

Indicative of his origins in western Anatolia, Poulos recorded several songs in the *zeybek* (*zeibekiko*) dance form, two of which, "Aptal havasi" and "Chakiji," would remain standards in the Greek American community into the twenty-first century, although they were usually performed as instrumental pieces rather than as songs featuring vocals. Another traditional Asia Minor zeybek, "Pergamos" or "Bergama," was recorded under the title "Tabanjassi belinde" and classified as a canto. This might have happened because the addition of lyrics to a traditionally instrumental tune probably occurred in the urban musical theaters and music clubs.[6]

A few sides were recorded in both Greek and Turkish by a Soultana Poulou, who may have been Poulos's relative. Poulos had traveled from France in 1929, accompanying his niece, Soultana Casteliotou (later Costas), to America. She was listed as an "artiste" on the ship's manifest, which might indicate that Soultana Poulou was an adopted stage name. Poulou recorded two versions of the famous Constantinople kanto in çiftetelli dance form, "Kadife," once in Turkish as "Kadife yasdigim yok: bahrie cifte telli" and once in Greek as "Kadifes," both on the Pharos label.[7]

After Poulos's short but prolific recording career, in the late 1920s recordings of Turkish songs by Greek singers slackened off considerably. However, as many surviving family collections show, interest in Turkish song and music continued. Major recording companies—Columbia, Odeon, and Victor—would include Turkish song categories in catalogs published both in Greece and America.[8] Surviving catalogs show that the songs were recorded both in Turkey and in Greece. Most of the artists recorded were Turks, for example Hafiz Burhan Bey, who collaborated closely with the Greek Istanbul oud player Yorgo Bacanos (Yiorgi Batzanopoulos) and his brother, lyra player Aleko Bacanos. But they also included Greeks, such as the Cappadocia-born Theodoros Dermitzioglou, whose recording of "Kasap misak" enjoyed renown, especially among Armenian Americans.[9]

In the 1930s and beyond, many Armenian and other former Ottoman subjects would continue recording Turkish songs. Among the most well-known among

A. ZERVAS, Violinist
for METROPOLITAN and BALKAN Records

BALKAN Turkish Records

4001 OGLAN YALANLAR DUZME, Marko Melkon-Ince Saz Takimi

NAZLI KADIN, Marko Melkon ......Ince Saz Takimi

4002 CAPKIN CAPKIN BAKARSIN, Marko Melkon...Ince Saz Takimi

HANIM OYUNU, Marko Melkon .....Ince Saz Takimi

4003 OGLAN OGLAN ....Marko Melkon

CIFTE TELLI, Ut Ile ....Marko Melkon

4004 HALIS ARAP KIZI, Ince Saz Takimi - M. Melkon, Ut Garbis, Kanun - Zervas, Keman

BEYAZIN ADI VAR, Esmerin Tadi Var, Ince Saz Takimi - M. Melkon, Ut - Garbis, Kanun - Zervas, Keman

4005 CILE BULBULUM CILE, Ince Saz Takimi, L. Matalon Garbis, Kanun - Zervas, Keman - Veedi, Klarinet

NICIN BAKTIN BANA OYLE, Ince Saz Takimi, L. Matalon - Garbis, Kanun - Zervas, Keman - Veedi, Klar.

4006 NIHAVENT SARKI, Yanaklarin Gul Olsun, M. Melkon, Garbis, Kanun - Zervas, Keman - Arif Veedi, Klarinet Trambuka - Ince Saz Takimi

USAK SARKI GUZELSIN, Bir Gul Gibi, Marko Melkon Garbis, Kanoun - Zervas, Keman - Arif Veedi, Klarinet Trambuka - Ince Saz Takimi

4007 SEVDASI VAR BASIMIZDA ...Haydini Hoplarda Gel Garbis, Kanoun - M. Melkon, Ut - Zervas, Keman A. Veedi, Klarinet - Trambuka

CAMLARDA BEKLE BENI, Garbis, Kanoun - Marko Melkon, Ut - Zervas, Keman - Veedi, Klarinet - Tramb.

4008 KONYALI NANI BENIM ELLI ....Dirhem Pastirmam Louis Matalon, Ince Saz Takimi - Garbis, Kanoun - Ut Can Papa, Klarinet - Trambuka

AYVA YOLLA YAR YOLLA BIR, Sevdali Yar Yolla Louis Matalon, Ince Saz Takimi - Garbis, Kanoun - Ut Can Papa, Klarinet - Trambuka

— 16 —

4009 AMAN KASAP, L. Matalon, Ince Saz Takimi - Garbis Kanoun - Keman - Ut - Can Papa, Klarinet - Tramb.

SALLA SALLA MENDILINI ...Louis Matalon, Garbis, Kanoun - Keman - Ut - Can Papa, Klarinet - Tramb

4010 BAGLAMAMIN DUGUMU, Ince Saz Takimi ...Garbis Kanun - M. Melkon, Ut - A. Zerva, Keman

GELIN GELIN, Ince Saz Takimi ....Garbis, Kanun M. Melkon, Ut - A. Zerva, Keman

4011 EGE ZEYBEGI, Modern Turk Orkestrasi ...T. Agabey

HARMANDALI, Zeybek ......Modern Turk Orkestrasi

4012 TAVAS ZEYBEGI, Modern Turk Orkestrasi..T. Agabey

SARI ZEYBEK, Modern Turk Orkestrasi ....T. Agabey

4013 CAKICI, Zeybek, Modern Turk Orkestrasi...T. Agabey

ARABAMIN ATLARI, Karsilama, Modern Turk Orkestrasi - T. Agabey

★★

METROPOLITAN Spanish Records

VICTORIA HAZAN — Turkish Melody
NICK DONEFF — Orchestra Trio

3001 MEKEMI Y ME IFNLAMI ....Victoria Hazan

NON RIYAS CON MI ....Victoria Hazan

3002 UN ANIO AY ....Victoria Hazan

MIS PENSERIOS, Gazel ....Victoria Hazan

3003 UN DIA YO BEZI ....Victoria Hazan

TODAS MIS ESPERANSAS ....Victoria Hazan

3004 LAGRIMAS VERTERE ....Victoria Hazan

SEDA AMARILLA SON ....Victoria Hazan

3005 CANTE POR LA VICTORIA (Victory Song) .V. Hazan

SABAH GAZEL - NO AY LUZ ....Victoria Hazan

★★

BALKAN Spanish Records

SPANISH ORIENTAL

6001 VEN CANARIO, Jack Mayesh Oriental Orchestra-Violin Ut - T. Kappas, Kanoun

PORQUE NOME AMATES, J. Mayesh Oriental Orchestra Violin - Ut - T. Kappas, Kanoun

6002 NO SEAS CAPRITCHOZA Jack Mayesh Oriental Orch. Violin - Ut - T. Kappas, Kanoun

DE TUS LAVOIS CORRE MIEL ....J. Mayesh Oriental Orchestra - Violin - Ut - T. Kappas, Kanoun

6003 ONDE QUE TOPE UNA QUE ES PLAZIENTE ...Jack Mayesh Orch. - Violin - Ut - T. Kappas, Kanoun

MOSTRAME GRACIOZA, Jack Mayesh Oriental Orch. Violin - Ut - T. Kappas, Kanoun

— 17 —

Figure 57. Metropolitan Kaliphon Balkan general catalog, 1937. Balkan Record Company, New York, 14–15. Courtesy of Meletios Pouliopoulos.

Greek Americans would be the already mentioned Markos Melkon. In 1937 he recorded the song "Oglan Oglan" for Victor. The rousing tsifteteli would become quite popular and remain a standard among many Greeks through the 1970s. Melkon recorded dozens of songs both in Turkish and in Greek—having grown up in Smyrna, he was fluent in both. Victoria Hazan, a Sephardic Jew from Kasaba just east of Smyrna, also recorded in Turkish, Greek ("Omorfo hariklaki," "I trata," "Na se haro hasapaki"), and her ancestral Ladino. Although few Greeks were Turkish-language vocalists on recordings during that period, they remained prominent as accompanying musicians. Among them were the clarinetists Gus Gadinis and John Pappas, violinists Alexis Zoumbas and Andreas Poggis, *kanun* player Theodore Kappas,[10] and others. At least two of the above, Gadinis and

157

Zoumbas, were born in territory that at the time was Ottoman but was eventually incorporated into Greece as a result of the Balkan Wars. The former was from Siatista, Macedonia, and the latter from Epirus. Both were experts in the folk music of their native region and were knowledgeable about Ottoman and Turkish music. Also prominent in the mixed ethnic orchestras was the Bulgarian-born violinist Nick Doneff, who often appeared on Greek recordings as simply Nikos D. These musicians were regularly featured in the 1940s and early 1950s on several smaller ethnic-owned labels such as Metropolitan, Virginia, Kaliphon, Me-Re, Balkan, and Pharos. Based in New York City and owned and operated by the Albanian Ajdin Asllan and the Greek John Gianaros, the Balkan Record Company became the chief venue for Turkish-language recordings.

The mixed ethnic orchestras flourished not only in the recording studios but also in the increasingly prolific ethnic music clubs in New York, Chicago, Boston, and elsewhere. Greek, Turkish, Arabic, Armenian, and other types of music, often generalized as Middle Eastern, attracted not only immigrants and their offspring from the eastern Mediterranean but also a growing mainstream American audience. The flourishing of these clubs can be attributed to the general economic stability won by the first generation of Greek and other eastern Mediterranean Americans and reflects a continuing pride and participation in their cultural heritage.

By the mid-1950s and through the 1960s, the center of the Greek music scene in New York was the corner of West Twenty-Ninth Street and Eighth Avenue in Manhattan, a neighborhood called "Greek Town." There, clubs with names such as Port Said, Egyptian Gardens, Britania, Arabian Nights, Ali Baba, and Kifissia not only hosted the many American-based immigrant musicians but also sponsored visiting (often quite long-term) musicians and singers from Greece and elsewhere. Turkish and Greek tunes predominated. They were played both in a style and with orchestration reminiscent of the older urban Ottoman traditions, sometimes still referred to as *incesaz* or *psila organa*, or in a style and orchestration informed more by the contemporary late rebetika/laïka scene of 1950s Greece with a bouzouki-based orchestra. Often the two would mix. In fact, in several 1950s recordings, popular contemporary laïka compositions from Greece would be reinterpreted with violin, oud, and kanun rather than the usual bouzouki, baglamas, and guitar. Virginia Magkidou's "Bir Allah" and Roza Eskenazi's "Ase me ase," both zeibekika, are examples of this.[11] The clubs would inevitably feature one or more belly dance shows with a long medley of tunes (Turkish, Greek, Arabic), usually progressing from fast to slow, to taximi, to drum solo, to fast again—and often with a coda in the karsilamas dance rhythm of 9/8. A fine example is the medley "Belly Dancer's Delight" on the first volume of Alector's *Greek Town USA* series (1960). It featured Greek musicians Bebis Stergiou (bouzouki), Stelios Lazarou (violin), and Tassos Halkias (clarinet), and Turkish kanun player Emin Gunduz. The introductory melody, which became a standard, was an instrumental version of the Turkish song "Bahcelerde ben gezerim," recorded earlier by Markos Melkon and Nick Doneff.

In the 1960s, a few Turkish songs became well known and standard in the Greek American repertoire, notably the karsilamas dance tune "Rampi rampi" but also songs such as "Adanali" and the older "Oglan oglan."[12] These and others were included on several 1960s LPs with mixed ethnic orchestras playing a mixed generalized Middle Eastern and Greek repertoire. Among the LPs were Gus Vali's *All Points East* and *All Ports East*, Cretan lyra player Harilaos Piperakis's *Mr. Lyra in Port Said*, and big band–sounding LPs by Peter Kara (*Music of Greece*) and Mike Hart (*Night Life of the Greeks* and *Greek Fire*). The Turkish singer Cihan Isak recorded two LPs of Turkish songs; one of them, *Flame of Istanbul*, featured the Greek musicians Petro Loukas Halkias, Vasilis Saleas (clarinet), Elias Platanias, and Stelios Lazarou (violin), as well as Armenians, Turks, and Arabs. Several of these same musicians as well as others were also featured on the Balkan LP *Love to Istanbul* with the Turkish singer Lütfi Güneri.

Many Turkish songs became well known in Greek America through the back door, so to speak, as originally Turkish songs given Greek lyrics. As noted earlier, this trend, observable quite early,[13] had already become standard in the recording studios of Greece in the late 1920s and 1930s and became increasingly more common in the post–World War II era among Greek Americans. Turkish-language songs flourished in Greece around 1960 with a series of RCA 45-rpm records featuring singer Ali Ugurlu and violinist Dimitris Manisalis, available as imports in Greek American record stores, as well as a series of Turkish songs recorded by the extremely popular laïko singer Stelios Kazantzidis.[14] It seems, though, that the origin of numerous Greek "copies" of Turkish songs released in the 1950s and 1960s was unknown to many if not most Greek Americans, who were then second and third generation. Examples include one of the era's most recognizable "Greek" songs, "Nina nai nai" ("Siko horepse koukli mou"),[15] as well as such songs as "Fige fige," "Mia melachrini," "Mes tis polis ta stena (Karapiperim)," "Exo dertia ke kaimi," and many others. In fact, Greek hits included not only songs of Turkish origin but also songs from Egypt and other Arab countries, as well as Indian and Hindu cinema compositions (Abatzi and Tasoulas 1998).[16]

This highlights the fact that Greeks drew musical inspiration from neighboring peoples and countries. This is especially true in terms of countries to its east, with whom they shared a common musical subculture. Although there are many stylistic permutations in local guise, the music (especially in its urban forms) was and is familiar enough that Greeks and most other post-Ottoman peoples are comfortable with each other's tunes and melodies.

I will end this short introductory survey of Turkish song and music in the Greek American community with the decade of the 1970s. As a young follower of the Greek and Middle Eastern music scene in the greater Boston area, I frequented the many venues including restaurants, clubs, and rooms that offered a variety of Greek, Turkish, Arabic, and Armenian song, such as the Averof, Sheraton, Athenian Corner, Bishops, and others. Shared songs were heard frequently, such as when an Armenian oud player might sing "Ushakli kiz" in Turkish one night, while a bouzouki player might sing the Greek version, "Mia melachrini," another night. An Arab American might sing Manolis Angelopoulos's hits "Ta mavra matia sou" and "Ta filia sou einai fotia" in Greek because the majority of the patrons were more familiar with the Greek versions, even though the originals were in Arabic.

In many ways, the intersection of Greek and Turkish (and to a lesser extent Arabic and Armenian) song in America throughout the twentieth century kept alive the cosmopolitanism of the old Ottoman Empire long after the empire's demise, with the attendant horrors accompanying the forced separation of peoples and the rise of exclusive nation-states. Turkish song itself never rose above a marginal level in terms of the size of the repertoire in the complex of Greek American music as a whole. But its influence and inspiration have remained strong and profound, contributing significantly to popular urban music usually referred to as laïka. Future studies may find it fruitful to examine this phenomenon when considering issues of Greek American identity.

Notes

1. The catalog in its entirety was reproduced and included as a supplement in the periodical *Laïko Tragoudi*.

2. The titles of recordings will appear as on the label. The orthography does not necessarily match that used in modern Turkish, especially since many recordings were made prior to the switch from the Arabic to Latin alphabet for Ottoman and modern Turkish.

3. This information is taken from personal family histories, for instance the Bilides family.

4. Demoticism refers to a linguistic and cultural movement in Greece that championed the common vernacular spoken language (demotic) for writing over the artificial, purified, and archaizing language (*katharevousa*)—although it did accept certain katharevousa phrases into demotic. Demotic Greek became the official standard in 1976.

5. Poulos's personal history was found in documents through Ancestry.com. His relationship with Markos Melkon was recounted by Melkon's daughter, Rose, in liner notes to the CD *Marko Melkon* (Traditional Crossroads 4281). Special thanks to all those who over the years have sent me copies, cassette or digitized, full or partial, of their personal libraries of Achilleas Poulos 78s: Dino Pappas, Charlie Howard, Dean Lambros, and Stavros Kourousis.

6. "Aptal Havasi" was also recorded in Turkish in Greece in the late 1920s by Smyrna-born Lefteris Menemenlis and Constantinople-born Dalgas. Several instrumental pieces were subsequently recorded in Greece in the 1920s and 1930s. Later, Greek lyrics were recorded by Roza Eskenazi and Duo Stamboul, but it became familiar mostly as an instrumental piece in versions by Andonis Sakellariou and orchestra in New York in 1928 and in the 1940s by Greek American clarinetists Kostas

"Gus" Gadinis and John Pappas. The circa 1960 recording with violinist Stelios Lazarou on volume 1 of Alector's *Greek Town USA* series was a standard among Greek Americans for many years. In Greece, the Hellenized title "Aptalikos" (Giorgos Mitsakis's 1961 bouzouki solo "Aptaliko"), for both the tune in question and the rhythmic type in general, gradually became more widespread than the Turkish "Aptal havasi" (The Crazy Man's Tune). In Turkey, this term is not known for the tune. What Greeks know as "Aptal havasi" most Turks know as either "Kordon zeybek" or "Karsi yaka souk suyu." The latter is the title used by Gus Gadinis, probably in imitation of the version by the famous Turkish clarinetist Sukru Tunar, whose recording was imported and made available in the United States.

Songs such as "Chakiji," "Tsakitzis," and "Cakici," better known among most Turks by their initial words "Izmirin kavaklari," extol the virtues of the Zeybek fighter and bandit Chakirdjali Mehmet Efe, who was considered a hero among the poorer Greek and Turkish peasants in western Anatolia. Other early recordings, sung in Turkish, include those by the Smyrna-born Lefteris Menemenlis, the Edirne-born Jew Haim Efendi, and, in the United States, by the female Shekar Hanim and later in the 1940s by the Armenian Ashot Yergat accompanied by the Greek kanun (*kanonaki*) player Theodoros Kappas. Instrumental versions were recorded by clarinetist Gus Gadinis and accordionist John Gianaros in the 1940s, and then in the 1960s by clarinetist Nick Rassias for the LP *Night Life of the Greeks*, and on bouzouki by the famous players Kostas Papadopoulos and Lakis Karnezis accompanied by clarinetist Tassos Halkias on volume 1 of the LP *Bouzoukee Boulevard* on the Alector label. Around 1953, Roza Eskenazi recorded the tune with Greek lyrics and Turkish refrain accompanied by the clarinetist Sukru Tunar in Istanbul for the New York–based Balkan Record label, which aimed at the Greek American market. In the 1930s, "I Stellitsa" was an earlier attempt to record the tune with Greek lyrics in Athens. It was written in the form of a dialogue between Roza and the singer Kostas Nouros, with lyrics totally unrelated to the *efe* bandit leader Tsakitzi. It did not seem to have much success. Another version with Greek lyrics, also extolling "Tsakitzi," was recorded in Greece in the 1960s by laïko singer Vangelis Perpiniadis.

Many versions of "Pergamos" were recorded both in Greece and America. They included an instrumental version, "I pergamia," with Alexis Zoumbas on violin and Louis Rassias on cimbalom on the small National label; a very early vocal version, "Chiotissa," with Greek lyrics sung by Kyria Koula circa 1920 in New York; another Greek vocal version, "Ousak smyrneiko," with Leonidas Smyrnaios in New York around 1927; and a later version, "Aman aman chiotissa," sung in Greek by Markos Melkon.

7. In the late 1920s and 1930s, several Greek-language versions of the song were recorded in Greece, mostly among Asia Minor artists such as Roza Eskenazi, Marika Politissa, Vangelis Sofroniou, Dalgas, Grigoris Asikis, and Dimitris Atraides, as well as in Istanbul by Kyria Pipina (Despina Kallergi). The lyrics of these versions differed in several places, although they seem to have drawn on older known couplets. More than likely, the tune was already well known, but mostly as the instrumental piece "Bahriye çiftetellisi." In the post–World War II United States, Virginia Magkidou recorded a version in Greek, "Den boro na katalavo," with the addition of a vocal amanes, and Markos Melkon recorded a version in Turkish with its standardized text. In Greece, the tune was also later adopted into some regional folk musics; on the island of Naxos, for instance, it is interpreted as a syrtos, the main dance of the island, rather than as a tsifteteli.

8. Full and partial Greek record catalogs from Greece can be found at the New York Public Library for the Performing Arts.

9. Theodoros (Todori) Dermitzioglou was born in the Cappadocian town of Semendere, from which a significant number of Greeks emigrated and settled in Michigan in the early twentieth century. Several copies of "Kasap misak" are in the library of the Armenian Museum in Watertown, Massachusetts. Thanks to curator Gary Lind-Sinanian for making this and other duplicates available to me.

10. Theodore Kappas recorded earlier, in 1919, accompanying Jemal Bey (vocals, oud) and Avny Bey (violin) on four Turkish songs on the Victor label (Spottswood 1990).

11. "Bir Allah," composed by Ioannis Stamoulis with lyrics by Haralambos Vasiliades, was first recorded by Sephardic Jewish rebetiko singer Stella Haskil in 1947. "Ase me ase me" ("Den thelis na me pandreftis"), composed by Giannis Papaioannou with lyrics by Kostas Manesis, was first recorded by Sotiria Bellou in 1950. Eskenazi's version with an *ala turka*–style orchestra was part of a larger series of recordings made by Balkan Records in Istanbul in 1953 or 1954. They recorded songs in Greek, Turkish, and both languages exclusively for the American immigrant and ethnic market. The recordings remained unknown in both Greece and Turkey until recently.

12. "Rampi rampi" was recorded by bouzouki player Giannis Papaioannou and singer Rena Dalia on the Nina label around 1955 as a 78-rpm record and was later reissued as a 45. Although sung in Turkish, it is obvious from Dalia's pronunciation that she was not very familiar with the language. The song was also included on Gus Vali's LP *All Points East* (United Artists, March 1960) and Mike Hart's LP *Greek Fire* (probably 1966), and appeared as "Rambe-rambe" on the 1963 LP *The Glorious Greeks* (Crescendo GNP-89) sung by Nitsa Grezi and accompanied by Yacoubian and Company: Hrach Yacoubian (Armenian) on violin, Yiannis Stamatis (bouzouki), Notis Issichopoulos (accordion), and famous drummer Bobby Morris. The song was one of several recordings by Roza Eskenazi and violinist Dimitris Manisalis, organized by Tetos Demetriades and released on his Standard label with the American market in mind, most likely in the late 1940s or early 1950s; it was probably the first recording of this popular karsilamas in Greece. "Rampi rampi" was recorded in Athens by Duo Stamboul (a male/female duet of probable Constantinople origin), with Greek lyrics ("I fotia p'oucheis anapsei"), around 1953–1954, and subsequently reissued on the LP *My Greece: Music of Athens Today* (Capitol Records) in 1956. This LP included other Turkish songs recorded by Duo Stamboul with Greek lyrics.

"Adanali" was recorded twice by Turkish vocalist and kanun player Emin Gunduz on *Greek Town USA*, vol. 2 (Alector ALP 5005) and *Greek Fire*. It was released earlier, in 1943, in Greek as "Adanato-poula" by Amalia Baka, whom we first met in the early 1920s. As an instrumental piece, it appeared with other well-known Turkish tunes such as "Doktor Doktor," "Kara Biberim," and "Konyali" on the LP *Anatolian Feast* with Spero Spyros and his modern Anatolian ensemble (Near East) in the late 1960s.

"Oglan Oglan" was included as an instrumental piece on *Mr. Lyra in Port Said* (Aris Records) circa 1960 with the famous Cretan lyra player Harilaos Piperakis. It appeared on Gus Vali's LP *All Points East*, sung in Turkish by Many Ayvas. Again it appeared as an instrumental piece on *Greece: Dimitri and His Ensemble* (Time Records) circa 1962, which probably included musicians Dimitris "Bebis" Stergiou (bouzouki), Tassos Halkias (clarinet), Emin Gunduz (kanun), and Stelios Lazarou (violin); and on *Greek Dance-Along with the George Stratis Orchestra* (Standard Colonial) in the late 1960s. "Oglan Oglan" was recorded with Greek lyrics as "Se zografisa vlacha m'" by Roza Eskenazi in the mid-1930s, and with different Greek lyrics by Kaity Giuli, but still titled "Oglan Oglan," on the 1963 Alector LP *Concerto for Bouzoukee*, vol. 2. It seems that none of the versions sung in Greek of the above songs overshadowed the popularity of the Turkish-language versions.

13. For example, the tsifteteli that is usually known today as "Tha spaso koupes" was recorded circa 1910 in Istanbul by Lefteris Menemenlis and Yiorgos Tsanakas, and the Smyrneiki Estoudi-antina version was recorded in Turkish at about the same time or earlier as "Tchiftetelli cantosu satchalar perischam" by Caragach Efendi. In 1928, Marika Papagika recorded a slower Greek version in New York City, and about the same time Kostas Karipis recorded a version in Athens. Since its revival in the 1980s by the popular singer Eleftheria Arvanitaki, "Tha spaso koupes" has remained a favorite tsifteteli.

14. Stelios Kazantzidis was the son of Pontian and Anatolian refugee parents. His mother, Ges-thimani, was a native Turkish speaker from Alanya on the south coast of Turkey.

Joseph G. Graziosi

15. The song was introduced to a wider American audience via a live television performance in 1966 by Nana Mouskouri, Danny Kaye, and Harry Belafonte. It appeared on numerous LPs during the 1960s, either sung (e.g., volume 1 of *Greek Town USA*) or as an instrumental piece (e.g., *Golden Greek Hits* with Teddy Kotsaftis and His Orchestra).

16. Among the more famous Greek "copies" of Indian film songs was "Oso axizis esi," one of Manolis Angelopoulos's greatest hits.

References

Abatzi, Eleni, and Emanouil Tasoulas. 1998. Indoprepon apokalipsi: Apo tin India to eksotismou sti laiki mousa ton Ellinon. Athens: Atrapos.

Baka, Amalia and Diamond. 2002. Amalia! Old Greek Songs in the New Land, 1923–1950. With liner notes and annotation by David Soffa. Arhoolie 7049. Arhoolie Records, El Cerrito, California.

Hatzipantazis, Thodoros. 1986. Tis asiatidos mousis erastai: I akmi tou athinaikou kafe aman sta chronia tis basileias tou Yioryiou A' [The Lovers of the Asian Muse: The Flourishing of the Athenian Café Aman in the Years of the Reign of George I; A Contribution to the Study of the Prehistory of Rebetika]. Athens: Stigmi.

Spottswood, Richard K. 1990. Ethnic Music on Records: A Discography of Ethnic Recordings Produced in the United States, 1893–1942. 7 vols. Urbana: University of Illinois Press.

PART TWO

Places

Survival of Greek Folk Music in New York[1]

—Sotirios (Sam) Chianis

Introduction

The folk music of Greece is related to both classical Greek and Byzantine church music. Certain folk dances as well as poetic and musical meters are directly related to classical traditions, while certain modes (scales), melodic characteristics, and ornamental devices are clearly derived from Byzantine ecclesiastical music. It would be erroneous, however, to speak of a specific type or style of folk music that can be considered common to the whole of Greece. Over the centuries, several stylistically distinct musical traditions have developed as a result of Greece's geographic position in relation to the other Balkan cultures and to those bordering the eastern Mediterranean Sea.

Music is found in every region and island of Greece and is a vital part of every event in village life. The bride and groom are taken to church with the sounds of processional music provided by local musicians. During the reception, the newly-weds are praised with songs of long life and prosperity. Villagers sing traditional road songs as they return home from a long day in the nearby fields or after a night of celebrating in the local coffeehouse. Mothers lull their babies to sleep with lullabies; the dead are mourned with laments. For village people, music not only serves as a means of self-expression but is truly an inseparable part of daily life.

In general, Greek folk music may be divided into two main classifications: the music of the mainland, and that of the islands. The mainland regions of Epirus, Macedonia, Thrace, Thessaly, Roumeli, and the Peloponnese are each considered distinct musical areas set apart from one another by regional customs, dialects, types and categories of folk songs and dances, modes (scales), accompanying rhythms, musical and poetic meters, melodic ornamentation, structural forms, and types and uses of folk musical instruments.

The folk music of Roumeli and the Peloponnese is rather similar in terms of melodic styles, repertoires, and dance types. While the *tsamikos*, *kalamatianos*, and *syrtos* are among the most common folk dances of the regions, klephtic songs constitute a large portion of the total repertoire. Performed in free meter and in a highly melismatic style, klephtic songs relate the heroic efforts of the *klefts* (freedom fighters) in battle against the Ottoman Turks. The typical folk ensemble of these regions consists of a clarinet, violin, *laouto* (lute), and *santouri* (hammered dulcimer).

Two characteristic instrumental forms of folk music from the region of Epirus are the *skaros* and *miroloi*. Both are extended improvisatory pieces set in pentatonic modes (five-tone scales) and performed in free meter over a drone on the tonal center. The most expressive types of dance music are *samandaka*, *berati*, *pogonisio*, and *singathistos*. These dance tunes are performed in a slow, deliberate tempo, while the rhythmic accompaniment is kept simple in order to allow the soloist as much melodic flexibility as possible. The most common folk ensemble is composed of a clarinet, violin, laouto, and *defi* (tambourine).

The region of Macedonia has some of the most interesting folk music and dances in all of Greece. In addition to the clarinet, violin, and laouto ensemble, instrumental groups consisting of the clarinet, cornet, trombone, and drums are highly characteristic in the vicinity of Kastoria and Kozani. In Naousa, however, a pair of *zournades* (singular *zournas*; a relative of the oboe) played to the rhythmic accompaniment of the *daouli* (a large double-headed drum) is typical. Numerous unique folk dances in complex asymmetric meters are among the distinguishing features of the central area.

Thrace possesses an extremely rich song tradition. Folk dances such as the popular *zonaradiko* are performed in a lively tempo. The *gaida* (bagpipe with a drone) and Thracian *lyra* (a type of bowed rebec), both accompanied by the daouli, continue to be a vital part of Thracian folk music. The musical style of Thessaly is a mixture of the bordering traditions of Epirus, Macedonia, and Roumeli. One of the most characteristic folk dances of this region is the *karagouniko*.

Island folk music, generally of a "lighter vein," is quite varied. One of the richest sources of music is found on Crete. The typical duo of lyra and laouto provides much of the island's lively dance music. Rhymed couplets or distichs, known as *kontylies*, are found in eastern Crete, while the *mantinada* tradition is popular along the northern coastal areas. From western Crete come the songs known as *rizitika*. These very ancient song forms use the decapentasyllabic (fifteen-syllable) text line, and their highly ornate and melismatic melodies are sung in traditional antiphonal style.

Typical of the Ionian Islands, along the western coast of Greece, is the *kantada* (serenade) sung in three- or four-part harmony and accompanied by violins, guitars, and sometimes mandolins. Distichs are preferred on the Cyclades and Dodecanese islands, where the typical folk ensemble consists of the violin, laouto, and santouri.

Figure 58. Advertisement for music lessons and performances offered by Giorgos "Nisyrios" Makrigiannis, New York. Courtesy of Panayotis League.

Greek Music in New York: Social Settings

During the first decade of the twentieth century, approximately 170,000 Greeks (95 percent of whom were males) entered the United States; many settled in New York. The typical immigrant belonged to peasant society, came from a small mainland village, was highly patriotic and individualistic, and was devoid of technical skills and knowledge of the English language. Furthermore, he was a product of a nation with a long cultural history richly endowed with folkloristic and religious traditions. Above all, he was accustomed to expressing his nostalgia, his love, and his sadness and happiness through music and dance (Chianis 1983, 3).

The Greek coffeehouse tradition was transplanted to America soon after the first immigrants arrived. The coffeehouse served as an important sociocultural center where males gathered to discuss current events and politics in Greece, their jobs, and common problems of adjusting to life in America, and to play cards, gamble, read Greek-language newspapers, and share news of their homeland with compatriots. But the coffeehouse was also a place where patrons could sing, listen, and dance to folk music from various parts of Greece. Music was often performed by the patrons themselves using folk musical instruments belonging to the coffeehouse. On weekends and on special holidays, enterprising coffeehouse proprietors would hire the services of well-known professional musicians. It is important to point out that many professional and semiprofessional folk

Figure 59. Mme. Koula, "I Malamo," 1920s. Panhellenion 8047-B.
Courtesy of Stavros K. Frangos.

musicians earned a living, cultivated their artistry, and expanded their repertoires by performing in coffeehouses. But eventually, as Theodore Saloutos notes:

> The coffeehouse eventually became a shadow of its former self, a memory of early immigrant days, even though in some communities it has survived to this day. One can only conjecture what the social life of the male immigrant would have been had it not been for the companionship and diversion provided by this very special Greek institution. (1964, 83)

Dancing was an integral part of engagement, wedding, and baptismal receptions as well as picnics, name-day celebrations, and religious and national holidays. It is interesting to note that, contrary to contemporary practices, musicians were seldom paid a set fee for their services. According to folk traditions brought from Greece, the lead dancer would request a particular dance type or a favorite tune. Because the leader was most often a male, he was then obligated to pay the musicians a fee, whatever amount he wished. If he happened to be an exceptionally good dancer, several of his friends would throw substantial amounts of money to the musicians. The length of a particular dance or tune largely depended on the amount of money given to the musicians. "Another custom in evidence at weddings [and most all types of celebrations] was the practice of wetting one-dollar and five-dollar bills with the tongue and sticking them on the foreheads of the musicians" (Saloutos 1964, 87).

Recognizing the supreme position folk music held in the lives of immigrants, the two giants of the recording industry, the Columbia Graphophone Company and Victor Talking Machine Company, began issuing 78-rpm double-sided ethnic music discs as early as the first decade of the twentieth century. Among these early recordings, of course, were numerous examples of Greek folk music featuring such outstanding immigrant artists as Athanasios Makedonas (violin), Christos Gamvas (violin), Andreas Patrinos (laouto), Lazarus Rassias and Stelios Melas (santouri), G. Kassairas and Yiannis Kyriakatis (clarinet), and the incomparable soprano voice of Kyria Koula (or Coula).

During the early 1920s, two privately owned Greek record companies were established. They devoted practically their entire output to Greek folk music. These historic firms were the Panhellenion Phonograph Record Company of New York and the Greek Record Company of Chicago. The latter, formed by two distinguished immigrant musicians, Spyros Stamos (cimbalom) and George Grachis (violin), quickly earned a national reputation by featuring prominent folk artists of the era. In addition to Stamos and Grachis, the artists included Amalia Baka (vocal), singer Aristotelis Katsanis (better known by the nickname Mourmouris), Angelos Stamos (vocal), Konstantinos Patsios (vocal), Marika Papagika (vocal), Epamenondas Asimakopoulos (vocal and laouto), Harilaos Piperakis (vocal and Cretan lyra), and the folk clarinetists Nikolaos Rellias and Konstantinos Filis.

In 1928, RCA purchased the famous Victor Talking Machine Company. Two years later Tetos Demetriades, with his expertise and vast experience as former head of Victor's foreign division, approached RCA with a truly historic proposal. Demetriades's plan was to record various categories of music in Greece and issue the discs in America. RCA, undoubtedly aware of the potential market for this music, agreed to underwrite the project. During his two-year stay (1930–1932), Demetriades managed to record some of Greece's finest instrumentalists and vocalists. Upon his return to New York, he began distributing these recordings on his famous Orthophonic label (which bore the note: "Manufactured by RCA Victor Company for the Standard Phono Company of New York").

Although the collection included some excellent Turkish music (recorded in Constantinople) and Albanian examples, the majority of the music was Greek. Demetriades judiciously catered to the highly varied musical appetites of the Greek immigrants. For example, in his general catalog of Orthophonic records dated June 1941, out of hundreds of Greek records, no fewer than 172 were of two-steps, tangos, foxtrots, and waltzes. All of these dance tunes were sung in Greek by artists such as Sofia Vembo, Kakia Mendris, Nikos Gounaris, and Demetriades himself. The collection also included Greek serenades (some

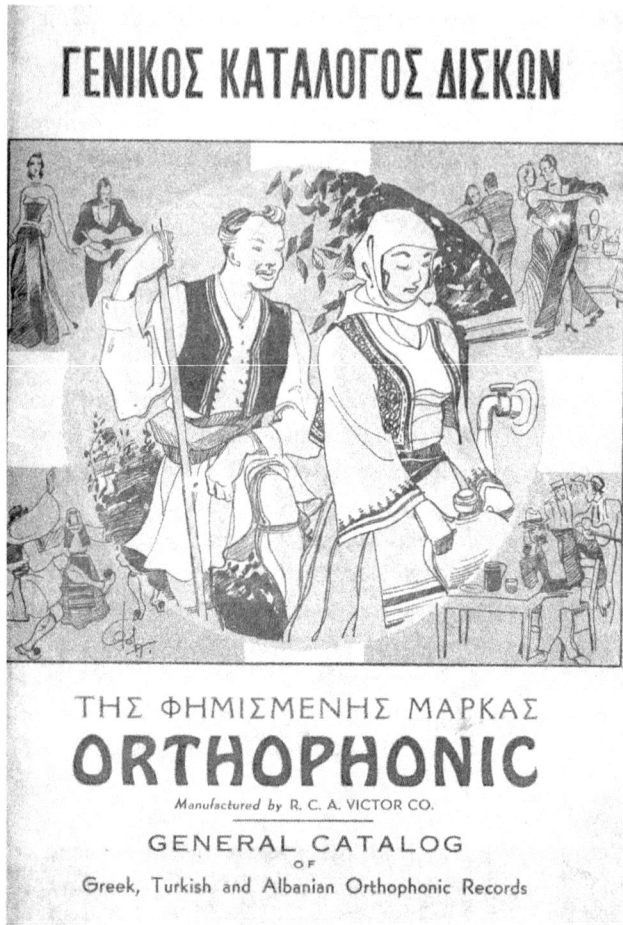

Figure 60. *General Catalog of Greek, Turkish, and Albanian Orthophonic Records*, Tetos Demetriades, title page, June 1941. Courtesy of Sam Chianis.

accompanied by Hawaiian guitars and mandolin orchestras), comical songs and dialogues (sketches), and examples of music of the Greek Orthodox Church.

But Demetriades's most important musical contributions were his recordings of rebetic music of the Greek subculture, Anatolian music (the musical traditions of Greeks residing in or originating from the Asian Minor cultural centers of Smyrna and Constantinople), and the folk music of Crete, Cyprus, and the Greek mainland. It should be emphasized that Demetriades's recorded collection of mainland folk music, made during an era that I like to refer to as "the golden age of Greek folk music," succeeded in capturing for posterity the unequaled artistries of such truly great professional folk clarinetists as Nikitas, Apostolos Stamelos, Nikos Karakostas, Konstantinos Karagiannis, Baios

Figure 61. *I Xeniteia me Hairetai: Songs of Greece.* Apollo Music Publishing Company sheet music, 567, New York. Courtesy of Meletios Pouliopoulos.

Malliaras, and Christos Margielis. Among the vocalists were Georgios Papasideris, Demetrios Benetos, and the immortal female voices of Rita Abatzi and Roza Eskenazi.

Recordings of Greek folk music in America and those imported from Greece are extremely important historical documents of a very rich and highly varied musical tradition. They also provide a remarkable opportunity for the study of styles, artists, instrumentation, melodic ornamentation and improvisation, and regional repertoires. Equally important is the fact that these recordings accurately reflect the types of live music that were performed at weddings and on name days in coffeehouses, and at picnics and holiday celebrations sponsored by churches and Greek societies.

Figure 62. George N. Helmis, *Greek-American Guide and Business Directory*. New York: Helmis Press, 1915, advertisement for Panagiotis Tzimis, an instrument maker, page 20. Courtesy of Meletios Pouliopoulos.

Greek Music in Print

Greek-language newspapers assumed an important role in the lives of immigrants. They provided news from villages and regions of Greece to those who had not yet learned to read English. Atlantis, the second Greek-language press in America, was founded in New York in 1894. It provided immigrants with books published in Greek in a variety of subjects, including folk music. Its first collection of music made its appearance in 1912.

In 1923, the Apollo Music Publishing Company of New York initiated a series of publications of Greek folk music for various instruments. The sheet music, composed mostly of dance tunes, offered the performer a choice of either playing the "simple melody" or the "artistic" one, the latter more closely approximating the melodic ornamental practices of folk musicians. Although these publications were of immense importance and were distributed throughout America, they were not intended as performance editions for professionals. They simply served the important task of acquainting immigrants and their offspring with the rich musical heritage of Greece.

The Apollo Greek Musicians Union

In October 1918, a group of immigrant musicians concerned about the state of Greek folk music in America gathered together in New York and organized a chapter of the Apollo Greek Musicians Union (Elliniki Mousiki Enosis en Ameriki "Apollon"), originally established in Chicago. It is important to note that the union's president, Ioannis Demetropoulos, the board of the directors, and the entire membership were actively involved in the performance of Greek folk music either as professionals, semiprofessionals, or amateurs. The organization's prime objective was to preserve Greek folk music in America. Unfortunately, the organization was dissolved in 1921.

The Making of Musical Instruments

Two of the most popular Greek folk musical instruments were the laouto and the santouri. Although most immigrant musicians brought their instruments with them, there soon was a tremendous demand for new ones. An outstanding craftsman of Greek folk instruments was Anastasios Stathopoulos of New York. Exactly when he began making instruments is not known; however, it is well known that his musical instruments were highly prized by folk musicians throughout America. I recently examined one of his laoutos (1915 vintage), owned by the late Charles Leounis of Binghamton, New York. Despite its age, it was in excellent condition. The sound hole or rose of the laouto is ornamentally carved from a separate piece of hardwood and bears the initials of the maker. The printed label inside the instrument gave the following information:

No. 5724   Date May 1915

This instrument is manufactured from materials that are especially selected and well-seasoned. Workmanship and construction are unexcelled. It is guaranteed against defects and remains climatically unaffected.

Stathopoulos
Manufacturer of Musical Instruments
New York, N.Y., U.S.A.

The Rise of Bouzouki Music

Until the end of World War II, Greek folk music in America as well as in Greece remained relatively unchanged. The prevailing musical style, repertoire of dance songs, and instrumental ensemble and its performance practices were definitely those of mainland Greece, because the majority of immigrants came from the regions of Roumeli and the Peloponnese. The clarinet and violin of the ensemble performed the melody in heterophonic style, the santouri added an additional layer of melody, and the laouto was limited to rhythmic and harmonic accompaniment. However, musical as well as extramusical events in Greece were to have dramatic effects on the people of Greece as well as the folk music in Greece and eventually in America.

Following the world war, Greece was devastated by a long and bitter civil war. Country folk abandoned their villages and flocked to urban centers to seek work and a "better" way of life. As a result, a huge urban middle class society was created. The folk songs and dance traditions that these people brought with them were considered inappropriate for city life. Also unsuitable was the rebetic musical tradition, left over from the prewar years, that spoke of misery, loneliness, poverty, pathos, and jail. What the middle class needed, then, was a type of music, dance, and lyric suitable to their social environment. The answer was the tradition known as bouzouki music or popular music. An ensemble included one or two amplified bouzoukis (a long-necked lute), an amplified guitar, drums, and other Western instruments. This music was so enthusiastically accepted in Greece that Greek entertainment clubs in New York and around the country began booking entire bouzouki ensembles directly from Greece for their Greek American clientele. Folk ensembles began borrowing its repertoire and instrumentation. When professional folk clarinetists Tassos Halkias, Apostolos Stamelos, and Vasilis Saleas came to America to perform in New York entertainment clubs, they brought with them a *new* folk performance style. The old folk ensemble of violin, santouri, and laouto gave way to an ensemble of amplified guitar, drums, and electric organ.

On very rare occasions, folk music programs in New York are still presented in the traditional style with traditional musical instruments. Most often however, folk and popular Greek music performed in New York and throughout America is provided by bouzouki ensembles. Populous cities throughout the state of New York have at least one such ensemble that performs music for weddings, church- and community-sponsored dances, and holiday celebrations. Churches now hold annual festivals and bazaars where one can sample food, enjoy listening and dancing to live folk and popular music, and witness young men and women performing all types of folk dances in national costumes. Greek Americans young and old take pride in preserving the rich folkloristic heritage brought to America by their parents and grandparents.

Conclusion

Being a professional Greek folk musician from a very young age, I had the distinct honor and pleasure of performing with numerous well-known folk musicians who we then called the older generation. I am sincerely proud of the fact that practically all of my repertoire of Greek folk music was acquired from these performing artists. They came to America during the first decade of this century, bringing with them the rich and varied folk musical traditions of their particular region of Greece. They played a variety of musical instruments such as the laouto, santouri, cimbalom, lyra, and violin. Others specialized in singing. They formed ensembles and performed in important gathering places such as the *kafeneio* and *cafés aman*, and provided dance music for baptisms, engagements, and weddings; for picnics, church events, and national holidays; and for any of the other numerous celebrations that called for music and dance. But, above all, they served as pioneers of Greek folk music in America, and the extremely rich legacy that they left behind for all of us must never be neglected or forgotten.

Notes

1. This chapter was first published in *New York Folklore* 14 (1988): 3–4, 37–48.

References

Chianis, Sotirios (Sam). 1983. "A Glimpse of Greek Music in America." In *Greek Music Tour*, 3–4. New York: Ethnic Folk Arts Center.

Saloutos, Theodore. 1964. *The Greeks in the United States*. Cambridge, MA: Harvard University Press.

Recommended Reading

Baud-Bovy, Samuel. 1935–1938. *Chansons du Dodecaneses*. 2 vols. Athens: Sideris.

———. 1972. *Chansons populaires de Crete occidentale*. Geneva: Minkoff.

Chianis, Sotirios (Sam). 1965. *Folk Songs of Mantineia, Greece*. Berkeley: University of California Press.

Frye, Ellen. 1973. *The Marble Threshing Floor: A Collection of Greek Folk Songs*. Austin: University of Texas Press.

Holden, Rickey, and Mary Vouras. 1965. *Greek Folk Dances*. Newark, NJ: Folkcraft Press.

Recommended Listening

Epirotika with Periklis Halkias: Greek Folk Music and Dances Recorded in New York. 1981. Folkways FSS 34024, 34025. Folkways Records, New York.

Folk Dances of Greece. 1956. Folkways FE 4467. Folkways Records, New York.

Folk Music of Greece. 1955. Folkways FE 4454. Folkways Records, New York.

Modern Greek Heroic Oral Poetry. 1959. Folkways FE 4468. Folkways Records, New York.

Communities Born in Song[1]

—Anna Caraveli

Part 1. The Symbolic Village: Community Born in Performance[2]

Being from Olymbos

"Being an *Olymbitis* [a resident of the village of Olymbos] shapes all your actions," said Kasos-born Captain Yiorgos of the *Panormitis* as our ship approached the island of Karpathos, "from the way you sit at the coffeehouse to the way you get married" (August 21, 1981). A few months later, Yiannis Sofillas, sitting in his Baltimore living room and looking at slides of his village taken on that 1981 trip, sighed and nodded his head knowingly. "Being an Olymbitis is a difficult art," he advised me. Then he proceeded to explain to me, as have so many of the Olymbos immigrants in this Baltimore community, the people, traditions, and rules of social conduct of the Olymbos he still revered more than ten years after emigrating. And so it is that conversations in many Olymbos and Baltimore coffeehouses, streets, and households frequently turn to discussions or arguments on the meaning of Olymbos identity and the changing boundaries of its universe.

The village of Olymbos (locally called Elymbos) perches dramatically on one of the highest mountains of the Greek island of Karpathos, set between the islands of Crete and Rhodes and part of a chain of islands known as the Dodecanese. Until sometime in the early 1970s, when a dirt road was constructed, contact with other parts of the island was accomplished by foot, animal, or boat.

Yet, while the village appears traditional and physically remote, change has confronted its small but diverse world in many forms and guises for many years, especially during the past two centuries. Multiple foreign occupations (Turkish, Italian) and reunification with Greece at the turn of the twentieth century were

178

among the historical events that helped to shape Olymbos's social and economic systems. Another significant force of change was the frequent contact with the outside world. While Olymbos's economy was "originally based on grain crops, pasture and forestry," and the major occupational groups were farmers and shepherds, agriculture and subsistence economy gave way to maritime trade and cash economy by the end of the eighteenth century (Philippides 1973, 32). Increasingly, the class of artisans became prominent, and Olymbites who were carpenters and stonemasons traveled to other parts of Greece or abroad, where they worked for several months or years. The Greek city of Piraeus, the Greek islands of Symi, Cyprus, and Rhodes, and cities in Asia Minor and North Africa were the most frequent destinations of these seasonal laborers, while some of those interviewed cite trips to places as distant as China, Iran, and other Asian countries.

The most profound and irrevocable agent of change, however, has been permanent emigration, a phenomenon that peaked in the 1950s and 1960s. Entire communities of Olymbites are now formed and scattered around the world, mainly in urban areas in Greece, especially Athens and Piraeus; the island of Rhodes; and US cities, especially Baltimore and New York.[3]

Far from being a static society, then, Olymbos is a place in which change and innovation have been absorbed continuously into the village's world view, the themes of its songs and daily conversations, its household interiors and architecture, and ultimately its concepts of self and community. Inside Olymbos homes, rows of imported plates, foreign objects, and old and new photographs taken in distant lands tell of their owners' journeys and returns and have continuously redefined local aesthetics. Traditional verbal art forms add new metaphors and images that reflect new experiences and explore the meaning of being from Olymbos.

For both those who have left and those who have remained, being an Olymbitis is an important identity, superseding in many ways that of being a Karpathiot, Greek, Greek American, or American. The total breakdown of the agricultural system, the Italian occupation of World War II, and the permanent emigration that started in the late 1960s (Philippides 1973, 94–120) dramatically hastened and deepened the rate and scope of change in the Olymbos world. Although regional identity has always existed, this historical moment of sudden and profound transition has heightened its importance, and the meaning of being an Olymbitis in Olymbos, Baltimore, or Piraeus often preoccupies young and old members of the Olymbos diaspora, both in the village itself and in its global settlements, as they reconstruct new systems of meaning and concepts of community from bits and pieces of disparate worlds. This daily process of negotiation often reveals an inexhaustible stream of creative solutions that are unique for each family, individual, or community and that produce endless combinations of tradition and innovation.

Definitions of Olymbos identity, varied as they are, generally involve the notions of discipline (*peitharhia*), strict adherence to moral rules of conduct (*afstirotis*), love of and loyalty to an idealized concept of "Olymbos" and its traditions, reverence for ancestral lands, honor, and a good name. For Sofia Kritikou, a resident of Piraeus, being an Olymbitisa additionally involves choice. Given a number of diverse lifestyles from which to choose, she consciously selects to live a traditional Olymbos lifestyle in order "to have something of my own, different from other Greeks and the rest of the world."

One of the few concessions Sofia makes to urban lifestyle is education, as she wants her only daughter to be university educated. In a complex and carefully thought-out plan designed to integrate village and city world views, she plans to marry her daughter, Anna, to an Olymbitis in a traditional arranged marriage before she is admitted to the University of Athens, where temptations for sexual freedom and nontraditional marriages abound. Part of the marriage contract, however, will be the groom's consent to Anna's university education while Sofia, as the grandmother, will help with the children.

Other solutions to the question of how to be an Olymbitis while abroad involve frequent visits to the village, especially in the summer months; maintenance of several households (both in the village and outside of it); participation in traditional celebrations and expressive events; marrying other Olymbites; and selecting a number of customs, decorative objects, and traditional festivities as identity symbols. For those remaining on the island, although dependent on financial aid from their émigré relatives and often viewing emigration as a distant dream for themselves, the role of encouraging the emigrant or returned visitors to follow local traditions is commonplace. The newspaper *I Foni tis Olymbou* (The Voice of Olymbos), published in Piraeus and contributed to by Olymbites worldwide, provides a vehicle for transcontinental communication, the maintenance of kinship and friendship ties, and the discussion of questions of identity and the boundaries of Olymbos.

A formalized arena for the expression of individual identity and the negotiation of community boundaries is a ritual celebration called *glendi*, performed both on the island and in one of its largest emigrant communities in Baltimore. An artistic extension of these informal conversations and quests for lifestyle, the glendi becomes a means of self-expression, of the creation of exquisite musical and poetic compositions, but also of forging important relationships and systems of meaning. Much like the beer-drinking events among the Iteso in East Africa, the glendi also provides a "synthetic image in terms of which [participants] represent to themselves contradictions in their social experiences" (Karp 1980, 83), as conflict, ambivalence, confusion, and the airing of grievances are accepted topics in their poetic discussions. Often the kind of poetry composed in glendia is published in *I Foni tis Olymbou*, while tape-recorded glendia are mailed from one

Olymbos settlement to relatives in another, thus expanding globally the sphere of participants in one celebration.

Barbara Kirshenblatt-Gimblett writes:

> [T]he study of ethnic folklore, which may also be defined as folklore on or about cultural boundaries, requires a shift in perspective. Rather than looking for a bounded and named "group"—the Poles in Chicago or Czechs in Texas—and studying the traditions of this group, we must look for settings, social occasions, and events in which boundary negotiation is an important activity. (1983, 45)

The glendi represents just such an activity. This chapter demonstrates how, through performance, the guests of a glendi symbolically recreate the parameters of the actual village or urban community in which the most important relationships are enacted and new ones are negotiated. Through the tape recorder and the print media, glendia further create a global community, one defined through activity and perception rather than bounded space or tangible objects, and one that can be conjured up repeatedly in ever-changing patterns. Far from being fixed, this symbolic Olymbos adapts age-old patterns for incorporating change in order to facilitate and make sense of the transitions facing the Olymbos universe.

Influenced by Victor Turner's notion of "processual analysis" (1974, 44) and informed by the local system of folk aesthetics, this study focuses on the glendi's process of gradual engrossment as its most salient element. By creating a context in which ordinary experience is heightened and the ordinary is transformed into the extraordinary, the boundaries of individual and community identity are challenged and renegotiated, while the processes that connect a temporal glendi event with the daily life of the community link individual performances to the larger, historical processes of creating a system of meaning.

The Rules of the *Glendi*

Throughout Greece (rural and urban), the concept of glendi defines one's notions of a "good time" when in the company of a compatible *parea* (circle of friends and/or relatives) and on an appropriate occasion (celebration of an event, or simply getting together).[4] Such glendia usually involve singing (often old, nostalgic songs) and exchanging jokes, as well as an increasing sense of camaraderie and abandonment to a state of mirth and heightened emotion called *kefi*. While a variant of this genre in a very general sense, the Olymbos glendi differs quite markedly in structure, rules of performance, content, tone, and, most significantly, in the meaning attributed to it by its participants in particular and the larger community in general. The glendi is often referred to as a "ritual" (*ierotelesteia*)

Figure 63. Olymbos *glendi*, August 14, 1988. Courtesy of Elaine Eff.

by Olymbites and as an event shaping and expressing one's identity. According to an experienced glendi performer, "An Olymbitis character becomes visible in a glendi" ("O haraktiras tou Olymbiti diakrinetai sto glendi").

Glendia are performed on formal occasions such as saint's day celebrations, life-cycle rituals, and religious holidays, as well as on informal occasions, roughly analogous to the notion of a "party." There are public glendia involving the entire community and private glendia held in homes and among small circles of friends. In all glendia, communication among participants is conducted through improvised, assonant couplets sung to the accompaniment of local musical instruments: a *laouto* (a type of lute), *lyra* (a vial-shaped, bow-stringed instrument), and occasionally *tsambouna* (bagpipe). Glendia today last between twelve and thirty-two continuous hours, with longer periods cited for successful glendia, especially those taking place in Olymbos. Glendia lasting for three to seven consecutive days were not unusual in years past.

While it is mainly men who sing and play musical instruments at glendia, women are far from passive. They prepare the food—an important element in a private glendi—and serve it. They listen attentively and critically, frequently writing down or tape-recording successful songs. They comment on the quality of performances and have a decisive role in transmitting good songs and in building or destroying the reputation of a performer. They compose and sing among themselves the kind of songs sung in a glendi, when alone or in each other's company. They dance at the end of a glendi. Finally, there are occasions on which it is appropriate for women to take part in the singing along with the men. The recent convention of composing traditional couplets and printing them in the newspaper the *Voice of Olymbos* has expanded women's roles in the glendi, as the print medium provides an additional outlet for poetic composition.

An intricate body of moral, social, and aesthetic rules underlies glendi performances and constitutes the rich system of local folk aesthetics. According to indigenous definitions, an important element in a good glendi is adherence to these rules. A good deal of folk criticism has to do with discussions and disagreements on the interpretation of rules, and well-known and respected glendi participants have been pointed out to me as being especially strict in the enforcement of rules (*afstiroi me tous kanones*). Insults, misunderstandings, and strong disagreements result from considered violations of rules, during or after a glendi. These rules shape and regulate five principal elements.

1. *Kefi.* In depicting the progress of an Iteso beer-drinking party, Ivan Karp cites the "increasing engrossment" of its participants as a key element (1980, 105). He goes on to say:

> The description of the party given by my friend is characterized by evidence of engrossment, and the party was punctuated by rituals that both highlighted and served to frame the engrossment. In our experience beer parties that were interpreted by Iteso as successful were characterized by the formalization of the evidence of engrossment. This engrossment not only had its own signs but was taken by Iteso in its turn as evidence of "much understanding." (1980, 108)

Similarly, for the glendi participants in Olymbos and Baltimore, the success of the glendi depends exclusively on the existence of kefi. In the context of Olymbos folk aesthetics, kefi refers to a heightened form of experience—far more transported and serious than the carefree and festive mood that the term connotes in other parts of Greece. It is not only common to see glendi guests weep, but weeping is expected of a true state of kefi: "The successful glendi is judged by [the amount] of weeping" ("To kalo glendi metrietai apo to klama").

Kefi is achieved methodically and systematically through drink, increasingly intimate subject matter in the songs sung, escalating expressions of feelings, and private relationships among the guests. When kefi is in full swing, glendi guests may display behavior seemingly out of control such as weeping, collapsing, shouting, pulling at their cheeks or hair, or embracing each other. Yet there are precise and well-articulated rules and patterns underlying kefi behavior dictating the timing, quality, and extent of the participants' actions when in the midst of engrossment. To an experienced glendi guest, it is immediately clear whether kefi behavior is wild (*exalo* kefi) and thus unacceptable or whether there is discipline and propriety in the manifesta-tion of engrossment. True kefi, consequently, involves formalized behavior and discipline (*peitharhia*).

2. *Meraklides*. Those knowledgeable about the complex rules of the glendi and capable of experiencing and conveying true kefi are called *meraklides*. While in the rest of Greece meraklis is primarily a performative category referring to the passion and skill displayed in performance, in the Olymbos glendi (*to Olymbitiko glendi*) it is a category combining aesthetic, moral, and ritual elements. A meraklis (known as *glendistis* or *idikos tou glendious*; a glendi participant or glendi specialist) is not a professional in the strictest sense of the word, but his skills accord him a position of honor in society, which, to some extent, can be passed down through generations. One is acknowledged as a meraklis on the basis of complex criteria beyond the abil-ity to simply sing well or compose fine poetry. One must couple knowledge of the glendi rules with an understanding of the social rules of the village universe before that person can be acknowledged as a good meraklis.

A capacity for serious commitment to the spirit of the glendi distin-guishes the true meraklis from the passersby (*perastikous*) who join the glendi during its initial stages only to have a good time. Meraklides instead give themselves (*dinonde*) without reservation or regard for their physical or emotional comfort. Interviews and folk commentary reveal that meraklides are judged to a great extent by their spiritual qualities. A meraklis has a deep sense of responsibility to the glendi and its participants, considering it his duty to lead them to a state of heightened kefi. Andreas Hirakis, one of the most famed meraklides in Olymbos, is said to have wept at a glendi in the 1970s when dawn arrived and he was still unable to bring himself to a state of kefi (*na erthi se kefi*). In addition, the meraklis must not only monitor what should be sung, to whom, and for how long but must also be sensitive to individual moods and knowledgeable about local and family histories. Addressing a personal concern such as impending emigration; encourag-ing a participant to express an issue of burning importance to him or her; noticing variations in mood so that, if appropriate, the glendi discussion can focus on it; making fitting allusions to a personal situation or past incidents from local history—all of these mark a meraklis's skill. Aesthetic, traditional, and historical knowledge coupled with the capacity for unusual psychological insights about the key glendi participants are considered essential for glendia to be held. Older Olymbites complain that one of the difficulties in having a proper glendi today is the lack of an adequate num-ber of good meraklides. "Otherwise," many have told me, "the burden falls on the shoulders of a few people, who cannot rest from their responsibilities for even a little while."

Generosity is another quality a meraklis possesses. Generosity is often directed toward the young and inexperienced, who must be encouraged to enter the discussion if the tradition is to continue, or toward the emigrant who has returned for a brief visit and must be made to feel at home.

While upholding and regulating difficult rules, the meraklis simultaneously encourages change, growth, and flexibility toward the exceptional and unexpected. At appropriate moments and situations, he might facilitate the entry of inexperienced performers or of a woman and encourage participation by a priest or someone in mourning.[5]

3. *Use of Space.* A strict hierarchy among the glendi participants exists within the glendi, which in part mirrors the social order outside it. Men sing seated around tables, while women sit apart, not directly participating. In Olymbos, when a glendi is held in a traditional Olymbitiko ("of Olymbos") house, most women sit on the *sofa*, a raised platform where the family sleeps. When the glendi is held at newly erected clubhouses (*megara*) in Baltimore or Olymbos, separate tables (or separate portions of the same table) serve to seat women apart from men.[6]

Seating arrangements further refine the existing social hierarchy honoring age, social status, and, above all, performance skill. In glendi, the most experienced and skillful performers cluster together so that they can listen to one another and respond properly, while the remaining guests' proximity to this prestigious group is proportionately related to the skills and age of each. The youngest and least experienced performers sit at the farthest remove from the meraklides, unless age, kinship ties, or social status mediate.

4. *Songs (mantinades).* The rhyming or assonant couplets encountered throughout the Dodecanese are the principal poetic form on the island of Karpathos. Rarely does one find a Karpathiot who has not at least dabbled in the composition of *mantinades* or adapted known mantinades of his village's repertoire (Mihailidis-Nouaros [1934] 1969, 26–27).

In an Olymbos glendi, almost all communication is conducted in the form of sung mantinades. These are freely improvised on the basis of conventional thematic, musical, and linguistic patterns.[7] The most successful among them become part of the village's oral repertory, a means of recording history and of linking people together through the shared body of allusion they can draw upon. Discussions as to what constitutes a successful mantinada are frequent and often passionate among the Olymbites at home and abroad. The standards applied form part of the intricate system of aesthetics used to judge the performance of both poetic and social relationships outside framed activities. A good mantinada must be rhythmically and metrically

Figure 64. Olymbos *glendi*, August 15, 1988. Courtesy of Elaine Eff.

correct, possess poetic excellence, and evince *noima* (meaning).[8] This meaning is judged by its performative and social appropriateness: was the timing right, did it correspond to a socially correct situation, did it serve as a fitting response to something said before, did it make an apt allusion to past events? Mantinades, therefore, are not judged by themselves but in relation to the entire glendi as well as to the larger social and historical context of the community. The height of the glendi blends the height of kefi with the height of "meaning" in the mantinades exchanged. A mantinada's success and a meraklis's art are judged in terms of how effectively they help achieve this ideal state in the glendi. Good mantinades, then, contribute to the progress of the glendi. Ultimately, individual participants, and musical, linguistic, and emotional components, are elements of a larger complex, working toward the heightening of ordinary experience.

5. *Tunes.* There is a set repertory of tunes to which mantinades are sung. People disagree as to the number of tunes known as recently as the 1940s, but all agree that many of the most complex tunes have been forgotten. There are many evocative associations connected with these tunes: happy or sad emotions, joyful occasions or upsetting ones such as emigration. Moreover, some tunes are associated with a particular meraklis and his family, as the tunes of his preference. These emotional, historical, or personal associations constitute a subtext unto themselves and can be manipulated

as a distinct language by a skillful musician. The combination of a sad tune with a happy theme can create ironic contrast, while a reluctant meraklis can be challenged to participate simply by playing the tune of his preference (Caraveli 1982, 138–39).

Conversation in Poetry: The Meaning of Glendi

One of the reasons the glendi is still viable in the changed world of Olymbos around the world, as well as in the village, is that it has historically accommodated both tradition and change, both "artistry" and the outside world that its guests must contend with. Although being from Olymbos and the Olymbos microcosm of the glendi are defined in terms of "fixedness" (rules, strictness, dedication, discipline), the Olymbos universe is a flexible one in which change has always been incorporated. Similarly, the glendi, viewed as a symbolic re-creation of the Olymbos universe, reflects indigenous patterns for accommodating change, irregularity, and exception that both parallel and reinforce a broader relationship between tradition and change in the village and its global settlements. Examined processually through repeated visits and a focus on the way actions and events unfold, the glendi reveals the dynamic elements within it as vital to the meanings it holds for its participants.

While rules are established and adherence to them is prized, interpretation, for example, can vary, and disagreement is widely tolerated. Only men can participate, yet exceptions are permissible, and folk commentary has it that "some of the best mantinades have been sung by women." The fixedness of the glendi structure, which constitutes one of its explicitly acknowledged attributes, is undermined in practice by folk terminology that uses metaphors of motion, fluidity, and interaction to describe it. Kefi is said to be *lepto* (delicate or fragile) and easy to destroy (*halai efkola*). The glendi as a whole has been described to me as "conversation in poetry" (Konsolas 1984), and as a "boat" with the meraklides as the helmsmen "steering it in the right direction" (Nikolaidis 1983).

An examination of structure and content alone points to a strictly secular event. From the standpoint of the participants, however, the process of increasing engrossment is as important as, and prerequisite to, content bordering on religious experience. "We may be Christian but the glendi is our religion," one meraklis said to me at the moment of total engrossment at a glendi. Thus, extraordinary and ordinary elements, ritual and secular realms, blend. For its guests, the experience of a glendi represents a journey of increased involvement, a journey through difficult emotional stages and thematic cycles of increased intimacy until new social, aesthetic, emotional, and moral balances are negotiated. It represents risks, as kefi might never be achieved or sustained and delicate aspects of private relationships might be exposed. The glendi's success and effectiveness, then, is not measured so much by what is said as by the nature of its progress: did a glendi achieve full kefi or not? It is through this gradual process of emotional engrossment and social involvement that the boundaries of the community and the identity of its members are symbolically dissolved and reconstituted, challenged, and fully experienced.

Anatomy of One Glendi: The Wedding of Hirakis's Son

I was led to Andreas Hirakis by a mantinada he had composed years ago, repeated for me by one of the young men in Baltimore who admired him greatly:

> I want to let out a shrill cry against the wind's backbone.
> I grieve, I weep, I cry out loud that old age has come.

Identifying people and events in Olymbos through mantinades recited about them in Baltimore was a procedure I learned to follow myself, one that facilitated my access to many households. Embedding mantinades in speech and using them as a code for communication as well as a sign for the importance of an event or person is characteristic of much of the conversation among Olymbites. Hirakis's family was impressed by my memory of mantinades and my understanding of them: "You understand, you sense, you grasp the meaning," I was told ("katalave-neis, niotheis, pianeis to noima").

A few days after my arrival in Olymbos, one of Andreas's sons, Yiorgos, married the daughter of another shepherd, like his father, in an arranged marriage.[9] It was August when I arrived in Olymbos that summer (1980). August has evolved into a month when many important festivities such as weddings and engagements take place.[10] Mobility among Olymbos settlements is very high. This generation of emigrants, for example, owns property in two or more émigré communities as well as in the village, with family members often scattered across two continents. Although active links among these communities are maintained throughout the year through travels, local publications with international circulation, and letters and tapes sent to and fro, August is the month when Olymbites residing outside the island return for short periods. Consequently, it has acquired special symbolic significance. Many glendia during this period have been endowed with new meaning as vehicles for welcoming the returnees, exchanging news, renewing ties, and conducting a number of diverse transactions, not the least important of which is the arrangement of marriages between emigrants and local brides and grooms.

Another wedding took place on the same day, and, as neither family would give in by choosing an alternate date, the village was divided between them. As the other wedding was to be blessed at the church, Andreas had his son's marriage blessed at home by the priest. The other wedding glendi took place at the club-house (*megaron*), a recent development decried by many Olymbites.[11] The glendi for Yiorgos Hirakis took place in the bride's parents' home. Both the megaron and the home were decorated with richly embroidered items of the bride's trousseau, hung from beams or walls.[12]

Following the brief religious ceremony, the tables were set and the guests were seated, with men sitting apart from women, while the groom's kin and the important meraklides occupied honorary positions. After a full course of meat, potatoes, and spaghetti, the tables were cleared and *krasomezedes* (snacks to accompany drinking) were served and continued to be served all night. Although wine was drunk in earlier times, the decline in wine production on the island, plus the higher status enjoyed by imported drinks, has led to imported beer and especially whiskey supplanting local wine.

The wedding glendi begins late in the evening, after the first course is cleared, with the priest chanting an appropriate hymn to bless the couple.[13] At the end of the hymn, he toasts one of the eldest and most experienced meraklides as a sign to him to begin the secular portion of the glendi. This section starts with the *syrmatika*, narrative songs with fixed texts and melodies.[14] Most syrmatika are sung at the beginning of the glendi, yet they are also interspersed throughout as a means of restoring tranquility after intense mantinades interchanges have taken place.[15] When the first sequence of syrmatika ends, another meraklis is toasted (*ton vriskoun*) as a challenge to him to begin the main portion of the glendi.

The wedding guests, actors in the soon-to-unfold drama, represented both the global dispersion of the Olymbites and the facility with which they return to participate in the village unit. Yiorgos, the groom, had not ventured far from the village, except for occasional trips to the other side of the island or to Piraeus for short-term work as a stonemason. His two best men, however, were dentists about to begin practice in major cities elsewhere in Greece. Similarly, the rest of the guests covered a gamut of social classes, from professionals to businessmen to farmers to laborers, and places of residence, including Olymbos, Rhodes, Piraeus, Baltimore, New York, South Africa, and Australia.[16]

One of the most outstanding returnees was Nikos A., an architect residing in Australia and returning to Olymbos for the first time after fifteen years of continuous absence. His status as a distinguished returnee was enhanced by another important status—that of a man of marriageable age. Even though Nikos was in his early forties and still single (because of family obligations), he was considered to be at a stage in his life when—free of economic hardships and pressing obligations—he was ripe for marriage.

A man of marriageable age is the focus of extreme attention in the Olymbos world. Faced with conflicting values and social systems challenging the "village units," home or abroad, this is a world in which quick adjustments and negotiations must be made continuously to accommodate both diversity and continuity. Continuity is synonymous with endogamous practices. A man marrying outside the village is "lost" to the community (although exceptions are tolerated increasingly). In the case of Nikos, a well-educated and tremendously successful man, the boundaries of the village world were sharply challenged. Guest after guest at the wedding discussed the necessity for Nikos to be married at home and the simultaneous fear that they didn't "have the right women to match him with." That the Olymbos world may not be able to accommodate a willing participant, thus forcing him to marry outside of it, was the cause for tensions played out intensely during Nikos's stay in the village. The dilemma, the suggested solutions, and the underlying doubts and fears about the inadequacy of the Olymbos unit were enacted during this glendi and during every subsequent glendi in which both he and I were present. Such interplay between individual concerns and the implicit larger social tensions or psychological dramas marked the slow unfolding of social relations, culminating in several climactic moments in the course of the glendi.

As in all glendia, in Yiorgos's wedding glendi the first *themata* (themes) dealt with the occasion itself: in this case, the wedding. Under the term "wedding themes" I group all those themes dealing directly with the wedding or with related themes that do not distract from the larger event of the wedding. This category includes praises and congratulations to the couple, their parents, and their relatives; discussions about the feelings of joy and sorrow the situation produced; broader philosophical discussions about the merits of a good life, of Olymbos traditions, of honor; and the like. Mantinades addressed to individual participants were sung, but the focus was not sustained for long. Among themes dealing with participants other than the married couple were those (traditional to weddings) describing the plight of the parents in raising their children and marrying them off well. In this wedding, the poverty and hardship of both sets of parents were the predominant topic. For example, Yiannis Fasakis, uncle of the bride, addressed the following to the bride's father:

You toiled in life to raise your daughter;
You've done well marrying her off to a good man.

Addressing the marriageable men was another topic. In this case, the two best men and Nikos A. were singled out with particular fervor. The situation of emigration (for Olymbites, the term is applied to those who live outside of Olymbos, whether elsewhere in Greece or abroad) has modified these themes in most glendia to stress advice: marry someone from Olymbos; keep up the customs; be successful outside but return to the traditions as a basis; and so on. Moreover, mantinades serving to make returnees feel welcomed at home are also new points of emphasis in the Olymbos glendia. Praise to returnees for their achievements outside the village, as well as for their respect for traditions, was meted out generously:

[Vasilis Kanakis]:
Good wishes to the best men for their turn to come;
May they and lovely brides join their bodies in marriage.
May this marriage take root, dear Niko Diakoyioryi;
And hurry up with your degree [in dentistry], for I have rotten teeth.
[Yiorgis Sakellis]:
May this marriage take root, and may you marry too!
But careful that you marry here in your fathers' land.
[Yiannis Fasakis to Nikos A., residing in Australia]:
We drink to your wedding, Niko, and may your turn come quickly;
Because I want to be present when this joyous moment comes.
The years pass quickly; they sneak by without us noticing;
Find a girl from our village and make her your wife.

The returnees at this point answered by expressing nostalgia and love for Olymbos, gratitude for the welcome by the community, and distress over the difficulties of living in "exile" (*xenitia*). Messages from one community to the other are customarily conveyed at this stage of a glendi through the returnees who replace absent parents, friends, or relatives and convey greetings, news, or congratulations on their behalf.

Any one of these themes can be developed more fully in later stages in the glendi. At this stage, however, the glendi consists of brief, unfocused, and disparate individual statements lacking sustained focus and the collective interest of the group. As the glendi progresses, individual themes tend to be sustained for increasingly longer periods of time, and the guests' attention intensifies.

The first sustained departure from the diffuse and generalized wedding themes occurred with the entrance of the village's president and his cousin, a well-known lyra player. The two men arrived a little before midnight as they had been at the other wedding glendi. A verbal duel ensued among newcomers and participants. The former apologized for being late but insisted that both weddings should be honored equally: "We expected we would be misunderstood though we love both couples equally well." The guests teased them about being so late, and their remarks became increasingly caustic. When the two newcomers defended their impartiality to both weddings, they were told sharply:

The elders had a few well-measured words for this:
Whoever goes after two hares at once, catches neither one.

With Andreas's (the groom's) father's mediating mantinada declaring that "I love all my friends equally," the tension eased. As Prearis, the late-arriving lyra player, was considered a good meraklis, the wedding themes picked up increased gaiety. When I asked if the participants had come to kefi, however, I was told that the level of the glendi was still "superficial" (*epipoleo*) and that many singers present "don't deal with themes in depth" ("den pianoun ta themata me vathos"). The new arrivals were considered *perastikoi* (passersby) and were not there to give themselves fully. This was gaiety (*efthymia*), I was told, not kefi. The wedding themes continued for a while, and the two men departed a little after midnight.

The second intense and extended interchange explored the topic of devastation of the neighborhood through emigration. As memories sketched out vividly through the mantinades the height and decline of the neighborhood (and, by implication, the village), the participants were choked with tears, interrupting their singing with sobs:

> [Yiannis Fasakis (brother of the bride's mother)]:
> In this neighborhood we're visiting, people have changed now;
> Old neighbors who have lived here come to my mind tonight.
> [Yiannis Diakoyeoryiou]:
> The neighborhood is wasted! Its mansions tightly sealed!
> And all those raised in its midst, scattered in foreign lands.
> I can't pass by this neighborhood anymore my friends!
> Deep sorrow shrouds my heart in black, heavy sheets.

The grievance over the decay of the neighborhood was mediated by themes of comfort. Many singers offered mantinades about summer returns as a solution, thus contributing to the new cycle of reconciliatory mantinades developed in the Olymbos glendia in previous years. In these mantinades, summer has taken on new symbolic significance.

> [Yiannis Diakoyeoryiou]:
> Cool breezes will always breathe through this neighborhood,
> And you must return each summer to take them in.
> [Yiannis Fasakis]:
> My heart, friends, has found no match anywhere else.
> That's why I return to the village each summer.

The return to the wedding themes was characterized this time by stylized challenges to the groom to sing. His sister Kalliopi entered the singing. Kalliopi was working as a waitress in Rhodes and raising her small son alone. Her arranged marriage to an Olymbitis culminated in tragedy as her young husband became mentally ill and was institutionalized. Everyone was familiar with Kalliopi's situation and with her great gifts in mantinada composition and performance. Kalliopi began by urging her brother to sing:

> Sing out your tune, Yioryi, like the trill of a bird,
> And for your own sake I will be filled with joy.

She continued with praises for the groom and his choice of a bride, and built up a subtly ironic contrast between the fragility of everything else (including marriage) and the stability of the household:

> Are you perchance proud for your tender youth or
> For the lovely partridge flown into your arms?
> At every hard moment, at every blow of wind,
> Turn to our home so the old man won't grieve.
> You are leaving and the joy is leaving our household;
> But take along our blessings for a faithful companion.

She ended this sequence with an allusion to her grievances and an implicit contrast between them and the festivities surrounding her:

> My darkly speaking kefi, I want you tonight: come!
> Wounded heart of mine, let yourself be moved to laugh!

The surprisingly long sequence of mantinades—the longest thus far—had a palpable effect on the participants, men and women alike. Kalliopi's mantinades were highly lyrical and metaphoric in content, flowed effortlessly—indicating and communicating the heightened emotional state of their composer—and alluded skillfully to a tragic situation known to all present. Her performance was at once passionate and restrained, reflecting both the quiet intensity of her personality and her respect shown to the male meraklides as a young, female performer. The excellence of the mantinades, the skillful timing and transitions of the sequence, the recognition that her state of mind was one of true kefi, and the seriousness of the grievances aired made her performance acceptable and effective even though she was a woman. The fact that it was a family celebration (*hara dikia tis*) and that she came from *yenia*—a long line of glendi specialists—further facilitated her acceptance as a performer.

With Kalliopi's singing, a tangible transition into a deeper and more intense level of kefi took place, which—with small interruptions—was to be maintained throughout the evening, escalating steadily. The exchange that followed featured Kalliopi at its center, with sympathetic guests trying to comfort her and urging her father to respond to her. The feelings expressed ranged from advice and comfort to anger at the unfortunate marriage match:

[Mihalis (brother)]:
I curse these relatives who came to your wedding
And drenched your heart in sorrow and grief, our child.

Or (as the exchange among family members intensified) anger at Kalliopi herself:

[Sofia (sister)]:
Why are you scratching at the wound that does not want to heal
And pour in it burning salt instead of soothing balm?

Kalliopi, upset by the sight of everyone weeping, indicated that it was time to change the subject, and the glendi returned briefly to the wedding themes. The singing of a syrmatiko (narrative) song mediated and restored some level of calmness after this intense interchange. A number of less intense communications followed, focusing on specific individuals or on relationships between them.

Remarking on the artistry of the glendi itself—its components or progress—is a conventional theme that can be sung about at any stage. In an adaptation of this theme, participants directed their mantinades at me and my role in the glendi as they perceived it. Mihalis Zografidis, son-in-law of Andreas Hirakis, began this sequence:

[Andreas]:
Look at the tape recorders taping away.
They've sent them from far to find you, Hirakis.
Ah but my damn kefi is stumbling somewhere tonight
Just when I wanted it to have so much success.
[Zografidis]:
Take down our tunes faithfully in your tape recorder
Because you'll never find the equal of the man singing here.
[Hirakis]:
Girl, coming from this far to take me along
Soon you will have the tunes I will compose for you.
[Zografidis]:
Take along our songs with you, but send them back to us,
And we will all remember you Anna when you leave.
[Hirakis]:
Modest scholar, pure Greek at heart!

I've admired the persistence I've seen in you tonight.
[Yiannis Fasakis]:
When you go to America and find our fellow villagers,
Take them greetings from all of us, greet them one by one.
[Hirakis]:
I feel the songs gathering in my mind for your sake,
Since you want me for your companion, my good folklorist.
[Fasakis]:
When you go to America where you will represent us,
Praise Karpathos to them well and tell them nice things.
[Hirakis]:
With all this machinery surely man can't die!
What if his body rots away, his voice will stay on!

The relationship singled out in the following sequences is that between
Hirakis and Nikos, each paying tribute to the other. The old, established meraklis welcomed and acknowledged the younger one and implicitly conveyed
to him that he was welcomed back as an honored and equal participant in this
important expressive event. Nikos protested that he was not worthy of being
considered on the same footing as Andreas, who had always been an inspiration and a companion to him in the "foreign land." He modestly and skillfully
shifted the focus from himself to the relationship between father (Andreas)
and son-in-law (Mihalis Zografidis). As the latter is a lyra player and a meraklis
(in fact, he played the lyra during most of the evening), the shift was not only
from friends to relatives but from one pair of old/young meraklides to another.
The new couple was encouraged to express their affection to one another, and
the father formally acknowledged the son-in-law as a worthy member of a family of meraklides:

With your sweet voice and your good lyra,
Even the dead, my eyes, are celebrating with you.

Kalliopi's reentrance acted as a signal for the intensification of mood and subject matter. Even before she made reference to her situation, her mere participation served as a code to her own suffering as well as to the broader topic of serious
grievances. Her brother-in-law addressed her:

[Mihalis]:
When I even hear your voice I'm overcome with bitterness
And feel my kefi for Yioryi rise at once.

The ensuing exchange took place between Kalliopi and her father, with her sister, Sofia, her brother-in-law, Mihalis, and a few other family members and friends serving as mediators and moderators of this poetic discussion. Kalliopi praised Mihalis and then her father. The father bitterly remarked to her: "[You] inherited my talent as if you were a boy." The daughter praised the father and went on to lament her own grief. The father wept and responded to her:

> Don't scold me, daughter, your pain is enough;
> Raise your child well and let him be your comfort.

Others echoed the father's point that her child should provide comfort to her and that she should not dwell in grief. Kalliopi recounted the course of her husband's mental illness and her feelings about it:

> I lost him, father, that proud young man.
> I lost him, father, before I got to know him.

All the guests were weeping and several asked her to change the subject. Kalliopi obeyed ("My spilled blood is streaming down the gully / Change the theme, the couple may be worried"). Praises for the poetic talent of the family further helped calm down the intensity of the interchange.

> [Sofia]:
> I am the child of the *protomeraklis* and I'll sign it formally.
> But when strong feelings move me, I lose my words completely.

Thus, mention of the harmony of family life, manifested in the continuity of talent from generation to generation, symbolically restored the order of the glendi. A brief return to wedding themes followed until the glendi was interrupted by the entrance of Yiannis, Hirakis's youngest son, who had been watching the sheep that night.

It was early morning by this time, and all signs of fatigue, shown earlier among the guests, had completely disappeared. The previous sequence was marked by intense concentration and profuse weeping. The one that followed was further intensified. Loud weeping could be heard throughout the house. The principal performers were now standing up as verbal exchanges were echoed by physical interaction (arms around each other, sitting on each other's lap, etc.). Many of the singers were weeping and trembling visibly while covering their eyes or pulling at their cheeks as they sang. There was one emotional and thematic focus in the room, with everyone present equally involved and fully engrossed. The original orderly seating arrangements had given way to disorder and listless movement to and fro.

The entrance of Yiannis, who was soon to be drafted in the military and—some feared—never to return, became the catalyst for a collective lament about the decline of the rural economy and the profound changes the village had experienced. The irrevocable loss of people and changes to lifestyles are all-consuming subjects to which Olymbites return glendi after glendi. The timing was now well synchronized and the pace faster, without gaps between mantinades or individual performances, so that a new event—the unexpected entrance of Yiannis—immediately passed into poetry, was fitted to what was said before, and was transformed into the most climactic moment of the glendi. The following exchange took place:

[Andreas Hirakis]:
You've come, child, from the mountains, my own two eyes, my light.
Soon others will snatch you away from me, and I'll be left alone.
[Mihalis Zografidis]:
How do you catch the flying birds crisscrossing the blue air?
How can you match your father's kefi tonight, show us!
How we long to hear you, relative, our dear co-in-law.
You've come from the barren mountains, sweet nightingale.
[Andreas Hirakis]:
And how did you find the fatted flock, tell me my little child?
Soon they'll be sold to the last one, my soul has told me so.
[Kalliopi]:
Tell us, little brother of the mountains, what garments are they wearing
Now that their shepherds are leaving them, casting their last glance behind?
[Andreas Hirakis]:
Daughter, the mountains are wasted and moss has blocked their paths;
And as I look at them like this, black tears shroud my eyes.
[Kalliopi]:
Father, give me back my shepherd's staff, if you have kept it still,
And I'll take to the mountains my old shepherd's chores.
[Yiannis]:
Damn those city jobs and those who invent them!
That will not let you take root, take sorrow and joy upon you.

By noon and early afternoon, the themes of grievance and loss had played their course. Some of the younger people who had left for a few hours to rest returned at this point. The girls were dressed in new finery and looked refreshed. The floor was swept and the seating order restored.

This portion of the glendi returned to wedding themes and was popular with the younger generation. The *kerasma tis nifis* (bride's treat) took place with the bride pouring wine for participants, in order of importance, and receiving praise mantinades in exchange. The last portion of the glendi, which extended into the next night, involved dancing and music and had more relevance for the young.

Analysis

Both the structure and content of the glendi reflect the continuous interplay between stability and fluidity, fixed structure and digression, calmness and engrossment. The wedding themes (or themes for the occasion for which a glendi is held), like the tonic of a musical composition, form the point of departure and return and frame digressions. I term the principal digressions from the wedding frame "social dramas," as they indeed represent sustained dramatic interchanges between two or more actors, or a focus on one person or intimate relationship.

I use this term in a somewhat different sense than Victor Turner.[17] While Turner's definition stresses conflict—"where conflicting groups and personages attempt to assert their own and deplete their opponent's paradigms" (1974, 15)— what I see as social dramas in the glendi microcosm represent a higher degree of intensity than that encountered in ordinary relationships.

As the kefi rises and participants become increasingly engrossed, casual exchanges of mantinades escalate into full-scale dramatic enactments of important relationships among them. While explicit conflict may not always be the topic of these interchanges, their thematic and emotional intensity makes them stand out, thus creating focuses of tension and individual emphasis within the glendi texture. As the wedding themes of joy and praise and the undifferentiated focus on the entire glendi community are the stated norm in a wedding glendi, these dramatic interchanges represent a breach of this norm—the first phase of social drama according to Turner (1974, 37–38). They direct attention to individuals and introduce serious themes of grievance, doubt, anxiety, or merely emotional intensity to the lighter tone of the rest of the glendi.

In the Hirakis glendi described, there were six principal social dramas:

1. Sakellis and Prearis's entrance and the ensuing verbal dueling.
2. The decay of the neighborhood and the comfort of summer visits.
3. Kalliopi's sorrow, her request to change the subject, and the singing of a syrmatiko.
4. Less dramatic focuses:
    a. I, as folklorist and mediator between Olymbos and Baltimore;
    b. Nikos A./Hirakis, that is, old and young meraklides; the one left behind and the one returning;
    c. Son-in-law/father-in-law.

5. Family interchange on the topic of Kalliopi's grievances. Blame, praise, reconciliation through praise of the family unit and the inherited talent.
6. Yiannis's entrance and the theme of social change.

Two modes of progress exist in the glendi: thematic and emotional. Thematically, the glendi as a whole is cyclical, from calmness to intensity back to calmness, from joy to grief back to joy, from relatively conventional themes to increasingly improvised and unexpected topics to the orderly and expected "bride's treat" and the final dance songs. There is, moreover, a shift in the ages that are dominant in each stage, although participation by age is not rigid. The initial and final stages of the glendi make the most references to the wedding event, the couple, the best men and bridesmaids, and therefore allow more participation by the young as these are more suitable topics for them. Although talented young people also participate, the middle part of the glendi is dominated by the older performers, as its themes of grief, anxiety, separation, and painful loss are born of experience and maturity. Each individual social drama also mirrors a similar cyclical progression from relative calmness to some form of symbolic dissolution of a given order (through conflict, grief, and a degree of intensity not encountered in everyday interaction) and a return to a newly restored and negotiated balance. With few exceptions, in a successful glendi such as this each social drama represents an escalation of intensity and engrossment over the one preceding it. "Cooler" themes or narrative songs provide occasions for respite from heated interchanges. Thus, the glendi moves through thematic plateaus of increasing intensity, emotional engrossment, and intimate social relationships, whose subjects, as the glendi progresses, tend to deal almost exclusively with the airing of grievances.

This thematic intensity is mirrored and paralleled by emotional intensity. The glendi at its most desirable height of kefi blends thematic with emotional depth, having progressed from stages of superficial gaiety to a state of complete engrossment. The articulated aesthetics of kefi describe high kefi (usually achieved at dawn) in terms of its seriousness and high quality (*to kefi tis avyis ine to kalitero*; the kefi of dawn is the best), its restraint (*ohi exalla pragmata*; not wild things), and its interactive quality, as meraklides are supposed to aid each other to achieve this stage. Emotional progress is also characterized by the movement from relatively disparate individual statements to increasing synchronization. At the highest moments of kefi, the group (*parea*) speaks almost as one coherent unit, sharing the same sense of timing, appropriateness, and meaning. Thus a community is formed in performance through symbolic action and a shared system of interpretation.

A similar transformation is visible in the space in which the glendi takes place. In the first portion of the Hirakis glendi, guests sat around rectangular tables, with most of the women seated on the *sofas*. As the glendi progressed, disorder reigned in the seating arrangement and the positions of various objects. People moved about freely, often embracing one another or occasionally sitting on each others' laps as they sang mantinades to each other; food and utensils were strewn in heaps on tables; discarded food such as nutshells lay on the floor; some people rested their heads on tabletops or on others' shoulders for a brief nap. At the end of the glendi, during the *kerasma*, guests awakened (some refreshed themselves and their appearance), and chairs and other objects were put in order. Before the dance started, the floor was swept, the tables and chairs removed, and attendees took new positions in the room. Thus the space of the glendi itself underwent a process of change mirroring the other types of transformation within the event.[18]

While a good deal of folk commentary as well as ethnographic descriptions (for example, Mihailidis-Nouaros [1934] 1979) stress the stable components of the glendi, close attention to folk criticism as well as participation in several glendia over time reveal the importance of digressions in them.[19] Thus, social dramas are the principal mechanisms for dynamic progress within a given event, while a process of increased engrossment on the part of the performers escalates their intensity and duration. Conversely, the more intense and intimate the dramatic interchange among the actors of these social dramas, the more transported the mood of the participants.

In spite of the traditionally conservative role of the glendi, its fluid, processual qualities define it for the Olymbos world: "Without kefi, a glendi cannot exist" ("Horis kefi, glendi den yinetai"). Moreover, it is precisely these qualities that render a traditional event capable of adaptation to drastically changed situations—from physical space to economic and value systems.[20] For the Olymbites of the village and those inhabiting Baltimore and other dispersed settlements, glendi performance re-creates the performers' memory or new interpretation of the village unit, thus constructing a community outside physical boundaries and markers.

Glendi and the Community beyond It

In addition to the progress within this glendi, we have seen another process at work blending events taking place in "ordinary" space and time outside the glendi into the mythic, extraordinary time and space of the glendi. Yiannis's return, for example, and his experience as a shepherd in the mountains—part of ordinary, everyday reality—were instantaneously turned into song and became the topics of a sustained exchange of mantinades. His return also functioned as an instrumental symbol, conjuring up the larger experience of loss, separation, and irreversible change in the community. Thus, an actual event taking place in historical time was instantaneously transformed into extraordinary experience.

Moreover, we saw that the glendi incorporated an intensified form of conversations already taking place in the community outside it: the role of men of marriageable age, the dilemma of global dispersion while maintaining intermarriage as a high value, the separation of friends and relatives, and the like. The more successful the kefi, the easier it is immediately to transform historical into extraordinary, social into aesthetic, ordinary into transported experiences. Several key conventions make possible a link between the glendi experience and the broader community, thus making it an important part of the process of creating community history and a collective sense of identity.

Repetition

The repeated recycling of a specific historical incident or of a type of relationship (those who stay behind and those who return, parents and children, people from Olymbos and outsiders or friends) into successive glendia over time builds additional layers of meaning and blurs the line between formal performance and outside world, experiential and historical understanding. Just as Albert Lord (1965) demonstrated that each performance is a new creation, glendia also make clear that each repetition of the same event or category of relationship becomes a new level of experience and creates additional nuances of meaning. The process of reexperiencing key historical incidents and categories of relationships continuously over time is important in building, experiencing, and reinterpreting collective identity.

The loss of Kalliopi's husband to mental illness, a man's losing an arm (as had the father of a bride in one case), the drowning of someone else's brother are experienced communally over and over again in glendia in which these people are present, or alluded to when they are absent.[21] Incidents that involved people's ancestors are similarly alluded to time and time again. New categories of relationships and situations enter the dramatic process of the glendi. Repeated performances and their symbolic reconstruction within the social dramas of the glendi negotiate new cultural solutions.

In the course of the Hirakis glendi, the most important relationships in the village unit were discussed and renegotiated after reaching a stage of emotional or thematic dissolution: relationships among family members, neighbors, old and young, men and women, man and land, individual and community, absent (or dead) and present. A number of new relationships—resulting from economic changes, primarily emigration—were prominent as well: exiles and those left behind, returnees and village residents, "link" individuals (travelers, ethnographers) and the community, community members and the changed land, new professions and old (dentists and farmers, for example).

It is significant that all these relationships are not merely discussed and enacted, nor simply enacted in an intensified context of tension and conflict. In each of the social dramas outlined above, instead, the symbolic dissolution is followed by a symbolic negotiation that represents a cultural solution. Social dramas 4b and 4c represent a potential conflict (in this case echoing an actual conflict between father and son-in-law) and a skillful solution by a meraklis. Nikos A. shifts excessive attention from Hirakis to himself to the relationship between Hirakis and his son-in-law, averting potential jealousy and proving himself a true meraklis in generosity and social judgment.

Enactments of new relationships in glendi performances provide the participants with the flexibility to deal with new and changing contexts in or outside the glendi proper. Further, sequences of mantinades develop suggestions for action and offer a variety of new solutions to accommodate the substantial changes of the past several decades.

Mantinades addressing the returnees, for example, praising their achievements abroad, making them feel welcomed, advising them as to how to marry and maintain their traditional customs, are not merely descriptive but reflective of a process of negotiation operating during the glendi. The solution suggested to them has to do with economic freedom and cultural retention: travel and achieve as much as you can, but marry here and be an Olymbitis. On a broader plane, the very fact of communication between returnees and villagers, emigrants and those who stayed behind, explores the terms of a new and difficult relationship: the settlements and the homeland, the symbolic center of the village unit and its diaspora. Whether in Olymbos or in any of the settlements, a glendi becomes an important vehicle for such transcontinental communication, in which messages are conveyed metaphorically or in person from one settlement to another and the symbolic composition of a global Olymbos, both at home and in exile, is discussed and constructed.

Another relationship, encompassing in actual performance a cultural solution, is the one between community and "link" people—those who steadily bridge the distance between its confines and other communities of Olymbites or, in general, the outside world. My participation in the glendia has generated a new cycle of mantinades in which my role is described but in which I am also asked to mediate distance and historical diaspora in two specific ways: (1) by representing them correctly to the world, and (2) by conveying messages to friends or relatives on the other side of the Atlantic. My delivery of messages in rhyming couplets to one settlement from another has been met with a combination of gratitude and bemusement, but what is significant is that a cultural solution has been incorporated into my role.

The convention of airing grievances is often exploited to express the sorrow and dislocation of emigration and to reconcile the experience with a variety of solutions. Transcontinental communication through the glendi is one such solution. Themes of comfort offer other solutions such as the comfort of return, the ability to maintain customs even abroad. Elaborate metaphors are developed in mantinades of reconciliation, expressing the relationships between homeland (actual or symbolic) and new settlement, old and new. In addition to the significance of summer months and the return visits of the emigrants, the mutual benefits of emigration to homeland and emigrants alike have evolved into another thematic convention, as demonstrated by the following mantinades addressing an emigrant Olymbitis sung at the wedding of Popi Sofilla in August 1981.

[Lendakis (to Pistolis, residing in Rhodes)]:
Cuttings from our plants take root in other lands,
But we enjoy their shade when the summer comes.
[K. Pavlidis]:
When you come, flower gardens blossom children of our land ...
[A. Pavlidis]:
Cuttings from our land have sprouted new branches.
Pistoli, what joy I feel that you come each year.
[K. Pavlidis]:
This way our land's value can never be lost.
Your return, friends, has deep meaning for us.

Thus, emigration can be profitable to the homeland, which shares in the maturity and success of the returnees, while the value of Olymbos is transferred via its customs and the loyalty and perseverance of its people—creating an endlessly renewable and adaptable value loop.

Symbolic Extension

Finally, we have seen another relationship between glendi and community: the extension of symbols and expressive tools of the mantinades sung at a glendi years ago became a means of identifying community members, of establishing my own identity within the community as well as my role in it, and of signaling shared associations for the Olymbos world. Similarly, when I showed slides of the island to community members in Baltimore, they identified places by remembering and reciting mantinades that individual meraklides had sung for them in the past, contributing to a heightened sense of sharing a common identity as well as of experiencing Olymbos.

Kalliopi and I became friends in the course of her brother's wedding glendi. Our relationship was shaped by the aesthetic and moral rules of the glendi. Of all the women, her passion for mantinades and her opinions as to who the best meraklides were came closest to mine. We enjoyed the same type of commitment to the glendi and were among the few women who endured all night long and all through the next day without a break. We wept together and were moved by the same "themes." This relationship carried through to other glendia on the same basis. When I left Karpathos, I started corresponding with her. Kalliopi wrote to me in mantinades, continuing some of the same themes on which we established bonding: the lament for her losses and those of women in general; the love of her father as a meraklis, which we shared; praise of me as a folklorist; affirmation of her friendship; expression of a desire to have been educated herself. Over time, I attempted to respond to her in mantinades also. She answered back, and a pattern of mantinades exchange was established between us.

The newspaper the *Voice of Olymbos*—published in Piraeus but circulating in all settlements—became an additional context for our communication, as Kalliopi published in it mantinades in which she alluded to our friendship. Thus, a relationship that had started in the glendi was expanded beyond it in time and place, yet it remained within the aesthetic and moral parameters defined by it. Not only were content and world view connected to glendi but format as well, as I reluctantly became a participant—something I could not do orally.

The Olymbos glendi has been examined as an expressive unit unto itself but also as a window into a community in the process of dramatic transition engaged in the redefinition and negotiation of personal and collective identity.[22] In the absence of physical signals for, and boundaries of, the Olymbos world, the glendi becomes a symbolic village, reconstituted over and over in repeated performances. The ideology of the "Olymbos world," which constitutes a focal point for the definition of identity for this generation of Olymbites, has no physical reality in the changed village of Olymbos or in the ethnic communities of Baltimore and other urban centers. It is constructed and continuously renegotiated in performance and extensions of performances, yet it becomes the principal mediator among disparate cultural systems and symbols, making sense out of apparent confusion and contradiction.

Close attention to the gradual unfolding of one glendi and its interpretation through folk criticism reveals the importance of its fluid elements rather than its fixed structures. The conventions for accommodating the spontaneous, unexpected, and exceptional on the basis of age-old patterns for dealing with change render the glendi a potent instrument for coping with the transitions faced by the community and the existential issues of identity and daily experience faced by community members. Through the process of gradual engrossment and transformation of ordinary into extraordinary, the glendi is linked to the surrounding reality, forging new systems of meaning and relationships or renewing old ones, while its performers become the agents of change of their world and the creators of continuously new communities, communities born not out of land or neighborhood but of action and perception.

Part 2. "Scattered in Foreign Lands": Olymbites in Baltimore in the 1980s

---

> The neighborhood is wasted! Its mansions tightly sealed!
> And all those raised in its midst, scattered in foreign lands.
> **—Yiannis Diakoyeoryiou,** Olymbos

The fluidity and role of glendia in constantly enacting and renegotiating individual and community identity are especially evident in the Olymbos communities of the diaspora. While historically Olymbos was both deeply traditional and physically remote, change and exposure to other cultures have been constant whether due either to the island's successive foreign occupations or to reliance on foreign economies for work and subsistence. Maria Nikolaidi, a seventy-five-year-old woman living in Baltimore, tells me how she was born a Turkish citizen, then became successively an Italian, Greek, and finally American citizen.

In 1947, Nikolaos Mastromanolis arrived in the United States from Olymbos and settled in Baltimore. In 1954, he was joined by his wife and three children. The emigration of entire families was a momentous event of important historical implications for Olymbos. Moreover, it affected significantly the composition of Highlandtown, a neighborhood in southeastern Baltimore where the family resided and where many others were to join them in the next few decades.

With entire families emigrating together, Olymbos became increasingly deserted even though links with the homeland remained; for example, most Olymbites in Baltimore maintained households on two continents and in two or three separate cities. However, although many claimed that they would return one day, most recognized emigration as irrevocable. Each passing year, investments in increasingly expensive private homes as well as in the purchase of a building for the headquarters for the Olymbian Brotherhood, the association of Olymbites in Baltimore, solidified and made permanent the community's ties with the city. Unlike earlier generations migrating for purely financial reasons, these more recent immigrants chose Baltimore as one out of a number of available options, attracted by new and better educational and professional opportunities for their children.

Glendia in Baltimore are not merely sentimental recollections of the past. They reflect and articulate a particular moment of disruptive change in the history of the community and give voice to the questions, contradictions, values, and personal and collective struggles that go into the making of a new identity. They become platforms for exchange, shared experiences of community and identity in the process of change.

Evolving Definitions

Being an Olymbitis is not a linear representational identity, connected to a geographic region or the mere memorization of rituals. Grappling with its meaning is coming to terms with an existential sense of self: who are we apart from our external identifiers (geography, jobs, status, social mores, etc.)? What remains constant and authentic when all else is gone? What does it mean to be an Olymbitis in Baltimore, Athens, or Melbourne? What stays and what goes? What is essential, what is expendable, and how can value from one realm be converted into different value in another?

Olymbites have been in the process of symbolically re-creating a new "Olymbos" both in the village and in its settlements around the world, with music, language, and art serving as the primary vehicles for reenactment and negotiation. A distinct sensibility and view of the world—and a mastery of history, musical and artistic traditions, rules of social conduct, and ritual events—are among the characteristics of a true Olymbitis. Yet the rules and their applications are constantly reinvented in different contexts and times. In both Baltimore and Olymbos itself, this distinct identity is reflected in daily aesthetic choices and experienced in its most intensive and complete form in the traditional ritual celebration of the glendi.

Journeys and Returns: Making a Home in Baltimore

Olymbos's home interiors make important statements about the identity of their residents as well as the way they want others to perceive them. They encompass vital aspects of family and local history and reflect aesthetic patterns and values that are reiterated in other spheres of life, such as song or daily conversation. Far from being fixed and unchanged, home interiors in the village itself have always incorporated both continuity and change by reflecting their owners' journeys and returns. Rows of imported plates as well as other objects manufactured outside the village, for example, become part of the traditional home decor of Olymbos households. Travels abroad and, more recently, emigration to America have enriched the women's traditional Olymbos dress with new and elaborate designs, colors, and fabrics.

In Baltimore's Highlandtown, while signs of Greek and Greek American culture are evident in storefronts, streets, and front porches, the distinctive Olymbos presence cannot be detected in public spaces, outside homes. Yet, once inside an Olymbos household, its statements of Olymbos identity and aesthetics are immediately apparent to an Olymbitis or to one familiar with Olymbos's culture, distinguishing it from other Greek American or ethnic Baltimore homes.

Individual objects, but mainly their aesthetic arrangement and the meaning their owners attach to them, encapsulate the experience of Olymbites in Baltimore and mark tangibly their existence in the city. Community members brought with them few traditional folk objects and family heirlooms, in part because they envisioned their stay in Baltimore as temporary. As years passed and their residence in the city acquired a permanent tone, a process of "re-creation" of traditional material culture began.

Objects, seemingly disparate to the eye of an outsider, are grouped together on the basis of conventional aesthetic village patterns, rules, and designs. Displays of silver, Japanese lacquerware, and other decorative items are combined with clear symbols of Olymbos identity such as a low-relief wood carving of a map of the island of Karpathos.

In Baltimore and New York, a series of non-Greek stores—from discount department stores to fabric shops in Queens—have been identified by Olymbites as sources for the re-creation of the Olymbos aesthetic. What to the outsider are commercial objects or material reveal to the Olymbitis parallels to village aesthetics in color, texture, design, or value and are utilized to construct and alter at the same time traditional items. In spite of the Olymbos ethos of strictness and adherence to tradition, there is no stigma attached to the use of a sewing machine to enhance the endurance or complexity of design. Embroideries in traditional women's dresses frequently combine machine-made and handmade stitches. Thus, the community appropriates and transforms foreign and commercial elements into building blocks for larger aesthetic architectures anchored in traditional culture and principles.

Modern urban and traditional village worlds are not mutually exclusive, then. Instead, through the act of creative selection, Olymbites interweave elements from both into patterns that are continuously changing, to define new dimensions of their experiences.

In much the same way, the tape recorder, the print media, and later social media have been incorporated into the process of oral transmission and folk criticism, as they can rapidly convey the content of the glendia from one community to another and expand participation beyond physical space. Rather than standing apart from the life outside, glendia express and synthesize the often divergent realities of the worlds with which Olymbites have contact.

In Baltimore, one of the public settings for community celebrations is a building on Eastern Avenue in Highlandtown referred to as the "mansion," the megaron. The mansion is a narrow brick row house flanked by commercial establishments on a noisy street. The ground floor is a dark and mostly barren hall with depressing brown, paneled walls and a serving bar at the end. When a glendi takes place there, however, it is transformed. Smaller tables are pulled together to form a long, communal table that stretches from one end to the other. Guests are spread in three concentric circles. Due to the narrowness of space, the musicians, usually a lyra player and a laouto player, sit atop the table in the middle. The rest of the people sit around the table. Soon, a third circle of dancers forms around the seated guests, for most of the evening moving to the rhythm of the music almost hypnotically, in slow, graceful, small steps. The music, the brilliant colors of women's traditional dresses, the fragrances and textures of the constantly replenished spreads of sumptuous dishes covering every inch of the table, transform the passive space into a community born in interactive performance.

The singing often begins with a low-key mantinada that establishes the context and sets the tone:

Even here, in this foreign land, it is good when we are together,
and it's deserving to preserve intact our own customs.

At a public glendi (as opposed to those taking place in homes), like one held during the carnival season before Orthodox Lent, topics are more likely to revolve around shared grievances such as emigration, loss, and old age; the occasion of the glendi; or humorous barbs among participants, than to focus on a family or personal drama:

Olymbos has affection for all its old customs.
Though far and exiled from home, we must keep them forever.

As in the glendia in Olymbos, the intensity of emotion and depth of thought escalate as the evening turns into night and night into dawn and as alcohol and music take increasing hold of the guests' emotions. This is seen in the sequence below—with singers differentiated by letters of the alphabet:

C. The passing years have brought on this uprooting upon us, and one by one, and slowly, we've all come to Baltimore.
B. This Sunday before Lent, breaking on us this dawn
is giving birth to old thoughts inside of me, my friends.

A. Neither here nor there can the soil nourish us; for us years pass by—solitary and bitter.

B. All years, past. Years, good years I remember!

Yet I curse them all a thousand times! They've made me an old man.

A. I grieve and cannot decide; I grieve and my mind is muddled.

It seems that if I'm still alive, I should return one day.

B. All of us should love our land's traditions

and keep them up as we found them ever from this far.

Again, as in Olymbos, glendia remain viable because they accommodate both change and tradition. The very folk terminology defining the aesthetics of the glendi contradicts fixedness in that it employs metaphors of fluidity: "Glendi is a boat and meraklides the helmsmen." A finely articulated system of folk aesthetics presents the glendi as a process from mirth to grief, from calmness to a state of emotional engrossment, from general themes to themes of a private, often painful and intense nature. The course of the glendi event is one of journeying through intricate emotional stages and a network of complex social relationships, to arrive at a newly defined social and emotional state.

Layering of Worlds: The Triple Wedding

The 1980 wedding of Popi Sofilla, daughter of one of the main meraklides in Baltimore and sister of one of the best lyra players, Manolis Sofillas, is an excellent example of both Olymbites' sense of community and identity and the vital role of the glendi in this process. The marriage was arranged following the traditional Karpathiot practice, but its celebration veered from tradition. To accommodate additional dimensions of the Olymbos-Baltimore identity, the wedding required three different festivities.

It began with a church ceremony and the bride dressed in white (as opposed to the embroidered wedding dresses worn by brides in Olymbos). The religious celebration combined traditional Byzantine chanting with the use of an organ—an addition introduced by the first generation of Greek Orthodox churches in the United States in an attempt to downplay their "foreignness" and emulate mainstream Protestantism. Following the ceremony, a reception was held at the Holiday Inn, mostly indistinguishable from mainstream American banquets except for the Greek American band, which played a mélange of popular Greek and American tunes.

The dancing that followed in the social hall in the basement of the church included, in typical Greek American fashion, a combination of ballroom and popular dances, with a smattering of Greek folk dancing. At 3:00 a.m. these festivities ended, and most of the guests went home. But it was in these early morning hours that the generic Greek American conventions gave way to a true glendi in which the Olymbos guests could behave as Olymbites.

The Olymbos community gathered at the megaron—the community clubhouse—for the "real" wedding celebration. Although a full banquet had been served at the Holiday Inn, the elaborate dishes prepared and served at the megaron did not seem to acknowledge this fact. Steaming platters of regional dishes kept alternating for hours, followed by trays piled with mountains of desserts that continued arriving into the morning as if the previous banquet had never taken place.

A major identity switch seemed to have taken place, signaled by the change of costume from Western to Karpathiot by some of the ladies; the realignment of social roles, with the meraklides occupying positions of honor; and the establishment of a new social hierarchy (indicated in part by the seating arrangement). Most importantly, however, there was a different mode of aesthetic expression and communication, now centered around the sung exchanges of mantinades, which brought out deep emotions and intensified the expression of various types of relationships.

In place of pleasantries and toasts, the evocative sound of the lyra signaled a shift in tone and invited guests to channel their most intimate thoughts into song. The father of the groom started the first sequence of mantinades:

Joy and sorrow are joined together, battling inside my body;
I put aside all cares tonight for my child's wedding

After the first few words, there was not a dry eye in the house. Parents identified with the father's emotions; the groom was moved by his expression of love to him; and some of the guests, reflecting on their own lives and relationships, responded to the father with their own mantinades. With each passing hour, the artistry of the performances, depth of expression, and intimacy among guests increased, taking a life of their own whose meaning extended far beyond the celebration of a wedding.

A year later, Mr. and Mrs. Sofilla commented on this triple wedding—a common practice among Baltimore Olymbites. Asked why he couldn't just have a Karpathiot wedding celebration, Mr. Sofilla responded that his social life and work involved him with the larger Greek and American communities and that he had incurred obligations he should reciprocate. He and his wife stressed the enormous physical and financial drain this triple wedding celebration entailed. "Twice as much money, twice the amount of preparation. I shudder to think about it."[23]

The practice of the dual wedding and other types of celebrations in bicultural communities is not unique to immigrants from Olymbos. The role of the ritual

Figure 65. Wedding *glendi* at the Olymbian Brotherhood clubhouse in Baltimore, following the church ceremony and catered reception at a nearby hotel. In Anna Caraveli, *Scattered in Foreign Lands: A Greek Village in Baltimore* (Baltimore: Baltimore Museum of Art, 1985). Photo courtesy of Liliane de Toledo.

glendi of Olymbos's communities of the diaspora is not only to present dual traditions but also to draw out the deepest expressions of personal and community identity through music and song and to provide a platform for their evolution and reinvention.

At Popi Sofilla's wedding, the church celebration and the reception that followed fulfilled religious and social obligations and certainly provided enjoyable experiences for the guests. However, the ritual glendi went beyond social obligations and fun. The stylized exchange of improvised couplets—praising the couple and the parents, bringing messages from those absent, remembering the dead, making allusions to generations of family history—allowed guests to experience and affirm a sense of self in its fullness and in relationship to the community. The context of increasing engrossment helps shed inhibitions and create intimacy, enabling guests to air grievances, reconcile conflicts, express affection, and negotiate change in a way no other celebration could. As Antonia Zografidis from Olymbos put it:

Love and separation, joy, grief and passion—
All flow together in the mantinada's stream.

The re-created "Olymbos" of the diaspora, and also of the village itself, is a community not of fixed structures and static symbols but one of action and emotional engagement; one that uses music, poetry, and a process of emotional engrossment to experience and redefine a sense of meaning and identity.

Notes

1. This work is based on two previously published but related pieces: "The Symbolic Village: Community Born in Performance," *Journal of American Folklore* 98 (1985): 259–86; and *Scattered in Foreign Lands: A Greek Village in Baltimore* (Baltimore: Baltimore Museum of Art, 1985).

2. Part 1 is based on a lecture delivered at the University of Pennsylvania in the fall of 1982. Fieldwork for this article was conducted in both Olymbos and Baltimore from 1979 to 1985. After January 1983, research and documentation was made possible through the generous support of the Folk Arts Program of the National Endowment for the Arts. In July 1984, this project received additional funding from the National Endowment for the Humanities for further research and the implementation of an interpretive ethnographic exhibition with a catalog, which opened at the Baltimore Museum of Art in July 1985. I am deeply grateful to the two endowments for this support which—in addition to the exhibition—provided me with new data and material for analysis. I also received invaluable help from the codirector of the exhibition, Elaine Eff, and the members of our advisory committee—Ivan Karp, Barbara Kirshenblatt-Gimblett, Diskin Clay, Maria Nikolaidis, and Minas Konsolas—in developing and refining my thesis and general methodology. I am also indebted to the National Center for Urban Ethnic Affairs in Washington, DC, for support and administration of this project, and to the American Folklife Center of the Library of Congress (especially Carl Fleischhauer) for loans of recording equipment, gifts of tapes, and substantive advice and interest. My biggest share of gratitude goes to the village of Olymbos and the community of Olymbites in Baltimore—especially our community advisers Manolis Diakomanolis, Nikolaos Nikitas, Emmanuel Nikolaidis, Yiannis Dargakis, and Kostas Nicolaidis—for their generous hospitality, advice, and encouragement during my work among them.

3. For a history of the Greek neighborhood of Highlandtown in Baltimore, see Prevas 1982 and Demetriades 1978.

4. There are changing attitudes toward definitions of a "good time" and use of leisure time in Greece. The notion of glendi as described here applies primarily to the old, middle-aged, or, generally, more tradition-minded Greeks. Among Olymbites, however, young people, especially those born in Olymbos, usually participate actively in glendia.

5. While persons in recent mourning do not participate in glendia, meraklides may encourage the ending or breaking of a mourning period by urging them to participate. While some priests are known as meraklides, open participation by them in glendia is not deemed socially acceptable, but exceptions are tolerated. It is often the most important meraklides who may give the signal for a rule to be bent and an exception to be allowed.

6. For a description of the traditional Karpathiot house, see Mihailidis-Nouaros (1934) 1979, 350–63; for the seating hierarchy of a traditional Olymbos wedding, see Mihailidis-Nouaros (1934) 1969, 96. For new settings for public glendia performances, see Simon Karas 1979, 99. Using his field notes, Karas describes the new hall (*megaron*) built with money Olymbos emigrants sent home.

7. For a comprehensive analysis of the process of oral formulaic composition, see Albert Lord 1965. Lord explores the relationship between improvisation and traditionally dictated patterns with regard to the composition and performances of epic songs. For a variety of theoretical perspectives

on folk song compositions and performances, see Caraveli 1982, Beaton 1980, Finnegan 1977, and Glassie, Ives, and Szwed 1971; for a broader perspective on performance, see Bauman 1977.

8. For an excellent analysis of Greek folk aesthetics and indigenous definitions of meaning, see Herzfeld 1981b. For a discussion of the process by which a song is rendered meaningful to the community in which it is generated, see Caraveli 1982. See also Danforth 1982 for a further examination of indigenous "meaning" in the relations between traditional aesthetics and social context.

9. Marriages in Olymbos and the Olymbos community in Baltimore are still arranged for the most part. Ancestry, wealth, education, and reputation are among the qualities considered when arranging a marriage. This practice, however, is weakening. Marriages to non-Olymbite Greeks, although frowned upon, have been made, and young people often have a more active role in selecting a spouse than they did in the past.

10. An important festival took place in a monastery near Olymbos on Saint John's Day, enhancing the opportunities for communal celebrations and reunions. For a study of the summer cycle of celebrations and festivals throughout Greece and the effect of tourism and other social and economic changes on them, see Loukatos 1981.

11. Simon Karas describes the glendi that took place in Olymbos to celebrate the opening of the megaron there, built with the financial contributions of emigrant Olymbites. He also discusses briefly the relationship between emigrants and the village (1979, 99–103).

12. These traditional items of a bride's trousseau are made to be used within the traditional Olymbos home interior. Their value has come to be increasingly symbolic rather than functional, especially in the case of couples living outside the village in nontraditional homes. Whether these items are used in a home or not, however, they are still painstakingly embroidered for years before a girl's wedding day (in Olymbos and abroad) and given to her as an important part of her dowry.

13. For a description of a traditional Olymbos wedding and comparisons with wedding customs in other villages on Karpathos, see Mihailidis-Nouaros (1934) 1969, 78–97.

14. Variants of what Olymbites call syrmatika are sung in other parts of Greece as well. Some collections of folk songs refer to them as *epitrapezia* or *tis tavlas*, while Mikail Mihailidis-Nouaros cites a few under the category *diiyimatika* (narrative songs) ([1934] 1969, 9–18).

15. For a comprehensive study of the folk songs of the Dodecanese, the island group to which Karpathos belongs, see Baud-Bovy 1935.

16. Although traditional Olymbos has been a class-based society in which possession of land and education defines one's standing within it (see, for example, Agapitidis 1979, 33–56), the glendi is considered to be an equalizer of classes (*isopedoni*). Emigration to Greek urban centers and abroad has added a wide variety of occupations to the traditional ones of farmer, shepherd, artisan, priest, and teacher. (See, for example, Karayeoryi-Halkia 1981, 253–88, for an analysis of social and economic developments on Karpathos.) In today's glendia, both in Olymbos and abroad, the composition of the participants is very diverse in terms of occupation, financial standing, and place of permanent residence, and thus the relationships negotiated are complex and challenging.

17. "Social dramas, then," Turner concludes, "are units of a harmonic or disharmonic process, arising in conflict situations" (1974, 37–38). He goes on to define what he sees as "four main phases of public action, accessible to observation": the "breach" of "regular, norm-governed social relations"; the "phase of mounted crisis"; "redressive action," which "limits the spread of crisis"; and the phase of "reintegration of the disturbed social group of the social recognition and legitimization of irreparable schism between the contesting parties" (1974, 37–42).

18. For an analysis of concepts of space and their relationship to culture and society, see Tuan 1977. For local concepts of space and attitudes toward the land, see Philippides 1973.

19. For an analysis of the role of digressions in the Greek folk song tradition, see Caraveli 1982, esp. 146–53.

20. On social change observed on a larger scale, Victor Turner notes:

The functionalists of my period in Africa tended to think of change as "cyclical" and "repetitive" and of time as structural time, not free time. With my conviction as to the dynamic character of social relations I saw movement as much as structure, persistence as much as change, indeed, persistence as a striking aspect of change. I saw people interacting and, as day succeeded day, the consequences of their interactions. I then began to perceive a form in the process of social time. This form was essentially *dramatic*. (1974, 32)

I see the same dynamic relationship between tradition and change, fixed form and fluid elements such as emotional state, aesthetic rules, and allowable exceptions to them within the Greek folk song tradition and in the social context of formal events (see, e.g., Caraveli 1982). Far from being antithetical, "fixed" traditional elements contain within them mechanisms for change, while there is a pattern in expressive processes such as kefi or various digressions to expressive events.

21. There is a traditional interrelationship between laments and wedding songs, death and marriage, in the Greek tradition. See, for example, Caraveli-Chaves 1978; Alexiou 1974, 120–22; Herzfeld 1981a; and Danforth 1982, 74–90.

22. For comparative purposes, see Timothy Rice's analysis of the Macedonian celebration *sobor*. Rice discusses issues of changing values, social conditions, and symbolic boundaries and concludes that "the sobor is one way for village society to assert its hold on all generations, living and dead" (1980).

23. Marina Sofilla, conversation with the author, Baltimore, October 4, 1981.

References

Agapitidis, Sotirios. 1979. "I ikonomikes drastiriotites stis parimies tis kinotitos Olymbou, Karpathou." In *Karpathiakai meletai*, vol. 1. Athens: Etairia Karpathiakon Meleton.

Alexiou, Margaret. 1974. *The Ritual Lament in Greek Tradition*. Cambridge: Cambridge University Press.

Baud-Bovy, Samuel. 1935. *Chansons du Dodecanese*. 2 vols. Athens: Sideris.

Bauman, Richard. 1977. *Verbal Art as Performance*. Prospect Heights, IL: Waveland Press.

Beaton, Roderick. 1980. *Folk Poetry of Modern Greece*. Cambridge: Cambridge University Press.

Caraveli, Anna. 1982. "The Song beyond the Song: Aesthetics and Social Interaction in Greek Folksong." *Journal of American Folklore* 95: 129–58.

———. 1985a. *Scattered in Foreign Lands: A Greek Village in Baltimore*. Baltimore: Baltimore Museum of Art.

———. 1985b. "The Symbolic Village: Community Born in Performance." *Journal of American Folklore* 98: 259–86.

Caraveli-Chaves, Anna. 1978. "Love and Lamentation in Greek Oral Poetry." PhD dissertation, State University of New York at Binghamton.

Danforth, Loring. 1982. *The Death Rituals of Rural Greece*. Princeton, NJ: Princeton University Press.

Demetriades, John. 1978. "A Brief History of the Saint Nicholas Parish." In *25th Anniversary: Saint Nicholas Greek Orthodox Community*. Baltimore: n.p.

Finnegan, Ruth. 1977. *Oral Poetry: Its Nature, Significance and Social Context*. Cambridge: Cambridge University Press.

Glassie, Henry, Edward D. Ives, and John F. Szwed. 1971. *Folksongs and Their Makers*. Bowling Green, OH: Bowling Green State University Popular Press.

Herzfeld, Michael. 1981a. "An Indigenous Category of Meaning and Its Elicitation in Performative Context." *Semiotica* 34: 113–41.

———. 1981b. "Performative Categories and Symbols of Passage in Rural Greece." *Journal of American Folklore* 94: 44–57.

Karas, Simon. 1979. "I Karpathos kai ta tragoudia tis." In *Karpathiakai meletai*, vol. 1. Athens: Etairia Karpathiakon Meleton.

Karayeoryi-Halkia, Fotini. 1980. "Kinoniki kai ikonomiki anaptiksi nisou karpathou." In *Karpathiakai meletai*, vol. 2. Athens: Etairia Karpathiakon Meleton.

Karp, Ivan. 1980. "Beer Drinking and Social Experience in an African Society: An Essay in Formal Sociology." In *Explorations in African Systems of Thought*, edited by Ivan Karp and Charles S. Bird, 83–119. Bloomington: Indiana University Press.

Kirshenblatt-Gimblett, Barbara. 1983. "Studying Immigrant and Ethnic Folklore." In *Handbook of American Folklore*, edited by Richard M. Dorson, 39–47. Bloomington: Indiana University Press.

Konsolas, Minas. 1984. Interview with Anna Caraveli, Baltimore, July 9.

Lord, Albert Bates. 1965. *The Singer of Tales*. New York: Atheneum.

Loukatos, Dimitrios. 1981. *Ta kalokairina*. Athens: Filippotis.

Mihailidis-Nouaros, Mikail G. (1934) 1969. *Laografika symmikta karpathou*, vol. 1. Athens: Syllogos Apandahou Karpathion.

———. (1934) 1979. *Laografika symmikta karpathou*, vol. 2. Athens: Syllogos Apandahou Karpathion.

Nikolaidis, Ilias. 1983. Interview with Anna Caraveli, Baltimore, November 14.

Philippides, Demetrios Agamemnon. 1973. "The Vernacular Design Setting of Elymbos: A Rural Spatial System in Greece." PhD diss., University of Michigan.

Prevas, Nicholas M. 1982. *History of the Greek Orthodox Cathedral of the Annunciation*. Baltimore: John D. Lucas.

Rice, Timothy. 1980. "A Macedonian *Sobor*: Anatomy of a Celebration." *Journal of American Folklore* 93: 113–28.

Tuan, Yi-Fu. 1977. *Space and Place: The Perspective of Experience*. Minneapolis: University of Minnesota Press.

Turner, Victor. 1974. *Dramas, Fields, and Metaphors: Symbolic Action in Human Society*. Ithaca, NY: Cornell University Press.

Musical Practice and Memory on the Edge of Two Worlds: Kalymnian *Tsambouna* and Song Repertoire in the Family of Nikitas Tsimouris[1]

—Anna Lomax Wood

Our bride is the thunder that comes with the storm.

Give them as many sweet years

As there are shoots on the mint.

—From "Parianos," a Kalymnian wedding dance

Nikitas Tsimouris (1924–2001) was one of a few Dodecanese bagpipers still practicing at the end of the twentieth century. Experts—who are as rare as the pipers themselves—considered him a master of his instrument, the *tsambouna*. He was loved and revered in his family and community as a bringer of joy and keeper of tradition and was a living treasure of his adopted home, the state of Florida. Nikitas and his instrument were, however, the standard bearers of a whole universe of song, dance, and poetry shared and often governed by the women of his family, which spilled out of their own intimate circle into the Kalymnian communities of Tarpon Springs and abroad.

It is my purpose to conjure up that world from the behavior and memory of this immigrant family and at the same time to draw attention to the importance of vocal music and its relation to instrumental music in this and by extension other Balkan and Mediterranean village traditions. Additionally, I propose this work as an example of cultural feedback falling within the realm of that rich and diverse field known as public folklore, in which the researcher collaborates with informants to galvanize musical memory, enrich cultural identity, and preserve the more subtle and fleeting—and often neglected—aspects of tradition.

The tsambouna is a small bagpipe with two chanters found in the Dodecanese (principally on Karpathos and Kalymnos), Crete, Pontic Turkey, and Thrace, and nearly identical to the sort played in North Africa and the Middle East. It is one of two variants known in Greece, the other being the *gaida*, which has a single chanter and is used in Thrace, mainland Greece, and elsewhere in southeastern

Europe. The term "tsambouna" (pronounced "tsabuna") derives from the ancient Greek word for harmony, an agreement of sounds (*simfonia*). Being a difficult instrument to master and tune, the tsambouna is not widespread. During the Greek junta of 1967–1974, it was banned as a primitive relic, but it continued to be held in high esteem by cultural insiders. Representing as it does a link with deep tradition, the tsambouna is still in demand, and there are now some fine young performers in Kalymnos and abroad.

It is often assumed that the tsambouna is an instrument for solo playing or formal display, but I learned early on in this study that this is by no means so. An audience of sheep and goats would have been the most common beneficiaries of a solo bagpipe performance, but far more often the tsambouna, like the gaida, served to lead dancing and accompany singing of all kinds; this was their main function. Instrumental music generally was almost entirely a male activity, while women and girls chiefly performed the social and ritual songs it accompanied. Nikitas's sisters and wife often sang while he played. His daughters, grandchildren, and others present clapped and beat the rhythms with their feet while dancing, augmenting the orchestra and spurring on the group to greater heights of *kefi* (joyfulness) and inspiration, creating the spirit of *glendi*.

Nikitas Tsimouris

Nikitas was born in the village of Hora on the island of Kalymnos and emigrated to the United States in 1967. Mountainous, near-barren Kalymnos had been the center of Aegean sponging, an activity known since antiquity. The island also prospered through trading and boatbuilding and was famed for its citrus groves. As Mediterranean sponge fisheries became depleted in the early twentieth century, Kalymnians emigrated in large numbers to Darwin and Melbourne, Australia; the Bahamas; Campbell, Ohio; and Tarpon Springs, Florida—first establishing the sponging industry in Tarpon and later developing a lucrative niche in industrial bridge painting nationwide.

Kalymnians were reputed to be wealthy among Aegean islanders, but the years encompassing the two world wars and the Depression, straddled by the Italian occupation of the Dodecanese from 1912 to 1947, were anything but prosperous. Nikitas was one of eight children. His father, a sponge fisherman and citrus sharecropper, was also a bagpiper, and the family was known for their love of music and dancing. After the third grade, Nikitas went to work in the mandarin orchards and the sponge fisheries to help maintain the family and earn dowries for his sisters, as was the custom. Upon his own late marriage, Nikitas received twenty sheep and goats as a dowry from his wife's family, which he sold in order to provide a dowry for one of his sisters. Even so, two sisters had gone

Figure 66. Nikitas Tsimouris playing the tsambouna for dancers, Tarpon Springs Centennial, March 1987. Courtesy of the City of Tarpon Springs.

into permanent service with well-to-do families as children and could not marry. Nikitas's father died in 1942, during the worst starvation years of World War II.

Once in the United States, Nikitas worked briefly on the Tarpon sponge boats, as a short-order cook and dishwasher in a Greek restaurant, and then in the stucco plastering trade. In later years he served as custodian of Saint Nicholas Greek Orthodox Cathedral. He was a short, rather stocky man, with the large, pale-blue eyes of the dawn sea and a phlegmatic, slightly mischievous air—not above being a tease to exasperate his wife, who, having the care of three daughters, was of a serious turn of mind. For the last ten years of his life, the effects of smoking left him unable to play his bagpipes without the aid of a compressor. Nikitas retired several years before his death in 2001. He rarely left home except at Christmas and Easter, allowing his wife and daughters to represent him at church and at parties. When not refurbishing his bagpipes or tending his tiny orchard of perfumed Kalymnian mandarins and the herbs and flowers planted round his modest house, he sat at the kitchen table listening to the Greek radio station and silently rehearsing the lyrics of the old songs.

At the end of his life, Nikitas Tsimouris was heaped with honors. First recorded and brought into the public eye by musicologist Theodore Grame of Tarpon Springs, he came to the attention of folklorists from the Florida Folklife Program, which produced a film about the family and their folkways (*Every Island Has Its Own Song*, 1988). This was followed by a 1989 Florida Folk Heritage Award; participation in the Florida Folk Festival and in the Florida Folklife

Apprenticeship Program as a master artist; and numerous magazine and newspaper articles. In 1991, Nikitas became the first Florida recipient of a National Heritage Fellowship from the National Endowment for the Arts. Nikitas is featured in the *Florida Encyclopedia* (1993), and one of his bagpipes is part of the permanent collection of the Museum of Florida History.

The *Tsambouna*

The airbag (*touloumi*) of the tsambouna is made of untanned kidskin (*trageois*) softened and airproofed with mixtures of honey, milk, olive oil, and sometimes chemicals. It is turned inside out, and the neck, tail, and two leg openings are tied shut with string. Tightly affixed with string to the remaining two leg openings of the bag are a mouthpiece and blowpipe made of olive wood, and a double chanter made of two pieces of bamboo (cane or rush are also used) pierced with a heated metal rod and bound together with string and beeswax. The mouthpiece and tube, which is serrated at one end, are made of olivewood that is carved and burned with geometric designs. Nikitas received his from his grandfather, dating it to the nineteenth century.

The parallel chanters, each having a single reed, are fitted into a single olivewood tube and sealed there with wax. One has five and the other three finger holes, and no thumbholes. To tune them, the piper adjusts the reed lengths with a piece of string and reduces the size of certain holes with bits of beeswax. As noted by Wolf Dietrich (1976), air leaks are stopped up with bits of beeswax, and air is kept from escaping out of the mouthpiece by an onionskin flap affixed on the inside with beeswax.

Nikitas filled his bag with air and squeezed it with his arms, forcing air through the chanters to produce sound. He played standing up, with his arms around the bag, keeping pace by tapping his feet. By varying the air pressure in the bag, he was able to "bend" notes—that is, to ornament the basic melody with flurries of grace notes. He would also occasionally hold the air pressure with his arms while singing a line or two of a song. Although the tsambounas of Crete and the Cyclades are similar, the manner of playing in the Dodecanese, particularly on Karpathos and Kalymnos, is unique:

I]t cannot be classified among either bagpipes with a fixed drone nor those which are solely melodic. In fact, the right pipe completes the hexatonic scale and can, at the same time, find itself in unison with the second degree of the scale, thus covering both melodic and accompaniment functions. The tsambouna's tuning system possesses qualities which are completely particular, of which the most obvious is the tonal "ambiguity" of the third degree (in relation to the lowest note of the scale).[2]

Melodies played on the instrument consist of one to two phrases—basically a litany—with variety and excitement created by patterns of trills, mordents, pulsing vibrato, and other bitonal effects. These are executed on the second (left-hand) pipe by the index finger, which "can create separate acoustic images and more complex rhythmic structures" (olymbos.org). *Lyra* players employ a similar technique, producing trills and tremolos with the left fifth finger. Using a multi-tiered method of coding each melodic segment, Haris Sarris, Tassos Kolydas, and Panagiotis Tzevelekos (2008) have studied melodic/rhythmic flow in Dodecanese instrumental music, focusing in one instance on a recorded performance of the "Pano hobos" played in Karpathos on the lyra (a pear-shaped rustic violin with three strings, held upright and bowed across). The authors make the interesting point that if the lyra came into play in the Aegean after the bagpipe, as they believe it did, the way it was played was imitative of, and was circumscribed by, the musical range of the tsambouna.

The limitations of the tsambouna are similar to those of the gaida: the musician lacks contact with the reeds, so he cannot modulate the continuous flow of sound through them by tonguing, "nor can he play pauses or rests, staccato, or even the same note twice in succession. Furthermore, bagpipes do not have a range of dynamics. Generally speaking, the higher the note, the greater the volume, so the loudest note is E5, while the least sonorous is E4" (Sarris and Tzevelekos 2008). As these authors also point out, the higher registers are the most sonorous.

Transmission and Performance Practice

The chanters traditionally were passed from father to son, and they are inserted into the skin when a new bagpipe is made. These are learned first, before progressing to the full bagpipe. Nikitas's chanters were made by his father. With this small instrument, which Nikitas began playing at the age of eight, he learned first to play the drone and then gradually to produce ornamented melodies before attempting to master the ensemble of airbag, mouthpiece, and chanters all together. Similarly, when Nikitas's nephew, Nikitas Kavouklis, showed an interest in the instrument, he made him a pair of chanters.

Nikitas learned to play the tsambouna from his father and other male relatives, who played the instrument to pass the hours while watching their animals. Mrs. Tsimouris's father had been a *megalos voskos* (a shepherd owning a large flock) on Kalymnos and also a bagpiper, and she recalls that family and neighbors often gathered to dance and sing in their courtyard. Nikitas played in the citrus orchards he tended and on the sponge boats he manned seasonally in the Aegean, to entertain the crew and pass the time. When he settled in the tightly

Figure 67. Nikitas Tsimouris with his nephew, Nikitas Kavouklis. Photo by Anna Lomax Chaire-takis Wood.

knit Greek community of Tarpon Springs, he was followed by his sisters and wid-owed mother, and they all took houses around one shady block between Banana, Lime, and Oakwood Streets in the "fruit salad" district of town. In the evenings, they came together with their growing families in one or another's dusty front yard, or in Nikitas's mandarin grove, to summon up the pleasures of their earlier lives on Kalymnos with laughter, music, and dancing.

Singing Style

Sarris and others have begun to look closely at how gaida/tsambouna/lyra play-ing and singing mirror one another in Thrace and Crete. What is the nature of this symphony, and how might it have evolved? In my view, one of the crucial topics to investigate in the folk music of the eastern Mediterranean is precisely the synergy between singing and instrumental music and its possible relation-ship to pastoralism.[3] Cantometrics (Lomax 1976) furnishes an effective system for profiling singing style and vocal qualities in a comparative framework. With general reference to this method, Kalymnian singing style as manifested by the Tsimouris family is rather loud and medium- to high-pitched, nasal, noisy, and forcefully accented. It uses melisma and vowel prolongation; a slow to moderate tempo; narrow intervals and melodic range; simple melodic forms with considerable variation; and long phrases. Instrumental and vocal preludes and many songs are in free rhythm. I heard only solo and individualized (raggedly blended) monophonic unison singing with occasional passages of heterophony. At least a quarter of the text is repeated throughout most songs.

The Documentation Project

I met Nikitas Tsimouris in the early 1990s with my late husband, William Chairetakis. He was introduced to us by my aunt, Bess Lomax Hawes, whom he had come to know at the National Heritage Awards. He took it as his personal obligation to befriend and look after us, both as compatriots (with the distinct plus that Bill was from Crete, a place and culture high in Greek esteem), and as a mark of respect for my aunt. By then, the first generation of Tsimourises had become stately older parents, uncles and aunts with several grandchildren and more on the way. The old musical pastimes had for the most part been incorporated into weddings, christenings, and other life-cycle parties, now big catered affairs, as well as into community festivals, dances at the Saint Nicholas Parish hall, and the Greek nightclubs in the Sponge Docks district of Tarpon. The tsambouna and the old songs had assumed iconic status and were foregrounded at climactic moments in the order of events.

When Bill died in 1992, Nikitas combined with my father to convince the priest to say the liturgy at the funeral home, which was quite irregular. In a gesture of remarkable solidarity, Nikitas attended with his wife and daughters and played the *mirologia* (laments). A few months later, I moved with our young son to Tarpon Springs. Invited into the society of our kind Greek friends, I noticed that village-style dancing thrived, but music and singing had become the province of popular entertainers—dazzling electric bouzouki players and clarinetists, and velvet-throated singers—as was also the case in Greece and southeastern Europe. As in many parts of the world, the unaccompanied singing tradition was being laid aside, both repertoire and style.

Noting a decline in the repertoire, I proposed a documentation project to the City of Tarpon Springs and the National Endowment of the Arts, with the object of capturing on tape the complete range of vocal music and dance still practiced in the Tsimouris family, and of learning more about both instrumental and vocal genres as they functioned in performance practice and in the life and memory of the community. This would be one of the few recorded studies made of singing and tsambouna together in a naturalistic setting, with fairly sophisticated equipment. It would also be a continuation of the work of cultural feedback begun by the Florida Folklife Program, aiming to consolidate and reflect back to the community, as well as to the Tsimouris family, a rich and relatively unexplored vein of their culture.

Nikitas readily acquiesced to the idea of a recording project, as did his sister Theia Nomiki, who had kept up her singing, but the married women in the family were reluctant at first, having lost the habit of singing regularly. Mrs. Tsimouris's responsibilities would not to allow her to give herself over entirely to frivolities. Nevertheless, she and Nikitas's other sisters, Theia ("aunt," also a term of respect applied to older women) Maria Ellinas and Theia Fotini (Fokaina) Skandaliaras, tentatively agreed to help out. Unlike the children of the Italian immigrants I had worked with several years earlier, who were shamed by their parents' music because it lacked support or context in the community, the Tsimouris's children and grandchildren were proud to assist and did so with verve.

We began in early fall 1994. The setting we chose for recording was one in which these activities had often taken place and in which everyone felt most at home: the Tsimouris's kitchen. I used a TEAC portable DAT recorder on loan from the Florida Folklife Program and Sennheiser stereo cardioid microphones. Achieving a perfectly balanced microphone placement for the bagpipes, vocals, and percussive dancing was beyond my competence, but we concocted a setup that worked fairly well.

Almost at once Nikitas's breath began to fail him. Not one to be frustrated, he devised an auxiliary for his weakened lungs. By trial and error, he had a mechanic friend build him a compressor that would generate a flow of air roughly equivalent to his own breath. To this he attached plastic tubing, and, after trying various sizes and lengths for the amount of flow needed, he attached the other end to the air pipe of his bag. Although the compressor was penetratingly loud, if placed at a distance of several feet behind a closed and sealed door, it was drowned out by the sound of the bagpipes and was undetected even by my sensitive microphones. Compressor and tubing, mike stands, recording cables, and improvised baffling; extra people, children, chairs, and stools; and the bulk of the aunts—all had to be accommodated in the Tsimourises' small, agreeable kitchen.

A trickle of cognac, introduced at our first meetings, overcame the reticence of the aunts and gave me the courage to plunge ahead, in spite of my limited knowledge of both Greek folk music and digital recording techniques. On September 18, October 7, 15, and 17, and November 2 and 29, 1994, and on March 26, 1998, we recorded five hours of music and commentary, as well as fairy tales told by Fokaina Skandaliaras. One session took place on the stage of the Tarpon Springs Cultural Center.

A Greek American folklore student from the University of South Florida made a first pass at the song lyrics. I thought that being able to review them at

length with the performers would solve the problems of transcription and translation, but Nikitas and his family were not able to fill in all the gaps and had
little patience for the task. The following summer I consulted my mother-in-law,
Maria Chairetakis, in Greece, who understood the Kalymnian dialect and knew
many of the songs. With her help, a near-complete set of lyric transcriptions in
Greek was produced. The subsequent theft of the computer containing this work
was so discouraging that I put the project aside until 2009.

Repertoire and Song Typologies

The family's repertoire of songs and instrumental pieces consisted mainly of social
music but also included the cycle of wedding songs; cradle-rocking verses (lullabies); and emigration songs, also called mirologia. We recorded twenty-six different songs plus variants—all the songs that the participants could recall at the time
with the exception of funeral laments, which are held to be inauspicious to perform
out of context, and *kalanda* (carols), of which those the Tsimouris family knew
were virtually identical to those sung throughout Greece. Work songs they scarcely
recollected, but they said that bagpipe tunes applying to social occasions were used
to enliven the men on the sponge boats, the shepherds on the hillsides, and the
farmers and laborers in their orchards, and further that the songs used to accompany work were love songs. Although forgotten songs and lyrics later surfaced, the
family's core repertoire—at least as it survived and continued to play a part in social
life in this country—appears to have been covered. Comparison of this with other,
broader collections of Kalymnian songs made in Greece indicates that there may
have been gaps and substitutions in the lyrics as sung by the Tsimourises.

The performers described their songs in ways that might be familiar to scholars of Greek music but were new to me, and contrasted with what I had learned
about musical typology in southern Italy, where in a given territory a handful of
melodics and a characteristic performance style accompanied scores of eight-line
lyric poems, many of them unique, others more widely known. Nikitas explained
that some Kalymnian songs apply to specific social functions and ritual occasions, but they are classified primarily by rhythmic motif and melodic mode.
Melody and rhythm identify songs more than do specific texts; the same verses
and refrains turn up in many songs. With Nikitas's help, I prepared the following
overlapping classification scheme so as to illustrate how Kalymnians variously
describe and order their songs.

   1. Social occasion, sequence of activities, and/or mood:
     • Table songs (*tou trapeziou*)
     • Dance songs (*yia horo*)

2. Rhythm/dance steps:
- Issos/Sousta
- Kalamatianos
- *Syrtos*

3. Tempo (corresponding to rhythm/dance steps):
- Slow
- Moderate
- Fast

4. Place of origin:
- In the eastern Aegean cultural and commercial universe: Kalymnos, Kos, Crete, Kefalonia, Kalamata, Halki, Kasos, Leros, Paros

5. Social function:
- Social songs:
  Erotika (love songs)
  Pismatika
  Mantinades
  Serenades
  Kantades (composed popular songs that entered the folk repertoire primarily from Kefalonia and the Ionian region of Greece)
- Ritual songs:
  Yia gamous (wedding songs)
  Mirologia (funeral laments)
  Yia apokries (carnival songs)
  Kalanda (carols)
- Songs associated with work and household tasks:
  Nanourismata (cradle songs)
  Other songs not remembered
- Patriotic songs:
  Epic narrative fragments (*akritika*, or border guard songs from the Byzantine period)
  Songs of emigration, also called *mirologia* (laments)

6. The way lyrics are deployed:
- *Skopos* (mode, melodic motif) with signature opening verses plus improvised and stock verses added on at will (the more common type)
- *Skopos* with fixed, designated texts

A song is identified primarily by its skopos, a term more or less signifying "mode" and designating a melodic motif, pattern, or scale. Traditional Greek instrumentalists rely upon it to describe their pieces, but few sources deal with the concept. A Macmillan music study guide provides an explanation that fits the approach to musical production by the tsambouna player: "The skopos is built upon a melodic skeleton from which the pitches are connected by ornaments and played in a fixed or free meter." In both multi-instrumental and vocal performances, "a group of musicians called a *parea* [company, group] play the tune in heterophony, meaning that they interpret the same melody in slightly different ways."

Specific texts, sequences of verses, and story lines are secondary to the skopos. Most songs in the category of social music have a few verses—sometimes only one or two—that are specific to one tune. The remaining verses are "migratory," as Nikitas put it, drawn by the singer(s) from a common pool, as their feelings and memories inspire them. However they begin, the singers often shift to *pismatika* (see below), when the verses belonging to their original song are exhausted while the singers are still warming up. Thus, many songs last as long as the singers wish to sing them. Often, too, when the tsambouna is being played, one tune will transition into another, and that tune into yet another, producing a continuous stream of music lasting for as long as thirty and forty minutes or more, with singing weaving in and out of the drone of the pipes, quieting down and heating up, emerging into the foreground and receding again.

Even as lyrics are handled in this pragmatic and flexible way, they are prized for their poetic content. Nikitas would say that he kept a light heart because the scores of verses he knew "lived in his mind." "The songs of then were really into love," said his daughter, Irene, then about twenty. "They're romantic, like Romeo and Juliet. They touched a woman's feelings."

Love Songs

"Pantote ta tragoudia itan yia tous erotes"—All [our] songs were about love—Mrs. Tsimouris said. Love songs are a category that embraces nearly all others—dance songs, table songs, pismatika, kantades, songs for working, wedding songs—if nothing else by means of verses of love and courtship "thrown in" to other songs. "O Potamos" (The River), in *syrtos* rhythm, may also be used as a table song. Its refrain addresses the river: "Oh River with your waves, your whirling waters." Fokaina Skandaliaras led the singing, with the group repeating each line.

> *Opening refrain: E . . . Potame, ta kimata sou*
> *A ta strifo—, ta strifoyirismata sou*
> *Tsakisma: Ela ela me ta mena, ki as' ti mana pou se yenna (2)*
> *M'ithela, m'ithela to sti zoi mou (2)*
> *Ach, na se ka, na se kano teri mou (2)*
> *Tsakisma: Ela ela ela pali, hiotiko mou portokali (2)*
> *Na sou stro—, na sou strono na kimase (2)*
> *Aspro peristeri mou, na sou n'a tairi mou (2)*

226

Tsakisma: Ela ela me ta mena, ki 'as ti mana pou se yenna (2)

Ta mata—, ta matakia sou ta mavra (2)

Sung as refrain: *Ta matakia sou ta mavra, pou na t'akhases na ta vra (2)*

To matio, to matio sou to triyiri

okai tou erota pechnidi (2)

Tsakisma [refrain]: *Ela ela me ta mena, ki as' ti mana pou se yenna (2)*

M'ipa sou, m'ipa sou to skilla kori (2)

Sto yialo, sto yialo mi katevis (2)

Yiati tha—, yiati thalassas fortouna

Tha se pa—, tha se pari na pniyis

K'an me pa—, ki'an me par pou tha pao? (2)

Mesa sta, mesa sta vathia nera (2)

Kano to, kano to kormi mou varka (2)

A kai ta he—, kai ta heria mou koupia (2)

Ta mallia, ta mallia tis kefalis mou (2)

Alisi—, alisides kai skinia (2)

Tsakisma: Ela ela ela me ta mena, ki 'as ti mana pou se yenna (2)

Eh . . . River, your waves

Your whirling—, your whirling and spinning

Come, come with me and leave the mother who bore you

He wanted me, he wanted me so much all my life

Ah, to be—, to be my mate

Come, come, come again, orange from Chios

I will lay—, I will lay you down to sleep

My white dove, to make you my mate

Come, come to my side, and leave the mother who bore you

Your eyes, your pretty black eyes

Your pretty black eyes

Where did you lose them so I can find them?

Your eyes, your dark eyes

Your eyes, and your playthings of love

Come, come to my side, and leave the mother who bore you

I told you, bad girl

Don't go down to the seashore

For the sea, the sea is rough

It will take—, it will take you and drown you

And if you take, and if you take me where will I go?

Down into, down into the deep waters

I will make, I will make my body into a boat

And my hands, and my hands into oars

The hair, the hair of my head
Into chains, into chains and ropes
Come, come to my side and leave the mother who bore you.

"Magdalini," a family favorite, is a satirical, playful love song.

O Magdalini Magdalini
Kateva kato stin avli
Na se do, na se gnorizo
Kai na se glikofiliso
Tsakisma: *Och aman, och aman Magdalini* [Repeat all]
Magdalini, ton andra sou (3)
Vale to sto zebilli
Kai kremase ton sta psila (3)
Na min ton fan i psili
Tsakisma: *Och aman, och aman Magdalini*
Den isoun esi pou mou 'leges (3)
San den me dis pothenis
Kai tora perpatas kai les (3)
Pou m' ides pou de me kseris
Miskokarfia mou kokkini (3)
Me ta saranda filla
Tsakisma: *Och aman, och aman Magdalini* [Repeat all]
Saranda s'agapisane (3)
Mono ego se pira.

Oh Magdalini, Magdalini
Come down in the yard
So I can see you, so I can know you
So I can sweetly kiss you
Oh *aman* [expression of sorrow], oh *aman*, Magdalini
Magdalini, your husband
Put him in your carrying hod
And hang him up high
So the fleas don't eat him
Oh *aman*, oh *aman*, Magdalini
Wasn't it you who was telling me
That without seeing me you die
And now you walk around and say
That you see me and don't know me
My scented red carnation

228

With forty petals
Oh *aman*, oh *aman*, Magdalini
Forty men loved you
I alone snared you.

Pismatika

Song lyrics also have a powerful in-the-moment social dimension. Pismatika (which can be translated as "back talk") are teasing couplets usually exchanged by a group of three or four women, followed by a refrain. The verses are improvised as well as pulled from a common reservoir and may be gossipy or competitive, but the spirit is mainly one of fun, intended to provoke friendly laughter and amusement. I asked why the women so often shifted from other songs into the pismatika mode. "Because that's what comes up," was the reply—"Ti allo tha peksoume?" (What else are we going to play at?). It was evident that pismatika are indeed a form of play and that these island women relished the game, as they returned to it again and again.

The pismatika are a manifestation of the poetic duel, the contest in song, which is one of the most fertile veins in the oral traditions of West Africa, Central Asia, southern Europe, and the Caribbean. Of great resilience and apparently long use (judging by its diffusion among ancient pastoral peoples), the practice may be employed in displays of ethnic supremacy and male proficiency, stamina, and valor. It is used in courtship and as a means of social and political criticism. Its functions may be those of social control or revenge; of harmonization or the provocation of conflict; of winning patronage or respect, or gaining the advantage in a love match. Verses can be boastful, flirtatious, teasing, slanderous, admonitory, insulting, or obscene; and no subject or target is sacred. The central Italian *contraste* were witty exchanges setting forth in song the opposing views and feelings of the participants. Examples of the type range from the toasts of Georgian mountaineers, the lengthy song duels of Sardinian shepherds, the *botta e riposta* of central Italy, the *controversia* and *decima* of the Spanish-speaking Caribbean, to calypso and many more. Even where there is only one singer, many songs of the circum-Mediterranean region seem to represent one side of a conversation, argument, or act of persuasion or vilification.[4]

In Kalymnian pismatika, singers take turns leading with the verses they prefer or that come to mind. The couplets and refrains are sung in tonal unison with some rhythmic heterophony. Often, the voices in the refrains overlap in such a way as to create rhythmic tension and syncopation so that the pismatika go into overdrive, becoming a kind of rapping, in spirit and musical effect. Watching the two Nomikis and Fokaina lean into the singing circle one by one with their verses, it occurred to me that "playing at" pismatika could be a pleasurable way of working through tensions and contradictory emotions arising from continuous proximity and interdependence among women confined to a small group of kinsmen and neighbors, as they had been.

"O Voskos kai o Vassilias" (The Shepherd and the King) is a dialogic song in the *issos* (slow and even) rhythm that was used in Kalymnos during carnival, when bagpipers and little groups of revelers went busking from house to house. The performance recorded by the Tsimourises, which morphs into pismatika, exemplifies the protean character of Kalymnian folk singing. The shepherd lover and his charms is a motif that recurs in a number of songs in the family's repertoire. Alternating solo voices, or solo alternating with group, repeat each verse.

> *First motif, refrain (repeated twice):*
> *O voskos, amani, aramani*
> *O voskos, vosko ki' o vasilias*
> *Second motif (repeated twice):*
> *O voskos, voskos ki' o vasilias, stekima ivasane*
> *Stekima, amani aramani*
> *Stekima, amani vasane*
> *Stekima ivasane, kai stekimatizane*
> *Voskos:* "*Pes mou afendi vasilia, ti pou vazeis stekima?*"
> *Vasilias:* "*Vazo ti amani aramani,*
> *Vazo ti vasilissa*
> *Vazo ti vasilissa, me to vasiliki tis.*"
> *Vasilias:* "*Pes kai esi, amani aramani,*
> *Pes kai esi, kale voske,*
> *Pes kai esi, kale voske, ti pou vazis stekima?*"
> *Voskos:* "*Vazo hi—, amani aramani*
> *Vazo hi—, hilia provata*
> *Vazo hilia provata, me ta aryirokoudouna.*"
> *Voskos:* "*Vazo kai, amani, aramani*
> *Vazo kai ena kalo arni*
> *Vazo kai ena kalo arni, me metaskoto malli.*"
> *Vasilissa:* "*Ach, ki' as i—, amani aramani*
> *Akh, ki' as i—, imoun komissa*
> *Akh, ki' as imoun komissa, n'amou kai tirokomissa.*"

> *Additional verses:*

> *Vasilissa:* "*Na tiroko—, amani, aramani mou*
> *Na tiroko,—komou to mandri*
> *N'avgazo kalo tiri kai mizithra drosiri.*"

The shepherd
The shepherd, shepherd and the king
The shepherd, shepherd and the king made a bet
Wager, *amani aramani*
Wager, *amani* they laid
They laid a wager and they bet
Shepherd: "Tell me, my lord king, what are you betting for?"
King: "I'm betting, *amani aramani*
I'm betting the queen."
"I'm betting the queen and her prince."
King: "Now you tell me, *amani aramani*
You say, good shepherd
Now you tell me, good shepherd, what you're betting on."
Shepherd: "I'm wagering a thousand sheep, *amani aramani*
I'm wagering a thou—, a thousand sheep
I'm betting a thousand sheep, with their silver bells."
Shepherd: "And I'm throwing in a nice lamb, with hair of silk."
Queen: "Ah, if I were only, *amani aramani*
Ah, if I were only a goatherd
Ah, if I were only a goatherd, I could be a cheese maker too."

Additional verses:

"If I could be a cheese—, *amani aramani*
If I could make cheese with my flock
I would make good goat cheese and fresh *mizithra*."

This song transitions naturally into "Ala Roudja Voskaroudja." The Tsimourises explained that *ala roudja, roudja, roudja* (or, *routsa*), the typical refrain of the pismatika, resembles *mana, mana, mana* (Mother, Mother, Mother), a common interjection in Greek folk and *rebetika* music. Irene Tsimouris and Nomiki and Petroula Sazalis (Nikitas's daughter and granddaughters, of similar age) were present and danced throughout this recorded sequence. The kitchen was packed with family and guests, dancing, stomping, whistling, and singing pismatika. After the leader, the chorus repeats each couplet and the last two lines of each tercet as well as the refrain.

Panathena ti mana sou,
Kai me tin edikia mou
Kai me tin edikia mou,
Kai den mas ipandrevgane
Na 'sou tora diki mou

Tsakisma (refrain): *Ela ela me ta mena, na pernas haritomena*
A, to voskaroui sto vouno
Sfirizi kselakoni
A, sfirizi kselakoni
Ki' i erimi tou i sfiria
Ta mesa mou ta lioni
Tsakisma: *Alla roudja roudja roudja, ta mikra ta voskaroudja*
Kardia an eisai apo yiali
Vasta kai mi ragisis
Vasta kai mi ragizis
Kai an eise apo sidero
Kala na yondisis
Kai an eise apo sidero
Kala na yondisis
Agalia galia me kero
K' i ora den ichathi
K' i ora den ichathi
Kai me ta votana tis yis
Yiatrevonde ta pathi
Tsakisma: *Ela ela me ta mena, ki 'as ti mana pou se yenna*
Matia kai fridia kai mallia
Pou t'achei to pouli mou
Pou t' achei to pouli mou
Ma ene kai pismatariko
K' ikopse ti zoi mou
Tsakisma: *Ela ela me ta mena, ki 'as ti mana pou se yenna*
A, ta matia sou einai kafenes
Ta fridia sou balkoni
Ta fridia sou balkoni
Pou 'rchonde kai glendizoune
I meraklides oli
Tsakisma: *Ala roues roues roues, i mikres o voskaroues*
Sto meraklido ta chartia
Eime ki' ego grameni
Eime ki' ego grameni
Eime sta chili yelasti
kai stin kardia kameni
Tsakisma: *Ela ela me ta mena, ki 'as ti mana pou se yenna*

Curses on your mother
And on mine too

And on mine too
They should have married us
So you would now be mine
Come, come with me, to live happily
Ah, the shepherd on the mountain
Whistles to gather his flock
Ah, he whistles to gather his flock
And the call of his whistling
Melts my insides
Alla roudja roudja roudja, that little shepherd girl
Heart, if you are made of glass
Hold it so you won't shatter
Hold on so you won't break
But if you're made of iron
You can take it
Slowly, slowly and with time
Time won't be wasted
Time won't be lost
For with the greens of mountain soil
The passions heal
Come, come with me and leave the mother who bore you
The eyes, brows, and hair
My sweetheart has!
That my sweetheart has
But she's stubborn and whatever she says goes
That she scares me half to death
Come, come with me and leave the mother who bore you
She scares me half to death
Ah, your eyes are brown
And your brows are balconies
Your brows are balconies
Where are all the enthusiasts going to party?
Ala roues roues roues, the little shepherd lads
On the roll of the partygoers
My name is written too
My name is written
And my lips are smiling
But my poor heart is burning
Come, come with me and leave the mother who bore you.

Table Songs

At festivities and gatherings, the men and women and friends of the family would sit together after eating to sing table songs in quiet gaiety with wine, spirits, nuts, and fruits before them: "Kathomaste to yiro, pinome krasaki, kai leme kathe tragoudi" (We sit around the table, drink a little wine, and sing all of our songs). Of old, the Tsimourises would gather every Sunday afternoon to sing, consuming several gallons of retsina between them. The singing of table songs is more than casual merrymaking. It has a quasi-ritual character clearly evident in the *kathisto glendi* (all-male seated glendi with singing only) in the conservative villages of the island of Karpathos, as well in the toasts and table singing of the Caucasus and the Balkans. For the Tsimourises, as for many Greeks in new lands or for those left behind, table singing served the purpose of integrating cultural memory with present experience, of sharing the experience of personal and historical loss as well as the pleasure of the occasion.

"Varkamou Boyiatismeni" (My Painted Boat) was a favorite of Nomiki A. Tsimouris, who used to sing it to me over the phone, and led it in this recording:

Main motif
Nomiki A.: E . . . kaimeni mou kardia, krata kai mi ragizeis
Group: O . . . kaimeni mou kardia, krata kai mi ragizeis
Refrain motif
Leader: Varka mou boyia—, varka mou boyiatismeni
Sta kaponia, sta kaponia kremasmeni
Group: Varka mou boyiatismeni, sta kaponia kremasmeni (sung as above)
Main: [Omitted: Kardia mou, an ise apo sidero]
Kai . . . an . . . vasana ta, kala na t'ayodiseis
Ela me to ga—, ela me to gazolini,
Pou einai i thala—, pou einai i thalassa galini
E . . . den ne boro ta matia mou psi—, psila na ta sikoso
[Kai tis kaimenis mou kardias, parigoria na doso]
Den s'arnioume, de—, de' s'arnioume, den s'arnioume
Mono sou para—, mono sou paraponioume
Kai . . . kai tis kaimenis mou kardias tha—, parigoria na doso
To matio sou, to ma—, to matio to mavradi
Zotani me—, zotani me pa' ston Adi
A . . . dos mou Thee mou eponomi os e—, os edoses stin petra
A . . . kai Panayia, Panayia mou parigora
Tin kardia mou, tin kardia mas afti tin ora
A . . . os edoses tou aidoniou chri—, sa ftera ki' peta
A . . . Panayia mou ki' as—, Panayia ki 'as provale
Na to do ki 'as figi pali

Akh . . . Thee mou, m' ida sou kana kai me pedevis toso
A . . . Panayia mou do—, Panayia mou dos tous chronia
San tes lemo—, san tis lemonia ta klonia
An ene yia pandotina, pare me na glitoso na glitoso
A . . . sti yi pato, sti yi pato ki i yis vronda,
A . . . ki iyis ta pathi mou rota (cuts off before group repetition)

Eh . . . My poor heart, bear it, don't break
Oh . . . my poor heart, bear it, don't break
My painted boat, my painted boat
Tied up at the dock
[*Omitted*: Heart, if only you were made of iron
So you could better bear your troubles]
Come bring the gas—, come bring the gasoline
For the sea, the sea is milky blue
Eh . . . I can't raise, I can't raise my eyes
[*Omitted*: I must give my poor heart consolation]
I'm not denying, not, not denying you, not denying you
I'm only complaining to you
Your eyes, eyes, your black eyes
They send me straight to Hell [Hades]
Ah . . . give me patience, my Lord, like you gave to the rocks
Ah . . . and Holy Mother give hope
To my heart, to my heart, right now
Like you gave to the nightingale
Golden wings so it could fly
Ah . . . my Holy Mother, Holy Mother as he comes
See how he goes away again
Ah . . . my God, what have I done that you torment me so?
Ah . . . my Holy Mother, give them, give them years
As many as the lemon trees, the lemon trees have branches
If it's forever, take me and caress me
Let the deep ground, let the deep ground of the earth
Let the earth swallow up my pains.

Table singing is essentially serious and spiritual, a collective, vocalized meditation. The company gathers as though to perform devotions to the emotional-poetic aspect of being. In isolated, conservative villages such as those on Karpathos where pastoralism has been the main source of livelihood, the singing of mantinades was almost exclusively an intensely male ritual (Caraveli 1985; Kavouras 1993). The men expressed their views and feelings on a variety of topics, addressing the company in fifteen-syllable rhymed couplets appropriate to the occasion. "This form of poetic expression occurs in the context of a sit-down musical celebration . . . amongst a group of men. It often happens spontaneously in various settings while wine and food are served" (Apella Nota 2008).

Even during celebrations, a gathering inward of thought and emotion is mustered for the performance of these songs (olymbos.org). Most table songs are in issos rhythm, and some may be danced as well. They are often preceded by introductory phrases sung in free rhythm, or played on the bagpipe if accompanied. These are the rhythmically free passages of melody preceding an instrumental piece, known in Arabic, Turkish, Persian, and Urdu as *taksim* or *makam* and in Greece as *taximi*, introduced there by Turks. The lamentations are called *amanes*, signifying "Alas!" or "Have pity!," from the Turkish, and also form a subcategory of table songs.

Mantinades were similarly sung in the homes and coffeehouses of Kalymnos, where, however, pastoralists in patri-groups (kin groups related through paternal lineage) intersected with a more uxorious horticultural, sponging, mercantile culture. Immigrants have led the way in bringing women increasingly to the fore in family and community life. In gatherings of the vivacious Tsimouris family, the female voice prevailed even during table singing. A song about immigration, "Marouli," is one about which Mrs. Tsimouris commented: "Aftos einai skopos varismenes"—This is a very heavy [grave and sad] song.

> *Leader 1: E . . . o kaimeni Kalimnos,*
> *Group: Kaimeni Kalimnos*
> *Leader 1: E . . . kaimeni Kalimnos,—to marouli*
> *Group: Mavrisan ta vouna sou (2)*
> *Group, Leader 2: O kaimeni Kalimnos, marouli,*
> *Leader 2: Mavrisan ta vouna sou*
> *Kai efigan, vlepe tous, Panayia mou*
> *Efigan ta levendopedja [sic]*
> *A ki' efigan leve—ndopedja, marouli*
> *Efighen ki i chara sou*
> *Efe—to pedja, marouli*
> *Kai 'fighen ki i chara sou*
> *Thee, kai megalo,—odiname*
> *Thee megalodiname*
> *Thee megalodiname, ach marouli*
> *Megalo t' onoma sou!*
> *Megalo diname, ach marouli*
> *Megalo t' onoma sou*
> *E . . . filo den pefti apo dendri*
> *Filo den pefti apo dendri*

O filo de pefi—apo dendri, ach marouli
Dichos to thelima sou
Filo de pefti a—po dendri, marouli
Dichos to thelima sou
E . . . opios 'gapa me—lachrino
Opios agapa melakcrino
Opios 'gapa me—lachrino, marouli
Prepi na to diloni
Opios agapa melachrino
Prepi na to diloni
Kai yiati echei ston ero—ota
Kai yiati echei ston erota, marouli
Logariasmo na dosi.
Opa! Clapping

Additional verses:

Figane ta omorfia sou
Pali figane i chara sou
O kaimeni Kalimnos, marouli
Mavrisan ta vouna sou.

Eh . . . unlucky Kalymnos
Poor Kalymnos
Eh . . . unlucky Kalymnos, *ola roula*
Your beloved mountains are in mourning
And they've gone, look at them, Holy Mother
Your fine young men have gone, *marouli*
And your fine young men
Your joys have departed *marouli*
The flower of your youth, *marouli*
And your joys have fled
God almighty
Oh God, great and strong
God, great and strong, ah, *marouli*
Great is Thy name
All mighty, ah, *marouli*
Great is Thy name
Eh . . . the leaf doesn't fall from the tree
The leaf doesn't fall from the tree
The leaf doesn't fall, from the tree, ah, *marouli*

Against Thy will
The leaf doesn't fall, from the tree, ah, *marouli*
Against Thy will
Eh . . . whoever loves a dark-haired man
Whoever loves a dark-haired man
Whoever loves a dark-haired man, *marouli*
Better declare it
Whoever loves a dark-haired man, *marouli*
Better declare it
Because when you're in love
When you're in love, *marouli*
There's a price to pay

Additional verses:

Your beautiful ones have gone
And your joys have also fled
Oh poor Kalymnos, *marouli*
Your mountains are in mourning.

Dance Songs and Metric Forms

Table singing may be punctuated with dancing, or vice versa. At the Tsimouris home, bagpiping inevitably led into dancing, in the measured issos meter, or with slow songs being sped up to transition into a *sousta*. All dances are performed by two or more dancers—often a roomful—progressing with linked arms counterclockwise in an arc.

Tsambouna music is played primarily for dancing, and Nikitas paced along with the dancers as he set the complex seven- and thirteen-beat rhythms. From our first recording session in the Tsimouris's kitchen, it was clear that he was at his best when playing off of the singers and dancers. Nikitas explained that a bagpiper should stand in the middle of the dancers and keep pace with the leader so that the leader would not lose his steps. This places the orchestra at the center of the dance, a typically African arrangement. "At a dance the bagpiper is supposed to control the dance, and listen to the singer and watch the singer. He measures himself with the singer, who dances and sings at the same time."

The Tsimouris family sang as they danced, their stamping feet, clapping, rhythmic whistling, and calls of "opa" making up the rhythm section of their little orchestra. The pismatika also provide rhythmic texture and drive, and the women often broke out into pismatika rapping in the excitement of dancing. Occasionally, Nikitas would hold the air pressure with his arms while singing a line or two of a song himself. As mentioned above, singing while playing is also common in the gaida music of Thrace and Bulgaria.

Dances are named and classified by rhythm, and every tune has a rhythmic designation. They are also described by the number of steps in each measure. The issos has five steps and is written in 2/4 time. Its tempo is slow to very slow. It is danced smoothly ("flat"), without any bounce. The sousta is a speeded-up version of the issos and is danced with short, springing hops and kicks; it can become quite wild. The word "sousta" derives from an Italian word for the springs of a carriage (Dietrich 1976). The issos and the sousta have become the typical dances of the Dodecanese, but each island has its own style.

The *kotikos* or *yialla* is a dance and song from Kos in issos meter. Nikitas and his sisters said that "yialla" was an old form of greeting. Because the song is from Kos, which was under heavy Turkish occupation and influence, there is an outside possibility that the phrase derives from the Arabic *Ya Allah*, which means "Dear God" or "God help me," a form of salutation. Alternating leaders and chorus sing while dancing and clapping.

Tsakisma [refrain]: *E . . . dos tous, Pana—yia mou, dos tous chronia*
San tis lemonias ta klonia
Leader 1: *E . . . Thee megalodiname*
Yiala! Megalo t'onome, megalo to onoma sou
Leader 2: *E megalo diname*
With group: *Megalo to onoma sou!*
Leader 1: *E . . . dos tous, Pana—yia mou, dos tous,*
T' achei o nous to logismos tous
Group: *Dos tous, Pana—yia mou, dos tous,*
T' achei o nous to logismos tous
(Each couplet is repeated by the leader, then a second leader and/or the group:)
E . . . filo den peftei apo dendri, yiala!
Horis to theli—, horis to thelima sou
E . . . s'agapo yia—ti ise oreos
O den tou miazi allos neos
Opa!
Echoun kero ta matia mou, yiala
Na doune ta, na doune ta dika sou
E . . . ela me to tachidromo
O pou 'nai grigora sto dromo
E . . . ki' echoun parapono frichto, yiala
Na klapsoune bro—, na klapsoune brosta sou

E . . . ela ela, me ta mena
E ki'as ti mana pou se yenna!
Opa!
Kho!
A . . . stin emprostela tou horou, yiala
Kai paraki, kai paraki ligaki
[Omitted] *Stekete mia miskakarfia / Me to mesimeraki*
A . . . Ki' vlepe mou tous, Panayia mou
O pou n'einai i pa—rigoria mou]
A . . . stekete mia ga—, garifalo,
Me to mesime—, me to mesimeraki
Stekete mia ga—, garifalo, yiala
Me to garifale, me to garifalaki
Op!
A . . . dos tis, Panayia, chronakia
San tou diosmou, o ta klonaikia
(Dancing and clapping continues)
Op!
Op!
Op!
Op!
Op!
Opa!
Op! Opa!
Op!
Opa, opa, opa!

Eh . . . give them, Holy Mother, give them as many years
As the lemon tree has branches
Eh . . . almighty God
Yialla! Great is your name, great is your name!
And great is your power
Great is your name!
Eh . . . give them, Holy Mother, give them
Give them reason in their minds (repeat)
Eh . . . A leaf doesn't fall from the tree, *yialla!*
Without, without Your wish
Eh . . . I love you because you're handsome
Oh other youths don't compare with you
My eyes have time to look at you, *yialla!*
To see, to see what's theirs
Eh . . . let the mail come soon

Oh may it be quick upon the road
Eh . . . and they [my eyes] have bitter complaints
To weep to you
Eh . . . come, come to be mine [come to me?]
Eh . . . and leave the mother who bore you
Ah . . . at the edge of town [there's a guy], *yialla*
And just over there, just over there a little
Stands a carnation
With a sunflower [?]
Ah . . . and watch over him, my Holy Mother
Oh, for he's my consolation
There stands a carnation
With the scented blossoms [?]
Ah . . . give them, Holy Mother, as many of those years
As the mint has little shoots

Also notable was an issos performed one evening when the group met at the little theater of the Tarpon Springs Cultural Center. Here, their serpentine line dancing had full scope, and one can hear the sounds of their feet measuring the 2/4 beat of the issos on the boards. The prolonged, haunting prelude functions to stabilize the airflow from the bag through the pipes, creates suspense and anticipation, and allows the singers to prepare.

They followed this with a sousta performed on tsambouna, with clapping, dancing, stamping, loud whistling, and singing pismatika:

Opa
Opa
Leader: *Den eimai se diathesi*
Yia na tragoudiso
Hatiri tis pareas mou
Pali tha to kiniso (2)
Group: *Pali tha to kiniso*
Ela ela ela, mikri mou ela
Ela pou na se feroune
Nekro sti yitonia mou
Kai na se saranone
Ta cheria ta dika mou (**Repeat verse**)
Christe mou ki as iprovale
Ena voskarouaki
Me to mantili sto lemo
Kai me t' aginaraki
Pismatika kai pismata

Se mena den pernoune
Yiati ime elefthero pedi
Kai me parakouloune
Den eimai se diathesi
To kefi mou ine ligo
Yiati den to 'da simera
To kokkino mou milo
Matia fridia kai mallia
Pou t'achi to pouli mou
Ine kai pismatariko
Kai 'kopse ti zoi mou
Thee megalodiname
Pou miazis tis kardias mou
Kane ta sinefa vrochi
Na svisis ti fotia mou
Coda: *Osi den horevoune*
Ine pou zilevoune.

I'm not in the mood
For dancing
But to bring enjoyment to my companions
I will do it anyway
I will do it anyway
Come, come, come, my girl, come on
Come on, let them bring you
Dead into my neighborhood
So I can wrap you with mourning bandages
With my own hands
My Christ I wish he would appear
A little shepherd lad
With a scarf around his neck
And a staff in his hand
Your wisecracks and retorts
Don't bother me
Because I'm a carefree guy
And they're begging me [to marry their daughters]
I'm not in the mood for dancing
I'm not feeling very inspired
Because today I haven't seen
My little red apple
The eyes, brows, and hair
Of my little bird

They are something to talk about
And they tear me apart
God all mighty
Who knows my heart
Make the clouds rain
To put out my fire
Those who don't dance
Don't dance because they're jealous.

The syrtos uses twelve steps and is in 4/4 time, making a slow three-beat and quick two-beat pattern. Of ancient origin and enjoyed also by the Ottomans, it is popular throughout Greece and the diaspora; each island, region, and city has its own variant. The *kalamatianos* syrtos originated in the southern Peloponnese, where the first battles for independence from the Ottomans were fought, and is one of the oldest Greek dances. It uses the same steps and slow three-beat, two-beat two-beat rhythm as the syrtos but is in 7/8 time—one of the complex additive rhythms used in Greece and the Balkans. In some areas, the syrtos is performed by couples dancing in a circle. The Kalymnians have their own version, but Nikitas preferred the *kritikos* syrtos from Crete. In "To Argalio" (The Loom), each line is sung by a leader and repeated by the group.

Kori pou fe—, kori pou fenis st'argalio (2)
Kai fenis kai ksefenis, kai to nou mou esi ton pernis (2)
Spase, Thee-, spase Thee mou t'argalio (2)
N'avgo na kano volta, na tin ne do stin porta (2)
Kori, s'an pas, kori s'an pas stin ekklisia (2)
Proskena kai yia mena, proskena kai yia mena (2)
Yia na sothoun, yia na sothoun ta pismata,
Pou s'oukho kano mena, proskena kai yia mena (2)
Panathema, panathema tin mana sou (2)
Kai mena tin dikia mou, kai emena tin dikia mou (2)
Kori pou fe-, kori pou fenis t'argalio (2)
Kai fenis kai ksefenis, kai to nou mou esi ton pernis (2)
Pismatika, pismatika kai pismata (2)
Se mena den pairnoune, se mena den pairnoune (2)
Yiati ime, yiati ime elefthero paidi (2)
Kai me perikaloune kai me perikaloune (2)
A pane na pis, pane na pis sti mana sou (2) **(Man to woman or vice versa)**
Na kani kai alli yenna, na kani alli yenna (2)
(Laughter)
Yia na kapsei ki' a-, na kapsi allinis kardia (2)
Os ekapse emena, na kani alli yenna (2) **(Or repeat 1st phrase of line)**

(Discussion)
(Man says to girl:)
Panathema, panathemame kai an holio (2)
Pou s' icha k' ichasa se, pou s' icha k' ichasa se
Mono holio, mono holio, tous kerous mou
To diko mou k' icha s' ase, pou s' echa k' ichasa se
Pou 'rchomoun ki' vriskase

Additional verses:

Panathena ti mana sou kai mena, kai mena ti dikia mou (2)
Pou den mas padrevase, na sou tora dikia mou (2)

Pismatika:
Kai me parakaloume
Pane na pis stis mana sou
Na kani kai alli yena
Yan a kapsi ki'allinis kardia
Os ekapsen emena

O girl weaving, weaving at the loom
Your constant weaving drives me crazy
Break, break the loom, Lord
So I can go out and see her at her door
Girl, if you go to church
Bow down and pray for [to?] me too
So they'll talk, talk and gossip
About what I've done to you, that you bow to me
Curses, curses on your mother
And on mine, and on mine
Girl, girl, weaving at the loom
You weave and weave and you take over my mind
[Talk, talk and wisecracking
Don't bother me]
[Look at me!] I'm a single man
And they're begging me [they're after me]
Ah, go tell your mother
To give birth to another like you
So she can burn another heart
The way mine burns—let her make another like you
Damn me if I'll grieve—
I had you and then I lost you

I only regret my old times
And the one I had that I lost
Damn your mother and damn mine
For not marrying us so you would be mine now

Wedding Songs and Cradle Songs

The traditional wedding cycle was long and many faceted, extending over days and weeks. We recorded as much of it as the family remembered, beginning with "Penemata tis Nifis" (In Praise of the Bride), a song addressed to the bride before her wedding. Early in the morning before proceeding to the church, female relatives and friends go to the bride's house and gather in her bedroom while she dresses or is being dressed by an experienced woman. At another point in the preparations, praises are also sung to the groom (*gambros*). The women sang unaccompanied, with leaders and group in alternation; Nikitas joined in at the end.

I nifi mas i omorfi ipofaneromeni (2)
Epire 'n andra emorfo, tin ekhei haidemeni (2)
I mana ta se yenise evriskonda sta ori
Ki' troye rises tou vounou kai kame tetia kori (2)
Gambros einai o neo aetos ki' i nifi peristeri (2)
Kai ta anikta garifala i nei simpetheri (2)
Nifi to velos sou evales, vale kai ti tsimpida (2)
Ki' omorfia sou graftike kai mes tin efimerida (2)
Gabre mou drosere flaste n'apo ton abelona
Na se hari i nifi mas s' ollo o neona (2)
Nifi, s'an se stoulosane stis ekklisias sti mesi (2)
Kouniodou o polieleos sti yi kato na pesi (2)
Gabre zouboulli chiotiko nifis smirnias vio—lenda (2)
Nifi tis fronimades sou tis kanane kouvenda (2)
Nikitas: *Nifi s'an se stolisane stis ekklisias sti mesi (2)*
Mikri megali t'opane hara tis pou ton echei (2)
Nikitas: *Gabre tin nifi n'agapas kai na mi tin egogizeis (2)*
San to vasiliko tis yis na tin drosologhizeis (2)
Fokaina: *Tha poume alli?* [**spoken:** Shall we sing another verse?]
Gabre ti nifi n'agapas kai mi ti ne malonis
Kai na travas to paploma kai na ti koukoulonis (2)
(Laughter)
Nomiki A.: *Kala ikseromi.* [We remembered well.]
Our beautiful bride is shown everywhere
She got a handsome husband, and he has her spoiled

The mother who bore you was found in the mountains
Eating mountain roots, and she made such a daughter
The groom is the young eagle, the bride is the dove
And the new in-laws are the carnations in bloom
Bride you wore your scarf—put on your veil as well
And they will write about your beauty in the newspaper too
My groom is a fresh grapevine in the vineyard
Let him give joy to our bride all of her life
Bride, if they stood you in the middle of the church
All the hanging oil lamps would fall to the ground
Groom, blooming flower of Chios; bride, violet of Smyrna
Bride, they are extolling your virtues
Bride if they stood you in the middle of the church—
Young and old, we would all wish him happiness
Groom, you better love your bride and not mistreat her
Water her like the basil plant
Groom, you better love your bride and don't scold her
Cover her up in a quilt and cuddle her

The first dance of the wedding is the issos. The very last dance is the *parianos*, also in issos rhythm. It is a rite of farewell to the bride in which she crosses over to the groom's side. Originating from the island of Paros, it is a very slow dance, similar to the issos but sung only at weddings in the early morning hours. First the bride's family dances, then her husband's goes: the father of the bride begins, then the bride dances, followed by the bride's mother, her mother-in-law, and lastly the other relatives. In the parianos, improvised and stock verses are followed by refrains, here repeated to the near exclusion of other text, leader and group singing each line twice in alternation.

> *E . . . i ormorfi pou einai nifi mas, melachrini komati (2)*
> **Tsakismata:** *O Panayia dos tous chronia / San tis limonias ta klonia (2)*
> *O san ta triandafila, trianda—fila podio sto mati (2)*
> **Tsakismata:** *Dos tous Panayia mou chronia / San tis limonias ta klonia (2)*
> *Vrisko vayia sto gabro louloudi ton angelo (2)*
> *Panayia mou, Panayia mou, dos ayera tis kardias mou (2)*
> *Malamatenia einai klidi pou aniyi to evangelio (2)*
> **Tsakismata:** *Panayia dos tous chronia / San tis limonias ta klonia (2)*
> *I nifi mas einai frondi pou erchete me ti vora (2)*
> **Tsakismata:** *Dos tous Panayia chronaikia / San tou diosmou ta klonakia (2)*
> *San strapsis stin anatoli tha feksi mesa i hora*
> **Tsakismata:** *Panayia mou pou t' avlaki, me to neo zevgaraki (2)*

246

E ... i mana sa se yenise evrisketo sta ori (2)
Tsakismata: Panayia dos tous chronia / San tis limonias ta klonia (2)
Kai etroye ri—ses kai stou vounou ki 'kame tetia kore (2)
Tsakismata: Panayia mou, Panayia mou, dos aera tis kardias mou (2)
E ... Apo mesa pou ti Kalimno irthe ena peristeri (2)
(Sung like refrain:) *To matio sou to mavradi, zotani me pai ston Adi*
E ki' fanose i perdika kai yina nea tairi (2)
... (cuts off)

Additional verses, omitted:

E ... tin omorfi tis yitonias t'ipofaneromeni
E simera fanoseme perdika ploumismeni
Kai smikse me ti perdika ka yinei san tairi
Panayia, pou khorizei, vlepetei pou kseyorizei]

Eh ... How beautiful is our bride, our dark-eyed one
Tsakismata: O Holy Mother give them years
As many as the lemon tree has branches
Oh like two roses, her eyes are two roses on a stem
Tsakismata: O Holy Mother, etc.
[*Vrisko vayia sto gabro louloudi ton angelo* (untranslated)]
Tsakismata: My Holy Mother, Holy Mother, give my heart ease
Golden are the keys to the Gospels
Tsakismata: Holy Mother give them years, etc.
Our bride is the thunder that comes with the storm
Tsakismata: Give them as many sweet years
As there are shoots on the mint
Like lightning in the east, she lights up the town
Tsakismata: My Holy Mother on the porch
With the new young couple
Eh ... your mother gave birth to you, and [they found you] in the mountains
Tsakismata: Holy Mother give them years, etc.
Eh ... Down into Kalymnos came a dove [young man]
(*Sung like refrain:*) The pupils of your eyes
Send me straight to Hell [drive me crazy]
Eh, a partridge appeared and there was a new mating

Additional verses, omitted:

Eh ... the beauty of the neighborhood, and one who shows the most

Eh, today a plumed partridge appeared
And alighted with the [female] partridge and became her mate
Holy Mother, why part them? She's the most beautiful.

The *kritikos skopos* (Cretan rhythm) segues from the parianos. Sung by the group, with clapping, laughter, and pismatika, this table song in the form of Cretan-style mantinades is very popular in Kalymnos. It is another song that comes at the end of weddings, when the family sits around the bride and groom and sings to them. Two leaders alternate, sometimes with the group coming at the end of a line or repeating each single line. These are couplets, of which each line is repeated, and sometimes the last phrase of the first line is repeated yet again by the leader. "Every word has a special meaning [*echoun noima*]," said Mrs. Tsimouris.

Refrain (**with laughter**):
Leader 1: A, na ne stenakso ithela (2)
Kai fovoume a mi pothano [sic] (2)
Leader 2: Ida ton kosmo hano (3)
Leader 2: M' archise glossa m' archise, tragoudise kardia mou (2)
Leader 2: Tragoudise kardia mou,
Leader 2: Yia na penes—, yia na penes, (**with group:**)*—so to kormi mou (2)*
Pou ine dipla mou
Leader 1: Tralalala lalala
Leader 1: Kenouria agapi ka pallia me valane sti mesi (2)
Leader 3: Strifoyirizo [kai vlepo] *ti palia, kenourio den m'aresi (2)*
Otan matia ti kardia rotoun, "Kardia mou 'nta 'chis lipi?" (2)
"Kardia mou 'nt 'acheis lipi?"
"Stravaste kai de' vlepete t' ateri mou pos lipi?" (2)
Matia kai fridia kai mallia, kai zakharenio stoma (2)
Leader: Kai zakharenio stoma
Group: E, lala lalu lulula, tralalala lalala
Nato i thalassa steria na echei kai parathiria (**twice, with leaders alternating**)
Kai ela ela na, na echei kai parathiria
Na vlepa to poulaki mou, sta matia kai sta fridia (2) (**girl talking about a man**)
Nato i thalassa steria na tin iperpatousa (2)
Na tin iperpatousa
N' archomouna na se damona chili kai me kratousa
As imouna aeroplano na peto ston aera (2)
Na peto ston aera
N' archomouna se damona mia n'ora tin i mera (2)
Vasanismeno mou kormi, tiranimeno soma (2)
Tiranimeno soma
Pote tha se skepasone i petres kai to homa? (2)

Otan se protognorisa "thio" m' iches fonaksi (2)
Kai tora ti kardoula mou m' echis katasparaksi (2)
Tralalala . . . **(laughter)**
Ta matia sou einai kafenes, ta fridia sou balkoni (2)
Pou 'rchounde kai glendizoune i meraklides oli (2)

Additional verses:

Archise glossa mou, archise, tragoudia n' aradiazeis
Kai tin kali parea mas na tin diaskedaseis.

I wanted to sigh
And I was afraid I would die
I saw I was losing the world [losing my mind]
I brought forth my words [loosened my tongue] and my heart sang
My heart sang
In praise of that being who is beside me
Tralalala lalala
Between a new love and an old one they put me
I twist and turn to look at my old love
And I don't care about the new one
When my eyes ask my heart,
"Heart, haven't you missed her?"
"Heart, haven't you missed her?"
"Are you blind, don't you see my mate [the girl's heart] is missing?
And eyes, brows, and hair, and mouth sweet like sugar
And mouth sweet like sugar
Eh, lala lala lalala, tralalala lalala."
If the wide sea had windows *(twice, with leaders alternating)*
And come on, come on, if it had windows
So I could see my little bird [my man], his eyes and his brows
If I had to journey the wide seas
If I had to journey far
I would come to meet you even if a thousand held on to me
If I were an airplane taking off into the sky
Taking off into the sky
I would come to meet you for an hour every day
My being is troubled, my body is tormented
My body is tormented
When will they throw stones and earth on you?
When I first met you, you called me "Uncle"
And now you have broken my little heart

Tralalala
Your eyes are brown, your brows are balconies
Where the devotees go and party

Additional verses:

Start singing, bring forth a song
So this good company of ours can be entertained

One of the most beautiful songs in the family's repertoire, remembered only by the older women, was the wedding serenade, "Mera Merose" (Day Has Dawned), here performed as a table song by the group accompanied on the tsambouna. Niki Sazalis explained that a mixed group of five to ten singers, unaccompanied or with *violi*, performed this ritual serenade at dawn at the bride's house (usually given to her by her father), in which the bride and groom spent their first night together. It can also be sung when the wedding is over and the guests have left. In that case, the closest relatives and friends sit in a circle around the bride and groom and process through these long poetic lines. Its fifteen-syllable lines are sung in the meter of classical Greek song. The heavily accented irregular rhythm, and the prolongation of lines and verses by means of partial repetition of the text, mark an antique style that is fast becoming a rarity. Group singing was led by Fokaina Skandaliaras and Nomiki A. Tsimouris.

Sose
Mera merose tora ki'—, tora ki' avyi harazi
Tora ke— [—laidoun], tora ta,
Tora ta poulia
Tora ta
Tora ta, tora ta
Tora ta poulia
Tora ta helidonia
Tora i pe—
Tora i pe—, tora i perdikes
Tora i pe—
Tora i pe—, tora i perdi—kes,
Tora i perdikes, tora i perdikopoules
Tora ke—
Tora kela—
Tora kelaidoun
Tora ke—,
Tora kela—aidoun
Tora kelaidoun, tora—laloun kai lene
Ksipna, afe—

Ksipna, afe—, Ksipna, afendi mou
Ksipna, afe—, Ksipna, afendi mou
Ksipna, afendi mou
Ksipna, kale mou afendi
Ksipna anga—
Ksipna angalia—
Ksipna angaliase
Ksipna anga—
Ksipna angalia—ase
Ksipna angaliase
Kormi kiparissenio
Ki' aspro le—
Ki' aspro mele—
Ki' aspro melemo
Ki' aspro mele—mo
Ki' aspro mele—mo
[Stithuria] san to hioni
Aspri li—, aspri lighe—, aspri ligeri

Day is breaking, and now dawn comes
And now they call out
Now the birds
Now the
Now the, now the
Now the birds
Now the swallows
Now the partridges
Now the pa—
Now the pa—, now the partridges
Now the partridges, now the little partridges
Now they cr—
Now they cr—
Now they cry out
Now they cry—
Now they call out
Now they cry, now they call out
Awake, lord
Awake, lord, awake, my lord
Awake, lord, awake, my lord
Awake, my lord
Awake and em—
Awake and embrace

That body like a cypress tree
And white thro—
And white marble throat
And white marble throat
And white marble throat
And breasts like the snow
White form, white form (*ligeri* untranslated)

The daughters and granddaughters of the Tsimouris family were raised with *nanourismata*, cradle-rocking songs, and say they sing to their own babies.[5] "I was in kindergarten," young Irene recalled, "and if my mom or dad didn't come up and tap me and sing [lullabies] to me, I wouldn't go to sleep. My dad used to tell me stories about *o yeros* ['The Old Man,' a child's fable]." In peasant homes, the baby slept in a wooden cradle that hung from a rope suspended across the matrimonial bed so that he or she could be near the parents and could be rocked easily during the night. Sleep is personified as in many southern European lullabies and is called to take the child away and bring him back "refreshed and tall like a cypress tree." Fokaina takes the lead in singing the verses of a nanourisma in alternation with the two Nomikis. Between verses, Nikitas, Fokaina, and others present make joking comments and mimic the baby's cries. Unaccompanied solo, with occasional group singing in alternation.

Kai yemises tous korfous tou me triandafila kai roda yia na kani
(adult mimicking baby cries)
Ela Ipne mou, kai par to kai pare to sta pervolia
(cries)
Apo kato pou ti lemonia, na kovi ta lemonia
Nani nani nani na—ani
To moro mou ya na kani [sic]
Ipne pou pairnis ta mora, pa—re kai to diko mou
Na mou ton fernis drosero, psilos san kiparissi
Nana nani, nani na—ni
To pedaki mou na kani
Nikitas (spoken): *Vre yineka, ti ha kanis? Tha merosis to pedi—ti tha kanis?*
(laughter)
Na mou to fernis drosero, psi—los san kiparissi
Nikitas (spoken): *Piase rizase to!*
Na mou ton **(breaks off laughing)**
(Various comments)
Na mou to feris drosero psi—lo san kiparissi
Kai na mou to zilevoune s' anatoli kai disi
Nani nani, to moro mou, na kimiso to mikro mou
(cries)

Nikitas (**spoken**): *Alakse to moro! Katouremeno ine, mori!*
Ela Ipne mou, pare to pa—ne sta pervolia
Apo kato tis lemonies, na pezi ta lemonia
Nani nani to moro
E . . . eh!
Nomiki A. (**spoken**): *Sava, . . . (inaudible) nanourisma na kimate*
Nani nani to 'Rinio mou
(**cries**)
Fokaina (**spoken in falsetto**): *Sopa na kimithis, kane nani, kanenani!*
Nani, tou riga tou pedi, tou vasilia t' angoni
Na to kounia i Pana—yia, me to chriso sendoni
Nani nani to pedi mas
Na mi kopsi ti zoi mas
Nikitas (**spoken**): *"Klei kai den boro na kimitho, den katalevenis?"*
Fokaina: "Ti tou kano tora to pedi? To riksome okso?"
Nikitas: Grepsato!
Fokaina: To kero pou t' ekanes den to ikseres? Theli na kimithi. Pas stin alli kamera ki' eki kimitho!"
(**laughter, whispering**)
Kimate o ilios sta vouna, ki' perdika sto dasi
Kimate to pedaki mou, ton ipno na hortasei
Nani nani nani na—ni
To pedaki mou to ka—ni
(**spoken**):
Nomiki A.: Endaksi
Nikitas: Kai katourise pali.
Nomiki A.: Pa na to sfougizeis!
Kimate o ilios sta vouna, ki' perdika sta dasi
Kimate to Ianaki mou, ton ipno na hortasi
Nani nani nani na, ipno elafri na kani
Nani nani nani nanaki
Ela Ipne sti kounia tou, stavre stin kefali tou
Ki' Ai mou Pandelemona fil—ayie ti zoi tou
En an a-a-a-e . . .
Kamu e-e-e . . .
Ai mou Pandelemona kai—si Kira Psili mou
Vlepeis to Savaki mou pou—kopse ti zoi mou
Kami e-e-e-e!
(**spoken**): *Etsi tha kimisi tora, kakomira . . .*

And you filled his bodice with roses and pomegranate flowers
So that he would sleep

Come my Sleep, and take him, take him to the orchard
Under the lemon trees, so he can cut lemons
Sleepy, sleep sleep
Let my baby sleep
Sleep, you who takes all the babies, take mine
Bring him back to me fresh, tall as a cypress tree
Sleep, sleep, sleep
Let my little one sleep
Nikitas: Woman, what are you doing? Will you quiet the child?
Bring him back to me fresh, tall as a cypress
Nikitas: Take him and give him the breast!
Bring him back—
Bring him back fresh, tall as a cypress
So they'll envy me him from east to west
Sleep, sleep my baby, let my little one sleep
Nikitas: Change the kid! He peed himself!
Come, my Sleep, take him to the orchard
Under the lemon trees, to play with the lemons
Sleep, sleep, the baby
E . . . eh!
Nomiki A.: Lullaby to sleep . . .
Sleep, sleep my Rini **(teasingly to Irene, her teenage daughter)**
Fokaina: Come now, sleep! Go on off to sleep!
Nanni, child of the lord, grandchild of the king
Let the Holy mother rock him, in golden sheets
Sleep, sleep, our own child
Don't scare the life out of us
(spoken):
Nikitas: He's crying and I can't sleep, don't you see?
Fokaina: What do you want me to do with the child? Throw him outside?
Nikitas: Get rid of him!
Fokaina: The time you made him didn't you realize? You want to sleep—go into the
other room and sleep!
The sun is sleeping in the mountains, the partridge in the woods
My little baby's sleeping, let him sleep until he's satisfied
Nani nanni nanni na—ni
My little baby's sleeping
(spoken):
Nomiki A.: Alright . . .
Nikitas: Now he's peed again!
Nomiki A.: You wipe him up!
The sun is sleeping in the mountains, the partridge in the woods

My little Johnny's sleeping, let him sleep until he's satisfied
Sleep, sleep, sleep, let him have a carefree sleep
Nanni nanni nanni nannaki
Come, Sleep, into his cradle, make the cross on his forehead
And my Saint Panteleimon [saint of healing] watch over him
En an a-a-a-e . . .
Go to e-e-e
My Saint Panteleimon, and you my Tall Lady[6]
See my little Sava, who gives me such a fright
Go, go to sle-e-e-ep!
(**spoken**): There, he'll sleep now, poor thing . .

Immigration

"Diosmari" is a sorrowful lament to Kalymnos addressing the loss of the island's young men, its most precious resource, to emigration. Its poetry is laid out on long melodic phrases carried forward by strong, irregular pulses, in which held notes and melismatic passages alternate with triplets. The text also belongs to "Marouli" (see the translation above), a table song usually accompanied on tsambouna or violi. Nomiki A. Tsimouris's renditions of this song were much requested at Kalymnian parties. I first heard it when a visiting radio producer requested an immigration song. I thought I had heard all of the family's songs, so this was a reminder of the surprising depths of the folk repertoire in long-continuous, stable traditions such as that of the Dodecanese, where there is always more poetry, always another song.

A mou kaimeni Kalimnos
Diosmaraki mou
O, mavrisan ta vouna sou
Sigana, sigana, sigana kai tapina
Efige i levendia sou
Efige i chara sou
Sigana, sigana, sigana kai tapina
Den boro ta matia mou
Diosmaraki mou
O psila ta sikosa
Sigana, sigana, sigana kai tapina

Ah, my poor Kalymnos
My sweet mint
Your mountains have turned black

255

Softly, softly, softly I tread the earth
Your young men have departed
My sweet mint
Your heart's joys have fled
Softly, softly, softly I tread the earth
My eyes can't bear it
My sweet mint
Oh I grew them tall,
Softly, softly, softly I tread the earth

Of Songs and Sponges

"Why do Kalymnians sing songs from other islands?" I asked Nikitas as he sat at the kitchen table one afternoon. "Long ago, Kalymnians were sponge fishermen [*sfoungarades*]," he replied. "They sailed to all the islands and brought their songs back to Kalymnos, and we made them our own." Nikitas continued:

In those years, in the days of my father, when they came back from the sponge fisheries in September bringing in the sponges, they would bring a song—one each year. All the songs that they sing in these islands around, we sing better in Kalymnos, because the Kalymnians knew how to party [*glendousane*], and they especially liked to dance. In Kos, for example, they did not. The Kotes sang these songs differently.... These are simple songs, not made by educated people. But they are better, because all that you have inside of you, you put into song. My grandmother lived to ninety-nine years and she danced the sousta. If you want to live a long time you must sing inside yourself. You must not be sorrowful. You must know all the songs, and keep them in your mind. That is the way I am.

(recited:)

Den kleo ego ton pethameno	I don't weep, for the dead
Oute otan pethano	Not even when I die
Kleo monacha leyo	I only weep when I wonder:
Edo sta skotina monachos ti tha kano?	Alone in the dark [of hell], what shall I do?
Etsi to apofasisa	And so I decided
Kai etsi tha to kano	And that's what I will do:
Tha pino kai tha tragoudo	I will drink and I will sing
Eos sou tha pethano.	Until the day I die.

Anna Lomax Wood

Cultural Transmission: The Ebb and Flow of Greek Life in Tarpon Springs

With over a hundred kinfolk and relatives by marriage in Tarpon Springs alone, the Tsimourises do not lack for society, and they circulate in a continual round of life-cycle celebrations, church lunches, and Kalymnian Society dinners and festivities. When I met them they were living in very modest circumstances and worked hard, but they were serene and exuberant and projected a sense of enormous satisfaction with the progress of their lives. When I asked Mrs. Tsimouris, who was the conscious keeper of the family ethos, about the source of their happiness, she attributed it to their fulfilling their duties as Kalymnian Greeks in the familial, community, and spiritual arenas, and particularly with respect to the conduct of courtship, marriage, and observances for the dead.

The family saw themselves as doubly fortunate to be directly engaged with the artistic traditions that symbolize and reinforce their Dodecanese heritage and identity as well as their ties to Kalymnos. These they have repeatedly renewed through extended stays and new bonds of marriage. Their circumstances allowed them to initiate a new coming-of-age rite, in which the young girls of the family were taken to Kalymnos when they were of an age to begin thinking of courtship and marriage. Whether this produced marriages or not, it had the effect of further binding the young Greek Americans to their Greek identity. It also brought them into generational synchrony with the youth culture of Greece in ways that were highly rewarding and pleasurable. Even the conservative Mrs. Tsimouris fully collaborated in allowing the young people a full and fairly unrestricted nightlife of clubbing and dancing, both in Tarpon and on Kalymnos. A more effervescent group of young people, or more fulfilled adults, would be difficult to find in the United States.

Thus the Tsimourises are energetic, engaged, and upstanding people. They raised flourishing, happy children who have tried new paths but have remained securely anchored in the family and community orbit. Inveterate Greek traditionalists, they are at the same time adaptable and flexible, always learning how to make the best of several worlds and how to make their island culture work in interesting ways wherever they are.

Does this sound too good to be true? Of course, like any other, the family has had its dramas and its problems, but while I lived among the Tsimourises as neighbor, quasi-family member, and ethnographer over seven years, they manifested a high level of functioning. It must be said, however, that I entered their orbit at a particularly happy conjunction between the degree of assimilation the family had achieved in the United States and the degree to which Greek village custom had, for them, maintained its moral force and idealized appeal, but had lost most of its fearsome disciplinary power. The Florida community was small, low key, and physically and socially unified, yet it had few of the inconveniences and restrictions of village life in Greece. These conditions and balances will inevitably change, but the people who lived through this phase of Kalymnian adaptation will influence at least two more generations.

The Greeks of Tarpon Springs are active in and on behalf of their traditions. Children are immersed in the Greek Orthodox religion, in Greek language taught daily at the church school and often spoken at home, and in Greek regional folk arts, particularly dancing, with several dance groups practicing and performing in the community at any one time. However, the little lyra, violi, or tsambouna orchestras with singing that used to accompany dancing have been replaced by pan-island and Panhellenic electric popular live and recorded music. Tsambouna music is considered antiquated, but at least as long as Nikitas was alive it continued to serve as a focal point at weddings and other community events. Much more endangered was the beautiful and unusual repertoire of vocal music and accompanying poetry performed in an antique style. The women who knew the songs were growing old, and the younger ones were only learning them partially at best.

Even so, there is continued interest in traditional music among some young Greek Americans in Tarpon Springs. It would therefore still be possible to encourage the Kalymnians to incorporate the songs and singing styles represented in this collection into their repertoire and performance practice, which could in consequence become more meaningful and interesting. One immense educational and spiritual benefit would be that of learning and absorbing the prosody of the singing and the poetry of the lyrics.

Public Outcome

The National Endowment for the Arts funded my original research project as documentation with a public outcome. Accordingly, the recording phase was followed by a period of public outreach resulting in more exposure for the folk artists and their musical traditions both locally and abroad. Nikitas and his family were featured in newspaper articles and a television program on ethnic traditions. During the much-celebrated Greek Independence Week of 1995 the Tsimourises performed at the Tarpon Springs Cultural Center, introduced by Nikitas's daughter Irene. Nikitas Kavouklis, a beginning Florida Folklife Program apprentice under his great-uncle, played tsambouna. At the 1996 Florida Folk Festival, the two demonstrated the outcome of the apprenticeship. The family performed at the Pinellas County Heritage Park Festival in Largo in September 1996, and again in May 1997 at the Florida Folk Festival in White Springs. One of their recordings was included in *The Florida Music Train*, a curriculum with CD for schools arranged by the Florida Folklife Program. The program notes for these presentations were made available to the family and presenting organizations for their future use. Copies of the original recordings were placed in the archives of

Figure 68. Nomiki Makarounes Tsimouris (left) singing with Nomiki A. Tsimouris (middle) and Fokaina Tsimouris Skandaliaras (right). Photo by Anna Lomax Chairetakis Wood.

the City of Tarpon Springs and of the Florida Folklife Program, and copies of the recordings and photographs were given to the participants.

About the Singers

The main ensemble of singers and bagpiper consisted of Nomiki Tsimouris, Nikitas's wife (vocal and clapping); Nomiki A. Tsimouris, Nikitas's sister (vocal and clapping); Fotini (Fokaina) Skandaliaras, youngest sister (vocal, songs, and stories); and Nikitas Tsimouris (tsambouna). Dancers, who also provided musical accompaniment with their stamping feet, whistles, and calls of "opa," were Nikitas's daughter Irene, who lived at home; sometimes his married daughter, Niki Sazalis, and/or her children, Nomiki and Petroula (Patty) Sazalis; and other visitors.

Nomiki Tsimouris née Makarounas was born in Skalia, Kalymnos, in 1935. She came from a shepherd family and village, and her father had a flock of three hundred sheep. In Tarpon Springs, Nomiki worked for many years at a small warehouse cutting sponges and as a housekeeper in a hotel, rising at 3:00 a.m. to make bread and cookies at a local bakery. She is known for her firm religious principles, her observance of custom, and her propriety and correctness in family and social affairs. She has four children, ten grandchildren, and three great-grandchildren.

Nomiki Antoniou Tsimouris (1928–2010) was born in Hora, Kalymnos. She went to work as a maid for a well-to-do family at age six and was not sent to school.

Unable to raise a dowry, she stayed single and cared for her mother, who died in Tarpon Springs at age eighty-two. Nomiki emigrated to Tarpon Springs in 1970, where she worked for many years cutting sponges. She retired in 1992, supplementing her tiny income by taking care of elderly people, boarding the occasional sponge buyer or visitor, and cooking for parties, where her singing was in demand.

Fotini (Fokaina) Skandaliaras née Tsimouris was born in Hora, Kalymnos, in 1931 and emigrated to Tarpon Springs in 1970. Her husband, like many Kalymnian men, made a good living as a bridge painter, traveling on jobs all over the country. They had four children. Fokaina, who rarely went out except to church, was shy and soft spoken. She had a special gift for remembering and telling fairy tales, the lives of saints and holy men, and stories about the old days, *ta chronia*.

Another sister, Maria Ellinas, was an approving and supportive presence at the recording sessions even though, being a widow, she could not be persuaded to fully join in. Her husband had been known for being a great singer and merrymaker. He organized all the family's evening glendis, which the young people remembered with great joy, and his early death blighted these happy gatherings.

Maria lived with her daughter and three grandchildren, all of whom attended college with scholarships. Both grandsons learned to play the tsambouna with Nikitas, who was a patient and encouraging teacher. "Little" Nikitas Kavouklis was awarded a Florida Folklife Apprenticeship to study the instrument and participated with his great-uncle in the Florida Folk Festival, planning at one time to continue the family tradition. The elder Nikitas estimated that between Kalymnos and Tarpon Springs there were perhaps ten tsambouna players, but only two or three of any merit, some of the more accomplished being younger men.

Like Nomiki, the youngest sister, Sevasti Tsimouris was sent to work as a live-in housekeeper at an early age. Although she, too, never married, she was able to get some schooling and the opportunity to travel, and became the most worldly of the four sisters. Considered the best singer in the family, with the finest voice, Sevasti visited Tarpon once a year and was sought after at parties for her singing.

Note on the Lyric Transcriptions and Translations

The transcriptions and translations were begun with Maria Chairetakis in 2000 and finalized with Mrs. Nomiki Tsimouris in 2009. Niki Sazalis, Irene Rinios, and Katerina Hatzileris explained many idioms and Kalymnian turns of phrase, bridging the language and interpretive gaps between Mrs. Tsimouris and myself. The transcriptions and translations are a work in progress, however, there being a number of words and phrases that remain indecipherable or that may have been imperfectly translated. The Greek texts have been presented in the Roman alphabet because I could find no one to transcribe them into the Greek alphabet while keeping to Kalymnian dialect usage as sung.

Anna Lomax Wood

Acknowledgments

The Folk Arts Program of the National Endowment for the Arts provided funding for the recordings through the City of Tarpon Springs. Thanks to Kathleen
Monahan, director of Cultural and Civic Services of the City of Tarpon Springs,
for her support of the project, and to Theodore Grame, who first learned of
Nikitas. The Florida Folklife Program provided the DAT recorder, and Robert
L. Stone of the program kindly tutored me on its use. Kenith Crawford made
beautiful black-and-white photographs at some of the sessions. Katerina Gryp-
aris, Maria Chairetakis, and Mrs. Nomiki Tsimouris worked on the transcriptions and translations with me. Matthew Barton transferred the recordings to
CD. I thank Tina Bucuvalas, Geoffrey Clarfield, Judith R. Cohen, Ellen Harold,
and David Marker for reading and commenting on this paper. I am deeply grateful to Nikitas Tsimouris, Mrs. Nomiki Tsimouris (my *nouna*), and all of the Tsimouris family for their hospitality, patience, and trust. Nikitas will always remain
an icon in my heart.

Notes

1. Previously published in *The Florida Folklife Reader*, ed. Tina Bucuvalas, 96–153 (Jackson: University Press of Mississippi, 2012). Many thanks to Panayotis League for revising the transliteration of
songs in Kalymnian dialect.

2. This quotation, and some others from this chapter, are from a website that was once available at
www.olymbos.org but that, at time of publication, was under refurbishment. Therefore, I am unable
to determine the name of the author. Subsequent quotations in the text from this website will be
cited parenthetically with (olymbos.org).

3. It can often be noted that, here, traditional singing and/or reed instrument playing is imitative
of or harmonious with ungulate vocalization. Can it have played an ancient role in domesticating
and herding ungulates in the region? Systematic studies of ungulate behavioral and brain responses
to this and other kinds of music, and of singing styles and instrumentation in the oldest pastoral
regions of the Middle East and Mediterranean basin, are required.

4. Why so strong a predilection for challenge and debate in oral poetry arises in this region is
an interesting question. Verbal dueling may be explained on a case-by-case basis, but one might
also look for an explanation in the combination of competition for scarce resources in precarious
environments and weak statehood that has characterized these regions over most of their history.
Such circumstances seem to produce a sort of high individualism and an inclination for intragroup
displays of power and skill, particularly among males but also among family groups and, in the past,
"estates" (*états*), formally established classes of people—the knight and the squire, the peasant and
the nobleman, the rustic and the townsman—of sixteenth- through eighteenth-century literature, for
example. Michael Herzfeld's observations of a Cretan shepherd village (1985) generally support this
line of argument. Herzfeld makes the point that, as state government with its controls and subsidies
takes on more importance in villagers' lives, competition for cattle and status between agnatic groups
subsides, as do the poetic traditions that dramatize such tensions. The poetic debate, sung or recited,
has been known since antiquity around the Mediterranean Basin and the Middle East, and among
many societies in western Asia (Reinink and Vanstiphout 1991; Tributalo 2012). Following David
Anthony (2007), I have suggested that it may be associated with Bronze Age culture (Wood 2018).

5. I did not learn what lullabies they sing or how.

6. The Tall Lady, an apparition of the Virgin, is said to have appeared to Greeks fighting the Italians at Morova in 1940, among other places.

References

Anoyanakis, Fivos. 1991. *Greek Popular Musical Instruments*. Athens: Melissa.

Anthony, David W. 2007. *The Horse, the Wheel, and Language: How Bronze-Age Riders from the Eurasian Steppes Shaped the Modern World*. Princeton, NJ: Princeton University Press.

Apella Nota Folk Music Productions. 2008. "Τ' Άχολο περιστέρι" [The Carefree Dove]. Αστική μη Κερδοσκοπική Εταιρεία. At www.karpathos.net/ApellaNota.

Baud-Bovy, Samuel. 1935–1938. *Chansons du Dodecaneses*. 2 vols. Athens: Sideris.

Bulger, Peggy A., dir. 1983. *Every Island Has Its Own Songs*. Florida Folklife Program, Florida Department of State.

Caraveli, Anna. 1985. "The Symbolic Village: Community Born in Performance." *Journal of American Folklore* 98: 259–86.

Caraveli-Chaves, Anna. 1980. "Bridge between Worlds: The Greek Women's Lament as Communicative Event." *Journal of American Folklore* 93: 129–57.

Dietrich, Wolf, comp. 1976. *Musica popolare del Dodecaneso: Folk Music of the Dodecanese Islands*. Albatros VPA-8295. Albatros, Milan.

Herzfeld, Michael. 1985. *The Poetics of Manhood: Contest and Identity in a Cretan Mountain Village*. Princeton, NJ: Princeton University Press.

Kavouras, Pavlos. 1993. "Extempore Dialogical Song and the Symbolism of the Ghlendi at Olymbos, Karpathos." *Ethnologia* 2: 155–200.

Lomax, Alan. 1976. *Cantometrics: An Approach to the Anthropology of Music*. Berkeley: University of California Extension Media Center.

Reinink, Gerrit Jan, and Herman Vanstiphout. 1991. *Dispute Poems and Dialogues in the Ancient and Mediaeval Near East: Forms and Types of Literary Debates in Semitic and Related Literatures*. Leuven: Peeters Publishers.

Sarris, Haris, Tassos Kolydas, and Panagiotis Tzevelekos. 2008. "Parataxis: A Framework of Structure Analysis for Instrumental Folk Music." In *Proceedings of the Fourth Conference on Interdisciplinary Musicology*, edited by Emilios Cambouropoulos et al. Thessaloniki: Aristotle University of Thessaloniki

Sarris, Haris, and Panagiotis Tzevelekos. 2008. "Singing Like the *Gaida* (Bagpipe): Investigating Relations between Singing and Instrumental Playing Techniques in Greek Thrace." *Journal of Interdisciplinary Music Studies* 2, nos. 1–2: 33–57.

Sutton, David E. 1998. *Memories Cast in Stone: The Relevance of the Past in Everyday Life*. New York: Berg Publishers.

Tribulato, Olga. 2012. *Language and Linguistic Contact in Ancient Sicily*. Cambridge: Cambridge University Press.

Wood, Anna L. 2018. "Ritorno in Sicilia." Unpublished paper.

Alternate Resonances: Kalymnian Traditions in Tarpon Springs, Florida

—Panayotis League

The following chapter, divided into two complementary parts, explores the music and dance traditions of Kalymnos in the contemporary diaspora context of Tarpon Springs, Florida, home to the largest and most prominent Kalymnian community outside the island. The first part takes a wide view of the life of these traditions in Tarpon Springs, focusing on Kalymnian music and dance as a resonant means of belonging to a wider community, while the second presents a more pointed take on what these practices can tell us about the diversity of ways that Kalymnian Tarponites express their regional identity, and invites us to consider music and dance events not only as harmonious collective celebrations but also as dynamic sites of contest, conflict, and change.

Part 1. Living the Dance: Imaginative Journeys and Musical Movement in Tarpon Springs

---

It's starting to rain. Skinny drops splatter on the warm pavement under our feet; the smell of ozone is tinged with the salt of the Gulf at our backs. The energy flowing between our hands shifts, becomes slightly more urgent. The circle moves on against the stiffening breeze, and I see the boats hung with sponges framed against the darkening sky, tables and chairs spilling into the street a few feet from us, people drinking and eating, old men clicking worry beads, giggling children darting in and out. A slight change in pressure from the hand held in my right palm, and we shift to even out the spaces as one of the dancers is pulled out of line by the leader. She blushes and protests but makes her way to the front of the line, and accepts the leader's handkerchief with her left hand; it connects her to the second girl and to the rest of us. We feel how the balance shifts from one moment to the next as we are subtly repositioned in space. The girl puts her right hand on her hip and begins to lead the dance. The transformation is immediate and complete. Her back straightens; her waist seems to float above the ground and her feet almost not to occupy any space on the pavement. Her eyes are lowered, her face expressionless; an American teenager a moment ago, she has become a young Kalymnian woman, the Doric ideal of modesty and utterly composed competence. She begins to improvise graceful figures, her gaze drawn down toward her feet; I marvel at the brief glimpses I catch of how the slightly delayed variations of her steps anticipate and weave into the bagpipe's phrases. Suddenly, the girl on my left slides her hand out of mine. I look over—she's replying to a text message. She hits "send," puts her phone in her back pocket, and takes my hand again.

This chapter explores the imaginative journeys taken by practitioners of traditional music and dance in the Greek American community of Tarpon Springs, Florida. Specifically, I examine how many Greek Americans in Tarpon Springs use the performance of dances and music from the Greek island of Kalymnos to negotiate a holistic sense of identity and belonging in a multi-sited, transnational context. Taking as a starting point anthropologist Thomas Csordas's concept of the body as the "existential ground of culture" (1990, 5), I propose that these dancers and musicians in Tarpon Springs experience their bodies as a resonant, experiential bridge between various cultural allegiances: a mobile site of tension and transcendence, and a secure place to explore the seemingly disparate notions of identity and ownership that confront them in their daily lives.

My investigation here is guided by the concept of "intermediate states of being" suggested by anthropologist Lowell Lewis. Lewis describes body practitioners such as dancers and athletes as inhabiting an intermediate realm between relatively embodied and relatively disembodied states (1995, 230). In this intermediate mode, the body is both subject and object of noninstrumental action, action whose goal is inseparable from the body's own movement. For the Tarponites who are the subject of this study, this intermediate phenomenal state of being is both an apt metaphor for their location between competing ethnic and national identities, and a way of negotiating these identities. Positioned on a constantly shifting spectrum with small-town America on one side and a fiercely traditional Greek island culture on the other, intermediate states of being are, for them, a way of life, a shared experience that contributes to social cohesion and a way to locate the self in a world of perpetually blurred boundaries.

The narrative with which I began this chapter draws on my own experiences as a lifelong member of this community. Like many Tarponite Greek Americans, I grew up around Kalymnian music and dancing, and experience them as an anchor that helps me balance the Greek and American aspects of my own constantly evolving sense of self. Unlike most Tarponite Greek Americans, I am not myself of Kalymnian descent; but Kalymnian music and dancing are a fundamental part of my social, internal, and artistic life, as they are for my

Kalymnian friends. I play Kalymnian music on the three canonical instruments—the violin, *laouto* (a steel-string lute), and *tsambouna* (a double-chanter shepherd's bagpipe)—and frequently perform at festivals, weddings, and other community events in Tarpon Springs, Kalymnos, and elsewhere in the diaspora. This visceral involvement and deep-seated emotional investment has doubtless shaped the thinking embedded in this chapter. In fact, for me the physical sensation of playing Kalymnian music on these instruments is an analogue to the dance experience that my interlocutors describe throughout this chapter, and my own literally resonant means of straddling the charged divide between the Greek and American aspects of my life.

A Community Rooted in Movement

Located roughly thirteen miles north of Clearwater along old Florida Route 19, Tarpon Springs is nestled inside a network of saltwater bayous where the Anclote River meets the Gulf of Mexico. The initial group of five hundred Greek islanders arrived in the sleepy Gulf Coast fishing village in 1905 to establish what was soon to become the most powerful sponge-diving industry in the world. From the outset they were a numerical majority in Tarpon Springs, and the Greek community continues to play a decisive role in the social, political, and economic life of what is today a small city of some twenty-five thousand people. A steady stream of immigration, primarily from the Dodecanese island of Kalymnos just a few miles from the Turkish coast, has continued over the intervening century, allowing the community to maintain a synchronic and symbiotic relationship with the homeland and keep in touch with its cultural imperatives. Kalymnians continue to dominate Tarpon Springs's Greek community today, and their specific dance and music traditions are a highly visible and audible symbol of Greek identity in the town.

Public performance of these Kalymnian markers of identity has thus become synonymous with the assertion of Greek Tarponite identity, and this has affected both the internal dynamics of the community as well as its relationship with the mainstream of Greek America. Many non-Kalymnian Tarponites have found that participation in Kalymnian music and dance practices is an ideal way to transcend their minority status as *xeni* (foreigners or outsiders) and be accepted as "adopted Kalymnians." As I noted at the outset, this is one of the central features of my own personal relationship with Kalymnian music; although it is the style of Greek music with which I most identify, I myself am at most an "adopted Kalymnian," and the irony of my position as one of the principal bearers of the Kalymnian music tradition in the town is not lost on me. The public performance of Kalymnian music and dance, particularly by the community's

Figure 69. Kalymnian Society Agios Panteleimon, Tarpon Springs, Florida. Photo by Tina Bucuvalas.

Kalymnian-centered Greek dance groups, has also earned Tarpon Springs a reputation throughout the Greek American community as a site of authentic preservation of Kalymnian traditions—regardless of the actual regional affiliation of individual dancers and musicians—and made the town a focal point of dialogue among members of the Kalymnian diaspora.

Considering the degree to which many other long-standing Greek American communities have assimilated, how do we explain the current vibrant state of Kalymnian arts and culture in Tarpon Springs, more than a century after the community was founded? The answer lies partly in a revival sparked by the efforts of local dance and music enthusiasts starting in the early 1980s, made possible by the vital and unceasing connection between Tarpon Springs and Kalymnos through immigration and, just as significantly, seasonal migration and cultural tourism, particularly in the second half of the twentieth century. Facilitated by the increased ease and decreased cost of transatlantic travel, this constant flow of people in search of economic opportunities (in the sponging industry and, later, bridge painting and the tourist trade) and social and spiritual nourishment has enabled the Kalymnian community in Tarpon Springs to stay in touch with the cultural imperatives of the homeland while simultaneously forging its own distinctly American path.

Tarpon Springs and Kalymnos seem, in many ways, to be inextricably bound together, two sides of a coin at once rusted and ancient, glittering and modern.

This sense is officially acknowledged through the two municipalities' status as Sister Cities,[1] and unofficially in a myriad of expressions, including a popular T-shirt proclaiming Kalymnos as "K-Town, Greece" and Tarpon as "K-Town, USA." These two examples call to mind Benedict Anderson's discussion of the relationship between colonial settlements and existing cities in the homeland. "What is startling," writes Anderson, "is that 'new' and 'old' are understood synchronically, co-existing within homogenous, empty time. . . . London is there *alongside* New London . . . an idiom of sibling competition rather than inheritance" (1991, 187). Anderson posits that this synchronic innovation of the colonial imagination is only possible when large groups of people are "in a position to think of themselves as living lives *parallel* to those of other substantial groups of people . . . proceeding along the same trajectory," and requires that "the distance between the parallel groups be large, and that the newer of them be substantial in size and permanently settled, as well as firmly subordinated to the older" (1991, 188).

A fundamental consequence of the physical journeys of immigration and seasonal migration that founded and sustain Tarpon Springs' Kalymnian community is the set of metaphorical ones that inhabit them—ways of traveling, through participation in traditional music and dance, to imaginatively engaged places of origin and longed-for, otherwise inaccessible zones of emotional fulfillment. I term these acts of metaphorical travel "imaginative border crossings." In so doing, I make a clear distinction between the realm of the imaginary and the realm of the imaginative. Imaginary things do not exist; they are *exclusively* a product of the imagination, fantastical creations with no clear footing in objective reality. Conversely, an *imaginative* engagement with one's surroundings entails a visceral awareness of their everydayness, an understanding that they are rooted in lived, physical space, as well as a desire to establish emotional connections between these surroundings and other, longed-for settings or ideals. The process of imaginative travel—imaginative border crossings—constructs these connections and reinforces them through repeated interaction. The journeys explored in this chapter are emphatically not imaginary; for those who embark upon them, they are very real.

Central to my argument is a question posed by James Clifford, who asks: "What if travel were untethered, seen as a complex and pervasive spectrum of human experiences? Practices of displacement might emerge as *constitutive* of cultural meanings rather than as their simple transfer or extension" (1997, 3). I see all of the above forms of imaginative travel—the physical and the metaphorical—as fundamentally constitutive of everything that it means to be a Kalymnian Tarponite, an identity that is built from its very core on multiple levels of displacement and, consequently, a search for belonging. Kalymnian Americans in Tarpon Springs are displaced from the ancestral homeland, the rocky island of Kalymnos from which their forebears sailed; and they are displaced from the mainstream of

American life and identity by virtue of their intense identification with their ethnic heritage.[2] This very identification as "Kalymnian" first and foremost also displaces them from the mainstream of Greek culture, both in Greece and in the diaspora. These multiple displacements make the work of identification, belonging, and self-expression through imaginative travel all the more urgent and compelling.

Anthropologist Lucy Lippard, paraphrasing David Harvey, writes that traveling—moving from one place to another—"is about *becoming* rather than *being*" (1999, 11). I venture that all the diverse modes of movement introduced above, and discussed below, are similarly concerned not simply with expressing states of being, identifications, or affiliations but also with an ongoing process of creative self-exploration to which the media of music and dance are ideally suited. This process of using musical movement to become "who one wants to be"—a relentlessly evolving and changing entity in and of itself—lies at the heart of the issues explored in this chapter.

Musical Mobility, Aesthetic Empowerment

Greek Americans in Tarpon Springs live in an intermediate state of being between two distinct local realities: the Greek-speaking, predominantly Kalymnian environment of home, church, and primary social conditioning, and the English-speaking American environment of school, government, and secondary social relations outside their ethnic community. All of my interlocutors relate this local dichotomy to a physical and psychological distance between Greece and the United States. As one of them told me, reflecting on a visit to Kalymnos:

> You know, it's funny; in America, we tell people we're Greek. For the short time that I was in Greece, you're telling everyone you're American. So what are we? Well, the answer is somewhere in between. Both countries somewhat define who we are.

This statement eloquently summarizes the dilemma of intermediate cultural being and hints at a hybrid, composite reality of which I caught glimpses time and again during my conversations with these Kalymnian American dancers. My interlocutors, or their forebears, left Kalymnos, but not completely; not even in body, as they incessantly return, physically and metaphorically through musical movement, to their place of origin. Their gaze remains firmly trained on the homeland as a source of emotional nourishment and sense of belonging that promises to deliver them from what they fear most—anonymous assimilation and loss of their distinctive regional identity.

Feelings toward Kalymnos itself are complex, born out of an inherited and incessantly reinforced reverence for the homeland that often seems to come into conflict with personal experience when the two encounter each other in the realm of dance and music. Another of my interlocutors, a young woman of mixed Kalymnian and other island parentage, explains it this way:

> I know that half the people in this town would kill me for saying this, but I'm not a fan of Kalymnos. Yet, I love their dances. I remember the first time I learned the Kalymnian dance [the *issos*]. Any other dance is just a dance . . . which I find very odd, because I don't connect to Kalymnos. Yet I connect to the dance.

This young woman clearly views Kalymnos, and Kalymnians, as "others," as "them"; yet she feels an affinity for the island's dance tradition so intense that for her it exists in its own ontological category, something different from all the rest of the world's dancing. Kalymnian musicians, especially those who have been exposed to other regional styles of Greek island music, express analogous feelings about their own tradition, which shares much of its repertoire with neighboring islands but is characterized by a brash playing style that marries extreme instrumental virtuosity and subtle embellishments with a jagged aggressiveness that frequently surprises Greeks who are accustomed to the lighter commercial *nisiotika* or island music. A Kalymnian violinist who frequently visits Tarpon and other Greek American communities to perform for dancers commented to me at a music and dance festival while we listened to a Cycladic version of a tune also popular in Kalymnos: "It's amazing—everything about *our* music is so extreme. *This* is so polite in comparison."

The majority of Kalymnian dances are circular and cyclical, and participants clasp hands or hold each others' shoulders while moving counterclockwise, for as much as half an hour at a stretch, until a break in the music. By Lewis's definition, this extended, collective dance is an explicitly noninstrumental activity, but in this case seemingly designed to allow the participation of literally an entire village at once, joined together by an unbroken chain of hands. Ethnomusicologist Deborah Wong's eloquent description of the Asian American *taiko* jam is applicable here:

> The rules for . . . participation are clear: you *should* participate. . . . Individuality and its diffusion into the heterogeneity of the group are essential. . . . [T]he shared aim is to create something bigger than you; you know you literally *couldn't* do it alone. (2008, 87)

By definition a communal activity, Kalymnian dancing is at once greater than the individual dancer and dependent upon his or her adherence to its social, stylistic, and aesthetic rules if it is to be successful.

In my own ongoing experience with these dances, I am frequently struck by the momentary blurring of individuality that occurs when participants' bodily movement is particularly coordinated. My Tarponite dancer friends agree. Nearly everyone speaks of an all-consuming feeling of "being in the moment" while dancing, analogous to the phenomenological reduction cited by ethnomusicologist Jeff Todd Titon, the musician's awareness of "being-in-the-world" (2008, 32). One tells me: "When everyone's in sync, you're all on the same plane, there's a collective perception of what's going on—when it's really good, it's like an out-of-body experience." Similarly, another common theme expressed during interviews is, as one of my interlocutors puts it, a "feedback loop" between the musicians and dancers, by means of which *kefi* (high-spirited willingness) exponentially rises and each party encourages the other to reach new heights of expression that serve the collective as much as the individual.

Discussing styles of movement as a mode of distinction between social groups, anthropologist Jane Desmond points out that movement is "a primary, not secondary social 'text'—complex, polysemous, always already meaningful, yet continuously changing. Its articulation signals group affiliation and group differences, whether consciously performed or not" (1993, 36). Greek Americans in Tarpon Springs are intensely aware of these distinctions, expressed in ways of moving, speaking, eating, and, of course, dancing. Although most of the town's inhabitants were born or at least raised in America, Kalymnian culture is so dominant in Tarpon Springs that a certain degree of "foreign" status is attached to non-Kalymnian Greek Americans. According to feminist dance historian and philosopher Ann Cooper Albright, "behind every aesthetic orientation and style of movement within the field of dance dwells a view about the world that is transmitted (albeit often subconsciously) along with the dance technique" (1997, 32). In Tarpon, the world view encoded in traditional dancing clearly places Kalymnian culture and social codes at the center. This is apparent in the aesthetics and technical details of the dancing itself, which encourage specific gender roles and reinforce notions of communal behavior, as well as in its usefulness as a vehicle for social mobility and identity construction, as dancers move in and out of subculture groups—yet another layer of intermediate states of being—through their participation in Kalymnian dancing.

Non-Kalymnian Greek Americans in Tarpon Springs are acutely aware of their status as xeni within the Kalymnian-dominated community. One of my interlocutors, a young woman whose family hails from a neighboring island, puts it this way:

> Do you know how hard it is? It's not easy. It's taken me fifteen years now.... They're like any group, any nationality, you have to embrace their culture. The group can be a little [pause] ... rough.

Many non-Kalymnian Tarponites find that this "roughness," manifested as subtle (or not-so-subtle) social ostracism, can be subverted by active participation in and adoption of Kalymnian ways of being. Foremost among these ways of being is a demonstration of competence at Kalymnian dancing; this particular young woman feels that her participation in the local Kalymnian-dominated dance group, which occupies a place of primacy in the social life of its members, has enabled her to make the transition from xeni to what in Tarpon Springs is commonly called "adopted Kalymnian."

Albright maintains that the "body is where the two realms (of essential [genetically inherited] and constructed [socially formed] being) interact. It is a place where sensation, representation, and physical experiences are interpreted both symbolically and somatically" (1997, 32). For many of my interlocutors in this project, the bodily experience of dancing serves as a conduit for feelings and emotions deeply tied to a symbolic interpretation of their heritage and their identity as Greek/Kalymnian Americans. Statements such as "it's who we are, it's what our parents did, what our grandparents did, it connects you way back" and "these are songs (and dances) that define who we are" are common; Kalymnian music and dancing are consistently portrayed as a "mystical" bridge, a "connection" to an ancestral past, despite limited physical contact with Kalymnos or other, less resilient aspects of traditional culture. One of my interlocutors tells me that when he is dancing,

> I just think about grandparents, great-grandparents I've never met.... It's sort of a mystic way ... with as little physical contact as I've had, I'm just feeling that connection.

This connection with Kalymnian culture seems to reference a partly imagined, partly material world that exists somewhere between the past—perhaps the relatively recent past of emigration from Kalymnos, perhaps the more distant pasts when these dances and songs were created, developed, and lived, what one of my interlocutors referred to as "the Kalymnos of yesteryear"—and the present.

My own experience of playing and singing Kalymnian music speaks to this connection through time and lived-in, bodily places. On the one hand, the act of singing traditional songs in the Kalymnian dialect—whose accent and vocabulary are distinctive and in some ways radically different from standard Greek—is an obvious way to make an imaginative connection with the singers of yesteryear, shouting with one's own voice the pungently sibilant syllables of songs about shepherds, sponge divers, and characters whose exploits and distinctive mannerisms have gone down in history in the form of heroic or satirical verses. And singing in unison in large groups—the standard practice in the Kalymnian tradition, faithfully followed in Tarpon Springs—has much the same collective emotional and physical effect as dancing the same steps joined hand-to-hand. (In fact, the two actions—dancing and singing in unison—frequently happen together.)

Figure 70. Michalis Kappas and Panayotis League perform *pismatika*, with Skevos Karavokiros playing *tsambouna*, Kalymnian House, Tarpon Springs, Florida, March 8, 2010. Photo by Tina Bucuvalas.

On the other hand, the physicality of the musical instruments themselves, especially the tsambouna, viscerally connects the performer to the island. The tsambouna is constructed from four primary ingredients, all profoundly reminiscent of the distinctive Kalymnian landscape: the body of a young goat, the root of an olive tree (from which the chanter and blowpipe are carved), two river-cane pipes, and aromatic beeswax as a sealant. When a Tarponite tsambouna player inflates the bag with his (or, rarely, her) breath, he brings these organic pieces of the island back to temporary life in a bleating feast of strident sound—and, with them, a multitude of imaginative images and visceral memories. It is no mistake that the instrument is particularly beloved in Tarpon Springs, and not only by older Kalymnians who were born on the island and have personal memories of the tsambouna animating festive gatherings in their rural youth; third- and fourth-generation Kalymnian high schoolers are just as likely to respond to the tsambouna's sound with enthusiasm. In the words of one strapping varsity football player, as he listened admiringly to a recording of his uncle playing the instrument: "Yeah, dude. That's my jams."

The experience of music and dance, writes ethnomusicologist Martin Stokes, "evokes and organizes collective memories and present experiences of place with an intensity, power and simplicity unmatched by any other social activity," and is "socially meaningful . . . largely because it provides means by which people recognize identities and places, and the boundaries which separate them" (1997, 3–5). As one girl put it, "we're trying to hold on to the beauty of the island," a beauty that has been alchemized and transformed through separation, isolation, and its dialogue with an encroaching American identity, taking on a new set of self-sufficient meanings.

Stokes urges us to view music and dance as "a patterned context within which other things happen" and asserts that "what is important is not just . . . musical performance, but *good* performance, if music and dance are to make a social event 'happen'" (1997, 5). So what makes dancing *good* for my interlocutors in the Kalymnian American community of Tarpon Springs? Most frequently, I hear about *who* my interlocutors wanted to dance with. *Why* they prefer certain dance partners—fellow travelers on their imaginative journeys—is illustrative of their intermediate state of cultural being and hybrid sense of identity.

When asked about their ideal dance partners, my interlocutors express an overwhelming preference for a group of Kalymnian Americans from Tarpon Springs who know each other well socially and have a close relationship as people and as dancers, with a wealth of shared life experience. One dancer explains, "I prefer my friends from our group in Tarpon to even the best Kalymnian dancers from Kalymnos. We have a stronger bond because we've had to work for it, to transcend our 'American-ness.'" Another emphasizes the importance of *kali parea* (good company) in providing the level of comfort, shared experience, and social ease outside of dancing that makes good dancing possible. "You want to dance with people who take you for who you are, without judging," even in the absence of live music; "I've had great experiences dancing to the trunk stereo in the parking lot of the 7-Eleven."

Seen from this perspective, Kalymnian dancing functions as a vehicle for social and personal empowerment, a safe place to explore these questions of identity and states of being. Philosopher Susanne Langer proposes that "the primary illusion of dance is a virtual realm of Power, not actual, physically exerted power, but appearances of influence and agency created by virtual gesture" (1983, 29). This sheds light on comments made by one of my interlocutors, who spoke of the dance circle as a place of personal power, surrounded by trust and family. "It helps me break out of my shell," he told me. "When I'm dancing, I have an alter ego that's powerful, confident, and in control. I'm able to be my true self." The powerful "alter ego" awakened here—one that successfully straddles the boundaries between American and Greek identity—is perceived as the "true self," encoded in the virtual gestures of the dance and existing in a realm of creative possibility.

Emotional Journeys

For Kalymnian Tarponites, the folk traditions of Kalymnos also function as a means of metaphorical travel to other places or times, imagined or real, if only

in the idealized past. For some, particularly second- and third-generation Tarponites whose contact with Kalymnos has been limited, the songs and dances
of their ancestral homeland evoke sepia-tinged nostalgia, memories of deceased
grandparents, and tales of an agrarian past (what one of my collaborators identified as "the Kalymnos of yesteryear" in his father-in-law's songs and stories)—a
homeland that, despite its evident hardships and cruelties, retains in the telling
its idyllic charm. Songs of emigration, exile, foreign oppression, and the travails
of sponge diving are relevant to the Kalymnian American audience, and viscerally felt, if to varying degrees.

But for other members of Tarpon's Kalymnian American community, tangible feelings of longing, loneliness, anxiety, and emotional anguish are a very
real part of daily life. Many Kalymnian Tarponites have lost relatives or friends
to the dangers of the sea and of sponge diving, and the *sfoungaradika*—popular
Kalymnian songs about the lives of sponge divers—resonate sharply with them.
First-generation immigrants are often separated from parents, siblings, spouses,
or children for months or years at a time, and immersion in the experience of
music and dancing can be, for them, a way of being with distant or departed
loved ones and soothing, if only momentarily, the pain and longing of separation
and exile, as the following excerpt from my field notes illustrates:

> *M. gives me a nod and begins "Tis Galanuenas" (Galanouena's Song), one of the most
> difficult slow songs in the repertoire. He motions to R.; she gets up and walks slowly
> over to where we're sitting, in front of the speakers that are still on despite the nearly
> empty courtyard. She picks up the microphone, closes her eyes, lifts her chin, and begins.
> "Eeeeeeeeeeee . . ."*
>
> M' irthan boulatsa ts' ipan mou ta cheretismata sou . . .
>
> *(Little birds came and gave me your greetings . . .)*
>
> *She lowers the mic to her side, sways in time with the music, her left hand raised
> in the air, fingers tracing the contours of the melody as the instruments repeat the last
> phrase.*
>
> Tse tharou bos imilou mou ta chili ta dika sou.
>
> *(And I thought that it was your own lips that were speaking to me.)*
>
> *I can see her eyes water with the last syllable. She places the microphone on its stand,
> wipes her face with the back of her hand, and walks away.*

Another young woman, a talented dancer who sees her father only once a year
when she visits him in Kalymnos, tells me the following:

> My Dad, dancing, and Kalymnos. These are the three things that will make me happy
> in the world. Nothing else. It makes me so happy. It makes me think that everything
> is fine with the world, that there's peace. . . . When I do (certain steps of) the σούστα

[*sousta*] dance . . . I always watched my dad when he was dancing, at all kinds of weddings, he would do it so good, and it just inspired me. I love that picture, I can picture it right now. . . . When I do that part, I always think of my Dad. I just wish he was here. . . . But, I make him proud with that, just that one spot. I make him so proud. Dancing . . . let's just say dancing is my life.

For Kalymnian Americans suffering from such emotional ailments—the common casualties of transnational being—music and dance give voice to what might alternately be silent suffering, and act as their imaginative passport to otherwise inaccessible emotional states of fulfillment and joy.

Performing Gender

Like the women who are the subject of anthropologist Jane K. Cowan's ethnography *Dance and the Body Politic in Northern Greece* (1990), Kalymnian American women and girls confront asymmetrical gender relations both on and off the dance floor. As Cowan points out, the audience that critically reads the bodily signs performed by the dancing subject is informed by the social codes that govern gender roles and relations (1990, 190–91). Although the interpretive possibilities awakened by the bodily experience of dancing are not boundless, they do create opportunities for a creative exploration of specific gender roles when they come into contact with the gendered conventions of Kalymnian culture.

When asked to describe the dancing Kalymnian woman, my collaborators—both male and female—unanimously use words such as "strong," "powerful," "proud," "confident," "feminine," "stately," "subtle," and "in control." Men's dancing is also characterized as "confident," "proud," and "powerful," as well as "masculine," but also, particularly when describing the improvised figures performed by the *brostellatis* or leader, as "flashy," "athletic," "acrobatic," "arrogant," "showy," "exhibitionist," and even "crazy." These latter qualities are generally considered the exclusive domain of men, who are entitled (and entrusted) to express the bravado and daring so admired by Kalymnians and treasured as an integral part of their idiosyncratic regional identity.

Women, however, are taught to avoid ostentatious and unrestrained physicality on the dance floor, mirroring the behavior expected of them in everyday social life. The following description of ideal female comportment, offered by one of Cowan's interlocutors, is equally applicable to the Kalymnian context and further informs the impressionistic passage that began this chapter:

She should dance with confidence, she shouldn't be shy or embarrassed. With many tricks, with little movements. If you're embarrassed, you don't do anything! You want to make an impression, to show something, to differentiate yourself a little. But not too much. If she does, they will say she's "crazy," that she's dancing in a "frenzied" way. (Cowan 1990, 200)

Behavior that is admired and even expected in men, both as dancers and as social (and, as Cowan [1990], Caraveli [1985], du Boulay [1974], and others have pointed out, sexual) beings, is often considered vulgar and inappropriate in women: it is, by traditional Greek standards, morally and aesthetically flawed.

Under extraordinary circumstances, though, female Kalymnian Tarponites find themselves compelled to push against the gendered boundaries prescribed by social convention. Yet another young woman, discussing dancing's meaningful role in her relationship with her father, a skillful dancer who lives and works in Kalymnos most of the year, tells me in typically macaronic fashion:

When I dance with my dad . . . he always wants me to be next to him, *na kano tis figoures* [to perform the improvised figures]. . . . You can see in his eyes he's so proud, and he's kind of like a *fiakas* [show-off], he's like "Hey, look at my daughter," [she's] dancing so good, "*pire apo 'mena*" [she took after me]. He sees me when I dance and he just goes crazy, super happy. And *ine toso eftichismenos mesa tou* [he's so happy inside], just being there together, 'cause most of the time we're not, and when we are, we're complete. 'Cause now, I'm half . . . it doesn't feel the same.

Here, her father's presence and encouragement make it socially acceptable for her to perform steps usually reserved for men, the elaborate improvisations of the leader. But during the long months of longing and separation, she uses the embodied memory of her father's dancing to simultaneously bring him closer and transcend the gender role normally expected of her:

But when I dance, especially *andrika* (masculine) Kalymnian dances, like the *thimariotiko* (a dance traditionally off-limits to women) . . . when I dance that, I feel like I'm a guy. I do the same steps, the same style like my dad. Sometimes I wish I was a guy. I would have done this so much better than everyone else here.

In the moment of performing dances like the thimariotiko, normally associated with men, she temporarily *becomes* an empowered masculine figure through her father's steps and in so doing issues a challenge to the men whose position of privilege she envies. Only her gender prevents her from being openly acknowledged as their superior on the dance floor, and she is thus compelled to find subtly subversive ways to use her advanced knowledge and skills.

The creative exploration of gender norms exemplified here is made possible, in part, by the multicultural American context in which Kalymnian dancing is embedded in Tarpon Springs. Every single one of my American-born collabora-tors, while expressing a clear preference for Kalymnian dancing, also reported experience with other types of dance, from regional and contemporary Greek styles to the relatively free, individualistic dancing practiced at area nightclubs. Indeed, at large, formal dance events such as the annual New Year's and Epiph-any balls, live Kalymnian music typically alternates with a local DJ spinning Greek, European, and American pop, techno, classic rock, and oldies, attempt-ing to cater to the multiple generations and cultural orientations present. I have watched the same dancers perform an impeccable Kalymnian *issos* to live violin and laouto, suggestively writhe to the latest *tsifteteli*,[3] toss their hair and wave their arms to Lady Gaga, and do the twist to Chubby Checker—all in the same eve-ning, with comparable enthusiasm, and without a touch of irony. Yet despite this wide variety of experience, most Kalymnian Tarponites seem to have embodied their native dance technique to such an extent that I perceive a clear Kalymnian "accent" in all of their danced movements, regardless of the style they are per-forming. They bend knees, shift weight, and delay steps in ways that immediately call to mind the most traditional Kalymnian dances, subconsciously articulating, after Jane Desmond (1993, 36), their group affiliations and differences.

Resonant Bodies

All of these ideas about the importance of Kalymnian music and dance in Tar-pon Springs can be summarized with a brief exploration of what happens to the body and mind of initiated dancers in the moment they come in contact with the music that drives the dance. Writing of the ecological model of perception, musi-cologist Eric Clarke suggests that "(p)erception is a self-tuning process, in which the pick-up of environmental information is intrinsically reinforcing, so that the system self-adjusts so as to optimize its resonance with the environment" (2005, 19). In Clarke's model, our consciousness hunts until it achieves clarity, like a dig-ital tuner. Ethnomusicologist Greg Downey, discussing Brazilian *capoeira*, puts it in more embodied, less mechanical terms: "Practitioners' lived bodies, fashioned by patterns of acting in relation to the music, respond almost involuntarily to the sonic texture" (2002, 500). These two perspectives on embodied perception resonate forcefully with my interlocutors' comments about the experience of physical contact with the music they love.

From the first moment of recognition, the music triggers the rich storehouse of lived experience into action and immediately transports the dancers into the realm of movement and all that it holds for them. One Kalymnian American dancer says, "When I hear Kalymnian music, I remember the first time I danced in Kalymnos, when I really understood that I was part of something thousands of years old, that these dances and songs make me who I am as a person. . . . It's where I come from." Continuing, he reflects: "Then I think of all the good times we've had dancing here in Tarpon with guys from the group, my cousins, my *thia* [aunt] . . . and that's what makes me want to get up and dance." For him, the synthesis of past experience, visceral understanding, and the opportunity to put that understanding into practice drive him to musical movement. Another dancer tells me: "I just get goosebumps thinking about it. When you hear those opening notes of the issos and somebody just screams out "Kalymniko!" [the colloquial name for the popular issos dance] . . . all of a sudden the *pista* (dance floor) just fills with people."

I viscerally understand what he meant: although—or perhaps because—I have played and danced to it thousands of times, when I hear the characteristically brash rhythm of the issos dance I get chills over my entire body and absolutely *have* to move. My other Kalymnian American friends agree: "I get that feeling every time," says one, a feeling beyond enjoyment—a mixture of ownership and responsibility, as if the music and the dancing were a part of his body. Elaborating on the experience of dancing to Kalymnian music—an experience repeated countless times since earliest childhood, and one that has become a defining feature of her life—one of my interlocutors simply shrugs and says: "When we dance Kalymnian . . . we're just living the dance."

The pavement is almost empty, more abandoned bottles and cans than people. The breeze has shifted, taken on the characteristic chill that signals the deepest part of night, just before the sky begins to blue with the first hint of dawn. We've gone through all the slow songs that we can think of since the dancing stopped several hours ago; the remaining hard core of revelers has gathered their purses, coats, keys, and sleeping children, and congregated around the instruments, long relocated from the abandoned makeshift stage to the center of the courtyard. The violinist starts "Mera Merose," the song that definitively marks the end of the glendi, from which there is no return until the next time we come together. As we sing, people kiss goodbye, wish a good rest, a good new day; remind of appointments, errands, church duties; promise to call tomorrow, to stop by for coffee.

Almost imperceptibly, someone begins to sway to the slow, stately pulse of the song, and gently, like a flower opening, those still present join arms and glide into the steps of the issos.

Conclusion

For Kalymnian Americans in Tarpon Springs, intermediate states of being are definitive, a reality of daily life. Existing in a state of multiple displacements— from their ancestral homeland of Kalymnos, from the mainstream of American life and identity, and from the mainstream of Greek diaspora culture—they turn to their inherited music and dance practices in search of social and internal resonance, using their bodies and imaginations as a way to travel across the sometimes yawning gaps between the various identifications that pull at them, and at times push them away. In the process, simultaneously wrestling with and celebrating a shared artistic heritage that carries the weight of centuries-old social codes and yet dissolves differences in moments of collective action, they find a variety of ways to navigate the various paths available to them. Whether experienced as personal empowerment, a mystical bridge to the past, or an expression of unity that either reinforces or defies ethnic affiliation, the music and dance traditions of Kalymnos are central to the Greek American experience in Tarpon Springs, and serve as a resonant passport for the perpetual boundary crossing in which their practitioners are daily called to engage.

Part 2. Interrogating "Authenticity" in the Kalymnian Diaspora

---

In the first part, I discussed how some Kalymnian Americans in Tarpon Springs use their music and dance traditions as a resonant bridge between competing cultural affiliations, as well as how these traditions function for them as a means of imaginative and emotionally fulfilling travel. In this part, I focus on the dance, song, and instrumental performance of Kalymnian, and specifically Tarponite Kalymnian, identity as a marker, simultaneously, of belonging and distinction. Exploring these manifestations of an identity that is both transnational and intensely local, I highlight the ways in which Kalymnian Americans in Tarpon Springs use music and dance performance to distinguish themselves from other members of the Kalymnian diaspora. In addition, I examine how affiliations with different manifestations of Kalymnian music and dance illustrate the diversity of ideas about what it means to be Kalymnian in Tarpon Springs.

These inquiries are framed against the backdrop of the Pan-Kalymnian Federation of America's annual convention, held in Tarpon Springs on January 5–8, 2012. The site of this gathering rotates among various locales in the United States with large Kalymnian populations and with organized Kalymnian philanthropic societies or social clubs; analogous conventions are also held in Australia, which has a large Kalymnian population, and in Kalymnos itself. The 2012 convention, hosted by Tarpon's Kalymnian Society Agios Panteleimon, was attended by representatives from Kalymnian communities in Ohio, New York, Washington, DC, Indiana, and the Bahamas, as well as a dignitary sent by the mayor of Kalymnos itself. The timing of the convention was deliberate, coinciding with Tarpon's renowned Epiphany festivities, which annually draw thousands of visitors from all over the world. Accordingly, the convention featured nightly events with live music, social dancing, and performances by visiting and local Kalymnian dance groups, giving Tarpon's Kalymnians the opportunity to showcase local iterations of Kalymnian traditions and assert their community's strength and prestige on a pan-diasporic stage.

As we have seen, Tarponite Kalymnians are fiercely proud of their heritage and distinct regional identity, which they frequently invoke to distinguish themselves from other members of the Greek diaspora. Their command of the Kalymnian dance idiom is usually ascribed, by both themselves and other observers, to the relatively homogeneous cultural makeup of their community and to their exposure from birth to primarily Kalymnian influences. For them, according to one,

> when you're dancing to Kalymnian, it comes instant. You don't have to think about it, you don't have to think about what your feet are doing, or what the person next to you is doing, you're just in that moment because you already know that step, you know everything about that style. You adapt to that style so much by being here that you don't even have to [think]. . . . Say you're doing a Pontian dance, you have to think, "Oh, I have to bend my knees because I have to bob." With Kalymnian, you don't have to think, it just comes like that. [snaps fingers]

This naturally embodied fluency in Kalymnian traditions has served to distinguish the local dance groups, Levendia and the now-defunct Tzivaeri, from their peers in other Greek American communities during Greek dance festivals and church-sponsored competitions throughout the southeastern United States. Levendia, the more active of the two groups, consistently wins first place for dancing, singing, and style at nearly every such competition, and the group's members see these activities as an assertion of who they are and where they come from. "When we're up there dancing," one of my collaborators from Levendia tells me, "we're representing Tarpon Springs, our families, our friends. . . . It's almost like we're the ambassadors of the city." Others explicitly make more ambitious claims, speaking of representing not only Tarpon but Kalymnos itself, which is certainly how the group is perceived in the wider Greek American community.

But what, if anything, gives Tarponite Kalymnians the authority to speak for or define what it means to be Kalymnian, and not just Kalymnian in Tarpon Springs? The 2012 Pan-Kalymnian convention gave Tarponite Kalymnian dancers and musicians the opportunity to explore this question in dialogue with other localized versions of diasporic Kalymnian identity as embodied by their guests. Through their virtuosic performance of commonly recognized markers of Kalymnian being—particularly music and dance—the Tarponite hosts sought to distinguish themselves from their peers and defend their reputation as privileged bearers of "authentic" Kalymnian tradition.

Invitation and Challenge

The Tarponite Kalymnians' commitment to virtuosic and authoritative performance of Kalymnian identity was apparent from the inception of the 2012 Pan-Kalymnian convention. The opening night's social event was held at the Kalymniko Spiti or Kalymnian House, headquarters of Tarpon's Kalymnian Society. Local women cooked copious amounts of traditional Kalymnian delicacies such as *fila* (boiled grape leaves stuffed with rice, ground meat, and onions), *arvitsa* (chick peas and tomatoes cooked in a clay oven), and *keftedes* (fried meatballs). His Eminence Nikitas Lulias of Dardanellia, a Tarpon-born bishop of Kalymnian descent who was the Greek Orthodox Church's inaugural metropolitan of Hong Kong and Southeast Asia—the highest ecclesiastical rank to be held by a Kalymnian—gave the blessing, and his cousin, Congressman Gus Bilirakis, another Tarpon-born Kalymnian who holds the highest political office of any Kalymnian American, contributed opening remarks. Even before the music and dancing began, Tarpon's Kalymnian community asserted its gastronomic, religious, and political authority to all present.

My friend M. (a native of Kalymnos) and I were responsible for providing the music for the event on violin and laouto. Significantly, this opening night, on which the local Kalymnians aimed to set the tone for the conference, was programmed to exclusively feature live traditional Kalymnian music, rather than the customary alternation between the band and a DJ, which would be the standard for the rest of the weekend. Tables and chairs were set up outside in the Kalymnian House's spacious flagstone courtyard; ringed by a tall white fence and imposing oak trees hung with Spanish moss, the setting was reminiscent of a *panigiri* or religious celebration in a church courtyard in Kalymnos. The crowd was near capacity, two hundred people or more at its height; roughly half were local Kalymnians, and the rest were visitors, mostly Kalymnians from Ohio and New York. We set up with our backs to the whitewashed wall of the main building, and after fiddling with the ancient PA system—the same crusty Peavey sound board and speakers that Levendia used at their first dance thirty years earlier—we started to play.

The night was warmer than we were expecting, but still cool enough to see our breath when we sang, and for our hands to numb slightly if we took a break for more than a few minutes. Ouzo was fetched to warm us and smooth our voices, and after about an hour of playing slow instrumental pieces as background music for dinner, we started "Yiala," an iconic issos, and a group of local college students

from Levendia got up to dance. The loose and noisy atmosphere changed immediately, as it often does when the first dancers hit the floor; everyone's attention
focused for a moment on the bouncing, swaying line, people craning their necks
or standing to catch a glimpse of the footwork. One of Levendia's dance instructors grabbed my microphone and sang the long, drawn-out "Eriiiiiiiiii" that
introduces the traditional verses of welcome:

> *Chilia kalos evrethime, chilia kai dio hiliades*
> *San karavoli prasinoi mesa stis prasinades!*
> *Yia des trapezia arhontika, potiria kroustallenia*
> *Agapita prosopata sto yiro kathismena.*

> A thousand, two thousand times well we've come together,
> Like green snails in the verdant places!
> Look at these noble tables with crystal glasses
> And beloved people seated around them.

Her gesture of hospitality—*Welcome, Kalymnian brothers and sisters! As your
hosts, we offer you abundant food, drink, and entertainment*—contained within
it an assertion of authority, and a friendly challenge, especially considering the
presence of the visiting Kalymnian dance groups. *This is how we do things here,*
she seemed to say. *We are the first to get up and dance, the first to sing, and will do
so with impeccably traditional style until the music stops. What about you?*

This gesture set the tone for the rest of the evening. Roughly half a dozen Tarponites spontaneously came up to the microphone and sang at different times,
reeling off *mantinades* and rhymes to their friends' cheers and whistles. The
members of Tzivaeri and Levendia repeatedly requested specific songs that they
all knew by heart, having learned them for performances or competitions, and
belted them out with coordinated passion, stamping their feet and stabbing the
air with their hands to emphasize the accents. At one point there were so many
people dancing, and so little available space to fit them, that they were knocking
over our microphone stands as they passed in front of us, and we had to hastily
squeeze together against the wall. When the dance floor was completely full, M.
and I sat glued together, our thighs touching, clouds of warm breath mingling in
the frigid air, his bow occasionally smacking into the face of my laouto. The atmosphere was one of almost maniacal merriment, shouts and ear-piercing shepherd's
whistles giving way to hysterical laughter at improvised satirical verses. After a
particularly scandalous rhyme, one old lady rushed forward in mock horror to
throw a handful of pepper in my mouth as punishment for the "spicy" lyrics.

At the midpoint of the evening, around 11:00 p.m., M. and I took a break
so that a choir of current and former members of Levendia could perform a

Figure 71. Pan-Kalymnian Federation dance at the Kalymnian House, Tarpon Springs, Florida, January 5, 2012. Photo by Tina Bucuvalas.

traditional Kalymnian Epiphany carol; afterward, the visiting dignitary from Kalymnos and the convention's organizing committee addressed the crowd and raffled off a pile of luxurious sponges. Following this pause in the festive dancing, M. and I convinced Skevos Karavokiros, Tarpon's lone remaining tsambouna player, to fetch his instrument from home. As he hooked his tsambouna up to an air compressor to help his weakened lungs keep the bag full, murmurs of surprise and delight ran through the crowd of visiting Kalymnians, many of whom had never seen a tsambouna outside of Kalymnos. Despite his initial bashfulness, Skevos played old shepherd melodies for over an hour, drawing a circle of dancers around him with his own unique sousta melodies and inspiring an impromptu duel of *pismatika* (satirical couplets) between M. and me. His daughter, son-in-law, nieces, and nephews watched proudly, clapping their hands and singing along, and the visitors marveled at what one told me could have been a scene from Skevos's native village of Vathis a hundred years earlier.[4]

Significantly, nearly everyone who danced at the opening night event was a Tarponite. The visitors from Ohio, New York, and other Kalymnian enclaves stood or sat in small groups, watching and listening, and until the very end almost none of them joined in the dancing. I wondered if they were intimidated, and I thought of a comment made by a non-Kalymnian member of Levendia, who said that before he joined the group and got to know them, they reminded him of a swim team from another school: cool, competitive, and aloof. When I later pointed out the visitors' lack of participation to one of the local dancers

283

and organizers of the event, she frowned. "To be honest with you, I didn't really notice," she said. "I hope it's not because they were being competitive." Although I was initially puzzled by this remark—if anyone was being competitive, it seemed to me to have been the hosts, not the visitors—upon further reflection, her perspective made sense. The local Kalymnians were simply doing what they do: pouring their hearts into the music and dancing that they love. To them, their behavior was as much an invitation as a challenge. From the Tarponite point of view, if the visitors were intimidated and chose not to participate, it was simply because of their own insecurity, inexperience, or inability to perform up to the standard established by the locals.

Performing Authority

These same issues of competitive performance of identity came to the fore a few nights later at the convention's main social event, the Epiphany ball. Held in the spacious function hall owned by Tarpon's Saint Nicholas Greek Orthodox Cathedral, the ball had a markedly different character from the event at the Kalymnian House. After a formal dinner and lengthy speeches, Kalymnian Americans in suits and ties and party dresses danced to DJ-spun Greek and American nightclub music in between long sets of live Kalymnian violin and laouto provided by M. and me. There was much more participation by the visiting Kalymnians than at the previous event, perhaps due to the more familiar setting, and regardless of the music being played the dance floor was continuously full from 10:00 p.m. until close to 2:00 a.m. Most of the middle-aged to elderly attendees danced primarily to the Kalymnian music, while the younger dancers stayed on the floor for most of the night, greeting the laouto and violin with as much noisy enthusiasm as they summoned for the DJ's pounding bass beats. Unlike at the Kalymnian House, dissenting attitudes were more freely expressed; I heard several visiting Kalymnian Americans express frustration at the emphasis on so much folk music. Conversely, many older attendees complained about the ear-splitting volume of the DJ's sets and what they termed the "undanceable" music that he was playing.

In addition to dinner, social dancing, awards, and speeches by the consul general of Greece, the Kalymnian mayor's representative, and other politicians—during which one proclaimed "To Tarpon Springs ine i defteri Kalymnos!" (Tarpon Springs is the second Kalymnos!)—the ball featured performances by visiting Kalymnian dance groups from elsewhere in the diaspora, as well as Tarpon's own Tzivaeri. M. and I were originally to play only for Tzivaeri's performance, having rehearsed with them in the morning; but when the other two groups realized, minutes before the show started, that we were accompanying Tzivaeri, they both asked us to play for them too. As we hastily talked through their chore-ography, they realized with alarm that they were both planning on performing the exact same program of dances, in the same order: "Dirlada" (an up-tempo couple's dance), the "Michanikos" (a relatively recently invented dance in which the leader mimics a crippled sponge diver), and the iconic pairing of issos and sousta. After some tense discussion and half-joking accusations about stealing each other's programs, the group set to perform second decided to change one of their numbers, substituting a *syrtos* for "Dirlada."

Both visiting groups entered to warm applause and performed reasonably well. However, the performance of the "Michanikos," an extremely difficult dance that requires focused concentration on the part of the lead dancer and nuanced communication with the musicians, was in both cases fraught with problems. The Michanikos, developed in the mid-twentieth century, is one of the few choreographed Kalymnian dances and the only one in circulation that is unique to Kalymnos. The musicians both follow the lead dancer's tortured move-ments as he mimics the paralyzed diver's labored attempts to walk, and cue the changes between the dance's different sections. Each dancer has his own person-alized way of playing the role of the crippled diver, and the climax of the dance, when the leader drops his walking stick and falls to the ground, is designed to be a moment of high drama, a cathartic communal experience through which the Kalymnian audience remembers and honors their own divers who have died or been paralyzed by decompression sickness. A highly skilled dancer and accom-panying musicians can spontaneously perform the dance if they pay close atten-tion to each other and correctly read each other's cues, even without rehearsal, but the musicians must know on what repetition of the main melodic theme the dancer plans to collapse. Before the visiting groups' performances, we agreed when each respective lead dancer would fall, but they both failed to give us the cue or pick up on those that we tried to convey. Both performances consequently fizzled out without great impact, and though the crowd cheered politely, it was obvious that they were underwhelmed. I spoke with the lead dancers from the respective groups afterward, and I gathered that in the heat of the moment they had simply forgotten where they were in the dance, whether from nerves or lack of experience.

Tzivaeri was the last group to perform. As soon as they entered the hall, dressed in the traditional costumes that their mothers, grandmothers, and in some cases they themselves had made, the atmosphere changed dramatically. Their energy and confidence were palpable, and an excited murmur spread through the crowd even before the music began. Once they started dancing, it was obvious that they were not only twice as large a group as the previous two but that they were far superior in experience, style, and stage presence. Their kefi (energy) was tremendous; whereas the other groups relied on tricky choreography that did

Figure 72. Tarpon Springs Kalymnian dance group Tzivaeri performing at the Pan-Kalymnian Federation's Epiphany ball, January 8, 2012. Photo by Eleni Christopoulos-Lekkas.

not always work, Tzivaeri just danced. They were relaxed, joyful, and supremely confident, the women seeming to float above the ground in their long *kavadis* (colored skirts), the men gliding effortlessly in and out of their figures. Their choreography was simple and elegant—they avoided dances with a performative, soloistic nature such as "Dirlada" and the "Michanikos"—and they executed it flawlessly. The performance felt like a particularly resonant glendi, one of those rare moments when dancers and musicians are so locked in that for a moment the boundary between them blurs. When they finished their last number—all thirty of them dancing a syrtos and singing at the top of their lungs in perfect unison— the applause was deafening, and it went on for roughly a minute.

Later in the evening, near the height of the glendi, with the members of all three groups dancing together to Kalymnian music, a young woman from Tzivaeri came up to the stage and asked for the "Michanikos." As we finished the previous tune, the floor cleared, everyone standing to the side to make room for a Tarponite college student and his parea, six or seven men from the dance group. He hoisted the walking stick and gave us a nod; as we began to play, cell phones and cameras came out to record the moment. His performance was relaxed, controlled, and unpretentious despite the dramatic shaking and twitching as he mimicked the crippled diver, and his timing was perfect: he reacted to all of our musical cues within a split second and fell to the ground at exactly the right moment. When the music changed to signal the last section, he leaped up, throwing off the hand that was helping him to his feet; he tossed aside the walking stick and went into a series of acrobatic squats and foot-slaps that electrified the crowd gathered around the dance floor. When the music stopped, he wiped his brow, nodded us an acknowledgment, and disappeared into the crowd.

It was clear that this virtuosic performance of the most recognizable danced marker of Kalymnian identity was intended both for his friends and peers from Tarpon, as a celebration of skill and shared history, and for the members of the visiting dance groups. To the latter, his relaxed, commanding performance said: *Look, this is how you dance the "Michanikos." I can do it twice as well as you, with more style, more energy, more kefi, even after having danced nonstop for three hours. Even out of costume, out of the formal spotlight, I'm closer to the prototype, more authentic.* While he danced, the dancers from the visiting groups who had performed the "Michanikos" earlier stood silently, arms folded across their chests, watching. It was less a challenge than a lesson, and they seemed to take it graciously. When the applause died down and we began the next tune, a light *kalamatianos* dance, they joined hands with the rest of the dancers as they spilled back onto the floor.

Watching the crowd throughout the evening, I noticed that every time we started up the issos—frequently described by Kalymnians as their "national anthem"—so many people rose to their feet to dance that there were often multiple circles on the dance floor, bumping into each other, weaving in and out, an ordered confusion of bodies and sounds moving through space. In the context of the Pan-Kalymnian convention, with Greek and American flags prominently displayed, citizens and officials from both nations' Kalymnian communities in attendance, and expressions of solidarity alternating with assertions of primacy and authority, the social and political dimensions of this "national anthem" are striking. In the Kalymnian diaspora, musical movement functions as a way to engage in dialogue within the collective body politic, a fluid means of exploring the constantly shifting hierarchies and degrees of cultural affiliation that play such a decisive role in the lives of these citizens. Responding to the hymn of their nation-across-nations by not only rising to their feet but moving hand-in-hand in noisy, joyful dance, they pledge allegiance to a common cultural ideal that allows them to individually interpret what it means to be Kalymnian.

Alternate Realities

After a week and a half of teaching and performing traditional Kalymnian music to enthusiastic and knowledgeable crowds at events organized by the members of Levendia and Tzivaeri, M. and I were invited to play at a baptism the night before our departure from Tarpon Springs. We were hired by a relative of the newly christened child, an acquaintance of ours from Kalymnos who was excited at the prospect of having traditional music at the event. Upon sealing our agreement, she even made a point of proclaiming, "Tha pexete mechri to 'Mera Merose'!" (You'll play until it's time to sing "Mera Merose"!), referring to the traditional last song of the glendi, sung at dawn. We expected a similar experience to what we had been having since we arrived and were looking forward to a long night of enjoyable music-making and dancing to cap off our time together in Tarpon. What actually awaited us was an exclamation point to my fieldwork, a surprising experience that eloquently summarized the diversity of interpretations of how, and what kind of, music and dance signify Kalymnian being in Tarpon Springs.

We were not acquainted with either side of the celebrating family, as they were not involved with the traditional music and dance scene in Tarpon. A friend had told us to expect extremely loud music from the DJ who would be playing during our breaks; she had overheard the child's mother say that she wanted the reception to be like a nightclub. As we set up on the floor in front of the DJ, we looked around, searching the crowd for familiar faces. We recognized a few people we knew from their peripheral involvement with Levendia, as well as several members of one of the visiting dance groups, but by and large the attendees were strangers to us. We started with an issos; after a week and a half of playing together hours a day, we were in perfect synchronization, and the music was ferociously good from the first note: gnarly, old-fashioned, and traditional. I looked up, expecting to see the dance floor packed in response to our performance of the Kalymnian national anthem, but to my surprise only the immediate baptismal party—ten people or so—was dancing. When we transitioned to a fast sousta, half of them dropped out, and the rest stopped dancing after just a few minutes. We played "Varka yialo," the most popular syrtos in Tarpon; nobody got up to dance. We switched to another tune, and another, songs that on previous nights had turned dozens of ecstatic faces our way and inspired rollicking sing-alongs, but to no avail. Our music elicited hardly a response.

While we were playing, perplexedly searching for the key to unlock a door that had so readily swung wide open for us until this moment, I noticed the father speak into the DJ's ear. As soon as we ended our medley of syrta, the DJ hit a button on his console, and out of the speakers came none other than "Varka yialo," the very tune we had just been playing. This version, though, was as different as could be: firmly rooted in a style popularly (and dismissively) known as *skilonisiotika* (a hybrid term that references both *nisiotika*, or generalized island music, and the "trashy" *skiladika*[5] style common in Greek nightclubs), it featured keyboards, electronic drums, and melody played by an electric violin that was barely distinguishable from a synthesizer. The singer, while using typical skiladika vocal technique, was obviously Kalymnian, judging by his accent.

On the whole, the contrast between the DJ's version of "Varka yialo" and the one we had just been playing could not have been greater, and neither could the audience's reaction. As soon as they heard the recording, the entire roomful of people got to their feet and rushed to the dance floor to salute this iteration of the Kalymnian national anthem. M. and I watched in shock as they danced away with evident pleasure, knees bent and arms waving in the Kalymnian style, tossing money at the DJ and on the floor. The father took us aside and told us that he did not want his guests to go home, so it would be best if we stopped playing for the night. "These are young people, not old-timers," he explained. He paid us half of the fee that we had asked for to play all night and told us we could leave. Standing there in a daze, our ears acclimated to the sound of the violin, and we recognized, through the ornamentation, who it was: the young grandson of the same old master violinist whose austerely traditional style we have spent out lives learning.

As we packed up our instruments, I reflected on what I had just experienced. The guests at this event obviously identify strongly with and deeply love the music that narrates their idea of what it means to be Kalymnian. To them, the modern, nightclub versions of the music are authentically Kalymnian in a way that ours are not: they resonate with their life experiences, expectations, and idea of a good time. It occurred to me that perhaps the musical events run by Levendia and Tzivaeri are not as representative of the community's tastes as I had previously thought. When the members of the traditional dance groups organize affairs, the music is oriented toward the old, traditional style because that is what they, through participation in these groups and reinforcement through association with other like-minded individuals, are accustomed to and associate with Kalymnian identity. When they are the dominant force at an event—such as the dances at which we had been playing over the previous ten days—people follow their lead and participate. But despite their high level of organization and prominence as public figures, it could very well be that they are a numerical minority in the Kalymnian community, and it is clear that their version of what it means musically to be a Kalymnian Tarponite is not universally shared. The musical aesthetic of their grandparents' generation, which they consider a vibrant link to a beloved past and an invaluable resource for re-creation and the attainment of self-knowledge, is to others stodgy, boring, and utterly incapable of producing the excitement and kefi that drives the dance.

On our way outside, we ran into the woman who had hired us. She was very apologetic and obviously embarrassed, and offered an excuse that further illustrates the divide between versions of authentic Kalymnian being in Tarpon. Gesturing dismissively toward the hall, she told us: "Ine oli panomerites, yi'afto" (They're all *panomerites*, that's why). The term *panomeritis*—"person from up-over-there"—is used colloquially in the Dodecanese to denote a foreigner or stranger, someone not from one's own community.[6] On its face, this comment seemed nonsensical: nearly all the guests were Kalymnian, and many of them were her own relatives. But on further reflection, it is clear to me that, in her mind, the various types of belonging as a Kalymnian are directly related to participation in and embodiment of ways of acting and being Kalymnian. As an older and more traditionally minded native of Kalymnos, she had grown up hearing the old-fashioned music that we play and associates authentic Kalymnian being with those sounds; the nightclub or skiladika aesthetic that resonates with the guests at the baptism strikes her as foreign. As we have seen time and again, music and dance practices are foremost among the means by which Kalymnian Tarponites perform their identity, and read others' performance.

Later, deconstructing the experience of the baptismal reception over margaritas at a Chili's on Route 19—as far as we could get from the Kalymnian enclave— M. mused that perhaps our intense disappointment at what had happened was of our own making. "Maybe it's our fault," he said. "Maybe we're too musically conservative, we're behind the times." All of those intricate laouto trills and special bowings, he suggested, mean nothing if people don't know how to read them and react to them, if they don't resonate with people. After all, he pointed out, the majority of what one hears at events in Kalymnos these days is exactly what the guests at the baptism wanted, and what the DJ gave them—not the music that we play and that our friends from the dance groups prefer. Our parea, our group of close friends, insists on the old-fashioned music and the personal relationships and communication between musicians and dancers that it requires; they listen to old tapes of tsambouna, violin, and laouto in their cars, at work, at home; and they appreciate the nuances of our bowing, strumming, and improvised poetry. But their prerogative, and ours, is not the only one. Indeed, it may not even be the most widely held, even in Tarpon, a place that we, and many others, think of as a hotbed of traditional Kalymnian culture.

There is clearly a multiplicity of ideas at work in Tarpon Springs concerning Kalymnian identity. What it means to embody that identity, to be Kalymnian, shifts according to one's surroundings and the company one keeps; when music and dance are the medium of this embodiment, this shifting is even more fluid, and the specific social context in which a given event or situation is embedded, the collective goal of a gathering of people, influences how identity and belonging are performed. Kalymnian music and dance traditions are a surprisingly supple and varied way for Kalymnian Tarponites to explore, through virtuosic performance, the various options of identification available to them, and give them the option to engage in a dialogue with each other and their shared heritage that references the past, illuminates the present, and points, inevitably, toward the future.

Notes

1. Tarpon Springs also has a Sister City relationship with the Dodecanese islands of Halki and Symi—the ancestral homes of a sizable minority of Greek Tarponites who also made significant contributions to the sponging industry—as well as with the city of Larnaca, Cyprus.

2. Reflecting regionalist tendencies, most Kalymnian Americans in Tarpon Springs—even members of the third or fourth generation since immigration—explicitly identify themselves as "Kalymnian" rather than "Greek" or "Greek American."

3. Tsifteteli is an improvised women's dance featuring subtle movements of the hips, arms, and hands, popularly associated with seduction and the Ottoman sultan's harem.

4. Like many Kalymnian men of his generation who grew up herding goats in the mountains, Skevos learned to play the tsambouna at an early age. He has many stories of making and playing the instrument in childhood, as well as entertaining his fellow sponge divers while working on sponge boats off the coast of Benghazi as a teenager. He emigrated to Australia in the 1950s, married, and eventually stopped playing, even losing his tsambouna. When he moved his family to Tarpon Springs in 1973, he was reunited with his childhood friend, tsambouna player Nikitas Tsimouris, but did not take the instrument up again until much later. Skevos is a humble and quiet man, and his own children had no idea that he played tsambouna until his daughter brought one back as a souvenir from her honeymoon in Kalymnos. Thinking that her father would perhaps like to hang it on the wall, she was surprised when he inflated it and began playing in the baggage claim area of Tampa International Airport. Since then he has not only resumed playing tsambouna but has also taken up the violin, laouto, lyra, and clarinet, in order, as he tells me, "to pass the time."

5. *Skiladika* means "dog music," presumably because the vocal style typical of the genre is often compared, pejoratively, to a dog's whine. Generally featuring electrified bouzouki, keyboards, and drums (or drum machine), skiladika is characterized by the excessive use of audio effects, ear-splitting volume, melodramatic lyrics, and a social environment that encourages the conspicuous flaunting of wealth and sexuality, real or imagined.

6. In colloquial Greek, the directional adverbs *kato* (down) and *pano* (up) take on meanings of proximity and distance, and thus familiarity and foreignness, respectively. Greek speakers will thus refer to their hometown or native country as *kato*—reminiscent of the English "down home"—and to a nonnative locale, such as a city or country to which they have relocated for work, as *pano*. For Kalymnian Americans in Tarpon, the frequently asked question "Tha pas kato to kalokeri?"—literally, "Will you go down this summer?"—means "Will you go to Kalymnos?"

References

Albright, Ann Cooper. 1997. *Choreographing Difference: The Body and Identity in Contemporary Dance*. Middletown, CT: Wesleyan University Press.

Anderson, Benedict. 1991. *Imagined Communities: Reflections on the Origin and Spread of Nationalism*. London: Verso.

Caraveli, Anna. 1985. "The Symbolic Village: Community Born in Performance." *Journal of American Folklore* 98: 259–86.

Clarke, Eric. 2005. *Ways of Listening: An Ecological Approach to the Perception of Musical Meaning*. Oxford: Oxford University Press.

Clifford, James. 1997. *Routes: Travel and Translation in the Late Twentieth Century*. Cambridge, MA: Harvard University Press.

Cowan, Jane K. 1990. *Dance and the Body Politic in Northern Greece*. Princeton, NJ: Princeton University Press.

Csordas, Thomas. 1990. "Embodiment as a Paradigm for Anthropology." *Ethos* 18, no. 1 (March): 5–47.

Desmond, Jane. 1993. "Embodying Difference: Issues in Dance and Cultural Studies." *Cultural Critique* 26 (Winter): 33–63.

Downey, Greg. 2002. "Listening to *Capoeira*: Phenomenology, Embodiment, and the Materiality of Music." *Ethnomusicology* 46, no. 3 (September): 487–509.

Du Boulay, Juliet. 1974. *Portrait of a Greek Mountain Village*. Oxford: Clarendon Press.

Frantzis, George T. 1962. *Strangers at Ithaca: The Story of the Spongers of Tarpon Springs*. St. Petersburg, FL: Great Outdoors Publishing.

Langer, Susanne. 1983. "Virtual Powers." In *What Is Dance? Readings in Theory and Criticism*, edited by Roger Copeland and Marshall Cohen. Oxford: Oxford University Press.

Lewis, J. Lowell. 1995. "Genre and Embodiment: From Brazilian *Capoeira* to the Ethnology of Human Movement." *Cultural Anthropology* 10, no. 2 (May): 221–43.

Lippard, Lucy P. 1999. *On the Beaten Track: Tourism, Art, and Place*. New York: New Press.

Stokes, Martin. 1997. Introduction to *Ethnicity, Identity and Music: The Musical Construction of Place*, edited by Martin Stokes. New York: Berg Publishers.

Titon, Jeff Todd. 2008. "Knowing Fieldwork." In *Shadows in the Field: New Perspectives for Fieldwork in Ethnomusicology*, edited by Gregory Barz and Timothy J. Cooley, 25–41. New York: Oxford University Press.

Wong, Deborah. 2008. "Moving: From Performance to Performative Ethnography." In *Shadows in the Field: New Perspectives for Fieldwork in Ethnomusicology*, edited by Gregory Barz and Timothy J. Cooley. New York: Oxford University Press.

PART THREE

Delivering the Music: Recording Companies
and Performance Venues

Greek Record Making in the Early Days, 1896–1937

—Dick Spottswood

After Thomas Edison created the sound recording and reproducing device he called the phonograph in 1877, he set about developing it as a dictation machine with possibilities for education and other practical applications. In the 1880s, his device languished until others sought to develop it further, and he then focused on it once more. By 1889, it became clear that the phonograph had more potential as a conveyor of music and entertainment than in offices, and coin-operated phonographs were soon popular and profitable in amusement arcades. By the mid-1890s, spring-wound table phonographs retailing from fifteen to fifty dollars were available for use at home or anywhere else. Edison and Columbia phonographs accommodated music on wax cylinders, and Emile Berliner's Gramophone (or Gram-O-Phone) came with seven-inch single-side gutta-percha disc pressings. Originally, "phonograph" and "gramophone" designations indicated cylinder and disc players, respectively, but, as cylinders became obsolete, a "phonograph" in the United States was any device that could reproduce sound from prerecorded discs.

As the fledgling industry began to grow at the end of the nineteenth century, English and German entrepreneurs set out to create new markets for machines and records throughout Eurasia. Portable equipment and technicians (called "recordists" or "experts") traveled to urban centers near and far to capture local and regional music, setting up recording equipment in hotel rooms and other rentable spaces. Phonograph companies correctly assumed that if familiar and appealing music was available, customers would buy records and phonographs to play them on. Hand-wound acoustic phonographs required no external power source and could be operated anywhere. These conditions prompted the production of an extensive body of folk, classical, popular, and religious music from many locales. Surviving early recordings give us valuable insights into the kaleidoscopic world of local, regional, and international music, languages, and performance styles from the first years of the twentieth century.

The first phonograph companies were in the United States. The earliest cylinder phonographs could record as well as reproduce, and in the 1890s local agents

Figure 73. Yiorgos Tsanakas, "Fa Majore," 1908. Victor Records
63544-A. Courtesy of Meletios Pouliopoulos.

in large American cities could make new records of local talent and duplicate them for sale. But their sound was poor and the wax cylinders fragile; few locally made records from the early years have survived.

Overseas, the Gramophone Company (aka His Master's Voice, or HMV) in England was first out of the gate, and surviving documents show how quickly recording expeditions were launched throughout Europe. The first were in 1899 and 1900, to Leipzig, Budapest, Stockholm, The Hague, Berlin, Milan, Madrid, Paris, Bucharest, Belgrade, Saint Petersburg, and Constantinople, producing seven-inch, single-sided discs that played at approximately 70 rpm for around two minutes, matching the playing time of cylinders.

Hugo Strötbaum has noted that before World War I, Gramophone Company recording teams from England and Germany regularly visited Constantinople and occasionally Athens (1909), and Smyrna and Thessaloniki (1909–1911), to capture the music of Greek and Turkish singers and musicians. The Favorite Company made Greek-language records in Constantinople in 1905, 1910, and 1911–1913, and in Smyrna and Thessaloniki in 1912. Other active companies in the region included Lyrophone and, later, Odeon. Ten-inch records became the standard size for popular records, replacing seven-inch discs by 1906. Around 1910, Victor began to reissue Gramophone masters from Greece and Turkey. Many were anonymously credited to Helleniki Estudiantina, Estudiantina

Figure 74. Tetos Demetriades, "Yiati, Yiati, Yiati," 1936. Orthophonic S-358-A. Courtesy of Meletios Pouliopoulos.

Grecque, or simply to "Tenor," "Baritone," and the like. A handful of performers, like Lefteris Menemenlis, Yiangos Psamatianos, and Yiorgos Tsanakas, occasionally appear on reissues, but others from the 1900–1912 recording era remain to be documented in depth.

World War I disrupted recording activity throughout Europe and temporarily ended Middle Eastern expeditions. Favorite's last records are from 1912–1913, when it was absorbed into the Carl Lindström group in Germany. Gramophone made no records in Constantinople after 1912 until 1927. After Greeks were expelled from Turkey in 1922, Gramophone recorded Greek music in Athens, where visits occurred in 1922 and annually after 1926, with more frequent stops after 1929. Electrically made records replaced wooden-horn acoustic records in the summer of 1927 and were used exclusively thereafter.

In 1929, Victor Records began to reissue Gramophone masters in America to supplement Victor's domestic catalog. In 1930, producer Tetos Demetriades sailed to Athens to commission records exclusively for the US market. They were made by Gramophone recording engineers from London and included singers Dalgas (Antonis Diamantidis) and Kostas Karipis, violinists Ogdondakis (Ioannis Dragatsis) and Salonikios (Dimitrios Semsis), accordionist Papatzis (Antonis Amiralis), kemençe (Turkish lyra) player Lambros Leondaridis, and oud player Agapios Tomboulis. All but Semsis had been born in Turkey in the nineteenth

297

Figure 75. George Helmis. *"Ax Mari!* Ah Mary!," 1918. Columbia
E-4206. Courtesy of Meletios Pouliopoulos.

century and were among Greece's finest performers in the style we call *rebetika* today. Record sales in America justified return trips to Athens by Demetriades in 1931 and 1932 for further sessions. When Victor stopped releasing new Greek and Turkish records in 1933, Demetriades produced them on his own Orthophonic label while still employed at Victor. The company reissued new material in many languages from Gramophone through the 1930s, continuing to press both Victor and Orthophonic records.

The earliest known Greek-language records were made in May 1896 by the tenor Michael Arachtingi for the Berliner company in New York, the first to publish disc records. Initially Berliner competed with Edison and Columbia cylinders until around 1910, when it was clear that the disc format would prevail. Around then, a hundred or so Greek records from Gramophone and Favorite in Europe were reissued in America by Victor and Columbia, and many remained available through the early 1920s. In the 1910s, most Greek records made in New York were performances by concert-style tenors like John Pavolvits, Marios Lyberopoulos, and George Helmis. Columbia took the next step in 1916, recording singer Kyria Koula (or Coula) (Kyriaki Antonopoulou, ca. 1880–1954) with violin, *laouto*, and *santouri* in Anatolian style. She sang in both Greek and Turkish, and her records sold well. She left Columbia to form her own Panhellenion label in 1919, and it thrived until patent-protected electrical recording technology put hers and other independent labels out of business after 1925.

Beginning in 1918, both Columbia and Victor recorded Marika Papagika (1890–1943) from the island of Kos. She recorded popular, demotic, rebetic, and even a few Turkish songs through the 1920s, and her records were even more popular than Mme. Koula's. After February 1925, they were made exclusively in the twelve-inch size, allowing an extra minute or so for each performance. Many were reissued in Greece in the days when local record making was infrequent. They set a standard for other prominent women singers, especially Rita Abatzi (1903–1969) and Roza Eskenazi (ca. 1895–1980), whose 1930s records were popular in Greece and America, dominating both markets until the bouzouki-based Piraeus underworld music of Markos Vamvakaris, Yiorgios Batis, Stratos Pagioumtzis, and Vassilis Tsitsanis eclipsed the older Anatolian style.

Bouzoukis were considered low class and were rarely on record before 1932, when Ioannis Halikias (Jack Gregory, born in Sparta, 1897–1958) recorded two celebrated solos in New York that made the instrument fashionable enough to be recorded extensively in Greece. The roughneck and outlaw Piraeus songs associated with bouzoukis were tolerated until 1936–1937, when the Ioannis Metaxas regime proscribed lyrics dealing with hash dens, prostitution, prison, and other underworld themes, and banned so-called eastern elements from the music. Although bouzouki-based rebetika continued, it dealt with safer themes and flourished alongside romantic tangos, waltzes, *kantades*, and other cosmopolitan styles that were less threatening and more upscale.

Earlier in 1931, Electric and Musical Industries (EMI) in England consolidated the Columbia and Gramophone labels. Although it continued to produce Gramophone (HMV), Columbia, Odeon, and Parlophone records as separate entities, all operated under a single roof. Greek artists in Athens often recorded for more than one of them, and their records were reissued in America by Victor (Gramophone), Decca (Odeon and Parlophone), and Columbia. After EMI built a permanent studio in Athens in 1936, record making there became as professionalized, industrialized, and monopolized as it was in London, New York, Paris, and other major culture centers. Influenced by the Metaxas ban, the music stressed international appeal at the expense of earlier styles, and new records from Athens became as popular in America as they were at home.

Recommended Reading

Gronow, Pekka, and Ilpo Saunio. 1998. *An International History of the Recording Industry*. London: Cassell.

Holst, Gail. 1975. *Road to Rembetika: Music of a Greek Sub-Culture*. Athens: Denise Harvey.

Spottswood, Richard K. 1990. *Ethnic Music on Records: A Discography of Ethnic Recordings Produced in the United States, 1893–1942.* 7 vols. Urbana: University of Illinois Press.

Strötbaum, Hugo. 1993. *Seventy-Eight Revolutions per Minute in the Levant: Discography of Favorite's Oriental Recordings.* 3rd ed. Privately published.

———. 2015. *Dating Oriental Recordings of the Gramophone Company According to Matrix Number (1900–1919).* Privately published.

Record Reissues

JSP Records (London) is producing an ongoing series of reissues from 78-rpm original discs in private collections, including these titles:

JSP7776   *Rembetika: Music of the Greek Underground*
JSP77105   *Rembetika 2: More Music of the Greek Underground*
JSP77111   *Vassilis Tsitsanis: Important Pre-War Rembetika, 1936–1940*
JSP77123   *Vassilis Tsitsanis: The Postwar Years, 1946–1954*
JSP77132   *Markos Vamvakaris: Master of Rembetika, 1932–1938*
JSP77146   *Apostolos Hadzichristos: Selected Recordings, 1937–1953*
JSP77152   *Women of Rembetika: Traditional Greek Music, 1908–1947*
JSP77165   *Rembetika 8: Have They Got Hashish in Hell? Rare Greek Cuts, 1920–1957*

These inexpensive sets usually contain four CDs and brief annotations. There are additional JSP collections of Turkish, Epirot, and demotic music.

Greek Music Piano Rolls in the United States

—Meletios Pouliopoulos

In the fall of 2014, Chris Pantezelos,[1] a luthier in the Boston area, called to say that someone had walked into his store with a box of piano rolls. He said that they were Greek and asked if I knew anything about them. At that time I knew little about player pianos, and nothing about Greek piano roll music. What I was soon to learn is that the Greek piano rolls are among the earliest recordings of Greek music in America.

Because there was so little information on Greek piano rolls, I decided to undertake a limited study. I examined forty-two such rolls—most from the early to mid-1920s. To date them, I referred to the surviving QRS productions books (QRS being the largest manufacturer of piano rolls at the time), the 1923 QRS Greek piano roll catalog, and the May 29, 1926, edition of the newspaper *Kaliphornia* (published in San Francisco by Bill Roumpogiannis and Cer. Tsapralis), which has an advertisement that includes a QRS catalog.[2] I also consulted the 1927–1928 general catalog of Atlas Department Store located at 25 Madison Street in New York: on page 27, they ran a full-page advertisement listing the Greek QRS rolls available through them.[3]

Player pianos were popular in United States in the late nineteenth and early twentieth centuries, reaching their peak in 1923 (Roehl 1961). The traditional player piano, or pianola, contained a pneumatic mechanism that ran with air generated by pumping the foot pedals. The music was recorded or set on a paper roll with perforations, with each perforation corresponding to a key on the keyboard. Piano rolls were sometimes produced with song lyrics, so that one could sing along as the roll played. The rolls might be thought of as an early form of karaoke.

Now located in Buffalo, New York, the QRS company has been producing rolls daily for over 100 years. At the peak of production in 1923, they had twelve locations in the United States and Canada. In April 1923, QRS published an eleven-page catalog with all titles in Greek and English. In that catalog, 60 percent of the piano rolls offered for sale featured non-Greek music—mostly classical plus some popular and patriotic songs. And 40 percent of the company's

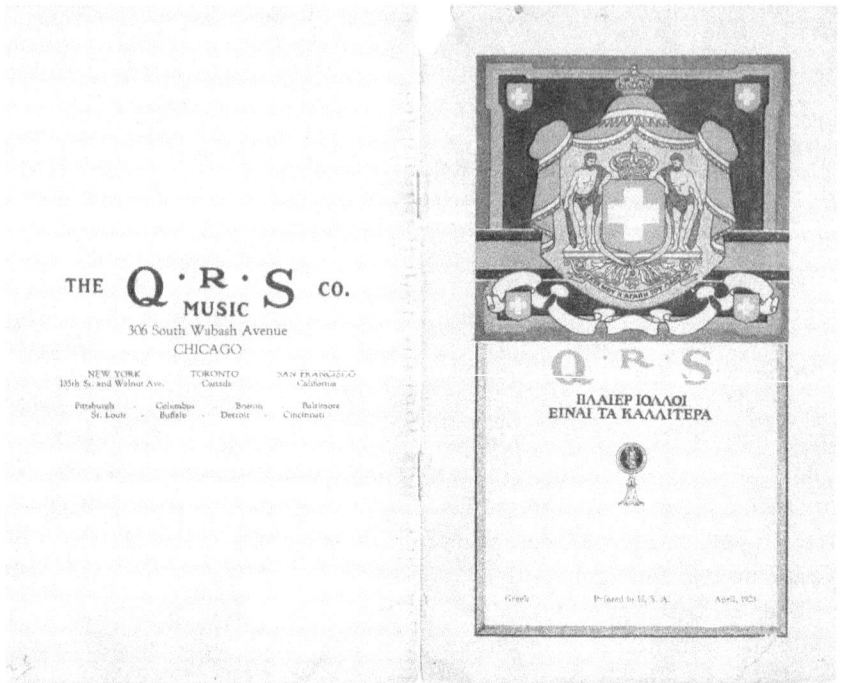

Figure 76. QRS, *Plaier iolli einai ta kallitera*, April 1923. QRS Company, Chicago. Courtesy of the Bob Berkman Collection/Pianola Enterprises.

offerings was Greek titles, mostly folk music from the mainland and Asia Minor, music from Greek operettas, and a few patriotic songs.

In order to bulk up their ethnic market catalogs, QRS included standard classical pieces and popular American and foreign numbers that were recorded for the mainstream American market, and then simply relabeled them with Greek titles in order to target the Greek market. Sometimes the lyrics were direct translations, but more often they were adapted. The popular Neapolitan song "O sole mio" (My Sunshine), composed by Eduardo di Capua, was released on a Greek QRS word roll (WF-7227) with the title "Μαρκαν και αν εισε," which translates as "If You Are Away." This lyrical adaptation was recorded by Tetos Demetriades in New York in 1926 on Columbia Records (7032-F/107314–2).[4]

Classical music popular in the latter part of the nineteenth century and early part of the twentieth century appeared not only in the early Greek piano roll catalogs but also in the early Greek 78-rpm discography. One such song, whose title was altered, is the "Blue Danube Waltz." QRS released piano roll F-60511, "Ο κυανους Δουναβις" (The Blue Danube). Columbia Records released the song on a 78 in its Ethnic Records series with the title "Τα κυματα του Δουναβεως" (E-2896), which was the title of another composition, "Waves of the Danube."

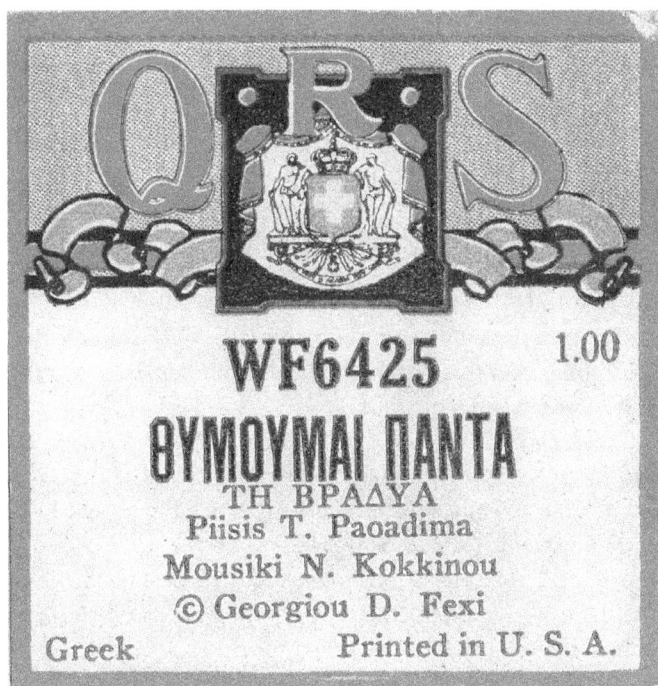

Figure 77. "Thymoumai panta ti vradia." Lyrics by T. Papadima. Music by Nikos Kokkinos. Published by George Fexis. QRS WF-6425. Courtesy of Meletios Pouliopoulos.

Within a few short years after releasing the 1923 Greek piano roll catalog, QRS abandoned their marketing of classical pieces to the Greek market.

Documenting Greek piano rolls presents many challenges. Bob Berkman, who currently owns Pianola Enterprises, is a retired QRS employee who continues to serve as the company's official historian. According to Berkman, none of the original masters of Greek piano rolls from the 1920s and 1930s survive in the QRS archives (2015). In the past, it was common practice to retain a master word roll for reference, but as soon as a roll was discontinued, the master would be destroyed. As for the Greek rolls and QRS's business records pertaining to them, all are gone with the exception of scattered entries in few pages of production logs from the late 1920s and early 1930s. These logs generally listed the title of the recording, the copyright owner's name, the assigned catalog number, the tempo, the layout date, and the date the recording was shipped from New York to Chicago for duplication.

Unlike standard procedures for commercial 78-rpm records, QRS did not use a matrix numbering system for dating their piano rolls, and their numbering systems for Greek rolls changed over the years. The earliest Greek rolls produced by QRS had five-digit numbers—as did the non-Greek rolls. By the time the

1923 Greek catalog was released, four-digit numbers were being assigned with either an *F* prefix for foreign or a *WF* indicating a foreign word roll. The older five-digit numbered Greek recordings did not appear in the 1923 catalog or in the reviewed listings thereafter, and they apparently were never assigned new four-digit numbers.

QRS would often take a non-Greek title and issue it to the Greek market with a different catalog number and a Greek title. The catalog numbers that QRS assigned were not reserved for a particular ethnic market. For example, catalog numbers 9890 through 9990 may have included Spanish, French, and Greek titles. In addition, as a manufacturer of piano rolls, QRS would often produce rolls for other companies that carried their own branding. In these cases, the roll numbers were blocked and sequential.

Piano rolls were usually more than just a recording of one person performing on a piano. Arrangers could do whatever they wanted, with several keys playing at the same time. Usually, sheet music was provided to produce the roll, and employees would then hand-punch paper based on the sheet music. The music produced on early Greek piano rolls often followed specific Greek recordings that were released in the United States on the Columbia, Victor, and Panhellenion labels. Other early rolls were based on sheet music published in both Greece and the United States.

In cases when early Greek piano roll songs had not previously appeared on 78-rpm records but rather came from published sheet music or were transcribed from oral tradition, they were the earliest known recordings of these works. In the early 1920s, when radio was popular, these unique recordings found their way to homes across America.

At least two Greek publishing houses (among probably others) were credited on some of the early QRS piano rolls: Μυστακίδου & Μακρή (Mystakidou and Makri) and Γεωργίου Δ. Φέξη (Georgiou D. Fexi), both based in Athens. QRS word roll 6215, "Εμβατήριον Βενιζέλου" (Venizelos's March), was composed by Σ. Καισαρη (Spyridon Kaisari) and published in Greece by Γ. Φέξη (G. Fexi) with the title "Ο γυιός του Ψηλορείτη." It honored Eleftherios Venizelos, a Greek statesman who served as prime minister from 1910 to 1920 and again from 1928 to 1933. In the United States, there are no known 78-rpm recordings of this song.

One multisong roll that was not included the 1923 catalog or subsequent listings, QRS F-42103, was titled "Four Greek Selections: (1) National Hymn, (2) Dance Kalamata, (3) For the Country, (4) Awaken Do Not Sleep." Two of these songs were easily identifiable. The national anthem of Greece, "Hymn to Liberty," a poem written in 1823 by Dionysios Solomos and set to music in 1865 by Nikolaos Mantzaros, was recorded on this roll as the first selection. The folk song now known as "Mantili kalamatiano" is the roll's second selection. The other two numbers have not been identified. While the "National Hymn" was beautifully

Figure 78. "Paidia m san thete leventia." Transcription by Nikos Kokkinos. Published by George Fexis. QRS WF-6259. Courtesy of Meletios Pouliopoulos.

rendered, "Dance Kalamata" unfortunately was not. Perhaps this explains why the roll was soon discontinued. By 1923, "Hymn to Liberty" had been released on QRS word roll WF-6082, and a new rendition of "Dance Kalamata" was produced as "Kalamatianos horos" on QRS F-6522.

The song "For the Country" from "Four Greek Selections" was published by G. Fexi, although the publisher was not credited. It was written by Spyridon Kaisari with sheet music published in Greece in 1902[5] and released around 1911 on 78 rpm on Columbia Records (E-834).

Certain Greek dances did not translate well on the QRS rolls. The *tsamikos* rhythm, usually in 6/4 or 3/4 meter, did not produce well on the piano rolls that were sampled. Most likely this was due to the non-Greek staff at QRS, who were unfamiliar with Greek music. Both "(1) Platanos, (2) Harem Dance" (QRS F-32843) and "Enas aetos" (QRS F-6523) were in this category—the melody was in the rendering, but without the familiar traditional rhythm it was impossible to dance to the music. However, many other Greek rhythms, such as the *syrtos, kalamatianos, zeibekiko*, and *aptalikos*, translated quite well in the piano rolls that were reviewed.

In "Παιδιά μ' σαν θέτε λεβεντιά" (QRS word roll WF-6259), the transcription credit was given to Nikos Kokkinos and the publisher listed as George Fexis.

Traditional songs such as this often do not credit a composer, but sometimes they note the person who transcribed the sheet music. The popular traditional song "Παιδιά μ' σαν θέτε λεβεντιά" was released on several early 78-rpm records including Columbia Records (E-7715 and E-7746) by Marika Papagika, Panhellenion Records (8004) by Kyria Koula, and Victor Records (63546) by P. Zorbanis. Set to the rhythm of a tsamikos dance, the song did not render well on the piano roll. The melody is there, but it lacks the essential tempo. Such appears to be the case with "To tsompanopoulo" (The Shepherd Boy) (QRS F-32819), a song written by Nikos Kokkinos with sheet music published by Fexis. The alternate title for this song is "Τσομπανάκος είμ' ο δόλιος."

Several Greek recording artists created arrangements that appeared on early Greek piano rolls. Markos Sifnios, a cellist who recorded in the 1910s and 1920s, arranged "Ta oula sou" (QRS piano roll F-6995), a traditional song from Asia Minor. He also recorded this song with Marika Papagika in July 1919 on Columbia Records (E-5193). On the label of the piano roll, his name is incorrectly spelled as "Tifnios."

Lukianos Cavadias, a pianist born in 1879 in Istanbul, recorded extensively for Columbia Records. He arranged and played "Alem Dag zeimpekiko" (QRS piano roll F9170). The title, which was written in Greek on the label, could not be matched to any 78-rpm Greek record that was released in the United States or in Greece. After much investigation, the song was identified by Athena Labiri, a young musician in Greece, as "Rast nikrîz zeybek" by Tanburi Cemil Bey. Bey was a celebrated composer and virtuoso musician from Istanbul and a contemporary of Cavadias. Allemdag is a mountainous area to the east of Istanbul, and also the name of one of the districts in the city.

Cavadias, who arrived in New York in 1913,[6] often signed the piano rolls that he produced. When someone signed a roll, it usually meant that he or she was involved in the recording or rendering process. Through his piano rolls, Cavadias brought several songs to America from Asia Minor. Along with "Alem Dag zeimpekiko" was "Re minore symrnaikes manes" (QRS F-9172), which was not included in the 1923 catalog. These songs have no known recordings in the Greek American 78-rpm discography. "Ti se meli esenane" (QRS F-9166) is a popular syrtos from Asia Minor. Cavadias's rendering is beautiful and contains an entire section that I had never previously heard. Signed by Cavadias, the piano roll states that it is played by him. The roll that I reviewed was hand-stamped "Litsas & Malicoutis Bros., 195 Broadway, Boston, Mass., Tel. Hancock 1679." Years after the release of the piano roll, in 1927, Marika Papagika recorded the song on Columbia Records (F-56061). Since then, the song has gained enormous popularity in the United States and is still being performed and recorded today.

Other traditional songs from Asia Minor can be found among the early Greek piano rolls. QRS piano roll F-42166, "Drunk Again," is the familiar song "Pali methismenos eisai," which was recorded by Marios Lyberopoulos on Columbia (E-3611). The song also is known by the title "To koutsavaki." Other songs were recorded on 78 rpm with the same name, but they are different songs.

In attempting to understand the music recorded and produced on Greek piano rolls, it is impossible to rely on titles alone. Some titles on the piano roll labels were in Greek and others in English. Sometimes they appeared as Greek words with Latin letters, other times just by the dance they represented. However, the labels often provided other clues, such as the composer or lyricist, and they occasionally contained a publishing line. Indeed, there were Greek piano rolls that were altogether mislabeled in title, song, and credit.

Piano roll QRS F-32843 was labeled as "(1) Platanos, (2) Harem Dance," but it appears that the numbers were reversed in order. It began with an unfamiliar song, presumably "Harem Dance" as given in the title. After a short break, "Platanos" was revealed as the familiar traditional song "Ναχει καει ο πλατανος." After another break, the two songs were repeated in order. Simple, perhaps low-budget piano rolls would sometimes be extended by repeating previous sections in the production. Such appears to be the case with this unfortunate roll, which was not included among the offerings by the time QRS published its 1923 catalog. It is curious, though, to wonder where "Harem Dance" came from. Was it perhaps a song taken from old sheet music? Or a melody passed down from oral tradition that was transcribed?

The Greek piano rolls also included operettas, a genre that was popular in the early part of the twentieth century. Although the genre has died out, many of the songs found their way into Greek popular music and rebetika—and some still survive today. Several songs from the operetta Οι Απάχηδες των Αθηνών (The Apaches of Athens) were produced on piano rolls and recorded on 78-rpm records. The first known performance of the operetta was in Athens in 1921. By the 1928 Atlas catalog, the QRS piano roll "Ποσο σ'εχω συμπαθησει" by Nikos Hatziapostolou (WF-7407) was released. There were multiple 78-rpm releases of operetta songs in America, including Marika Papagika on Columbia (7006F), Menelaos Theletridis on Panhellenion (346), and Tassia and Tetos Demetriades on Victor (68830). Demetriades also released "Ποσο σ' εχω συμπαθησει" on Columbia (7029F). Although very popular in its day, the song has fallen out of the current Greek repertoire.

Two other songs from the operetta The Apaches of Athens were mislabeled in the QRS Greek piano rolls. On the piano rolls, both were called " Οι Απάχηδες των Αθηνών," but QRS word roll WF-6744 has the song "San oneiro" by Theophrastos Sakellaridis, and QRS word roll WF-7088 has the song "Mono me sena" by Nikos Hatziapostolou. "Mono me sena" was recorded many times over the years, and revived and made popular again by Nikos Gounaris and Eva Styl in the early 1950s on Liberty Records (141). The song "Οι Απάχηδες των Αθηνών"

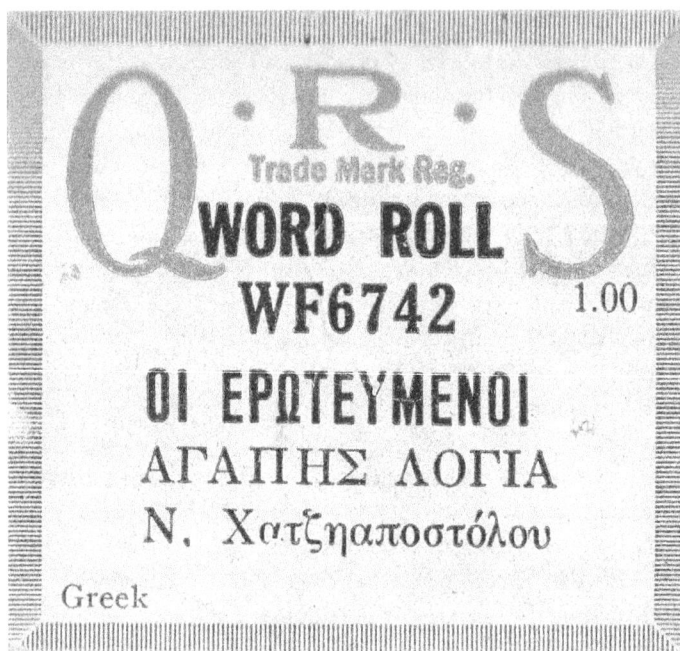

Figure 79. Nikos Hatziapostolou, "Oi eroteumenoi: agapis logia." QRS WF-6742. Courtesy of Meletios Pouliopoulos.

was released on 78 rpm first as an instrumental on Panhellenion Records (326) and Okeh Records (82022), and then in 1922 as a vocal version with Maria Smyrnaiou on Victor Records (73314).

Music from the 1919 operetta *O arlekinos* (The Harlequin) by Theophrastos Sakellaridis also suffered various mislabelings in the piano rolls and the 78-rpm discography. QRS piano word roll WF-7087, "Ο αρλεκίνος," was listed with transposed numbers "7078" in the 1923 QRS catalog. The numbers were fixed by the 1928 listing in the Atlas catalog, where the song appeared as "Πω! Πω! Πω! (Ο αρλεκίνος)." In the 78-rpm discography, the song was released with the title "Po Po Po" as an instrumental on Panhellenion Records (8063) and on Columbia Records (56174F). Tetos Demetriades created a vocal version on Victor Records (73347) with the title "Ο Μόρτης (Πω, Πω, Πω)," also performed by Marika Papagika as "Po po po (O mortis)" on Columbia (7003F). More recently, some rebetika bands have revived the song and are reintroducing it to Greek American audiences.

The music of Theophrastos Sakellaridis can also be heard on QRS piano word roll WF-7185, "I glykeia Nana," from the operetta of the same name. The publishing credit for the sheet music is given as "Z. Marki." In piano roll listings, this work appeared with a different catalog number: WF-6991. On record, it was released in the United States on Victor (73754) by Petros Zounarakis.

Another piano roll song from an operetta was "Οι ερωτευμενοι—αγαπης λογια" (The Lovers: Words of Love) (QRS word roll 6742), by Nikos Hatziapostolou from the operetta Οι ερωτευμενοι. Listed in the 1923 catalog as "Οι ερωτευμενοι," by 1928 the title had changed to "Αγαπης λογια." Several versions of the beautiful song were released on 78-rpm recordings. Panhellenion Records issued it twice: catalog number 312 with Vivi Antonopoulou and Tetos Demetriades, and catalog number 328 with only Vivi Antonopoulou. Marika Papagika recorded the song for Victor Records (73137), and two versions were released on Columbia Records, by Giorgos Kanakis (E-7676) and as an instrumental played by a mandolin orchestra (56296F).

Greek player piano rolls were available in department stores such as Prodromidis in New York, in smaller variety shops that also sold records, and in traditional piano stores. Stores frequently hand-stamped the rolls with their name and address. One store stamp found on several rolls was from the Daynes-Beebe Music Company, located at 61-63-65 Main Street in Salt Lake City. Their tagline read, "Largest Player Roll Department in the West."

Greek piano rolls ranged from approximately three to five minutes in length and cost between $.60 and $1.25—about the same price as a 78-rpm record at the time. The piano roll normally featured one song, but on the older five-digit number rolls, two to four shorter songs would be inscribed as separate pieces. Piano roll manufacturers were responsible for obtaining a mechanical license for the use of copyrighted materials. They obtained the licenses from the Harry Fox Agency in New York, and the rate was two cents per song from 1909 to 1972. At the present time, the mechanical license rate is about nine cents per song (Berkman 2015).

In addition to QRS, other companies produced and branded their own Greek piano rolls. On March 28, 1938, the Greek department store Prodromidis, located at 616 Eighth Avenue in New York, produced Greek piano rolls that were manufactured by QRS in a series numbered P251 to P272. Seven of these rolls were listed in the surviving QRS production logs from 1938:

- P266: Μη με στελνεις μαννα στην Αμερικη
- P267: Μυλωνας
- P268: Ελενακι μου
- P269: Κουραστηκα να σ'αγαπω
- P270: Εθνικος υμνος
- P271: Συγγνωμην σου ζητω
- P272: Θα γυριζης

Although no other credits were noted in the QRS production logs or on the piano roll labels, some believe that the Prodromidis rolls were the work of J. Lawrence Cook, a prolific piano roll artist who worked for QRS for nearly fifty years.[7]

Another company that produced Greek piano rolls was Alector. The Alector rolls were stamped with their logo showing a drawing of a rooster standing on a piano roll in front of a solid circle. Two Alector rolls are included in this study: Alector 604, "Ethnimisou sklira," and Alector 542, "I gynaika pou skotonei."[8]

In the 1930s, the Apollo Music Company, located at 301 West Forty-First Street in New York, published sheet music of much of the decade's popular piano music;[8] Apollo had begun publishing sheet music in 1920. Because the piano was often the centerpiece of entertainment in the American home throughout the 1920s and 1930s, piano music gained in popularity during this time.

Player pianos were initially marketed as easy to play, and advertisements depicted toddlers pushing the pedals to illustrate the point. By 1909, Alfred Dolge, an importer and manufacturer of piano-related materials, foresaw the need for the proper teaching of player piano technique. To play well on a player piano required more skill than simply pumping pedals. One could play loud or soft, and one could accent the sound with finger keys that were mounted in front of the keyboard. Instructors offering classes in the proper techniques of the player piano soon emerged, and QRS issued an educator set of piano rolls.

By the 1930s, machines had been developed for home use allowing enthusiasts to punch out their own piano rolls. The rolls then could be taken to a company such as QRS for mass production (Berkman 2015). So far, we have not seen any Greek music rolls of this type, but they may exist in private collections or misplaced in a mislabeled box.

The Greek piano rolls of the 1920s and 1930s represent some of the earliest recordings of Greek music. They carry the songs of genres such as operetta and patriotic marches that are rarely heard today. They hold some of the earliest forms of folk music, with melodies that have long been lost, dating back to a time when pianos and specifically player pianos were popular features in Greek homes. Perhaps it was the rise of the radio and the phonograph record player—less expensive mediums of entertainment—that replaced player pianos in homes.

Today, new piano roll players no longer require a full-size piano with someone pumping pedals to move the keys and augment the sound by hand controls. With this automation, we have lost a certain personalization in the performance of piano roll music.

Greek piano rolls are no longer being produced. The old catalog of piano rolls has long been retired and the master rolls destroyed. It is my great hope that the Greek piano rolls of yesteryear, and all the music they hold, will one day be heard again.[9]

Notes

1. Thanks to Chris Pantezelos, luthier and owner of Spartan Instruments in Lowell, Massachusetts, who provided the initial set of piano rolls for this study.

2. Thanks to Bob Berkman of Pianola Enterprises for the QRS production logs, the 1923 QRS Greek piano rolls catalog, and the 1926 clipping from *Kaliphornia*—research that he obtained from Sotirios (Sam) Chianis.

3. Thanks to Stavros K. Frangos for the piano roll listing from the 1927–1928 Atlas catalog, which he obtained from Helen Zeese Papanikolas. This catalog is included in the Helen Zeese Papanikolas Papers at the University of Utah Library in Salt Lake City.

4. All dates, catalog numbers, and matrix numbers are taken from Spottswood 1990.

5. Friends of Music Society, Lilian Voudouri Music Library of Greece, at http://www.mmb.org.gr/megaro/page/default.asp?la=2&id=4, accessed June 13, 2016. This organization provides information and produces study materials on Greek music. Among their focuses are Greek art music from antiquity and the Byzantine period to the present, and Greek folk music including *rebetika*.

6. The July 28, 1913, passenger manifest for the SS *Patris* sailing from Piraeus shows both Cavadias's birthdate and arrival date in New York.

7. Bob Berkman, conversation with the author, October 14, 2014.

8. Thanks to Stavros K. Frangos for the Apollo Music Company sheet music that I referenced for this study.

9. Special thanks to Bob Berkman for our recording session on September 28–30, 2015, in Buffalo, New York, when we recorded all of the piano rolls in this study, including several from Bob's personal collection.

References

Berkman, Bob. 2015. Interview with Meletios Pouliopoulos, Buffalo, New York, September 28.

Roehl, Harvey N. 1961. *Player Piano Treasury: The Scrapbook History of the Mechanical Piano in America as Told in Story, Pictures, Trade Journal Articles and Advertising.* New York: Vestal Press.

Spottswood, Richard K. 1990. *Ethnic Music on Records: A Discography of Ethnic Recordings Produced in the United States, 1893–1942.* 7 vols. Urbana: University of Illinois Press.

Encountering Greek American Soundscapes

—Anthony Shay

In this chapter, I will look at Greek American music making through the eyes of a non-Greek who, beginning in my teen years, have enjoyed and sought out this musical tradition for more than fifty years, primarily as a folk dance enthusiast and later in my career as a choreographer with two major folk dance ensembles.

For the international recreational dancer, Greek music has rich melodic lines and many different rhythmic patterns (5/8, 7/8, 9/8, etc.) that have attracted many Anglo Americans like me to learn them. This was especially true in the 1950s, 1960s, and 1970s, when recreational and performance folk dance consti-tuted a major leisure activity for hundreds of thousands of mainstream Ameri-cans who did not identify with any specific ethnic background but still longed for the warmth and conviviality to be found in folk dance events, such as those found in Greek American environments (Shay 2008). Another attraction for dancers, especially at certain events like church-sponsored festivals and in the *taverna* (the Greek equivalent of a nightclub), is that conviviality rules and, as such, the event is accompanied by delicious food and drink; engaging, light-hearted conversation; compelling music; and appealing dances—a far cry from the bland American popular music and food with which I grew up (Shay 2002). As I later researched and wrote, it became clear that the Greek American experi-ence, as with other immigrant groups, was different from that of the home coun-try. In some instances, there was not a critical mass of compatriots who shared an immigrant's local or regional music and dance traditions, and that person thus had to learn more common Panhellenic dances.

When searching for where Greek Americans and, to a lesser extent, non-Greeks encounter Greek music in America, one must look first into the con-texts in which Greeks listened to music, sang, played musical instruments, and danced in their home country, and then to look at patterns of Greek immigra-tion to the United States. These two factors determine the types of music one encounters in several different contexts in the new country, who is playing or singing each of the musical genres and the attitudes that people have toward them, and, finally, who makes up the audience in each context. Much of this has changed over time, and yet some musical and dance practices have remained the same, and many individuals derive comfort from familiar performance genres and locales.

When people leave their homes for an unknown and unfamiliar destination, many, if not most of them, feel a great need to surround themselves with the familiar, and this was true for the Greeks who came to America—a place that could turn hostile to early immigrants who arrived toward the end of the nineteenth century (Shay 2006, 94–95). This is especially true for the many genres of music and dance because of their potential for nostalgic connections with the homeland, which can bring fond memories of life in the old country because they are generally associated with happy occasions that broke up the ceaseless toil that characterized Greek village life. Thus, music and dance can bring comfort and solace in a new environment in a special way tied to warm memories. For later generations, music and dance provided a means of constructing their identity as Greek Americans, a process that continues even today in the context of formal, staged folk dance programs, as I will describe later.

Music in Greece

Greece has generated three basic types of music: church music of Byzantine origin, mainland and island folk music, and urban music largely developed by the sophisticated Greek populations of Athens, Piraeus, Smyrna, and Constantinople. Greeks from the latter two cities brought urban music to Greece after the population exchanges between Greece and Turkey in 1922–1923, while some musicians from those locations bypassed Greece, where work was scarce, and went directly to the United States, Canada, and other countries.

Greek Church Music

Most Greeks and Greek Americans hear Byzantine ecclesiastical music for liturgies and special ceremonies like marriages throughout their lives. This musical genre is exclusively vocal. Unlike in the Roman Catholic Church, Greek Orthodox musical practice never included instrumental music. This is true both in Greece and in America, where I first heard this enchanting music echoing in the large Saint Sophia Cathedral in central Los Angeles in the early 1950s while attending a liturgy with my friend Efstathios Gourgouris. That music is beyond the scope of this chapter, but it certainly is an important part of the Greek American soundscape, as it is in Greece.

As I have noted elsewhere (Shay 2006), immigration patterns for many ethnic and national groups determine which musical genres are brought to the New World. Typically, most Greek immigrants at the beginning of the heaviest period of Greek immigration, around the turn of the twentieth century, were men, sometimes 90 to 95 percent of the total (Hecker and Fenton 1978; Jones 1990). Many of them came to make enough money to buy land back home, intending to return to Greece to marry and raise a family. Frequently, individual immigrants or, later, families, would arrive from different villages. As a result, much of the music that was regionally or locally specific would no longer be performed in the New World because individuals would have no one with whom to dance or sing, nor would they find instrumentalists who knew the regional or local repertoire with which they were familiar. A sufficient number of Cretans and Cypriots came to certain urban locations in the United States and Canada and thus were exceptions in that they continued to practice their regional dances in those cities, where they founded lodges and clubs.

In Greek villages prior to World War II, when roads were few and poor, many communities lived in extreme isolation. "Before extensive road-building programs after World War II, treacherous, mountainous terrain on the mainland separated regions and often nearby villages. Unpredictable seas isolated Greece's fourteen hundred islands" (Cowan 2000, 1007). This isolation resulted in the creation of more than eighty specific regional music and dance styles throughout the islands and mainland of Greece—the number provided by Alkis Raftis, president of the Dora Stratou Greek Folk Dances Theatre (1998, 296). In these regions local musicians, either Greeks or Roma, played for *panigiria*, local festivals and weddings, and market days. They played a variety of local instruments; the most popular and widespread are described by Raftis (1987) and Jane Cowan (2000).[1]

The multitude of music and dance styles found in these eighty regions were for the most part, with the exceptions noted above, not brought to the United States and Canada because the individuals who performed them were often single individuals or families who were the only persons emigrating from that specific region. Instead, once they reached the United States, they learned the four or five dances that the majority of Greek Americans performed: the *syrtos*, *kalamatianos*, *tsamikos*, and *hasapiko*, the so-called Panhellenic dances.[2] Most regional, locally specific music and dance forms remained in Greece.[3] Many Greeks, both those who relocated to cities elsewhere in Greece or emigrated abroad, tried to return to the natal villages of their families, especially on the village's patron saint's day, to bathe and breathe in the familiar dances and music of their ancestors. Raftis notes: "Emigrant villagers will travel for hours or even days to attend their village feast; expatriates from Canada, Australia, the United States and other far-flung corners of the globe delight in bringing their families to this event" (1987, 40). Music and dance, and ties to one's natal village, continue to hold deep meaning for Greeks.

The salience of dance and its deep meaning, which resonates in Greek rural life, is underscored by Cowan's description: "[D]ancing at festive events remains a highly structured social practice, whose rules vary from one locality to another. In addition to striving for an exuberant high (*kefi*), which comes from copious wine and conviviality, people 'perform' gender, class, political, and regional identities, negotiate power relations, and express solidarity or rivalry, with kin, neighbors, and friends" (2000, 1017). Cowan's magisterial study of dancing events in northern Greece amply demonstrates her way of describing the many ways in which dancing is entwined in Greek life and constitutes a vehicle for identity construction.

Given that these dances and musical traditions were specific to a small area, the traditional instruments associated with these regional styles—a wide variety of bagpipes, double-reed *zournades*, *lyras* and other stringed instruments, and percussion instruments usually crafted by local instrument makers—generally remained behind as well. The musicians of these traditions generally did not emigrate. Local amateur musicians in Greece, according to ethnomusicologist Sotirios Chianis, "held a high social position within their respective villages" (1983, 27). Chianis mentions local professional musicians, also described by Raftis, who study with older professionals to attain their status. Raftis points out that even professional musicians had to maintain a second trade like blacksmithing to make a living. Raftis differs from Chianis in his assessment of the social status of local music and notes that village parents, in general, did not want their sons to become musicians, considering them on a par with the lowest social figures in rural life: the Roma (gypsy) professional musicians.[4] Raftis observes: "Parents often actively dissuade or even violently prevent their son from learning an instrument, even when there are other musicians in the family. To play an instrument for one's own amusement is a waste of time, to play for money at feasts and ceremonies is considered the work of inferiors" (1987, 63).[5]

As has been noted, many urban people in Greece can still dance because dance is taught in the schools (Blau et al. 2002, 83). In addition, as Kevin Dawe reminds us, people often return to past styles of music and dance. This tendency originates in attempts to recapture a golden age that never actually existed, in a village that they would never think of living in again. "Interest in regional music seems to have been given renewed profile as the legacy of a conscious and serious exploration of roots by younger musicians and scholars in Greece during the 1980s" (Dawe 2007, 177). Dawe thinks that such a music revival might have originated "as a consequence of neo-nationalism, nostalgia, novelty-seeking and exoticism" (2007, 177). This time period coincides with the founding of the

Greek Orthodox Youth Folk Dance Festival organization in the United States in the mid-1970s. Music and dance can serve as a vehicle for identity construction, and the current popularity of regional folk music, both in Greece and in North America, point in that direction for both Greeks and non-Greeks who are fascinated with the rich music and dance traditions of Greece. Dawe makes one final point that gives hope: "[T]he younger generation in Greece—many of whom are now growing up in a cosmopolitan urban-based culture—are much more accepting of the cultural affinities that connect the Balkan nations and are rather tired of the politicking that divides the region" (2007, 177). In addition, one must note that modern classical and jazz musicians often turn to folk music for inspiration for their new compositions.

Urban Music in Greece

Unlike specific local and regional rural music, around the turn of the twentieth century many urban Greek musical styles appeared in large Greek cities, and in cities overseas with large Greek populations. Studies tracking the development of urban music in Greece and the Aegean coastal cities of the Ottoman Empire vary in detail and terminology. This variance has consequences for scholarly perceptions of the soundscapes encountered in US and Canadian cities. Gail Holst-Warhaft notes: "We may argue about origins and precise chronology, but we can broadly agree that the rebetika were popular with a fairly large audience of Greeks, most of whom were urban and not wealthy, from the early decades of the twentieth century until the early 1960s" (2003, 172). She also notes that, like regional folk music of Greece, rebetika music experienced a revival in the 1970s and became popular with a new audience, including many tourists and interested foreigners (2003, 172). We must keep this in mind, because music revivals contribute to the preservation and development of music traditions like rebetika.

In the late nineteenth and early twentieth centuries, there were two types of nightclubs in Athens and other Greek urban centers in the Ottoman Empire, especially Smyrna and Constantinople: the *café chantant* and the *café aman*. The former, modeled on the French café, featured music that was clearly Western and attracted Western-facing intellectuals. The café chantant need not detain us in our discussion of traditional Greek music.

The café aman, however, became a phenomenon that appeared not only in Greece but in the United States among Greek immigrants. Sotirios Chianis notes: "As early as 1910 the café aman and its strong traditions sprang up in numerous large urban areas such as New York City, Boston, San Francisco, Baltimore, and Chicago. . . . Mirroring the café aman tradition in Greece, musicians in America would perform the *Smyrneïka* (Smyrna) tradition." (1983, 3). That tradition was named for the frequent refrain "aman" (which can be roughly translated as "woe

316

is me") found in the vocal style *amanedes*, a highly melismatic type of formalized musical lament. The typical instruments of the café aman, according to Holst-Warhaft, a leading authority on Greek rebetika, were "the violin, santouri, cello, cymbalum and 'ud and women singers seem to have been at least as popular as men" (1998, 115). This latter observation is pertinent because Greek instrumental music is very gendered, played almost exclusively by male musicians, both in rural and urban contexts.[6] I observed in the early 1950s in tavernas that a woman vocalist might play the tambourine or finger cymbals while dancing the *tsifteteli* (a kind of belly dance performed by both men and women).[7]

As a direct result of the catastrophic population exchange throughout 1922 and 1923 in which a million and a half Anatolian Greeks were exchanged for the Muslim population who been living in the Greek nation-state, the musical style known as *Smyrneïka* (from Smyrna, now İzmir) was brought to Greece by professional musicians who established nightclubs and developed a musical genre known as *rebetika*. This was the music of the down-and-outers and socially disenfranchised: "Originating in the tavernas and coffeehouses frequented by sailors, peddlers, the jobless, and petty criminals, rebetika lyrics lament frustrated loves, idealize bravado, and reject bourgeois values" (Raftis 1998, 298). The *manges* (tough guys) who frequented these haunts displayed their hypermasculine bravado to confront an uncaring world in which poverty and misery were the lot of the victims of the population exchange (Shay 2002).

The development of the café aman and rebetika traditions was extremely important because they not only were established in a more congenial American taverna environment but also became the dominant music among generations of Greek Americans. In their new environment in the shantytowns of Athens, the displaced musicians from the former Ottoman Empire quickly established themselves. "The musicians among the refugees did not move into a musical vacuum, but they brought with them a level of professional skill unusual on the mainland. . . . [T]here was a revival of oriental, or what would retrospectively be designated, 'Smyrna-style' music" (Holst-Warhaft 1998, 115). Such revivals occurred both in the mid-twentieth and early twenty-first centuries.[8]

In the 1930s in Piraeus, the seaport of Athens, a new style of rebetika music arose with lyrics that celebrated the underworld and hashish, and complained bitterly about hard-hearted, betraying women. This latter topic was also a major theme of tango, jazz and blues, and flamenco lyrics—other genres of music and dance that developed in similar environments. As Joseph Graziosi notes: "During the 1930s, under the influence of the composer and performer Markos Vamvakaris, the bouzouki came out of the prisons and hashish dens and became the accepted instrument of the *taverna*-style nightclub" (1983, 20). The style of singing was raspier and became less and less oriental. As time passed, "[c]omposers increasingly replaced Turkish modes, known in Greece as *dromoi* (roads), with the diatonic major and minor scales of European popular music. . . . [The oriental] became a conventionalized 'orientalism'" (Cowan 2000, 1020). This was the music that I first encountered in the mid-1950s before the fame of the movies *Zorba the Greek* and *Never on Sunday* popularized rebetika music for both Greeks and, for the first time in larger numbers, non-Greeks.

The bouzouki, a mandolin-like relative of the *baglamas*, a stringed instrument popular in the café aman, was largely electrified by the time I encountered it in the early 1950s in the Greek Village club on Hollywood Boulevard in Los Angeles. It provided the distinct sounds that became for the world the quintessential Greek music heard in *Never on Sunday* (1960, music by Manos Hadjidakis) and *Zorba the Greek* (1964, music by Mikis Theodorakis). The music became the driving force for many middle-class Greeks, as well as many non-Greeks, to emulate the machismo, the perceived unsuppressed joy of life, and the freedom that the films' characters represented. As Cowan observes: "These characters' penchant for abandoning themselves to song and dance signals their otherness, for films portray Greeks as an emotional people who have retained a spontaneity and naturalness that people in more industrialized societies have lost" (2000, 1007). One must not underestimate the influence of this film music, and the many songs and dances in the same style, in the history of the Greek American taverna. Even in mid-2015, when I revisited Athens in the midst of the economic crisis that had struck Greece, the nightclubs and tavernas that provided a venue in which people could pursue the Zorba image were still flourishing.

In discussing Greek music in any context, there has been an unfortunate avoidance by some scholars to come to grips with the music's Turkish/Ottoman origins. Instead, some scholars search for ancient Greek or Byzantine elements. While there may well be Byzantine elements in Greek folk and urban music, most observers, especially non-Greeks, find that it is characterized by what Holst-Warhaft (following Nikos Kazantzakis) terms "oriental bowels" (1998, 113). Ethnomusicologist Bruno Nettl also notes that while Greek music may have ancient Greek elements, "Greek folk music seems to show the influences of centuries of Turkish and Muslim occupation" (1990, 100). And Jane Cowan adds that "classifying Greek music as a branch of Near and Middle Eastern music makes common sense" (2000, 1008). This is especially true of the music of the café aman, which utilizes the Turkish *makam* system of modes and tonal intervals that feature microtones. Greek café aman musicians had a common repertoire with Turkish, Armenian, and Jewish musicians in Smyrna and Constantinople, and several of the records they made had both Turkish and Greek versions (Holst-Warhaft 2003, 172). Holst-Warhaft notes that in the early music that preceded rebetika, the more oriental features seem "gradually to have died out" (1998, 113).

In Athens and other large Greek cities where people from different parts of Greece congregate, including large numbers from the countryside, several types of music are generally available to them. Raftis notes: "In general, Greeks distinguish between bouzouki tavernas with rebetiko music, clarinet tavernas with traditional music from the mainland, and violin tavernas with music from the islands and the coasts" (1998, 299). Greek audiences, like people in other cultures, enjoy listening to a wide variety of musical genres.

Rebetika and eventually laïka music later dominated the Greek American taverna, while demotic clarinet and *santouri* ensembles could be heard in the family, church-related events that I experienced in Los Angeles. As Holst-Warhaft points out: "[T]he characteristic instrumentation, rhythms and vocal quality of the rebetika have remained intrinsic to Greek popular music for approximately seventy years, and the revival of older style rebetika that began in in the 1970s is still going on" (Holst-Warhaft 1998, 125). The sounds and rhythms of Greek music can still be heard in the New Age music of Greek composer and musician Yanni (Yiannis Chryssomallis), particularly in blockbuster concerts with full symphony orchestra that he performs in historical sites the world over, including his award-winning concert appearance at the Acropolis.

An Eager Young American Encounters Greek Music

Fifty years after my first encounters with Greek music, I can still remember the excitement of the music. I heard two types of urban music in Los Angeles, and the context of the performance largely determined the types of dances that one saw. The first context was the public dances that were featured at family- and church-oriented events such as picnics. Among the earliest memories I have is listening to the amazing virtuoso playing of Sotirios (Sam) Chianis on the santouri (a trapezoid-shaped hammered dulcimer, probably Persian via the Ottoman Empire in origin, although the Greek version is much larger), and the distinctive oriental sound of the clarinet, as well as other instruments like the *laouto* (a kind of lute) and violin. In this family-oriented context, one could see and dance the syrtos, the tsamikos, the hasapiko, and the kalamatianos, all group dances that are performed in semicircles with a leader. These dances were suited to events celebrating patron saints' days, often called *panigiria*. These large events were held outside, often in a park, with large numbers of people participating in the dancing.

In describing the instruments heard in any of these contexts, I name a variety of instruments that might be found. This does not mean that every group of musicians played the same instruments but rather that new members with different instruments would sometimes join an orchestra to provide a range of sounds.

The other context in which I encountered Greek music was the tavern. The Greek Village, a nightclub on Hollywood Boulevard, was my first such experience. There, one encountered a very different crowd from the family events:

Figure 80. Left to right, Peter Mangalousis (standing) with Sam Chianis, Andrew Chianis, and Tom Kappas, playing for the American Hellenic Educational Progressive Association dance, Long Beach, California, 1948. Courtesy of Sam Chianis.

except for a belly dancer and vocalist, all of the clientele were men. The instruments were the (sometimes) electrified bouzouki, often a clarinet, and other string instruments, and the female vocalist played the tambourine (*defi*). The dances were the *zeibekiko*, a solo men's dance; the slow (*vari*) hasapiko, with two or more men holding shoulders; and sometimes a tsifteteli. Jane Cowan, in her study of dancing in northern Greece, has vividly described the perils of performing the tsifteteli in the wrong context, especially for women (1990). These dances were not considered suitable for public family social events, and instead of under the sunshine of the outdoor events, they took place on the dimly lit dance floors of the early tavernas.

The many tavernas I have danced in for over fifty years all over the United States—Los Angeles, San Francisco, Boston, New York, Chicago, Minneapolis, Salt Lake City, Washington, DC—all looked alike in many ways, or at least they blur in my memory. The Greek Village did not have much decor and was dimly lit, whereas later tavernas that I experienced decked the stage, walls, and wooden arbors with plastic grapevines, glittery bandstands, painted scenes from Greece, colorful tablecloths in red and white checks or Greek key designs, and brighter lighting as befitted a space welcoming families and female patrons. They all, whether simple or fancy, had a stage or performance area for the orchestra, dancing space, and tables and chairs for patrons. In these later incarnations, it was not unusual for the waiters to dance.

Figure 81. Nikos Pourpourakis playing bouzouki at the Athenian Gardens, Los Angeles, 1970. Archives of Nick Pourpourakis (Nick Dakis).

The Greek Village, the Athenian Gardens, and, less well-known to the general population, Intersection, which catered to lovers of Greek folk and taverna dancing (as well as Balkan and Israeli dancing), were places that I frequented over many years. The Greek Village was my earliest hangout. In my first visits, I probably should not have been there at all, since I was still in my late teens and very much underage, but fortunately I never requested a drink. I was there for the music and the dancing, which was often performed by Greek sailors who had made their way to Hollywood from the docks of San Pedro, the port area of Los Angeles. The Greek Village provided a relatively comfortable space, and, in the mid- and late 1950s, was strictly a male hangout that provided recent Greek immigrants with the comfort of soulful music and the Greek language. The only women that I recall were the vocalist, who sat on the stage with the orchestra and sang and played the *defi*, and the belly dancer, usually not a Greek. I often became friends with these women, like Jamila Salimpour, whom I knew from my student days at Los Angeles City College. Unlike in the rebetika clubs and tavernas of Greece, where tsifteteli dancing predominated, belly dancers in Los Angeles and other American cities danced Egyptian-style cabaret belly dance. The *bouzoukia*, or bouzouki-dominated orchestra, featured male singers as well as female vocalists.

The Athenian Gardens came later, after the fame of *Never on Sunday* and *Zorba the Greek* popularized Greek dancing and music. The club flourished into the 1990s, after which I no longer heard about it. The club's bouzouki orchestra catered to middle-class Greek American and non-Greek audiences, which then, in contrast to the Greek Village, included many women. It played many renditions of the *syrtaki*, the dance made famous by *Zorba the Greek*. The syrtaki morphed from other slow Greek dance forms: "[T]he music speeds up so that the rebetika rhythm of hasapiko becomes a hasaposerviko [indicating a fast style] and the syrtaki is born" (Holst-Warhaft 1998, 111). In the 1990s, the Athenian Gardens very much catered to those men who wanted to act out their inner Zorba. Food and conviviality were a large part of its attraction.

A final source of Greek music for me was the large number of phonograph recordings that I acquired at record shops or was given as gifts. Beginning in my late teens, as a recreational folk dance enthusiast, I listened to Greek music on records several times a week. I was especially grateful for a wonderful retrospective of early café aman and rebetika singer Roza Eskenazi that my friend, dance scholar and tsifteteli dancer extraordinaire Stavros Stavrou Karayanni, gave me as a gift. I still treasure and frequently listen to the soulful songs of Stelios Kazantzidis that I have collected over the years. Finally, during my career as a choreographer, the several Greek folk and urban dances that I prepared for the companies that I directed, the AMAN Folk Ensemble and the AVAZ International Dance Theatre, remain precious memories.

Notes

1. There is an excellent small museum of traditional musical instruments of Greece located in the Plaka District of Athens. See Cowan 2000 for musical varieties; see also Petrides 1975a, 1975c; and Holden and Vouras 1965 for the many types of regional folk dances.

2. Raftis vigorously refutes the notion of Panhellenic dances: "[T]here is the conviction that there exist panhellenic dances. . . . Nowadays, however, there is no excuse for perpetuating this misconception of the so-called 'panhellenic' dances for these are simply the dances of 'Old Greece' [the original regions that formed the independent Kingdom of Greece after its liberation from the Ottoman Empire] which have been transplanted by civil servants and government officials into those regions liberated later" (1987, 37). School officials introduced them into the school curriculum in order to foster a national, as opposed to local, identity. This practices continues. These were the dances that most Greeks in America danced almost exclusively until the late 1970s, and in social settings they continue to be popular.

3. Athan Karras, who taught Greek dances, recalled how he had been "thrown out of the church by the priest" for attempting to teach other than the Panhellenic dances (Karras 2000). This situation changed in the years following the founding of the Greek Orthodox Youth Folk Dance Festival, in which young people in different age cohorts prepare costumes and dances to win prizes. As language skills declined among succeeding generations of young Greek Americans, preparing staged folk dances and offering prizes to the best group in each age category became a vehicle for the Greek Orthodox

Church to keep young people close to the church and encouraged marriages among participants in the older age categories. Each year, the various groups choose a different area of Greece to represent, requiring the choreographer and those preparing the costumes to find information, since neither they nor their families came from these regions. Sociologist Caterina Pizanias observes: "When we Greeks go 'out' into the 'multicultural' we take with us dances from places in Greece we know little about" (1996, 41). These groups frequently turn to the Dora Stratou Greek Folk Dances Theatre for help in their research (Raftis 2000). While most Greek Americans enjoy the festivals, not everyone is enthusiastic. Pizanias observes: "What mattered was the performance event, the daughters staying in the fold. . . . All that was needed were mechanical execution of steps and spectacular costumes. All they [Greek Canadians] could see was [that] the most spectacular tourist summer show in Athens was Dora Stratou's, and the most spectacular amateur dance troupe at the Heritage Festival was ours—the most Stratou-like one" (1996, 17). See also Bloland 1994; and Shay 2006, 91–105. When dance becomes competition, it frequently departs, often rapidly, from the original forms in seeking spectacular elements with which to impress the judges and the audience, as Pizanias notes.

4. For a detailed description and analysis of the Roma musicians and their social status in Greece, see Blau et al., who note that the Roma "had no strategy for removing the stigma from their 'ethnicity'" (2002, 144). They sum up: "Roma are different, somewhat less than Greek as citizens and somewhat more than Greek as musicians" (2002, 95). See also Papakostas 2008.

5. One can encounter a similar situation in Iran. Unless a member of a musical family, it is not unknown for a parent to disown a child for becoming a *motreb* (public entertainer), and several Iranians have related to me experiences of parents destroying musical instruments to prevent them from playing (Shay 2014, 23).

6. For the gendered aspects of Greek music and dance, see Cowan 2000; Holst-Warhaft, 1998, 2003; Shand 1998; and Shay 2016.

7. On tsifteteli, Angela Shand notes: "Despite its overwhelming popularity, tsifteteli is problematic for many Greeks, along lines of identity, gender and the body" (1998, 127). The dance is considered Turkish, its movements provocative, and many of the contexts for performances transgressive, as Cowan (1990) vividly describes (see also Karayanni 2004). It is also associated with the Roma, who are sometimes professional belly dancers, which adds to the way in which it is evaluated. Blau et al. note that the Roma consider the dance their own: "In Jumaya [Greek Macedonia] Roma call the tsifteteli dance 'our bread,' 'ours,' or 'our dance,' expressing their love for it" (2002, 292n14). The Roma in Turkey constitute the primary professional dancers of the *çiftetelli* (tsifteteli). The Roma of southern Serbia, Kosovo, and the Republic of Macedonia also perform the tsifteteli, which they call *čoček* (Silverman 2008). I would, however, question the notion posited by Blau et al. that "all these so-called belly dances have their origins in the fertility rites of the primitive peoples of the Eastern Aegean" (2002, 292n14). Dance scholars have long abandoned the idea that ancient origins can be found for any dance genre— they are unknowable. That having been said, professional dancers, usually of slave origin, indeed existed in ancient Greece and Rome who performed erotic dances with articulations of the shoulders, torso, and hips; however, they were not associated with fertility but with sex (Shay 2014).

8. For a detailed account of dancing in rebetika clubs, see Cowan 1990; Holst-Warhaft 1998; Petrides 1975b; and Shay 2016.

References

Blau, Dick, Charles Keil, Angeliki Vellou Keil, and Steven Feld. 2002. *Bright Balkan Morning: Romani Lives and the Power of Music in Greek Macedonia*. Middletown, CT: Wesleyan University Press.

Bloland, Sunni. 1994. "Sixteenth Annual California Greek Orthodox Youth Folk Dance Festival: A Social and Artistic Extravaganza." In *Proceedings of the Seventeenth Symposium of the Study Group on Ethnochoreology, Nafplion, July 2–10, 1992,* edited by Irene Loutzaki, 25–28. Nafplion, Greece: Peloponnesian Folk Foundation; International Council for Traditional Music.

Butterworth, Katharine, and Sara Schneider, eds. 1975. *Rebetika: Songs from the Old Greek Underworld.* Athens: Aiora Press.

Chianis, Sotirios (Sam). 1983. "A Glimpse of Greek Music in America." In *Greek Music Tour,* 3–4. New York: Ethnic Folk Arts Center.

Cowan, Jane K. 1990. *Dance and the Body Politic in Northern Greece.* Princeton, NJ: Princeton University Press.

———. 2000. "Greece." In *Garland Encyclopedia of World Music,* vol. 8, *Europe,* edited by Timothy Rice, James Porter, and Chris Goertzen, 1007–28. New York: Garland.

Dawe, Kevin. 2007. "Regional Voices in a National Soundscape: Balkan Music and Dance in Greece." In *Balkan Popular Culture and the Ottoman Ecumene: Music, Image, and Regional Political Discourses,* edited by Donna A. Buchanan, 175–90. Lanham, MD: Scarecrow Press.

Graziosi, Joseph. 1983. "Urban Music." In *Greek Music Tour,* program, Fifteenth Annual Winter Folk Festival, 18–20. New York: Ethnic Folk Arts Center.

Hecker, Melvin, and Heike Fenton. 1978. *The Greeks in America, 1528–1977: A Chronology and Fact Book.* Dobbs Ferry, NY: Oceana.

Holden, Rickey, and Mary Vouras. 1965. *Greek Folk Dances.* Newark, NJ: Folkcraft Press.

Holst-Warhaft, Gail. 1998. "Rebetika: The Double-Descended Deep Songs of Greece." In *The Passion of Music and Dance: Body, Gender, and Sexuality,* edited by William Washabaugh, 111–26. New York: Berg Publishers.

———. 2003. "The Female Dervish and Other Shady Ladies of the Rebetika." In *Music and Gender: Perspectives from the Mediterranean,* edited by Tullia Magrini, 169–94. Chicago: University of Chicago Press.

Jones, Jayne Clark. 1990. *Greeks in America.* Minneapolis: Lerner.

Karayanni, Stavros Stavrou. 2004. *Dancing Fear and Desire: Race, Sexuality, and Imperial Politics in Middle Eastern Dance.* Waterloo, Ontario: Wilfrid Laurier University Press.

Karras, Athan. 2000. Interview with Anthony Shay, Los Angeles, April 27.

Nettl, Bruno. 1990. *Folk and Traditional Music of the Western Continents.* 3rd ed. Englewood Cliffs, NJ: Prentice Hall.

Papakostas, Christos. 2008. "Dance and Place: The Case of the Roma Community in Northern Greece." In *Balkan Dance: Essays on Characteristics, Performance and Teaching,* edited by Anthony Shay, 69–88. Jefferson, NC: McFarland.

Petrides, Ted. 1975a. *Folk Dances of the Greeks.* Jericho, NY: Exposition Press.

———. 1975b. "The Dances of the *Rebetes.*" In *Rebetika: Songs from the Old Greek Underworld,* edited by Katharine Butterworth and Sara Schneider, 27–33. Athens: Aiora Press.

———. 1975c. *Greek Dances.* Athens: Lycabetus Press.

Petropoulos, Elias. 1975. "Rebetika." In *Rebetika: Songs from the Old Greek Underworld,* edited by Katharine Butterworth and Sara Schneider, 11–15. Athens: Aiora Press.

Pizanias, Caterina. 1996. "(Re)thinking the Ethnic Body: Performing 'Greekness' in Canada." *Journal of the Hellenic Diaspora* 22, no. 1: 7–60.

Raftis, Alkis. 1987. *The World of Greek Dance.* Translated by Alexandra Doumas. Athens: International Organization of Folk Art.

———. 1998. "Greece: Dance in Modern Greece." In *International Encyclopedia of Dance,* vol. 3, edited by the Dance Perspectives Foundation and Selma Jeanne Cohen, 296–301. New York: Oxford University Press.

———. 2000. Interview with Anthony Shay, Athens, February 21.

Shand, Angela. 1998. "The Tsifte-teli Sermon: Identity, Theology, and Gender in Rebetika." In *The Passion of Music and Dance: Body, Gender, and Sexuality*, edited by William Washabaugh, 127–32. New York: Berg Publishers.

Shay, Anthony. 2002. *Choreographic Politics: State Folk Dance Companies, Representation, and Power.* Middletown, CT: Wesleyan University Press.

———. 2006. *Choreographing Identities: Folk Dance, Ethnicity, and Festival in the United States and Canada.* Jefferson, NC: McFarland.

———. 2008. *Dancing across Borders: The American Fascination with Exotic Dance Forms.* Jefferson, NC: McFarland.

———. 2014. *The Dangerous Lives of Public Performers: Dancing, Sex, and Entertainment in the Islamic World.* New York: Palgrave Macmillan.

———. 2016. *Ethno-Identity Dances for Sex, Fun, and Profit: Staging Popular Dances around the World.* London: Palgrave Macmillan.

Silverman, Carol. 2008. "Transnational Čoček: Gender and the Politics of Balkan Romani Dance." In *Balkan Dance: Essays on Characteristics, Performance and Teaching,* edited by Anthony Shay, 37–68. Jefferson, NC: McFarland.

Bouzoukis and Belly Dancers, Drinkers and Dreamers: A Look at Greek Nightlife at the Crossroads[1]

—Nick Pappas

It is one o'clock in the morning in the Grecian Cave in New York's Greek Astoria. Under the expensive, multitinted spotlights of one of the Western Hemisphere's most famous Greek nightclubs, Greek singing stars Giota Lydia and Dimitris Xanthakis entertain a capacity all-Greek audience of several hundred people, most of whom are recent immigrants. The Grecian Cave (Elliniki Spilia) is located on the lower level of a catering establishment called the Crystal Palace, the hub of much of New York's Greek social life. Although located in America, the scene at the Grecian Cave is entirely Greek—decor, language, food, audience, and performers—particularly at the bar, where young men jam the railing raptly surveying the scene.

Characteristically short for the most part, many wearing high-heeled shoes and open-necked shirts, and dateless on a Saturday night in a country still strange to them, their lonely eyes devour the kaleidoscope of sight and sound in this transplanted piece of the Greece they miss so much. And though they don't pay the higher cover and minimum of those at the tables, they nevertheless reflect the market on which the greatly troubled entertainment-oriented Greek nightclub business depends in America.

Like Plato's flickering wall shadows in his Allegory of the Cave, what these men, and others in similar clubs across the country, are watching is the expensive illusion produced by the owners, who put in sixteen-hour days, seven days a week, to create an expensive club, good food, beautiful lighting, and a great sound system, and to import polished stars who deliver the latest song hits. Behind the illusion, though, a shadow lurks, for the Grecian Cave is one of the few remaining clubs of its kind in America.

The high cost of bringing Greek stars here, and the unwillingness of the essentially working-class market to pay the high cover and minimum in some of the clubs, has reduced the number of such clubs from about ten in the United States

Figure 82. Imported Greek talent at the Neraida in Astoria, 1981. Photo by Odette Lupis. Courtesy of the *National Herald*.

Figure 83. Lost in the sea of a great city, men newly arrived from Greece find solace from their homesickness in the tavernas and nightclubs, 1981. Photo by Odette Lupis. Courtesy of the *National Herald*.

and Canada to just three, with two of them in New York. It will be no great surprise if that number is further reduced in the near future.

In his office in the rear of the Grecian Cave, which has been in existence since 1966 and at its present site since 1979, owner Costas Pavloyianis says:

> Ninety percent of our patrons are Greek, and seventy percent of those are recent immigrants. They couldn't afford to see the big stars in Greece, so they come here to see them and throw flowers and plates. But it's becoming an impossible situation. Until the Neraida supper club [a competitor] opened a few months ago, the fifteen or so top Greek stars asked $1,200 or $1,300 a night. Now they're aware of the competition and ask $2,000 and $3,000 a night. They don't like to come here to begin with, agreeing only if there's spare time in their schedule. Some of them, from poor village backgrounds, used to be warm and a pleasure to deal with. Now they've got arrogant, swelled heads, and ask far more than they're worth.

At the nearby Neraida, owner Dimitri Papadopoulos, whose other business is jewelry, agrees:

> It's very hard, running around trying to sign the stars, fighting the competition. The stars are asking too much to come here, and I suppose you can't blame them. They're asking what they think the market can afford, except they keep asking more and more and the people just won't pay the high prices you have to charge because of expenses. Our patrons are mostly recent Greek immigrants, working people who come here just once a week, on Friday or Saturday. But you've got to pay your expenses the other nights too.

One can accept these interpretations. But it also seems a simple case in which entrepreneurs misread the market that developed with the new wave of immigrants of the past ten or fifteen years. Rightly, they assumed that these people would like to hear the latest hits sung by Greece's top stars, whom they had only heard through records or Greek radio; stars like Gregory Bithikotsis, Dimitris Mitropanos, Yiannis Parios, Rita Sakellariou, Manolis Angelopoulos, and Vicki Moscholiou.

What the owners failed to foresee was the competitive situation that would develop, driving the salaries of the stars through the roof. Also, with just a few exceptions, the singers don't like to come to the United States, and only that extra dollar can entice them to cross over. Finally, the limit appears to have been reached as to what the Greek immigrant public will pay to support high-salaried performers.

Just across the river, though, in Manhattan, as well as in hundreds of other places in the United States and Canada, a different kind of Greek supper club is flourishing—partly because they emphasize cuisine and a more universal kind of

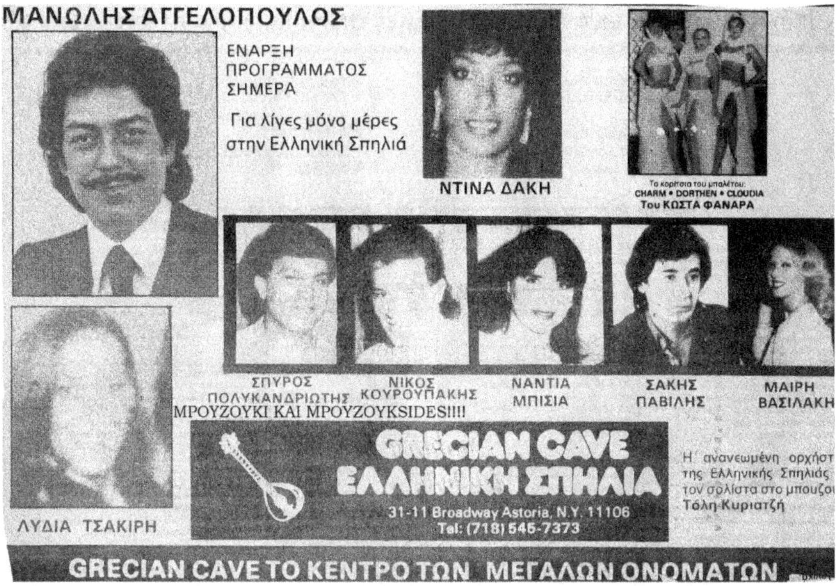

Figure 84. Advertisement for Grecian Cave/Elliniki Spilia, Astoria, with Manolis Aggelopoulos and others, ca. 1980s. At http://mpouzouksides.blogspot.gr/2015/02/polykandriotis-music -family.html. Courtesy of Spiros Stamoulis.

Greek entertainment that appeals to all tastes, and partly because their strategy and location result in half their patrons being non-Greek, which makes the market limitless. In these clubs, you will not see tieless working men with shirt collars outside their jackets, but successful men and women wearing the latest fashions.

Manhattan boasts a number of such clubs, ranging from S'Agapo, which features live entertainment and disco dancing and attracts personalities such as Telly Savalas and Sophia Loren, to the quiet piano and guitar at the Orpheus. Dino's Taverna features Greek food upstairs, Greek and American food downstairs, and live music, while Rita Dimitri sings everything from Mikis Theodorakis to Edith Piaf at La Chansonnette, earning her the billing "the French Greek Singing Star."

Another example is the Lawrence Supper Club in lower Manhattan, a small, softly lit room whose decor includes plants and tasteful Greek artifacts. Where Neraida patrons look and listen, Lawrence patrons smell and feel. The food is good, and low-key music and singing by small groups center around the bouzouki, an instrument that cuts across nationality and racial barriers.

Owner Johnny Kotsifakos, who moves lovingly from table to table seeing to the needs of his patrons, says: "Unlike Astoria, we concentrate on food and on creating that warm special mood for which Greece is famous."

The same feeling pervades the Estia Supper Club in uptown Manhattan, owned by Vasilis Moschonas and Andreas Ortigas. In operation for ten years, the Estia, like the Lawrence, has the advantage of a Manhattan location and a longer history. A taverna-type club, its name means, roughly, "a warm meeting place for dining and talking." Half the customers are non-Greeks, and patrons have included ambassadors, shippers, and luminaries such as Aristotle Onassis, Anthony Quinn, Irene Papas, and Melina Mercouri. Here, too, the emphasis is on low-key music, singing and dance, and, mostly, food. The Estia's menu, featuring dozens of outstanding items, received rave reviews in the *New York Times*, *Gourmet* magazine, and *Harper's Bazaar*.

Of the star-oriented clubs, Moschonas, who sings for his guests, says gently:

> I don't know Astoria too well, but there has to be a club or restaurant for each taste, and every person has to find the one he's comfortable in. Sometimes a patron will combine the two, have dinner here and then catch a star in Astoria. We mix old and new songs, trying to read the mood of the patrons, aiming for a soft, appealing mix, without microphones, that you can only get in a small club.

Audience contact is crucial to the success of this style of supper club and has a strong advocate in the owner of Manhattan's Sirocco Supper Club, Aris San (born Aristides Saisanas). In existence for ten years, the Sirocco's continental thrust, with Greece as a base, results in a patronage that is 70 to 80 percent non-Greek. San says:

> I learned that you can't survive if your market is just Greek. That's why the great old clubs like the Adonis, Dionysos, and Mykonos failed—they got too Greek. The advantage I had was that I left Greece when I was seventeen, I went to Israel and other places, where I learned how to sell Greek music and food to non-Greeks, looking for the universal nerve. I backed that up with Israeli, French, and Spanish numbers and menu items, creating the balanced atmosphere most patrons like. I prefer American-born Greeks to recent immigrants, because they are more sophisticated in their tastes. And the best part of my show is the audience, when they get up to dance and participate. To watch them is my greatest pleasure.

Proof of the effectiveness of this approach was seen on a recent snowbound night, when the Sirocco show, headed by Aris San himself, entertained a near-capacity crowd that looked like a United Nations banquet. In the air hovered the presences of Sirocco regulars such as Anthony Quinn, Roger Moore, Telly Savalas, Harry Belafonte, Natalie Wood, and Aristotle Onassis.

All club owners, though, whether of a nightclub in Astoria or a supper club in Manhattan, remain constantly preoccupied with the needs and moods of their patrons, good and bad. In Manhattan, the owners are happy with their so-called class patrons and are always alert for any trouble that might disrupt their delicately balanced atmosphere.

Estia owner Moschonas speaks of the bad effect liquor has on some otherwise fine people. The Lawrence's Kotsifakos says: "A few times some singer attracted some rowdy Astoria types here, and I had to put my foot down. Another time, in another Manhattan location, I befriended some down-and-out Canadian Greeks with food and money, and they robbed me. I'm happy to say they were caught, and that we don't have the problems I hear Astoria clubs have."

Of those problems, Grecian Cave owner Pavloyianis is bluntest:

> Many recent immigrants are idle, arrogant people who think they own the place. A lot are gamblers, and others come in and shoot off guns into the ceiling. They come once a week to harass the stars, demanding certain songs, and as soon as they have a few drinks they change into monsters. Sailors are particular problems, very arrogant and superior-acting.

Others who prefer anonymity agree. "We know cops from four or five precincts who served in Astoria," one source says, continuing:

> They say the Greek element is worse there. In the clubs everything's a rip-off, with waiters and bartenders walking around with their hands out all the time. One cop called it the "Greek ghetto." It seems the change started in the late sixties, when the junta took over in Greece. They drove all the bad elements out, many of whom came to America. In a nightclub atmosphere, they're at their worst.

A one-sided view perhaps, and a little too harsh a judgment. Maybe the recent immigrants are not as staid as our parents and grandparents were when they came over. But Greece has suffered significantly since the 1930s, with war, occupation, and revolution, and the new Greek immigrants merely reflect those hardships. If the big nightclubs seem profit oriented, one must remember that they paid plenty to bring that big name across an ocean. You cannot expect to see Sinatra for the same price as an unknown singer.

In trying to make that profit and survive, the big clubs are constantly cutting costs. A regular patron will note that with each visit some new amenity is missing or changed; five musicians instead of twelve, no chorus line, one man handling both sound and lighting, and two captains at the door instead of five. Struggling to make the equation work, they are apparently doomed to failure unless the big stars agree to take less or some alternative form of entertainment is developed, neither of which seems likely.

Nonetheless, the owners maintain a deep love and commitment for the business of entertaining and feeding human beings. Neraida owner Papadopoulos was one of the most frequent patrons of other clubs, a true Greek who threw flowers and plates with the best of them. In his own club now, he obviously enjoys each show as much as any of his patrons. He says: "Even though I was never in this business before, I felt that New York needed a large club, with class, where people could see their favorite stars with the best lighting and sound just like in a big Las Vegas hotel. It remains a labor of love for me."

Grecian Cave owner Pavloyianis, in the business longer than most, fits the same mold, and he was a pleasure to watch one evening as he lovingly orchestrated his daughter Dian's early-evening sweet sixteen disco party, deftly maneuvering her friends and incoming club patrons in time to start the big Greek show.

That same love pervades the Manhattan operations. The Estia's Moschonas says:

> It takes time to learn how to be a good supper club host, how to read the mood not only of an entire room, but individual tables as well. But if you've got the feeling, then you can do it. I used to go to a lot of Greek nightclubs myself, and saw that people forget their troubles at night, and smile more. So I decided that's the kind of business I'd like to be in. I'm very happy here.

Lawrence owner Kotsifakos used to go to the so-called Greek belly joints on Eighth Avenue three times a week, and he is now ecstatic in his work. Very simply, and meaning it, he says: "If I make enough money to pay my bills and please my customers, that's enough for me."

In their pursuit of individual fulfillment, the men and women who operate the clubs work with a Greek product whose component parts are history, food, music, dance, hospitality, and other ephemeral qualities that give that product its universal and eternal appeal. The skill with which these ingredients are mixed determines an operation's success or failure.

The big, entertainment-oriented nightclubs pluck mainly music from this repository of riches, presenting it, by necessity, in a big, impressive nightclub setting that is proving too expensive to maintain. Many clubs have folded, others might follow, and those that survive will have to talk the stars, in their own best interests, into lowering their fees. Perhaps Rita Sakellariou, who likes America so much she is thinking of buying a home here, and Manolis Angelopoulos, who after seven visits calls the United States a second home, will take the lead in informing the stars in Greece of conditions here. Otherwise, the owners must develop alternative forms of entertainment that might include Greek American singers delivering the latest hits for $500 a week instead of $2,500 a night. Either way, one does not envy their dilemma.

The chances for supper clubs like the Lawrence, the Estia, S'Agapo, Dino's Taverna, the Orpheus, and others like them across the United States and Canada are much better. With costs more under control, they feature a product whose market is as broad as the human race: top-notch food, presented within that whole frame of Greek history, decor, music, dance, and, mostly, Greek soul. It's an irresistible combination for Greeks and non-Greeks alike.

Notes

1. Previously published in *Greek Accent*, February 1981, 28–31.

PART 4

Profiles

Figure 85. Giorgos "Nisyrios" Makrigiannis. Courtesy of Panayotis League.

Giorgos "Nisyrios" Makrigiannis (1875–1933)

—Panayotis League

The Dodecanese are home to some of the most complex and virtuosic violin music in Greece, blending the sophisticated repertoire of Smyrna and other urban centers of Asia Minor with indigenous folk tunes and scattered melodies culled from other Greek, Balkan, Arabic, and European traditions. The music of the region is tremendously varied in both style and repertoire; yet violinists from Kalymnos, Leros, Kos, Rhodes, Patmos, Symi, Nisyros, and other neighboring islands all point to Giorgos Makrigiannis, or Nisyrios ("the Nisyrian"), as the dominant influence on modern Dodecanese violin style and the musician who largely determined the course that their local traditions have taken over the past century—a course that was largely plotted in the United States.

Giorgos Makrigiannis was born in the Nisyrian expatriate community of Constantinople in 1875 and spent his childhood in the Ottoman capital. He was doubtless exposed during his formative years to the immense variety of musical genres, forms, and playing techniques in circulation in the city's multiethnic music scene, and upon his family's return to Nisyros in the last decade of the nineteenth century he consolidated his mastery of the dance tunes popular among Dodecanese musicians. Like many other virtuosos of the era, Makrigiannis traveled widely throughout Greece, Egypt, Romania, and Asia Minor performing for Greek and perhaps other communities in major urban centers, and his vast repertoire and absolute command of his instrument allowed him to supplement his performer's salary with work as a violin instructor.

In 1916, Makrigiannis left Greece for the United States in search of a more lucrative means of supporting his large family. He settled in New York, where he began a relatively brief but brilliant and profoundly influential stateside career. He continued to perform throughout the Greek and Ottoman diasporas in the United States, moving with ease and grace between island dances, modal improvisations in the urban Asia Minor style, and the latest polkas, tangos, and foxtrots; and he taught an entire generation of Greek American violinists from his studio on West Forty-First Street between Eighth and Ninth Avenues. But Makrigiannis's most lasting impact on Greek music in the twentieth century—including his catalytic contribution to the development of the Dodecanese violin style in both Greece and the Greek diaspora—was as a recording artist.

Between 1917 and 1919, his Trio Makrigianni (with the accompaniment of G. Klosteridis on *santouri* or hammered dulcimer and V. Katsetos on *laouto* or steel-string lute) made twenty-four recordings for the Victor Talking Machine Company of primarily instrumental pieces. These selections not only showcase his brilliant tone, dynamic bowing, and delightful melodic sensibility but also provide tangible evidence of the diverse repertoire that professional Greek musicians active in early twentieth-century urban America were performing and that, judging by the presence of particular pieces in the commercial recording sessions, their patrons demanded. Unsurprisingly, these recordings include the *syrtos, issos,* and *sousta* dances that are still emblematic of the Dodecanese; but they also feature Asia Minor *zeibekiko* dances and a classic *rebetiko* or urban Greek song, a virtuosic imitation of the Cretan *askomandoura* or goatskin bagpipe (known in the Dodecanese as *tsambouna*), dances associated with the Vlachs of central Greece, a Romanian *doina*, a march, and cheeky, melodramatic polkas fit for the most respectable Edwardian drawing room.

Makrigiannis's recordings were tremendously influential in the crystallization of a number of local violin styles throughout the Dodecanese and, by extension, their diasporas in the United States. The most striking example is perhaps the dominant stream of traditional violin music on the island of Kalymnos, which has a large American diaspora community (largely concentrated in Tarpon Springs, Florida, and Campbell, Ohio) well known for its virtuosic dancing, singing, and instrumental music. Violinists in the Kalymnian tradition trace their artistic lineage directly back to Giorgos Makrigiannis through one of his prized pupils, Kalymnian musician Theofilos Magriplis, who passed on Makrigiannis's repertoire and idiomatic bowing technique to his nephew Mikes Tsounias (widely known by his nickname To Ennima). The two most recent generations of Kalymnian violinists have now internalized Tsounias's own idiosyncratic interpretation of Makrigiannis's approach to the instrument while at the same time returning to Makrigiannis's original recordings for further inspiration. Many of these younger musicians—myself included—have expressed amazement not only at Makrigiannis's breathtaking technique and inventiveness but at the uncanny similarity between the "old" Kalymnian versions of standard pieces in the local repertoire and Makrigiannis's recordings. It is clear that the musicians (Magriplis, Tsounias, and others) who developed the Kalymnian canon over the past century studied Makrigiannis's playing—most likely from his recordings—down to the smallest detail.

In Kalymnos and the Kalymnian diaspora today, the distinctive "Nisyrios school" of violin and laouto music is a prerequisite for weddings, baptisms, and informal *glendis* or musical celebrations. The folkloric dance group Levendia of

Tarpon Springs, largely composed of third- and fourth-generation Kalymnian Americans, routinely wins first place at major dance competitions singing and dancing to Makrigiannis's syrtos version of the Peloponnesian *kleftiko* ballad "Tou Kitsou i mana" (Kitsos's Mother) and his distinctive settings of the sousta dance. Makrigiannis's versions of these and many other tunes have recently been rerecorded by Kalymnian musicians active in the United States, and Kalymnian violinist Michalis Kappas—himself the foremost present-day practitioner of this style—frequently travels to Tarpon Springs to teach Makrigiannis's repertoire and technique to young Greek American musicians, perpetuating the Nisyrian's legacy of virtuosic performance and musical pedagogy.

References

Hatzitheodorou, Giorgos. 1980. *Tragoudia kai skopoi stin Kalymno*. Kalymnos, Greece: Ai Mousai.

Kappas, Michalis, Panayotis League, and Irene Karavokiros. 2016. *Traditional Music and Songs from Kalymnos*. MKPLIK1. Brookline, Massachusetts.

Makrigiannis, Giorgos. 2011. *Istorikes ichografiseis 1917–1919*. MPESN 1. Morfotikos Politistikos Eksoraitikos Syllogos Nisyrou, Nisyros.

Madame Koula (circa 1880–1954)[1]

—Stavros K. Frangos

Kyriaki Yiortzi Antonopoulou was the first internationally successful Greek female vocalist who made North America her permanent home. Known simply as Madame Koula (Koula being the diminutive of Kyriaki), sometimes spelled "Coula," this woman proved to be so popular that from 1916 to 1927 she recorded at least 199 individual songs. No other female vocalist of Greek heritage in North America made or sold as many records during this same period.[2]

In late 1916 or early 1917, Koula Antonopoulou entered the New York studios of Columbia Records and soon conquered the Greek music scene in North America. Given the technological limitations of the day, Mme. Koula sang through a megaphone, successfully recording thirty-four songs—or seventeen records—during her initial sessions. While we do not always know which instrumentalists played on each song, we do know that Athanasios Makedonas played the violin, Andreas Patrinos was on *laouto*, and Stelios Melas played the *santouri*. We should quickly note that the santouri is not present on all these Columbia recordings. Xenophon Mitchell, Antonopoulou's only grandchild, contends that Mme. Koula's husband, his maternal grandfather Andreas Antonopoulos, also played the laouto on some of these Columbia songs. Mme. Koula's first recorded song was "Eleni karsilamas" (Columbia E3324).

It is only when one listens closely to Mme. Koula on these Columbia records that it unexpectedly becomes apparent that she is not singing alone. Many of these early songs are more choral than individual renditions. As it was explained to me, the recording was meant to mimic the club conditions in which Mme. Koula performed. Unlike other Greek records available during this early period, Mme. Koula's records showcased the singing of audience members as they accompanied her performance. It is widely accepted that the unexpected and totally unprecedented success—in terms of overall sales—of just these thirty-four songs prompted all the major American record companies to immediately begin releasing Greek music with an eye to capturing part of this new market.

Mme. Koula and her *kompania* recorded songs of virtually every traditional and popular Greek genre. Regrettably, Antonopoulou is most remembered by

Figure 86. Kyriaki Antonopoulou (Mme. Koula). From "Gel Gel!"
advertisement, 1916. Courtesy of Meletios Pouliopoulos.

academics and record collectors for her Greek café music or *café aman*–style
records. *Aman* is the Turkish word for "mercy," as in calling out for one's life to
be spared, which also conveys the notion of "alas." The prominent repetition of
aman in the refrains eventually earned these songs the genre name *amanes*, and
so the locations where they were performed came to be known as cafés aman.
These cafés aman emerged during the second half of the nineteenth century in
the seaport towns of the Aegean and western Anatolia.

While Mme. Koula was certainly not the first Greek female vocalist to record
in North America, she was the first to become an unquestionable top-selling performer. Koula Antonopoulou was also the first Greek female vocalist to record in
Turkish. Mme. Koula's first vastly popular Turkish song was "Kioutsouk glastan
hiouzom," a *canto* (Columbia E3388). That Mme. Koula was simultaneously the
first top-selling female vocalist in both traditional Greek and Turkish music only
adds to her lasting fame.

Far from a naïve immigrant pawn in the hands of sophisticated American
record company executives, Mme. Koula was also the first Greek immigrant
musician to own (together with her husband, Andreas) and perform on her own
record company label, the Panhellenion Record Company of New York.[3] The
first credited Panhellenion studio recordings are cited as taking place in early
1919 somewhere in New York. While still a matter of continuing debate, scholars

generally recognize that either Panhellenion or the Greek Record Company of Chicago was the first Greek immigrant–owned record label in North America.

When discussing his grandparents' life and business ventures, Xenophon Mitchell was always careful to stress their early years together in Patras, Greece, and the eastern Mediterranean. This is worth noting, because a period of nearly three years separates the time when Mme. Koula made her Columbia recordings and when she began recording on Panhellenion. Mitchell recounted that he had been told that it was his grandparents' accumulated savings, from earnings in Greece and Egypt, coupled with sales revenue from the first Columbia records that collectively funded their venture into Panhellenion Records.

In fact, again according to Mitchell, immediately after his grandmother's success at Columbia Records, she and her husband started performing in clubs across North Africa. It was while in Cairo that the Antonopouloses became convinced that the best professional recording equipment in the world was to be found in Germany. At some point after their 1916–1917 Columbia Records sessions and before their return to the United States during 1918–1919, the Antonopouloses purchased German-made recording equipment with the express aim of establishing their own company. This very expensive investment was funded with their savings from both the Columbia Records remittances and touring. And it was while Mme. Koula was in Cairo, just before her return to North America, that local promoters crowned her as the "Kanarini," or canary, of Greek and Turkish song. This is likely why Andreas Antonopoulos chose a canary sitting on a record as Panhellenion Records' official trademark logo. In the late 1920s, the main offices of the Panhellenion Phonograph Record Company were located at 635 Eighth Avenue in New York.

Among the many pioneering credits due to Mme. Koula and her Panhellenion Record Company is the first mother and daughter duet in the history of modern Greek music in North America. In June 1919, Koula and her daughter Paraskevi recorded "Kamariera" (Panhellenion 7000). For the eighteen-year-old Paraskevi, this was also the first documented occasion on which the child of a Greek immigrant musician recorded on a family-owned label. Mme. Koula is also the first Greek female vocalist to have a marked rivalry with another popular singer in North America, in her case Marika Papagika (1890–1943). For these reasons (and many others), Mme. Koula is often referred to as the "first" or "the best of the early" Greek female vocalists in North America.

In 1927, with the unexpected death of her beloved husband, Mme. Koula, out of grief, closed the Panhellenion Record Company and announced that she was retired. It must be stressed that, whatever might happen in later years, in the late winter of 1927 Mme. Koula was the biggest-selling Greek recording star in all of North America. It was at this precise moment that Tetos Demetriades (ca. 1891–1971) stepped in. Sometime in the early 1920s, the first records that Demetriades ever released appeared on the Panhellenion label. "Ela" and "Se agapo" (Pan-hellenion 307) featured him singing a duet with a young woman known only in published sources as "Vivi." The couple went on to record two more songs, "Agapis logia" and "I glentzedes" (Panhellenion 312). Xenophon Mitchell identi-fied "Vivi" as the diminutive of his mother's given name, Paraskevi. Obviously, Demetriades's professional and, we can assume, private connections with the Antonopoulos family extended over many years.

On October 25, 1927, at the RCA Victor recording studios in Camden, New Jersey, Mme. Koula recorded four songs with Demetriades in the studio. They were not what we would consider her most accomplished performances. The songs were "Tis nifis i tsembera" (The Bride's Veil, a *syrtos*) with the B-side "Stis mantzouranas ton antho" (The Flowers and the Trees, a *tsamikos*). Together, these songs are found on Victor Talking Machine Company 68910-A/B, released in twelve-inch deluxe format. Mme. Koula was accompanied by two unidentified musicians, a clarinetist and a cimbalom player.

What is especially interesting about "Tis nifis i tsembera," once we know some-thing of Mme. Koula's emotional state when it was recorded, is the disconcerting enthusiasm of Demetriades shouting "opa, opa" between the lyrical lines. It is as if Demetriades were trying energize Koula's obviously weak performance. The final two songs are "Agapo ena helidoni" (I Love a Blackbird [*sic*], a tsamikos) and "Kato ston Aspropotamo" (Down by the White River, Victor 68948-A/B). We should note that these songs were recorded with the latest recording technol-ogy of the day—an electric microphone.

On "Tis nifis i tsembera," Koula's voice is strained and, frankly, there is no color in it. At various moments, she attempts to give energy to the song, but in the end merely walks through the performance. "Stis mantzouranas ton antho," as a slowly metered tsamikos, allows Koula to render a dignified presentation. Then, between one lyrical line and another, we hear her call out to the other musicians in such a fashion that only they would understand: "Ach, ferao mavra, Panagia, yassas paidia, lao, yassas!" (Oh, I am in mourning black, Holy Virgin Mary, life to you my boys, I say, life to you!) Koula Antonopoulou never made a commercial record for a large record company ever again.

Sometime during the later stages of the Great Depression, Mme. Koula returned not only to commercial recordings but to touring the United States, giving live performances. In the late 1940s, based then in Lowell, Massachusetts, Mme. Koula started a second independent record label, the Panhellenic Record Company. This label did not restrict itself to just Greek and Turkish music but included Armenian and Arabic recordings as well. Mme. Koula had always per-formed with a host of different musicians. During this last phase of her profes-sional life, she spent a great deal of time performing and recording with Ashot Yergat, an Armenian vocalist and oud player. No other Greek musician from the senior generation of musicians, let alone a female, is documented as ever start-ing two independent record companies in North America. While Mme. Koula recorded in Greek and Turkish for her new label, the number of songs she ulti-mately recorded and how many records altogether were released by Panhellenic Records is not known.[4]

A bittersweet family memory distinguishes the last occasion on which Koula sang. In early 1954, she had to stop performing due to sustained heart troubles. Later that year, when Koula attended a Greek American child's birthday party down the block from her daughter's home, someone insisted that she sing. Unex-pectedly, she recovered her voice and gave a memorable performance. Mme. Koula was found the next morning in her bed, having died from heart failure. A vase of flowers given to her by the children at the party was next to her bed.

Notes

1. I want to acknowledge the many kindnesses shown to me by Xenophon William Mitchell (1918–2006) and his wife, Poppy Mitchell (1918–2012), during my visits to their home and his offices in Ottawa, Illinois. I made oral history recordings during my visits in the early 1990s and have kept these in my private collection.

2. All individual record citations such as titles, performers, record companies, dates, and other identification are drawn from Richard K. Spottswood, *Ethnic Music on Records: A Discography of Ethnic Recordings Produced in the United States, 1893–1942*, 7 vols. (Urbana: University of Illinois Press, 1990), unless otherwise noted.

3. *Editor's note*: Greek music historian Meletios Pouliopoulos pinpointed a recent online article in which author Antonis Boskoitis (Στα ίχνη της Κυρίας Κούλας: Η ζωη και το εργο τησ πρωτησ ρεμπετισσασ τησ αμερικησ, at http://www.lifo.gr/team/music/54645) learned that the Antonopoulo-ses had founded the Orpheum record company previous to Panhellenion, but it lasted only one year. More research is needed to confirm this information.

4. My deep thanks to Nick Topping (Topitzes) (1918–2007) of Topping and Company, a Milwaukee record store owner and music promoter, for his discussions with me on the Panhellenic Record Company and other topics related to the history of Greek music in North America post-1945. Although Mme. Koula was based in Lowell, Massachusetts, the Panhellenic Record Company's recording studio was located at 33 Columbus Avenue, between Sixtieth and Sixty-First Streets, New York.

George Dimitrios Grachis (1882–1965)[1]

—Sotirios (Sam) Chianis

My first meeting with George Grachis was truly a historic occasion. About 1960, he and Spyros Stamos were playing in the Greek *kafeneio* that was then located at Third and Folsom in San Francisco. I knew Stamos because I was studying cimbalom with him and I lived in his home in South San Francisco for almost a year.[2] I hadn't previously met Grachis, but I was well acquainted with his violin artistry through his recordings on the Greek Record Company label. During that evening in the kafeneio, I not only had the distinct honor of accompanying him on cimbalom but was honored to be in the presence of two of the patriarchs of Greek folk music in America.

In 1965, I conducted a series of all-day taped interviews in Greek with George Grachis and his wife in their home in San Mateo, California. In the atmosphere of genuine Greek hospitality, their frank and honest comments provided me with a wealth of historical materials that were simply unavailable elsewhere. From this voluminous information from the Grachises, and other materials in my possession, I have presented a few highlights of his long career as a Greek folk musician. I consider it extremely important to include as many of Grachis's comments as pertinent, exactly as he spoke them. This chapter is most sincerely dedicated to George Dimitrios Grachis for the important role he played in Greek folk music.

George Dimitrios Grachis

When George Dimitrios Grachis arrived in America in 1907, he was not only a master instrument maker who had learned his craft from his father but an accomplished violinist as well. Grachis was born on August 12, 1882, in the small Peloponnesian village of Ligourio, near the ancient amphitheater of Epidaurus. Grachis's father, Dimitrios, was born in Argos and had acquired the art of carpentry from his own father (who was born on the island of Spetses). Dimitrios learned to play violin as a young man and soon began making them in Ligourio.

345

Figure 87. George Dimitrios Grachis, Chicago, 1920. From the Terpandros instrument factory catalog. Courtesy of Sotirios (Sam) Chianis.

It was in Ligourio that fate spared the young George from death before he'd reached his tenth birthday. He related the tragic event:

> In Ligourio, my father had four children: me, another son, and two daughters. At that time a dreadful illness came along and my siblings contracted it. There were no doctors, no medicines, nothing in the village. As a result, my brother and two sisters died. I was the only one left. My father almost went crazy. So he took me and my mother to Argos. He sold our home in Ligourio and bought a small house in Argos. He made the move because he was afraid that I would die too. And that is how I survived.

From the time he moved to Argos until his arrival in America, George was not only performing professionally at weddings, festivals, church celebrations, and holidays in Argos, Corinth, Nafplion, Tegea, and other Peloponnesian cities and villages, but managed to master the art of instrument making. In Argos, he and his father specialized in making *laouta* and bouzoukia, which were in great demand in those years. During his adolescence and early adulthood, George met and performed with some of the finest musicians in Greece. "I played for many years with the clarinetist Nikolaos Souleimanis [1848–1921]," he said. "He was a Turk who was later baptized [1864] and became a Christian. He married a good woman [1892] and had a small house in Messolonghi. I took him along and we played in Patras, Corinth, the island of Aegina, and other places." It should be mentioned that Souleimanis is truly a legendary figure in Greece.

When I asked George if he knew the incomparable clarinetist Nikitas Kotsopoulos (1880–1947), he was quick to reply: "In fact Nikitas visited my home in

Argos with Spyros Stamos's uncle. Spyros had [a maternal] uncle, Alexandros Tsochos, who played violin. We knew each other from childhood and we would meet at festivals held in Corinth. He would say to Nikitas, 'Let's go to Argos and see George,' and they would come to see me."

During the late nineteenth and early twentieth centuries, Corinth and Argos were the principal performance centers of folk music in the Peloponnese. "During these festivals," Grachis informed me,

> we played all types of dance tunes: *kalamatiana*, *syrta*, *tsamika*, and *balla*. In Nafplion and Argos people loved to dance the ballos. We would start out playing a kalamatianos and then go into a lively syrtos. And from the syrtos we would play a ballos. The dance ended with the ballos. We also played the *berati* [also called *himariotiko*]. People danced the berati as a kalamatianos; however, in Epirus, it is danced differently, more in place.

The years spent in Argos provided Grachis with the opportunity to develop into a superb violinist and acquire an extraordinarily rich and varied repertoire that was to serve him throughout his entire life. He might very well have stayed in Argos had it not been for a single incident: a handshake.

Grachis's father had a violin student who came from a small village near Tripolis and lived in their home. During his stay, the student asked young George if he would be his *koumbaros* (the godfather of his first child). George agreed and made it official with a handshake. The student eventually traveled to America, opened a candy store in Chicago, accumulated a sizable estate, and returned to Greece to get married. When his marriage plans didn't work out, he passed by Argos and said to George's father, "Why don't I take George along with me to America, where my koumbaros will earn a lot of money with his violin. I'll pay for his passage." George's father approved. The year was 1905.

Grachis arrived in Chicago in 1906 as a twenty-three-year-old lad. His koumbaros's forecast proved to be correct. Grachis recalled those years for me:

> After a month or two in Chicago, I paid off my passage expenses and even sent money home to marry off my cousins. I was making a lot of money then with my violin. I would play for a wedding and earn $500 to $1,000. There were three of us in the ensemble and each would earn $300 to $400. We never earned less than $200. [By tradition, all tips are divided evenly among the musicians.] That was money! Life was inexpensive and you had money left over. You could buy the best suit of clothes for only $25, the best pair of shoes for $6, and a dozen bananas cost only five cents. I was constantly invited months in advance to play on Sundays in certain saloons. And when we went and played we would make money by the sackful. After about a year or a year and a half, I received a letter from a compatriot of mine who lived in Salt

Lake City, Utah, inviting me to play for his sister's wedding. I arrived in Salt Lake City with my trio consisting of Theodoros Smyrnis (who played the santouri), my uncle Kosta Pantelopoulos on laouto, and myself. It is not a lie that we made $1,500 at the wedding. There were many Greeks in Salt Lake City because they worked in the mines outside the city and also on the railroad. One day a person approached me and said, "why don't you open up a kafeneio," and I did.

In November 1907, a short but critical financial crisis known as the Panic of 1907 caused widespread failures of banks and business concerns. Many Greek immigrants along with other foreigners lost their jobs. And when the crisis reached its climax, numerous anti-Greek incidents occurred around the country. These circumstances had a devastating effect on Grachis and his kafeneio. He lost everything and decided to return to Chicago with his ensemble. They played in cities along the way to pay their expenses.

Arriving back in Chicago, Grachis decided to return to Greece in order to bring his father and mother to America. Before leaving, however, Smyrnis suggested that he bring back a woman who could sing and dance, "so we can open up a *café aman*." Grachis was able to bring his parents as well as a singer/dancer from Athens, named Kleoniki. It was a historic occasion. Grachis, Smyrnis, Pantelopoulos, and Kleoniki constituted the first Greek *kompania* (musical group or ensemble) to perform in a café aman atmosphere in Chicago. "Whenever we played," said Grachis, "people went wild, they loved us."

Cafés aman were venues where a kompania (consisting of several instrumentalists and one or two female vocalists) could perform. As Grachis explained: "You must have a large repertoire for the café aman because you don't know who you have to please. They'll come to you with a five or ten dollar bill and say, 'play this tune' or 'that tune.' And if you don't know it you lose the money. In the café aman we played music from the islands, Epirus, and the mainland. We played many *tsiftetelia* and *karsilamades*, even Turkish tunes. In those days I was an expert. Whatever people requested, we would play it." A typical café aman would open between 7:00 and 9:00 p.m. and close at 1:00 a.m.

Grachis was continually performing during the years he lived in Chicago. In fact, he played with virtually all of the outstanding Greek folk instrumentalists and vocalists then performing in America.

The Terpandros Musical Instrument Factory

In 1910, Grachis and his father established the first Greek musical instrument factory in Chicago. Located at 606 South Morgan Street, the factory was aptly given the name Terpandros after Terpander of Lesbos, a legendary patriarch of

Greek music. It was here that they began making their first musical instruments in America, including the santouri, laouto, bouzouki, mandolin, and guitar. Terpandros was a complete music store that not only supplied Greek and other musicians with all types of musical instruments, strings, reeds, instrument cases, and the like but also offered expert instrument repair services. In 1915, the factory was moved to 608 Blue Island Avenue and renamed Ellinikon Ergostasion Mousikon Organon (Factory of Greek Musical Instruments).

Page 13 of Grachis's new thirty-three-page catalog (published in 1915) includes the following description: "Our bouzoukia are exceptional in every aspect. They have been made with the latest techniques, with the very best of materials, well-constructed, and have a sweet and clear sound." Two different types of bouzoukia were made. Although each had a pear-shaped body, a rounded back made of several ribs (staves), a long fretted neck, and three double courses of strings, it was the construction of the soundboard (on the top) that distinguished the two. In one, the soundboard was flat (as on a laouto or guitar); this version was called a *misolaouto* (half laouto). In the other, the soundboard bent downward below the bridge; this style was called a *mandola*. Bouzoukia ranged in price from $15 to $50. Bouzouki strings sold for five cents apiece, or twenty-five cents for a full set of six. The price of a santouri ranged from $50 to $75. Those readers who are acquainted with the name "Buffet" will appreciate the following statement from the catalog: "All Buffet clarinets pitched in either A, B-flat, C, or E-flat have the identical price of $34.50." The lowest-priced Grachis laouto sold for $50, while the most expensive model went for $90.

There is no doubt that virtually all the hundreds of instruments made by the Grachises had exceptional tone qualities and were truly masterpieces of workmanship. George Grachis had gained such a remarkable reputation in America as well as in Greece that he became known as the Stradivari of Greece. A phenomenal number of musical instruments were produced at the factory. According to Grachis, he made about eighty-five santouria, more than three hundred bouzoukia, and approximately one hundred laouta. "Many of my bouzoukia and laouta were taken to Greece by musicians," Grachis said. "In fact, a few years ago here in San Mateo, I came across a photo in an American magazine that showed instrumentalists and dancers in Greece. And the person with the laouto was playing one of my instruments. I recognized it!" Grachis continued making bouzoukia in San Mateo. "I made eight of them here," he said, "and I have only two left. Just leave them for my children and grandchildren."

It was Grachis who was responsible for making Spyros Stamos's first cimbalom, during 1920–1921. When Stamos arrived in America as a young man, he was an established virtuoso santouri player. Both the santouri and cimbalom are trapezoidal in shape, classified as struck zithers and played with two cotton-covered sticks. The prime difference between the two instruments is the arrangement of the strings and the placement of the bridges. The tuning (arrangement of strings) of the santouri is commonly referred to as *ala turka* and the cimbalom *ala franka*. "When Stamos wanted to begin learning the cimbalom," Grachis said,

> he didn't have one. So I told him that I would make one for him, and I made him one. It was a good cimbalom and he learned to play on it. At that time, another person and I owned three movie theaters and Stamos would practice all day in one of them. I organized an ensemble consisting of two violins, cimbalom, and piano, and we would perform in the theater in the evenings. We played all kinds of overtures and opera selections that we learned from music. After performing for about a year, Stamos left to play elsewhere and I finally sold the theaters [in 1922]. . . . I've performed for over twenty-five years with Stamos, traveling all over America. We were very good friends and I loved to perform with him and he with me.

The Apollo Greek Musicians Union

In 1965, I visited Spyros Stamos at his home in Mountain View, California. During the course of our conversation pertaining to Greek folk musicians in America, he said: "By the way, here is my Greek union book." I was taken completely by surprise, for I was unaware of the fact that Greek folk musicians had a union. Stamos added: "Mr. Grachis started it and did everything." Stamos also gave me a clipping from the Greek-language newspaper *Atlantis* (first published in New York in 1894) announcing the dissolution of the union in 1921.

During my lengthy interviews with Grachis, I mentioned what Stamos had related about the existence of a Greek union and that he had given me his union book. "You want to know how it came about," Grachis said, "I'll tell you." He continued:

> We Greek musicians had problems with the women (who had the role of vocalists and dancers and constituted an important part of the musical ensemble). Musicians were constantly arguing with them. The women wanted to be free to have lovers. But the musicians didn't want this situation to continue. The musicians didn't want the women to seem dirty because it had a degrading effect on their profession as musicians. A solution had to be found. So I gathered together those musicians who I knew were sympathetic in order to discuss the problem and the idea of a union. "If there is a union," I said, "a person cannot perform unless he or she is a member. You can establish rules and punish their inappropriate behavior." The union idea pleased the prospective members, who saw that it was a practical solution. We wanted to establish moral principles among the musicians as well as the women. We wanted the women to act as human beings, to be ethical. In reality, they did become ethical.

The union, called the Apollo Greek Musicians Union, was established in Chicago on October 3, 1918 (the English translation of the bylaws specifies October 31). Moral and ethical principles were so important that the first of twenty-one articles contained in the bylaws included the following statement: "The object thereof shall be: first, to encourage and strengthen the relations between Greeks and Americans in general; second, to secure their cooperation; and third, to protect and to advance the moral and material interests of the Greek musicians in the United States, whatever be their citizenship." Article 3 was concerned with the conduct of the membership: "Any member whose conduct is opposed to the best interests or to the dignity of the Association may be expelled from the Association by decision of the Assembly, if accused on oath by three members of the Association of some misdeed." It is interesting to note that Article 11 begins: "Musicians of either sex are eligible to membership in the Union, men having the right to vote and to be candidates for office a week after their matriculation while women have only the right to vote." According to Article 16, musicians were obligated to donate each year the proceeds of two or more of their performances to the union.

I asked Grachis whether the musicians liked the idea of a union. "They loved it," he said, "because they saw that it was good. As a result of the union, problems with the women were solved. But the women didn't catch on to our purpose. Even today, they still don't know. But now the union no longer exists. I've only related this to you so you'll know why the union was organized. It was I and not any other person who organized the union."

When asked if all Greek musicians in the Chicago area were members of the union, Grachis replied:

Yes, all the instrumentalists! New York City soon established a [local] chapter of the union with a president and everything along the same lines as ours, and it flourished. Musicians could not work without being members. In fact, they were forced to join the union. A member of the Chicago Local could work in New York City, while a member of the New York City Local was permitted to perform in Chicago. It was the same union with different chapters.

The Greek Record Company

Among Grachis's and Stamos's numerous and important contributions to the Greek folk music scene in the United States was the creation of the Greek Record Company (Elliniki Etairia Diskon Fonografou) of Chicago. Grachis established the company and Stamos served as its director. A careful examination of all the documents (both published and oral histories) clearly indicates that the company was established during 1922–1923.

An advertisement (in Greek) announcing the Greek Record Company's products stated:

> The new phonograph records that have just been released by the Greek Record Company have as their featured performer, of Panhellenic fame, George Grachis, who initiated the Greek Record Company and who with his violin artistry promises to offer numerous Greek phonograph record customers faithful renditions of our national songs and immortal folk music. On some discs he is accompanied by the lyrical voice of Angelos K. Stamos [brother of Spyros], and on all of his discs he is accompanied by the world-famous cimbalom artist Spyros Stamos.

The thirty ten-inch and twelve-inch 78-rpm phonograph records issued by the Greek Record Company featured outstanding Greek instrumentalists and vocalists from the Chicago area. The extremely rare catalog (generously given to me by Spyros Stamos) lists a variety of selections intended to please every taste: kalamatiana, syrta, tsamika, klephtic songs, *taximia*, amanedes, *zeibekika*, a waltz, rebetika, *hasapika*, *sarki*, and even a two-step performed by the Trianon Orchestra of Chicago. The performance of the dance tune "Beratiano" (catalog no. 515), featuring George Grachis on violin, Spyros Stamos on cimbalom, and Angelos Stamos singing, is an absolute classic! The catalog also includes portraits of many of the artists. Artists featured on the recordings included vocalists Amalia Baka, Marika Papagika, Aristotelis Katsanis (Mourmouris), Angelos Stamos, Kleoniki, Eleni Arapakis, and Epamenondas Asimakopoulos; musicians Konstantinos Filis (clarinet), Nikolaos Rellias (clarinet), Konstantinos Patsios (clarinet), Harilaos Piperakis (Cretan lyra); and directors J. B. Lamp (Trianon Orchestra) and Spyros Becatoros (chorus). The chorus included John Kouvarakos (tenor), Angelos Stamos (secondo), Spyros Stamos (secondo), Theodoros Diakos (baritone), A. Speh (baritone), and Demetrios Tsatsis (bass).

Conclusion

Over the years, I've often listened to the tapes of my interviews with George Grachis and his wife. Each and every time I listen to them I am overtaken with profound nostalgia. He was truly an extraordinary man who gave so generously his time and was so genuinely interested in what I was attempting to do. By the time of my interviews he was an elderly man to be sure, but when he spoke so enthusiastically about his love of Greek music and instrument making, Greek musicians of the past, and his lifetime of experiences, he seemed to grow young;

for it was quite evident that he was thoroughly enjoying every moment of the two full days of interviews. Because he knew of my interest in instruments and instrument making, he spent many hours painstakingly explaining exactly how a laouto is constructed, the types of wood to be used, the finish, and other details. When he explained how one performs a taxim (a solo improvisation) in a given mode, he would pick up his violin and demonstrate. However, he was quick to apologize for his playing by saying: "Now my bow arm does not move synchronously with my fingers. Do you understand? That's why I'm distressed and I don't want to play. I don't want to hear myself play! It seems as though someone else is playing—as if a student is playing—like someone who is just starting to play violin." Finally, he expressed extreme concern about the future of Greek folk music, the music that was his life. "If the young generation doesn't learn to play and sing our folk music," he said, "our music will die out."

Notes

1. *Editor's note*: This chapter is a substantially edited combination of two previously published essays: "George Demetrios Grachis: America's Greatest Greek Violinist and Instrument Maker," part 1, *Laografia* (September–October 1994): 2–6; and "George Demetrios Grachis: America's Greatest Greek Violinist and Instrument Maker," part 2, *Laografia* (May–June 1995): 9–14.

2. Spyros Stamos was an exceptional musician and a true artist. He played in some of the best nightclubs and exclusive restaurants in Chicago and later in San Francisco, and made numerous appearances as a solo artist with some of America's finest symphony orchestras. I am especially honored and proud to say that he was my cimbalom teacher.

References

Mazaraki, Despina. 1959. *To laïko klarino stin ellada* (The Folk Clarinet in Greece). Athens: French Institute of Athens.

Saloutos, Theodore. 1964. *The Greeks in the United States*. Cambridge, MA: Harvard University Press.

Harilaos Piperakis (1888–1978)

—Panayotis League

Harilaos Piperakis was born in 1888 in the village of Xirosterni (or Viola) in Apo-koronas, an area of the western Cretan province of Chania that was a strong-hold of the *lyra* (an upright bowed fiddle) in a region otherwise dominated by the violin. He grew up with the sounds of both instruments, and his long career would be marked by his study of these and many other Aegean and Middle East-ern musical traditions. Indeed, his first instrument was the violin, but he soon switched to the lyra after his family temporarily relocated to the Cretan capital of Heraklion and he was exposed to that city's many great exponents of the latter instrument. By the age of fourteen, Piperakis's natural talent and single-minded dedication had made him one of Crete's finest lyra players, and as a young man he emigrated to the United States to begin a career as a performer and recording artist that would last for more than seventy years.

In many ways, Harry Piperakis (as he was known in his new home) was typi-cal of the many migrant musicians of his time and place: he spent more than half a century performing extensively throughout North America at weddings, nightclubs, and other musical venues and made roughly two dozen commercial recordings for Pharos and Columbia Records. What set him apart from his peers and what continues to call attention to his music was not only his remarkable technical prowess—he greatly expanded notions about the Cretan lyra's capabili-ties by modulating with ease between different scales and modes and routinely playing in the extreme high range of the instrument, reminiscent of a violin—but also his insatiable appetite for musical knowledge and his remarkably expansive familiarity with a wide range of Aegean and Middle Eastern traditions. Although he was most renowned in the Cretan diaspora and was an unparalleled expert in performing the traditional dances of the island (accompanied for many years by the great *laouto* or steel-string lute player Giorgos Gobakis from the village of Babakados Selinou in Chania province), he was equally adept at playing music from many other regions of Greece and was in constant demand in the Arabic, Turkish, and Armenian expatriate communities as well. His intimate knowl-edge of the modal Arabo-Turkish *makam* system allowed him to freely perform

HARILAOS PIPERAKIS & Lyra
Plays and Sings for KALIPHON Records
D-758 · D-759 · D-760 · D-761

Figure 88. Harilaos Piperakis. From the Kaliphon Records catalog. Courtesy of Meletios Pouliopoulos.

improvisations or *taximia* alongside the great oud (fretless bowl-back lute), *kanun* (plucked zither), and violin players active in the Middle Eastern nightclub scene, and he was known for being an assiduous student of the subtle differences between regional styles, taking care to adjust his intonation to conform to his colleagues' particular interpretation of the microtones and embellishments characteristic of each stream of modal music.

Piperakis also remained a student of his native tradition well into his adulthood. Sometime during 1926–1928, on the cusp of middle age and already a seasoned and established professional, he made a special trip from his home in California to the village of Drapania in Kissamos in the extreme west of Crete in order to study with the famed violinist Giorgis Marianos. The violinist taught Piperakis a wealth of old *syrtos* melodies and instructed him in the intricacies of the Chania violin tradition—which Piperakis adapted to his lyra. Piperakis returned to Crete several times to learn new music and play with old friends. On another such trip—probably in 1928—he visited the legendary violinist Nikolaos Charchalis in his home village of Charchaliana, Kissamos, in order to ask permission to record Charchalis's composition "Lousakianos syrtos." Charchalis agreed, in exchange for permission to record Piperakis's famous "Xirosterianos

355

syrtos," composed in honor of his home village and still one of the most popular syrtos dance tunes in Crete.

Piperakis's recordings were also unusual—and enjoyed unusually wide popularity in several different diaspora communities—because of his expansive aesthetic and open-mindedness as an arranger and bandleader. While most Cretan recording artists in the early and mid-twentieth century preferred to limit their recordings to the "traditional" pairings of lyra or violin with laouto—regardless of actual performance practice—Piperakis routinely collaborated with singers and instrumentalists from Arabic, Armenian, Turkish, and other backgrounds, and his records featured accompaniment by instruments like the oud, *santouri* (hammered dulcimer), and *dumbek* or *toumbeleki* (goblet drum). His live performances frequently involved background singers, dancers, kanun, oud, and drums—a lineup calculated to offer maximum flexibility and the ability to conform to the tastes of almost any audience from the wider Mediterranean region.

Piperakis lived most of his life in the United States. He recorded several songs dealing with explicitly American themes or chronicling the Greek immigrant experience in the country, including several in the urban *rebetika* style (including the first commercial recordings of a Cretan lyra playing melodies in the heavy *zeibekiko* rhythm). Perhaps his most famous recording in this vein, later rerecorded by the great Smyrna-born Armenian oud player and singer Markos Melkon, is "To ouest" (The West), which mentions boomtowns in the American West like Sacramento, Vallejo, Lodi, San Francisco, Salt Lake City, and Butte, and chronicles the typical trials of Greek immigrants who flocked to work the mines, ranches, farms, and factories of the expanding Pacific coastal and mountain states.

Despite his popularity in his adopted country, and regardless of his frequent trips back to his native Crete, Piperakis's commercial recordings were never a tremendous success in Greece during his most active years as a recording artist and performer. Perhaps the eclectic nature of his selections and his gleeful mixing of sounds from various distinct musical cultures alienated an audience that had grown accustomed to a conscious separation between Greek, Turkish, Arabic, and other related traditions. And, like many other Cretan artists who recorded in the early decades of the twentieth century, many of his arrangements were rerecorded by later musicians who failed to give him credit. The most famous example is perhaps Rethymno lyra player Andreas Rodinos's tremendously influential 1933 recordings of "Apokoroniotikos syrtos" and "Kissamitikos syrtos"—two old syrtos melodies that Piperakis had learned from Chania violinists, adapted to the lyra, and recorded back in 1919.

Piperakis died in 1978 in Fairfield, California, at the age of ninety. He left behind a remarkable legacy whose importance in the history of Cretan, Greek, and Middle Eastern music grows greater with each passing year, as more and more musicians from all over the region discover his thoroughly modern sensibility and recognize him as their artistic forebear.

References

Deiktakis, Athanasios P. 1999. *Xaniotes laïkoi mousikoi pou den iparchoun pia*. Kastelli Kissamou: Athanasios P. Deiktakis.

Stilianakis, Giorgos. 1999. "Apochairetismos s' ena megalo kallitechni." In *Xaniotes laïkoi mousikoi pou den iparchoun pia*, by Athanasios P. Deitktakis, 183–86. Kastelli Kissamou: Athanasios P. Deiktakis.

I am also grateful for personal communications from Nikolaos Manias (September 2003), Ross Daly (August 2004), Emmanouil Manioudakis (June 2006), and Dimitris Rapakousios (July 2015).

Marika Papagika (1890–1943)[1]

—Stavros K. Frangos

At Marika's

In his excellent liner notes for *Greek Oriental Smyrnaic Rebetic Songs and Dances: The Golden Years, 1927–1937* (Folklyric 9033), Martin Schwartz wrote about Marika Papagika's musical development:

> Marika Papagika was born on the island of Kos near Turkey. Her recording career began in the US c. 1918 along with that of her husband Gus, with whom she made the majority of her recordings, and the brilliant Makedonas. She also recorded with such great talents as the Epirot violinist Alexis Zoumbas and the clarinetists Peter Marnakos and Nikos Rellias. Papagika's early recordings include old rural folksongs and light or sentimental European-style numbers but she eventually focused on the Smyrnaic-rebetic genre, including old songs about hashish, prison, and street life. Much of her repertory corresponds to that of her predecessor Coula (who recorded c. 1914–1921), who sang in a less refined voice. Papagika's repertory and style is comparable to those of Amalia Baka and Angeliki Karagianni, who recorded well into the 40s, whereas Papagika seems to have stopped in the 30s. (Schwartz 1993)

What Schwartz did not mention is the issue of audience. In the Balkans and Asia Minor before 1920, mixed-language songs and songs sung in languages other than Greek were typical of the musical traditions found in the *cafés aman*. While it is fashionable today to write of "old songs about hashish, prison, and street life," the non-Greek elements found nightly in the clubs are rarely discussed. The constant ethnically diverse patronage in the American cafés aman also explains why Greek 78-rpm records sold out of proportion to the Greek immigrant population, for Greeks were not the only people buying the records.

The first café aman to open in New York was a second-floor walk-up called Marika's, located at Thirty-Fourth Street between Seventh and Eighth Avenues. The club was named after its owner and principal performer, Marika Papagika. Using the income gained from nearly six years of commercial record sales, along

Figure 89. Kostas and Marika Papagika, ca. 1920s. Courtesy of
Katerina Papagika.

with savings from touring throughout the country, Papagika and her husband set
up Marika's in 1925. It was the fifth year of Prohibition (1920–1933), and Marika's
was not just a café aman but a speakeasy. It is also significant that the thirteen years
of Prohibition coincided with most of Papagika's eleven-year recording career.

Marika's attracted not only Greeks as regular patrons but also Albanians,
Arabs, Armenians, Bulgarians, Syrians, and even the occasional Turk. The majority of regular patrons on any given night at Marika's were not Greeks, in fact,
but Armenians. After Marika's opened, other cafés aman soon appeared in the
Jewish section on the Lower East Side of Manhattan near Delancey and Cherry
Streets—which included a Romaniote Greek Jewish community. Within less
than fifteen years there were an additional six to eight cafés aman in the Eighth
Avenue area as well, all within four or five blocks of Marika's. They included the
infamous Port Said, Arabian Nights, and Omar Khayyam's around Thirty-Ninth
Street and Eighth Avenue (Frangos 1991a, 1991b, 1991c, 1993a).

The cosmopolitan nature of these cafés cut across social as well as ethnic lines. In Greece, the cafés aman were visited by the intelligentsia and the wealthy. In New York, Chicago, Detroit, and elsewhere, non-Greek Americans were often a part of the audience. The American poet e. e. cummings, for instance, recorded his experiences in "one April dusk the" (Cummings 2013, 84).

Overlooking the mixed audience forestalls discussion of non-Greek and mixed-language records produced by Greek artists. A case in point is Papagika's Turkish songs. The first for which documentation exists is the August 1919 song "Ne itsoun saidin," released as Columbia E4878. Next is "Kioutsouk hanoun" (June 1922), which Columbia issued as two pressings, Columbia E5272 and Columbia 75022-F.[2] In September 1922, she recorded "Ben yarimi giordoum" (Columbia E9030); and in 1923 "Channakale" and "Sinanaiwere" were released together as Columbia E5283. Papagika was not alone—other Greek female vocalists recorded Turkish, Armenian, Ladino, Arabic, and mixed-language songs in America between 1911 and 1933.[3]

Non–Greek language songs were not restricted to records. In keeping with pan-Balkan and Anatolian performance traditions, Kostas (Gus) Papagikas may have written the song "Armenaki" (The Little Armenian) in response to that segment of the club's regular nightly, standing-room-only audience. According to John K. Gianaros, a Greek musician of that generation, the song was first sung publicly in Armenian. The lyrics on the Victor record are sung in Greek, but the melody is Armenian.[4] Gianaros relates:

> I was there when she introduced the song . . . because Armenians used to go to the cabaret she had. At this time those places [ethnic speakeasies] they used to call cafés aman. You know why? [It] was Prohibition. . . . You sit at a table and you told the waiters, "Café. Aman! Café . . . aman!" They didn't mean the place. . . . They'd put ouzo in the coffee cups and would bring it to them. That's why they called it café aman. (Gianaros 1987)

The slang usage here plays on *aman* as the Turkish word for mercy, for instance calling out and begging for your life. The implication is that the patrons petitioned to be served and saved from "dying" of thirst. When asked why Greeks would want what seemed to me non-Greek music, Gianaros replied: "Because in those *kafenions* used to go all kinds of nations . . . Turkish, Arabians, Bulgarians, Yugoslavians." When asked who owned those places, he said, "only Greeks" (Gianaros 1987).[5]

Recordings

Not being familiar with other Greek female vocalists who sang from 1911 to 1929, many consider Papagika as the era's premier Greek singer in North America.

With no detailed general histories of Greek music and musicians, it is also understandable that writers since the 1970s have focused almost exclusively upon *rebetika*.[6] Given the genre's historical importance, it logically followed that, when articles on Greek music in America finally began to appear, they initially focused on rebetika in the early twentieth century (Gauntlett 1982–1983; Smith 1991a; Pappas 1992).[7]

Marika Papagika's career lends itself to this interpretation of Greek music history. In May 1928, the first record documented with the word *rebetiko* printed on the label was released—Papagika's "Sti filaki me valane" and "I mavromata" (Columbia E56117-F). The unintended consequence of bestowing the honor of "first rebetika song on commercial record" is that it belittles a significantly more interesting career. This one rebetika record is certainly less important than a body of 226 known commercial records. Papagika's role in the history and transformation of modern Greek music is ultimately far more significant than one word on any single record label! The problem with current scholarship on the history of Greek music since 1896 is that it is limited to fragmented and segregated encyclopedia or journal articles about folk music or Byzantine music; biographical entries on internationally known Greek composers; and the occasional book on rebetika.

Rebetika in its blazing bouzouki incarnation of the 1970s is very much a tourist phenomenon. The difference between music created for the consumption of foreign tourists and the music Greeks listen to regularly is indeed a vast divide. Likewise, most articles and books written on rebetika pander to the foreign market. Instead of expanding readers' perceptions about the Greek version of "world music," writers have domesticated the genre by reducing its complexity and taming its stark beauty. Most writers introduce the genre to the world by stating that it sounds "like the blues" (cf. Butterworth and Schneider 1975; Holst [1975] 1989).

Few have listened to the full range of Greek musicians and musical genres available on commercial records since 1896, and fewer still attempt to understand Greek music in America in historical terms. It is important to place Greek music, wherever initially played or recorded, within the wider frame of the commercial record industry and its worldwide network. Marika Papagika was at the very heart of this world. Today, all we know of her early life is that on July 19, 1918, she entered the Victor Talking Machine Company studios in New York already an accomplished singer with an established *kompania* of instrumentalists. Like other Greek female vocalists who recorded between 1911 and 1926, she sang through a megaphone. On that bright July morning of her first studio session, only "Me xechasane" was recorded. No instrumentalists are identified by name, but a violin, *santouri*, and cello accompanied her. Company documents state that the session was a "trial." But less than three months later Papagika was back to record another trial record of "Me xechasane," this time with only piano accompaniment.

On December 4, 1918, Papagika successfully recorded her first commercial song, "Smyrneiko minore." It was released on at least three different record labels: Victor Talking Machine Company 72192, His Master's Voice A0343, and the small Greek specialty label Phalirea 22/23 (33). "Golfo kleftiko," allegedly a *kleftiko* song, is the flip side to the Victor and HMV releases. There is no information about what the flip side was on the Phalirea release, but it was common throughout this period to release a rebetiko on one side with a kleftiko on the other.

Conditions at Victor must have proved difficult, because Papagika did not record again for seven months, and throughout 1919 she and her kompania recorded only for Columbia. Between July and August 1919, Papagika, along with Athanasios Makedonas (violin), Markos Sifnios (cello), and Gus Papagikas (cimbalom), recorded thirty-five individual songs. That they were an instant success is obvious not just by the long list of recordings she was destined to make but because the Columbia executives decided to issue her records as both singles and multiple releases.

A select review of Marika Papagika's recordings will help determine her role in Greek music during the early 1900s. The breadth of themes found on her records spans the gamut of the collective hopes, dreams, and memories of Greek America from 1918 to 1929. We can roughly separate themes into three categories: patriotic songs and village Greece, European romance and the Roaring Twenties, and *Smyrneika* and rebetika songs.

Patriotic Songs and Village Greece

Because the words "Patriotic Song" appear on only four of Papagika's songs, why have a separate category? The classification is due in part to the phenomenal success of "Eleftheria," a song associated with Papagika ever since its release in 1919. The amazing energy she instilled in the song could only reflect the spirit of the Megali Idea among diaspora Greeks in the summer of 1919. Set to the tune of George M. Cohan's "Over There," its lyrics speak of the Greeks taking back Agia Sofia in Constantinople and planting their flag atop its dome. The first of many top-selling records, it was so popular that in 1922 a remake titled "To tragoudi tis lefterias" (Columbia E7707) set the pattern for a long string of top-selling kleftika and *dimotika* records.

Papagika's kleftika are still played at Greek American family parties. Usually overlooked is the fact that she recorded many more kleftika and dimotika than Smyrneïka. These popular songs (often in multiple releases) include "Kalamatiano"

(Columbia E5185, Columbia 56143-F, Columbia 11808); "Vangelo" (Columbia E478Z, Columbia 7738); "Oi Kolokotronaioi" (Columbia 56216-F); "Golfo" (Victor 72192, HMV A0343, Columbia K7305); and her vastly popular "Olympos kai Kisavos" (Victor 68596, Columbia 56009-F, Columbia 11667).

European Romance and the Roaring Twenties

This category separates the singing careers of Papagika and Mme. Koula Antonopoulou.[8] With the *ala franka* songs, we face difficult questions of creativity and cross influences. A random selection of releases includes "Tip-top-ah i ftohia" (Columbia E4968), recorded in October 1920; "To tsiganiko tango" from *O vaptistikos*, a musical revue composed by Theophrastos Sakellaridis (Victor Talking Machine Company 72976); "Ah Mari," composed by Eduardo di Capua and arranged by Nathaniel Shilkret (Victor 73082); "Tis maskas to foxtrot" (Columbia E7811); and "A Irene," also identified as a foxtrot (Victor 77767).

During the early days of Prohibition, Papagika sang two of the quintessential Greek American flapper songs: "To elektriko koritsi" and its flip side, the infamous "I gynaika pou skotonei," both recorded in April 1924 (Columbia 7009-F). This was far from an isolated turn to the flapper genre. Two years earlier, on October 18, 1922, she recorded "Glenti trelo" (Victor 73563), which is described as a foxtrot shimmy credited to Greek composer Nikos Hatziapostolou.

Smyrneïka and Rebetika

Some scholars have stressed that, in the latter part of her career, Papagika recorded Smyrneïka-style songs extensively. Why she made that choice had much to do with who her audience was on any given night. She and her kompania were working musicians who performed for a living. Recording Smyrneïka was not simply an artistic decision: Papagika made commercial records because they sold. But why were they popular in New York, Chicago, Salt Lake City, and Los Angeles? The number of Greeks from Anatolia, Cappadocia, and the Black Sea region was relatively small compared to the total population of Greeks in America, and they could never account for all the record sales. But we know that from the late 1900s to the early 1920s, the majority of Greeks in America were young men. They were lonely. They missed their homes and their families. The 1920s were years of social and economic hardship. So the loss of home that Asia Minor Greeks sang of so eloquently must have struck a chord in those young men, who also lived far from their homeland.

The problem with distinguishing between *amanedes*, *laïka*, rebetika, Smyrneïka, and zeibekika as musical genres on records produced between 1911 and 1929 is that the musicians who first performed these songs, the record company executives who produced them, and the immigrants who bought the records never made the categorical distinctions. This does not mean they did not know what kind of music they were playing, issuing, or buying. But the confusion arises from projecting current beliefs onto the past without solid historical documentation.

This situation becomes clearer if we look at the first appearance of the word *rebetiko* on a commercial record label. By taking this as a criterion for including specific songs within a genre, many songs obviously a part of the pan-Balkan/western Anatolian musical traditions can immediately be omitted. For example, Papagika's highly popular rendition of "Tha spaso koupes," a *tsifteteli* (Columbia F-56100 205806), is among a handful of songs directly associated with the Greek café music scene in Smyrna. Recorded one month before the appearance of the word *rebetiko* on the label, it is simply lumped together with Papagika's other Smyrneïka. Many other examples exist.

The nine Papagika songs marked "rebetiko" on their labels were, with one exception, recorded at Columbia Records' New York studios during 1928–1929, the last two years of her recording career. As mentioned earlier, the first record with the word "rebetiko" on the label—Papagika's "Sti filaki me valane" and "I mavromata" (Columbia E56117-F)—was released in May 1928.[9] While endlessly cited as the first rebetika songs to appear on a commercial record, Papagika may in fact have recorded the first rebetiko for Chicago's Greek Record Company. "Smyrneia" is cited as a "rempetiko" [*sic*] on the label, with "Armenaki-sousta mpalos" on the flip side (GRC 511). The difficulty with bestowing the title of "first rebetiko record" on this release, however, is that no exact chronology exists for records made by the Greek Record Company. Given the catalog number, the song must have been recorded sometime in the early 1920s, but no precise date can be attributed.

Papagika recorded and released the next two rebetika in 1928. "Dourou, Dourou," a rebetiko eventually issued as Columbia 56121-F, was initially recorded in June 1928. "Fotia ke niata," another rebetiko (Columbia 56128-F), was not recorded until sometime in October. Her next two rebetika releases were recorded in late 1928 or early 1929: "Ah! Giatre mou" and "To pismatariko" (Columbia 56166-F). Her last two known rebetika were recorded in 1929: "I flogeri sou i matia" (Columbia 56203-F) in January and "Fonias tha gino" (Columbia 56158-F, CBS 82303 [33], and Columbia 40–82303) in July. While she released no new rebetika records after 1929, record companies continued to reissue her rebetika.

Marika and Koula

A common misconception is that Papagika merely rerecorded Mme. Koula's best songs—but Koula also recorded songs that Papagika had released. For instance, Papagika recorded "Arap sousta armenaki" in July 1919, but Antonopoulou did not record "Armenaki sousta" until the early 1920s (Pan 5027). To give another example, Papagika recorded "Baglamades" twice before Antonopoulou did. Songs recorded by both singers include "Ayia Sofia," "Aidinikos," "Arahova," "Barba Giannis," "Beratiano," "Bournovalio," "To koutsavaki," "Diamanto," "Diamantoula," "Elenaki, "I Garifalia," "Golfo," "I Itia," "Kalamatiano," "Oi Kolokotronaioi," "Kovo mia Klara," "O Loulios," "Ta oula sou," "Sta salona," "Smyrneïkos balos," "Samiotissa," and "Yioussouf Arapis."

The two singers had a similar basic repertoire, and both recorded café aman music from the 1890s; their main difference was that Papagika is said to have had a more refined voice. Papagika's career differs from Antonopoulou's in that she recorded a much wider range of musical genres then popular within the Greek community. This in no way reflects negatively on her obvious command of traditional dimotika and laïka which can be heard on surviving 78-rpm records.

Papagika's commercial recording career only extended two years beyond Antonopoulou's voluntary withdrawal from Greek music in America. These twinned events suggest that the music they were singing was no longer of interest to the record-buying public. In America, an aesthetic shift was taking place, and Greek musicians who did not follow the new developments no longer recorded. Such singer/composers as George Katsaros and Tetos Demetriades, who kept up with stylistic changes, continued to record; vocalists like Mme. Koula and Marika Papagika did not.

Papagika returned only once after July 1929 to record for a major record company. None of the comeback songs were from the Smyrneïka or rebetika genres. On February 15, 1937, she sang "Xyna Megale Constantine" and "Ehasame ton stratigo Kondili" (Orthophonic S-727). Then, on March 30, she recorded "Ton Venizelo hasame" and "I Souliotises" (Orthophonic S-733). Given these songs, I can only conclude that in 1937 Marika Papagika determined that the best way to revive a recording career was to perform dimotika and not Smyrneïka or rebetika.

Conclusion

Some of the finest expressions of Greek music on commercial records were made in New York and Chicago between 1911 and 1929. A solid historical approach to the development of the international music industry will unquestionably throw further light onto the careers of Greek musicians and vocalists such as Marika Papagika, who performed in America during that era.

Notes

1. This profile is based on my earlier essay, "Marika Papagika and the Transformations in Modern Greek Music" (1994). Aside from available publications, I relied heavily upon my review of the seven hundred Greek 78-rpm records at Indiana University's Archives of Traditional Music (see esp. ATL nos. 89-050-F/C and 89-182-C). Both Dan Georgakas and Neni Panourgia commented on an earlier version of the 1994 essay, and I profited greatly by their observations and suggestions. I am also indebted to Dick Spottswood's fine discography of ethnic music recorded in America.

2. I often use song title transliterations as they appear in Dick Spottswood's discography (1990). Because Spottswood is a recognized reference source, I did not want to depart too far from his spellings in fear of losing readers unfamiliar with Turkish or Greek. For an opposing opinion, see Smith 1992. However, in cases when titles would be more readily understood using more current Greek transliteration methods, I have changed them to reflect this.

3. Did Marika Papagika ever record a mixed-language song? Again, as with all other Greek female vocalists who recorded in America between 1911 and 1929, no public archive has all the commercial records she recorded. I sound this now familiar lament because she released her version of the popular "Neo hanoumaki" (Columbia E4495) in August 1919. Unfortunately, I have never heard this version. In Roza Eskenazi's recording, the lyrics are a mix of Greek and Turkish (Orthophonic 317-B). Papagika may have also recorded this song with such a language mixture.

4. Marika recorded at least two versions of this hit song. The first may well have been for the Greek Record Company of Chicago, for whom she released "Armenaki" as a *sousta ballo* sometime in the early 1920s (GRC 511). The better-known version of "Armenaki" was recorded in New York on November 17, 1926, and was a multiple release (Victor Talking Machine 68790, CBS 82290, and Victor 40-82290). It may be that "Armenaki" or an earlier version was recorded before the two 1920s versions. Documentation exists for "Arap sousta Armenaki" (Columbia E4780), which she recorded in July 1919. Again, without having heard it, I cannot tell whether it is the same song.

5. An earlier description of the multiethnic composition of the café aman and the nearly exclusive role of Greeks as their owners appears in an eyewitness report by Macedonian American writer Stoyan Christowe on the introduction of belly dancing in the United States (1930).

6. The meaning of the term *rebetika* has generated considerable discussion (Morris 1981; Gauntlett 1982–1983, 1985). The argument has usually been one-sided, with an emphasis on events in Greece after 1922. This position is similar to one taken by neo-klezmer writers who see the music from Ottoman territories as being strictly the province of Jewish musicians. If we take the history of the international recording industry from 1880 to 1900 as a guide, it's easy to see the multicultural reality of the Ottoman Empire (cf. Gronow 1975, 1981, 1982).

The question of when the term *rebetika* appeared is given a new twist if we consider Kyriaki Antonopoulou's song "Panayia mou Despina," an island *syrtos* (Panhellenion 8023 A). On this record, in between the lyrical lines, we hear Mme. Koula and the musicians call out to each other. The shouts of praise from one musician to another are typical of live Greek performance. Halfway through "Despina" we hear a male voice call out, "yassou Koula." We then hear her say, "tha zisoune, tha zisoune." And almost immediately afterward, we hear what may be the most significant aside in modern Greek music: Koula calls out, "yassou Yiannis, tis rebetis." While we don't know the exact date for this song, it was recorded in New York between 1920 and 1925. Until further evidence proves otherwise, this is the first use of the word *rebetis* on record.

7. To underscore this direct association, we need only note that a film titled *Rembetika: The Blues of Greece* (dir. Phillipe de Montignie, 1982) was based on Gail Holst's book *Road to Rembetika* ([1975] 1989). See Loring Danforth's review of the film (1985).

8. For a treatment of the life and career of Mme. Koula, see my profile in this volume.

9. I am limiting my review of Papagika's rebetika songs to those cited in Spottswood (1990) or at the Archives of Traditional Music at Indiana University (ATM). The 1927–1928 New York–based Atlas catalog has four separate listings of Papagika's songs; only two are listed as rebetika. One song, "E Kairiani," is not among the records at the ATM, nor is it listed in Spottswood. While reference to these national Greek American catalogs is essential to underscore the availability of these records to Greeks and any other interested customers literally anywhere in North America, they are not infallible sources of information. I also do not want to fall into the pointless search for the rebetika ur-record (Smith 1991b; Pappas 1992). With that being said, I must thank Helen Zeese Papanikolas for allowing me to make a research copy of her original 1927–1928 Atlas catalog.

References

Butterworth, Katharine, and Sara Schneider, eds. 1975. *Rebetika: Songs from the Old Greek Under-world*. Athens: Aiora Press.

Chianis, Sotirios (Sam). 1988. "Survival of Greek Folk Music in New York." *New York Folklore* 14, nos. 3–4: 37–48.

Christowe, Stoyan. 1930. "Kyotchek." *Outlook and Independent* 155, no. 2 (May): 48.

Cummings, E. E. 2013. *Complete Poems, 1904–1962*. New York: Liveright.

Danforth, Loring. 1985. Review of *Rembetika: The Blues of Greece. American Anthropologist* 87, no. 4 (December): 991–92.

Frangos, Steve. 1991a. "Large Record Collectors: The Unrecognized Authorities." *Resound* 10, no. 2 (April).

———. 1991b. "The Many Traditions of Greek Music." *Greek American*, March 23–May 25.

———. 1991c. "Greek Music in America: John K. Gianaros, Musician and Composer." *Greek American*, September 14–November 23.

———. 1993a. "Yiorgos Katsaros: Last of the Greek-American Café-Aman Singers." *Greek American*, December 24–June 12.

———. 1993b. "Portraits in Modern Greek Music: Rosa Eskenazi." *Resound* 12, nos. 1–2 (January–April).

———. 1994. "Marika Papagika and the Transformations in Modern Greek Music." *Journal of the Hellenic Diaspora* 20, no. 1: 43–64. At https://www.researchgate.net/publication/265362198_Marika_Papagika_and_the_Transformations_in_Modern_Greek_Music.

Gauntlett, Stathis. 1982–1983. "Rebetiko Tragoudi as a Generic Term." *Byzantine and Modern Greek Studies* 8: 77–102.

———. 1985. *Rebetika Carmina Graeciae Recentioris*. Athens: Denise Harvey.

Gianaros, John K. 1987. Interview with Steve Frangos, Tarpon Springs, Florida, April 13. Archives of Traditional Music, Indiana University (ATL no. 89-049-C/F).

Gronow, Pekka. 1975. "The Record Industry, Multi-National Corporations and National Music Traditions." *The Canada Music Book/Les Cahiers canadiens de musique*, nos. 11–12: 175–81.

———. 1981. "The Record Industry Comes to the Orient." *Ethnomusicology* 25, no. 2: 251–84.

———. 1982. "A Checklist of 78-rpm Foreign Language Records." In *Ethnic Recordings in America: A Neglected Heritage*, 1–49. Washington, DC: American Folklife Center, Library of Congress.

Holst, Gail. (1975) 1989. *Road to Rembetika: Music of a Greek Sub-Culture*. 4th ed. Limni, Euboea, Greece: Denise Harvey.

Morris, Roderick Conway. 1981. "Greek Café Music with a Listing of Recordings." *Recorded Sound* 80 (July): 79–117.

Pappas, Dino J. 1992. "The Rebetiko Genre." *Laografia* 9, no. 4: 11.

Schwartz, Martin. 1993. Liner notes to *Greek Oriental Smyrnaic Rebetic Songs and Dances: The Golden Years, 1927–1937*. Folklyric 9033. Arhoolie Records, El Cerrito, California.

Smith, Ole L. 1991a. "Rebetika in the United States before World War II." In *New Directions in Greek American Studies*, edited by Dan Georgakas and Charles C. Moskos, 143–51. New York: Pella.

———. 1991b. "The Chronology of Rebetiko: A Reconsideration of the Evidence." *Byzantine and Modern Greek Studies* 15: 318–24.

———. 1992. "New Evidence on Greek Music in the U.S.A.: Spottswood's *Ethnic Music on Records*." *Journal of the Hellenic Diaspora* 18, no. 2: 97–109.

Spottswood, Richard K. 1990. *Ethnic Music on Records: A Discography of Ethnic Recordings Produced in the United States, 1893–1942*. 7 vols. Urbana: University of Illinois Press.

Theodotos "Tetos" Demetriades (1897–1971)

—Stavros K. Frangos

Theodotos "Tetos" Demetriades, a Greek immigrant from Constantinople, was a musician, composer, and record producer of incredible importance not simply to the history of modern Greek music but also to the production of ethnic music in the United States. Perhaps not unexpectedly, then, we find that a great deal has been published about this man in Greece and across the Internet. Unfortunately, much of the material found on the Internet is contradictory, while that available from Greek sources often borders on the fantastic. Nevertheless, there are reliable public documents published during Demetriades's lifetime as well as other primary source materials in public archives that can offer a reliable sketch of his professional life.

As far as can be determined, Demetriades's first known commercial recordings in the United States were made for Columbia Records sometime in April 1922: "To proto randevou" (The First Rendezvous) and "Theo na do ton Papa" (I Want to See the Pope) on Columbia E7635 A/B.[1] Moving from one company to another, Demetriades began recording exclusively for the Victor Talking Machine Company in 1927. Although he is credited with more than 250 known individual recordings, it is hard to determine an exact number of his records due to his use of pseudonyms. Given his acute awareness of niche marketing, Demetriades recorded under personas including Takis Nicolaou, Nontas Sgouras, and others when performing particular songs or genres. He was also known for his covers of popular American songs of the day.[2]

Demetriades proved especially successful at choosing top-selling song titles, musicians, dance instrumentals, and genres for the wide array of Greek regional musical traditions. His ability to select best-selling music was not limited to Greek and Balkan music. For decades, he proved a master in selecting and recording popular music for more than twenty different ethnic groups in the United States. While at the Victor Talking Machine Company, Demetriades was appointed executive producer for the foreign language division. The appointment is all the more significant because at that particular moment, Victor was the world's largest manufacturer of commercial music.

Figure 90. Tetos Demetriades. Orthophonic record catalog, 1941. Courtesy of Stavros K. Frangos.

Demetriades is particularly recognized for his recording trip to Greece between March 1930 and late 1931, during which he engaged in a singular field collection project that coincided with a significant historical moment. Following World War I, strict government restrictions in Greece, Turkey, the Balkan nations, the Middle East, and North Africa prohibited the performance and recording of mixed-language songs and/or songs that mentioned drugs. Depending on the country in question, various ethnic groups, such as the Roma or Sephardic Jews, were prohibited from recording altogether. One of the cultural consequences of the political breakup of the Ottoman Empire was that the newly formed countries (inclusive of Turkey) would not allow any "foreign music" to be recorded within their recently drawn borders. The obvious problem with this policy was that the Ottoman Empire had always been a polyglot, multicultural, and religiously diverse entity.

During his stay in Greece, Demetriades recorded music by Greek, Turkish, Albanian, Armenian, Roma, Sephardic Jewish, and other musicians. Consequently, Demetriades left Greece with a wide selection of some two hundred individual recordings of the prohibited genres, instrumentals, and musicians. Ship records report that he returned from Patras to New York City on November 4, 1931. Upon his return, Demetriades arranged with RCA Victor (RCA had purchased the Victor Talking Machine Company two years earlier) to issue the Greek, Turkish, Ladino, and other recordings exclusively on the company's Orthophonic label.

The unintended cultural outcome of Demetriades's strictly commercial endeavor was the preservation of time-honored musical traditions, musicians, and performative styles. It also preserved the mixed-language public performances that remained prohibited and were not commercially recorded for several decades in Greece and the eastern Mediterranean after the breakup of the Ottoman Empire. After Demetriades's field collection trip, he returned to his dual role as music producer and recording artist.

During this same time period, Demetriades produced and shot two Greek-language films in New York, *I grothia de sakati* (1930) and *Afti einai i zoi* (1931). They were the first two Greek-language sound films made anywhere in the world. Both films are lost, and documentation on them is very slim at best (Georgakas n.d.). As advertising attests, after 1934 Demetriades continued to own and operate a fully appointed record store at 305 West Twenty-Third Street in New York. Whether he also co-owned a store in Athens with other members of his family is a question for future research. Given the number of references to Demetriades as a bandleader, he must have performed in such a capacity. Around this same time, he also recorded Greek-language comedy records.

Given that Demetriades crisscrossed so many musical traditions, those who follow the history of American popular music are likely familiar with yet another aspect of his recorded music. On many of his recordings, especially those featuring cover songs, Nathaniel Shilkret (1889–1982) and the Victory Orchestra accompany him. Shilkret was a musical child prodigy who first performed in professional orchestras at the age of thirteen, continuing until his death. A star of radio, Broadway, record company studios, and even Hollywood, Shilkret did a yeoman's labor in professional music circles. If we are to believe the *Discography of American Historical Recordings* website, Shilkret as a conductor recorded over 135,000 individual songs.[3]

There can be no question that Demetriades learned a great deal working with a musician of Shilkret's caliber. Not only did Shilkret serve as conductor for the vast majority of his cover songs, but the duo also issued some unique recordings. "Original Greek Blues" (Victor V-41) credits Demetriades and Shilkret as cocomposers. "Teresina," recorded by a group called the Four Sicilians on December 12, 1931, features Shilkret, R. Palumbo, Nikos Hatziapostolou, Demetriades, and George Mavaveas. Most notably, Shilkret conducted the orchestra for Demetriades's rendition of "Misirlou."

Even a casual consideration of Demetriades's career highlights the many different aspects of the music industry in which he was not only an accomplished authority but a true visionary. A case in point is his September 26, 1942, *Billboard* article titled "The Importance of International Music to Music Machines," in which he discussed his involvement with the top-selling version of "Beer Barrel Polka." Will Glahe, a German-born accordionist and composer, achieved the pinnacle of chart success in 1939 through his rearrangement of "Polka of Modrany." Yet Demetriades is credited with changing the name to "Beer Barrel Polka." Next, he violated all record-marketing rules and insisted that initially the song only be available on jukeboxes. As the popularity of the song grew, so did its potential market. Consequently, when finally released to the general public, it became an overnight best seller.

In 1945, Demetriades left RCA Victor to establish his own independent record company, Standard Phono Company, with its Colonial and Standard labels. In time, this company would feature titles in more than twenty languages including Greek, Turkish, Albanian, Arabic, French, Irish, Lithuanian, Norwegian, Polish, Slovenian, and Swedish. Such was Demetriades's overall success and unique approach to record sales that *Billboard* ran the following review of his methods on April 15, 1950:

> Disk sales and merchandising in the foreign field, [Demetriades] points out, varies [*sic*] considerably from accepted record business traditions. For instance, a good disk often starts slow, with perhaps a sale of 1,000 the first year. The second year it may sell another 2,000—and continue to build for years—finally becoming a solid catalog item. The philosophy of a rapid sale and quick death, so common in the pop field, is completely divorced from the foreign field. ("Lingo Disker" 1950)

In the early days of June 1950, Demetriades moved the Standard Phono offices and record plant from New York to his New Brunswick, New Jersey, farm. On July 1, 1967, Recordwagon purchased the Colonial Standard label. At the time of this sale, Demetriades's company featured 155 titles in twenty-one languages.

On November 26, 1971, Demetriades died at Englewood Hospital in Bergen, New Jersey, from throat cancer. He was buried at the Novo-Diveevo Russian Orthodox Cemetery in Nanuet, New York. As a musical artist, record producer, impresario, filmmaker, and field collector of rare music traditions, Tetos Demetriades led a full career, and his lasting cultural impact mandates extensive study.

Notes

1. All 78-rpm records citations follow Spottswood 1990.

2. In 1990, as a Helen Zeese Papanikolas Charitable Trust award, two of the largest commercial record collectors in the nation, Dino J. Pappas and Andreas Dellis, deposited rerecordings of the vast majority of Demetriades's commercial records inclusive of his many performances under pseudonyms. The rerecordings were accompanied by a full discography, English translation, and commentaries. The materials, along with other documents related to the history of Greek music in North America, can be found in the Helen Z. Papanikolas Oral Histories Collection at the Marriott Library, University of Utah, Salt Lake City. Two survey essays by Dino Pappas and Andreas Dellis announcing this deposit and its contents appeared in the journal *Laografia* (Pappas and Dellis 1991a, 1991b). See also Pappas's later article, "Tetos Demetriades: Blending Greek and American Music" (1995).

3. *Discography of American Historical Recordings*, s.v. "Nathaniel Shilkret (conductor)," at http://victor.library.ucsb.edu/index.php/talent/detail/20274/Shilkret_Nathaniel_conductor, accessed April 23, 2018.

References

Georgakas, Dan. n.d. "The Greek American Image in American Cinema." Center for Byzantine and Modern Greek Studies, Queens College, City University of New York. At http://www.qc.cuny.edu/academics/centers/byzantinegreek/Pages/news.aspx?ItemID=12. Accessed May 4, 2018.

"Lingo Disker Hits Bingo tho Biz Methods Nix Usual Rules." 1950. *Billboard*, April 15, 16.

Pappas, Dino. 1995. "Tetos Demetriades: Blending Greek and American Music." *Laografia*, February 12.

Pappas, Dino, and Andreas Dellis. 1991a. "An Expanded Discography of Tetos Demetriades, part 1, ca. 1920–1928." *Laografia*, May 8, 1–102.

———. 1991b. "An Expanded Discography of Tetos Demetriades, part 2, ca. 1928–1932." *Laografia*, May 8, 103–87.

Spottswood, Richard K. 1990. *Ethnic Music on Records: A Discography of Ethnic Recordings Produced in the United States, 1893–1942*. Vol. 3, *Eastern Europe*. Urbana: University of Illinois Press.

Amalia Baka (1897–1979)[1]

—David Soffa

Three days after her fifteenth birthday, traveling by herself on the largest sailing ship ever to fly the Austrian flag, Mazaltov (Mally) Matsa of Ioannina, Epirus, steamed toward the new land. Two weeks shy of a year later she married Jack Saretta, a fellow from her hometown. They set up housekeeping on Rivington Street in New York's Lower East Side, a short walk from the Kehila Kedosha Janina, the only Romaniote synagogue. She had work as a seamstress, and he made silk flowers for ladies' hats.

The Ioannina she left in 1912 was diverse, fractious, complicated, multinational, and multicultural, in many ways similar to New York. Romaniote Jews had lived in Ioannina for about 1,800 years. Life for Mally had been strictly defined by that tradition. In the Romaniote community, girls were born to a servile position in a male-dominated world, their births not recorded, their early education limited to that which would best serve their future husbands, and their worth reckoned in the end by the number of male children they might bear. A Romaniote girl was kept at home until her father chose a husband for her. When she married, she was sent to live in the home of her new husband.

Mally's marriage was certainly arranged before she left Ioannina. The home she made in the new land was intended to continue the old ways. The enumerator for the 1920 census found Mally and Jack with two daughters, Diamond and Esther Cleoniki, named after their grandmothers in the Romaniote tradition.

The old ways had a good foothold on New York's Lower East Side, although for Mally the pressures and freedoms to be found on foreign shores had shaped changes even before she landed. She had traveled by herself on the SMS *Kaiser Franz Josef I*, an immense, modern ocean liner, only months beyond its own maiden voyage. At Ellis Island, she was detained because she did not have the fifty dollars in cash required of new immigrants; after a phone call, she was sponsored by her Aunt Rachel. Life in New York demanded money, so Mally got a job sewing in a factory. Circumstances had forced her to accept a level of responsibility and independence forbidden to Romaniote girls in Ioannina, and with it came opportunities that were also customarily denied.

Figure 91. Amalia Baka on a Turkish-language poster. Courtesy of Emily Papachristou.

In Ioannina, Mally had lived within Jewish, Greek, and Turkish cultures, and threads of each are woven through her songs. About the only public or semipublic activity that Romaniote women could engage in was the keening of laments at the time of death. Romaniote religious ceremony is conducted in demotic (that is, everyday spoken) Greek instead of Hebrew, and Romaniote singing also borrowed traditional Greek melodies. The memory of these songs and laments was deeply instilled, and they would always be an important part of Mally's repertoire.

Mally sang all her life. Her talent for singing was "discovered" when she sang in the factory where she sewed, or when she sang while hanging up her laundry. Both stories are probably true. She sang in Greek and Turkish, and by the early 1920s had begun singing professionally as Amalia in Greek *cafés aman* and Turkish clubs. Her first recordings were eight Turkish songs for the M. G. Parsekian Record Company, across the Hudson River in Hoboken, New Jersey; then, in Chicago, she recorded six Greek and Turkish songs for the Greek Record Company of George Grachis and Spyros Stamos.

Amalia's independent spirit and emerging career caused trouble at home. In the old country, women who sang in clubs were considered prostitutes—fallen women at best. Jack divorced her, and Cleoniki was sent to live in Greece ("kidnapped," Diamond said).

In 1926, Mally converted to the Greek Orthodox religion in order to marry Gus Bakas, and she continued recording as Amalia Baka from 1927 to 1929. Gus worked in the restaurant business, and Amalia was herself involved in clubs and restaurants, both as owner and as headline entertainer.

Live performances in Turkish clubs, cafés aman, and restaurants were the mainstay of Amalia's singing career. She was always working, according to her daughter, Diamond, who from the beginning was with her at recording sessions and on stage, playing *toumbeleki*, encouraging her with "Yia sou, Mitera!" (Your health, mother!), and sometimes singing duets with her. Cafés aman were lively and numerous in Prohibition-era New York. Entertainment, atmosphere, and booze were a magic combination, and dozens flourished around Eighth and Ninth Avenues at Thirty-Third and Thirty-Fourth Streets, packed with people from all parts of the city. Amalia opened her own club, the Cafe-Aman Pavsili-pon, with, as Diamond remembers, "a few tables and a bottle of bootleg booze . . . little by little they were coming in . . . the priest came in, too."

Amalia did not record in the 1930s but traveled quite a bit, often with singer George Katsaros, and sang at clubs, restaurants, and resorts in an informal circuit that included New York, the Catskills and Finger Lakes areas of New York State, and cities with large Greek populations such as Detroit, Chicago, Gary (Indiana), and Philadelphia.

By 1940, Amalia and Diamond were living in Chicago, and Amalia was involved with a club/restaurant, the Pantheon, near Halsted Street in the heart of "the Delta," Chicago's old Greektown. The city's Greek restaurants were also bars and nightclubs, social watering holes with live entertainment, cadres of regulars, and many stories. Amalia was a spirited and memorable participant who helped lead the charge for about two decades, and she is still remembered with fondness and awe. "If she didn't like you, chairs would fly," recalled John Katsikas, a cimbalom and *santouri* player who accompanied Amalia. Her performance of "Bahaiotiko," a slow dirge, is remembered still, as is her prowess at poker and *barbouti* dice. To a patron who needed money to get married, she gave a gold ring from her own finger; "and she would swear like a man."

In the early 1940s, Amalia was recording again, this time for Ajdin Asllan's Me-Re/Balkan/Gadinis/Kaliphon/Metropolitan family of labels in New York, in which she also had part ownership. Her recording sessions in New York were with luminaries such as clarinetists Gus Gadinis, John Pappas, and John Dalas; kanunists Garbis Bakirgian and Theodore Kappas; and violinists Alexis Zervas and Nick Doneff.

During World War II, Greek music in the United States saw a revival of songs and styles that had originated or were popular in the late 1910s and early 1920s, the time of the influx of ethnic Greek refugees from Turkey into Greece as part of the 1922 League of Nations relocations. Over a third of Amalia's recordings from this period were old songs from her own or from pioneer Greek vocalist Koula Antonopoulou's early recorded repertoire. Mostly laments or songs that expressed resilience in the face of troubles, they offered some solace to expatriates horrified at the fate of Greece and of their families and friends there during World War II.

Amalia retired in the early 1960s. Chicago's redevelopment efforts had removed the heart of Greektown to make way for the University of Illinois at Chicago campus, and Amalia's home and the restaurants and clubs she sang in were destroyed.

Diamond had moved to Florida in 1960 and opened the New Hellas restaurant in Tarpon Springs, close to where the sponge boats docked. Amalia followed in 1974, moving to New Port Richey, just north of Tarpon Springs.

Amalia died in 1979. Her obituary did not mention that she was a singer, that one of the most fluid and evocative of Greek voices had been stilled.

Amalia lived and sang with great passion. Although her repertoire was very traditional, she made her songs her own by comments and ad libs while singing, by changing words, and by using songs to show what was happening in her life. She wrote "Elenitsa Mou" when she was baptized, taking the baptismal name Eleni, and she wrote and sang "Diamontoula Mou" for her daughter Diamond. Unlike her contemporaries Marika Papagika and Koula Antonopoulou, she did not sing much of the world of hash, *manges*, and *rebetes*—most of her recorded songs are about love.

In her long experience singing for live audiences in small clubs, she developed a very personal and intimate style. She understood and exploited the subtleties of the electric microphone from its first years in the recording medium to bring a palpable closeness and immediacy to her recordings.

Remarkable within ordinary circumstances, her story is almost incredible when her own background is considered. Uprooted and cast to sea on a floating skyscraper to make her way in a boisterous and challenging world, she responded with an indomitable, creative, and generous spirit that still lingers in her songs.

Notes

1. This essay was originally published as the liner notes to the CD *Amalia! Old Greek Songs in the New Land, 1923–1950: In Foreign Lands since My Childhood*, Arhoolie Records, El Cerrito, California, 2002.

Ioannis Halikias, aka Jack Gregory (1898–1957)[1]

—Aydin Chaloupka

Introduction

Before 1932, the bouzouki had only been recorded a handful of times commercially, but these recordings had little influence. The instrument still carried negative implications and, with the exception of performances by Thanasis Manetas in 1931, had not been recorded in Greece.

In 1932, Ioannis "Jack" Halikias (1898–1957), a Greek American, recorded "Minore tou teke," the first bouzouki solo and probably the most influential bouzouki recording ever made.[2] It was this record that was responsible for the decision to start openly recording the bouzouki in Greece. It also provided the opportunity for the rise of players like Markos Vamvakaris, Anestis "Artemis" Delias, Giannis Papaioannou, and Vassilis Tsitsanis. It was "Minore" that inspired Papaioannou to pick up the bouzouki:

> Listen then, how I got a bouzouki and became Papaioannou: One day I was sitting in the *taverna*, eating. I was wearing work clothes. I heard a record that Halikias made in America. It was a great hit from America, on one side there was a solo *minore* and on the other a solo *zeimbekiko*. Once I heard it, I went crazy. I got up to read the label and saw Halikias's name. It said "Giannis Halikias." It was the "Minore tou teke." I went crazy! A song like that will never be produced again in nature. No one else made a song like that. That is a symbol, which is untouchable by the whole world.[3]

For all the influence Halikias had in Greece, he spent little time there. He was born in the village of Logastra in Laconia in 1898, but after arriving in the United States in 1909, he never returned to Greece. His family gradually emigrated to New York, where Halikias and his brothers sold items such as candies and fruits from carts. Although Halikias's father, Dimitri, was a well-to-do merchant who contributed $10,000 toward the purchase of the building that became the Saint Nicholas Orthodox Church in New York, Halikias had a different calling. His uncle was a *mangas* who taught Halikias the bouzouki and the code of the *manges*

Figure 92. Ioannis Halikias. Courtesy of Jack Halikias.

when he was a boy. Halikias's father did not approve of his son's interest in the bouzouki, so Halikias would sneak out of the house to learn from his uncle on the streets and rooftops. The conditions were such that, at times, his twin sister Antonia had to hold up an umbrella to protect him from the rain while he practiced.

A Life of Crime

Along with his interest in the bouzouki, Halikias drifted into a life of crime, with which he was associated for most of his life. In his youth, he stole wallets in picture shows, and as an adult he ran the numbers in Harlem. In the words of his friend, musician and luthier Thanasis "Peiraiotis" Athanasiou, known as the *rebetis* of Aegina, Halikias was a "gentlemanly thief" (1997, 75). He was sentenced in 1927 for attempted grand larceny, his crime attributed to "easy money." For this, he served fifteen days in Sing Sing.[4]

After his sentence, Halikias was able to avoid further police trouble, and, with his business partner and *koumbaros*, *outi* player and violinist Tom "Lahanaras" Kokotos, got into bigger ventures.[5] They started with the black market—typically paying truck drivers to drop goods off at a warehouse, then abandon the truck by the docks and report that it had been stolen. Later, probably in the mid-1930s, after setting up black market and racketeering operations, they realized that they could buy grocery stores themselves. This remained a profitable venture, and Athanasiou reported that Halikias and Lahanaras made around $3,000 per day (1997, 72), a huge sum for the time equivalent to around $900,000 monthly today.

One story about Halikias concerning the incredible wealth he and Lahanaras amassed has been mistold many times. The story typically relates that, after Halikias's death, the police found that his closet was full of other people's wallets. This has no basis in truth; Halikias was a pickpocket only for a brief time in his youth. In reality, the penthouse that he owned with Lahanaras was robbed, and the thieves found a closet packed with cash, which they stole. What they did not notice, though, was that there was another closet filled in the same way. Such was the wealth of especially Lahanaras that Athanasiou said he was "like a pasha" (1997, 73).[6]

The racketeering business was incredibly profitable, but in the late 1940s Halikias and Lahanaras left it due to increased FBI attention. Lahanaras relied on his restaurants, hotels, and other businesses, while Halikias relied on his *kafeneia*, which also served as *tekedes* (speakeasies that provided hash) and gambling dens. As a professional gambler who specialized in sleight-of-hand tricks, this occupation served him well. In addition to gambling, Halikias also prepared the *nargiles*, played bouzouki, and cooked at his *tekedes*. During this time, he paid about $1,000 a month to an informer in the New York Police Department who told him when police officers were expected to raid his *tekedes*. On those occasions when the police were able to surprise him, he told the officers that the hashish being consumed was Turkish tobacco. Despite being a wealthy man, Halikias lived his life as a mangas, lending out money freely to his friends and those in need. Like most manges, he was a scofflaw—evidently he would ignore paying his parking tickets, and one anecdote describes how, on one occasion, he collected a pile of them, carried them to the courthouse, paid a large sum of money to clear the debt, and walked out. In another instance, on his 1927 arrest record, in a sarcastic gesture toward the police, he gave his alias as "Jack Hercules."

Music

Halikias was also known as Jack Gregory—"Jack" being a nickname and "Gregory" an Anglicization of his mother's maiden name, Grigoriou.[7] He assumed these names to appeal to American audiences, both Greek and non-Greek, with the dream of making the bouzouki known in the world of American music—especially jazz.

Living in the United States afforded Halikias exposure to many musical styles he may not have heard in Greece. He was a fan of jazz and went with his wife Hope to see Dizzy Gillespie, whom he greatly admired, at the Apollo Theater. Musically, Halikias's primary influences were not from other bouzouki players but rather from violinists, *santouri* players, *klarino* players, jazz musicians, and the like. That is in part why his sound was unlike that of any other bouzouki player.

It is unknown how Halikias became involved with the Columbia Record Company, although soon after recording "Minore tou teke" he became disillusioned with his contract situation. Initially, he had not realized that his contract did not allow him to earn anything from sales in Greece. In anger, he tried to record with other companies, without realizing that an additional clause stipulated that his Columbia contract was in effect for thirty years. Aside from these issues, Columbia also made Halikias tour for a year, something he hated. In 1933, Halikias recorded "Rast tou teke" and "Mourmouriko zeibekiko" without guitar accompaniment, merely so that he could satisfy his four-song contractual minimum. Other than these details, little is known of Halikias's activities during this period.

Postwar Years

After the death of his first wife, Halikias married Hope Xenos around 1950. She was a singer and often accompanied Halikias, whose playing she adored. Her admiration dated back to her childhood, when she and her sister would dance to a copy of "Minore" while their parents were away, as they had forbidden the girls to play it.

As always, Halikias continued playing the bouzouki. According to Halikias's guitarist and friend Alex Panos, in the prewar years Halikias was mainly playing a Grachis bouzouki. At some point he sold the Grachis, and around 1947 he bought a 1940 Zozef bouzouki from Thanasis Athanasiou, who also served as Halikias's bouzouki repairman. This bouzouki became his favorite.

Around 1947 or 1948, in violation of his contract with Columbia, Halikias released five records on Athena Records, his own label.[8] However, the company was not commercially successful, and very few of the acetates that Halikias and his friends made were pressed for release. Of those released, very few were made or sold. Because of this, Halikias abandoned the venture and began to record on a reel-to-reel tape recorder at his home rather than on the record lathe he had been using.

Aside from the abovementioned commercial recordings, during the 1953–1956 period Halikias performed on at least one other record. He appeared on the songs "To megalo psari" and "Den eisai besalou" with Giannis Papaioannou and Rena Dalia on Liberty 156, although he is uncredited.

Not only did Halikias produce relatively few records, but he did not like to play professionally. In 1949, at the urging of Lahanaras, he gave his last public performances at the Kismet Club with Markos Melkon and Andreas Poggis. He was booked for a period of six months, and an account of one of his performances is found in the *Metropolitan Host Weekly Guide to New York* of July 23, 1949. Halikias preferred to play at home and at house parties with his circle of friends, many of whom are, aside from their appearance on home recordings with him, discographically unknown.

Although he eschewed performing, Halikias regularly visited the clubs in New York and played with many local musicians based in the United States such as his friend Kostas Kalivas (best known for his work on the Grecophon label), Markos Melkon, George Katsaros, Andreas Poggis, Athanasios Zervas, Thanasis Athanasiou, Nick Yortamas, and Kostas Doussas (with whom he played in Chicago), as well as visiting musicians like Giannis Papaioannou, Roza Eskenazi, Manolis Hiotis, Rena Dalia, Poly Panou, and Giannis Tatasopoulos. Of these, he was especially close to Athanasiou, Melkon, Papaioannou, and Tatasopoulos (for whom he was a mentor).

There is an interesting anecdote pertaining to the visit of bouzouki virtuoso Manolis Hiotis, widely known for popularizing the four-string bouzouki. When Hiotis visited Halikias's house, the host asked him to play, but Hiotis replied: "I came to hear you play." Commenting on Halikias's virtuosity, Athanasiou said: "Even Hiotis could only play as Hiotis" (1997, 76).

Even though Halikias recorded so few records, with only one ("Minore" and "Mistirio") being released in Greece, his work remains foundational to the history of the bouzouki. His playing remains a standard that countless musicians have tried and failed to emulate. Today, there is a good degree of ignorance about just how much Halikias shaped the history and playing technique of the bouzouki. Were it not for his issues with Columbia and his death in 1957, just five years short of the end of his thirty-year contract, it is certain that he would have exerted a much greater influence on the development of bouzouki playing than he already had. Although currently very few recordings of Halikias are available to the public, his son, Jack Halikias Jr., possesses ten hours of home recordings by his father, a large collection of photographs, two of his father's bouzoukia, and his guitar. Hopefully, in the future, the public might gain access to the full extent of Halikias's virtuosity.

Notes

1. For the information in this chapter, I am indebted especially to Jack Halikias Jr.; Halikias's friend and guitarist, Alex Panos; Giannis Papaioannou's autobiography (1996); Thanasis "Peiratiotis" Athanasiou's autobiography (1997); and private correspondence with Gail Holst-Warhaft and Stavros Kourousis, both of whom knew Athanasiou. I also wish to acknowledge the late George Manikas Kalevas, who, at an advanced age, took time to tell me about his life and the history that he lived; and Christian Baskous and his family for providing me with more information about Halikias's activities in Schenectady, New York.

2. The flip side was "To mistirio," also a popular recording of a tune still performed today, but "Minore" was the main attraction.

3. I accessed this quotation from an online excerpt of Papaioannou's autobiography at the website of the Spoudastirio Neou Ellinismou at http://www.snhell.gr/testimonies/content. asp?id=123&author_id=88. See Papaioannou 1996 for the original publication.

4. For an image of the Sing Sing receiving blotter, see https://www.facebook.com/133891123347 459/photos/pb.133891123347459.-2207520000.1457910269./926023640800866/?type=3&theater.

5. In the *mangika* lexicon, *lahanara* means "wallet." In everyday Greek, it means "cabbage."

6. While Halikias was also affluent, he lived humbly, drove a Buick, and dressed plainly but elegantly.

7. Interestingly, on pressings of "Minore" made in the United States, Halikias's name appears as Jack Grigoriou in Greek and Jack Gregory in English. On Greek pressings, it appears as I. Halikias. On the record "Raste tou teke," which was only released in the United States, his name appears as Jack Halikias (Stavros Kourousis, e-mail message to the author, April 9, 2015).

8. Most of these records have yet to be reissued and will be included in a project that I am working on. Later in the later 1950s, another label called Athena appeared, but it was under different ownership and produced records with a yellow label, whereas Halikias's company used a red label.

References

Athanasiou, Thanasis. 1997. *Auti einai i zoi mou*. Aegina, Greece: Athanasios Athanasiou.
Papaioannou, Giannis. 1996. *Doumpra kai starata: Autobiografia*. Athens: Kaktos.

John K. Gianaros (1904–1998)

—Stavros K. Frangos

John K. Gianaros was a professional musician who performed with some of the most notable Greek, Armenian, Turkish, Albanian, and Sephardic musicians of his generation. Over his long career he was a musician, composer, and record producer whose work crossed not only ethnic boundaries but also public venues.

Gianaros was born in 1904 on a boat en route to Piraeus. His father hailed from the Dodecanese island of Astypalaia, while his mother came from Syros in the Cyclades. After Gianaros came to the United States in 1922, he "fell in love with the accordion."[1] In 1927, he began studying music and not only learned to play it but to read and transcribe it in twelve-note scales. He took particular pride in being a lifelong member of the Associated Musicians of Greater New York, Union Chapter 802.

For almost forty years, Gianaros performed with various bands across the United States. As a working professional, he played at private parties, hotels, church events, weddings, christenings, name-day celebrations, radio programs, clubs, and Catskill Mountain resorts. According to Gianaros, the standard orchestra for all such venues consisted of clarinet, violin, oud, *santouri*, and drum. The drums were sometimes an hourglass-shaped *toumbeleki* and other times a standard American drum set. Musicians were paid $55 to $60 per week plus tips. During this same period, the average New York City musician only made about $35 per week. Regardless of the venue, most instrumentalists worked from 8:00 p.m. until at least 2:00 a.m., and some nights much later. These groups would regularly perform with between two to four belly dancers and two or three singers.

In 1929, Gianaros joined the AM Popular Orchestra, named after the founders Andy and Manuel Andipas. Stamos of the WWRL Greek Hour approached the orchestra to perform live every Friday night from 10:00 to 11:00 p.m. under the sponsorship of the Beech-Nut Gum Company. Gianaros contended that the AM Popular Orchestra was the first Greek orchestra to regularly perform live on New York radio. This exposure proved to be the orchestra's big break: they began to receive bookings every night of the week for weddings, baptisms, dances— anything and everything.

Figure 93. John K. Gianaros, accordion player and songwriter, ca. 1920s. Courtesy of Stavros K. Frangos.

In the 1930s, Gianaros began playing with the Arnold King Orchestra, which performed almost exclusively for the Greek Jewish community of New York. When asked how often he played for this community, Gianaros replied: "That's how I made my living!" Elaborating later, he estimated that during a typical season in New York, he spent at least half his time performing at events hosted by Greek Jews.

"Me and Charlie, we played the Macedonia music," is how Gianaros described his seventeen-year partnership with clarinet master Konstantinos (aka Gus, Costas, or Kostas) Gadinis (ca. 1885–1987). Gadinis was born in the town of Siatista, western Macedonia, from where he immigrated to the United States around 1915. A folk musician in the truest sense, he never learned to read music but always played by ear. Beginning his professional recording career in the early 1920s, Gadinis was another musician who regularly performed for a wide variety of ethnic groups. He was known by a host of names: Charlie Gadinis, Charlie Macedonos, and the "Greek Benny Goodman." By whatever name, he was recognized as the premier ethnic clarinetist of New York City.

Standard record company policy during this era stipulated that any individuals or groups who wished to record should submit written sheet music for the songs to be recorded. After checking to see that the submitted music had not been previously recorded, the company would invite the musicians to come to the studio and record. In this fashion, Gadinis and Gianaros recorded roughly from the late 1930s into the 1950s for Columbia, Victor, Orthophonic, Capitol, and small independent companies such as Liberty, Kalos Diskos, Metropolitan, and Mastertone. For an unspecified period of time, Gianaros and Gadinis produced their own small independent label, NIKI. Royalty checks were based on the individual's role in the recording.

Musicians were paid $45 for each set of four songs recorded—a four-song set being the minimum. Whoever wrote the music received from one to five cents per record sold. Whoever wrote the lyrics received two cents per record. Because Gadinis did not know how to write music, he would split the money with Gianaros, who transcribed whatever Gadinis had composed.

There was a twist to this process when an instrumental dance record was released under a different name by the same company. Gianaros's claims for this practice is documented in Dick Spottswood's *Ethnic Music on Records* (1990). As a case in point, Spottswood notes that some instrumentals recorded by the C. Gadinis Popular Dance Orchestra were reissued by Victor but credited to the "Jewish Orchestra" with the new numbers V-9050, V-9084, 25-5017, and 25-5046. Spottswood adds that "a fourth title, (BS 060728–1R) 'Lechayim' (Good Luck), released on Vi V-9084 and Vi 25-5046-B, is dubbed from another untraced Gadinis recording."[2]

At some point in 1935 or 1936, Gianaros invested in the independent Balkan Record Company of New York. It is unclear exactly when Gianaros was involved with this company. During recorded interviews, Gianaros frequently moved back and forth across time, performers, and especially popular records and business woes (Gianaros 1986–1987; Gianaros 1987). What is clear is that Ajdin Asllan (Aidinidis Aslanidis, 1895–1976), an accomplished musician on the oud, clarinet, and laouto, was the sole owner when Gianaros joined the label. A polyglot, Asllan was an Albanian immigrant who was highly valued for his ability to communicate with a host of ethnic groups. The Balkan Records store and the record company of the same name operated at 42 Rivington Street in New York.

Gianaros first knew Asllan as a musician when performing with him at Albanian American events and on commercial records. As an example, on May 1, 1942, as the Gus Gadinis Trio, Gadinis performs on clarinet with Gianaros on accordion and Asllan on oud on the recordings "Istambul Zeybek" (Orthophonic S-584-A). "Pireotikos ballos" (Orthophonic S-584-B). "Mes t' Agianiou ton platano" (Orthophonic S-585-B). and "Ena dio tria" (Orthophonic S-585-A).

Gianaros asserted that he was responsible for the production of at least sixty records (120 songs) in Arabic, Albanian, Armenian, Greek, Ladino, and Turkish during his involvement with the Balkan Record Company. Given the financial considerations of this independent label, no more than five hundred records were pressed per song. Acutely attuned to the diversity of their respective audiences, Gianaros and Asllan took niche marketing to an entirely new level. The Balkan Record Company printed a general catalog that showcased particular artists and musical traditions under different specialty labels, such as Metropolitan and Kaliphon. Under these subsidiary labels, the Asllan/Gianaros partnership recorded and then target-marketed very distinct groups and genres of music to the public. Gianaros's time at Balkan (and its various guises) is especially notable for the wide array of stellar singers and instrumentalists who recorded for him. A few such notable musicians included Ed Bogosian, Nick Doneff, Victoria Hazan, George Katsaros, Virginia Magkidou, Markos Melkon, and even Roza Eskenazi on Balkan's special Constantinople label. Within roughly three years, Gianaros was forced to leave the Balkan Record Company because of Asllan's failure to set aside funds for taxes.

From 1947 to 1957, Gianaros performed nightly at resort hotels in the Catskill Mountains. The season began anywhere from the end of May to June 15 and would end around Labor Day weekend. All union musicians received the standard $45 per week. As a family man with two small sons, Gianaros would simply not sign a contract with any resort unless he received a rent-free room with two double beds in addition to his regular salary. At the end of each season, he signed the contracts for the next year. Over the decade that Gianaros played in the Catskills, he appeared at the Monte Carlo, the Summer House, and the Grand Hotel—all Greek resorts.

In 1963, Gianaros retired to Tarpon Springs, Florida. While technically retired, Gianaros continued to write and perform. He was a favorite at various celebrations in Tarpon Springs and at other Greek American gatherings in Florida. During this period, Gianaros founded Astro Records, his last record label. At this late stage of his career, he composed "Big Sponge Boy," a song about sponge divers in Tarpon Springs. In 1994, he received a Florida Folk Heritage award. John K. Gianaros passed away in 1998, at age ninety-four, and is buried next to his wife, Helen, in Cycadia Cemetery in Tarpon Springs.

Notes

1. Unless otherwise noted, the information and quotations attributed to John Gianaros are from my recorded interviews with him. Listening copies of my 1986 and 1987 John K. Gianaros interviews are held at the Archives of Traditional Music, Indiana University, Bloomington (ATM 89-049-C/F). The 1987 tapes are available online through Florida Memory, State Library and Archives of Florida, series S1708, tapes 19–20, at https://www.floridamemory.com/items/show/236619.

2. Some of these labels can be viewed online through Florida Atlantic University's Judaica Sound Archives; see Jewish Orchestra 1941(?).

References

Gianaros, John K. 1986–1987. Interview with Steve Frangos, Florida Folklife Program/Folk Arts Survey, Tarpon Springs, Florida, November 17, 1986; April 13, 1987. Available online at the Archives of Traditional Music, Indiana University, Bloomington (89–049-F/C ATL). At http://www.iucat.iu.edu/catalog/5738433. Accessed July 2, 2016.

———. 1987. Interview with Steve Frangos, Florida Folklife Program/Folk Arts Survey, Tarpon Springs, Florida, April 13. Available online at Florida Memory, State Library and Archives of Florida, series S1708, tapes 19–20. At https://www.floridamemory.com/items/show/236619. Accessed June 30, 2016.

Jewish Orchestra. 1941? Lechayim. RCA Victor-5046-B. Florida Atlantic University Libraries, Recorded Sound Archives. At https://rsa.fau.edu/track/4802. Accessed May 3, 2018.

Spottswood, Richard K. 1990. *Ethnic Music on Records: A Discography of Ethnic Recordings Produced in the United States, 1893–1942*. 7 vols. Urbana: University of Illinois Press.

Pericles Halkias (1909–2005)

—Jim Stoynoff

As one of the few remaining Greek folk musicians of his generation, Pericles Halkias was the subject of several interviews and studies in his later years. Living in Astoria, New York, since 1962, thousands of miles from his native region of Epirus in northwestern Greece, he came to be viewed by researchers as a "laographic" gem.

Although Halkias's recordings and personal biography have been well documented, it is only recently that his deep knowledge of Epirot musical tradition has been explored. This is particularly relevant given that he witnessed its most dynamic phase of evolution, a period marked by more changes than in all the decades preceding his time.

I had the privilege of studying with Halkias in the early 1980s, a learning process grounded in oral tradition and an absence of musical notation. There are unique advantages to this model of learning. In my case, it provided insights into the historical context of the repertoire and mentoring to achieve nuanced embellishment and coloration of musical phrases, along with many anecdotes, mostly didactic and some humorous, too! Much of what I share in this chapter is based on Halkias's recounting of his musical life and the conditions that affected the music of his native Epirus.

Epirot Clarinet Music

Musical practice in Epirus at the turn of the twentieth century was shaped by the social environment during and after Ottoman rule. Significantly, the adaptation of the Western clarinet to Greek folk music during the Ottoman years facilitated greater technical artistry as well as the formation of regional musical groups, setting the course of Epirot music well into the 1960s, a point in time that Halkias feels marked the beginning of the end for many cherished musical traditions. To understand the significance of Halkias's recollections and his views on these trends, they are presented here in the context of relevant historical background, beginning with his instrument, the clarinet.

Figure 94. Halkias Family Orchestra, ca. 1982. L-R, standing, Achilleas Halkias, Petros Halkias; seated, Pericles Halkias, John Roussos, Lazaros Harisiades. Photo by Jack Mitchell. Courtesy of the Center for Traditional Music and Dance.

The clarinet is believed to have first appeared in northwestern Greece around 1830–1835 and perhaps a bit earlier in neighboring northern Epirus (today, southern Albania). Although its potential use in folk music was quickly recognized, the cost and relative scarcity of the instrument made it difficult for most musicians to acquire, a factor that inhibited its widespread use in Epirot music until the beginning of the twentieth century. Halkias tells of how his grandfather fashioned a homemade clarinet, as did many players who could not afford to purchase one in those years.

Usually made from either *tsimtsidi*[1] or *abanoz*,[2] these instruments were referred to as *tzourades* (from *jura* in Turkish) because of their small size. Since hardware to hold keys in place was not readily available, protrusions of the wood stock would be carved to serve as posts and forged keys mounted on metal "rods" to allow motion. Spring action for the keys was provided by using thin strips of semithick copper, bent in order to provide leverage. Mouthpieces were carved from similar woods, and reeds from bamboo cane.

Halkias notes that no two such instruments were alike, and because standard tuning had not yet been established, it was impossible for two clarinets to play together with the same accompanying *laouto* (lute) or violin. In fact, tuning these clarinets to string instruments was often impossible due to their inconsistent intonation—the primary factor that deferred the formation of musical ensembles featuring the clarinet until a time when factory-made instruments from France and Belgium became accessible.

Without exception, these were early Albert system clarinets having as few as five keys, and therefore they were more difficult to play than the modern seventeen-key Boehm system instruments. Since forked fingerings available on the Albert system were similar to those found on the *flogera* (shepherds' flute), players found transition to the clarinet a natural extension of fingering techniques that they had already developed. In fact, the Albert system is still preferred by folk clarinetists throughout Greece and Turkey.

Because of the clarinet's greater tonal range and technical capabilities compared to the flogera, more complex embellishments of traditional melodies became the norm, exemplified by such masters as Selim, Aslanis, Birbilis, Kitsos Harisiades, Nikola Batzis, Nikola Ninou, Demos, and Dinos o Koulos, all predecessors of Halkias. This is especially evident in the Zagori village dance pieces by Nikola Ninou and the highly ornamented pastoral "Skaros" as recorded by Harisiades, recognized as the greatest technician of his time.

Halkias notes that over the years, clarinets in various pitches were popular. Traditionally, clarinets in the key of C became popular during the 1920s and remained so until the late 1960s, when the trend moved toward a lower, darker tone. This era saw a widespread use of lower-pitched clarinets in B-flat, A, and G, which incidentally is still preferred by Roma in Macedonia and Turkey. Currently, the B-flat clarinet is the most prolific in vocal accompaniment as well as in solo performances. A visit to Halkias's workshop revealed a treasure trove of vintage clarinets that he had acquired over the years. He had also built several instruments in novel pitches, such as soprano G.

Halkias related how, in the years preceding the use of sound systems (around the 1960s), clarinetists achieved a primitive form of amplification by carefully lining the inner chamber of the mouthpiece with candle wax. This served to dramatically increase the clarinet's volume, important for outdoor performances, which were very common in villages. Interestingly, a similar technique has been used by New Orleans clarinetists, who would apply a layer of chewing gum for the same purpose.

Halkias's early recordings were performed with a C clarinet, typical of that era. As he points out, C clarinets were used by such early players as Selim and Birbilis. With their clear, brilliant tone and strong projection, they were ideally suited to outdoor use. Also, violinists and *santouri* (hammered dulcimer) players preferred tuning to a C clarinet to avoid transposing.

Parallel to the centuries-old custom in Epirus of unaccompanied polyphonic singing was the emerging prominence of the clarinet and ultimately the formation of the typical *ziyia, kompania,* or *takimi*[3] consisting of clarinet, violin, laouto, and *defi* (tambourine), with the santouri added around 1900.

According to Halkias, the Batzis family of Tsarapliana was the first to form such a kompania in his region of Pogoni. They composed countless ballads and dance tunes based in large part on the polyphonic singing of elders. In fact, the family's identification with local musical tradition was so great that patrons would request a *batzitiko*, which had become synonymous with *pogonisio* (songs indigenous to Pogoni), a practice still common today among older patrons.

Prior to the liberation of Epirus from the Turks in 1912, travel to northern Epirus was not restricted, and the Halkias and Batzis families as well as others often traveled into Albania to perform for Turkish beys for celebrations known as *ramazania* and *sinetia*.[4] They also performed for the beys in the Delvinaki and Filiates areas of southern Epirus.

According to Halkias, all the players of this era were influenced by Birbilis, Selim, and the latter's son Aslanis, who came from Leskovik and Argyrokastro (Kastro; today, Gjirokastër) in southern Albania. They were noted for their solo clarinet *mirologia* (laments) as well as Arvanitic dance pieces, all of which predate recording. Halkias related how as a young man he once walked two days from his village in Pogoni to Kastro to hear Selim play. He sat close by during the two-day festival and tried to memorize as many musical phrases and techniques as possible. He was especially moved by one *miroloi*, and as he returned home he would sing the melody repeatedly so as to not forget it. Many years later in New York (ca. 1963), he recorded this miroloi and titled it "Vorioepirotiko miroloi, Selimos" (North Epirus Lament, Selimos). It is probably the only approximation of Selim's style we are likely to ever hear, since he himself was never recorded.

Out of Epirus

In the late 1920s, Greece's emerging recording industry provided unprecedented opportunities for Epirot clarinetists, yet many of them refused to be recorded, fearing that they would no longer be in demand for live performances. Because of this reluctance, there were numerous players such as Vasili Bitas of Metsovo and Tsoutas of Konitsa whose fame never reached beyond their hometowns and surrounding areas.

The Pogoni district alone has approximately 160 villages, which until the 1960s represented a vast number of regional musical styles and repertoires known only to local musicians. Halkias and noted contemporaries such as Filipas Roundas and Tassos Halkias among others became the beneficiaries of this rich oral tradition, which fortunately is preserved in their extensive discographies. Halkias began recording in 1947 for Columbia and His Master's Voice, and continued to record into his late seventies.

During the 1930s, Halkias moved to Athens, where he played at the prestigious Elatos and Zhangos *tavernas*. Although he worked as a blacksmith during World War II—sometimes playing for a military audience—he resumed performing in Athens during the 1940s and 1950s. During the summers he returned to Epirus to play for community and family celebrations.

After settling in America, Halkias was the most sought-after Epirot clarinetist in New York City. At one time or another, he played at most of the nightclubs on Eighth Avenue and performed for many years at Epirot organization events, weddings, baptisms, patron saint's day celebrations, and on several occasions at the funerals of compatriots—where he played soul-wrenching laments that he had learned as a young man.

In the early 1980s, he formed the Halkias Family Orchestra, which played traditional music for Epirot events. The group was also part of the 1982 Greek Music Tour that brought together several legendary Greek musicians, including the laouto player Lazaros Harisiades, with whom he had performed at countless events in Epirus in the early years. His most significant recognition outside the Greek community came in 1985 when he was awarded a National Endowment for the Arts Fellowship.

Epirot Music Today

It is ironic that while Halkias was being so honored in the United States for preserving, teaching, and performing in the finest Epirot tradition, dramatic changes adversely affecting folk music were gaining momentum in Greece. Increasing commercial demands by the recording industry for innovative interpretations of traditional pieces prompted younger folk artists to seek out new elements that could be incorporated into their performances. This resulted in the incorporation of Turkish, Arabic, Slavic, and Indian elements at the expense of tradition. Similarly, migration to urban areas by the younger generation exposed them to many nontraditional genres, alienating them from the traditional music of Epirus much as Halkias had lamented in the late 1960s.

The good news is that since 2010 there has been a strong resurgence of interest in traditional folk music on the part of younger audiences and players in Greece. This is evident in the number of performing groups emerging from Epirus and other regions of Greece. Halkias's son Petros is now considered the "patriarch" of Epirot clarinet, and other senior legends such as Grigoris Kapsalis and Stavros Kapsalis also perform regularly on national TV and at concerts and festivals. Among the younger generation of Epirot clarinetists is the incomparable Nikos Phillipides, who in turn mentors students. This trend also serves to energize the many folk dance groups that have existed in the United States for decades and accounts for the increasing number of new members of all ages and ethnic backgrounds.

To what extent the trend will be sustainable remains to be seen, but it is encouraging that a resurgence has occurred and remains strong. One example is the weekly TV program *Alati tis gis* (Salt of the Earth), which features an hour of live folk dance music with audience participation including a significant number of young people. In speaking with folk music performers and students in Greece today, the consensus is that while the current enthusiasm may ebb in time, traditional music will not fade into oblivion. I was reminded by those with whom I spoke of the age-old phrase, "Ta dimotika einai athanata": folk music is eternal!

Notes

1. *Tsimtsidi* is from the Turkish *shimsir* (boxwood).

2. *Abanoz* is the Turkish word for ebony.

3. A musical ensemble was referred to as a *ziyia* or *kompania* (company) and in some locales *takimi*, from the Turkish word *takim* (group or band).

4. *Ramazania*, from the Turkish *ramazan*, is the word used by Greeks for any type of Moslem festival. *Sinetia* is the plural of the Turkish word *sünnet* (circumcision celebration).

Steve Zembillas (1923–2002) and the Grecophon Record Company

—Stavros K. Frangos

From 1946 through 1954, the Grecophon Record Company of Gary, Indiana, issued recordings of traditional Greek island music that had its American roots in Tarpon Springs, Florida. Founded by Skevofylax (Steve) Zembillas from Kalymnos, Greece, this small, independent label showcased a host of rarely recorded music.

In the 1930s, most Greeks living in Tarpon Springs were the families of sponge fishermen who came principally from Kalymnos, Symi, Halki, and other Dodecanese or Saronic islands to work the rich sponge beds of the Gulf of Mexico. In 1937, when Zembillas arrived in Tarpon Springs, nearly one thousand men in hundreds of Greek-style boats were plying the rich sponge beds. "I was crazy for that music," Zembillas said, describing his response to the Greek musicians he found playing in the coffee shops along the Tarpon Springs sponge docks.[1]

Ten years later a red tide (a colloquial term referring to a variety of naturally occurring harmful algal blooms that may have a reddish color) began to sweep through the Gulf waters, killing the fish and sponges and so destroying the Greeks' livelihood. Throughout the late 1940s, hundreds of Kalymnians from Florida, in a chain migration, moved to the northwestern corner of Indiana. It is estimated that nearly 90 percent of the Kalymnians now living in Indiana arrived there as a result of the sponge industry's collapse.

The Grecophon Record Company's history reflects this wider background of events. In 1946, Zembillas's love for Greek music led him to buy a Wilcox-Gay portable phonograph, and he recorded local Tarpon Springs Greek musicians at his studio in the family gift shop at 530 Athens Street (Galoozis 2016; Ioannidis 2016). Over the next six months, Zembillas produced private recordings requested by local Greeks who placed their orders at his small storefront record shop. The musicians were paid a dollar per record. Producing the records, one at a time, Zembillas sold them for three dollars each.

As the list of requests grew, Zembillas realized that there was a vacuum for island music, since the big Greek record companies would not take the time to

395

Figure 95. Steve Zembillas. Courtesy of Harry Zembillas.

record and release island music commercially. Zembillas then recorded what he always contended was the best music he ever produced on his Wilcox-Gay machine. With Elias (Louis) Peronis, Tarpon Springs' finest violinist, a local *laouto* (lute) player, and himself on vocals, Zembillas recorded such traditional island songs as "Panayoti" and "Perivolla." Next, he traveled to New York City with eight original celluloid discs and the aim of convincing Tetos Demetriades, the largest manufacturer of Greek records in the nation, to release the songs on his Standard Colonial Phonograph label. Demetriades agreed and filled out the contracts, allowing five cents per record for each performer's royalties. The Tarpon Springs musicians, who had expected to receive thousands of dollars for these records, never signed the contracts, and the records were never released.

Zembillas always regretted his failure to release this specific group of recordings. Yet they served as the catalyst for the professional formation of Grecophon Records in 1947. At a Chicago recording studio near Ontario and Ohio Streets, Zembillas produced the initial eighteen records that would be the founding legacy of Grecophon Records. Expenses were considerable: $100 an hour for the studio, with an average of three hours needed for the production of four records. Realizing the small scale of the business, the musicians charged only $100 per record, $50 below union scale. The manufacturing cost averaged fifteen cents per record. The records wholesaled at forty cents, and retailed at between seventy-five cents and a dollar. For a press run of just under two thousand records, Zembillas's total production cost for a single ten-inch 78-rpm record averaged a little above $2,000.

Distribution for Grecophon was divided between record stores and mail orders. Standard orders on records from the distributors were in units of twenty-five. Despite the fact that Grecophon produced nearly exclusively Greek island music, these records proved quite popular, and so Greek record stores in places such as Detroit, Boston, Chicago, New York, San Francisco, and Youngstown, Ohio, regularly sought out the company's latest releases. With the national circulation of the New York–based Greek newspapers *Atlantis* and the *National Herald*, Grecophon advertisements brought in a brisk mail-order trade.

Zembillas states emphatically that, with a single popular record, there was "no problem selling ten thousand records in those days, no problem." His problem was the unpopular records. "I used to make money on one, then lose it on the next and have to start all over again." One best seller was the dance song "Afto to vradi to skotino" (This Dark Evening, GR 11A), with George Katsaros doing vocals and guitar accompanied by Kostas Kalivas on bouzouki. Three thousand copies of this record were sold in the Boston area alone.

Still, predicting musical hits was a tricky business. Zembillas had judged that "Kalymnos essos," a traditional Kalymnian dance tune (GR 10A), would be an extremely popular dance selection and only put "Kalymnaki" (The Kalymnian Youth) on the record's B-side as a novelty. However, more than five hundred copies of this record sold in Tarpon Springs alone because "Kalymnaki" proved so popular.

Using a popular Greek melody of the day, Zembillas himself wrote the lyrics of "Kalymnaki" as a love song with the Tarpon Springs Greeks in mind. The opening lines are:

Ena kaiki apo to Tarpon
Yia ta sfoungaria anahorei,
Ki ena naftaki pou einai mesa
Anastenazi kai te steria thorei.

A sailboat from Tarpon
Sets off for sponge fishing,
And a young sailor on board
Sighs and looks back at the shore.

Released just a few years after the 1947 red tide, this romantic song of lost love was immediately associated with the loss of the Kalymnians' way of life along the Florida bayous.

On April 25, 1955, Zembillas married Stamatia Georgiades (September 20, 1928–April 7, 2015) at Saint Nicholas Greek Orthodox Cathedral in Tarpon Springs. Also of Greek descent, she was born and raised in Tarpon Springs (*Times of Northwest Indiana* 2002). The couple was destined to have six children together. Realizing he now had a family to support and given the overall uncertainty of the record business, Zembillas decided in early 1955 to close down Grecophon Records. For the next twenty-seven years, he owned and operated Gold Coast Finer Foods in Gary. On November 24, 2002, Zembillas passed away in Crown Point, Indiana, surrounded by his loved ones (*National Herald* 2015).

In my conversations with Zembillas, he always returned to those lost recordings he took to Tetos Demetriades in the summer of 1946. They were his lost dreams, the music he believed Grecophon Records could have preserved. "At least the Kalymnians would have had something to be proud of today when it comes to their music." Despite his disappointment, the musical heritage of the Kalymnians (and several other Greek island musical traditions) is not entirely lost. Grecophon Records is that heritage. The most easily recognized trademark for those in search of Greek island music remains an island with a bird high above in flight, the label of Grecophon Records.

Notes

1. In 1985, I deposited interviews with Steve Zembillas and rerecordings of original Grecophon 78-rpm records at the Archives of Traditional Music, Indiana University, under accession number 85-268-F/C. See also Frangos 1985.

References

Frangos, Steve. 1985. "Songs of an Indiana Island: The Grecophon Record Company of Gary, Indiana." *Resound* 4, no. 3 (July).

Galoozis, Sevasti Smolios. 2016. Interview with Tina Bucuvalas, Tarpon Springs, Florida, June 8.

Ioannidis, Anna Smolios Kouskoutis. 2016. Interview with Tina Bucuvalas, Tarpon Springs, Florida, December 7.

National Herald. 2015. "Stamatia Georgiades Zembillas, Met. Savas' Mother, Is Mourned by Community." *National Herald* (New York), April 9. At http://www.thenationalherald.com/81299/. Accessed May 30, 2016.

Times of Northwest Indiana. 2002. "Nov. 26 Obituaries (N-Z)." *Times of Northwest Indiana* (Crown Point, IN), November 26. At http://www.nwitimes.com/news/local/obituaries/nov-obituaries -n-z/article_c73170bc-ed23-5c91-a402-8e7dc20d33ab.html. Accessed May 30, 2016.

Nicholas "Nicos" Tseperis (1923–2010) and Nina Records[1]

—Meletios Pouliopoulos

Musician, entertainer, and business owner Nicholas "Nicos" Tseperis was born in Athens. He first came to the United States in 1956, aboard the ill-fated luxury ocean liner *Andrea Doria*. By the time he arrived, he had already established himself as a highly celebrated singer with performances in Istanbul and Athens, and a six-month run at the Cannes Casino in Deauville, France. As a recording artist and performer, he was regarded as one of the great troubadours of Greek music.

In the United States, Tseperis began performing at the Athenian Corner in Fort Lee, New Jersey, a popular nightclub that featured live music seven nights a week. He sang not only in Greek but in five other languages. At the famous Molfetas club in Hackensack, New Jersey, Tseperis appeared several times in the late 1950s with Manolis Hiotis and Mary Linda. Other notable performances in New York include the Hotel Statler on November 23, 1956, with George Stratis, and in 1957 with Nikos and Katina Pourpourakis at the Zappion Pavilion in Astoria. On September 22, 1957, he returned to the Manhattan Center at Thirty-Fourth Street and Eighth Avenue for a "Farewell Performance" for Rena Dalia. Performers included Dalia, Giannis Tatasopoulos, Thodoros Kavourakis, Manolis Hiotis and Mary Linda, Kostas Kaplanis, Demetris Frantzeskakis, George Stratis, Mitsakis Orfanidis, Petros Nikolaou, and Kostas Sevastakis.

In the 1950s through the end of the 1960s, Tseperis performed in many places outside New York and New Jersey, notably in 1957 with violinist Fred Elias and Hiotis at the Club Zara in Boston. He played in Cleveland at the Doric Restaurant in December 1963, and in Canton, Ohio, at the Onesto Hotel in March 1964 as part of the Greek American Progressive Association's Greek Independence Day celebration. From 1961 to 1962, Tseperis performed regularly in Baltimore with Giannis Tatasopoulos at the Istanbul. In December 1969, he returned to Baltimore to play for the Laconian Association's local chapter ("Lycourcos") along with George Kent and his Greek American Orchestra, and the "Aidoni" of Greek song, Miss Zorba. He was especially proud of his performances at the

Figure 96. Nicos Tseperis. Courtesy of Virginia Tseperis.

Sydney Opera House and at Carnegie Hall, where he performed in December 1967 with esteemed Greek musician Harry Lemonopoulos. He also enjoyed touring Europe, Japan, and Australia with the Trio Bel Canto in the 1970s. In addition to live musical performances, he appeared on the Mike Douglas and Dick Cavett television shows.

Tseperis was known for his beautiful singing voice and range. Shortly after his arrival in America, he began a career at Nina Records, then owned by George Valavanis (1920–2012) and located at 312 West Fifty-First Street in New York. His first Nina LP, *Festival in Greece* (Nina Records L-61), was released in 1959 and favorably reviewed by *Billboard* on September 28, 1959. It included a variety of traditional, modern, and classic songs such as the *kantada* "Stis nychtas ti Sigalia," written by Hermes Poggis in 1918. The songs were beautifully arranged and orchestrated by Michel Assael, who also collaborated with Tseperis for his second LP, *The Songs of Nicos Tseperis* (Nina Records L-71, 1960). These first two albums were unique in the early Nina catalog (which usually carried contemporary *laika* and traditional folk music), and were colorfully nostalgic in sound, bringing listeners back to the songs and traditions of yesteryear.

Tseperis was also a successful businessman and record producer. He became the manager of Nina Records years before he purchased the company from Valavanis. Nina was first incorporated in New York in December 1957 but was actually in operation as early as 1955. Valavanis brought the top artists from Greece to record, including such well-known composers and performing artists as Giannis Papaioannou, Giannis Tatasopoulos, and Manolis Hiotis. The records were of such a high quality, employing the best recording techniques and physical materials, that they have stood the test of time.

Shortly after Tseperis purchased Nina Records in March 1971, he formed a partnership with Polydisc Records of Greece to distribute their recordings in the United States. For the nearly twelve years that Tseperis owned Nina, he expanded the catalog to include Greek satire, contemporary folk, *rebetika*, and even children's records. Some examples of rebetika LPs released in the 1970s on the Nina label include two records by singer Apostolos Nikolaidis, *Otan kapnizei o Loulas* (Nina 402) and *Ston adi adamosoume* (Nina N-2650), as well as *Proi proi me ti Drousoula* by Nikos Papadatos and Litsa Zanet (Nina N-415) and *Chronia ston Peiraia* by Spyros Zagoraios (Nina N-642).

Tseperis had the gift of recognizing talent in others, and he produced records for many artists under the Nina label, across various genres of music. He brought the folk singer Grigoris Maroulis to record *Giorti tou horou* (Nina LS-321) with Giannis Tatasopoulos's orchestra, including Kostas Sevastakis on clarinet and the up-and-coming artist George Soffos on bouzouki.

During the 1970s while operating Nina Records, Tseperis continued performing, recording, and entertaining. He had a brilliant sense of humor and was often called upon to serve as master of ceremonies for various events. With the release of his first satire album in 1972, *Nicos Tseperis Satires* (Nina 469), he conveyed his comic genius with words and music—explaining in the cover notes that he had wanted to do satire for many years. Due to the album's enormous success, it was the first in a series released by Nina. *Nicos Tseperis Satires No. 2* (Nina 621) was the second in the series. In the album credits, he thanks songwriters Nikos Routsos, Kostas Kofiniotis, and Manolis Spyroglos and musical directors Gerasimos Giannatos and Demetris Frantzeskakis. On *Nikos Tseperis Satyrikes Parlates* (Nina N-647), he credits the writer as humorist Christos Pyrpasos. In the cover notes to his fourth satire record, *Nikos Tseperis: Satires no. 4* (*Kosmiki Kinisis*) (Nina N-2651), he states: "Tested in front of an audience of four thousand listeners in Sydney, Australia, and in all major cities there."

Tseperis produced two children's LPs in the 1970s. The first, *Greek Tales in Two Languages* (Nina N-1650), featured the fairy tales "The Magic Cones" and "Adventures of Little John." The tales were told in Greek and English by professional actors and set to music. The second children's record, *Greek Tales in Two Languages* (Nina N-1651), related "The Servant and the Master" and "The Proud

Hare." The children's recordings were also available in 8-track and cassette tapes, which were packaged with a booklet. Sometime in the mid-1970s, Nina ceased production.

In the 1970s, while recording and producing his four satire records and running Nina Records, Tseperis was a frequent performer at various Greek resort hotels in New York State's Catskill Mountains. He performed at the Starlite Motel in Big Indian, the Sunset Springs Hotel in Hensenville, the New Olympia Hotel in Wyndham, the Rivera Hotel in Summitville, and the Monte Carlo Hotel in Monroe.

From 1978 to 1981, Tseperis operated a specialty shop, Nico's Gift and Music Center, at 31-12 Twenty-Third Avenue, Astoria. In 1978 and 1979, Tseperis broadcast a weekly Greek radio program in New York on WHBI, 105.9 FM, on Sunday afternoons from 3:30 to 4:00 p.m. His program contained a wide variety of music, local advertisements, and community announcements and featured short, original comedy pieces.

It is difficult to imagine such a talented musician, consummate performer, and successful businessman as Nicos Tseperis. Listening to his music recordings—to his beautiful voice and masterful guitar—or to the brilliance of his satire, you will get a glimpse of this great and much-loved artist.

Notes

1. Special thanks to the daughters of Nicos Tseperis, Virginia Tseperis and Danielle Tseperis Kalas, for invaluable input for this study through personal communications from 2012 through 2016, and in-person interviews at their homes in New Jersey on February 14 and 15, 2016.

Sotirios (Sam) Chianis (b. 1926)

—Tina Bucuvalas

Ethnomusicologist and musician Sotirios (Sam) Chianis is one of the foremost authorities on Greek folk music as well as an excellent performer on the *santouri*, the Greek version of the cimbalom.[1] Chianis's father, Ioannis, was born in 1890 in the village of Valtetsi, in the Arcadia region of the Peloponnese, and came to America during the first decade of the twentieth century. His mother, Kalliopi Dimas, was born in Thessaloniki in 1900 and raised thirty kilometers north of that city in the village of Assiros. When her father passed away, her uncle brought Kalliopi and her mother to Santa Barbara, California, in 1923. Ioannis and Kalliopi met and were married there in 1923. Chianis's brother Andrew was born in 1925, Sotirios was born in 1926, Constantina in 1928, and the youngest sister, Athena, in 1935. Kalliopi passed away soon after giving birth to Athena, so the young family moved with their maternal grandmother to Long Beach, where Ioannis's brother lived.

The Santa Barbara Greek community was large and close—Chianis remembers that it seemed like one huge family. His father taught Greek school three times weekly, excelled at singing Greek folk songs, and urged his children to learn Greek songs and dances. Chianis remembers loving the sound of the santouri in the trio that traveled from Los Angeles to Santa Barbara to perform for weddings and picnics. During this period, the santouri was an important instrument in Greek folk ensembles, including those that performed *rebetika*.

When the family moved to Long Beach in 1935, Ioannis encouraged Andrew and Sotirios to learn and perform Greek folk music. Chianis heard the santouri played quite often at community events and was fascinated by the instrument. Although they were extremely poor, his father bought him a small santouri when he was in the fifth or sixth grade, and Andrew acquired a clarinet. Ioannis taught them many dance tunes, which they eventually performed at local events. He also enjoyed singing with them, but not at formal performances. Both brothers became excellent musicians. Chianis also took clarinet lessons during junior high school, and his brother learned to play the bouzouki.

Figure 97. Spyros Stamos and Sam Chianis at the Balalaika, San Francisco, 1949. Courtesy of Sotirios (Sam) Chianis.

Their intensely Greek life was interrupted while the Chianis boys served overseas during World War II. After graduating from high school in June 1944, Chianis joined the army and was sent to the Philippines. When he was discharged and returned home in 1947, he found that most of the local professional musicians had retired. Thus, the Chianis brothers formed a trio consisting of clarinet (Andrew), santouri (Sam), and *kanun* and vocals (Tom Kappas); a couple of years later, they were joined by accordionist John Manolis. The group played almost every weekend for Greek communities and societies from Santa Barbara to San Diego during the late 1940s and 1950s. Their repertoire consisted primarily of folk music that had been brought to America by Greek immigrants during the first decade of the twentieth century. Dance scholar Anthony Shay recalls that in California, Greek picnics were usually community dance events: "The orchestra that I most often encountered in these events consisted of various ensembles of a clarinet, bouzouki, and santouri, a large cimbalom-like instrument. For several decades in the 1950s and 1960s, the orchestra led by Sam Chianis and his brother, played a large repertoire of scores of melodies for these dances for many years in Southern California" (Shay 2006, 96).

Chianis had never taken formal lessons on the santouri, but he wanted to do so. The santouri player in the trio Chianis had listened to before the war had returned to Greece, but he heard that the eminent cimbalom player Spyros Stamos had moved from Chicago to San Francisco. Chianis had bought a cimbalom from a Hungarian player, but he didn't have a teacher. He decided to travel the 450 miles from Long Beach to San Francisco to ask Stamos to teach him. Chianis took weekly lessons from Stamos for about a year and a half beginning in 1948. Unfortunately, that entailed taking the overnight Greyhound at 7:30 p.m. Saturday and arriving in San Francisco at 8:00 a.m. Sunday. After breakfast, he walked to the Balalaika, where Stamos performed every evening, and practiced on his cimbalom until early afternoon. Stamos then gave him a two-hour lesson, after which Chianis boarded the 7:00 p.m. bus and arrived back in Long Beach at 7:00 a.m. Monday morning. Finally, he moved into a shack in Stamos's backyard in San Francisco and found a job at Bank of America. Although Stamos had played on hundreds of 78-rpm recordings of Greek music in America, he never taught Chianis any Greek songs. Instead, his lessons were drawn from a method book written by the famous Hungarian cimbalom player Géza Allaga—the same method book that Stamos had used when he came to America around 1910. For a year, Chianis devoted every free minute to playing and practicing; then he returned to Long Beach. Although he continued playing the cimbalom, he decided to return to college and finish his music studies.

As an accomplished musician, Chianis played the santouri on several recordings throughout his career. The albums included *Epirotika: Greek Folk Music and Dances from Northern Greece* (Folkways, 1981); *Ravi Shankar: Portrait of a Genius* (World Pacific Records, 1964); and two classical recordings. In addition, he appeared as a guest soloist on the santouri and cimbalom with the Boston Symphony Orchestra, the New York Philharmonic Orchestra, the Northeastern Pennsylvania Philharmonic, and other groups. He also played on radio and TV in Athens, and worked for years as a musician in some of the largest Hollywood television and movie studios, including Universal, MGM, Columbia, Walt Disney, and Paramount.

Chianis received both a BS and an MA in music from Long Beach State College before enrolling in ethnomusicology/musicology at the University of California, Los Angeles. While still a doctoral student, in 1958 he received an invitation from George Spyridakis, director of the Folklore and Folk Song Archives at the Academy of Athens, to conduct research on Greek folk music. In order to acquire the knowledge necessary to complete his dissertation, it was essential for Chianis to make extensive field recordings in remote villages. Using the Hellenic Folklore Research Center of the Academy of Athens as his base for field research, he recorded the vocal and instrumental repertoires of the Peloponnesian villages of Chrisovitsi, Valtetsi, Dara, Nestani, Vytina, Kandyla, and Ligourio.

Throughout his life, Chianis often returned to Greece for new field recording expeditions, usually working closely with the Hellenic Folklore Research

Center. He recorded extensively in the village of Elias in eastern Crete; Orchomenos and Martino in Roumeli; Volos and the Vlach region in Thessaly; Kozani, Macedonia; and Agia Eleni (Anastenaria), Thrace; and on the Aegean islands of Kythnos, Andros, Amorgos, Skinousa, Koufounisi, Keros, Sifnos, Skyros, Kasos, and Samothrace. He donated copies of his recordings to the Greek Folk Music Recording Archives, where they have proved to be an invaluable resource for generations of researchers.

Ethnomusicologist Michael Kaloyanides notes that, before Chianis,

> [e]thnomusicological analysis was limited and often colored by the dogmatic belief that true Greek music was descended purely from ancient and Byzantine Greek traditions. Influences from other traditions were considered contaminations, so scholars often resorted to creating twisted and strangely grafted musical family trees to show the supposedly pure ancestry of modern rural and urban Greek music. I must acknowledge Sotirios (Sam) Chianis who, beginning in the late 1950s, introduced a more expansive and deep ethnomusicological methodology to studying Greek music and influenced a generation of scholars. (Kaloyanides 2001)

After finishing a dissertation titled "The Vocal and Instrumental Tsamiko of Roumeli and the Peloponnesus," Chianis received a PhD from UCLA in 1967. While still a graduate student, he had begun teaching courses in Greek and Balkan folk music; he further directed performance groups at UCLA from 1961 to 1967 and at Long Beach State University from 1965 to 1967. In 1967, Wesleyan University's World Music Program in Ethnomusicology invited Chianis to give intensive courses to doctoral students during a year-long field expedition to the island of Samothrace. The island was selected for its isolation and the lack of previous recordings. He both taught and supervised students, whom he placed in several of the island's villages for two months to record music and related folklife materials.

In 1968, Chianis joined the faculty of the State University of New York at Binghamton as the first staff ethnomusicologist in the SUNY system. He established a graduate program in ethnomusicology and taught courses in world music, including Greek folk and popular music. He also taught instruments such as the santouri, laouto, and bouzouki, and directed performance groups. Chianis served as a full professor and chair of the Department of Music, and is today an emeritus professor.

Outside of the academy, Chianis worked closely with Greek officials to bring traditional musicians, singers, and dancers to the 1976 Bicentennial Festival of American Folklife in Washington, DC. He also received grants to conduct musical research in the Dodecanese islands in 1969 and 1972. Closer to home, Chianis served as the secretary and president of the American Hellenic Educational Progressive Association (AHEPA) chapter in Binghamton.

Chianis has written extensively about Greek and other types of traditional music. Below are some selected publications:

"George Demetrios Grachis: America's Greatest Greek Violinist and Instrument Maker," part 1. *Laografia* (September–October, 1994): 2–6.

"George Demetrios Grachis: America's Greatest Greek Violinist and Instrument Maker," part 2. *Laografia* (January–February, 1995): 9–14.

"Survival of Greek Folk Music in New York." *New York Folklore* 14, nos. 3–4 (1988): 37–48.

"Greek Folk Music: Style, Repertory, and Instruments." In *Greek Music Tour*, program, Fifteenth Annual Winter Folk Festival, 25–33. New York: Ethnic Folk Arts Center, 1983.

An Introduction to Greek Folk Music: Analytical Notes, Transcriptions and Bibliography. Thirty-page booklet accompanying two volumes of recordings. New York: Folkways Records, 1982.

"Neohellenic Folk Music." In *The New Grove Dictionary of Music and Musicians*, edited by Stanley John Sadie, vol. 7, 675–82. London: Macmillan, 1980.

"The Vocal and Instrumental Tsamiko of Roumeli and the Peloponnesus." PhD diss., University of California, Los Angeles, 1973.

Folk Songs of Mantineia, Greece. Berkeley: University of California Press, 1965.

"Aspects of Melodic Ornamentation in the Folk Music of Central Greece." *Selected Reports*, 89–119. Los Angeles: Institute of Ethnomusicology, University of California, Los Angeles, 1960.

In recent years, Chianis has written a series of books based on his early field-work expeditions:

Folk Songs from the Central Peloponnesus, Greece. Athens: Hellenic Folklore Research Center, Academy of Athens, forthcoming.

Folk Songs from Dara, Arcadias. Athens: Hellenic Folklore Research Center, Academy of Athens, 2016.

Folk Songs from Vytina, Arcadias. Athens: Hellenic Folklore Research Center, Academy of Athens, 2013.

Folk Songs from Valtetsi, Arcadias, vol. 1. Athens: Hellenic Folklore Research Center, Academy of Athens, 2010.

Folk Songs of Skyros, Greece. Athens: Peloponnesian Folklore Foundation, Hellenic Folklore Research Center, Academy of Athens; Rethymno, Greece: University of Crete, 2004.

Produced in collaboration with the Hellenic Folklore Research Center, these studies take a multifaceted approach that includes discussion of the folk cultural context and analysis of musical structure and expression. Each song is presented with complete text and musical script, and the books contain CDs with the recordings. Thus they are an invaluable resource not only for those who enjoy traditional music but also for scholars and researchers.

Throughout his long life, Sotirios Chianis has shown remarkable dedication and skill in both the study and performance of Greek music. He has been, and still is, a force to be reckoned with.

Notes

1. The difference between the cimbalom and the santouri is in the arrangement of the strings. The santouri's arrangement is chromatic and highly adapted to Greek folk melodies. The cimbalom's arrangement was devised to play Hungarian folk and classical music. The concert cimbalom is about three times larger than the santouri, sits on four legs, and weighs about two hundred pounds. The Greeks called santouri tuning (arrangement of strings) *ala turka* and cimbalom tuning *ala franka* (Western or European).

References

Kaloyanides, Michael G. 2001. Review of *Mousiki Thisavri tis Kritis (Musical Treasures of Crete)*, no. 9, *75 Years*, by Yiorgos Tzimakis and various artists, Cretaphon 01409 (1997); and *Vocal Music in Crete*, by various artists, produced by Tullia Magrini, Smithsonian Folkways SFW CD 40437 (2000). In *Music and Anthropology* (University of Bologna), no. 6. At http://umbc.edu/MA/index/number6/cdrev/cdrev.htm. Accessed April 14, 2016.

Shay, Anthony. 2006. *Choreographing Identities: Folk Dance, Ethnicity, and Festival in the United States and Canada.* Jefferson, NC: McFarland.

Ilias Kementzides (1926–2006)

—National Endowment for the Arts

Ilias Kementzides was born April 2, 1926, in Kazakhstan in the Soviet Union, of Greek parents from Sampsunda, Pontus. The Pontic Greeks lived from ancient times in the Pontus area of Asia Minor, on the southeastern coast of the Black Sea. The community resettled in Greece as part of the compulsory exchange of populations between Greece and Turkey in the early 1920s, but some families also relocated into areas under Soviet rule.

Kementzides began playing the Pontic *lyra* (a bottle-shaped violin with three strings) when he was eight, learning from his uncle, who was a professional musician. About his upbringing, Kementzides said:

> In Russia, every weekend the whole neighborhood would gather in the courtyard. There was nothing else to do, no theater, no movies, only music. If someone heard an instrument starting up, everyone would come running. It was joyous. That's how it was in Greece, too. Not a blade of grass could grow in our courtyard, there was so much dancing.

In 1940, Kementzides moved with his family to Greece and settled in a small town near Thessaloniki, an area heavily populated by Pontic Greeks. During World War II, this region of Greece was occupied by the Germans, and during this difficult period, Pontians were often treated as outsiders, even by the Greeks, forcing the Pontian community to bind more closely together to preserve its cultural traditions.

Kementzides became a professional musician, playing at social clubs and theaters. He also farmed a small plot of land but eventually realized that he could not make enough money in Greece to support his family. He was determined to emigrate to the United States, and in 1974 he and his wife and three children settled in Norwalk, Connecticut, where he found employment in an electronics factory.

In Connecticut, Kementzides began playing almost at once at Pontic social occasions. Word spread quickly throughout the Greek community that a powerful new musician had arrived who was a talented dance musician and a strong

Figure 98. Ilias Kementzides. Photo by Panos Papanicolaou.
Courtesy of the Center for Traditional Music and Dance.

singer with an extensive repertoire of songs in the Pontic dialect. In addition, he was fluent in Greek, Turkish, and Russian and made his own instruments. Kementzides was invited to perform at weddings, christenings, baptisms, and other events in his community, most notably those held at the local Pontic American Club of Astoria in Queens, New York. Typically, the lyra heads a three-piece orchestra ensemble, but Kementzides has also preserved the strong solo lyra tradition he learned as a child.

In 1989, Kementzides received a National Heritage Fellowship from the National Endowment for the Arts—the highest award in the United States in the traditional arts. A man of strength, dignity, and compassion, he died in his home on November 11, 2006, surrounded by his children, grandchildren, and close friends.

Giannis Tatasopoulos (1928–2001)

—Tina Bucuvalas[1]

During the post–World War II era, Greek music in America underwent major changes. Among those leading the way was outstanding musician/composer Giannis Tatasopoulos. Considered the finest bouzouki player of his generation in America, he developed a unique style that was distinguished by remarkable dexterity, phrasing, and instrumental tone. He also was a leader in the exploration of different musical genres with the bouzouki.

Tatasopoulos was born Kifissia, a suburb of Athens, on January 7, 1928. His father was from Pyrgos in Constantinople. He was an excellent oud player and vocalist, although he did not perform professionally. His mother came from an ethnic Greek village in what is today southern Albania. From both his parents, Tatasopoulos inherited knowledge and appreciation of their different regional music traditions.

Tatasopoulos first played guitar, which he began to learn at eight years old. When he took up the bouzouki, his first teacher was the renowned *rebetika* musician and composer Anestis Delias (aka Artemis). His second teacher was Manolis Hiotis, one of the most gifted bouzouki musicians of all time. Tatasopoulos began playing professionally at the age of twelve with Dimitris Arapakis (Dimitrios Kalinikos), the great singer and *santouri* player, at the famous *I Μπυρα Του Πιχινου* taverna in Athens's Thisio district.

By the 1950s, Tatasopoulos was one of the most popular musicians in Greece. From 1946 to 1955 he worked as one of the primary session musicians for Columbia Records, performing as musician and vocalist on more than three hundred recordings. In addition, he was placed in charge of auditioning new talent. Several of Tatasopoulos's recordings hit the top of the Greek charts, and he appeared in several films. His compositions were sung by many of the most popular vocalists of the period such as Marika Ninou, Stelios Kazantzidis, Prodromos Tsausakis, Kaiti Grey, Giota Lydia, Sotiria Bellou, Ioanna Georgakopoulou, Anna Chrysafi, Stella Haskil, Poly Panou, Rena Dalia, and more. During this era his friends, coworkers, and influences included the performers he most admired: musicians Manolis Hiotis, Dimitris "Bebis" Stergiou, Harry Lemonopoulos,

Figure 99. Giannis Tatasopoulos. Photo taken for the album *Musical Odyssey*, Nina Record Company (NL-1269), 1966. Courtesy of Tina Bucuvalas.

Giannis "Sporos" Stamatiou, Yiorgos Tsibidis, Giorgos Mitsakis, Giannis Papaioannou, and Vassilis Tsitsanis; singers Stratos Pagioumtzis, Antonis Diamantidis (Dalgas), and Dimitris Arapakis; and others from outside Greek music.

The postwar era was an economically difficult time in Greece. In the mid-1950s, many of the top bouzouki musicians emigrated to or undertook lengthy tours of US diaspora communities for financial reasons. Tatasopoulos settled in New York in October 1955, where he recorded on Nina Records and worked with many Greek musicians in clubs. Among those with whom he recorded were Rena Dalia, Poly Panou, Thodoros Kavourakis, and Axiotis Kehagias. He later toured to Boston, Chicago, Detroit, and Philadelphia.

In addition to playing on many recordings, Tatasopoulos was a prolific songwriter. Except for a few recordings he made in Greece in 1958, after 1955 he recorded entirely in the United States. He recorded dozens of his compositions during the 1950s and 1960s, including "Hanoumaki mou" (Nina 642-A, with Axiotis Kehagias and Rena Dalia); "Μου στειλαν δεκα προξενια," with lyrics by Nikos Routsos, a huge hit (Nina Records, with Rena Dalia); "Παπαδοπουλα" (Nina Records, with Rena Dalia); "To teleftaoi randevou" (Nina Records, 1959, with Stelios Kazantzidis and Marinella); "Afou den me theleis" (Nina Records, with Poly Panou); "Polles manades klapsane" (Nina Records, with Kazantzidis);

and "Glykoharazei, O Avgerinos" (Liberty, lyrics by Nikos Routsos, sung by Marika Ninou).

Popular Tatasopoulos compositions recorded in America by other artists included "Ελα σηκω χορεψε το" (Kalos Diskos 1953, sung by Thodoros Kavourakis and Angeliki Pallagoudi); "Ο καταδικοσ" (Kalos Diskos, with Kavourakis and Pallagoudi; "Εισαι γυναικα φιλου μου" with lyrics by Nikos Routsos (Virginia Records, sung by Virginia Magkidou); and "Το αρζαν" (Aristophone, with Tasos Rigopoulos and Ioannis Marki).

In 1960, Tatasopoulos moved to Washington, DC, where he and his *koumbaros* George Harris opened the well-known Port Said Club on I Street. It was reported to be the first in the city to feature a multiethnic ensemble and belly dancers—and by all accounts they staged a fantastic and wildly popular show. He later played at other area clubs including the Astor and Black Ulysses.

One of the reasons that Tatasopoulos preferred to stay in America was the greater freedom of musical expression. Like many bouzouki musicians, he was knowledgeable about classical music as well as Romanian and Spanish musical genres. In addition, he had a passion for Middle Eastern music and was undoubtedly influenced by the classical Arabic and Turkish music to which he listened. By 1960, he was beginning to seriously collaborate with musicians playing in other genres. His first commercial release on this trajectory was the Nina album *Musical Odyssey* (1966), on which he appeared with Armenian American trumpeter Roger King Mozian (one of the early greats of Latin music) and his orchestra, which included Cuban musicians. Their collaboration marked an important moment in the use of the bouzouki in Latin-Greek musical fusion.

From 1969 through the 1970s, Tatasopoulos collaborated on a series of five albums with Lebanese violin virtuoso Fred Elias.[2] The ensemble included both Greek and Armenian musicians, notably veteran musicians and brothers George (keyboard) and Nick Kokoras (guitar, bouzouki), and talented percussionist Arthur Chingras, who appeared on the first two records. On the recordings, Tatasopoulos explored the possibilities of utilizing the bouzouki as part of a hybrid genre of Middle Eastern and Greek music. The Fred Elias ensemble appeared at the Philharmonic Hall and Lincoln Center in New York, the Chicago Opera House, and throughout the United States. At the same time, Tatasopoulos also was among the first to experiment with technical innovations, such as effects pedals, on the bouzouki.

In the 1980s, Tatasopoulos played at the Astor in Washington, DC. His performances were enormously popular, with lines sometimes extending around the block waiting to see him play with famous visiting vocalists from Greece. When the Astor closed, he played a variety of club dates, such as at the Averoff and Fantasia in the Boston area. In the early 1990s, he began to play with his son Nikos, a remarkable bouzouki musician in his own right. Tatasopoulos never returned to reside permanently in Greece, although he toured there occasionally. At his last appearances in Greece, in December 1996, he performed with Sporos Stamatiou and Babis Goles. In the United States, he continued performing until 1998, when he began to have health issues.

Giannis Tatasopoulos died in October 2001, but his son and his many students and protégés have carried on his stylistic and experimental legacy. Born in America, Nikos Tatasopoulos first played bouzouki on stage with his father when he was three years old. In recent decades, he has made his home in Greece and become an internationally respected bouzouki musician in his own right. In 2011, he supervised the Ellopia Media Group production of the CD Οσα χρονια κι αν περασουν, on which many stars of the Greek music world performed as a tribute to his father's compositions and musical artistry.

Notes

1. I would like to thank the great Greek music veterans George and Nick Kokoras for sharing information about the gigs they played and the albums they recorded with Tatasopoulos over the course of thirty years.

2. Among the albums were *Mystical Temptations* (Intrasonic IS-1001, 1969); *Artistic Moods for Dance*, vols. 1, 3 (Intrasonic IS-2002, 1975; Intrasonic IS-2004, 1978); and *Golden Hits of John Tatassopoulos* (Intrasonic IS-2005, 1979).

Gust J. (Dino) Pappas (1931–1999)

—Stavros K. Frangos

Personal interests and wider historical events converged in the life of Gust J. (Dino) Pappas. From roughly 1940 onward, he passionately collected ethnic commercial records and, in so doing, sought to learn everything he could about the complex musical traditions of Greece, the Balkans, the Ottoman Empire, and the eastern Mediterranean in general. Well before middle age, he had amassed what many believe to have been the largest such collection of its kind in the world. With more than ten thousand 78-rpm records (and other musical formats), Pappas spent hour after hour, year after year, listening intensely to this ocean of music. Coupled with Pappas's avid (some might say near-microscopic) attention to the music was his daily life, which gradually and naturally included ever-increasing meetings and conversations with traditional musicians, record store owners, record company producers, noted dancers, other large record collectors, and eventually academics from around the world. As the son of Greeks from the 1880–1924 wave of immigrants, Pappas, who was fluent in Greek, actively sought out anyone who had experienced this music in its original setting in order to extend his knowledge of the wider musical scene and to gain additional insights into its original aesthetics.

During the last three decades of his life, Pappas's role evolved from record collector and music aficionado to public speaker, record producer, and, ultimately, recognized music authority. A sure method that he adopted early when discussing some musical point was not to argue but to go directly to his collection and pull out one or more records and play them. Adapting this technique to his ever-growing series of lectures and interviews, Pappas would record ahead of time a series of musical segments to highlight his presentations. From university lecture halls, to folk music and dance gatherings, to radio programs in the United States and in Greece, Pappas's method, while not original perhaps, provided a level of authenticity to his presentations that few have subsequently matched.

It can be argued that Pappas changed forever the deep divide between academic researchers and music lovers. The divide revolves around the two opposing claims: that academics do not have a solid grounding in the existing sources

Figure 100. Dino Pappas delivering a lecture. Courtesy of Stavros K. Frangos.

of traditional music, while music lovers are reputed to know nothing but the recorded music. And, given the rarity of commercial records and other supporting ephemera, researchers quickly question the basis for many claims made by those devoted solely to the music. Pappas, unknowingly perhaps, bridged this gap by turning the question back on to the researchers. Any assertion that Pappas made could be verified by the music. He also freely shared this audio evidence with academics, musicians, folk dancers, and music lovers alike. While not a startling insight today perhaps, in the early 1980s his focus on the actual records (and other ephemera) at the high level of expertise at which he publicly presented them had no equal.

On August 1, 1931, Dino Pappas was born in Detroit to Greek immigrant parents Xenofone Papakonstantinou, who hailed from Roumeli, and Zenovia (née Gzindzienoglou or Gingigloglou) from Constantinople. Baptized as Constantinos J. Papakonstantinou and raised during the Great Depression, Pappas remembered his family as poor but not desolate in spirit. He recalled many times when friends or family would come by with nothing more than some halva or feta with bread, and the gathering of adults would soon be singing, laughing, and dancing. Music was a part of his everyday life. For his ninth birthday, his parents each gave him a 78-rpm record—his mother bought him a Turkish record and his father a Greek record. For whatever reason, this simple gesture triggered Pappas's ambition. Until his death, he kept not only his parents' original Victrola in a place of honor in his living room but also their original collection of Greek and Turkish 78-rpm records. His ninth birthday presents were always among them.

Pappas graduated from high school, served as a US Marine, and then became a Detroit policeman. His most memorable experience as a police officer was during the 1967 riots in Detroit. In 1974, Pappas took early retirement, in part due to his wife's declining health. He cared for her and their two children until his death.

Throughout his life, Pappas assiduously amassed one of the world's largest collections of 78-rpm commercial records showcasing Greek, Turkish, Armenian, Albanian, Arabic, Sephardic, and other ethnic musics from the Balkans, the Ottoman Empire, and the eastern Mediterranean. At its height, he claimed to have gathered some 7,000 Greek 78-rpm records with an additional 3,000 78s that were a mixture of Turkish and Armenian. Aside from these, Pappas collected 2,000 45-rpm records as well as some 2,500 Greek, Turkish, and Armenian LPs. In his ever-systematic search, he accumulated other musical formats such as piano rolls, 8-track tapes, and CDs. Striving for as complete a collection of these musical traditions as possible, Pappas also made rerecordings of records when he could not obtain an original.

During the years that Pappas was collecting music, local ethnic stores existed across North America. He was able to regularly buy records and collect a huge amount of music-related ephemera such as catalogs, price lists, posters, and other items, while quizzing all the store owners about their dealings with local musicians, record companies, and so on.

Beginning in the early 1980s, Pappas's quest for records and information about music became widely recognized. Musicians, record collectors, producers, record companies, and academics from around the country as well as in Greece sought him out. It is no exaggeration to say that he became a kind of nexus for music from Greece, the Ottoman Empire, and the Balkans.

Pappas's encyclopedic knowledge drew innumerable individuals to his home. He regularly made customized rerecordings from his record collection for musicians, researchers, and music lovers alike. A short list of such visitors who spent time in his basement listening to music includes George Chittenden, Jane K. Cowan, Joel Bresler, Stavros K. Frangos, Carol Freeman, Joe Graziosi, Gail Holst-Warhaft, Michael G. Kaloyanides, Stewart Mennin, Martin Schwartz, Sophia Bilides, and Zora and Tony Tammer. He also carried on a lengthy correspondence with Greek music scholar Elias Petropoulos.

During the last three decades of Pappas's life, more and more original commercial recordings, sheet music, music-related ephemera, and oral history recordings were deposited in public institutions. Even so, Dick Spottswood, compiler and author of the monumental series *Ethnic Music on Records: A Discography of Ethnic Recordings Produced in the United States, 1893–1942* (1990), felt compelled to spend many days in Pappas's basement documenting a host of Greek and Turkish records that he could not find elsewhere.

Pappas's knowledge was sometimes expressed in curious ways. For example, through the good offices of actor and dancer Athan Karras (1927–2010), he provided the Greek music used in the all-too-brief Greek dance scene in Bob Rafelson's 1981 remake of the film *The Postman Always Rings Twice*.

In 1990, Pappas along with fellow record collector Andreas Dellis received a Helen Zeese Papanikolas Charitable Trust award. As two of the largest commercial record collectors in the nation at that time, Pappas and Dellis deposited rerecordings of the vast majority of Tetos Demetriades's commercial recordings (inclusive of his many performances under pseudonym) into the Helen Z. Papanikolas Oral Histories Collection at the University of Utah's Marriott Library. Pappas and Dellis wrote two survey essays announcing their deposit and describing its contents (1991a, 1991b).[1]

In 1997, musician Ara Topouzian produced three CDs on the American Recording Productions label (Farmington Hills, Michigan) that were drawn from recordings in Pappas's collection: *Vasilios Saleas*; *Sukru Tunar: Legendary Clarinetist of Turkey*; and *Yiorgo Anestopoulos*. Topouzian recently wrote the following about his relationship with Dino Pappas:

> Recently I was listening to the *Fresh Air* program on NPR and they had a great story about an author who wrote a book about collecting the most rare 78-rpm recordings from around the world. Recordings that would be over 100 years old from different countries. Amanda Petrusich discusses what record collectors will do to go to great lengths in finding these old recordings. "Some," she says, "have been known to take jobs specifically because they allow access to strangers' basements, where rare records may be collecting dust."
>
> I could not help but to be immediately reminded of an old friend of mine named Gust J. "Dino" Pappas. . . . He was a proud Greek American and his first passion was for the music that his parents and grandparents grew up listening to in "the old country." First and foremost, Dino loved his Greek folk music. Equal to the music of his country he loved to listen to both Turkish and Armenian music. He never mixed politics with music and even though he was passionate about the atrocities the Greeks endured by the Turkish government, he still loved the music.
>
> He was well known throughout the country as "the" record collector in many circles including the Greek dance community. He most possibly had the largest col-

lection of Greek, Armenian, and Turkish 78-rpm records in the world. At one time he told me that he had 10,000 records in his collection. . . .

Dino was ever so colorful in his conversations with me and I always enjoyed his frankness and sometimes inappropriate comments. Some have said he could be rough around the edges but to me, we had a good relationship. Here was a guy that thoroughly loved to listen to music and he could do it all day and night. It was more than a hobby of his, it truly was a passion and something that gave him a great amount of joy.

He was an encyclopedia of knowledge when it came to Greek and Turkish music. Way before computers Dino would document every recording with hand written notes that included catalog numbers, record label names, and performers. Dino even would write down how he came to own a particular record! He used to write them on loose leaf paper and put them in three ring binders which were carefully placed on bookshelves in his basement. He knew where to find any song within his collection.

Those visits are still vivid in my memory. His basement was wall-to-wall recordings. He had CDs, cassettes, and even rare Greek piano rolls. If that wasn't enough, he would have duplicates of some of his more precious or favorable recordings. I can still picture it today sitting in a metal folding chair in his basement for 7 to 8 hours while he sat and DJed for me anything I wanted to hear. We never came up for air— he had a full bathroom in [the] basement and so there was almost never a need to see the sun! Many times when we would emerge from the basement, it was pitch dark outside. On occasion, he would yell up to check on his wife.

Fluent in Greek, it was extra special to hear him play a record and translate the lyrics to me. Musicians from around the world would contact him as he was considered a major resource for music. Several CD releases include his name in the credits for providing material to musicians in order to learn songs. If the singer was looking for a folk song or instrumentalist was looking to learn different forms of music, Dino was the guy. (Topouzian 2015)

On August 8, 1999, Pappas died at his home in St. Clair Shores, Michigan, of a stroke. He was buried at Cadillac Memorial Gardens in Clinton, Michigan. At the gravesite, his family placed one of the 78-rpm records from his parents' old Victrola player cabinet in the coffin with him.

According to Hank Bradley in his article "An Approach to Playing Violin in *Rebetiko*," the Dino Pappas collection is now housed in the basement archives of the Hellenic Society for the Protection of Intellectual Property and is open to the public.[2] Audio and video recordings of Pappas's lectures and interviews are held at the National Hellenic Museum in Chicago, the Archives of Traditional Music at Indiana University, the Michigan Room at the Grand Rapids Public Library, and elsewhere.

Since his death, many of Pappas's friends and admirers have written about him at various websites, in the Greek American press, and other places. While various academics and music collectors have publicly noted his aid in helping them achieve a better historical understanding of the history of Greek and Turkish music production in North America, some notable figures have not acknowledged his valuable assistance. Whatever the case, there is little question that Dino Pappas gave more to the world than was given to him.

Notes

1. See also Pappas's later 1995 article, "Tetos Demetriades: Blending Greek and American Music."

2. The Hellenic Society for the Protection of Intellectual Property, which protects intellectual property rights for Greek music and musicians, is located at Fragoklisias and Samou 51, Athens, telephone 210-685-7494, at http://www.yppo.gr/1/e1540.jsp?obj_id=811, and is recognized by the Greek Ministry of Culture as a Greek royalty-collecting organization. Sotiris Lykouropoulos is in charge.

References

Bradley, Hank. 2003. "An Approach to Playing Violin in Rebetiko." At http://ilma.orgfree.com/HydraGathering/bradley2003.html. Accessed June 11, 2016.

Pappas, Dino. 1995. "Tetos Demetriades: Blending Greek and American Music." *Laografia*, February 12.

Pappas, Dino, and Andreas Dellis. 1991a. "An Expanded Discography of Tetos Demetriades, part 1, ca. 1920–1928." *Laografia*, May 8, 1–102.

———. 1991b. "An Expanded Discography of Tetos Demetriades, part 2, ca. 1928–1932." *Laografia*, May 8, 103–87.

Spottswood, Richard K. 1990. *Ethnic Music on Records: A Discography of Ethnic Recordings Produced in the United States, 1893–1942.* Vol. 3, Eastern Europe. Urbana: University of Illinois Press.

Topouzian, Ara. 2015. "Basement Records: A Story about Dino Pappas." *HYE Times*, September 4. At https://hyetimesmusic.com/2015/09. Accessed June 11, 2016.

Harilaos Papapostolou (1932–1998)

—National Endowment for the Arts

Harilaos Papapostolou was born April 22, 1932, in the city of Agrinion in west-central Greece, a longtime center of Byzantine chant. He came from a long line of priests, including his father. He apprenticed with a traditional *psaltis*, or chanter, at age five, and eventually spent long hours each day mastering the enormous liturgical repertoire that was part of the day-to-day liturgical cycle.

Papapostolou held degrees in both Byzantine and Western music from the Conservatory of Athens and a theology degree from the University of Athens. This knowledge was a crucial factor that provided the insight he needed to understand and interpret the ecclesiastical hymns of the Orthodox Church.

In his hometown, Papapostolou became the head chanter (*protopsaltis*) of the cathedral. He also founded and directed a musical conservatory and directed performances of both sacred and secular music on the radio and in public concerts. In the mid-1960s, Papapostolou accepted the position of protopsaltis at Saint Sophia Cathedral in Washington, DC, where he remained for thirty-two years. In the United States, he found that the Western-based four-part-harmony choral style with organ accompaniment had nearly eclipsed the more traditional chant, which is marked by a single melody line juxtaposed with a drone voice, or *ison*. The melody is governed by a complex system of eight modes, or scales.

The chanter improvises an interpretation of the melodic skeleton, applying melodic ornamentation and other nuances of performance that express *ifo*—a mood that reflects the meaning of the sacred text, the liturgical movement, and the immediate context. In the words of Papapostolou, the chanter directs his creativity to the purpose of devotion, creating "the sound that facilitates prayer, that becomes the bridge between man and God, not a showcase for the performer." Ironically, the complex "Oriental"-sounding modes and melodies were thought too "primitive" by many Greek Americans, who had little prior exposure to the tradition.

"We have really strayed," Papapostolou said. "On the one hand, we are the Orthodox Church, and we have our own tradition in all aspects: iconography, church art, and architecture from the chandelier and candles to the priest's robes,

Figure 101. Harilaos Papapostolou. Courtesy of
Rena Papapostolou.

the music ... but we have remained Orthodox in name only. In everything else,
we have lost our tradition."

Papapostolou played a large part in the revival of Byzantine chant, which is
rooted in the music of medieval Byzantium. He taught dozens of apprentices and
offered public demonstrations. He has received the highest praise from connois-
seurs for his expressive ability.

In addition to his chanting responsibilities, Papapostolou became the choir
director and the principal of Saint Sophia's Greek-language school. His wife,
Rena Papapostolou, also taught language and established Return to Origins, a
dance troupe that performed at cultural events. The Papapostolous were also
known for Greek Echo, a family band that performed at the Smithsonian Folklife
Festival, the Corcoran Gallery of Art, and numerous Greek festivals, weddings,
and baptisms.

The National Endowment for the Arts awarded Papapostolou a 1998 National
Heritage Fellowship for his skill in Byzantine chant. Sadly, he died only a month
later on November 30, 1998.

Kay Skordilis (b. 1936)

—Tina Bucuvalas

In addition to the artists themselves, there are others whose lives are anchored in the world of Greek American music. During her teenage years, Kay Skordilis was a vivacious New York club kid whose social life centered around Greek music and its stars. She has spent most of her adult life married to two prominent artists, Spiros Skordilis and Thodoros Kavourakis, and as a valued friend to innumerable other musicians and vocalists over the past half century.

Born Kalliope Gavokosta on March 20, 1936, in Thessaloniki, Kay, in her childhood, endured the extraordinarily difficult circumstances during World War II and the Greek Civil War. In 1939, her mother, Evlambia, was pregnant with Kay's brother Kosta when her husband, Panagiotis Gavokostas, was drafted. He was killed fighting in the Albanian conflict. Kay remembers that, during the war, water and food were rationed and the streets were closed at dusk. Kosta died of starvation at three years old, and the family had to take shelter from bombardment three times as they trudged to the cemetery to bury him in his makeshift coffin.

Evlambia married Vangelis Kalimtgis in early 1946. During the ravages of the Civil War, he was jailed and sentenced to a concentration camp. Because he had been born in the United States, Evlambia notified the American consulate in Thessaloniki, which secured his release. In May 1946, the family journeyed two weeks on an American navy ship, eventually arriving at Ellis Island. They settled on Eighth Avenue and Forty-Fourth Street in Manhattan, but life was not easy. Kalimtgis suffered from a bullet wound, the bullet still in his leg. After four years of hospitalization, his leg was finally amputated. Meanwhile, Evlambia worked as a fur finisher.

Kay completed high school in New York, but on weekends she often danced the night away with friends at Greek nightclubs such as the Britania, Port Said, and Molfetas. In the clubs, they left their struggles behind and enjoyed the era's major stars, such as George Katsaros, Giannis Tatasopoulos, Kostas Kaplanis, Stavros Tzouanakos, Marika Ninou, Rena Dalia, Giorgos Zambetas, Manolis Hiotis, Mary Linda, Bebis, and Nikos Pourpourakis. Kay formed friendships

Figure 102. Kay and Spiros Skordilis with Tango. Courtesy of Kay Skordilis.

with the stars and sometimes attended the recording sessions of Tatasopoulos, Dalia, Pourpourakis, and Kavourakis. Her life changed dramatically when she married singer and recording artist Thodoros Kavourakis at the age of fourteen.

Kavourakis was born in the central Rhodian village of Malona during the 1920s. There, he married and had three children, but left for America after the war. He soon launched a singing career in New York. By the mid-1950s, he was a widely popular vocalist who recorded on the Nina, Kalos Diskos, Grecian Artists, and Aristophone labels with such artists as Roza Eskenazi, Rena Dalia, Giannis Tatasopoulos, Demetris Frantzeskakis, John Gianaros, Nikos Pourpourakis, Andreas Poggis, Antonis Loris, and Axiotis Kehagias. Although Kavourakis was respected among Greeks Americans, he never achieved the same level of prestige in Greece. He returned to his natal village at the end of the 1980s, where he resided until his death in 2016.

Kay often accompanied Kavourakis to club dates and recording sessions, where she became friends with many luminaries in the Greek music world. Together, the couple opened two successful restaurants in Manhattan. They also enjoyed spending time on their yacht, once accompanying the famous swimmer Jason Zirganos as he circumnavigated the island of Manhattan. Kay particularly remembers a party they gave that was attended by Manolis Angelopoulos and his band, who were then playing in the city. In 1972, they sold everything and moved to Tarpon Springs, Florida, but they divorced in 1974.

Kay remained in Tarpon Springs, where she volunteered at her daughter Tammy's high school and worked to sustain various Greek fraternal organizations. One night in 1977, she joined friends at the local nightclub to hear recently arrived bouzouki player/singer/composer Spiros Skordilis and his wife, vocalist Lena Daina.

Spiros Skordilis (1930–2013) was born in Athens. He learned to play guitar from his father but later transitioned to the bouzouki. At eighteen, he formed the popular Laiki Orchestra. Five years later he founded the Blue Trio, which played *kantades* and European-style music in Plaka *tavernas*. By 1958, he was appearing nightly at the Vachos Taverna with other respected musicians. Skordilis soon signed a contract with RCA, for which he recorded original compositions including his most famous hit, "Oti arhizei oraio" (When Something Beautiful Begins, 1961)—which remains a standard. While the junta was in power in Greece, Skordilis's song about miniskirts ("To mini mini") was banned. He and his wife left Greece to perform in Canada and the United States.

Kay enjoyed meeting the couple and listening to their music. Two weeks later, she observed several musicians leaving Saint Nicholas Greek Orthodox Cathedral in Tarpon Springs and learned that Daina had died suddenly from an aneurysm. When she next saw Skordilis, she expressed her condolences and offered to help him with legal paperwork, since he knew little English. They developed a relationship, and in 1978 they were married at Saint Nicholas.

In the ensuing years, the Skordilises traveled throughout the United States as Spiros toured extensively from Tarpon Springs to Daytona Beach, Astoria, Chicago, Houston, Phoenix, and places in California. While Spiros performed, Kay found jobs waitressing in the nightclub or at a nearby restaurant so that they could be together. Their nomadic life was often plagued by financial difficulties when employers did not pay or provide promised amenities. After many years, they returned permanently to Tarpon Springs.

Skordilis played for Tarpon Springs–area clubs, restaurants, and festivals for more than thirty years. In addition, he taught bouzouki to students through the City of Tarpon Springs' Folk Arts in the Schools program at Tarpon Springs Elementary School during the early 1980s. He appeared at the Florida Folk Festival and in 1987 participated as a master artist in the Florida Folklife Apprenticeship Program—and several students went on to play in local Greek bands. For many years, he also conducted the Prometheus Hellenic Cultural Center Chorus. During their years in Tarpon Springs, the Skordilises were close to many other musicians and vocalists who resided permanently or temporarily in the area, including George Katsaros, Stelios Kazantzidis, Jim Apostolou, Dimitris Tzaras, and George Soffos.

Throughout their marriage, the couple collaborated in songwriting—with Kay writing the lyrics and Spiros the music. Kay also actively promoted her husband's music through CD production and early Internet marketing. In addition, she dealt with copyright issues and record companies, becoming quite savvy about royalty matters.

The Skordilises spent many happy years together before Spiros's health declined; he died in 2013. At his burial in Cycadia Cemetery, a contingent of local musicians bid him farewell by singing his most beloved song, "Oti arhizei oraio." Today, Kay remains an essential part of several local Greek organizations while continuing to work at her daughter's travel agency. Nevertheless, she always has time to support the work of local musicians, with whom she has maintained strong ties. She is highly respected not only for her many kindnesses but as an eyewitness to Greek American musical history.

References

Marmarinos, Stavros. 2015. "Kay Skordilis: My Life with Music Composer Spiros Skordilis (*Oti Arxizi Oreo*)." *National Herald*, April 1.

Peter Stephen Kyvelos (1943–2017)

—Michael G. Kaloyanides

In a modest and unassuming storefront on a major thoroughfare in Belmont, Massachusetts, Peter Kyvelos plied his trade as a master luthier. Although his bread and butter was the repair of violins, violas, cellos, basses, and other Western chordophones, his passion and greatest artistry was crafting the oud, the short-necked plucked lute found throughout Greece, Turkey, western Asia, and North Africa. Kyvelos was called "the Stradivari of the oud," as he was widely accepted as the premier maker of the instrument in the Western Hemisphere. He was a gregarious and bigger-than-life craftsman always willing to engage those who entered his workshop, particularly on his two biggest passions: the oud and fly fishing.

Peter Stephen Kyvelos was born in 1943 in Fitchburg, Massachusetts, to Greek American parents, Angela Petalas Kyvelos and Stavros George Kyvelos. His father had immigrated to the United States and became a master candy maker, opening a business in the 1920s with a cousin in Greenport, Long Island. Kyvelos recalls his father as someone who liked to work with his hands and took pleasure in woodworking; he taught Kyvelos how to work with tools. From a very young age, Kyvelos enjoyed carving things out of wood.

Kyvelos's father was also an amateur musician, playing rural and urban Greek music on violin, and Kyvelos was intrigued both by the music his father played and by the sounds and songs he heard on his father's 78-rpm recordings. He took lessons on violin for a short time but, attracted by 1950s rock and roll, took up the guitar and taught himself to play. Yet he continued to be intrigued by the plaintive sound of a particular instrument on the old 78s that his father could not help him identify. A turning point came in his life when Kyvelos went to a dance with an Armenian friend and finally experienced firsthand the mysterious instrument he had previously only encountered in 78-rpm soundscapes: the oud. Mesmerized by the live performance, he realized that this was the instrument he had been looking for. "I just had to have one. It was love at first sight—or sound." Kyvelos acquired his first oud at age sixteen and taught himself to play it and repair it.

Kyvelos soon mastered the oud and began performing professionally. He moved to California in 1962 and studied at Oakland City College, Merritt

Figure 103. Peter Kyvelos, Boston, 2001. Photo by Tom Pich.

Campus, and San Francisco State University. He helped pay his way through school by performing with his own group, the Anatolians, in nightclubs in the North Beach section of San Francisco, and by doing instrument repair work. To learn to repair and build violins, Kyvelos spent considerable time observing the internationally known violin maker Albert Muller as he constructed his violins. In 1970, Kyvelos returned to Massachusetts and began an instrument repair business in his mother's house.

In 1971, he opened his Belmont, Massachusetts, shop with the business name Unique Strings and thereafter worked out of that facility. Kyvelos soon attracted the attention of string players in New England and across the country who sought him out for repairs for their instruments. He did considerable work for the Boston Symphony Orchestra and was entrusted with both Amati and Stradivarius violins. Unique Strings developed into a mecca for aficionados of the musics of the eastern Mediterranean and western Asia, particularly the oud and other instruments. In his time at Unique Strings, Kyvelos made more than two hundred ouds. With excellent craftsmanship, beautiful design, and spectacular sonic qualities, his creations are masterpieces, highly sought and coveted. Among the great artists who have performed on Kyvelos ouds are Mal Barsamian, Al Gardner, Charles Ganamian, and Richard Hagopian.

National and international recognition came in 1989 when Armenian American oud player Richard Hagopian was awarded a National Heritage Fellowship and performed with one of Kyvelos's ouds. It was during these festivities that

Hagopian called Kyvelos "the Stradivari of oud making." And in 2001, Kyvelos himself was awarded a National Endowment for the Arts National Heritage Fellowship for his artistry as an instrument maker and musician, and he performed on one of his instruments at that year's National Heritage Foundation concert. Documentary Arts, a nonprofit organization based in Dallas and New York, also named him a Master of Traditional Arts.

Perhaps less known than Kyvelos's work as an instrument maker was his excellence as a performer on the oud. Kyvelos's delicate and sophisticated technique was evident is his interpretation of Greek, Armenian, and Turkish rural and urban musics. He performed at dances, clubs, and festivals and in concerts and recitals throughout the United States. In the Boston area, his performance venues included Symphony Hall and Harvard University's Sanders Theatre.

I am indebted to Peter, Virginia, and Matthew Kyvelos for information they provided in various communications in 2016.

References

Alarik, Scott. 2000. "Their Mission: To Keep Folk Crafts Alive." *Boston Globe*, May 28.

Holtzberg, Maggie. 2008. *Keepers of Tradition: Art and Folk Heritage in Massachusetts*. Amherst: University of Massachusetts Press.

Montgomery, Maurice R. 1998. "A Journey through the World of Greek Music." *Boston Globe*, April 3.

Trio Bel Canto and Takis Elenis (b. 1948)

—Tina Bucuvalas

After World War II, new forms of instrumental music, song styles, and dance emerged in Greece. In response to the international trend highlighting Latin American music, one popular musical form consisted of trios producing a sound that fused the early twentieth-century *kantades* of the Ionian Islands and Athens with Latin American trios. Performing Greek music for American audiences with polished vocal harmonies and strong musicianship, the Trio Bel Canto became arguably the most popular Greek American band of all time. Their blend of new Greek hits and updated bouzouki interpretations of traditional music became the standard for most Greek musical events that are staged today. Among the Trio's musicians, the most notable was the outstanding bouzouki player Takis Elenis, who performed with them at their pinnacle before pursuing a solo career.

The original Trio Bel Canto started out in Greece in 1948 with friends and classmates Evangelos Metaxas and Bobby Tsobanakis, bouzouki players and vocalists who joined with guitarist John Papamakariou to form a trio. Originally the Trio Coumbatsero, they became the Filoi tou Bel Canto (Friends of the Belcanto) in 1950—joining many other groups who serenaded diners in the outdoor cafés and tavernas. Under that name, the group recorded numerous 78-rpm records with Mimis Plessas and Giorgos Mouzakis, but in 1952 they started calling themselves the Trio Bel Canto. Simultaneously, entertainment promoter Giorgos Economidis started booking them at popular clubs, and they gained popularity throughout the 1950s. In 1956 the Trio, along with the Giorgos Mouzakis Orchestra, were invited to perform in America by the American Hellenic Educational Progressive Association (AHEPA). Shortly after their return to Greece, Bobby Tsobanakis left the group and was replaced by Michael Matheos. Throughout the remainder of the decade, the Trio Bel Canto continued entertaining at well-known clubs in Athens, Cyprus, and Thessaloniki. In addition, they released records, appeared in numerous shows and events with the popular musicians of the time, performed on radio, and were featured in Greek films.

In the 1960s, after touring Israel and Lebanon as well as around Greece, the Trio Bel Canto rose to fame in the United States—establishing permanent

Figure 104. Trio Bel Canto, *Me Agape: With Love*, 1973. Peters International, PILPS 92. Takis Elenis is on the left. Courtesy of Meletios Pouliopoulos.

residency in 1966. In 1962, revered singer Nikos Gounaris invited them to join him at the Monte Carlo Hotel in the Catskills, which was famous for hosting evenings of Greek music and dance. Their enormously popular performances influenced the direction of Greek dance music. The Trio would learn new hits sent to them from Greece, then release covers in their lively, upbeat style.

After Gounaris's death in 1965, the Trio started working regularly with the popular Greek American orchestras led by Gus Vali and George Stratis. They also expanded their repertoire to include modern, sophisticated versions of *rebetika* and other classic traditional songs appropriate for dancing and for the increasingly popular *bouzoukia*—and their modern approach appealed to urban and young Greek Americans unfamiliar with older styles. The Trio performed at prominent nightclubs (e.g., the Athens Club, Chicago; Carson's Supper Club, Detroit; and the Salomé Night Club, Astoria), theaters (Carnegie Hall, and Philharmonic Hall at Lincoln Center in New York), local dinner-dance events (*horoesperides*) for Greek churches and organizations, and Johnny Carson's *The Tonight Show* (May 1963). At Carnegie Hall, they appeared with singers Jim

Apostolou and Eva Styl as well as the Vali and Stratis orchestras. They made a second appearance at Carnegie Hall in December 1967 with renowned bouzouki musician Harry Lemonopoulos.

The Trio Bel Canto issued numerous albums during the 1960s and 1970s, many of which became extremely popular. Their mixture of modern hits with interpretations of folk classics struck a chord with most Greek Americans. The Trio also intuitively understood that Greek audiences wanted to participate in the music, so albums such as *Sing and Dance with the Trio Bel Canto* (Fiesta Records/Grecophon 1966) became enormous hits that were found in most Greek American homes and spun at many community events.

When Michael Matheos left in 1971, the group discovered Takis Elenis—an exceptional bouzouki player whose precise yet passionate style further enhanced the Trio Bel Canto's standing. In particular, Elenis ably reinterpreted many rebetika standards by Giannis Papaioannou, Vassilis Tsitsanis, Markos Vamvakaris, and other greats. During the 1970s, the group played at every major Greek festival or event across the United States and traveled to the Caribbean, Australia, Panama, and Canada. They performed a third time at Carnegie Hall in early 1970s and made frequent appearances on Maria Papadatos's television show, a popular variety program for Greeks in New York. In addition to live performances, they continued to record albums and cassettes, returning to Greece in 1979 to cut the *Road of Return* album. Their popularity peaked in the 1970s—they were undisputedly the top Greek band in the United States and one of the top Greek bands in the world.

The Trio Bel Canto continued to play an important role in the Greek American music scene in the 1980s. They toured nationally and internationally, often appearing with other Greek artists. Takis Elenis left the group in 1986 to pursue solo interests, and the excellent bouzouki player George Vlismas joined in his place. However, Elenis's departure marked a turning point, and from 1988 until 1995 the group performed primarily at New York City venues, clubs, dinner dances, and festivals. Gradually, Greek dinner theaters and nightclubs began to close, until only a handful were left in major cities—and they often hired disc jockeys as an economic strategy. Live performers were only booked for special events that would ensure a profit. Greek cassettes and CDs became more widely available in the United States, and popular singers and bands from Greece made frequent American tours. With the simultaneous formation of more Greek bands, the Trio lost their competitive edge, although they continued to be a popular attraction.

In the 1990s, the Trio Bel Canto continued to perform primarily in New York. George Vlismas left the group in 1997, after which the Trio hired a variety of different players/vocalists. In 1998, Metaxas, Papamakariou, and Aggi Giannopoulos attempted a comeback in Greece. Unfortunately, the music business had moved on, and the Trio found a plethora of young stars fighting for recognition in new musical styles. Discouraged, Metaxas returned to the United States, but Papamakariou decided to remain in Greece—ending a fifty-year partnership. Metaxas brought in his son, Kyriakos (Chuck) Metaxas, an accomplished guitar player who quickly learned the repertoire. As Trio Bel Canto: The Next Generation, the group now includes lead vocalist Evangelos Metaxas, Kyriakos Metaxas (guitar and second vocals), and Nick Mandoukos (lead bouzouki and third vocals). Today, the Trio continues to delight audiences at festivals, concerts, dances, weddings, baptisms, and other events.

Takis Elenis

Elenis was born on November 22, 1948, on the tiny Dodecanese island of Lipsi. In 1960, his family relocated to the largest island in the Dodecanese, Rhodes, so that his father could find work. Three years later they emigrated to the United States, where his father found employment in the construction industry in the New York City area.

When he was a child, Elenis frequently practiced his bouzouki four to five hours a day in order to achieve his goal of becoming a good musician. Although he never took formal lessons, he visited an acquaintance several times in order to learn scales. Elenis learned to play bouzouki by listening to recordings and live music, but he did not learn to read music. It is worth noting that, even today, few musicians playing Greek traditional and popular music rely on sheet music.

As a young man, Elenis started working in construction, but he did not care for it and soon quit. In 1968, he started performing in the clubs on Eighth Avenue in New York—especially the Britania and Ali Baba. There, he backed up famous singers from Greece including Kaiti Grey, Poly Panou, Vangelis Perpiniadis, Manolis Angelopoulos, Rena Koumioti, and Giannis Floriniotis. Later in Astoria he performed at Skorpios and then the Grecian Cave alongside such stars as Stelios Kazantzidis.

Elenis never wanted to be a traditional bouzouki player—he always had an interest in incorporating jazz or other elements. In terms of personal style, he says that he stole bits from such bouzouki greats as Manolis Hiotis and Giannis Palaiologou, blended everything together, and made the mix his own. His friend Al Di Meola used to come to his house, and they would practice together for their own enjoyment. Di Meola invited Elenis to tour with him, but he declined. Elenis also acknowledges inspiration from rock and roll—which he believes emerges when he plays a *tsifteteli*. Among his eclectic influences were rock guitarist Eddie Van Halen, flamenco guitarist Paco de Lucía, Al Martino, Al Di Meola, Maharishi, and Ravi Shankar.

On one occasion when Elenis was playing at the Britania, an employee of Monitor, a company producing international records, was in the audience. Elenis was playing an instrumental program early in the evening while the patrons ate dinner. The Monitor representative asked if his company could make a live club recording, and the resulting album was the very popular *Dance the Greek Way* (Monitor 1971). Monitor wanted him to continue recording with them, but Elenis was unable to do so after he signed with the Trio Bel Canto.

The Trio stumbled upon Elenis quite by accident. In 1972, they visited the home of Elenis's grandmother, where they saw a photo of him playing bouzouki. When they asked about him, his grandmother told them that he played on Eighth Avenue with vocalist Kaiti Grey. After hearing him play at the club, they asked him to join the group. Elenis performed at innumerable events, toured nationally and internationally, and recorded five albums with the Trio during the fifteen years that he was a member.

After Elenis left the Trio in 1987, he worked at Hackensack, New Jersey's famed Molfetas for eight years. He subsequently performed at New York's well-regarded Estia Restaurant, and then at the Vraka in Astoria for four or five years. For a brief period, he joined a group that entertained at weddings and other events. Afterward, he played for visiting Greek vocalists at a variety of New York clubs, community events, weddings, and other venues. Although Elenis currently considers himself retired, he now has the time to practice more sophisticated pieces for his own enjoyment. He sometimes posts them to YouTube—making many younger players jealous of his still remarkable speed, expression, and precision. He also occasionally joins friends and colleagues who invite him to play with them at venues or events—but just for fun.

References

Elenis, Takis. 2016. Telephone interview with Tina Bucuvalas, June 4.

Karras, Athan. "Trio Bel Canto: The Next Generation." Hellenic Communication Service. At http://www.helleniccomserve.com/trionextgeneration.html. Accessed June 3, 2016.

Trio Bel Canto. Website. At http://www.triobelcanto.com. Accessed June 3, 2016.

George E. Soffos (1953–2013)

—Tina Bucuvalas

George Soffos was a musician's musician with an amazing mastery of the bouzouki. With lightning speed, excellent phrasing, and a repertoire that included
thousands of songs, he was a performer of the highest caliber. Beyond technical
mastery, he played from the heart, infusing his performances with exquisitely
expressed emotion. Many considered Soffos the best bouzouki player born in the
United States.

Soffos's repertoire was extremely broad. As a consummate professional, he
understood the necessity of playing to the tastes of the audience and often to
specific individuals in the audience. He performed not only the *nisiotika* (island
music) of the Dodecanese, from which his family came, but other genres including *rebetika*, *Smyrneïka*, and *dimotika*. In addition, he flawlessly played Greek
popular urban music (*laïka*) and art music (*entechno*), when demanded by the
performance context.

Soffos found enormous joy in music. It was a calling and it defined him. He
loved to bring the same joy to others. Greek music plumbs the depths of the pro-
foundest emotions—love, joy, longing, and despair. By plucking the strings of his
bouzouki, Soffos could flood the hearts of listeners with those feelings.

Beginnings

During the late nineteenth and early twentieth centuries, immigrants flocked
to the steel mills in Ohio. Migration chains concentrated together Greeks from
the same village, island, or region, and Warren, Ohio, was home to many from
Rhodes. In the 1940s and 1950s, most members of the tight, interrelated Rhodian
community lived in same neighborhood, where they maintained many aspects of
traditional life while acclimating to American society.

George's father, Constantinos Soffos, was born in the village of Asklipios in
southern Rhodes. He emigrated to the United States as a young man and worked

Figure 105. George Soffos (1953–2013), Tarpon Springs, Florida, 2012.
Photo by Joann Biondi.

thirty years at Republic Steel in Warren. His wife, Stella (Stamatia), was born to parents from the southern Rhodian village of Katavia.

Soffos was born on November 6, 1953, the youngest of five children. All three of his brothers worked in the music industry, but only he turned to Greek music. His mother was very involved with a local Greek organization, and the family often hosted visiting musicians. When major Greek stars toured America, they attended performances in midwestern and East Coast cities. As a result, Soffos met many notable musicians at a young age. When he was only six years old, while attending New York's Britania Café with his family, he decided to be a musician.

Soffos started playing music on a plastic guitar when he was ten, and his parents bought him a bouzouki when he was twelve. The Louis Fatimus Orchestra was the premier local Greek band at the time; Fatimus and singer Maria Paxinou were family friends, and they often encouraged Soffos to play a few songs with the orchestra while Maria sang. Soffos took bouzouki lessons from Fatimus, but he also learned from records and live performances. As he developed his skills, his mother was his biggest supporter.

When he was fourteen, Soffos played his first paid gig for a Greek night at Cleveland's Blue Chip. He joined the Grecian Lads, led by Parry Tsangaris from

Youngstown, which played at local dances and conventions. Long-time friend Stan Harris remembers being astonished to see him play the bouzouki behind his head, a la Jimi Hendrix. Tsangaris remembers, "George was one of those people that had the music in him. You could tell that he had a lot of raw talent. He wasn't always musically correct, but he had speed and he felt the music. He was exciting to people."[1]

Bouzoukia

As a teenager, Soffos decided to leave high school and play the bouzouki professionally. His parents were appalled, but eventually they asked family friend Giannis Tatasopoulos if he could help their son. At sixteen, Soffos moved to the Washington, DC, area to study with Tatasopoulos, the most highly regarded bouzouki player of his day. At first he lived with cousins in Baltimore and was ferried daily to Washington, then later he lived with Tatasopoulos himself. Soffos played with Tatasopoulos at the Black Ulysses Restaurant in 1970–1971. During this time, they played together on *Giorti tou horou* (Nina LS-321), a recording by singer Grigoris Maroulis.

When he was seventeen, Soffos began his career as an independent headliner in *bouzoukia* throughout the country. He started at the Astor Restaurant and Club on Fourteenth and M Streets in Washington, which featured a large and talented ensemble, including Nikos Zervas on drums. At nineteen, Soffos accepted a job at the Golden Dolphin in Atlanta, owned by singer George Evagoras. He performed on Evagoras's album *A Grecian Evening with George Evagoras*, along with Golden Dolphin musicians Yiannis Tziotis (drums), George Platanias (keyboard), and Kostas Milonakos (guitar, bass).

Soffos began to attract attention. Legendary country music songwriters Boudleaux and Felice Bryant heard him play, then brought him to Nashville and wrote a song featuring a duel between bouzouki and banjo. "EmmyLou the Belly Dancer" was recorded by British country music duo Lynch & Dawson but was never released in the United States. During that period, Soffos also was invited to apply to the New England Conservatory of Music but declined because he was enjoying life in Atlanta. He later said that it was the one thing that he regretted.

"I'm Not Your Traditional Kind of Player"[2]

During the early 1970s, Soffos bounced around the country, playing limited engagements in Las Vegas, Silver Spring (Maryland), New York City, and California. He left Atlanta permanently in 1975 to work in the San Francisco Bay area, with occasional gigs in Chicago and Greece. In California, he formed Apollo's Children with guitarist Ari Harmandas and drummer Panos Lemonidis. They played at various venues, including a long stint at Lewis "Louie" Gundunas's popular Balkan Village in Los Altos. Not surprisingly, in the early 1970s Soffos's music and techniques reveal significant influences from rock and roll, including the use of distortion effects.

From the 1950s to the 1980s, celebrated Armenian violinist Hrach Yacoubian led a popular orchestra that played Greek, Armenian, Middle Eastern, and classical pieces. Yacoubian invited Soffos to join after hearing him play, and in 1977 he moved to Los Angeles. He was delighted that Yacoubian encouraged him to spend several months just listening to classical music and learning to read music in order to master the orchestra's eclectic repertoire. Soffos performed with the group in Los Angeles and Las Vegas for two years.

Although he continued commuting to gigs in other locations, Soffos settled in Chicago in 1980. He performed regularly at famed Greek restaurant and cultural center Deni's Den in 1979, 1985–1986, and 1992–1994. Musician Maria Sklavounou Broude recalls his remarkable artistry:

> The very first time I heard him was at Deni's Den—the song: "Epefte bathia siopi" by [Mimis] Plessas. He played the bouzoukee solo in such a way that it made my hair stand up straight—I was transported beyond this earth—it was such an ecstatic experience. Later, I thought it was just my imagination. Over the course of my life, I had heard so many bouzoukee performers—but none resonated with me the way his playing did. Every time I heard him play, I felt the same way. And then, he left Chicago and he left a deep void in the city. . . . I always thought he was close to God.[3]

From 1989 to 1992 he and several other musicians (Demetri Xydas/keyboard, George Papadatos/drums, Vasilis Roussis/bass, Panos Lambropoulos/vocals and *baglamas*) co-owned the Neon Greek Village. The Neon musicians were an accomplished group who not only accompanied celebrated visiting and local vocalists but also played solid instrumental laïka and pop pieces. Soffos also performed and toured with renowned vocalist and musician Vasilios Gaitanos.

In Chicago, Soffos occasionally worked with highly respected clarinetist Jim Stoynoff, who observed: "You noticed the ease with which he would start a phrase. And then he would layer up the complexity of what he would play. It's not very simple . . . and his improvisations were very thoughtful, very structured." Stoynoff noted their similar responses to the evolution of Greek music:

> When we first started playing in the sixties, you were looking at predominantly Greeks and first generation people that were very much in sync with the music and the interpretation that we were raised with. And as intermarriages became more

prevalent and the style of music in Greece changed and . . . was being disseminated in America, those changes were significant in terms of their departure from the traditional styles that we were raised with. It presented a challenge for George and myself, and for every other Greek American musician that had their roots in that style. What he did (and I found it inspirational in the context of *klarino* playing) starting to accommodate the likes of the newer audiences but not completely abandoning the traditional way; finding ways to still incorporate some of those characteristics of flavor, color, and emotion that are so characteristic of the style as we learned it from oral tradition, and yet still having some flair. (Stoynoff 2013)

While living in Chicago and later Florida, Soffos periodically played at Molfetas in New Jersey, where he accompanied singer Nikos Kritikos, on whose album he played (*Den Eisai Ekeini*). Other musical colleagues there included Takis Elenis, Ari Harmandas, Vasilis Roussis, Nikos Zervas (1980s), and later Dimitri Matsis (1998). He also played at the Grecian Cave in Astoria, New York, with singer Manolis Angelopoulos, and at the Bouzoukia Lounge and the Mykonos in Detroit. Internationally, Soffos performed in Montreal, Toronto, and numerous Greek cities. He often provided instrumental backing for Greek singing stars such as Marinella, Rita Sakellariou, Poly Panou, and Katerina Topazi, who sometimes requested that he accompany them on US tours. He performed at countless festivals and special events, such as the Rembetika Music Program organized by Stoynoff at the Chicago Public Library for the Chicago Arts Council in 1991.

Moving toward the Sun

Soffos moved to Florida's Tampa Bay area in 1994—he loved the climate, and his brothers Jimmy and Michael lived there. He briefly co-owned the Mirabella Restaurant near St. Petersburg with family members, but when it closed he returned to performing in Florida, nationally, and in Greece. Soffos was diagnosed with throat cancer in 1997. Initially the cancer responded to radiation treatments, but in 1999 it returned. He underwent a tracheotomy and ceased performing for several years.

When Soffos resumed playing in 2003, he became the most sought-after performer at clubs and events in central Florida, an area with a strong Greek cultural presence. Between 2003 and 2008, he performed periodically at Zorba's Restaurant and Lounge in Tarpon Springs with keyboard player Rhodell Fields. They also appeared at Pappas Restaurant and Limani in Tarpon Springs, until Fields moved to New York in 2009.

In 2009, Soffos joined vocalist Elias Poulos and keyboard player Dino Theofilos to create Ellada. The band was quickly booked for events throughout the state and around the country. Most performances focused on old favorites to which the crowds could dance, but because the Tarpon Springs Greek community was initially settled by Dodecanese islanders, the band incorporated many traditional nisiotika in its repertoire.

Although Soffos had occasionally taught when younger, in later years he developed a strong interest in passing his knowledge to the younger generation. In addition to private lessons, he taught bouzouki classes through the City of Tarpon Springs. He became a mentor to many aspiring musicians and was deeply gratified to see several students show the promise of future careers in Greek music.

During his final years, Soffos was accorded broader recognition. He received a Florida Folk Heritage award in March 2011. In July 2011, the National Council for Traditional Arts included him in the Guitar Masters program at the Lowell Folklife Festival in Massachusetts along with several National Heritage Fellows. He was designated a master artist through participation in the Florida Folklife Apprenticeship Program from 2011 to 2012, and was the top-rated candidate for the 2013 Florida Individual Artist Award in Folk Arts, awarded by the Florida Division of Cultural Affairs.

George Soffos died unexpectedly of a heart attack on January 8, 2013. He was intricately woven into the fabric of Greek music in America in terms of performances, repertoire, venues, and professional relations with other musicians. In many ways, his life represents the history of Greek music in this country since the 1970s. As an exceptional musician and a fine person, he brought great joy to many; his early death was a tragic loss for us all.

Notes

1. Parry Tsangaris, e-mail message to the author, July 15, 2013.
2. The quotation is taken from an interview; see Soffos 2010.
3. Maria Sklavounou Broude, e-mail message to the author, July 2, 2013.

References

Soffos, George. 2010. Interview with Tina Bucuvalas, Holiday, Florida, October.
Stoynoff, James. 2013. Interview with Tina Bucuvalas, Chicago, May 21.

APPENDIX
Greek Music Collections in the United States

—Stavros K. Frangos

Given the enduring popularity of Greek music performed, produced, and target-marketed to an array of audiences in the United States since 1896, it is difficult to understand why no systematic compilation of this complex of musical traditions is currently available. What follows is a review of Greek music known to exist in collections available to the public. All forms of traditional music, popular urban music, amateur performers/performances, liturgical music, and oral history interviews, as well as all manner of commercial recordings, are cited below.[1]

Between 1896 and 1942, at least two thousand individual commercial recordings of Greek music were produced in the United States (Spottswood 1990). What we do not know is how many commercial recordings of Greek music were imported during that same period. Given economic and psychological factors, Greeks in the United States proved to be avid consumers of Greek music during this period. A further dimension to this broader puzzle is that the accepted figure of two thousand individual records does not include the output of all the small, independent companies in operation in the United States prior to 1945, because no one can honestly say how many small companies in fact existed. We have learned about these obscure, small companies only from odd bits of surviving ephemera and chance remarks during oral history interviews.

Dick Spottswood's phenomenal seven-volume masterwork, *Ethnic Music on Records: A Discography of Ethnic Recordings Produced in the United States, 1893–1942* (1990), lists sound recordings produced by or for minority groups issued in the United States. Volume 3, which includes data on Greek music, is the primary published source documenting the existence of the two thousand recordings made from 1896 to 1942. Without going into detail, the Albanian, Sephardic Jewish, and Turkish discographic entries are also related to the Greek section. This watershed publication was drawn from years of research based on record company documents, private collectors' holdings, and visits to public institutions around the country. For ethnic music in the United States prior to World

War II, no other study matches it in detail or scope. Now that we know which records were produced and released, the question becomes, where are they?

No private collectors or public institutions claim that they possess all known early recordings. Nor can these same sources shed light on the total number of imported or target-marketed recordings, small-company inventory, and related questions. However, from the record company catalogs issued at the same time as the actual music, we can compile a broader picture—dating from as far back as 1910—of far more than simply two thousand individual recordings.

To the best of my knowledge, there is no annotated guide to the locations or holdings of Greek music. The vignettes offered below represent my best assessment of existing collections that include folk, urban, and living expressions of Greek music in America since 1896. The collections vary widely for many reasons. For example, not all archivists hold the same theoretical position on commercial records as documents of traditional musical forms, and archival collections are organic entities subject to changes in the thinking of those who preserve them. Other factors influence the ongoing existence of these materials such as allocated monies, spatial concerns, and other extremely pragmatic issues.

Collections

Library of Congress
101 Independence Ave. SE, Washington, DC 20540
https://www.loc.gov/folklife/archive.html

The Greece Collections in the American Folklife Center's Archive of Folk Culture offer a complex array of sound and print materials related to Greek cultural traditions. Anyone interested in this broad-based collection of Greek materials is best served by consulting the online reference "Finding Aids to Collections in the Archive of Folk Culture" compiled by Vivy Niotis (http://www.loc.gov/folklife/guides/Greece.html). The collections found in this guide are not limited to music produced by or commented upon by Greeks living in the United States. Music collected in Greece, commercial records produced in Greece, and oral histories collected in Greece and in the United States from temporary or permanent residents are also part of this overall collection. A quick review of the guide reveals dozens of field recordings, commercial records, and oral history accounts related directly to Greek music as it is and was performed, produced, and recalled in the United States. Among the sound documents are extremely rare interviews with professional musicians, extended collections of Greek-language radio programs, and recordings of amateur Greek American performers from various communities around the country.

From the folk songs and oral history accounts collected by the Works Progress Administration (WPA) in Florida during 1929–1940 to the 2001 live musical performance at the Coolidge Auditorium at the Library of Congress, this collection is a far more rich and complex body of material than Niotis's citations convey. To cite an example of its complexity, the Library of Congress's AFC 1939/026 Alton C. Morris Collection of Florida WPA Recordings contains information not simply on Morris's *Folksongs of Florida* (1950; reprinted 1990), but also on the related Alton Morris/George Herzog correspondence in the Archives of Traditional Music (cited below). The correspondence reveals that Greek materials were not included in Morris's book because Herzog did not complete the transcriptions and translations.

Of special note in this broad-based collection is the James (Demetrios) A. Notopoulos Collection of Greek Poetry, Music, and Tales. An invaluable source of field recordings of traditional Greek music and oral accounts made in 1952–1953, its relationship to Notopoulos's field collections among Greek Americans has as yet to be determined.[2]

Hellenic College and Holy Cross Greek Orthodox School of Theology
50 Goddard Ave., Brookline, MA 02445
617-850-1223; http://www.hchc.edu/library/

The Archbishop Iakovos Library and Learning Resource Center holds innumerable volumes, manuscripts, recordings, and other materials related to the liturgical music of the Eastern Orthodox faith. It houses more than sixty thousand monographic volumes, over four hundred active serial titles, and a large number of audiovisual materials. In addition, the holdings include a rare book collection. Materials related to the history of Greek Orthodox music in the United States are to be found scattered throughout the wider collection. Of special interest is the wealth of materials related to individual parish music.

Historical Society of Pennsylvania
1300 Locust St., Philadelphia, PA 19107
215-732-6200; www.hsp.org

Obtained in 2006 from the Balch Institute of Ethnic Studies, items in the Balch Institute Sheet Music Collection (Collection 3141) document the diverse cultures and peoples of Philadelphia. The merger of the Balch Institute and the Historical Society of Pennsylvania resulted in the division of various collections. In 1992, the Balch Institute held some 325 individual pieces of Greek sheet music including Greek folk songs in Gary, Indiana (1956–1961), from the Attikon Music Company of Astoria, New York; two pieces from the Colonial Music Company,

New York; one piece from Cosmopolitan Music Publishers (1945); one piece from L. Cavadias Publishing (1933); one piece dated 1943 from Argyriou Brothers, Newark, New Jersey; and two pieces dated 1912 from the Atlantis Company of New York. For more information, see the Balch Institute's reference guide, "Ethnic Sheet Music Collection at the Balch Institute for Ethnic Studies," by Deborah Wong (August 25, 1984).

Archives of Traditional Music, Indiana University
Morrison Hall 117, 1165 E. 3rd St., Bloomington, IN 47405
812-855-4679; atmusic@indiana.edu

This collection holds arguably the broadest representation of folk, urban, and oral histories in the United States, and the largest number of commercial recordings in all formats. In the documentation that accompanies each collection, the researcher will find a considerable mix of ephemera and other documents.

In chronological order, the Greek American collections focusing on music are: Greeks of Florida (Accession no. 54-066-F); folk songs sung by Georgia Tarsoulis (54-295-F); Greeks in Indiana folk song, 1951 (54-295-F); Greek folk songs in Gary, Indiana, collected by Harriet Munn (61-068-F); Greek folk songs and folktales collected in Indiana and elsewhere (061-9-14); the Pittsburgh Greek Festival (70-132-F); Detroit radio broadcast, 150th anniversary of Greek independence (71-311-B); the Marsha Penti-Vidutis Collection (76-128); the Gary Project (Greek American collections 76-135t-B, 76-135c-F, 76-135h-F, 76-135f-F, 76-135j-F); the Sylvia and Jack Cohen family record collection (79–110-C); Greek bands and Byzantine choir music, Indianapolis (84-1431-32-F); the Matina and John Costakis family record collection (85-456-C); Skevos (Steve) Zembillas (85-268-F/C) and Bucuvalas and Frangos (86-033-F); oral history/music from the Calumet region (86-003-F); the Pappas/Sloane record collection (86-102-F/C); interviews and recordings by Greek and Macedonian musicians in Indiana (80-106-F, et al.); interviews with Greek musicians George Katsaros and John K. Gianaros by Steve Frangos (89-049-C/F); the Greek American family record collection (89-050-C); and the Liberty record collection (89-182-C).

An example of documents mixed in with recorded music and interviews is the collection of forty-five letters and cards from July 1937 to March 1941 between Alton Chester Morris and George Herzog (1901–1984), then director of the ATM, concerning Greek music recorded by Morris in Florida.

Appendix

Grand Rapids Public Museum
272 Pearl St. NW, Grand Rapids, MI 49504

Among the oral history collections gathered during the National Endowment for the Humanities–funded 1980 museum exhibition, *The Greek American Family: Continuity through Change*, are discussions of the public presentation of Greek dance in the early 1920s by women in the dance troupe who presented traditional Greek dances as well as interpretations of classical Greek dances following the example of Isadora Duncan. Other oral histories review the establishment of the Hellenic Festival and music related to the annual event. See "Finding Aid for Hellenic Horizons: The Greek American History of Grand Rapids, Michigan Collection 277," at http://grplpedia.grpl.org/wiki/images/f/f9/277.pdf.

National Hellenic Museum
333 South Halsted St., Chicago, IL 60661
312-655-1234

The institution holds uncounted numbers of commercial recordings in all formats produced in the United States and imported from Greece. Musical instruments, sheet music, and Victrola- and other music-related materials are part of the larger collection. There are audio and video recordings of musicians such as John Katchikas (*santouri*) and Jim Stoynoff (clarinet), audio recordings of interviews with fabled record collector Dino Pappas accompanied by musical examples that illustrate interview topics, and many others. Documentation related to the 1995 *Return to Our Roots* exhibit, curated by Stoynoff, is in the museum's files. *Return to Our Roots* chronicled more than one hundred years of Greek music as it came to life in the homeland and later grew in many places where Greeks migrated, such as Chicago's Halsted Street. Individual collections worth attention are the papers and commercial records in the Nick Topping Collection as well as the handbills, posters, and other ephemera for musical events produced by local printers. Unfortunately, given the sheer volume of materials and the lack of dedicated funds and expert personnel, these materials are not currently available to researchers.

Jane Addams Hull-House Museum
University of Illinois at Chicago,
800 South Halsted (M/C 051), Chicago, IL 60607-7017
312-413-5353

The Jane Addams Hull-House Museum is on the campus of the University of Illinois at Chicago. Wallace Kirkland (1891–1979) was a social worker and professional photographer, and his photographs are divided between the museum

445

and the university's archive on the fifth floor of the main library. Kirkland first worked at Hull-House in the early 1930s and, in the course of his duties, began teaching photography at that time. He took a wide array of black-and-white images of Chicago's Halsted Street area, which at the time was home to the largest Greek neighborhood in the city. Kirkland eventually became an internationally known Time Life photographer and donated prints and negatives from his long career to the Hull-House Museum and the university archives. Researchers must visit both the museum and the university archives to survey the entire collection of Kirkland photographs and other documents.

During the 1930s, Kirkland took photographs of the Mouzakiotis brothers' storefronts at their Halsted Street and Blue Island locations. The photographs show records hanging in the windows along with instruments, Victrolas, and other items. Other images show Holy Friday processions in the Halsted Street area with hundreds of parishioners carrying and accompanying the Epitafios. To best of my knowledge, no researcher has surveyed all of Kirkland's images.

Immigration History Research Center Archives
University of Minnesota, 219 Elmer L. Andersen Library
222 21st Ave. South, Minneapolis, MN 55455
612-625-4800

Scattered across the center's collections are books and papers related to Eastern Orthodox liturgical music in North America. See especially the materials related specifically to Greek liturgical music.

Helen Zeese Papanikolas Papers (1954–2001)
Special Collections, J. Willard Marriott Library, University of Utah
295 South Campus Dr., Salt Lake City, UT 84112
801-581-3886; http://www.lib.utah.edu/collections/special-collections/

The Papanikolas collection holds a diverse array of music-related materials. Among these documents are forty-five hours of rerecordings of Greek music recorded in the United States from the early 1900s until the post–World War II period. Another source for music-related information is a 1927–1928 Atlas Import/Export catalog, which features some sixty pages of music materials.

In 1990, Dino Pappas along with fellow record collector Andreas Dellis received a Helen Zeese Papanikolas Charitable Trust award. As two of the largest commercial record collectors in the nation at that time, Pappas and Dellis deposited rerecordings of the vast majority of Tetos Demetriades's commercial recordings (inclusive of his many performances under pseudonym) into the

Papanikolas collection. Pappas and Dellis published two survey essays announcing this deposit and describing its contents (1991a, 1991b).[3]

University of California, Santa Barbara, Library
525 UCEN Rd., Santa Barbara, CA 93106-9010
805-893-5444

One of the library's most notable music-related holdings is the only Greek musical cylinder noted in the public record, "O yero Demos" (Old Man Demos) by George N. Helmis, released in 1911 (Edison Blue Amberol: 11804/Edison Amberol: 11562; reissue of Edison four-minute Amberol 11562: Greek series). The piece is a tenor solo with piano accompaniment and is held in the Blanche Browning Rich collection (http://www.library.ucsb.edu/OBJID/Cylinder1434).

A second holding of interest at this library is the Kutay Derin Kugay collection, which consists of some 429 Turkish and Greek 78-rpm recordings spanning the period between 1906 and 1963. Again, this is a mixed collection of commercial records, with some produced in the Ottoman Empire and released by commercial European companies and others produced in the United States. This rare collection of materials will undoubtedly be of service to any number of future researchers, especially those interested in select recordings of Greek and Turkish music produced, performed, and recorded in America.

Florida Memory, State Library and Archives of Florida
500 South Bronough St., Tallahassee, FL 32399-0250
850-245-6700; https://www.floridamemory.com/

In 2005, a team of specialists in education and preservation at the State Archives of Florida completed a project to enhance access to and provide educational tools based upon the Florida Folklife Collection. The materials consist of field notes, images, and sound recordings created by folklorists with the Florida Folklife Program from the mid-1970s through 1995. Many materials were added to the Florida Memory website. In addition to these research files, the collection also includes recordings and images gathered by Works Progress Administration programs and from the annual Florida Folk Festival, the nation's longest-running continuous folk festival. Florida Memory's website includes audio, photographic, and visual materials of Florida resident artists such as George Katsaros, Nikitas Tsimouris, John K. Gianaros, Dimitris Tzaras, Spiros Skordilis, Phil Demas, Kostas Maris, and others.

Other Potential Sources

Those seeking local Greek American organizations that may hold musical materials should consult the umbrella group Preservation of American Hellenic History (pahh.com). Greek churches, fraternal organizations, and independent organizations have since the 1980s formed historical societies, museums, and archives, and many hold materials related to music.

Various documentary films feature Greek music in North America. *Every Island Has Its Own Songs: The Tsimouris Family of Tarpon Springs* (dir. Peggy Bulger, Florida Department of State, 1988) showcases the life and artistry of Nikitas Tsimouris (1924–2001), a Kalymnian *tsambouna* player and National Heritage Fellow in Tarpon Springs.[4] Also in 1988, filmmaker John Cohen released *Pericles in America*.[5] The website AllMovie reports:

> Greek-American clarinetist Pericles Halkias has received the National Heritage Award from the National Endowment for the Arts and is responsible for trying to preserve traditional Greek music forms both in the U.S. and in Greece. Part of the film concerns the musician and his family, who live and celebrate their Greekness in Astoria, Queens. Another part of the film is a docudrama concerning a young Greek American who returns to Greece in order to find himself a bride in his parent's native village. The docudrama is filled with exactly the kinds of music the clarinetist is trying to preserve and shows it being performed in the context of everyday Greek life. (Fountain 2016)

The unquestionable beauty of Greek music informs the creativity of musicians across the planet. Hopefully, the information here will allow many more to hear and learn more about the music as it has existed in America since 1896.

Notes

1. Unfortunately, many subjects related to Greek music are seldom or never studied, despite the popularity of Greek music produced for and/or targeted to a Greek audience in the United States. These subjects include sheet music, instrument makers, the lives of professional musicians, the functions of amateur musicians in their home communities, the enduring role of Greek cafés and restaurants in American life, the continuing importance of music among Greek Americans, and related issues. Although the number of rereleases of older recordings, whether on CD or in digital format, is unknown, it is apparent that many non-Greeks have been actively involved in this resurgence. By virtue of the growing number of rereleases, we are able to gauge that the music has gained in popularity among not simply Greek and non-Greek Americans but also a broader world audience.

2. In "Tragoudia Dodekanesion tes Amerikes," noted classical scholar Demetrios A. Notopoulos (1957) presents lyrics from songs he collected among Greek sponge fishermen in Tarpon Springs,

Florida. The author provides a sound discussion of the relationship of these Greek American forms to the musical traditions of the island of Kalymnos and elsewhere in Greece.

3. See also Pappas's article "Tetos Demetriades: Blending Greek and American Music" (1995).

4. *Every Island Has Its Own Songs* can be streamed at http://www.folkstreams.net/film,136.

5. *Pericles in America* is distributed by the University of California Extension Center for Media and Independent Learning, at http://www.berkeleymedia.com/product/pericles_in_america/.

References

Fountain, Clarke. 2016. "Synopsis, *Pericles in America*." AllMovie. At http://www.allmovie.com/movie/pericles-in-america-v176377. Accessed July 2, 2016.

Notopoulos, Demetrios A. 1957. "Tragoudia Dodekanesion tes Amerikes" (Songs of the Dodecanesians in America). *Laografia* 17: 22–29.

Pappas, Dino. 1995. "Tetos Demetriades: Blending Greek and American Music." *Laografia*, February 12.

Pappas, Dino, and Andreas Dellis. 1991a. "An Expanded Discography of Tetos Demetriades, part 1, ca. 1920–1928." *Laografia*, May 8, 1–102.

———. 1991b. "An Expanded Discography of Tetos Demetriades, part 2, ca. 1928–1932." *Laografia*, May 8, 103–87.

Spottswood, Richard K. 1990. *Ethnic Music on Records: A Discography of Ethnic Recordings Produced in the United States, 1893–1942*. 7 vols. Urbana: University of Illinois Press.

CONTRIBUTORS

Tina Bucuvalas is curator of arts and historical resources for the City of Tarpon Springs. She previously worked for the Florida Folklife Program (1996–2009), serving as director and state folklorist, and coordinated the Folklife Program and curated the Object Collection at the Historical Museum of Southern Florida, Miami (1986–1991). She served as exhibition review editor for the *Journal of American Folklore*, Florida Folklife Council member, and Florida Folklore Society president. As a Fulbright Scholar (2006–2007), Bucuvalas traveled throughout Greece researching public folklife programs. She wrote *Greeks in Tarpon Springs* (2016), edited *The Florida Folklife Reader* (2011), coauthored *Just Above the Water: Florida Folk Arts* (2006) with Kristin Congdon and *South Florida Folklife* (1994) with Peggy Bulger and Stetson Kennedy, published numerous articles on Florida folklife, and curated many exhibits. She holds a PhD in folklore from Indiana University.

Anthropologist **Stavros K. Frangos** is an independent scholar who has worked on museum exhibitions, archival collections, and oral history projects since the 1980s. His writings include *The Greeks in Michigan* (2004); "The Greek Slave," in *Founded on Freedom and Virtue*, edited by Constantine G. Hatzidimitriou (2002); with Alexandros K. Kyrou, "Diaspora Studies: Hellenic Diaspora," in *Greece in Modern Times*, edited by Stratos E. Constantinidis (2000); articles in the *Journal of Modern Hellenism*, the *Journal of the Hellenic Diaspora*, and others; and more than five hundred newspaper and magazine articles on the Greek experience in North America. In 2010, Frangos received the American Hellenic Educational Progressive Association's Academic Achievement Award.

Anna Caraveli has a PhD in comparative literature and folklore from Binghamton University. She has done extensive research and published on women's ritual laments in Greece; Byzantine chanting performance in the United States; and ritual, verbal art on Greek islands and the Greek American community in Baltimore. Later in her career she researched and wrote about peer, customer, and professional communities; organizational culture; and leadership. She is managing partner of the Demand Networks, LLC, and author of *The Demand Perspective: Leading from the Outside In*.

Aydin Chaloupka recently graduated from high school and received an associate degree. At eleven years old, he discovered *rebetika* through his interest in the music of the former Ottoman Empire. A year later he was given a bouzouki by his friend, Greek folk musician Christos Govetas. Through his research, he discovered Ioannis Halikias (Jack Gregory), who became his favorite bouzouki musician, and soon thereafter he located Jack Halikias Jr. on a bouzouki forum. They still communicate frequently, which has assisted in Chaloupka's continuing research.

Sotirios (Sam) Chianis is one of the foremost authorities on Greek folk music. He is also an excellent performer on the *santouri*, which he studied with the eminent Spyros Stamos. Chianis received a PhD in ethnomusicology/musicology from the University of California, Los Angeles. Since 1958, he has recorded the vocal and instrumental repertoires of villages throughout Greece—returning frequently for field recording expeditions and working closely with the Hellenic Folklore Research Center at the Academy of Athens. After teaching at Wesleyan University and elsewhere, he joined the faculty at Binghamton University in 1968 as the first staff ethnomusicologist in the State University of New York system. Chianis has played the santouri for recordings including *Epirotika: Greek Folk Music and Dances from Northern Greece*, *Ravi Shankar: Portrait of a Genius*, and two classical albums. He was a guest soloist with the Boston Symphony Orchestra, the New York Philharmonic, and others; played on radio and TV in Athens; and performed for Hollywood television and movie studios such as Universal, MGM, Columbia, Disney, and Paramount.

Born Photios Despotopoulos in Cleveland, Ohio, **Frank Desby** (1922–1992) was a seminal figure in the revision of sacred music throughout the Greek Orthodox Archdiocese of North and South America. He developed an interest in Byzantine chant while his family temporarily resided in Greece, and later received a PhD in music from the University of Southern California. While based at Annunciation Greek Orthodox Church and then Saint Sophia Cathedral in Los Angeles, Desby studied chant, the liturgical music of western Europe, and Russian choral music, then used the knowledge to create new compositions. By distributing his book *Choral Music to the Divine Liturgy for Mixed Voices*—which included reworked versions of John Sakellarides and some original material—through regional music conferences sponsored by the archdiocese, Desby influenced the subsequent development of Greek American liturgical music.

Stathis Gauntlett is a Fellow of the Australian Academy of the Humanities and currently a senior research associate of the University of Melbourne, where he was first appointed to the foundation lectureship in modern Greek in 1973.

He retired from the Dardalis Chair of Hellenic Studies at La Trobe University, Melbourne, in 2006. Among his publications are books on *rebetika*, articles on Greek literature and oral traditions, and literary translations, most recently an annotated translation of *The Last Varlamis* by Thanasis Valtinos (University of Birmingham, 2016).

Joseph G. Graziosi has done extensive research on regional dance in Greece and among Greek communities in the United States. In 1982, he codirected the Greek Music Tour sponsored by the National Endowment for the Arts and Ethnic Folk Arts Center, and he coauthored the accompanying booklet. Graziosi has taught throughout the world for community groups, universities, and folk dance camps, including the Balkan Music and Dance Workshops, since 1982. He cofounded both New York's Greek American Folklore Society, where he taught throughout the 1980s, and the annual World Music and Dance Camp. He has served as judge and adviser for the Greek Orthodox (San Francisco Metropolis) Folk Dance Festival since 1984, and more recently for the Atlanta Metropolis's Hellenic Dance Festival. He also produces CD compilations of rare regional dance music.

Gail Holst-Warhaft is an adjunct professor in the Departments of Comparative Literature and Biological and Environmental Engineering, member of the Graduate Field of Music, and director of the Mediterranean Studies Initiative in the Institute for European Studies at Cornell University. She lived for several years in Greece, where she played with composers Mikis Theodorakis, Dionysis Savvopoulos, and others. She was appointed Poet Laureate of Tompkins County, New York, for 2011 and 2012. Her books include *The Fall of Athens* (poems) (2016), *Penelope's Confession* (poems) (2007), *The Cue for Passion: Grief and Its Political Uses* (2000), *Dangerous Voices: Women's Laments and Greek Literature* (1992), *Theodorakis: Myth and Politics in Modern Greek Music* (1980), and *Road to Rembetika* (1975). She coedited *Losing Paradise: The Water Crisis in the Mediterranean* (2010) and *The Classical Moment* (1999).

Michael G. Kaloyanides holds a PhD in ethnomusicology from Wesleyan University. He has conducted extensive field research in the rural and urban music of Greece and Turkey and recorded Greek and Turkish music albums for Lyrichord Records. He has published in *Ethnomusicology*, the *Yearbook for Traditional Music* of the International Council for Traditional Music, *Essays in Arts and Sciences*, the *New Grove Dictionary of Music in the United States*, and *Music and Anthropology*. In addition, he composed and produced the film scores for the PBS documentaries *The Royal Archives of Ebla* and *Arts in the Workplace*. An Emeritus Professor of Music at the University of New Haven, he also taught at Yale University, the Hartt School of Music, and the Institute for Shipboard

Education's Semester at Sea program. Kaloyanides is a classically trained percussionist who has played bouzouki in Greek ensembles, drums in West African drumming groups, and guitar and keyboards in blues and rock bands.

Panayotis League is an ethnomusicologist and performer specializing in the music and oral poetry traditions of the Greek islands, northeastern Brazil, western Ireland, and their diasporas. He holds a PhD in ethnomusicology from Harvard University, where he wrote a dissertation on the Anatolian Greek diaspora community in the greater Boston area and the island of Lesbos. He has published articles and reviews in *Ethnomusicology*, the *Journal of Modern Greek Studies*, the *Journal of Greek Media and Culture*, and *ReVista: The Harvard Review of Latin America*. He also contributed chapters on Greek music to *The Ethnomusicologist's Cookbook*, vol. 2, and translated Greek folklorist Nikolaos Nitsos's *Tales, Rituals, and Songs*. He directed the Harvard Libraries/Hidden Collections project "Sounds and Moving Images of Greek Shadow Theatre" and is currently the James A. Notopoulos Fellow at the Milman Parry Collection of Oral Literature, Harvard Library. He performs, records, and teaches Greek, Brazilian, and Irish music on violin, various lutes, accordion, *tsambouna* bagpipe, and percussion.

Roderick Conway Morris graduated from the University of Cambridge, and did postgraduate research in *rebetika* and Asia Minor lyrics and music at the School of Oriental and African Studies in London as well as in Greece and Turkey. He learned to play the *outi* in Athens with the veteran refugee musician Yannis Soulis. For more than twenty-five years, he has been writing about European art and culture for the *International New York Times* (formerly the *International Herald Tribune*), the *Spectator*, and the *Times Literary Supplement*. He wrote the entries for Greek and Turkish instruments in *The Grove Dictionary of Musical Instruments* and the sections on the Ottomans and Moghuls for the Time-Life History of the World series. He is also the author of a novel, *Jem: Memoirs of an Ottoman Secret Agent*, which has been translated into French, Turkish, and other languages.

Meletios Pouliopoulos is a Greek music historian and archivist who has documented and archived thousands of recordings for more than thirty years, including 78-rpm records, field tapes, and interviews. In Boston, he spent five years producing the radio show *For the Record: The History of Greek Music* and also coproduced the *Live and Unplugged* program. He researches Greek music, consults on Greek music programming and legal issues, and lectures on Greek music in America. In 2015, he served as a consultant for *Greek Music in America*, an exhibit about Greek music from 1880 to the present produced by the City of Tarpon Springs, Florida. He is the president of Greek Cultural Resources, a nonprofit organization that preserves and documents Greek music and related traditions.

Anthony Shay is associate professor of dance and cultural studies at Pomona College. He was founding artistic director/choreographer of the AMAN Folk Ensemble and AVAZ International Dance Theatre. Shay wrote *Choreophobia: Solo Improvised Dance in the Iranian World* (1999); the award-winning *Choreographic Politics: State Dance Companies, Representation, and Power* (2002); *Choreographing Identities: Ethnicity, Folk Dance, and Festival in North America* (2006); *Dancing across Borders: The American Fascination with Exotic Dances* (2008); *The Dangerous Lives of Public Performers: Sex, Dance, and Entertainment in the Islamic World* (2014); and more than fifty essays. He edited *Balkan Dances: Essays on Characteristics, Performance, and Teaching* (2008); and coedited *Belly Dance: Orientalism, Transnationalism, and Harem Fantasy* (2005), *When Men Dance: Dancing across Cultural Borders* (2009); and *The Oxford Handbook of Dance and Ethnicity* (2016).

David Soffa writes: A long-time music collector, I came across a pile of Greek records at the flea market. To my unaccustomed ear, they sounded like cats being slowly run over by cars. Continued listening, however, revealed a new world of sounds, and I began looking for more. I was surprised that none of the singers on my records were available on reissues. I felt that the three main immigrant female vocalists, Marika Papagika, Amalia Baka, and Mme. Koula, deserved a wider audience, and began research. This introduced me to many fascinating stories. When I met Greeks in the course of my research, they asked three questions: Are you police? No . . . Are you Greek? No? Then, why are you asking about this? I told them it was in memory of my Lebanese grandmother, of whom I had never asked enough questions and who had taught me how to cook Greek food. That usually did it. So research continued. I searched for obscure stories and obscure 78s and published them on obscure CDs. I am very happy those CDs have somehow continued to have some life!

Dick Spottswood included a discography of early Greek American records in *Ethnic Music on Records, 1893–1942* (1990, 7 vols.). He has assembled anthologies of early Greek, Turkish, Jewish, Irish, Slavic, and Caribbean music and collections of American jazz, country, and blues. He is coauthor of *Country Music Sources: A Biblio-Discography of Commercially Recorded Traditional Music* (2002). *Banjo on the Mountain* (2010) is a biography/discography of Wade Mainer; *The Blue Sky Boys* (2018) recounts the story of the North Carolina country band. His weekly *Dick Spottswood Show* (aka *Obsolete Music Hour*) features vintage recorded performances and streams online from www.bluegrasscountry.org.

Jim Stoynoff (Dimitri Stoyanoff) specializes in the research, preservation, and performance of Greek folk music, with emphasis on regional clarinet styles in

Epirus, Macedonia, central Greece, and Turkey. He studied with masters of the Greek folk clarinet including Yiorgo Anestopoulos, Apostolos Stamelos, and Pericles Halkias, as well as Turkish master clarinetist Saffet Gundeger. Since 1965, he has performed regularly for Greek, Armenian, and Turkish communities throughout the United States. In Chicago, he played with the Chicago Symphony Orchestra at the World Music Festival, performs with the Chicago Immigrant Orchestra, appears at Chicago Cultural Center events, and was part of Yo-Yo Ma's Silk Road residency (2006–2007). He designed and curated the National Hellenic Museum's *Road to Rembetika* exhibit (2007) and currently works on their archives and music exhibit. He also lectures, performs, and publishes essays about the Balkan clarinet.

Anna Lomax Wood is an applied and theoretical research anthropologist and project manager. A Grammy Award winner, she is also a writer, editor, translator, and lecturer with a research focus on the music and folk poetry of Italy and Greece, as well as on microcultural variation and its importance to international disaster management and recovery. A speaker of Spanish, French, Italian, and Greek, Wood contributes to the field of Mediterranean folklore as a working scholar. As executive director of the Association for Cultural Equity, Wood facilitates of all aspects of the Alan Lomax Archive, especially community repatriation of specific collections, and directs the multidecade Performance Style and Culture Project. Daughter of Alan Lomax and granddaughter of John A. Lomax, she is the third generation of Lomaxes who have dedicated their careers to cultural preservation and equity. She holds a PhD from Columbia University in cultural anthropology.

INDEX

Page numbers in **bold** refer to illustrations.

www.ingramcontent.com/pod-product-compliance
Lightning Source LLC
Chambersburg PA
CBHW030855270326
41929CB00008B/427